Bridging Two Dynasties

Memorable Teams in Baseball History

Bridging Two Dynasties

The 1947 New York Yankees

Edited by **Lyle Spatz**

Associate Editors: **Maurice Bouchard and Leonard Levin**

Published by the **University of Nebraska Press Lincoln & London,** and the **Society for American Baseball Research**

© 2013 by the Society for American Baseball Research

A different version of chapter 22 originally appeared in *Spahn, Sain, and Teddy Ballgame: Boston's (Almost) Perfect Baseball Summer of 1948*, edited by Bill Nowlin (Burlington MA: Rounder Books, 2008).

All photographs are courtesy of the National Baseball Hall of Fame Library, Cooperstown, New York, unless otherwise indicated.

Player statistics are courtesy of Baseball-Reference.com. Final standings in chapter 60 are courtesy of Retrosheet.org.

Library of Congress Cataloging-in-Publication Data

Bridging two dynasties: the 1947 New York Yankees / edited by Lyle Spatz; associate editors, Maurice Bouchard and Leonard Levin.
pages cm. — (Memorable teams in baseball history)
Includes bibliographical references.
ISBN 978-0-8032-4094-0 (pbk: alk. paper) 1. New York Yankees
(Baseball team)—History—20th century. I. Spatz, Lyle, 1937–
GV875.N4B75 2013
796.357'64097471—dc23   2012044734

Set in Sabon by Laura Wellington.

Table of Contents

Acknowledgments

This book is the result of the work of many members of the Society for American Baseball Research (SABR). Mark Armour, chairman of SABR's Bio-Project Committee, and Bill Nowlin, in charge of team projects, first had the idea for books devoted to specific teams.

I thank all the contributors, those who wrote player biographies and those who wrote articles, for their patience and cooperation. I offer my grateful appreciation to Len Levin and Maury Bouchard. Len and Maury read every word of the text and made numerous corrections to both language and statistics. Tom Bourke researched the genealogical history of every player and in many cases spoke to their descendants. Stephan Saks of the New York Public Library helped track down some difficult-to-find 1940s New York newspaper stories.

Rugger Ardizoia, Dr. Bobby Brown, Allie Clark, Don Johnson, Randy Gumpert, Mel Queen, Phil Rizzuto, and Dick Starr, all members of the 1947 Yankees, were most generous in sharing their remembrances of their careers, as were the friends and families of many of the players.

The National Baseball Library and Archive in Cooperstown, New York, provided various authors access to their subjects' player files. Patricia Kelly, of the National Baseball Library and Archive, furnished all the photographs that appear in the book except for that of Frank Colman. Scott Crawford, of the Canadian Baseball Hall of Fame and Museum, provided the Colman photo.

Introduction

Marty Appel

The 1947 Yankees always seemed to stand "alone" to me among the litany of champion Yankee clubs—neither a Joe McCarthy team nor a Casey Stengel team, carrying over some wartime players and introducing some guys that, frankly, did not feel like Yankees.

I mean, what were George McQuinn (a St. Louis Brownie!), Bobo Newsom (who played everywhere!), and Aaron Robinson (a catcher who was neither Dickey nor Berra) doing in Yankee pinstripes?

And for that matter, what was Bucky Harris doing managing the Yankees? As Larry MacPhail was remaking the team following his purchase of the club in 1945 (with Dan Topping and Del Webb), this made little sense. Harris was a career American Leaguer with little connection to MacPhail, and even less a connection to the Yanks. This was the man who would manage the team? You thought of Harris, and you thought of the Senators. The Yankees?

It all seemed so strange.

McQuinn, for example, was best known for holding down first base for the pennant-winning Browns in 1944—their only pennant—but even then, he was a .250 hitter of rather pedestrian skills.

Newsom! Don't get me started! He had this clownish nickname, and he was so un-Yankee, having started playing pro ball in 1928 and pitching for Brooklyn, the Cubs, the Browns, the Senators, the Red Sox, the Browns again, the Tigers, the Senators again, the Dodgers again, the Browns again, the Senators again, the Athletics, and the Senators again, before waking up and finding himself in baseball heaven, the Yankees. He had lost twenty games three times. This was not a classic Yankee pickup.

Yet there was Bobo, thirty-nine, taking the mound as a starting pitcher in his baggy gray New York uniform, starting Game Three of the 1947 World Series in Ebbets Field, the park where he had broken in at age twenty. His teammates then included Dazzy Vance, Davey Bancroft, and Max Carey, and his manager was Wilbert Robinson, who broke in in 1885! He had more than five thousand professional innings under his belt, and there he was—a Yankee starting pitcher in a World Series, surrounded by Joe DiMaggio, Tommy Henrich, and Phil Rizzuto.

This would be the game in which Yogi Berra, pinch-hitting for Sherm Lollar, lofted a pinch-hit home run in the seventh inning off Ralph Branca, which would, incredibly, be the first pinch-hit home run in World Series history.

Yes, there was something very interesting about this team. There was Snuffy Stirnweiss at second base, a chance to prove he was not just a "wartime" player, as he paired with Rizzuto to form an excellent double-play combination. And there were Allie Reynolds and Vic Raschi, not quite the Reynolds-Raschi-Lopat trio who would prove so dominant in coming years, but enjoying their first year as teammates and picking up World Series rings in the process. Reynolds came from Cleveland for Joe Gordon and won nineteen, while Raschi, homegrown and signed by Lou Gehrig's scout, Paul Krichell, came up from Portland in July and went 7-2.

Fireman Joe Page was a special figure in 1947, a

relief pitcher before there was glamour to the role, winning fourteen and saving seventeen (although saves were not an official statistic back then), and Joe enjoyed the good life, perhaps more than he should have. But to be young and a Yankee and to hang out with Joe DiMaggio—life was good.

Fans were still basking in the postwar era of good feelings, packing Major League ballparks, and enjoying the return of the "real guys" after enduring years of 4-F players. DiMaggio, who had hit just .290 in 1946, needed to prove that he was still Joe D., and he did, with his third MVP Award. He got out of the gate quickly and peaked at .368 on June 3. Now thirty-two, there certainly loomed large questions over whether his skills were gone. Everyone—Yankee fans or not—breathed a collective sigh of relief when it looked like indeed, his game had returned.

Given little chance to displace the powerful defending champion Boston Red Sox, this blend of veterans—along with rookies like Frank Shea, Yogi Berra, and Bobby Brown—compiled a record-tying nineteen-game winning streak as they romped to the American League pennant. They then defeated the Brooklyn Dodgers in a classic seven-game World Series that included two of the most memorable incidents in Series history—both at the expense of the Yankees.

It was in the 1947 World Series, the first to be televised, that Brooklyn's Cookie Lavagetto broke up Bill Bevens's attempt at the first World Series no-hitter, when, as Red Barber announced, "here comes the tying run and here comes the winning run!" And Al Gionfriddo was the Brooklyn outfielder who Barber told us went "back, back, back, back, back . . . oh doctor!" in robbing DiMaggio of what would have been his only World Series home run in Yankee Stadium. (Neither Bevens, Gionfriddo, nor Lavagetto ever played in the big leagues again after that Series.)

"Every kid has a dream, right?" said Bevens. "Mine was to meet Babe Ruth, be a Yankee and

pitch in a World Series. Well I reached all three so how can I complain? Of course, it would have been nice to know all those years ago that Lavagetto couldn't hit a low inside pitch. But what the hell."

Bucky Harris deserved a better fate. With MacPhail gone in '48 after one too many drinks and one too many punches at the World Series celebration party in '47, Harris could not survive finishing two and a half games behind the following year, despite winning ninety-four games. Had he been spared, as good logic suggests, he might have been the man to win five straight world championships starting in 1949, as Casey Stengel did. And then we would be speaking of Harris in the opening paragraph when we write of the greatest managers in history.

Yes, the '47 Yanks were the team that did not quite connect with the team's past, but one that made its fans feel terrific—the war was over, and the Bronx Bombers were back on top. Real life had officially returned.

And all was right with the world.

Chapter 1. The Yankees' Ownership

Mark Armour and Dan Levitt

What came to be known as the Yankees Dynasty began under the twenty-four-year stewardship of Jacob Ruppert. Known as "Colonel" because of his prior service in the National Guard, Ruppert owned and operated a profitable brewery, served four terms in the U.S. Congress, and in 1915 purchased half of the New York Yankees. His co-owner, Tillinghast L'Hommedieu Huston, rose to the rank of lieutenant colonel in the army during the First World War. Colonel Ruppert bought out Colonel Huston in 1923, by which point the Yankees were the class of the American League.

Ruppert's willingness to invest in his team led to the purchase of several players from the Boston Red Sox, most notably Babe Ruth, and the new talent helped win a string of pennants. In the fall of 1920 the Yankees' owners hired Ed Barrow as one of baseball's first general managers. Two and a half years later the team christened the massive Yankee Stadium, with nearly sixty thousand seats, which became the country's most venerated sporting facility. In 1932 Ruppert hired George Weiss to create and run one of baseball's first and best farm systems, ensuring the continuation of the dynasty.

At the time of Ruppert's death, in January 1939, the club had won ten pennants and seven World Series. Ruppert had no children; he left his entire estate, including his brewery and the Yankees, in a trust for the benefit of two nieces and the daughter of a deceased friend. Barrow and manager Joe McCarthy continued to ably run the club, and the team made four more World Series appearances (winning three) in the next six years.

Meanwhile, Ruppert's trustees were faced with a large estate-tax burden and not enough cash to settle it. There were also disagreements between the government and the trust as to the value of its assets, including the Yankees. When Ruppert bought out Huston in 1923, the team had been valued at $2.5 million, but the government now assessed it at $5 million. The estate chose to litigate the valuations of both the team and the brewery, which had the benefit of postponing the tax payment for a few years. Nevertheless, in order to raise the funds to settle the tax burden, the eventual sale of the team was inevitable.[1]

In 1941 the country was drawn into the Second World War, and most of America's non-war-related financial activity came to a halt. The Yankees were now administered by the Manufacturers Trust Company, which was actively trying to sell the team. With a war going on, though, there were few willing and able buyers around.

One interested buyer was Larry MacPhail, the former general manager of the Cincinnati Reds and Brooklyn Dodgers, now working in the War Department. In early 1943 MacPhail put together a syndicate to bid on the Yankees. The most prominent moneyed member of his group was John Hertz, a taxicab and rental-car magnate in Chicago. In February 1944 Commissioner Kenesaw M. Landis put the brakes on the deal because Hertz owned several thoroughbred horses, and Landis wanted to avoid any relationship between baseball and gambling interests. While MacPhail backed away, Ed Barrow looked for another buyer.

Barrow, now seventy-five years old but still running the club and wishing to continue, had two big reasons to disapprove of a sale to a MacPhail group. First, Barrow owned 10 percent of the club, and

MacPhail's offer ($2.8 million for the 96.88 percent of the stock owned by the Ruppert estate and Barrow) represented little profit on Barrow's investment more than two decades earlier. The team had enjoyed tremendous financial success in the intervening years, always pouring its profits back into the ball club, and now also owned several Minor League teams and Yankee Stadium. Moreover, MacPhail was a loud, domineering man who would surely want complete control over the operation of the club. Barrow would be out, he knew.

Barrow tried to interest his friend Tom Yawkey, owner of the Boston Red Sox, in purchasing the Yankees, which would necessitate Yawkey's finding a buyer for his own club. It is not known how seriously Yawkey took Barrow's suggestion, but in any case, nothing ever came of it. Barrow also turned to James Farley, a former postmaster general, but that also went nowhere.

As the pressure grew on the trust to pay the estate tax, MacPhail learned the trust was still willing to accept the original terms if he could come up with the money. He soon did so, more successfully this time, lining up two investors from his original syndicate to put up most of the money: Dan Topping, a sportsman-playboy who owned a professional football team in Brooklyn, and Del Webb, a construction and real estate magnate from Arizona. Once Barrow realized the sale was inevitable, he arranged separate meetings with Topping and Webb to stress the importance of maintaining stability in the organization. Both men assured him they intended to keep the team running as it always had.

The sale of the Yankees to MacPhail, Webb, and Topping was announced in January 1945. Shortly thereafter the trio acquired the small remaining interests held by others, giving the three men complete ownership. MacPhail borrowed most of his share of the purchase price from the other two and, as the baseball man in the group, was named club president. Topping, Webb, and Weiss were

elected vice presidents. Barrow was made chairman of the board, an empty title with no duties. MacPhail was in charge.

During the long reign of Ruppert and Barrow, the Yankees had been a businesslike, drama-free operation. Ruppert gave Barrow control over the team, and the two men managed to keep any disagreements they may have had out of the newspapers. In 1931 they hired Joe McCarthy to manage the club and granted him autonomy over the players. They deftly sidestepped Babe Ruth's annual lobbying (with the backing of many fans and writers) for the Yankees' managerial post. Ruppert put off his star until Ruth could no longer help the club on the field and then sold his contract to the Boston Braves.

Ruppert and Barrow wanted to win and were not driven by concerns about public relations. Both men, along with Weiss and McCarthy, lived quiet lives off the field and proved frustrating to the press corps. Despite the assurances to Barrow by Topping and Webb, Larry MacPhail made news wherever he went and would not change just because he was taking over the hallowed and conservative Yankees.

With the war going on and many baseball players in the service, there was little opportunity for reconstructing the ball club. Much of MacPhail's energy was instead directed toward the day-to-day activities of the team, which did not sit well with Joe McCarthy, who had won seven World Series as the Yankees' manager. McCarthy had always been a drinker, but during the relatively calm days working with Ed Barrow he had managed to keep his habit in check. In 1945, though, his problem worsened, and he left the club on July 20 to return to his Buffalo home. (The press was told he was battling health issues.) He tried to resign, but MacPhail encouraged him to stick it out, and he returned on August 9. During McCarthy's absence MacPhail had jettisoned his best pitcher.

On July 27 MacPhail sold Hank Borowy, the

club's most effective pitcher, to the Chicago Cubs for ninety-seven thousand dollars. This was somewhat shocking, as the Yankees did not seem to be in need of money. MacPhail feebly noted that Borowy was a poor second-half pitcher, but the hurler finished 11-2 for Chicago and helped lead them to the National League pennant.[2] MacPhail, it was assumed, just wanted to shake up his team and to show the troops who was boss. The Yankees were 4 games behind the Tigers at the time of the sale and finished 6½ back.

In 1946, with the war over, MacPhail was ready to make more of an impact. He installed lights at Yankee Stadium, as he had done in Cincinnati (the first in the Major Leagues) and Brooklyn. He added a new Stadium Club (which offered more luxurious seating and brought in five hundred thousand dollars before the season even started), reinstalled fifteen thousand seats, and added more promotional events. The Yankees drew an all-time record 2,265,512 customers in 1946, a sign that much of MacPhail's work was paying off.

On the field the Yankees won 87 games, well short of the powerful Boston Red Sox. Joe McCarthy again had to leave the team for "health" reasons, and this time he did not return. Longtime catcher Bill Dickey took over the club in May, but quit in September when he realized that MacPhail would not renew him for 1947, admitting that getting along with MacPhail was a challenge.[3] Johnny Neun finished out the year, but left after the season to manage the Cincinnati Reds. MacPhail then hired Bucky Harris, a managerial veteran of twenty seasons.

MacPhail made two important moves during the off-season. First, he traded second baseman Joe Gordon to the Cleveland Indians for pitcher Allie Reynolds. The thirty-one-year-old Gordon had hit just .210 in 1946, and MacPhail probably thought he would not recover his prewar form. In fact, Gordon did bounce back to give the Indians a few excellent seasons and help lead them to

their 1948 pennant. Nonetheless, Reynolds's eight stellar years anchoring the team's pitching staff made this an excellent deal for MacPhail. In January 1947 MacPhail signed veteran first baseman George McQuinn to take over for the disappointing Nick Etten. McQuinn was nearly thirty-seven and was coming off a poor season with the Philadelphia Athletics, but he still had one excellent season left.

In the spring of 1947 Larry MacPhail was involved in a bit of drama whose echoes would be felt throughout the season and beyond. During spring training the Yankees and Dodgers played a series of exhibition games in Havana, Cuba. After one of the contests, Dodger president Branch Rickey told the press that there were "notorious gamblers" sitting in MacPhail's box. Dodger manager Leo Durocher had been warned by Commissioner Happy Chandler about his own off-the-field associates, so Rickey, and Durocher in a subsequent newspaper column, wondered why the rules were not the same for MacPhail. The angry Yankee boss denied that he even knew the people who were sitting near him and demanded a hearing with Chandler. At the two meetings, both Durocher and Rickey apologized for their apparent mistake, and MacPhail walked over to Leo and hugged him, saying, "You've always been a great guy with me, and you always will be a great guy. Forget it buddy, it's over."[4]

Unfortunately, Commissioner Chandler did not agree, suspending Durocher for the entire 1947 season for his unnamed nefarious off-field activities (none of them related to the MacPhail matter). The Dodgers were flabbergasted, as was MacPhail, who spent most of the rest of the year trying to get Durocher reinstated. Chandler demanded that no one in the hearing talk about what went on, a demand MacPhail ignored. MacPhail had been the man most responsible for Chandler's becoming commissioner in 1945, but the Durocher decision so angered him that it effectively ended their friendship.

Meanwhile, the Yankees surged to ninety-seven wins and won the pennant fairly easily. After their dramatic World Series victory over the Dodgers, ending with a Game Seven win in Yankee Stadium on October 6, the Yankees' front office had every reason to feel satisfied with their accomplishment and their future.

Yet MacPhail's bizarre reaction to the club's victory would ultimately take over the story. Just minutes after the final game, he stormed into the team's clubhouse and announced his resignation, a decision first thought to be fueled by emotion (he was reportedly crying) and alcohol. A few hours later, MacPhail arrived at the Biltmore Hotel, in Manhattan, where the three owners were hosting a lavish "Victory Dinner." The press was waiting for him, but he angrily shouted, "Stay away or get punched." Sid Keener, of the *St. Louis Star-Times*, managed to get a few quotes. "I'm simply tired of it all," said MacPhail. "Too much worry. The critical New York press gets me down. Besides, there are a lot of guys in baseball I don't like—and don't care to associate with." He specifically mentioned Chandler and Rickey. "Well, I gave New York another championship, didn't I? And what are they saying about it around here? That I'm nothing but a big popoff. Maybe I am, but I deliver the goods, don't I?"[5]

It later came out that MacPhail had been flustered by a brief exchange with Rickey after the final game, before MacPhail entered the Yankees' locker room. MacPhail offered his hand, which Rickey took while saying, "I'm shaking hands with you because a thousand people are looking on, but I don't like you." Rickey later acknowledged this conversation.[6]

When he finally made it inside to the dinner, MacPhail only made things worse. He stumbled drunk around the dining room, alternating between bouts of sentimental crying and irrational raging. He slugged John McDonald, former traveling secretary with the Dodgers, who had made a complimentary remark about Rickey. MacPhail then accosted Weiss, who was sitting with his wife, eventually firing the Yankees' accomplished farm director. When Dan Topping tried to intervene, MacPhail shouted at his partner, "You're just a guy who was born with a silver spoon in your mouth and never made a dollar in your life." As MacPhail walked away, Topping grabbed him, saying, "Come here you. . . . I have taken all of this I am going to take." Topping forced MacPhail into an adjoining kitchen and closed the door.[7]

Mrs. MacPhail was in tears. "What's Danny doing to him?" she cried. "He's a mighty sick, nervous man." Topping emerged alone, having forced the somewhat calmer MacPhail out a side door. MacPhail returned sometime later, freshened up with neatly combed hair. He berated at least one Yankee player after his return, but the drama was largely over.[8]

Topping and Webb quickly assessed the situation and concluded that they could not leave their investment in the hands of the obviously unstable Larry MacPhail. The following day the Yankees announced Webb and Topping had bought out MacPhail's shares for $2 million. Topping was elected president, and Weiss was named general manager. "MacPhail's connection with the Yankees is ended," said Topping. MacPhail had turned his initial $250,000 investment into $2 million in less than three years, but he would never work in baseball again.

Dan Daniel, writing in the *Sporting News*, summarized the dramatic events this way: "After three years of turbulence and equivocation under the sometimes inspired, and often much less than that, administration of Col. Leland Stanford MacPhail, the Yankees have returned to quiet and the peaceful pursuit of baseball happiness."[9] The team of Webb, Topping, and Weiss would remain in place for thirteen years, capturing ten pennants and seven World Series titles.

Chapter 2. **How the 1947 Team Was Built**

Lyle Spatz

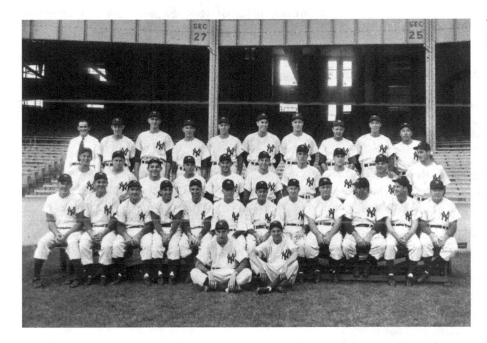

The 1947 world champion New York Yankees.

Pitchers

SPUD CHANDLER: Signed as an amateur free agent in 1932.

BILL BEVENS: Signed as an amateur free agent in 1936.

BUTCH WENSLOFF: Signed as an amateur free agent in 1936.

MEL QUEEN: Signed as an amateur free agent in 1938.

KARL DREWS: Signed as an amateur free agent in 1939.

RANDY GUMPERT: Acquired from the Philadelphia Athletics in July 1939 in a Minor League transaction.

AL LYONS: Signed as an amateur free agent in 1939.

RUGGER ARDIZOIA: Purchased from the Hollywood Stars of the Pacific Coast League (PCL) on August 13, 1940.

TOMMY BYRNE: Signed as an amateur free agent in 1940.

JOE PAGE: Signed as an amateur free agent in 1940.

FRANK SHEA: Signed as an amateur free agent in 1940.

VIC RASCHI: Signed as an amateur free agent in 1941.

DICK STARR: Signed as an amateur free agent in 1941.

BILL WIGHT: Signed as an amateur free agent in 1941.

DON JOHNSON: Signed as an amateur free agent in 1944.

ALLIE REYNOLDS: Acquired from the Cleveland Indians in a trade for second baseman Joe Gordon on October 11, 1946.

BOBO NEWSOM: Purchased from the Washington Senators on July 11, 1947.

Catchers

AARON ROBINSON: Acquired from the Snow Hill (North Carolina) Billies of the Coastal Plain League in 1938.

RALPH HOUK: Signed as an amateur free agent in 1939.

KEN SILVESTRI: Acquired from the Chicago White Sox in a trade for infielder Bill Knickerbocker on December 31, 1940.

YOGI BERRA: Signed as an amateur free agent in October 1942.

SHERM LOLLAR: Acquired, along with infielder Ray Mack, from the Cleveland Indians in a trade for pitcher Gene Bearden, pitcher Al Gettel, and outfielder Hal Peck on December 6, 1946.

Infielders

FRANK CROSETTI: Acquired from the San Francisco Seals of the Pacific Coast League on August 23, 1930, for $100,000, three Minor League players, and a player to be named; in 1931 the Yankees sent third baseman Julie Wera to San Francisco to complete the deal.

BILLY JOHNSON: Signed as an amateur free agent in 1936.

PHIL RIZZUTO: Signed as an amateur free agent in 1937.

GEORGE STIRNWEISS: Signed as an amateur free agent in 1940.

JACK PHILLIPS: Signed as an amateur free agent in 1943.

BOBBY BROWN: Signed as an amateur free agent in 1946.

RAY MACK: Acquired, along with catcher Sherm Lollar, from the Cleveland Indians in a trade for pitcher Gene Bearden, pitcher Al Gettel, and outfielder Hal Peck on December 6, 1946.

GEORGE MCQUINN: Signed as a free agent on January 25, 1947.

JOHNNY LUCADELLO: Purchased on waivers from the St. Louis Browns on March 1, 1947.

TED SEPKOWSKI: Purchased from the Cleveland Indians on June 3, 1947.

LONNY FREY: Purchased from the Chicago Cubs on June 25, 1947.

Outfielders

JOE DIMAGGIO: Acquired from the San Francisco Seals of the Pacific Coast League for five players and cash on November 21, 1934.

JOHNNY LINDELL: Signed as an amateur free agent in 1936.

TOMMY HENRICH: Signed as a free agent on April 19, 1937.

CHARLIE KELLER: Signed as an amateur free agent in 1937.

ALLIE CLARK: Signed as an amateur free agent in 1941.

FRANK COLMAN: Purchased from the Pittsburgh Pirates on June 17, 1946.

Chapter 3. The Hiring of Bucky Harris

Art Spanjer

The announcement on November 5, 1946, that Bucky Harris would manage the 1947 New York Yankees was almost a foregone conclusion. "The announcement scarcely bowled over anyone with surprise," one newspaper commented.[1] Still, the circumstances that led to the hiring were anything but mundane.

The process began early in the 1946 season. That season was a managerial turnstile for the Yankees' second-year co-owner Larry MacPhail (who was also the team's president and general manager). Joe McCarthy, who had been the manager since 1931, abruptly left in May after 35 games. He was succeeded on May 24 by fan favorite Bill Dickey, whose "managerial contract," the club said, "would run through 1947."[2] Dickey managed the team for 105 games and quit on September 12. Later it was disclosed that Dickey had never signed a contract, a detail that paved the way for his quick exit with 14 games left in the season.

Dickey's departure and the hiring of Harris had to do with both on- and off-field issues. In 1946 hundreds of baseball players were returning from World War II. Evaluating new players and reevaluating veterans took tremendous time and energy. This placed a huge burden on Major League teams' front-office and scouting staffs. Scouting was less highly developed then, with nothing like the complex, computer-driven systems of the modern baseball era. With the sudden influx of veterans, teams were pressured to assess large numbers of players in a very short time.

On the field the Yankees languished in second or third place for most of the 1946 season. The impulsive and outspoken MacPhail was strident in

New York Times columnist Arthur Daley called Harris "an eminently sound choice."

his demands that the Yankees finish no lower than second place. Predictably, Dickey and MacPhail had several rough patches during the season. Dickey threatened to quit at least four times, only to be dissuaded by MacPhail.

Then, in a surprise press conference on September 9, MacPhail introduced Stanley Raymond "Bucky" Harris as an executive hired without a title and with a vague job description. MacPhail commented to Roscoe McGowen of the *New York*

Times that he and the Yankees' farm director, George Weiss, were stretched to the limit because of the scouting burden. "Bucky will be the contact between myself and the club, doing a job that I have found neither myself or [nor] George Weiss has had time for this year."[3]

Harris was a longtime player and manager. He made his managerial debut in 1924 when the Washington Senators added field management to their second baseman's responsibilities at the astonishingly young age of twenty-seven. The Senators won the pennant and World Series in Harris's first year, earning him the sobriquet "Boy Wonder." In 1946 Harris, after twenty years of managing several teams, was the general manager of the Buffalo Bisons in the International League, a farm club of the Detroit Tigers. MacPhail had not met Harris until a couple of months before he hired him. Ed Barrow, who had preceded MacPhail as the Yankees' general manager, and Clark Griffith, owner of the Washington Senators, convinced MacPhail that Harris would fill a hole in the Yankees' organization. "'There's not a sharper, shrewder appraiser of young talent in the majors than Stanley Harris," Barrow said.[4]

When he introduced Harris at the September 9 press conference, MacPhail said he would be an executive aide hired to help in the evaluation of talent and to bolster scouting. MacPhail's first directive to Harris: "Join the Yankees, follow them around the circuit. I want you to get acquainted with the American League again."[5] Harris himself said he had no desire to return to managing, that his assignment was to be solely administrative.

Near the end of the press conference a sportswriter asked MacPhail who would manage the Yankees in 1947. MacPhail replied, "That hasn't been decided. I haven't given it any thought."[6] When Dickey was informed of MacPhail's statement, he immediately went to the Yankees' executive offices on Fifth Avenue in Manhattan. He confronted MacPhail and asked for a clarification of the president's remark, apparently to no avail. Then, early on the morning of September 12, while the Yankees were in Detroit, Dickey telephoned MacPhail and took himself out of managerial consideration for 1947.

The timing of Dickey's announcement apparently astonished MacPhail.[7] He had assumed Dickey would finish out the year. For Dickey to call him from the road, on the eve of an important series with Detroit, whom the Yankees were battling for second place, was more than MacPhail could take. The next day Dickey was gone, and Johnny Neun was named interim manager.[8] The speculation that Bucky Harris would be the 1947 manager was now growing, even though both MacPhail and Harris continued to assert that Harris's role with the Yankees would remain off the field.

Behind the scenes, though, MacPhail began to press Harris to be the manager for 1947. But the Yankees' boss was also considering another candidate, Brooklyn Dodgers manager Leo Durocher. When MacPhail was the general manager of the Dodgers before leaving to serve in World War II, Durocher was his manager, and the two had great respect for each other. MacPhail was also not fond of Branch Rickey, who had succeeded him at the helm of the Dodgers.

MacPhail and Durocher met in mid-November, but the facts are somewhat cloudy as to what took place. Durocher told the *Washington Post*, "About a month before the season ended Larry MacPhail asked to see me. I went over and he offered me the Yankee job. I told him I had a verbal agreement with Mr. Rickey and couldn't take it. That was the last I heard of it."[9]

MacPhail denied he had offered the job to Durocher. According to MacPhail, Durocher had sought out Yankees part-owner Dan Topping in early August and expressed interest in the manager's job. Then, in October, Harris, after scouting Brooklyn's playoff series with the Cardinals, recommended Durocher for the job. MacPhail took Harris's recommendation "under advisement," but five days later, on October 8, told the Yankees' board of directors he was recommending that Harris be hired.[10]

The story then turns a little strange. Apparently, Harris and MacPhail had agreed to terms on October 21 for Harris to manage the 1947 Yankees. Two days later, on the twenty-third, Harris and Dodgers coach Charlie Dressen signed contracts, and MacPhail called Durocher to inform him of the decision. MacPhail told the *New York Times* that Durocher had said he would "consider it a favor" if MacPhail could hold the announcement for a few days, to give Durocher some leverage in his negotiations with Branch Rickey over a new contract. MacPhail agreed, but called Durocher again on October 26 and told him that he "could not wait any longer."[11] Durocher and MacPhail subsequently agreed to a date of November 5 for the announcement. (Based on the previous history of their relationship, MacPhail appeared to be tweaking Rickey and the Dodgers by insinuating that he withheld the Harris announcement in order to give Durocher leverage in his negotiations with Rickey and the Dodgers.)

Durocher said he was "surprised when Dressen signed with MacPhail and hasn't heard from Dressen since."[12] Jack Hand, an Associated Press sportswriter, commented, "This situation, following on the heels of Dressen's 'jumping' the Dodgers, could be the foundation of an honest-to-goodness feud.[13] However, it should be noted that the two teams jointly announced three exhibition dates in Havana and another three to be played at Ebbets Field."[14]

Sportswriters for the most part lauded MacPhail's choice of Harris, but many criticized MacPhail's seemingly impulsive, haphazard decision-making process. *New York Times* columnist Arthur Daley called Harris "an eminently sound choice" and said he would take no "nonsense"

from MacPhail "if that impulsive character ever should try to stick his finger in the pie."[15]

There was one more twist to the saga of Harris's hiring: at the winter baseball meetings in California, even though Harris had already signed with the Yankees, the Tigers offered him their general manager position, which they termed "the job of a lifetime." Yet one has to question why the Tigers did not go after Harris earlier, when he was leaving Buffalo and not yet hired by the Yankees, especially since the Bisons were a Detroit affiliate. Harris nevertheless was forced to reemphasize to the press his commitment to the Yankees. MacPhail also jumped in to allay any rumors, telling the press that the job had been offered to Harris and he spent some period of time considering it, but ultimately rejected it.[16]

Harris's final determining factor in accepting the job as Yankees manager may have been money. It was speculated in the press that when Harris was hired as a special assistant to MacPhail, his salary was put at twenty thousand dollars, and when he was made the manager it was raised to thirty-five thousand dollars. Others also mused that once a talent like Harris was bitten by the managerial bug, the wound ran deep and a return to the position was inevitable. One sentiment everyone could agree on when it was obvious that the Yankees had something special happening in 1947: "Well, it couldn't have happened to a nicer guy."[17]

Chapter 4. Yankees Spring Training in 1947

Walter LeConte and Bill Nowlin

The spring of 1947 was one that saw the three New York–area baseball clubs range far and wide geographically. The New York Giants held their spring training in faraway Phoenix, Arizona—the first Major League club to be based in Arizona. (The Cleveland Indians moved to Tucson that same spring.) The Brooklyn Dodgers ran their exhibition season out of Havana, Cuba. The Yankees were situated once again in their usual St. Petersburg, Florida, home where, save for the war years, they had trained since 1924—but they also played five games in Puerto Rico, six games in Venezuela, and three games in Cuba.

The Yankees were not looking for a new home so much as they were looking for a return to the top of the standings. The Yanks had missed only one pennant from 1936 through 1943, and in six of those seven seasons they had won the World Series. But in 1944, 1945, and 1946, they had come in third, fourth, and third again.

The '47 Yankees had a new manager in Bucky Harris. Joe McCarthy's remarkable run of fifteen-plus seasons at the helm had ended on May 23, 1946. Bill Dickey and Johnny Neun had skippered the team through the balance of the season, but Harris was in place at the start of spring training. His coaching staff consisted of Johnny Schulte, returning for his fourteenth season, and the newly hired former Brooklyn Dodgers Red Corriden and Charlie Dressen. To round out the staff, Frankie Crosetti, a Yankee since 1932, would serve for the first time as a player-coach.

The team faced a number of decisions at the start of training, with only four positions locked in place: shortstop (Phil Rizzuto), left field (Charlie Keller), right field (Tommy Henrich), and center field (Johnny Lindell, because Joe DiMaggio was out with a heel injury).

Harris had twenty-game winner Spud Chandler, Bill Bevens, and Joe Page returning for another season, along with Allie Reynolds, acquired in a trade with the Indians. Rookies Frank "Spec" Shea and Don Johnson were poised to challenge for places in the starting rotation.

Aaron Robinson figured to retain his role as the first-string catcher, with Yogi Berra, Ralph Houk, Charlie Silvera, Gus Niarhos, and Sherman Lollar competing for the backup position.

Veteran first baseman George McQuinn had been released by the Philadelphia Athletics in January and signed by the Yankees. He took over for Nick Etten, whom the Yanks would sell to the Philadelphia Phillies the day before opening day.

Joe Gordon had been traded to the Indians for Reynolds, so second base again belonged to Snuffy Stirnweiss, who had played the position in 1944 and 1945.

With the shift of Stirnweiss to second base, the competition for the third base job was the most active one of the exhibition season. Rookie Bobby Brown and veteran Billy Johnson were pitted against each other for the position. Johnson got the nod from Bucky Harris just before the season opener.

Fifteen-year veteran Joe "Ducky" Medwick was released by the Brooklyn Dodgers in October 1946 and signed by the Yankees later that December. Although he had an impressive spring, making the final roster cut, Medwick would never play a game with the Yankees and would finish the last two seasons of his phenomenal career with the St. Louis Cardinals.

In July 1946 Yankees president Larry MacPhail had announced his team would begin spring training in San Juan, Puerto Rico, starting on February 15. There were thirty-three players in the "Caribbean contingent," although some rookies and invitees were left behind to work out under Crosetti in St. Petersburg. It was not the first time the team had spent part of spring training outside the United States; in 1946 they had spent a few days in Panama. The visit to Puerto Rico was sponsored by the Don Q distilleries.

The team flew the sixteen hundred miles from LaGuardia Airport in New York to San Juan, Puerto Rico, in a chartered Constellation, arriving on Valentine's Day. The first day of workouts saw a frustrated Harris threaten to leave the island, after a reported three thousand Puerto Rican youngsters swarmed in the outer reaches of the outfield and made off with as many as five dozen balls hit out there. He did not blame the kids for acting like kids, but decried the lack of police protection.

After a week's preparation, the Bronx Bombers played their first game on February 22 against the San Juan Senators, beating them handily, 16–3. The next day they took on Caguas in a 10:30 a.m. Sunday game and beat them, 6–5. Caguas was a team that the *New York Times* said was composed entirely of "Negro stars." The third team to challenge the Yankees was Ponce, who bombarded the visitors, 12–8. The Yanks lost again the next day, the twenty-fifth, this time in twelve innings to a team of Puerto Rican All-Stars, 7–6. The biggest news of the day was that Joe DiMaggio, who had been hobbling around on crutches following a bone-spur operation on his heel, had to return to New York for further treatment. He missed all of spring training.

There was one more game in Puerto Rico, and the Yankees prevailed over the All Stars, 8–6, thanks to a four-run outburst in the top of the ninth. The game scheduled for the twenty-seventh was rained out.

After flying to Caracas, Venezuela, the Yankees played on March 1 against the Vargas club and lost, 4–3, when Vargas scored twice in the bottom of the ninth. The major story of the day, however, was the jailing of two Vargas pitchers for refusing to pitch in the game. The two, Ed Chandler and George Brown, said they were under contract to Brooklyn and that Branch Rickey had ordered them not to play. The Yanks then ran off back-to-back wins. Ralph Houk's ninth-inning hit broke a 4–4 tie against the Magallanes team, and on March 3 they defeated the Caracas All-Stars, 9–2.

There followed three games, all in Caracas, against the Brooklyn Dodgers and all played under lights. Some ten thousand spectators saw the Yankees win the first game, 17–6, and then fall, 8–7. The deciding game of the "Venezuelan Cup" went to the Yankees, 4–0. Both teams flew to Havana; for the Dodgers it was a return to their spring-training home park at Gran Estadio de la Habana.

Three Brooklyn pitchers combined to no-hit the Yankees for nine innings, yielding one in the top of the tenth. The Dodgers got two of their five hits in the bottom of the tenth and won, 1–0. Four in the fourth gave the Yankees all they needed for a 4–1 win on March 9. When the Dodgers boarded a plane for the Panama Canal Zone on the tenth, MacPhail blasted them for walking out on the third game (which had indeed been listed in all the printed schedules and the program for the three days). The Yanks instead took on a team of Cuban All-Stars, and lost, 2–1.

Local teams from Puerto Rico, Venezuela, and Cuba had each won a game or two from the visitors, but the Yankees held an 8–6 edge in games played to this point. On March 12 the traveling team reunited with those under Crosetti's charge in St. Petersburg, and the brand-new Al Lang Field was opened with a game against the St. Louis Cardinals. The Yankees had played fourteen games on their Caribbean tour, with an 8-6 record (3-2 versus Brooklyn and 5-4 against various Caribbean clubs).

In Grapefruit League action, New York played against the reigning world champion Cardinals, the reigning American League champion Boston Red Sox, and the Cincinnati Reds, Detroit Tigers, and Philadelphia Phillies. They dropped the first four games, but finished the spring season 9-9 against those five teams.

Before breaking camp, DiMaggio had a full workout on April 3 for the first time all spring and gave his teammates a show from the batting cage. On Spud Chandler's first pitch, Joe whacked a towering shot, albeit foul. Because of his heel injury, DiMaggio would miss the first three regular-season games before his first appearance, pinch-hitting on April 19.

In early April the Yankees beat the Class Double-A Atlanta Crackers in two games at Atlanta and then beat the Class B Norfolk Tars in Virginia. In the first game at Atlanta, Yogi Berra was 5 for 6 with four runs scored and five RBIs in the 14–1 drubbing of the Crackers. In the April 7 contest at Norfolk, he was 3 for 6, with six runs batted in. His 450-foot home run over the center-field wall gave him three round-trippers in two days. If there had been an award given to the top rookie in spring camp, Yogi would have won it hands down.

The next day New York beat the Class Triple-A Orioles in Baltimore, 7–3, before ending with three games against the Dodgers, all at Ebbets Field, where they lost the first one and won the next two. In thirty-nine spring games, it was reported that the Yankees attendance was 265,130, an average of almost 6,800 per contest. Overall, the team came out of spring training in good shape to start the regular season.

Chapter 5. Yankees Involvement in the Suspension of Leo Durocher

Jeffrey Marlett

"For *what*?"

Such was Leo Durocher's first response to the news on April 9, 1947, that Commissioner Albert "Happy" Chandler had suspended him from baseball for the 1947 season.[1] The response was uncharacteristically short for Durocher, known throughout baseball for his verbal barbs. However, Commissioner Chandler had, upon pain of further suspension, requested silence from all parties involved in a series of clashes between the Brooklyn Dodgers and the New York Yankees. Chandler had fined both teams, fined a Dodgers assistant for the column he ghostwrote for a Brooklyn paper in Durocher's name, and suspended Charlie Dressen, a Yankees coach, for thirty days. Leo's suspension certainly appeared out of proportion.

The facts seem clear enough. The yearlong suspension resulted from several years of Durocher's riotous behavior. Dodgers general manager Branch Rickey once said that Durocher "possessed an infinite capacity for immediately making a bad thing worse."[2] As first a player and then a manager, Durocher had built a reputation as a big-spending, womanizing loudmouth. Routinely overextending his finances, Durocher maintained his job security with his slick fielding and fiery competitiveness. He often survived through timely and repeated interventions by his superiors. The pattern started during his playing days with the Yankees and continued during his stints with the Cincinnati Reds and the St. Louis Cardinals. Before the 1938 season, Durocher moved to Brooklyn, where he joined Larry MacPhail, the team's mercurial president (and former Rickey protégé). MacPhail named him manager before the 1939

season; nevertheless, Leo's lively gambling ways continued. This taste for the fast lane came at a cost. By 1944 Durocher had burned through two marriages, both of which had flashed brightly at first but then languished for years.

Commissioner Kenesaw Landis had warned Leo about the damage his gambling friends could do, but Landis died in November 1944 and was replaced by Chandler. In October 1946 New York papers started associating Durocher again with a minor Hollywood actor, George Raft, who knew mobsters like Lucky Luciano and Owney Madden. Nationally syndicated columnist Westbrook Pegler led the charge with three columns indicting Durocher for his fast life and criminal associations. At Rickey's request, Chandler summoned Durocher to discuss the matter, and Durocher duly apologized. Then, embodying Rickey's statement that he could make any situation worse, Leo proceeded to tell the commissioner about his burgeoning love affair with actress Laraine Day, who was still married. The news stunned Chandler, but he did not threaten Durocher with suspension. The Brooklyn Catholic Youth Organization (CYO), though, had seen enough and on March 1 withdrew its members from the Dodgers' Knothole Gang.[3]

The events that actually caused Leo's suspension came a week later. The Yankees, then owned partially by MacPhail, and the Dodgers were scheduled to play two spring-training games in Havana, Cuba. Just days before, Durocher had published a diatribe needling MacPhail (ghostwritten by Dodgers staffer Harold Parrott) in the *Brooklyn Eagle*. On March 8 Durocher spotted nightclub owner Connie Immerman and racing handicapper Memphis Engelberg sitting near MacPhail. Both men counted among those Landis and Chandler had warned Durocher to avoid. Rickey publicly echoed Leo's belief that a double standard existed: "one for Durocher and another for MacPhail."[4] The Yankees' owner then declared that Rickey and Durocher had libeled him and demanded that Chandler act.

Over the last two weeks of March Chandler organized two meetings: The first, on March 24 in Sarasota, Florida, featured all those involved — Durocher, Dressen, MacPhail, Rickey, his assistant Arthur Mann, and the Dodgers' legal representative, Walter O'Malley. A second meeting, four days later in St. Petersburg, included MacPhail, Yankees assistant Arthur Patterson, Rickey, Mann, and O'Malley.

Chandler ran the proceedings, asking most of the questions. Durocher noted that the "trial" bore little resemblance to constitutional freedoms. Patterson noticeably dodged Chandler's question about the source of Engelberg's and Immerman's tickets. After the second meeting, Chandler casually asked Rickey, "How much would it hurt you folks to have your fellow out of baseball?" Rickey was astonished, but still thought the commissioner was bluffing. The Dodgers expected that Leo might receive a minor fine and perhaps a short suspension. The yearlong suspension left them flabbergasted.[5]

Two figures provide the connections between the Yankees and Durocher's suspension: Charlie Dressen and Larry MacPhail. Both shared relationships and character traits with Durocher. In 1982 Red Barber wrote, "Try to untangle Durocher from either Rickey or MacPhail and it's no story."[6] Barber could easily have added Dressen to the tangle of clashing personalities and jealousies. Like Durocher, Dressen was a diminutive, working-class Catholic. Both Dressen and Durocher enjoyed sporting pastimes like cards — especially bridge — and betting on horses. Consequently, both tended to manage their baseball teams with a healthy dose of hunch playing and intuition. Finally, Dressen and Durocher knew each other quite well professionally. The two played together for two seasons in Cincinnati (1930 and 1931). They reunited in Brooklyn in 1939 when Durocher, in one of his first acts as Dodgers manager, named Dressen as one of his assistants.[7]

Nonetheless, Dressen initiated Yankee involvement in what would become Leo's suspended season. In September 1946 he gave Rickey a verbal commitment to return to the Dodgers for the next season. Two months later he and another Dodgers coach, Red Corriden, joined the Yankees as coaches for new manager Bucky Harris. Rickey and Dressen did not get along well, largely because of Dressen's gambling. Rickey even briefly fired Dressen as punishment in 1943, only to rehire him a few months later. Dressen tired of such lessons and rejoined MacPhail. Dressen's culpability led to his own thirty-day suspension.

But it was MacPhail who played a direct and, in the eyes of Brooklyn fans, malicious role in securing Durocher's yearlong suspension. MacPhail matched Durocher's panache and dramatic flair. He was "the swashbuckling marauder, dressed to the nines in expensive but garishly loud suits . . . who thought his day was not complete unless he had done something worthy of mention in the press." MacPhail had characteristically alienated three managers (Joe McCarthy, Bill Dickey, and Johnny Neun) in the 1946 season, so he needed a replacement. Rumors simmered that he had even approached Durocher during the season. In November he finally persuaded Bucky Harris, the former Washington Senators, Detroit Tigers, Boston Red Sox, and Philadelphia Phillies field boss, to take control.[8]

MacPhail's blustery entrepreneurship — familiar to fans of all the teams he had owned — set the stage. Contacting Durocher midseason would have constituted tampering, a suspension-meriting offense. Brooklyn fans were certainly accustomed to Durocher-MacPhail spats, but these were almost always patched up within a day. Now MacPhail had gone too far. Public protests by the Yankees' owner himself that he had not intended Leo's suspension did not help. Making things worse was the widespread belief that Chandler owed MacPhail a favor for winning him the commissionership.[9]

Consequently, Chandler's own position in the Durocher maelstrom underwent intense scrutiny. A Brooklyn policeman mused that Chandler must have possessed special testimonial evidence; otherwise, "how could he do such a thing?" A Brooklyn bartender exemplified the extent of the borough's sense of injury: "We had bad teams until Durocher came along. Lippy put Brooklyn on the map all over the world and that's no way to treat a man who does that."[10] *New York Times* columnist Arthur Daley argued that Chandler had reprimanded the wrong man. "The entire business was so childish as to be ridiculous. The unhappy Happy should have spanked them all and sent Rickey and MacPhail packing off to bed without their suppers."[11]

Chandler had misgauged the combative atmosphere of New York's sports and media culture. Pegler's 1946 columns certainly stirred up controversy. Pegler had earned his muckraking credentials legitimately. He won the 1941 Pulitzer Prize for uncovering shady union practices, and in 1951 he was the first to name Bill "Mr. Big" McCormack as the crime boss controlling New Jersey's shipping ports.[12] Nevertheless, within New York's fevered sports and media climate, Pegler was but one, albeit widely read, voice. Years later Durocher himself said, "If a man dropped down from Mars and read nothing except Pegler's columns for a month, he couldn't help but believe the two great enemies of the Republic were Eleanor Roosevelt and Frank Sinatra."[13] From Chandler's perspective, though, Pegler's work ignited the notion to remove Durocher.

Likewise, Chandler's claimed communica-tion with U.S. Supreme Court justice Frank Murphy seems unfounded. During the two late-March "trial" days, Chandler mentioned that "a big man" in Washington had read Pegler's columns and then wrote to demand Durocher's lifelong suspension. This turned out to be Murphy.[14] Two Brooklyn Catholic priests, Vincent J. Powell and Edward Lodge Curran, had spearheaded the Brooklyn CYO's opposition to Durocher, so Murphy's call for suspension did not portend well for Leo. Harold Parrott went so far as to blame Walter O'Malley, whose connections among Brooklyn's Catholics could have stopped the witch hunt.[15]

However, the Catholic-conspiracy theme seems dubious. Murphy's most meticulous biographer does not focus on sports at all, even on an explosive character like Durocher.[16] Furthermore, attempts to see collusion between Murphy and the Brooklyn diocese overlook Murphy's own ambivalence toward his church's clergy. Though certainly devout, Murphy also exhibited an independent streak counter to the then stereotypical "pray, pay, obey" image of Roman Catholics.[17] Furthermore, presuming that Murphy did in fact contact Chandler, connecting the judge to Pegler in anything other than timing lacks evidence. Pegler and Murphy might have indeed both condemned Durocher's behavior, but only Chandler melded their separate concerns into a singular moral argument. For his own part, Durocher claimed that Murphy soon distanced himself from Chandler's claim.[18]

Almost immediately after the news of Durocher's suspension broke, Red Smith of the *New York Herald-Tribune* wrote, "As baseball commissioner charged with administration of the national game, Chandler works for the people, the millions of baseball fans in the land. He does not, whatever his decisions may suggest and whatever his own opinion in the matter may be, work for Larry MacPhail."[19]

Chandler's demand for absolute silence from the event's participants provided the stigmatization necessary to fuel conspiratorial thinking. In Smith's column the MacPhail-Chandler relationship provided the real reason for Durocher's suspension, not Chandler's official conclusions. Chandler's refusal to publicize his evidence indicated fear and possibly even guilt, argued Smith. Baseball fans deserved better, he said. "They have a right to study the evidence which convinced Chandler that Durocher was guilty and MacPhail innocent of conduct detrimental to baseball. The Brooklyn club, as defendant in the case, has a right to have that evidence made public."[20] Arthur Daley agreed: "If the Flatbush Faithful mutter bitterly today 'We wuz robbed,' their grief is understandable."[21] Some Brooklyn fans even burned Chandler in effigy. The sentiment did not die quickly. In late April, before celebrating Babe Ruth Day, Chandler had to stare down an initially hostile crowd at Yankee Stadium. Sportswriters in other Major League cities, though not Durocher fans, argued that the punishment went too far.[22] Fifteen years after the suspension, columnists still accepted Chandler's guilt in the matter. Writing from Los Angeles, Jim Murray reminisced that Durocher "got set down one whole year just for standing next to a gambler. Baseball paid him off on the q.t. because the action was as illegal as lynching and everyone knew it but the commissioner, Happy Chandler, who had read one too many chapters of the life of Judge Landis."[23]

However, other interpretations have detected conspiracy behind Durocher's suspension from the increasingly bitter relationship between Rickey and MacPhail. Peter Golenbock dates the conflict to spring training 1939 when Durocher started Pete Reiser, then a Minor Leaguer whom MacPhail had agreed to "hide" as a favor for Rickey (an offense worthy of suspension itself), when Rickey was still running the Cardinals. Rickey accused MacPhail of reneging on their secret deal and, in 1942, believed MacPhail had ruined Reiser's once promising career.[24]

Geography and demographics also contributed to conspiratorial thinking behind Durocher's suspension. Within New York's five boroughs, Brooklyn stood out as a rough-hewn also-ran. A strident antitriumphalism thus quickly emerged among the borough and its team's fans. In 1947 MacPhail, who had created Durocher's pennant winner in 1941, now stood victorious on the other side. Along the way he had swiped away Dressen. Durocher's suspension seemed the pinnacle of MacPhail's perfidies—all committed with the hated crosstown rival Yankees. Rickey was so distraught by the loss that, when confronted by a jubilant MacPhail after Game Seven, he broke all ties, severing a professional relationship that dated to 1930. MacPhail then went famously on a drunken binge wherein he retired from baseball, fired Yankees executive George Weiss, and scuffled with his fellow team owners.[25]

Forty years later Durocher still harbored animosity, refusing even to speak Chandler's name when interviewed. Durocher indicated that although he maintained his silence publicly, he repeatedly chewed off Chandler's ears over the telephone. In Leo's view his suspension's cause, if it had any at all, rested solely with the commissioner.[26]

As Leo himself said of MacPhail, "He did things, and when you do things, other things, unexpected things, are always happening around you."[27] Something was bound to happen, and it did. But Durocher and MacPhail had accepted each other's apologies in the March 24, 1947, meeting, so in their minds the matter was settled. The unexpected thing, Leo's suspension, came from Chandler, whose appointment MacPhail orchestrated.

Most figures involved suspected Durocher would return to baseball, which he certainly did. Harold Parrott asserted that the manager "led a charmed life, walking the tightrope across problems with women, money, umpires, and Unhappy Chandler."[28]

Chapter 6. **Bucky Harris**

John Contois

The New York Yankees of 1946 had many of the same stars who made them the dominant team of the pre–World War II years, but they finished in third place, seventeen games behind the Boston Red Sox, under three different managers. After the season, Bucky Harris, an experienced and well-traveled skipper, was brought in to lead the team in 1947. Harris had previously managed in Washington, Detroit, Boston, and Philadelphia, but after his success with the Senators in his first two seasons, he had a sub-.500 record as skipper. Despite the losing record, Harris was well respected among his peers and his players, with a reputation as a smart and savvy manager.

Harris first earned fame as the "boy manager" of the 1924 Washington Senators. Washington had failed to field a competitive team through a succession of managers until owner Clark Griffith boldly named the twenty-seven-year-old second baseman with five years of Major League playing experience, but none as a manager, to lead the team. The Senators won the pennant and the World Series in his first year and repeated as pennant winner the next year.

Stanley Raymond Harris, son of Thomas Harris, a native of Wales, and Catherine (Rupp) Harris, was born on November 8, 1896, in Port Jervis, New York, an area where New York, Pennsylvania, and New Jersey meet. His father was a coal miner for the Pennsylvania Coal Company and also worked at various times as a detective for the Erie Railroad, a patrolman for the Port Jervis Police Department, a police inspector for the Lackawanna and Western Railroad, and a police magistrate.

Bucky Harris led the Yankees to the American League pennant and victory over the Brooklyn Dodgers in the 1947 World Series, earning him the Manager of the Year Award.

Stanley was raised in Pittston, Pennsylvania, near Scranton. Brother Merle, seven years older, was a Minor League player. When Stanley was thirteen years old his father abandoned the family, and young Stanley quit school to help his mother. A neighbor, W. P. Jennings, superintendent of a Pennsylvania Coal Company mine, gave him a job separating coal and slate. He worked nine hours a day for twelve cents an hour. It was hazardous work; accidents were not uncommon, with limbs getting caught and mashed by the crushing and sorting machines. After work he played baseball with other youngsters until dark, usually with a ball made by winding string around a rubber core and covering it with tape.

After six months Stanley became an office boy at the Butler Colliery for less pay but with a better chance for promotion. The following year he was promoted to assistant weigh master, tasked with keeping a check on the coal leaving the colliery. He was now earning $9.72 a week as a fourteen-year-old, and even though he weighed only about 100 pounds, he still yearned to become a professional ballplayer like brother Merle. He played basketball during the winter to keep in shape and build up his strength. There he earned his lifelong nickname. "I had a couple of players on my back in a rough game," he said. "When I shook them off and shot a basket [a friend] said I bucked like a tough little bronco."[1]

Still just fourteen, Harris earned a chance to play in the semipro Suburban League for $2 a game. He was the youngest player in the league and said in an autobiography written in 1925 that it was not talent that earned him the opportunity: "They were short on infielders, ability didn't turn the trick." But he found a mentor in another player, Tony Walsh, who worked with him to improve his game.

In 1916 Harris was invited to play for Scranton of the New York State League in an exhibition game against the Yankees. Manager Bill Coughlin put him in at third base for the last four innings of the game. Coughlin then offered Harris $125 a month—more than a year's salary in the mines—to play for Scranton, but the Detroit Tigers swooped in, signed him, and sent him to training camp in Waxahachie, Texas, and then to the Muskegon (Michigan) Reds of the Central League. He was released, re-signed when his replacement fared no better, and released again after finishing the season with a .166 batting average in 169 at bats and a poor fielding percentage.

In 1917 Harris played in sixteen games for Norfolk in the Virginia League before the league disbanded after the United States entered World War I. He played as a semipro again for a short while and then joined the Reading (Pennsylvania) Pretzels of the Class B New York State League. Manager George Wiltse thought he was hiring Merle but gave Bucky the opportunity to play, and Bucky played in seventy-five games, hitting .250. When the season was over, he went back to work in the mines.

The next year Harris played with the Buffalo Bisons in the International League. He still weighed only about 130 pounds, but he hit a respectable .241. After the season Harris joined the Baltimore Dry Dock Club, an exhibition team made up of Major and Minor Leaguers, and the advice he received from the veterans on the team helped him improve at the plate and in the field. He returned to Buffalo for the 1919 season, became a fixture at second base, and batted .282. Harris had a tryout at the Polo Grounds in front of New York Giants manager John McGraw. "Evidently I didn't make much of an impression," Harris recalled.[2] (The next time they met was in the 1924 World Series.)

Harris did, however, impress Senators scout Joe Engel. When playing a game for the Bisons in Binghamton, he was hit in the hand by a line drive, but played through the pain. Engel recommended him to Griffith, the club owner. Griffith went to see for himself, and the Senators purchased Harris's contract for $4,500. Harris made his debut on August 28, 1919, getting a single off the Yankees' Carl Mays in his first at bat to drive in two runs. Harris was still in pain, and X-rays showed that his hand was broken in three places. After eight games, he was done for the year.

After the season Harris played basketball to keep in shape. He went to spring training in 1920, competing to keep the second base job, and he

JOHN CONTOIS

worked hard to correct his weaknesses, the double-play pivot and getting under pop flys. He won the job and by going 4 for 4 on the last day of the season finished at an even .300. In 1921 he finished with a .289 average. The following season his average slipped to .269, but he rebounded in 1923, hitting .282.

Harris led the league in getting hit by pitches for three consecutive years starting in 1920, but it was in the field where he really earned his pay. After placing second in 1921 in putouts among American League second basemen, Bucky led the league in 1922 and 1923. He also ranked in the top three for assists and in the top five for fielding percentages for 1921–23, despite committing thirty or more errors a season. Harris simply got to more balls than just about anyone else.

After the 1923 season Griffith, who had tried three different managers in the last three seasons, fired the latest entrant, Donie Bush, and gave the job to Harris at a salary of $9,000. At twenty-seven he became the youngest noninterim Major League manager to that point; he was also the second-youngest starter on the team. (As of 2012 Lou Boudreau was the youngest manager, signing on to lead the Cleveland Indians in 1941 at the age of twenty-four.) Griffith said he had Harris in mind as a "manager in the making" for several years. "You're only a kid, as managers go, but I'm gambling on you having the right stuff," he told Bucky.[3]

Harris was a hardworking manager. In spring training he was diligent in drilling the team on fundamentals. He let the new players know what was expected of them, and he learned the strengths and weaknesses of all his players. He was proud that they had learned to work well together and that there was no dissension. And there was no interference from Griffith—this was Bucky's team.

Harris showed a gift for strategy and for handling his pitchers. Before spring training ended he sent Walter Johnson home to prepare for opening day. He decided that he would not be afraid to pull his starting pitchers when they were hit hard or if they did not have their best stuff, a change from the standard practice at the time. He had faith in his relief pitchers and made Firpo Marberry a closer, long before this practice became fashionable. (Marberry relieved in thirty-six games that season and finished thirty-one.) Despite the preseason predictions of a second-division finish, the Senators were contending by June, and the players' confidence grew. The Senators, who had finished under .500 the season before, won their first pennant, edging the Yankees by two games.

The World Series cemented Harris's reputation as a shrewd manager. Thirty-six-year-old Walter Johnson, who had led the league in victories, strikeouts, and earned run average (ERA), started Game One, but the Senators fell 4–3 in twelve innings to the Giants. By Game Five, Johnson's next start, with the teams tied at two wins each, Johnson was hit hard with a 6–2 defeat. For Johnson, playing in his first World Series after eighteen years in the big leagues, the losses were heartbreaking. But Harris knew that Johnson was still a great pitcher and gave him another chance in Game Seven—only not as the starter.

Harris planned to start right-hander Curley Ogden, but let him pitch to only one batter, then substitute left-hander George Mogridge. This would cause John McGraw to switch to his right-handed batting order and bench Bill Terry, whom Harris considered the Giants' most dangerous hitter. McGraw did pull Terry, in the sixth inning, and thus Terry's replacement, right-handed-hitting Irish Meusel, batted in the ninth inning against Walter Johnson with two on and two out, and grounded out.

Ogden struck out Lindstrom to start the game. Harris let him face Frankie Frisch, but he walked Frisch and was replaced by Mogridge. Mogridge pitched well until the sixth inning, when Marberry relieved him. Harris tied the score in the eighth inning with a bases-loaded single. (Earlier in the game he had hit his second home run of the Series.) In the ninth inning Harris called in Walter Johnson for one more appearance. Johnson gave up a one-out triple to Frisch, but he struck out George Kelly and got Meusel to ground out. Johnson pitched four scoreless innings, and the Senators won in the bottom of the twelfth. Harris had helped win the Series with his head and his bat, despite the Senators' being outhit and out-fielded by McGraw's Giants. Harris hit .333 and drove in seven runs with two home runs, as many home runs as he would hit in any single season. Harris became the youngest manager to win a World Series.

Bucky's success as the young player-manager of the Senators endeared him not only to the Washington faithful, but to Washington's young socialites as well. He met Mary Elizabeth Sutherland, daughter of a former Senator from West Virginia, and they married in 1926. The Harrises bought a home on Wyoming Avenue, in Washington's upscale Northwest section. They had three children: Stanley, Richard, and Sally. The couple was divorced in 1951.

The Senators repeated as American League champions in 1925, but lost a hard-fought World Series in seven games to the Pittsburgh Pirates. Harris's first losing season as a manager came in 1928, and after the season he was traded to Detroit and named the Tigers' manager. By this time he was almost exclusively a bench manager. In his five seasons with Detroit the team never finished higher than fifth. He resigned on September 23, 1933, after a Tigers victory over the Browns. Frank Navin, president of the Tigers, tried to dissuade him, but Harris would not be moved. Harris explained to the press that he felt someone else could perhaps do a better job, and he wanted to be fair to Navin. "Perhaps he [his successor] can do better," Harris said. "I am not going to sit around and blame the breaks," he continued. "I dislike to sever my connections with the Tigers, but under the circumstances feel that it is the only fair thing to do."

In 1934 Harris managed the Boston Red Sox, who were in full rebuilding mode under new owner Tom Yawkey, to a fourth-place finish. The next season Harris returned to Washington to lead the Senators for eight more seasons, never finishing higher than fourth. In 1943 he signed on as manager of the National League's perennial losers, the Philadelphia Phillies. Phillies owner William D. Cox fired Harris less than two months into the season. So popular was he with his players that they threatened to strike when he was fired. (After he was fired Harris told reporters that Cox had been placing bets on Phillies games. Cox was forced to resign and slapped with a lifetime ban from baseball.)

In 1944 and 1945 Harris served as manager and general manager for Buffalo, a Detroit Tigers affiliate, in the International League, before returning to the Majors in 1947 with the Yankees. He led New York to the American League pennant and victory over the Brooklyn Dodgers in the World Series, for which he received his second Manager of the Year Award. In 1948 the Yankees finished third despite a 94-60 record, and Harris was fired at the end of the year.

He managed San Diego of the Pacific Coast League in 1949, before returning to manage the Senators (1950–54) and the Tigers (1955–56), but with little success. Harris quipped of his three stints as manager in Washington, "Only Franklin D. Roosevelt had more terms than I did in Washington." He was remembered as a popular and knowledgeable manager who brought out the best in his players. Joe DiMaggio said, "If you can't play for Bucky, you don't belong in the major leagues." Goose Goslin called him "the best manager I ever played for."[4]

Harris had a career Major League batting average of .274. In 1,253 games at second base, he led the American League in putouts four times and in double plays five straight times (1921–25). In twenty-nine years as a manager he won 2,158 games and lost 2,219. With two World Series victories and the respect of his peers, he was voted into the Baseball Hall of Fame by the Veterans Committee in 1975. Harris will be remembered as a scrappy ballplayer known for his great defense, his hard-nosed play, his base-running skills, getting hit by pitches, and for his clutch hitting in the 1924 World Series. As of 2012 only Connie Mack, Tony LaRussa, John McGraw, and Bobby Cox had managed more games than Harris, and he ranked seventh all-time in managerial victories and third in losses.

From 1956 to 1960 Harris was assistant general manager and then general manager of the Boston Red Sox, and he finished his baseball career as a scout with the Chicago White Sox and then as a special assistant with the expansion Washington Senators of the 1960s.

In 1954, as manager of the Senators, Harris put Carlos Paula, a black Cuban, on the roster as the first black Senator. Harris was not an activist; he appeared to be motivated to field the best team possible, regardless of color. When Pumpsie Green became the first black player for the Red Sox in 1959, Bucky was the general manager.

Harris died on his birthday, November 8, 1977, at the age of eighty-one, of Parkinson's disease. Bucky, whose second wife, Marie, deserted him when he became seriously ill, is buried at German Protestant Cemetery in Hughestown, Pennsylvania.

Chapter 7. Charlie Dressen

Mark Stewart

Although common wisdom dictates that baseball games are won with bats, balls, and gloves, Charlie Dressen believed until his dying breath that any game could be won with brains. Well, any game could be won with *his* brains. And it is not hard to see why. Few field leaders had the percentages figured better than Dressen, he believed, and no one could match the sheer volume of retrievable information he accumulated during his five decades in baseball.

Charles Walter Dressen was born on September 20, 1894, in Decatur, Illinois.[1] He was the oldest of three children born to Phillip and Kate (Driscoll) Dressen.[2] As a young man he loved to race horses and for a time he considered becoming a jockey. His sharp mind and quick reflexes made him a standout in baseball and football, despite his small stature; he stood five feet five and weighed less than 150 pounds. While working as a switchman for the Wabash Railroad, he played for various football and baseball teams for whatever they were paying. The going rate to have him pitch was $7.50 a game. His arm was not quite good enough to impress the scouts, but his hitting and fielding were.

The right-handed batting and throwing Dressen's first organized baseball contract was a Minor League deal with the 1919 Moline (Illinois) Plowboys of the Class B Three-I League. He got into forty-two games with the Plowboys, playing mostly at second base. He returned to the Three-I League in 1920, this time as a member of the Peoria (Illinois) Tractors.

After the baseball season concluded Dressen returned to Decatur, where George Halas and

Charlie Dressen broke a cardinal rule of baseball by signing his 1947 Yankees contract while still an employee of the Brooklyn Dodgers.

Dutch Sternaman recruited him to play for the A. E. Staley Food Starch Company football team. He appeared in four league games in 1920 for the Staleys, a precursor of the Chicago Bears. Returning to Peoria in 1921, Dressen, who had played almost exclusively in the outfield in 1920, was shifted to third base. Toward the end of the season, he moved up to the St. Paul Saints of the American Association.

Dressen was the Saints' starting third baseman from 1922 through 1924, batting more than .300 all three years. His breakout season was 1923, when he led the club with 71 extra-base hits, including 50 doubles and 12 home runs.

After the 1922 and 1923 seasons, Dressen picked up extra cash playing pro football. He joined the Racine (Wisconsin) Legion and played quarterback for the club in seven games in 1922, running for two touchdowns. Dressen played one game for Racine in 1923, but apparently determined his future was in baseball, not football, and quit the club.

Dressen's instincts were correct. His average soared to .346 in 1924, and he led the Saints in virtually every offensive category, including RBIS with 151. That led the Cincinnati Reds to purchase his contract and send St. Paul a couple of Minor Leaguers to seal the deal.

Dressen made his big-league debut as a pinch hitter on April 17, 1925, and had his first hit nine days later, against Wilbur Cooper of the Cubs. He saw action at second, third, and the outfield for the third-place Reds, batting .274 in seventy-six games. A month into the 1926 season, Dressen took over at third base. He batted .266 and led the National League in assists at third base.

Dressen had his finest big-league season in 1927, batting .292 and finishing among the league leaders in doubles, triples, and walks. But by 1929 his average had dipped to .244, and in 1930 he lost his starting job to young Tony Cuccinello. He split most of 1931 between the Minor League Baltimore Orioles and Minneapolis Millers. He knew he was nearing the end of the line; unlike most ballplayers, however, he was prepared.

In 1932 Dressen was essentially without a job. When he learned in June that the Nashville Volunteers of the Class A Southern Association were in need of a new manager, he borrowed train fare from a friend and made Vols owner Fay Murray an offer he could not refuse. There were seventy-seven games left on the schedule. If Dressen failed to win

more than half of the remaining contests, Murray would not owe him a dime.

On the final day of the season, Nashville's record under Dressen stood at 38-38. Playing the Crackers in Atlanta, the Vols fell behind in the early innings. They rallied to win, so Dressen got paid. He also got a one-year deal to manage the club and play third base in 1933. It was as manager of the Vols that he earned a reputation for an encyclopedic knowledge of player tendencies and situational statistics.

In early September 1933, Dressen left the Vols to play third base for the New York Giants, with whom Nashville had a working arrangement. The Giants' third baseman, Johnny Vergez, had been stricken with appendicitis. Dressen played in sixteen games for the pennant-winning Giants, batting .222.

He was back managing Nashville in 1934, when in July, with the Reds twenty-nine games under .500, player-manager Bob O'Farrell was dealt to the Cubs. Dressen was offered the job. He quit his post at Nashville and took the managerial reins in Cincinnati. He did not do much better than O'Farrell, as the Reds finished in last place.

Dressen piloted Cincinnati to a sixth-place finish in 1935 and a fifth-place finish in 1936. In 1937 the Reds tumbled into the cellar again, and when Dressen demanded to know his status for 1938, he was let go with a month left in the season. Consequently, he returned to Nashville, now a Dodgers affiliate in '38, and guided the team to a second-place finish. Larry MacPhail, former Reds general manager and now in a similar role in Brooklyn, added Dressen to Leo Durocher's staff as a third base coach for 1939.

The 1939 Dodgers were a ball club on the rise. After a seventh-place finish in 1938, the 1939 team finished third, followed by a second-place finish in 1940. In 1941 the Dodgers outlasted the St. Louis Cardinals in a pennant race that went down to the wire. Durocher called the shots for this remarkable club, but rarely without input from Dressen. Although the Yankees defeated the Dodgers in the World Series, the news was not all bad for Charlie. After the season he married the former Ruth Sinclair.

Branch Rickey, who replaced MacPhail as Brooklyn's president after the 1942 season, apparently did not appreciate Dressen's fondness for horse racing. When Charlie refused to swear off gambling, Rickey fired him in November 1942. In July 1943, with Dressen staying away from the track, Rickey rehired him, and he remained with the Dodgers through the 1946 season.

After returning from military duty, MacPhail came into Dressen's life for a third time. He bought a piece of the Yankees and, in his dual role as general manager and president, immediately cast his eye on the Dodgers' coaching staff. MacPhail lured Dressen and Red Corriden to the Bronx, where the team's new manager, Bucky Harris, was trying to get the Yankees back on the pennant-winning track.

Dressen broke a cardinal rule of baseball, however, by signing his Yankees contract while still a Dodgers employee. That slip-up earned him a thirty-day suspension and one-twelfth of his salary.

One of Dressen's special talents was his ability to steal opponents' signs. From his vantage point on the coaching lines he was often able to make out how many fingers the catcher was putting down and then inconspicuously relay this information to the batter as the pitcher began his windup. This could be risky to the batter if the battery-mates became suspicious, particularly in the days before batting helmets. Once when Joe DiMaggio was at the plate, Dressen flashed the sign for a curve. The pitch was a fastball up and in; only DiMaggio's catlike reflexes enabled him to avoid a beaning. He cursed Charlie after the at bat and ignored his signs thereafter.

Besides manning the coaching box at third,

Dressen doubled as pitching coach. He set down a few rules and schedules and went over the hitters before each series, but did not offer much in the way of technical assistance. (Some pitchers thought he offered too much.) Dressen took an interest in some of the hitters, too, though there again his advice did not sit well with many of them.

The Yankees won the pennant and World Series in 1947. Charlie Dressen thus became the answer to a baseball trivia question: *Who was the only man in uniform for the city's three baseball teams—the Yankees, Dodgers, and Giants—when they clinched a pennant?*

The Bronx Bombers faltered in 1948, finishing behind the Indians and Red Sox. Dressen's protector, Larry MacPhail, sold his share in the team, so it came as no surprise when Charlie was let go by general manager George Weiss, who never really considered him "Yankee material." Harris was shown the door, too. The new hire was Casey Stengel, with Dressen grabbing the managing job Stengel left, with the Oakland Oaks of the Pacific Coast League. Dressen guided the Oaks to a second-place finish in 1949 and a PCL pennant in 1950.

That winter the call came from Brooklyn again. This time the Dodgers wanted Dressen to be their manager. He inherited one of the most talented rosters in National League history, one that included Gil Hodges, Jackie Robinson, Pee Wee Reese, Carl Furillo, Duke Snider, Roy Campanella, Don Newcombe, Preacher Roe, and Carl Erskine.

Dressen did much of his managing from the third base coaching box with the 1951 Dodgers. Under his guidance the team held a double-digit lead over the second-place Giants in mid-August. Then things began to tighten up. The Giants came roaring back, and, under pressure, the Dodgers dropped six of their last ten to finish the regular season in a first-place tie. A best-of-three playoff ensued, with a coin flip to determine who would get the rubber game if necessary. The Dodgers won, and Dressen opted to play the opener in Ebbets Field, giving the Giants the next two at the Polo Grounds.

After the Giants won Game One, behind Jim Hearn's five-hitter, the Dodgers came back to win Game Two, 10–0. The deciding game remains perhaps the most famous ever played. Newcombe held the Giants in check for eight innings, and the Dodgers were up 4–1 with three outs to go. The Giants scored a run against Newcombe and had two men on when Dressen called coach Clyde Sukeforth in the bullpen. Ralph Branca and Erskine were warming up. Sukeforth reported that Erskine had just bounced a curve. Despite the fact that the batter, Bobby Thomson, had homered off Branca in Game One, Dressen chose him to close out the Giants. The rest is history.

Dressen had better luck in 1952 and 1953. The Dodgers won the pennant both seasons. The '52 team won 96 games—exactly the number Dressen predicted prior to the start of the campaign. The '53 team won 105 games and finished 13 games ahead of the second-place Milwaukee Braves. The only smudges on Dressen's record of achievement in 1952 and 1953 were World Series losses to the Yankees—in 7 games the first year and in 6 the next.

Dressen had been working on one-year contracts with the Dodgers. During the off-season, he and Ruth composed a letter to Dodgers owner Walter O'Malley explaining why he deserved a three-year deal. O'Malley's response was that the Dodgers had probably paid more people for not managing than any other club in baseball, so it was one year or forget about it. When Dressen did not back down, O'Malley called a press conference to announce the hiring of Walter Alston as the team's new skipper.

Brick Laws, owner of the Oakland Oaks, snapped up Dressen to manage his club in 1954. He led Oakland to a third-place finish and in 1955 was hired to replace his old boss Bucky Harris as

skipper of the Washington Senators. The Nats lost 101 games in 1955 and 95 in 1957. Twenty games into the 1957 season, Dressen was relieved of his duties and replaced by Cookie Lavagetto.

In 1958 Dressen returned to the Dodgers for a third go-round, this time as a member of Alston's coaching staff. He helped preside over the move to Los Angeles, which resulted in a surprising World Series championship in 1959. Hot off this success, Dressen was hired by the Braves as their manager for the 1960 season. Milwaukee boasted two of baseball's most productive sluggers in Eddie Mathews and Hank Aaron and an ageless pitching ace in Warren Spahn. But the supporting players who helped the Braves win pennants in 1957 and 1958 were fading, and the farm system had little to offer. Milwaukee finished second in 1960 under Charlie. In 1961, with the team out of the pennant race by September, he was replaced by Birdie Tebbetts.

Dressen stayed with the Braves as a Minor League manager, taking over the Toronto Maple Leafs in 1962. The Leafs missed the pennant by 2½ games—quite an improvement from 1961, when they were a sub-.500 ball club. The Braves were not offering a big-league job in 1963, so Dressen went back to the Dodgers a fourth time and agreed to scout for them.

That job lasted until mid-June, when Dressen got a call from the Detroit Tigers to replace Bob Scheffing. In their final 102 games Detroit went 55-47. In 1964 the Tigers went 85-77 and returned to the first division with a fourth-place finish.

During spring training in 1965, Dressen suffered a heart attack. Bob Swift took over the Tigers for 42 games before Dressen felt well enough to return. Detroit finished fourth again. They got off to a 5-0 start in 1966, but a month into the season Dressen had a second heart attack. While recuperating he got a kidney infection and subsequently had a third, this time fatal, heart attack. He died on August 10, 1966.

Charlie Dressen's overall record as a Major League manager with five teams was 1,008-973. He managed two pennant winners, played for a world champion with the 1933 Giants, and coached on World Series winners in 1947 with the Yankees and in 1959 with the Los Angeles Dodgers. As a player Charlie was active in seven big-league seasons, was a regular for four years, and had a career batting mark of .272.

Although he was a nonstop talker and supreme egotist, Dressen was the flesh-and-blood epitome of a baseball lifer — single-minded, resilient, and always thinking three steps ahead.

Chapter 8. **Red Corriden**

C. Paul Rogers III

John Michael "Red" Corriden, the first base coach for the 1947 New York Yankees, was a baseball lifer. From 1908 until he retired from baseball after the 1958 season, a span of fifty-one years, Corriden served as a player, coach, manager, and scout.

The 1947 season was Corriden's first as a Yankees coach. He was brought to New York by new manager Bucky Harris after a six-year stay as a Brooklyn Dodgers coach under Leo Durocher. His role tended to be something of a father confessor, and he always encouraged the players, referring to everyone as "buddy boy." As the first base coach, his chatter was continuous. "Come on down to see me, buddy boy," he would yell to the batter. "I ain't mad at you. And when you get down here, please turn to your left. Nothing on your right but a lollypop stand."[1] Not surprisingly, the players affectionately called him Lollypop.

Corriden could, however, deliver a message rather directly when needed. Bobby Brown, a rookie with the '47 Yankees, recalled that early in the year Corriden said to him, "Buddy boy, lay off that high pitch. All you're doing is hitting fly balls to the warning track." Brown did not take Corriden's advice, and about ten days later Corriden again approached him, saying, "You're still hitting that high pitch. If you keep it up, you'll be hitting it in Newark."[2] At that point Brown got the message and started laying off the high ones.

Corriden was born on September 4, 1887, in Logansport, Indiana, where he was raised and attended elementary and high school. His parents were Michael B. and Catherine A. (Klein) Corriden. He grew up playing baseball and for a number of years had a paper route in Logansport,

In 1947 the Yankees hired Red Corriden away from the Dodgers to coach at first base.

which included the parents of future baseball commissioner Kenesaw Mountain Landis. One Christmas Eve Landis's mother summoned Red inside and stuffed his pockets with cookies and sweets and a snap-on bow tie. Corriden kept the tie for many years before presenting it back to Judge Landis's brother Fred at a banquet in Logansport many years later.

In 1908 Corriden broke into professional baseball as a twenty-year-old third baseman with the Keokuk (Iowa) Indians in the Class D Central Association. He hit only .209 and committed 40 errors in 95 games, but somehow he showed enough to be invited back for 1909. Corriden improved to .282 in 143 games, a good-enough performance for the St. Louis Browns to purchase his contract for 1910. The Browns farmed him to the Omaha Rourkes of the Class A Western League.

Corriden had an impressive season with Omaha, batting .308 and earning a call-up to the last-place Browns for the final month of the 1910 season. He hit only .155 in 26 games, but on October 9, the last day of the season, Corriden unwittingly found himself in the middle of a national firestorm. The Browns were playing the Cleveland Naps in St. Louis in a doubleheader. The games meant nothing in the standings, but the Naps' namesake, Napoleon Lajoie, was in a tight race for the batting title with Ty Cobb, with the winner to receive a new Chalmers automobile.

Browns manager Jack O'Connor, who, with many, had enmity for Cobb, ordered his rookie third baseman, Corriden, to play back on the outfield grass behind third base, ostensibly to avoid injury from one of Lajoie's vicious line drives. Lajoie slugged a triple over the head of rookie center fielder Hub Northen in his first at bat, but on his succeeding eight plate appearances, Lajoie bunted the ball in the general direction of third base. Seven of the eight bunts went for base hits, with one bunt being ruled a fielder's choice.

American League president Ban Johnson quickly investigated the suspicious affair and found Corriden not culpable because he was just following orders. He also declared Cobb the batting champion with a final average of .384944 to Lajoie's .384084. The Chalmers Company magnanimously gave both Cobb and Lajoie new cars, but manager O'Connor lost his job and was effec-

tively banned from organized baseball. In two years Corriden would find himself a teammate of Cobb.

Corriden did not stick with the Browns for 1911 and signed with the Kansas City Blues of the American Association. He batted .247 in 137 games and committed 64 errors at shortstop. He was back with the Blues in 1912 and raised his average to a sparkling .318, attracting the attention of the Detroit Tigers, who purchased his contract late in the season. But Red could manage only a .203 batting average in 138 at bats for the Tigers.

After the season the Tigers sold Corriden to the Cincinnati Reds, who then sent him to the Chicago Cubs. In 1913 Corriden batted just .175 in 46 games as a utility infielder for the Cubs. Nonetheless, when Al Bridwell, the Cubs' starting shortstop, jumped to the Federal League in 1914, Corriden replaced him, batting .230 in 107 games. He also made 46 errors in 432 chances at short for an .894 fielding percentage, lowest by twenty points among the National League regulars.

Red started the 1915 season with Chicago, but after only three at bats was sold to the Louisville Colonels of the American Association. Again he showed he could hit top-level Minor League pitching, batting a lusty .318 in 346 at bats. However, although he was only twenty-eight years old, Corriden's Major League playing career was over. He had appeared in 223 games and had hit only .205 in 640 at bats. Defensively, he had 90 errors in 900 chances.

Corriden was back with the Colonels in 1916 and became a member of Louisville's "Iron Man Infield." With Red at third, Jay Kirke at first, Joe McCarthy (later to become the Yankees manager) at second, and Roxy Roach at shortstop, the infield played every inning of every game of a 168-game schedule.[3] Corriden batted .277 as the Colonels swept to the American Association pennant.

After hitting .276 in 151 games for Louisville in 1917, Corriden played with St. Paul of the

American Association in 1918 and 1919. He sat out the 1920 season, which he spent at home in Logansport working as a machinist, but returned to play in 1921 for the St. Joseph (Missouri) Saints in the Western League. At the age of thirty-three, Corriden experienced a resurgence, batting a hefty .336 in 143 games, all in the outfield. He returned to St. Joseph in 1922 and put together another stellar year, hitting .331 in 160 games.

The Des Moines Boosters, who had finished in the Western League basement in 1922, hired Corriden to be their player-manager for 1923. The club improved to fifth place in the eight-team league, with an 87-79 record. At thirty-five Corriden could still play at that level. He penciled himself into the lineup every day and hammered out a .343 average. He returned to manage Des Moines in 1924, but the team slipped to seventh place, costing Red his job. He still had a terrific year at the plate, batting .338 in 126 games on thirty-seven-year-old legs.

In spite of his excellent year in 1924, Corriden never played another game in organized baseball. Thanks in part to his old Iron Man Infield mate Joe McCarthy, who was by 1926 managing the Chicago Cubs, Red spent a couple of years scouting in his native Indiana before joining the Indianapolis Indians of the American Association as a coach in 1928. He succeeded Bruno Betzel as manager in 1930, but the Indians finished dead last.

Rogers Hornsby had taken over from Joe McCarthy as manager of the Cubs at the tail end of the 1930 season and hired Corriden as one of his coaches for 1932. That would begin a nine-year run for Corriden as a Cubs coach, during which he also served under Charlie Grimm and Gabby Hartnett. It was a most successful decade for the Cubs, as they won pennants in 1932, 1935, and 1938 and finished in the first division every year but 1940.[4]

Once during those years on a train trip between Chicago and New York, Corriden, upon boarding, told the porter to be sure to tell him when the train pulled into Indianapolis because he planned a quick visit with relatives there. He promptly fell asleep in his Pullman berth. Hartnett had overheard the conversation and when the train pulled into Englewood on Chicago's South Side yelled, "Indianapolis!" Corriden shot out of his berth, yelling, "Why didn't you give me more time?" He raced off the train, hailed a cab, and gave the Indianapolis address of his relatives. By the time he realized he was still in Chicago, the train was long gone.

When Hartnett was fired after the Cubs' fifth-place finish in 1940, Corriden was canned as well. He was not out of a job long, however, as Leo Durocher quickly added him to his Brooklyn Dodgers coaching staff. Red was just in time to enjoy another pennant, but he remained without a World Series ring, as the Dodgers lost to the Yankees in five games.

Corriden remained with Brooklyn for six tumultuous years under Durocher. In 1946 his son John was briefly with the Dodgers, appearing in one game as a pinch runner. Bucky Harris was hired to manage the Yankees in 1947, and Larry MacPhail, the former Dodgers executive and now co-owner of the Yankees, hired Corriden away from the Dodgers to be his first base coach.

The 1947 World Series again matched the Yankees against the Dodgers, who had a second-year center fielder named Carl Furillo. After watching Furillo throw, Corriden advised against running on him, saying, "Furillo has a rifle hanging from his shoulder." Furillo thus became ever known as the "Reading Rifle," after his hometown and rifle-like arm. The Yankees beat Furillo's Dodgers in seven games to finally give Corriden his World Series ring.

Red remained with the Yankees through the 1948 season, continuing as first base coach. Although he was very popular with the Yankees players, he could occasionally rub them the wrong way. Fellow coach Charlie Dressen and Corriden were prone to go on about how they did things in the National League, where both had spent many years, implying that the National League was somehow superior. Bobby Brown remembers Joe DiMaggio remarking to him after one such episode, "Yeah, and we beat their asses every fall."[5]

When the Yankees slipped to third place in 1948, they fired Bucky Harris and replaced him with Casey Stengel. Harris moved to the Pacific Coast League in 1949 to manage the San Diego Padres and took Corriden with him.

Corriden was back in the big leagues in 1950, hired as a coach by Chicago White Sox manager Jack Onslow. Following a May 26 loss to the Cleveland Indians, the White Sox were in last place with only eight wins in their first thirty games. New general manager Frank Lane fired Onslow and named the sixty-two-year-old Corriden to his first and only big-league managing job. The club responded by winning its first game under Red, 6–1, behind the young southpaw Billy Pierce. The team was not a good one, however, and finished the season in sixth place, thirty-eight games behind the pennant-winning Yankees.

Under Corriden the club won fifty-two games and lost seventy-two. It was not enough to gain Red another year, and Lane brought in Paul Richards to manage for the 1951 season. Eddie Robinson, the first baseman on the 1950 White Sox, remembered that when Corriden would come to the mound to take a pitcher out of the game, he would inevitably say, "Buddy Boy, let's let somebody else try." When the new pitcher arrived, Corriden's advice was, "Buddy Boy, you've got to get this guy out." In general, Robinson thought Corriden was too nice a guy to be an effective manager.[6]

Indeed, Corriden's role in his many years as coach was as a buffer between salty managers like Durocher, Hornsby, and Hartnett and the players. In fact, his players often called him Uncle John in addition to Lollypop, and a 1947 newspaper article about him was headlined "Corriden Is Good Will and Good Humor Man."[7]

After his dismissal by the White Sox, Corriden became a scout for the Dodgers, a position he held until he retired from baseball after the 1958 season at the age of seventy-one.

One of the players Corriden had signed for the Dodgers during his scouting days was pitcher Larry Sherry. In the middle of the 1959 season, the Dodgers needed pitching help, and Sherry was one of their prospects, pitching in St. Paul. Dodgers general manager Buzzy Bavasi reportedly called Corriden to ask whether he thought Sherry was ready for the Majors. Corriden replied, "Lollypop, grab him fast."

Bavasi followed Corriden's advice, and Sherry was superb, winning seven games while losing only two and compiling a sparkling 2.19 earned run average while helping to push the Dodgers to a tie with the Milwaukee Braves for the National League pennant.

Unfortunately, the story has a very sad ending. Red Corriden was stricken with a fatal heart attack at his home in Indianapolis on September 28, 1959, while watching Sherry pitch for the Dodgers in a playoff game against the Braves. Corriden was seventy-two years old. He was buried in Mount Hope Cemetery in Logansport. He was survived by his wife, the former Ethel Shuman, whom he married in 1911, and sons John M. Jr., Richard, and Robert. John and Ethel's first-born, a daughter, Mary, died on November 8, 1912, the day she was born. With John Corriden's passing, baseball had lost one of its acclaimed good-humor men and goodwill ambassadors.

Chapter 9. Timeline, April 14–April 29

Lyle Spatz

Monday, April 14, at Washington—Rained out. 0-0, First (T).

Tuesday, April 15, vs. Philadelphia—Fifty-year old Bucky Harris made his debut as Yankees manager in a 6–1 opening-day loss to the Athletics. Right-hander Phil Marchildon, who served three years as a gunner with the Royal Canadian Air Force and took part in twenty-six missions against the Nazis, went the distance, limiting the Yanks to just six hits. Spud Chandler, the first of three Yankees pitchers, was the loser. With an injured Joe DiMaggio out of the lineup, Charlie Keller batted in the cleanup spot. Right fielder Yogi Berra's fly ball in the eighth inning drove in new Yankees first baseman George McQuinn with New York's only run. 0-1, Fifth (T), 1 game behind.

Wednesday, April 16, vs. Philadelphia—Rained out. 0-1, Fifth (T), 1 game behind.

Thursday, April 17, vs. Philadelphia—Bill Bevens's complete-game three-hitter defeated Philadelphia, 2–1, as the Yankees won their first game of the season and first under Bucky Harris. The A's gave pitcher Dick Fowler a 1–0 lead in the first inning that held up until the Yanks scored twice in the eighth. Tommy Henrich's double drove in Phil Rizzuto with the first run, and Henrich later scored on an error by rookie first baseman Ferris Fain. 1-1, Third (T), 1 game behind.

Friday, April 18, at Washington—President Harry Truman threw out two first balls, one left-handed and one right-handed, in the Senators' home opener at Griffith Stadium. Allie Reynolds, obtained from Cleveland in an off-season trade for Joe Gordon, made his Yankees debut a successful one with a 7–0 shutout. Charlie Keller, with a three-run homer off Nats starter Bobo Newsom in the third inning, and Yogi Berra, with four hits, led the offense. 2-1, Third (T), 1 game behind.

Saturday, April 19, at Washington—Washington's Sid Hudson allowed just two seventh-inning runs, both scoring on George McQuinn's double, in beating the Yankees, 4–2. Washington got four in the fifth, all charged to Yankees starter and loser Joe Page. The Yanks used five pitchers, including Frank Shea, making his big-league debut. Joe DiMaggio made his first appearance of the season, as a pinch hitter. 2-2, Third (T), 2 games behind.

Sunday, April 20, at Philadelphia (2)—Joe DiMaggio made his first start of the season and hit a three-run home run off Jesse Flores as the Yankees won the opener, 6–2. Spud Chandler avenged his opening-day loss to Philadelphia with a route-going performance. George McQuinn had three hits for the Yanks, and Bobby Brown had two. Mike Guerra and Pete Suder each had three hits for the A's, and Sam Chapman had a home run. New York also won the second game, 3–2, in ten innings. Twenty-year-old Don Johnson, making his Major League debut, outlasted Phil Marchildon, who had beaten the Yanks in the opener. Both men went the distance. Tommy Henrich's double scored Phil Rizzuto with the game winner. 4-2, Third, ½ game behind.

Monday, April 21 — Not scheduled. 4-2, Third, ½ game behind.

Tuesday, April 22, vs. Boston — The Yankees had only three hits in defeating the Red Sox, 5–4. Trailing 4–3, they scored two runs in the home eighth. Charlie Keller's first-inning home run with two men on had provided New York's first three runs. The defending American League champion Red Sox got home runs from Ted Williams, Sam Mele, and Rudy York. Bill Bevens went all the way for the Yanks. 5-2, Second, .286 percentage points behind.

Wednesday, April 23, vs. Boston — Allie Reynolds pitched his second consecutive shutout, a two-hitter, to down the Red Sox, 3–0, and move New York into first place. Rudy York had both hits off Reynolds, a seventh-inning double and a ninth-inning single. Catcher Aaron Robinson drove in the first two Yankees runs off loser Dave Ferriss, one on a home run, and George McQuinn drove in the third. 6-2, First, 1 game ahead.

Thursday, April 24, vs. Boston — Tex Hughson of the Red Sox allowed only two hits — a Joe DiMaggio double and an Aaron Robinson single — in beating the Yankees, 1–0. Frank Shea allowed only three hits in his first start. Boston scored in the fifth on a pair of walks and Sam Mele's fly ball. 6-3, First, ½ game ahead.

Friday, April 25, vs. Washington — Rained out. 6-3, First, ½ game ahead.

Saturday, April 26, vs. Washington — Don Johnson made his Yankee Stadium debut with a five-hit, 3–1 win over the Senators. Washington's one run was unearned, attributable to a Johnson error. Charlie Keller had two runs batted in for the Yankees with a double off starter and loser Micky Haefner and a home run off Bobo Newsom. Catcher

Ralph Houk had a double, two singles, and a walk in his first Major League game. 7-3, Second, .014 percentage points behind.

Sunday, April 27, vs. Washington — A pregame tribute to Babe Ruth drew more than fifty-eight thousand to Yankee Stadium, but the Yanks lost, 1–0. Sid Hudson of the Senators and Spud Chandler of the Yanks both went the distance. Buddy Lewis's eighth-inning single drove Hudson home with the game's only run. Bobby Brown had three hits for the Yanks. 7-4, First, ½ game ahead.

Monday, April 28 — Not scheduled. 7-4, First, 1 game ahead.

Tuesday, April 29, at St. Louis — Rained out. 7-4, First, 1 game ahead.

Chapter 10. Yankee Stadium

Chris Kemmer

Between 1913 and 1922 the Yankees had played their home games at the Polo Grounds as a tenant of the National League New York Giants. After the Yankees acquired Babe Ruth for the 1920 season, their growing attendance infuriated Giants manager John McGraw, who "encouraged" the Yankees to find a new home. McGraw figured the Yankees would not be able to find a particularly suitable place to build and they would be out of his hair.

Yankees owners Jacob Ruppert and Tillinghast L'Hommedieu "Til" Huston did have some problems finding a site that met their demands, but ultimately were able to purchase a ten-acre parcel of land from the estate of William Waldorf Astor for $675,000. The Yankees were not moving far from McGraw—their new home was in the Bronx, just across the Harlem River from the Polo Grounds.

Under the direction of architects from the Osborne Engineering Company of Cleveland, the White Construction Company began work on the new ballpark in early May 1922. Within days, Ruppert bought out Huston, becoming the team's sole owner. The name Yankee Stadium was chosen by Ruppert (over the suggested House That Ruth Built) because he wanted the name to depict a grand venue that "would be made impenetrable to all eyes, save those of aviators."[1] Contrary to Ruppert's wish, games could be seen from passing elevated trains and from buildings later erected on River Avenue. The initial plan for the stadium to be roofed all the way around was dropped at some point during the planning phase, and on opening day the third deck did not reach either foul pole.

Before construction could start, 45,000 cubic yards of earth had to be removed. Construction materials included 3 million board feet of lumber, 20,000 cubic yards of concrete, 800 tons of rebar, 2,300 tons of mechanical steel, 13,000 yards of topsoil, 116,000 square feet of sod, 950,000 board feet of lumber for the bleachers, and 1 million brass screws.[2] The work was completed in 284 working days, in time for opening day, 1923.

On Wednesday, April 18, 1923, an estimated seventy-four thousand fans attended the first game at the new $2.5 million Yankee Stadium, located between 157th and 161st Streets on River Avenue. Grandstand seats cost $1. Governor Al Smith threw out the first ball, and then the Yankees beat the Boston Red Sox, 4–1, with the help of a three-run home run by Babe Ruth. The announced attendance was generally seen as an overstatement since there were only sixty thousand seats in the new ballpark, but it was still the largest crowd ever assembled for a baseball game up to then and more than twenty thousand fans were turned away.[3] For many years, it was assumed the stadium was actually built to accommodate seventy thousand fans, as the opening-day attendance estimate made its way into baseball folklore, giving the place even more perceived splendor.

The Yankees, however, drew fewer fans in 1923 than they did in 1922 at the Polo Grounds, which could seat forty-three thousand for baseball at the time. Yankees home attendance had declined each year since the peak in 1920 (Ruth's first year). The Babe's off-year in 1922, and perhaps the hangover from that in 1923, was not offset by the new stadium.

There were many firsts in the design of Yankee

Stadium. It was the first ballpark to have triple-deck stands (albeit not all the way around) and the first to sport an electric scoreboard. It gave the batting order; the inning-by-inning score of the game with runs, hits, and errors; the scores of other Major League games that day; and the pitchers for each team. It was all operated by electricity, with numbers and letters flashing out of a black background.[4] While the scoreboard was innovative for the times, the most recognized feature of the stadium was the sixteen-foot-tall copper frieze hanging from the roof of the upper grandstand.

The place was "huge," as Ruppert wanted, but the ballpark's size also made some of the seats not particularly appealing from which to watch a baseball game. Most of the sight lines gave an unobstructed view, but many of the seats were so far from the action that fans had a difficult time seeing what was happening on the field. Not only were the fans affected by the dimensions, but players encountered strange angles of sunlight and shadows that could affect their skills at different times during the day. Right fielder Ruth was actually accommodated by the dimensions and layout of the field. The Yankees insisted the new ballpark be oriented so the late-afternoon setting sun would shine in the eyes of left fielders, not right fielders.

Also, the right-field foul pole was just 255 feet away, with a low fence along the right-field grandstand, making it a cinch for the left-handed-batting Ruth to clear the fence with a good swing of the bat. The left-field line also measured 255 feet from the home plate. (In 1924 the distances down the foul lines were extended to 295 feet in right field and 280 feet in left field.) Straightaway center field was close to 500 feet from the batter's box, an almost impossible distance for most batters. In addition to the vast amount of territory a center fielder had to cover, the expanse was further complicated in the early years by a grass slope running up to the fences and in later years by the addition of the original Monument Park, which was placed within the field of play. The first monument, installed in 1932, was in tribute to the late manager Miller Huggins. Lou Gehrig was so honored in 1941 and Babe Ruth in 1949. Sometimes a hard-hit ball would rattle around the monuments of former greats while the current greats were trying to make a play. Casey Stengel once remarked, "Ruth, Gehrig, Huggins, someone throw that damn ball in here *now*."[5]

On September 4, 1923, the first no-hitter was thrown at Yankee Stadium, by Sam Jones, against the Philadelphia Athletics. The first season for the Yankees in their new ballpark ended with a 98-54 record and an American League pennant, their third straight, and for the third year in a row the Yankees' competition in the World Series was the Giants. Manager McGraw banned his Giants from using the Yankees' visitor's clubhouse, making them dress for their Yankee Stadium games in their own clubhouse at the Polo Grounds. The first game was won in the top of the ninth when, with two outs and the score tied at 4–4, Giants outfielder Casey Stengel hit a line drive into the gap in left field for an inside-the-park home run. Stengel homered again in Game Three, but the Yankees ultimately won the Series in six games. The Yankees had lost their previous two World Series against the Giants, so this win in their new home was sweet revenge and ushered in a new era for the Yankees.

In 1928 the seating capacity was increased when a third deck was added to the left-field stands. On September 9 of that year, a record 85,265 (81,622 paid) saw the Yankees sweep a doubleheader from Philadelphia.

In 1929 the Yankees wore numbers on their uniforms for the first time. The numbers were based on the player's spot in the batting order, which is why Babe Ruth was number 3 and Gehrig was number 4.[6] Also in 1929, two people died and sixty-two were injured during a "stampede" in the standing-room-only right-field bleachers.[7] Supposedly, this put a stop to the practice of selling more tickets than there were available seats.

In 1937 the right-field stands were also expanded to three decks, a concrete structure replaced the wooden bleachers, and the distance to the center-field fence was reduced from 490 feet to 461 feet. Remember that pledge to sell no more tickets than there were seats? It seems to have lasted not even a decade; on May 30, 1938, a reported 81,891 watched the Yankees win both ends of a doubleheader from the Boston Red Sox. On many other occasions reported attendance exceeded the number of seats.

Lou Gehrig gave his famous "luckiest man in the world" farewell speech at the stadium on July 4, 1939, and a week later, on July 11, the All-Star Game was held there for the first time, to coincide with the New York World's Fair. Almost 63,000 attended the game and saw the American League, loaded with Yankees, beat the National League, 3–1. With third-deck expansions in right and left fields, offset by a change from field bench seats to chair seats, seating capacity gradually progressed throughout the 1930s and '40s, stabilizing at 67,000 by 1947. Many other events were held in Yankee Stadium, including home games for the Black Yankees of the Negro National League, college football, and championship boxing matches.

April 27, 1947, was declared Babe Ruth Day throughout the Major Leagues, with a celebration held in the "House That Ruth Built." After more than a year in physical decline, Ruth appeared pale and thin and barely able to speak—but speak he did, thanking the fans and talking about youngsters starting out in baseball—"the only real game . . . , I think." Ruth died about sixteen months later, on August 16, 1948.

After the 1945 season Jacob Ruppert's heirs sold their interest in the Yankees for $2.8 million to a group that included Larry MacPhail, a former Cincinnati Reds and Brooklyn Dodgers executive. At both his former franchises MacPhail had intro-

duced night baseball, and he did the same with his new ball club, in spite of grumbling from Yankees traditionalists.[8] As part of a $600,000 renovation of Yankee Stadium for the 1946 season, lights were added to the ballpark along with auxiliary field-level scoreboards in right field and left field. The first night game at the stadium was played on May 28, 1946, when the Yankees lost to the Washington Senators, 2–1. MacPhail added a plush Stadium Club behind the grandstand, with four box seats selling for $600. Also in 1946, the home and visiting teams switched dugouts, with the Yankees moving to the first-base dugout. The team finished third in 1946; nevertheless, 2,265,512 people attended games at Yankee Stadium, a Major League record to that date. In 1947 the Yankees celebrated the stadium's twenty-fifth anniversary by winning their fifteenth pennant and eleventh world championship.

Chapter 11. **Spud Chandler**

Mark Stewart

AGE	W	L	PCT.	ERA	G	GS	GF	CG	SHO	SV	IP	H	BB	SO	HBP	WP
39	9	5	.643	2.46	17	16	0	13	2	0	128.0	100	41	68	0	2

Spurgeon Ferdinand "Spud" Chandler was a no-nonsense, take-charge hurler who went after opposing hitters as if they were mortal enemies. The intensity with which he patrolled the area around the pitching rubber sent a clear message to the batter: I will not lose. You will have to beat me. Despite a late start and an uncooperative elbow, the blue-eyed, blond-haired Georgian was on six World Series championship teams. He won an American League Most Valuable Player (MVP) Award and set a modern record for career winning percentage that still stands. Chandler threw just about every pitch, and he threw every pitch as if it might be his last, a possibility that loomed over him for most of his big-league career.

The boy everyone called Spurge and later Spud (which he preferred) was born on September 12, 1907, in Commerce, Georgia, a Jackson County agricultural community about sixty miles northeast of Atlanta. When he was a boy his parents, Leonard "Bud" Chandler and Olivia (Hix) Chandler, moved the family to Franklin County, Georgia. As a teenager Spurge played sports with a consuming passion that intimidated teammates and opponents alike. He did not mind the comparison to another Franklin County product, Ty Cobb. He said proudly throughout his life that he and Ty Cobb were the two most famous people to come from Franklin County.

In 1928 Chandler won a football scholarship to the University of Georgia, earned a spot on the team, and developed into a classic triple-threat (running, passing, kicking) back. Chandler also starred on the Georgia baseball team. The New York Giants and St. Louis Cardinals tempted him

Bill Dickey called Spud Chandler the best pitcher he ever caught.

with contract offers in 1929, but he chose to stay in school. He was having too much fun being a football star. Besides, his favorite team was the Yankees. He would wait to hear from them.

In November 1931 the University of Georgia football squad played New York University in front of sixty-five thousand people at Yankee Stadium. Chandler was one of the stars in a 7–6 victory. After the game he walked out to the pitcher's mound and began throwing footballs through the uprights. When teammates asked what he was doing, he responded that he wanted to get used to the place because he expected to be pitching there someday.

The following spring Chandler was the property of the Yankees. The Chicago Cubs actually had first crack at him, but a paperwork foul-up enabled New York scout Johnny Nee to swoop in and sign him. Chandler began his professional career at the Class B level with the Binghamton (New York) Triplets of the New York–Penn League. He went 8-1 for Binghamton and earned a promotion to the Class A Springfield (Massachusetts) Rifles of the Eastern League, where he was perfect in four decisions.

Chandler had a sinking fastball that worked best without a full follow-through. The pitch put undue stress on his right arm, already tender from a football injury. The resulting pain limited his availability and effectiveness for much of the 1930s.

Chandler was back in Binghamton to begin the 1933 season, as the New York–Penn League moved up to Class A status. He went 10-8 before finishing the season with the Newark Bears of the International League, the Yankees' top farm team. Spud struggled against the better competition. He pitched for Newark again in 1934 and also did stints with the Minneapolis Millers and Syracuse Chiefs. Elbow pain all but ruined his season, as he won just two games and had an ERA over 6.00.

The Yankees shipped Chandler to the West Coast in 1935. He played for Oakland and Portland in the Pacific Coast League, pitching in thirty-four games as a starter and reliever. In 1936 the Yankees brought him back to Newark on the word of his manager at Oakland, Ossie Vitt, who was also hired as the Bears' manager. Chandler went 14-13 for Newark with a fine 3.33 ERA.

He began the 1937 season with Newark, a club that featured young sluggers Joe Gordon and Charlie Keller. History would recall this team as perhaps the best ever assembled at the Minor League level, but Chandler was not on the roster long. He was called up to the Bronx in early May and made his big-league debut on May 6 in Detroit. He entered the game in relief of Frank Makosky in the eighth inning.

Makosky had failed to record an out starting the frame, and Spud did no better, giving up hits to both batters he faced. Three days later manager Joe McCarthy started Chandler against the White Sox in Chicago. Spud had better luck this time, settling into a pitchers' duel against Thornton Lee after allowing a first-inning run. The score was tied 1–1 in the seventh when he allowed a home run to Zeke Bonura that gave the White Sox a 2–1 win.

Chandler won his three remaining May starts, tossing shutouts against the White Sox and Cleveland Indians at Yankee Stadium and also beating the Philadelphia Athletics at home. McCarthy used him as a spot starter until a sore shoulder sidelined him in early August. Chandler did not pitch again during the regular season and was not on the World Series roster when the Yankees defeated their cross-river rivals, the Giants. Chandler finished 7-4 with a 2.84 earned run average in 82⅓ innings.

The next season Chandler cracked the regular rotation, which was led by the trio of Red Ruffing, Lefty Gomez, and Monte Pearson. He made twenty-three starts and completed fourteen in 1938, despite battling aches and pains throughout the season. With a lineup featuring Joe DiMaggio, Bill Dickey, and Lou Gehrig, his primary responsibility was to keep the games close. Chandler won his fourteenth game on September 5 and pitched once more before a sore elbow ended his season. For the second year in a row, he sat out the World Series.

In 1939 Chandler fractured his ankle before the season started and was not back in uniform until the end of July. By then the Yankees were well on their way to a fourth consecutive pennant. Chandler was used out of the bullpen in August and September, making eleven appearances mostly in mop-up duty. For the third straight season, he picked up a World Series check but did not participate.

It is difficult to say if Chandler's injury problems were a matter of bad genes, bad luck, or bad judgment. Certainly, there were times when he acted more like a college running back than a big-league pitcher. When Chandler came to the plate, he swung with great ferocity. He was a decent hitter, with a lifetime average above .200 and occasional home run power. As a base runner, the six-foot, 181-pound Chandler had more than a little Ty Cobb in him; several times a season he would get into pileups breaking up double plays. He maintained that he could beat any pitcher in baseball in a footrace to first base—a claim he continued to make as a coach and scout in his forties.

Fielders thought twice about blocking a bag when Chandler was steaming toward them. Even the umpires were not safe. In a game against the White Sox, on June 27, 1942, Spud raced to back up a throw to third base and slammed into umpire Harry Geisel with such force that Geisel later had to retire.

Chandler reclaimed his spot in the Yankees' rotation in 1940, starting twenty-four games. Detroit and Cleveland both had strong clubs, and the Yankees spent all year chasing them. In early September New York came within a game of the lead, but lost seven of nine games in midmonth and finished third. Pitching with varying degrees of discomfort throughout the season, Chandler was as much a part of the problem as the solution. He won only eight games against seven losses, and his ERA rose steadily throughout the season, ending up at 4.60. One redeeming moment for Chan-

dler in this disappointing campaign came on July 26, when he socked a pair of homers, including a grand slam.

The Yankees got back on track in 1941, winning the pennant by seventeen games over the Red Sox. Chandler took a while to get warm, performing as both a starter and a reliever in the first three months. He did not record his first victory until July, but won ten games in eleven weeks and finished 10-4.

Chandler started Game Two of the 1941 World Series against the Brooklyn Dodgers. He gave himself a 1–0 lead in the bottom of the second inning with an infield hit that scored Charlie Keller, but he ended up the loser, as the Dodgers came back to win, 3–2. The Yankees took the Series in five games to give Spud his fourth championship.

In 1942 Chandler finished 16-5 with a 2.38 ERA. He was selected to play in his first All-Star Game, held at the Polo Grounds. As the American League starter, he was the beneficiary of first-inning home runs by Lou Boudreau and Rudy York and was awarded the victory in a 3–1 win. He pitched four innings, allowing two hits and no runs.

In late July Chandler pitched back-to-back shutouts over the Tigers and Browns, the latter a three-hit masterpiece. The Yankees returned to the World Series, this time facing the St. Louis Cardinals. Ruffing, the Game One starter, entered the ninth inning with a 7–0 lead, but left after allowing a walk and four hits. McCarthy summoned Chandler to get the final out. Terry Moore and Enos Slaughter greeted him with singles to make the score 7–4 before young Stan Musial tapped a grounder in the hole that was gloved by Buddy Hassett. Chandler raced to the bag and took the throw from the first baseman to end the game.

The teams played four more close games, and each time St. Louis won to take the World Series four games to one. Chandler was an effective starter in Game Three, limiting the Cardinals to three hits and a run in eight innings, but Ernie White was better, blanking the New Yorkers, 2–0.

The 1943 Yankees found themselves without the services of DiMaggio, Ruffing, Hassett, Phil Rizzuto, and Tommy Henrich. The talent drain of World War II had turned baseball topsy-turvy, but in the end it was the Yankees and Cardinals repeating as pennant winners. Chandler enjoyed another injury-free year and was the talk of baseball. Pitching against lineups made up of prospects and suspects, he mowed down American League hitters with frightening efficiency.

Chandler went 20-4, while allowing three or fewer earned runs in all but one of his defeats. Five of his league-leading wins were shutouts, and four more were 2–1 games. Win number twenty, the pennant clincher, came in a fourteen-inning complete game. His 1.64 earned run average was the lowest for an American Leaguer since Walter Johnson in the Dead Ball Era. Never a strikeout pitcher, Chandler fanned 134 batters, equaling his 1941 and 1942 totals combined. He was the *Sporting News*'s Major League Player of the Year, and when the writers cast their votes for Most Valuable Player, Chandler's name was atop twelve of the twenty-four ballots. He out-pointed batting champion Luke Appling of the White Sox by thirty-one votes.

Chandler started the World Series opener in a rematch with the Cardinals and twirled a complete-game 4–2 victory. The Yankees had a 3–1 series lead when Chandler took the mound for Game Five in St. Louis. Time and again the Cardinals put runners on, but the Yankee ace escaped without allowing a run. Nine innings, ten hits, and two walks later, Chandler had a 2–0 shutout, and the Yankees were champs.

Uncle Sam caught up with Chandler after the Series. He was classified 1-AL, which meant he would not see combat because of a permanent injury. Ironically, the army listed this debilitating condition as limited movement of his right arm.

Chandler attended spring training in Atlantic City, New Jersey, and pitched one regular-season game before being called to active duty as an infantry private and shipped to Georgia for basic training.

Spud and his wife, the former Frances Willard, were expecting a child that spring. When she went into labor he was unable to be at her side. It was a difficult birth that required a C-section, and the baby died a few hours later. The couple did have two sons, Frank, born in 1941, and Richard, born in 1945. Frances had been a stewardess for National Airlines and had first met Spud in Chicago when the Yankees were in town. They were married in Athens, Georgia, in 1939.

Chandler trained at Camp Shelby in his home state of Georgia. Because he was too old and injured to qualify for combat, he hoped he might spend the war playing ball and serving as a fitness instructor. Many other baseball stars had pulled this type of duty. Although he did launch a few fastballs for the camp baseball team, Chandler spent most of his time there firing weapons.

Although he never saw overseas action, Chandler missed almost two full seasons. He was discharged in early September 1945 and made four starts for the Yankees, winning two and losing one.

Chandler was among hundreds of returning veterans hoping to make Major League squads in 1946. Some had lost their edge, while others had gained strength and toughness during their time in the military. Chandler blanked the Athletics on opening day and did not lose a game until mid-May. He finished 20-8 for the third-place Yankees, with a 2.10 ERA and a career-high 257⅓ innings pitched.

That October, Chandler joined the Bob Feller All-Stars, a barnstorming group made up of Yankees and Indians players. It was a chance to make a little extra cash and, as it turned out, do something he could brag about for years to come. Facing Satchel Paige's All-Stars in a game at Youngstown,

Ohio, on October 1, he hit a home run against Paige.

Chandler had turned thirty-nine in September 1946. Although his statistics were impressive, his right elbow was getting more troublesome with each start. There were times when he left the clubhouse with his collar unbuttoned and no tie—he was in too much pain to dress. The agony he endured only added to his aura in the Yankees' clubhouse. Known as an intense competitor (some said he was just plain mean) when he joined the club in the 1930s, by the late 1940s he would get so keyed up before starts that no one dared bother him. Milton Gross wrote a story for the *Saturday Evening Post* calling him the angry Yankee ace. Chandler always denied he was mean in the locker room, claiming he was just "determined." On the mound, however, he made no apologies for his behavior. He referred to other teams as the enemy and refused to give in to hitters. If he saw an opponent digging in, Chandler would likely sail a pitch at his chin.

After an operation in Atlanta to remove more than a dozen bone chips in his right elbow, Spud felt good enough to give it a go again in 1947. He started and lost the season opener in Yankee Stadium, yielding six runs to the Philadelphia A's. Five days later he avenged this defeat in Philadelphia. On April 27 Chandler hooked up with Sid Hudson of the Washington Senators in a thrilling pitching duel at Yankee Stadium. The two hurlers wriggled in and out of trouble but hung up zeroes inning after inning until Hudson singled in the eighth and later scored on a hit by Buddy Lewis for the game's only run. Hudson—who like Chandler lost key years to military service—later remembered this as his greatest game.

After five starts Chandler's record stood at a lackluster 1-3, albeit with a sub-3.00 ERA. This was unfamiliar territory for Chandler, who had yet to register a losing record as a Major Leaguer. Beginning with his next start, against the White Sox, he won eight of nine decisions. Pitching against the Tigers at Yankee Stadium on June 21, he fanned eleven batters, a career high.

On July 4 Chandler beat the Senators to raise his record to 9-4. He had already pitched 118 innings in the season, as manager Bucky Harris was riding his starters hard. In his first start after the All-Star Game, Chandler faced the Browns in St. Louis. With one out in the seventh inning, after yielding the tying run in a 3–3 game, he could throw no more. He gave way to Joe Page, who finished the contest and hit a game-winning homer in the ninth inning. Lost in the postgame celebrating was the fact that Spud Chandler might be through.

Chandler did take the mound again twice more, but he was ineffective in two September appearances, one in relief and one in a start against Boston. His final regular-season line was 9-5 with a 2.46 ERA in 128 innings. Not a bad way to say good-bye. Alas, it was not *quite* good-bye. The Yankees were pennant winners again, and Chandler pitched two innings and allowed two runs to Brooklyn in Game Three of the World Series.

The Yankees officially handed him his release in April 1948. Twice a 20-game winner, he won 109 games in all—26 by shutout. He lost only 43, for a career winning percentage of .717, the best ever by a modern-day pitcher with at least 100 victories.

Bill Dickey called it a pleasure to squat behind the plate with Spud on the mound. He claimed his teammate could spot seven different pitches—fastball, sinker, curve, slider, screwball, knuckler, and splitter—plus a couple more he never bothered to name. Chandler, Dickey insisted, was the best pitcher he ever caught.

In the years that followed Chandler stayed busy as a scout for several teams, including the Yankees, Indians, and Minnesota Twins. He managed for two years in the Minor Leagues. In 1954 he piloted Cleveland's Class D affiliate in Jacksonville Beach, Florida, and once put himself in a game as a pinch hitter.

The following year Chandler managed the Class B Spartanburg (South Carolina) Peaches, another Cleveland farm team. He appeared in two games as a pitcher at the age of forty-seven. He later served two seasons as the Kansas City Athletics' pitching coach.

Chandler retired from baseball for good in 1984, at the age of seventy-seven. In 1989 he fell and fractured his shoulder. Complications followed, and he suffered a heart attack in 1990. He was eighty-two when died on January 9, 1990, near St. Petersburg, Florida. He was survived by Frances and his sons.

Chapter 12. **Don Johnson**

Nicholas Diunte

AGE	W	L	PCT.	ERA	G	GS	GF	CG	SHO	SV	IP	H	BB	SO	HBP	WP
20	4	3	.571	3.64	15	8	4	2	0	0	54.1	57	23	16	1	0

"They've made a simple game complicated," Don Johnson said as he reflected on the changes he had seen in baseball. "When I was on the Yankees, we had a few trainers. If you got hurt on the mound, they said, 'Here, have a beer. You'll feel better.' That's all they told you. We didn't have video. We had a whirlpool. It's changed; baseball has changed. Now, you throw one hundred pitches; they want to get you out of there."[1]

Donald Roy Johnson was a product of humble beginnings. He was born on November 12, 1926, in Portland, Oregon, the only child of Swedish immigrants Gus and Judith (Bjorklund) Johnson. "I got my start playing ball in high school. I couldn't afford any baseball shoes or gloves. My dad got old pieces of leather and cut holes in it for a glove for me," Johnson said. "After a while, I finally got a pair of baseball shoes."

Johnson's patchwork equipment had little effect on his performance. He excelled at Jefferson High School and in American Legion ball, attracting the attention of Major League scouts at the age of sixteen. "I threw hard; I could fire that ball. I played high school ball and pitched six no-hitters in high school and American Legion ball. That's where Joe Devine, the Yankees' scout, along with five or six others, came after me."

A bidding war for Johnson's services ensued, and, in 1943, he accepted the Yankees' offer of ten thousand dollars. In 1944 the seventeen-year-old Johnson leaped the lower classifications of the Minor Leagues, debuting with the Kansas City Blues of the American Association. Despite Johnson's 3-11 record with the Blues, the Yankees moved him to the Newark Bears, where he did bet-

Don Johnson blamed his limited usage in the second half of the season on coach Charlie Dressen.

ter, winning six games and losing two in International League play. "I won two playoff games [for Newark]. Then I went into the army."

Johnson was sent to Fort Lewis, Washington, where he played for the base team, the Warriors, which was loaded with Major Leaguers, "guys like Danny Litwhiler of the Cardinals and Dom

Dallesandro of the Cubs. We won forty-six and lost none!"

Johnson spent a little more than two years in the military, moving to the Army of Occupation in Japan. Discharged before the 1947 season and still only twenty-one years old, he reported to Yankees spring training on a plane carrying celebrities Joe DiMaggio and Jack Dempsey and another rookie, Yogi Berra, who was wearing navy fatigues because "he didn't have any other clothes."

The upstart Johnson made the 1947 Yankees out of spring training. During the season he was befriended by DiMaggio, whom he called "the best player I ever saw in my life." The six-foot-three, two-hundred-pound Johnson made his Major League debut in the second game of a double-header on April 20, starting against the Philadelphia Athletics in Philadelphia. It was a memorable appearance; the Yankees won in ten innings, 3–2, and Johnson pitched all ten innings to earn the victory. "I was throwing good," he remembered.

Six days later Johnson followed his debut with another complete-game victory, this time 3–1 over the Washington Senators. The good fortune did not last, however. On May 3 Johnson yielded six runs in just four innings while losing to the Chicago White Sox. After that manager Bucky Harris used him sparingly, with mixed results. Following a June 29 win, he pitched only eight more times during the season and finished with a record of 4-3.

Johnson blamed his limited usage in the second half of the season on Charlie Dressen, one of Harris's coaches. "Charlie Dressen went and said, 'Don, you're lifting your leg too high.' I said, 'Stick it, man! I've got four wins.' I didn't pitch much after that. If you talk back to some of these big shots, you don't pitch anymore. That's it."

Johnson did not appear in the World Series against the Brooklyn Dodgers. In a sad turn of events, he said, he had to pawn his World Series ring the next year to fix his car after it broke down in Wyoming.[2]

During the spring of 1948 Johnson developed a sore arm and was sent back to the Minors, where he moved around in the upper levels of the Yankees' farm system. Playing with the Portland Beavers of the Pacific Coast League, as well as returns to Newark and Kansas City, he had a combined record of 7-17. He spent another season in the PCL to regain his arm strength, going 8-14 with the Sacramento Solons in 1949. Despite his losing record, he shaved nearly a full run off the previous year's ERA. Johnson felt good about regaining strength in his arm. "I threw hard, and we had a pretty good club" at Sacramento, he said.

Johnson returned to the Yankees in 1950, only to be sidelined with a skin disease, eczema.[3] "I went to the doctor, and he couldn't cure me." With Johnson pitching ineffectively, the Yankees sought pitching help elsewhere. They traded Johnson, along with infielder Snuffy Stirnweiss, outfielder Jim Delsing, pitcher Duane Pillette, and fifty thousand dollars to the cash-strapped St. Louis Browns for pitchers Tom Ferrick and Joe Ostrowski, plus infielder Leo Thomas.

"What a place!" he recalled. "We didn't win many games, but we had a lot of fun." Johnson appeared in twenty-five games, including twelve starts, for the seventh-place Browns; overall, he finished the season at 6-6, with a 6.09 ERA. Johnson hurled four complete games, all with the Browns, including a 6–0 shutout against Cleveland on September 8.

In 1951 Johnson was sold to the Washington Senators, managed by his old Yankees manager, Bucky Harris.[4] "We had a bad club," Johnson remembered. He won seven games and lost eleven, with his best outing coming on July 14 at Briggs Stadium in Detroit. The big right hander delivered a three-hit, no-walk shutout of the Tigers, while going 2 for 3 at the plate with two RBIs and a run scored.

Poised for a fresh start with the Senators in 1952, Johnson was injured again, this time in spring training. "I pulled a hamstring down in Orlando in 1952. Those hamstrings are tough. They don't get better. I was out practically all year. I didn't win a game that year." The Senators won sixteen more games in 1952 than the previous season, but Johnson went 0-5 in twenty-nine games, mostly in relief.

In 1953 the Senators sold Johnson to Toronto of the International League for fifteen thousand dollars.[5] He won fifteen games and lost twelve for the Maple Leafs and led the league with a 2.67 ERA and 156 strikeouts.[6] His performance attracted the attention of the Chicago White Sox, who purchased his contract. He pitched in forty-six games for the White Sox in 1954, both as a starter and as a reliever. For the first time since his debut with the Yankees, Johnson had a winning season, posting an 8-7 record with three shutouts and seven saves. "I had my best year in Chicago. We had a good team! We won 96 [sic] games and came in third. That's the year Cleveland won all those games and Willie Mays made that big catch on Vic Wertz."[7]

While Johnson was pleased with his performance, White Sox general manager Frank Lane was looking for help behind the plate. Lane shipped Johnson to the Baltimore Orioles in a seven-player deal that brought catcher Clint Courtney to Chicago.

Johnson was unhappy about the move. "I didn't want to go to Baltimore; I wanted to stay in Chicago. I had good friends on the White Sox, guys like Nellie Fox and Virgil Trucks." Johnson's memories of Baltimore are dark. "I got in trouble while I was over there. I got into a scrap at a hotel bar. You have to stay on the straight and narrow if you play big-league baseball." He also faced suspension by the team for missing a game against the Kansas City Athletics after discovering he was being sued for an accident he was involved in during the off-season.[8]

The 1956 season found Johnson back in a familiar place, Toronto, after the Orioles sold his con-

tract to the Maple Leafs. The return to Toronto rejuvenated Johnson's flagging career. He rolled off two consecutive winning seasons, going 15-9 in 1956 and 17-7 in 1957, and winning the league's Most Valuable Player Award in the latter year. Leafs owner Jack Kent Cooke went out of his way to give Johnson a little extra incentive during the season. "After every game there was an envelope for me in the clubhouse," Johnson remembered. "I was making pretty good money, about four thousand dollars per month."

Cooke was generous with his cash but took a hard line over Johnson's off-the-field antics. "I was with Toronto and got picked up for drunken driving. They threw me in jail in Vero Beach, Florida. I was in jail for six days with three murderers. They took good care of me. They put me on the chain gang with the snakes, cutting grass. Cooke told me to stay there until I changed my life and sobered up."

Cooke's patience with Johnson started to run thin after his MVP season. He had disappeared from the team four times in two seasons and was fined heavily upon his return.[9] In July 1958, after the fourth escapade, the Maple Leafs got rid of Johnson by trading him to the San Francisco Giants in exchange for pitcher Ray Crone. "[Manager Bill] Rigney and I didn't get along. I didn't pitch. I mopped up games," Johnson said of his tenure in the Bay Area. He was used exclusively in relief and was ineffective in that role, with an ERA of 6.26 in seventeen games. He also had a run-in with Willie Mays.

Johnson pitched with Toronto again in 1959 and closed out his career in Portland in 1960 after hurting his arm. After retiring from baseball, Johnson drove a cab in Portland, which provided at least one hair-raising—and almost fatal—experience.

[The dispatcher] sent me to this rough place in Portland. The guy looked like Yul Brynner. He told me to take him to the hospital as he had to start his wife's car. I sensed something suspicious. I took him to the parking lot, and he pulled that Beretta on me. He put it right in my neck and said, "I want your money." I had nineteen dollars cash, and the bastard shot me right through the head, the neck, and the clavicle tube of the spine. I fell out of the cab, and he came around and tried to shoot me again, and fortunately the gun misfired. Then he ran across the parking lot, and the cops caught him up the street. I almost died.

Luckily for Johnson, a few good Samaritans stepped in to save his life. "These two people that picked me up saw me lying on the street and thought I was drunk. They had a 1962 Buick with white seat covers. They took me to the emergency room only a block away. They called the priest. They read me the last rites in the hospital; they thought I was going to die as they couldn't stop the bleeding. Finally, they got this young doctor that came in and stopped it for me. I made a full recovery, but I get some little shocks in my system all the way up my neck and back."

Someone must have been trying to send Johnson a sign to change careers because his first day back driving a cab, another attempt was made on his life. "A guy held me up again," he said. "The guy pulled out something you cut grass with and said, 'I want your money or I'll cut your head!' Fortunately, there were two big ol' Irish cops, and they took him out and beat the crap out of him. A week later I got hit over the head with a wine bottle from a [drunk], and I said it was time to quit!" Johnson worked in the parks department for a while and then began to draw his Major League pension, while spending time with his wife, Betty, and children, Steve, Don, and Lori.

In 2010 Johnson was honored at a Yankee Stadium Old-Timers Day as part of a sixtieth-anniversary tribute to the 1950 Yankees team. He was featured in an article in the *New York Times* and once again was able to hear the cheers of the Yankee faithful. "I'm grateful I got to go back to the old-timers game. It was a hell of a deal. I saw some of my old cronies, Whitey Ford and Jerry Coleman, who I used to room with. I was the first one on the field from the 1950 team. I can't believe how New York has changed. It's a wall of people."

Despite the long travel from Portland, Johnson would welcome one more return to the Bronx. "If they have another one, I'd go. You walk out the elevator; there were five hundred people that wanted your autograph. I said, 'Hey, I ain't famous.' They said, 'Yeah, you played with the Yankees.'"

Chapter 13. George McQuinn

C. Paul Rogers III

AGE	G	AB	R	H	2B	3B	HR	TB	RBI	BB	SO	BAV	OBP	SLG	SB	GDP	HBP
37	144	517	84	157	24	3	13	226	80	78	66	.304	.395	.437	0	6	0

It was a long journey for George McQuinn to the 1947 New York Yankees where he became a key figure in their run to the pennant. In addition to his normal stellar play at first base, McQuinn batted .304 and drove in eighty runs, a significant upgrade from Nick Etten, a .232 hitter for the third-place Yankees in 1946. In late May he was batting a league-leading .392, and by the All-Star break he was still among the league leaders at .328. For McQuinn's efforts the fans chose him as the American League's starting first baseman for the All-Star Game. One sportswriter described his success as "the story book story behind the Yankees' surprising success . . . in 1947."[1]

McQuinn's contribution was perhaps equal parts unexpected and gratifying. It was unexpected because McQuinn had hit only .225 in 1946 for the cellar-dwelling Philadelphia Athletics, who gave him his unconditional release after the season. It looked as though at the age of thirty-six, without a job and with a bad back, his Major League career might be at an end. One article even referred to McQuinn as "the man nobody wanted."[2] New Yankees manager Bucky Harris, however, was an old fan of McQuinn's and the New Yorkers had a need at first base, so on January 25, 1947, the Yankees signed McQuinn as a free agent.

George Hartley McQuinn was born on May 29, 1910, in Arlington, Virginia, a suburb of Washington DC. His parents were William McQuinn, an electrician, and the former Ada Hartley, who was born in England but emigrated in 1899. The pair had seven children, five boys and two girls. George, the third son, began playing baseball at the age of seven. When he was twelve he bought

George McQuinn's success was the storybook story behind the Yankees' surprising success in 1947.

a George Sisler–model first baseman's glove, but McQuinn patterned himself after Joe Judge, the slick-fielding first baseman of the hometown Washington Senators.

McQuinn starred in basketball and baseball at Washington-Lee High School. He was a left-handed pitcher, but his high school coach began playing him at first base full-time. McQuinn had an offer to play baseball at the College of William and Mary but decided instead to try for a career in professional baseball.

In 1930 he was working as an elevator operator for the Chamber of Commerce in Washington and playing for a semipro team in northern Virginia. After a tryout arranged by his semipro manager, the New Haven (Connecticut) Profs of the Class A Eastern League signed McQuinn to his first professional contract. Playing time was limited, however, and the league was a fast one for a nineteen-year-old. McQuinn could manage only 2 hits in 19 at bats, and in May New Haven released him.

Fortunately, McQuinn had made an impression on Joe Benes, one of the veteran infielders for the Profs. Benes recommended him to Yankees scout Gene McCann, who signed McQuinn to a contract with the Wheeling (West Virginia) Stogies, the Yankees' farm club in the Class C Middle Atlantic League. McQuinn's .288 batting average for the Stogies earned him a promotion to the Scranton Miners of the Class B New York–Penn League for 1931, where he hit a strong .316 and drove in 101 runs while hitting just 5 home runs.

In 1932 McQuinn batted a combined .334 with 100 RBIs, while splitting the season between the Albany (New York) Senators of the Eastern League and, after the league folded on July 17, the Binghamton (New York) Triplets of the New York–Penn League. That performance earned him a spring-training invitation in 1933 with the International League Newark Bears, the Yankees' top farm club. The Bears, however, had the veteran Johnny Neun at first base, so McQuinn was shipped to the rival Toronto Maple Leafs. Despite an excellent start with the Leafs, he was sent back to Binghamton, where he batted a league-leading .357 and drove in 102 runs to win the league's Most Valuable Player Award.

McQuinn played a full season with Toronto in 1934, hitting .331 in 138 games, before fracturing an ankle sliding into third base in the Little World Series. By now some writers were wondering if the Yankees would consider trading Lou Gehrig to make room for McQuinn at first base.[3]

Yankees general manager George Weiss sent the Patient Scot, as McQuinn was sometimes called in the press, to Newark in 1935, where he hit .288, subpar for him because of a sore shoulder. Defen-

sively, he broke a twenty-two-year-old International League record for first basemen by fielding .997 for the year.

McQuinn had yet to be invited to a Yankees spring training, but he continued to attract attention from other organizations. Before the 1936 season the Cincinnati Reds, looking to replace Jim Bottomley at first base, purchased McQuinn conditionally, meaning they could return him to the Yankees up to June 1. McQuinn, still just twenty-five years old, finally got his big-league chance, and it was a flop. The Reds, under manager Charlie Dressen, immediately tried to get him to pull the ball rather than hit to all fields, as was his custom. He was unable to adjust and in 134 at bats hit only .201 with no home runs, prompting the Reds to send him back to the Yankees on June 1.

McQuinn returned to Toronto and hit a reaffirming .329 in 410 at bats. While there McQuinn met Kathleen Baxter, originally from Belfast, Northern Ireland, on a blind date at the ballpark. They married after the 1937 season and eventually had two daughters, Virginia and Victoria.

Kathleen knew little about baseball. The first time she saw a game in which it rained, she was perplexed about why the team had removed the tarpaulin when the rain stopped. After the game she asked George to explain why he had to play on a muddy field when it would have been so much cleaner to play on the canvas.

With Lou Gehrig still going strong for the Yankees, McQuinn found himself back with Newark in 1937. Playing for what is widely regarded as the best Minor League team ever, he batted .330 and stroked 21 home runs, as the Bears won the pennant by 25½ games. Under the rules then in place, McQuinn became eligible to be drafted by another Major League team after the 1937 season, if the Yankees did not place him on their big-league roster. As a result the St. Louis Browns selected McQuinn with the first draft pick and installed him at first base to begin the 1938 season.

McQuinn made sure he did not flub his second chance at the big leagues. On opening day he clubbed a single, double, and triple against one of the best pitchers in the league, Cleveland's Johnny Allen. Typically a slow starter, he hovered around the .270 mark for the first two months of the season, before improving to .300. Then, on July 24, he had 4 hits in 4 at bats against the Washington Senators, beginning a torrid 34-game hitting streak during which he batted .386. For the season he led the seventh-place Browns with a .324 batting average, while slugging 12 home runs and driving in 82 runs to lead the team in both categories.

The 1939 season brought more of the same, as McQuinn again led the Browns with a .316 average while playing in all 154 games. He improved his home run and runs batted in totals to 20 and 94, respectively, for the last-place Browns. For his efforts, McQuinn was named to his first All-Star team, although he did not appear in the game.

After the season the Yankees sought to trade for McQuinn, who had been blocked in the Minor Leagues by Gehrig for all those years, to replace the ill Gehrig at first base. The American League, however, had instituted a bizarre no-trade with the pennant-winner rule late in the year, which ended up quashing the deal. Yankees general manager Ed Barrow later lamented that the failure to land McQuinn had cost the Yankees their fifth straight pennant in 1940.

Thus, McQuinn found himself back with St. Louis in 1940. He slipped to a .279 average for the improved sixth-place Browns, but made his second All-Star team, although he again did not appear in the game. McQuinn, who was particularly adept at turning the 3-6-3 double play, also led American League first basemen in fielding average.

The Rawlings Sporting Goods Company began marketing a George McQuinn–model first baseman's glove. Years later it was reported that President George H. W. Bush, another slick-fielding first baseman from his days at Yale, kept his old first baseman's "claw" glove in his desk drawer in the Oval Office at the White House. It was a George McQuinn model.

McQuinn improved his batting average to .297 in 1941, with 18 homers and 80 runs batted in. The highlight of his season came on July 19, when he hit for the cycle. For the second consecutive year McQuinn led American League first basemen in fielding percentage. After the season he was to be included in what would have been a blockbuster trade with the National League champion Brooklyn Dodgers. The deal would have sent McQuinn and third baseman Harlond Clift to the Dodgers for reigning National League MVP Dolph Camilli, Cookie Lavagetto, and cash. McQuinn and Clift, however, could not clear American League waivers, and so the deal did not happen.

A back ailment that was becoming chronic hampered McQuinn in 1942 and 1943, as his batting average slipped to .262 in '42 and .243 in '43. It had gotten to the point that he needed to wear a brace to play. With World War II in full swing, McQuinn was ordered to take a preinduction physical in June 1943, but was rejected because of his back.

The Browns were a veteran team and would lead the league in 4-FS, medical discharges, and family-related deferments. While other teams were losing key players to the service, the Browns were relatively unaffected. As a result the 1944 Browns, playing in a weakened American League, won their first pennant.

The thirty-four-year-old McQuinn hit only .250, but his 11 home runs were second on the team, and he again led the league's first basemen in fielding average. He also made his fourth All-Star team, this time as the starting first baseman. He played the entire game, singling in the first inning off Bucky Walters to go 1 for 4, as the Americans went down to defeat, 7–1.

The Browns faced the St. Louis Cardinals, who had breezed to the National League pennant, in the only "All–St. Louis" World Series. In the fourth inning of the first game, with a man on, McQuinn blasted a towering drive off Mort Cooper onto the right-field roof to lead the Browns to a 2–1 victory. The Browns, however, hit only .183 for the Series and lost in six games. McQuinn was the one bright spot, batting .438 with seven hits, seven walks, and five of the team's nine runs batted in. His home run in Game One was the only one the Browns hit.

McQuinn was again called for a preinduction physical in early 1945, but was rejected under a new edict that ballplayers not fit for combat should not be drafted. McQuinn improved his batting average to .277, as the Browns finished a respectable third, six games behind the pennant-winning Detroit Tigers.

Shortly after the season, the Browns swapped McQuinn to the Philadelphia A's for first baseman Dick Siebert. The deal hit a snag when Siebert could not agree to terms with the Browns and retired from baseball, but Commissioner Happy Chandler ruled the A's could keep McQuinn nonetheless. The last-place A's may have regretted the commissioner's decision, as McQuinn had his worst year in baseball in 1946, hitting only .225, with three home runs and just thirty-five RBIs. He struggled through some long slumps and incurred the ire of the Athletics fans. At one point, after striking out four times and popping up three times in a doubleheader, McQuinn decided to quit the game, but Kathleen talked him out of it, telling him he had had too many good seasons not to be able to endure a bad one.

The Athletics gave McQuinn his unconditional release on January 9, 1947. Connie Mack, the venerable manager of the Athletics, was heard to remark that McQuinn had "played baseball one year too long."[4]

After McQuinn signed with the Yankees, he did not accompany the team on its spring tour through Latin America in 1947, joining them when they returned to St. Petersburg, Florida. By that time the Yankees' lineup looked set, with Tommy Henrich at first base and Yogi Berra in right field. Charley Keller, however, pulled a muscle in early April, sending Henrich temporarily to left field and giving McQuinn an opening at first base. He began hitting well immediately, including against left-handers, and soon took over the first base position, with Henrich occupying right field and Berra the catcher.

Early in the season McQuinn asked traveling secretary Arthur Patterson if he could room alone on the road. He was worried his chronic back pain, which made it hard for him to sleep at night, would disturb his roommate. He also found that being able to sprawl out in a double bed helped him sleep better.

With his back responding, the thirty-seven-year-old McQuinn got off to a great start and by early June was leading the league with a .354 average. Only a few months after being released by arguably the worst team in baseball, McQuinn was named as a starter for the American League All-Star team. He played the entire game at first base, going hitless in 4 at bats.

McQuinn had a reputation for being quiet and not very talkative. Teammate Bobby Brown remembered that his nickname on the Yankees was Si, short for "Silent." Brown recalled McQuinn as a great teammate and a very nice man. His typical postgame ritual on the road was to smoke an after-dinner cigar in the hotel lobby while watching the people go by and then head to bed at ten o'clock.

McQuinn tailed off late in the year to a final .304 average—second highest on the team—with thirteen home runs and eighty RBIs. Unlike 1944, however, he struggled in the World Series, hitting only .130 in 23 at bats as the Yankees defeated the Brooklyn Dodgers in seven games.

Although McQuinn would turn thirty-eight in May 1948, the Yankees wanted him back, and after a brief holdout, he signed for the '48 season.

He got off to another exceptional start. He was hitting .354 on May 31, and was again named the All-Star Game starter at first base for the American League, his sixth All-Star team. McQuinn played the entire game and was one of three players, along with Richie Ashburn and Stan Musial, with two hits as the American League won 5–2. He also set an All-Star Game record with 14 put-outs and 14 total chances. But he wore down over the long season and ended the campaign hitting .248 in 94 games as the Yankees finished third in a tight three-team pennant race.

The Yankees released McQuinn after the season, and he retired to Arlington, Virginia, to run a sporting-goods store bearing his name. He was lured back to baseball in 1950 by the Boston Braves organization with an offer to manage the Quebec Braves in the Class C Canadian-American League. The team finished first with a 97-40 record, won the semifinals four games to one, and swept the finals in four games against the Amsterdam (New York) Rugmakers. Along the way, McQuinn put himself into seventy-four games and hit .318.

The Braves switched to the Provincial League, also Class C, in 1951, as McQuinn again managed the team, this time to a fourth-place finish. Although he was now forty-one years old, he was still a playing manager, hitting .301 in 136 at bats. McQuinn was back managing Quebec in 1952 and guided the Braves to a second-place finish, while appearing as a pinch hitter twelve times, the final at bats of his playing career.

McQuinn continued to manage Quebec through the 1954 season with remarkable success. In five years leading the Braves, the club had finished first twice, second once, third once, and fourth once and won the league playoffs four times.

The Braves organization promoted McQuinn to manage the Atlanta Crackers in the Double-A Southern Association for 1955. With the club's record at 49-49 on July 16, McQuinn stepped down as manager. However, McQuinn's magic touch returned in 1956. On July 1 he took over the managerial reins of the Boise Braves in the Class C Pioneer League and led them to the pennant. McQuinn returned to Boise for 1957, but the team finished seventh.

Now forty-seven years old, McQuinn wanted to spend his summers closer to his Arlington home, and so he became a scout for the Washington Senators, concentrating on Virginia and West Virginia. He later scouted for the Montreal Expos before retiring from baseball in 1971 after forty-two years in the game. He published a detailed guide to playing baseball in 1972 and delighted in giving it to any youngster who expressed an interest.

In an interview late in life, McQuinn lamented that Lou Gehrig probably cost him four years of his big-league career. He expressed some bitterness that the Yankees had never taken him to spring training, despite his outstanding years in the Minor Leagues.[5] He also had little use for Commissioner Landis, who refused to act when told of the Yankees' undercover deal with the Browns in 1938.

But with the exception of his appeal to Landis, McQuinn was never one to make waves. During his Minor League career, his name was twice butchered by the teams he was playing for. In Scranton the public-address announcer called him Mike McQuinn, and later in Newark an error led him to be listed on the roster as Jack. He never corrected either mistake and for the rest of his life was known as Mike to those who had known him in Scranton and Jack to those from Newark.

McQuinn's Major League career spanned twelve years and four teams. He ended with a lifetime batting average of .276 with 1,588 hits in 1,550 big-league games. Although it was not as uncommon then as it is now, he walked more times than he struck out, 712 to 634. He is most remembered as a stalwart of some mediocre St. Louis Browns clubs in the late 1930s and early 1940s and as the star of the 1944 World Series. But he had a major impact on the '47 Yankees run to the pennant after Yankees manager Bucky Harris plucked him off the scrap heap.

McQuinn died on December 24, 1978, in Alexandria, Virginia, of complications from a stroke. He was sixty-eight years old.

Chapter 14. Allie Reynolds

Royse Parr

AGE	W	L	PCT.	ERA	G	GS	GF	CG	SHO	SV	IP	H	BB	SO	HBP	WP
30	19	8	.704	3.20	34	30	3	17	4	2	241.2	207	123	129	4	8

Because of religious strictures imposed by his parents, Allie Reynolds did not play baseball in an organized fashion until after he left high school. He overcame that handicap and had an outstanding thirteen-year career in the 1940s and 1950s as a pitcher with the Cleveland Indians and the New York Yankees.

Allie Pierce Reynolds was born in Bethany, Oklahoma, a suburb of Oklahoma City, on February 10, 1917, to David C. and Mary (Brooks) Reynolds; he was the eldest of three sons. Allie was three-sixteenths Creek Indian, descending from his three-quarters-Creek grandmother, Eliza Root Reynolds. He grew tired of explaining the three-sixteenths and often told reporters he was one-fourth Creek.

Allie's father was born in Indian Territory in 1890, attended Chilocco Indian School, and became a Nazarene preacher. Allie's parents lived strictly by Nazarene doctrine, staying away from movies and dances. One doctrinal stand that affected their athletic young son was the prohibition of playing sports on Sunday. From an early age, Allie loved baseball. Because most sandlot and semipro games were played on Sunday afternoon, he did not play baseball on a team until after high school, but turned to other sports, including softball, track, and football.

Except for football in the sixth grade, Allie did not play any school sports until he entered Oklahoma City's Capitol Hill High School in the fall of 1933 for his senior year. He weighed 145 pounds and saw only limited action as a back on offense and defense. The Capitol Hill Redskins were an undefeated team that claimed the national high

Allie Reynolds was the Yankees' best starting pitcher in 1947, with a 19-8 record and a .704 winning percentage.

school football championship by defeating Chicago's Harrison Tech, 55–13.

Allie had completed his high school class work by going to summer school in 1934, but he returned to Capitol Hill High School for one more semester to play football. As the starting quarterback, he led the team to an undefeated season that was marred only by two ties.

His father's meager income as a Nazarene minister meant Allie would have to earn his own way if he wanted to go to college. He was disappointed to learn football coaches at the University of Oklahoma were not interested in him because of his light weight. However, in January 1935, he accepted a track scholarship from Oklahoma A & M that paid twenty dollars a month toward his tuition and room and board. Also, because of his Creek heritage, he was granted a four-hundred-dollar loan by a foundation.

In May 1935 Allie was the Missouri Valley Conference's high-point man for Oklahoma A & M in the annual freshman track meet. His times in the 100-yard dash and the 220-yard dash and his distance in the javelin throw were comparable to those of the great Jim Thorpe in the 1912 Olympics.

On July 7, 1935, Allie married his Capitol Hill High School sweetheart, Dale Earlene Jones. He had a summer job slinging a sledgehammer and playing baseball in the outfield for an Oklahoma City oil-field equipment firm. Their first son, Allie Dale, was born on June 8, 1936. He died in an airplane crash in Wyoming in 1978.

In 1935 Reynolds was the leading ground gainer for Oklahoma A & M's freshman football team. For the next three seasons, he was the starting fullback and a tenacious defensive back on varsity teams that won only six games and lost twenty-four.

One afternoon in the spring of 1937, Oklahoma A & M's athletic director and basketball and baseball coach, Henry P. Iba, saw Reynolds throwing a javelin next to the baseball field. Iba asked the track and football star if he could help the baseball team by throwing batting practice. Allie agreed, and without any warm-ups, he started striking out batters, throwing as hard as he could. After a few batters Iba called him in and told him to go to the equipment room and get a uniform.

Allie was used primarily as a relief pitcher at the beginning of the season. In his first start as a collegian, he pitched all nine innings and hit a home run in a 3–2 victory over the University of Oklahoma.

In late June 1937 the need for a summer job took Reynolds to Colorado to play on the Leyden Coal Company's semipro team. With Allie pitching the championship game, Leyden Coal won Colorado's first statewide semipro championship.

Reynolds had a 5-2 record as Oklahoma A & M won another state conference title in 1938. On May 20 of that year, he and Earlene became the parents of a daughter, Bobbye Kay Reynolds. In 1939 Allie was elected team captain. He was 5-1 in his final college season, including a May 15 no-hitter against Southwestern Oklahoma State University.

Coach Iba advised Reynolds to consider a career in professional baseball and set up a meeting for him with Cleveland Indians scout Hugh "Red" Alexander. The Indians signed Reynolds, paid him a one-thousand-dollar bonus, and assigned him to their Springfield, Ohio, affiliate in the Class C Middle Atlantic League. Plagued by control problems, he nevertheless compiled an 11-8 record.

Because he had not yet completed his college education, Reynolds returned to classes at Oklahoma A & M for the fall semester of 1939. Later he took correspondence courses, completing a bachelor of science degree in June 1942.

Cleveland promoted Reynolds to the Cedar Rapids (Iowa) Raiders of the Class B Three-I League, where he had a 12-7 record for the 1940 season. On March 8, 1941, Earlene gave birth to their third and last child, James David. Reynolds opened the 1941 season at Wilkes-Barre, Pennsylvania, in the Class A Eastern League. He appeared in only three games with no decisions before being sent back to Cedar Rapids, where he had a 10-10 record.

As he had in 1941, Reynolds began the 1942 season with Wilkes-Barre. He became the Eastern League's premier pitcher with an 18-7 record, including eleven shutouts. He was named the right-handed pitcher on the league's all-star team (Warren Spahn was the left-handed pitcher). After the

Eastern League season ended, Reynolds was called up to the Indians, and he made his Major League debut on September 17, 1942, as a reliever against the Washington Senators.

As the 1943 season began, Cleveland had high hopes for Reynolds to replace Bob Feller, who was in the navy. The 1943 game that established the six-foot, 195-pound Reynolds as a coming star was a 12–0 shellacking of the Yankees on July 2 at League Park. He finished the season with an 11-12 record and a league-leading 151 strikeouts.

Pitching for a second-division ball club in 1944, Reynolds posted an 11-8 record, which gave him the best winning percentage among Indians pitchers. He was 18-12 for the fifth-place Indians in 1945, but led the league with 130 walks in 247⅓ innings. Reynolds got off to a great start in 1946, but he had to win nine of his final fourteen decisions to salvage an 11-15 record.

At the end of the 1946 season, Reynolds was the subject of trade discussions between the Indians and the Yankees. During a World Series game at Fenway Park, Larry MacPhail, the president of the Yankees, asked Joe DiMaggio which Cleveland pitcher would be best for the New Yorkers, Red Embree or Reynolds. DiMaggio said he could hit Embree but had never been successful against Reynolds. MacPhail made the trade, sending second baseman Joe Gordon to the Indians in exchange for Reynolds.

Allie started the 1947 season year with back-to-back shutouts, including a two-hitter against the Boston Red Sox on April 23. He duplicated the two-hit shutout against the Red Sox exactly a month later. He finished the season with a 19-8 record and a .704 winning percentage, the league's second best. The Yankees easily won the American League pennant and defeated the Brooklyn Dodgers four games to three in the World Series. Reynolds had a complete-game, 10–3 victory in Game Two and a no-decision in Game Six.

The Yankees acquired left-hander Eddie Lopat from the Chicago White Sox in 1948, and he, Reynolds, and Vic Raschi became a dominant pitching trio throughout most of Allie's remaining years in baseball.

Reynolds opened the 1948 season with five straight victories and finished with a 16-7 record for the third-place Yankees. He was 17-6 in 1949, as the Yankees edged Boston for the pennant on the last day of the season. In Game One of the World Series against the Dodgers, Yankees first baseman Tommy Henrich hit a ninth-inning home run off Don Newcombe to secure a 1–0, two-hit shutout for Reynolds. In Game Four Allie came into the game in the sixth inning and retired all ten batters he faced (including five strikeouts) to save Lopat's 6–4 win.

In the 1950 World Series the Yankees swept the Philadelphia Phillies. The Game Two starters were Reynolds, who had a 16-12 record during the season, and twenty-four-year-old future Hall of Famer Robin Roberts. The Yankees scored a run in the second, and Reynolds yielded a single tally in the fifth. The score held up until the tenth, when Joe DiMaggio homered against Roberts. Reynolds gave up a leadoff walk to start the bottom of the frame but then set down the Phils in order, winning 2–1. It was his third World Series victory without a loss.

Going into the 1951 season, Reynolds was the Yankees' main pitching concern. Doctors had told him he had several bone chips floating in his elbow and an off-season operation might be needed, but Reynolds chose not to have the surgery. To combat the pain in his back and elbow, allergies, and a tired feeling that may have been prediabetes, he started eating a prescribed four oranges per game.

If the Yankees were concerned about Reynolds for the '51 campaign, they need not have worried. The thirty-four-year-old right-hander had one of his finest seasons, which included pitching two no-hitters. On the night of July 12, in Cleveland, he topped Bob Feller in a 1–0 squeaker. Yankees center fielder Gene Woodling homered in the top of the seventh for the only score of the game. Allie ended it with a strikeout of second baseman Bobby Avila.

Going into the final weekend of the season, the Yankees led the Indians by two and a half games. The Yankees had four games at home against arch-rival Boston, including a Friday doubleheader. Reynolds faced eighteen-game winner Mel Parnell in the opener and had an 8–0 lead with two outs in the top of the ninth inning. He had issued four walks but not a hit as he prepared to face Ted Williams. Williams hit a towering foul ball behind home plate that was muffed by catcher Yogi Berra. Reynolds threw a second fastball in the same spot, and Williams popped it up again. Berra caught it for the final out of the game, preserving the no-hitter. When Raschi won the nightcap, the Yankees clinched the pennant.

Allie became the first pitcher in the American League to pitch two no-hitters in a season. After the second one Yankees broadcaster Mel Allen began calling Allie "Super Chief," a nickname that stuck.

Reynolds completed the 1951 regular season with a 17-8 record and a 3.05 ERA over 221 innings. He led the American League with seven shutouts and, showing his versatility, had seven (retroactive) saves. The Yankees met the New York Giants in the World Series. Riding the momentum of their amazing late-season surge capped by Bobby Thomson's storied home run off Ralph Branca, the Giants rolled over Allie and the Yankees in Game One, 5–1.

After the teams split Games Two and Three, Reynolds evened the Series by shutting down the Giants, 6–2, in Game Four. The Yankees took the last two games of the Series behind Lopat and Raschi to claim their third successive world championship. Reynolds won the Ray Hickok Award as the professional athlete of the year. The award was an alligator-skin, gold-buckled, diamond-studded

belt, which Allie kept in bank storage for years because it was too expensive to insure.

The Yankees were confident they could win a fourth consecutive pennant in 1952, a feat accomplished only twice before. The team started slowly but finished two games ahead of the Indians. Reynolds had the only twenty-victory season of his career at 20-8. He had a 2.05 ERA and six shutouts, and he led the American League in strikeouts with 160. His second-place finish in the MVP voting was the highest of his career.

In the World Series the Yankees and Dodgers squared off in Game One in Brooklyn. Reynolds pitched well but lost 4–2 to surprise starter Joe Black. Allie got revenge against Black with a masterful 2–0 shutout in Game Four that evened the Series. The Dodgers won Game Five to go ahead three games to two. Reynolds relieved Raschi with two outs in the eighth inning of Game Six and saved the Yankees' 3–2 victory. In Game Seven he relieved Lopat in the fourth inning. He gave up one run in three innings and was the winning pitcher in a 4–2 victory that gave the Yankees their fourth consecutive World Series championship.

Reynolds spent the winter in Oklahoma City building his oil business. As a prelude to spring training, he achieved a longtime ambition in mid-February by winning the National Baseball Players Golf Championship, beating Giants shortstop Alvin Dark, 1-up, in Miami, Florida.

The Yankees won their twentieth American League pennant in 1953. Reynolds, now primarily a reliever, had a record of 13-7 with thirteen saves. The Yanks defeated the Dodgers in six games for their record fifth consecutive world championship. Reynolds was the winning pitcher in Game Six after relieving Whitey Ford in the eighth inning.

By winning his seventh World Series game, Reynolds tied a record held by Yankees pitcher Red Ruffing. It was Allie's last World Series game. He went home to Oklahoma to trade his baseball glove for oil-field gloves. A successful winter in the oil business and an aging right arm combined to convince him that 1954 would be his last baseball season.

Reynolds continued to work as both a starter and a reliever in 1954. On September 23 he pitched his last Major League game, beating the Philadelphia Athletics at Yankee Stadium, 10–2. The Yankees closed the season with 103 victories, more than in any of their five previous seasons. But the Indians won 111 games for a new American League record. Reynolds finished with a 13-4 record and a .765 winning percentage, the best of his career. In his thirteen Major League seasons he had started 434 regular-season games and relieved in 309.

At season's end, he had not made up his mind about retirement. He continued his representation of American League players in talks with baseball management on pension matters. In an interview on February 25, 1955, with sportswriter John Cronley of the *Daily Oklahoman*, Allie announced his retirement from baseball.

Living in Oklahoma and working in the oil business all of his retirement years, Reynolds became the sole owner and president of Atlas Mud Company. His active participation in Oklahoma civic and charitable causes was extensive. One of his favorite causes was the YMCA baseball program. In 1960 he headed a fund drive to build a new YMCA in his hometown of Bethany. On April 24, 1982, the new baseball stadium at his alma mater, now called Oklahoma State University, was dedicated in his honor.

On October 28, 1983, Allie's wife of forty-eight years, Earlene, died after a lengthy battle with cancer. On November 16, 1991, Allie was inducted into the Oklahoma Hall of Fame. More than twelve hundred people attended the black-tie event that was televised statewide.

Reynolds was a member of the Yankees All-Star team selected by former manager Casey Stengel. In 1989 he was honored with a plaque in Monument Park at Yankee Stadium.

Reynolds did everything he could to promote his Native American heritage. He served as president of the National Hall of Fame for Famous American Indians at Anadarko, Oklahoma. His last public appearance was on October 3, 1994, when he was in Anadarko for the dedication of a portrait in bronze of Kiowa chief Stumbling Bear.

Suffering from lymphoma and diabetes, Reynolds entered Oklahoma City's St. Anthony Hospital in December 1994. He died on December 26, 1994, at the age of seventy-seven. He was buried at Oklahoma City's Memorial Park Cemetery after American Indian services celebrating his Creek heritage.

Chapter 15. Timeline, April 30–May 22

Lyle Spatz

Wednesday, April 30, at St. Louis—The Yankees began their first western swing with a 15–5 loss to the St. Louis Browns at Sportsman's Park. Jeff Heath with a grand slam, Walt Judnich with two home runs, and Vern Stephens with one led the assault on Allie Reynolds, Randy Gumpert, Joe Page, Mel Queen, Karl Drews, and Rugger Ardizoia, who was making his first and last big-league appearance. Denny Galehouse and Fred Sanford allowed the Yanks just five hits. 7-5, Second, .017 percentage points behind.

Thursday, May 1, at Chicago—Rained out. 7-5, Second, .017 percentage points behind.

Friday, May 2, at Chicago—New York moved into first place as rookie Frank Shea won his first Major League game, a 5–2 victory at Chicago's Comiskey Park. The White Sox scored both their runs in the eighth inning. The Yanks had scored one in the first and four in the third off Chicago's Edgar Smith. George McQuinn had three hits, including a double, and two runs batted in for New York. 8-5, First, 1 game ahead.

Saturday, May 3, at Chicago (2)—The White Sox took over the league lead by sweeping a doubleheader from New York, dropping the Yanks to fourth place. Left-hander Thornton Lee beat Bill Bevens, 2–1, in the opener. Charlie Keller's fourth-inning home run gave Bevens a lead, but the Sox rebounded with single runs in the fifth and eighth. Chicago pounded Don Johnson, Al Lyons, and Karl Drews for eleven hits to win the nightcap, 10–3. The Yanks had ten against Eddie

Lopat and Gordon Maltzberger, who pitched the last three innings. Tommy Henrich, Joe DiMaggio, Billy Johnson, and George Stirnweiss each had two hits for New York. Johnson had hits in his first two at bats but pulled a muscle in his side and had to leave the game in the fourth inning. Rookie catcher Ralph Houk was thrown out of the game by umpire Art Passarella in the first inning of the nightcap, becoming the first Yankee ejection of 1947. 8-7, Fourth, 1 game behind.

Sunday, May 4, at Detroit—A rainy day and muddy conditions at Briggs Stadium led to the game being called after six innings with the score tied at 2–2. Spud Chandler and the Tigers' Hal Newhouser went the distance. Eddie Lake had a home run for Detroit, and Joe DiMaggio had two doubles for New York. 8-7-1, Fourth, 2 games behind.

Monday, May 5, at Detroit—Rained out. 8-7-1, Fourth, 2 games behind.

Tuesday, May 6, at Detroit—Eddie Lake's eighth-inning home run, his second in two games, gave the Tigers a 3–2 victory. Allie Reynolds squandered a two-run lead as his record fell to 2-2. Hal White, who relieved starter Virgil Trucks in the seventh inning, got the win. Pat Mullin of Detroit extended his hitting streak to thirteen games. Tommy Henrich and Phil Rizzuto each had two hits for the Yankees. 8-8-1, Fifth, 2 games behind.

Wednesday, May 7, at Cleveland—Canceled because of cold weather. 8-8-1, Fifth, 2 games behind.

Thursday, May 8, at Cleveland (2)—Canceled because of cold weather. Pitcher Rugger Ardizoia and infielder Ray Mack were sent to the Minor Leagues. 8-8-1, Fifth, 1½ games behind.

Friday, May 9—Not scheduled. 8-8-1, Fifth (T), 2 games behind.

Saturday, May 10, at Boston—The Yanks scored four in the first and three in the second to defeat the Red Sox, 9–6, at Fenway Park. Frank Shea went all the way for the win, while Joe Dobson took the loss. Shea twice struck out Ted Williams in at bats where Williams represented the tying run, once with the bases loaded and once with two on. Bucky Harris's revamped batting order produced twelve hits. Yogi Berra, who caught Shea, had three hits and four runs batted in. 9-8-1, Fifth, 1 game behind.

Sunday, May 11, at Boston—The Red Sox scored six runs in the first inning against Bill Bevens and then held on to win, 8–7. Bobby Doerr's three-run homer was the big blow. Tommy Henrich, with a single, a home run, and three runs batted in, and pitcher Al Lyons, with two singles and two RBIS, led the Yankees' attack. 9-9-1, Sixth, 2½ games behind.

Monday, May 12, at Boston—The Yankees hit three home runs, but all came with the bases empty as they lost again to the Red Sox, 4–3. The blasts by George McQuinn, Yogi Berra, and pitcher Spud Chandler were negated by Boston's three-run uprising against Chandler in the eighth inning. The Yanks had now lost five of their last six games and had won only twice in the last nine. 9-10-1, Sixth, 3 games behind.

Tuesday, May 13, vs. St. Louis—Allie Reynolds's three-hitter defeated the Browns, 9–1, as the Yan-

kees returned home. The Yanks had four home runs, two by Charlie Keller and one each by Joe DiMaggio and Johnny Lindell. Keller's second, DiMaggio's, and Lindell's came in succession in the sixth inning off rookie Fred Sanford. New York pounded starter Sam Zoldak and Sanford for fourteen hits. Phil Rizzuto's fifth-inning steal of second was the Yanks' first stolen base of the season. 10-10-1, Fourth (T), 3 games behind.

Wednesday, May 14, vs. St. Louis—Rained out. First baseman Nick Etten and catcher Ken Silvestri were sent to the Minors to get the Yankees down to the twenty-five-player limit. 10-10-1, Fourth, 3½ games behind.

Thursday, May 15, vs. Chicago—The White Sox broke a five-game losing streak by pounding the Yankees, 8–2, in the first night game of the season at Yankee Stadium. The Yanks scored two runs against Frank Papish in the first inning before Joe Haynes relieved Papish and held New York scoreless the rest of the way. Right fielder Bob Kennedy with four hits led Chicago's sixteen-hit attack against Bill Bevens, Randy Gumpert, and Joe Page. 10-11-1, Fifth, 4½ games behind.

Friday, May 16—Not scheduled. 10-11-1, Fifth, 4 games behind.

Saturday, May 17, vs. Chicago (2)—New York won both ends of a doubleheader, each by a 4–3 score in front of a crowd of 66,666. Frank Shea, who had three hits of his own, went the distance to win the opener. Joe DiMaggio's leadoff home run in the ninth inning was the game winner. Chicago scored all their runs off Spud Chandler in the first inning of the nightcap, but Chandler shut them out the rest of the way. Billy Johnson's eighth-inning single scored George McQuinn, who had three hits in the game, with the winning run. Eddie Lopat of the White Sox allowed only eight hits, with Chandler's double being the only one for extra bases. 12-11-1, Third, 3½ games behind.

Sunday, May 18, vs. Cleveland—Former Yankees second baseman Joe Gordon made a triumphant return to New York in leading Cleveland to a 5–3 win. Gordon, traded to the Indians for pitcher Allie Reynolds, had two singles and two walks against Reynolds and a ninth-inning home run off Joe Page. Bob Feller, with ninth-inning relief help from Steve Gromek, was the winner. The Yanks had seven hits in the game, two apiece by Bobby Brown, Charlie Keller, and Joe DiMaggio. 12-12-1, Fourth (T), 4 games behind.

Monday, May 19, vs. Cleveland—The Yankees left nine runners on in losing to Cleveland, 5–4. Don Johnson, the first of four New York pitchers, was the loser. Rookie Bryan Stephens, with Steve Gromek again helping in relief, was the winner. Joe DiMaggio had two doubles for the Yankees, while Charlie Keller hit his seventh home run and Frank Colman his first. 12-13-1, Sixth, 4½ games behind.

Tuesday, May 20, vs. Cleveland—Trailing 2–0, the Yankees tied the score in the seventh, only to have Cleveland score two in the eighth to win, 4–2. The runs came against Bill Bevens, who suffered his fourth straight defeat. Don Black, the first of three Indians pitchers, was the winner. The Yanks again failed to get the big hit when it counted, leaving seven men on base over the final three innings. Charlie Keller had his eighth home of the season. 12-14-1, Sixth, 4½ games behind.

Wednesday, May 21, vs. Detroit—Frank Shea raised his record to 4-1, shutting out the Tigers, 5–0. It was Shea's fifth complete game in his five starts. The Yanks got three in the first off Hal

Newhouser on Joe DiMaggio's bases-loaded double and two more off Newhouser in the seventh. Meanwhile, Shea limited Detroit to just four singles. 13-14-1, Sixth, 3½ games behind.

Thursday, May 22—Not scheduled. 13-14-1, Sixth, 3½ games behind.

Chapter 16. **Ray Mack**

Joseph Wancho

AGE	G	AB	R	H	2B	3B	HR	TB	RBI	BB	SO	BAV	OBP	SLG	SB	GDP	HBP
30	1	0	0	0	0	0	0	0	0	0	0	—	—	—	0	0	0

"Ray Mack's Lunging Play Ends Classic" read the subheadline in the *Cleveland Plain Dealer* on April 17, 1940. The "Classic" was Bob Feller's no-hit mastery of the Chicago White Sox on a cold, raw opening day at Comiskey Park. Through 2012 it was still the only Major League no-hitter pitched on opening day.

Although Feller had his fastball humming, he was quick to give praise after the game to the defense behind him. "I had some pretty fancy support out there," he said. "Ben Chapman saved my bacon twice and Kenny (Keltner) and Ray (Mack) each made a couple of swell plays. Sure, I had pretty good stuff, but I was lucky too."[1]

Ray Mack had three assists at his second base position, and two of them were dandy plays, in the eighth and ninth innings. In the eighth he scooped up a slow roller off the bat of pinch hitter Larry Rosenthal, and his throw just beat Rosenthal to first base. In the ninth he went to his left, knocked down a line drive, retrieved it on the outfield grass, and threw out Taft Wright for the game's final out. "Mack came up with two as sweet plays as I've ever seen," Feller said. "He was way off balance when he scooped up Rosenthal's roller in the eighth, and how his throw ever beat Larry to the bag I don't know. And I don't know how he ever knocked down Wright's smash in the ninth, to say nothing of retrieving the ball and throwing the guy out."[2] For Mack, the sparkling performance launched his best season in a big-league career that lasted nine years and included one regular-season game with the world champion New York Yankees in 1947.

Raymond James Mlckovsky was born on

Ray Mack's only game as a Yankee was as a pinch runner on May 6, 1947.

August 31, 1916, in Cleveland, the older of two sons born to Joseph and Rose Mlckovsky. He grew up on Cleveland's East Side and attended John Adams High School. After graduation Ray entered the Case School of Applied Science (now Case Western Reserve University). Baseball was his first love, but Case did not field a team, so the six-foot, two-hundred-pound Mlckovsky turned his talent to football. He excelled at the game and quickly came to be known as the Case Ace. Primarily a fullback for the Engineers, he also passed, kicked, and started in the defensive backfield. He was named All-Ohio three consecutive years. But Mlckovsky shrugged off his success. "I never cared to play football," he said. "Baseball was the sport

I really loved. Why did I play football? Well, you know how it is; I had the size, was fairly fast, and could take it. I did not intend to play football when I entered Case. I was after my engineering degree and wished to play baseball in the summertime as Case did not have a baseball team. But the coaches and my fellow students got after me and I turned out for football, just to give my best for 'My Ole Almy Mammy.'"[3]

Picked by the Chicago Bears in the eleventh round of the 1938 National Football League draft, Mlckovsky bypassed pro football and instead played sandlot baseball in Cleveland in the summer of 1937. While playing for the semipro Poschke Barbecues, he was signed by the Cleveland Indians. Poschke manager Laddie Placek, who also scouted for Cleveland, persuaded Indians general manager C. C. Slapnicka to take a chance on Mlckovsky. "If I can make the big leagues, I will stick to baseball," Ray said. "If I see at the end of a year or so I cannot make the grade, I will go in for engineering. But I think I can make the big leagues."[4]

The Indians assigned Mlckovsky to the Fargo-Moorhead (North Dakota, Minnesota) Twins of the Class D Northern League for the 1938 season, where he passed his first test with flying colors. In ninety-four games, seventy-seven of them at shortstop, he led the league in batting, with a .378 average, and had thirty-two doubles, twenty-four home runs, and ninety-six runs batted in.

His performance earned him a call-up to Cleveland, where he played in two games, both at second base. He made his Major League debut on September 9 against the Detroit Tigers and made his second appearance in the last game of the season, the second game of a doubleheader, also against Detroit. In that game, his first Major League start, he went 2 for 4, with a triple and two RBIs before his hometown fans. His first big-league hit came off Tigers right-hander Bob Harris.

At Fargo-Moorhead he had started to use the name Mack instead of Mlckovsky, for the benefit of scorers and sportswriters. Later that year his father, Joseph Mlckovsky, got permission from a court for the family to change its surname to Mack. Joseph told the court Mlckovsky was too hard to pronounce and too easy to misspell.

Cleveland manager Ossie Vitt felt Mack could use more seasoning, so in 1939 he was farmed to the Indians' affiliate in the International League, the Buffalo Bisons, where he was teamed with shortstop Lou Boudreau. The pair became an effective double-play combination. Because of his size, Mack was difficult to move off the bag but still displayed excellent range. Boudreau and Mack formed a strong bond on the field, as well as a close friendship off it. Their relationship served them and the Indians well over the next several years.

Mack and Boudreau were both called up to the Indians on August 3, 1939, and made their season debuts on August 7. Cleveland was just four games over .500 when Mack and Boudreau joined the team, but was 36-20 the rest of the way. Though Mack hit just .152 in thirty-six games, and replaced the popular Odell "Bad News" Hale at second base, the hometown product quickly found favor with the fans.

The 1940 season started with Feller's masterpiece and escalated with a pennant race that went to the final week. Mack's first full season in Cleveland was productive. He was leading the team in hitting with a .318 average at the All-Star break and was selected for the All-Star Game at Sportsman's Park in St. Louis. (He struck out as a pinch hitter in the top of the eighth inning and played second base in the bottom of the inning.) His final average for 1940 was .283, a career high, but it was his work in the field that was making others notice. "Never saw anyone better on double killings than this Mack boy," said manager Vitt. "It's just swish, swish, swish, and two guys rubbed out."

The pitching staff was equally thrilled to have the young combo backing them. With Hal Trosky at first base and Ken Keltner manning third, the Indians' talented infield foursome earned praise. "How can you help winning when you've got an infield like that in back of you?" said left-handed starting pitcher Al Smith. "Why, they cut off more hits than if you had a picket fence on the edge of the infield."[5] Mack was third among regular second basemen with 109 double plays, but he was also second in errors and had the second-lowest fielding percentage.

But all was not rosy on the Indians' squad. The hypercritical Vitt often lashed out at his players, in private or in the press. Finally, several veteran players, looking for an opportunity to overthrow him, signed a petition urging that Vitt be fired. Mack and Boudreau were excused from participating because the veterans did not want to penalize the younger players by potentially ruining their careers. They appealed to owner Alva Bradley privately, but in the end Bradley backed his manager.

Word of the players' revolt reached the public, and soon they were dubbed the Crybaby Indians. They were ridiculed in the press and at every opposing ballpark. In spite of the turmoil the Indians were neck and neck with Detroit and New York the entire season. Trailing the Tigers by two games, Cleveland needed a sweep of the season-ending three-game series against Detroit at Cleveland Stadium. Feller, who led the league with twenty-seven victories that season, lost the first game, 2–0, to Floyd Giebell, a youngster who won the only two games he appeared in all season. Cleveland finished one game behind Detroit, one ahead of New York.

For Mack the 1940 season was the apex of his career as a batter. Although his defense remained solid, his offense never again measured up to his rookie year. In addition to his .283 batting average, he had twelve home runs and sixty-nine RBIS. Over the next five seasons, he averaged just .224 with four homers and thirty-two RBIS. Boudreau believed that being a local player hurt Mack. Every

coach or friend was close by to lend advice. And Mack tried to listen to them all. He became tense at the plate and could never find his groove. Mack had his own diagnosis for his hitting woes: "My big fault is that I take too many third strikes."[6]

On October 19, 1940, Mack married the former Jean Fisher, a classmate of his at John Adams High School and a schoolteacher in the Cleveland suburb of Cuyahoga Heights. They had three children, Judith, Tom, and Dick.

During Mack's remaining tenure with the Indians, the team did not come as close to winning a pennant as it had in 1940. Roger Peckinpaugh replaced Vitt after the 1940 season, and then he was replaced by Boudreau, in 1942. Although Boudreau and Mack remained friends, Lou's new status as player-manager removed most of the camaraderie they had shared before. As a manager he could show no favoritism to his buddies, like Keltner and Mack.

Because of his wife and their first child, Mack was classified 3-A by his draft board. Then he was reclassified as 1-A, but appealed it and in 1943 was again classified 3-A. After the 1943 season he took a job as a design engineer at Thompson Aircraft Products Company in Euclid, Ohio. Though Commissioner Kenesaw Mountain Landis had ruled that players doing war work could rejoin their teams in their spare time, Mack decided to forgo part-time baseball. "I'd like to play baseball when the war is over," he said, "But I think I can do more for the war effort by sticking to my job at the plant."[7] He changed his mind in June 1944, however, and joined the Indians on home dates and at weekend road games. In all he played in eighty-three games in 1944, while working full-time at the war plant. As World War II wound down, but manpower needs increased, Mack was inducted into the army at Camp Atterbury, Indiana, on April 17, 1945, and missed the 1945 baseball season.

When the war ended, Mack returned to the

Indians, but in a backup role. Cleveland had acquired second baseman Dutch Meyer from Detroit twelve days after Mack entered the army. Mack played in only sixty-one games in 1946 and posted his career-low batting average, .205. He did show off some of his old defensive flair. On April 30, at Yankee Stadium, Bob Feller was on the verge of achieving his second no-hitter. With the Indians leading, 1–0, the Yankees' George Stirnweiss was on third base with two outs when Charlie Keller hit a roller to second. Mack was playing on the edge of the grass and in his haste to field the ball fell to all fours. He recovered in time and threw to first base from his knees to get Keller for the final out.

On October 11, 1946, the Indians acquired second baseman Joe Gordon from the Yankees in exchange for pitcher Allie Reynolds. The addition of Gordon spelled the end of Mack's time in Cleveland, and on December 6 he and catcher Sherm Lollar were traded to the Yankees. "Mack is the second sacker we have been looking for as a stand-in for Snuffy Stirnweiss," Yankees manager Bucky Harris said.[8] Indians general manager Bill Veeck echoed Boudreau's concerns, saying, "I think Ray's only weakness was the fact that he was playing before his hometown friends. He's a good boy and I wish him all the success in the world—except of course, when he's playing against us."[9] But despite Bucky Harris's optimism, Mack was unable to win the backup role at second base. He got into only one game with the Yankees, pinch running for catcher Aaron Robinson on May 6. He spent most of the season with the Newark Bears of the International League. On September 7 the Chicago Cubs purchased Mack from Newark, and he ended the year starting in twenty-one games for the Cubs.

Mack was thirty years old when he retired after the 1947 season. He went to work as an executive at the Ohio Locomotive Crane Company in Bucyrus, Ohio. He took pride in his sons' accom-
plishments on the football field. Tom, an All-American lineman at the University of Michigan, played for the Los Angeles Rams for thirteen years and was inducted into the Pro Football Hall of Fame in 1999. Ray's other son, Dick, was a three-year letter winner (1972–74) at Ohio State University.

Ray Mack never lived to witness much of his sons' successes. He died on May 7, 1969, from complications of cancer. He often looked fondly at Feller's no-hitter in 1940 as the highlight of his career. "That was the greatest thrill I ever had in sports," he said. "If I had missed that play, I probably would never have forgiven myself."[10]

Chapter 17. **Bobby Brown**

Mike Huber

AGE	G	AB	R	H	2B	3B	HR	TB	RBI	BB	SO	BAV	OBP	SLG	SB	GDP	HBP
22	69	150	21	45	6	1	1	56	18	21	9	.300	.390	.373	0	4	1

More than seventeen thousand players have played Major League Baseball, but Dr. Bobby Brown's life story has no parallel. He played professional baseball on a team that won five world championships, was a practicing cardiologist in Texas, served as interim president of the Texas Rangers, and spent ten years as president of the American League.

Robert William "Bobby" Brown was born on October 25, 1924, in Seattle, Washington, to William and Myrtle (Berg) Brown. His father's career caused several cross-country moves, but Bobby excelled at baseball everywhere they lived. His father had been a semipro of some note with the Meadowbrooks in Newark, New Jersey. Bill Brown had even played against Lou Gehrig, when the latter played by the name of Lou Long.[1] Bobby always felt that his father wanted him to give baseball a whirl, if consistent with his college plans and medical hopes.

Young Bobby was only ten when he drop-kicked twenty-four field goals in a contest for youngsters staged by a Seattle, Washington, newspaper, which tested football kicking and throwing skills. At age twelve he was playing American Legion Junior Baseball; by the eighth grade, he went to the tryout camp at Ruppert Stadium in Newark for the International League Newark Bears; and at eighteen he was a freshman sensation at Stanford University, receiving offers from several Major League teams.

Bobby attended San Francisco's Galileo High School, the same school as Vince, Joe, and Dom DiMaggio and Hank Luisetti, who was once considered America's greatest basketball star. Brown was a straight-A student and president of the student body.

Bobby Brown had two doubles, a single, and a walk in four pinch-hitting appearances in the 1947 World Series.

In 1941, while a junior at Galileo, he was noticed by a Cincinnati Reds scout, who had seen the Galileo squad destroy the University of California freshman baseball team. After the game, the scout, who was also a professor at Berkeley, asked young Bobby if he would like to go to Cincinnati and work out with the Reds. Bobby, a shortstop, promptly agreed. That summer he took the train to Ohio and worked out for ten days with the Reds, followed by an additional three-day workout when the team went to Chicago. After graduation from high school, Bill Brown sent his son back east to work out with the Reds, Detroit Tigers, New York Yankees, Brooklyn Dodgers, and Philadelphia Athletics.

Brown entered Stanford in 1942, expecting to major in chemical engineering. While still at Stanford, he enlisted in the navy in 1943. Called up for duty on July 1, 1943, he was assigned to a naval unit at UCLA and given five semesters to finish his premed courses. Brown was at UCLA for one year, where he played baseball for the Bruins and was then assigned to San Diego Naval Hospital for temporary duty.

On December 1, 1944, Brown was assigned to Tulane Medical School and was given a midshipman's uniform. He played a year at Tulane, the 1945 season. With Brown on the team, the Green Wave had its most successful season to that point, winning 21 of 27 games, including 12 in a row, and Brown batted .444.[2] When he was mustered out of the navy in January 1946, the scouts came calling.

Brown convinced the dean of the medical school at Tulane that he could play ball and still go to medical school. On February 18, 1946, he signed a contract with the New York Yankees that stipulated he would receive $11,000 for 1946, $15,000 for 1947, $18,000 for 1948, as well as receiving a cash bonus of $10,000. According to Bobby, that was the second-highest bonus awarded up to that time. His highest per-season salary while playing was $19,500 (both 1952 and 1954), which was more than the dean at his medical school earned.[3]

Bobby was at Tulane when the 1946 season began and with the Yankees when it ended. He spent most of the year with Newark, the Yanks' top farm team, where he hit .341. Jackie Robinson hit .349 for Montreal, edging Brown for the batting title. Because of his great season for the Bears, Bobby was honored in January 1947 at the Newark Athletic Club as one of the top four outstanding New Jersey athletes of 1946.

Brown was called up to New York after the International League season ended. The six-foot-one, 180-pound youngster made his Major League debut on September 22, 1946, playing shortstop and batting third in the second game of a Yankee Stadium doubleheader against Philadelphia. He got his first big-league hit in that game, as did his roommate, Yogi Berra, also making his debut. Bobby appeared in 7 games, going 8 for 24.

In 1947 Bobby batted .300 in 69 games and then played an important role in the Yankees' 7-game World Series win against the Brooklyn Dodgers. The Yankees used the twenty-two-year-old left-handed-hitting Brown as a pinch hitter four times, and four times he came through: two doubles, a single, and a walk. His fourth-inning double in Game Seven tied the score at 2–2 and sent the eventual Series-winning run to third base.

In the 1949 World Series, Bobby had 6 hits in 12 at-bats, including a double and two triples, and he drove in 5 runs. Then in 1950, when the Yankees swept the Phillies in the Series, Bobby went 4 for 12, with a double and a triple. The next season brought a fourth trip to the World Series for Brown. In 5 games he had 5 hits in 14 at bats with 2 walks. He had also won four world championship rings by the age of twenty-six.

Between 1948 and 1951 Bobby averaged 104 games played per season, platooning with Billy Johnson (1948 to 1950) and Gil McDougald (1951) at third base. He was a steady contributor to the Yankee lineup. During this four-year span, Brown collected 364 hits in his limited time, sporting a .281 batting average.

In 1951 Bobby and his future bride, Sara Kathryn French, set their wedding date for October 12, 1951, which was shortly after the scheduled end of the World Series. The Yankees were playing in the Series against the New York Giants, but after Game Three there was a heavy downpour that threatened to continue for a few days. Bobby and his bride had not planned a huge wedding, inviting only family and close friends, so he called her and changed the date to October 16, giving enough extra time in case the weather combined with possibly 4 more games extended past the twelfth.

The Series lasted 6 games. Brown batted .357, and the Yankees won another title. Brown's .439 (18-for-41) career batting average in World Series play is the highest for batters with more than 20 at-bats.

Bobby and Sara were married at the Northway Christian Church in Dallas, Texas. Brown likes to tell folks that his was the only marriage postponed by rain. Following the honeymoon, he served as an intern at Southern Pacific Hospital in San Francisco.

On April 24, 1951, Bobby was shagging fly balls when he was called to the Yankees' clubhouse. He was asked to treat Casey Stengel, who was suddenly overcome with nausea. As it turned out, Casey had had a kidney stone.

When the Korean War broke out, Dr. Brown was eligible for the "Doctor's Draft," since he had not actually served overseas during World War II. Consequently, he was sent to Korea to serve with the 45th Division in the U.S. Army and was assigned to the 160th Field Artillery Battalion, heading the battalion aid station. After nineteen months of military service in Korea and at Tokyo Army Hospital, Brown returned to the Yankees in May 1954. The Yankees had lost 9 of their first 16 games, leading Casey Stengel to exclaim, "Boy, do we need a doctor!"[4]

While at Tokyo Army Hospital, Bobby joined Joe DiMaggio and Lefty O'Doul to give clinics to the Japanese teams who were in spring training. Joe had brought his bride, Marilyn Monroe, to Japan for their honeymoon. Joe told the press the only doctor who could treat Mrs. DiMaggio was Lieutenant Brown.

Bobby Brown retired from baseball in 1954 at the age of twenty-nine. He had spent parts of eight seasons in New York, but he felt the calling to become a full-time doctor, a decision he never regretted. In 1974 Dr. Brown wrote, "The only regret I might have is that I didn't play ball exclusively for two or three years. I'd like to know how well I could have done if I'd concentrated exclusively on baseball for several years."[5] His response is akin to Burt Lancaster's line in *Field of Dreams*, when Ray Kinsella asks Moonlight Graham if he ever regrets becoming a doctor and not playing baseball. Dr. Brown will tell you, "Not going to medical school would have been a tragedy."

After trading the bat and glove for a stethoscope and lab coat, Dr. Brown served his residency in internal medicine at San Francisco County Hospital from 1954 through 1957 (he was chief resident the last year). He then served a fellowship in cardiology back at his alma mater, Tulane Medical School, from 1957 to 1958. Following that he entered private practice in Fort Worth, Texas, on August 1, 1958.

In May 1974 Brown took a six-month leave of absence from his medical practice to become interim president of the Texas Rangers. Brad Corbett, a good friend, had purchased the team and needed Bobby's help. Coincident with his appearance, the Rangers moved into first place. "Modesty keeps me from taking the credit," Dr. Brown told the *Los Angeles Times*. "Modesty and Ferguson Jenkins and Billy Martin."[6]

Brown knew he had his work cut out for him. "Texas is football country," he once said. "We've got to get them interested in baseball." The 1974 Rangers finished above .500 after two consecutive one-hundred-loss seasons, but at the end of the '74 season, Dr. Brown returned to his practice.

When Bowie Kuhn retired as commissioner of Major League Baseball in 1984, the owners asked Bobby to interview for the job. However, the owners wanted a businessman to be the commissioner and offered Brown the job of president of the American League. It was a job he held for ten years, before Gene Budig replaced him on August

1, 1994. On August 10, Bobby got on a plane to fly home to Texas. That was the same day the players went on strike, a strike that would end the season and cancel the World Series.

Brown visited the U.S. Military Academy in January 2007, meeting with cadets who were students in a sabermetrics course. He was very candid in his remarks. Regarding the state of baseball at that time, Dr. Brown said television is driving the huge amount of money being given to players. Attendance is higher than ever, and millions of people are subscribing to teams' television networks.

He is amazed that the distances set up more than 125 years ago have proven to be "just right" — ninety feet between bases and sixty feet, six inches to home plate from the mound. They have raised and lowered the height of the mound, but the horizontal distances are "just right."[7]

The former American League president was proud of having very few controversies during his tenure, but a few incidents still stick in his mind. Dr. Brown's toughest cases involved two marquee players. The first was when Roger Clemens was ejected in a playoff game against Oakland in 1990 for arguing balls and strikes. He received an eight-game suspension for the next season. The second involved Albert Belle, who was discovered to have used a corked bat on July 15, 1994. Belle received a seven-game suspension.

Brown believed steroids were a huge temptation for ballplayers to perform better. Cocaine was a major problem in baseball when he became American League president. In 1984 he had suggested testing for illegal drugs four or five times per season. His proposal called for random testing with no identifying names on the specimen bottles, to simply determine the extent of the problem. The players' union refused.

Joe DiMaggio was the best all-around baseball player he ever saw, Brown said. Joe never gave inspirational talks, but he always played at 110 percent, so others played hard, too. In fact,

Bobby recalled that no player on the Yankees gave big inspirational speeches. "We all got along. At the end of the day, everyone knew who had played well in a game."[8] It was an eight-team league in those days, but Bobby felt that nobody stood out like DiMaggio. From 1937 to 1973, it was 457 feet to left-center field in Yankee Stadium. In any other ballpark, Joe might have hit well over five hundred home runs. Having said that, Bobby said Ted Williams was the best pure hitter he ever saw.

In June 1949 the *Sporting News* interviewed Brown about his future in both medicine and baseball. He replied, "The basic truth is this: Just as long as baseball wants me, I will want baseball. Inevitably, there will be a day when I will have to say to myself, 'The time has come. Hang up your spikes and your uniform, put away the bats, and get down to working out the Oath of Hippocrates.'" The article ended with the following: "The day we talked with Brown, he was batting .333, and moving along impressively. A fine youngster, a credit to baseball, and he will be a credit to medicine. As he left to go out on the field, Bobby laughed, 'Here are two more points. I will not wear a goatee as a doctor. And I am not engaged to be married.' The future Dr. Brown pulled on his glove and walked out on the field to do a little laboratory work under the watchful eye of Prof. Casey Stengel."[9]

Dr. Brown is a member of the Athletic Halls of Fame at Stanford, UCLA, and Tulane Universities, as well as those of Galileo High School, San Francisco Prep, and Greater New Orleans. He has received the Presidential Citation from the American Academy of Otolaryngology (1990) and the Branch Rickey Award for Uncommon Service to Baseball (1992) and has been awarded three honorary doctorates (from Trinity College, the University of Massachusetts, and Hillsdale College). He was awarded the U.S. Coast Guard Silver Lifesaving Medal and served our country proudly during World War II and the Korean War. He and Sara have three children and ten grandchildren.

Chapter 18. **Rugger Ardizoia**

Bill Nowlin

AGE	W	L	PCT.	ERA	G	GS	GF	CG	SHO	SV	IP	H	BB	SO	HBP	WP
27	0	0	.000	9.00	1	0	1	0	0	0	2.0	4	1	0	0	0

The steamship ss *Colombo* arrived in New York from Naples, Italy, on December 6, 1921, bearing a boy who had just turned two years old, Rinaldo Ardizzoia, accompanied by his mother, Annunziata (Mossina) Ardizzoia, a tailor from Oleggio, in northern Italy, where Rinaldo had been born on November 20, 1919. The mother and son were on their way to Port Costa, California, to join husband and father Carlo Ardizzoia, who had sailed to the United States thirteen months earlier.[1]

Twenty-six years later that same boy pitched in the Major Leagues for the New York Yankees. In a February 2010 interview, he was asked what brought his father to the United States, and he replied, "The man who owned the brickyard in Port Costa, he was from my home town and he invited a bunch of Italians over to come to America and have a job."[2]

In 1923 the family moved to San Francisco. Rinaldo had lost his mother two months after his sixth birthday to what he understands was double pneumonia. While living in San Francisco as a youngster, Rinaldo added the middle name Joseph—not Giuseppe; Joseph was a confirmation name. He thought he picked up his nickname around this time. "I was all by myself. My father was working and I was only six years old. I lived across the street from a playground and I used to go over there and play marbles and fool around and get in fights. Guys would chase me. We had a bunch of thistle back there that wasn't cleared and I'd run into the thistle and they wouldn't chase me. They'd say, 'You're a rugged little bugger.' I also played rugby and I was a Rugger there."

In 1931 the Catholic Youth Organization began

Rugger Ardizoia's Major League career consisted of two innings pitched against the St. Louis Browns on April 30, 1947.

a baseball team, and Ardizoia played for St. Theresa's Church CYO. Next came play in American Legion ball and at the High School of Commerce. He had favored football as a youngster and was a third baseman when he first started playing baseball. It was only in his junior year at Commerce that he took up pitching. He threw two no-hitters in high school, and in one of them opposing pitcher Art Gigli also threw a no-hitter. The game had to be called off because it ran too long, neither team ever getting a base hit.[3]

The day he graduated from high school in 1937, the seventeen-year-old signed a contract with the Mission Reds of the Pacific Coast League (the team represented San Francisco's Mission district). Actually, he had signed while he was still in high school, six months before his graduation. Offered a scholarship to Stanford University, he had to turn it down because he had already turned professional.[4]

Ardizoia's father was working as a warehouseman in 1937, earning $25 a week. His son now was making $150 a month. "That's when he quit," Rugger said of his father. "He said, like an old Italian, 'I supported you for seventeen years, now you support me, OK?' . . . Money was pretty good and so when I turned twenty-one, I bought this house. . . . I've been in this house here sixty-five years." On January 11, 1942, Ardizoia married a fellow Commerce student, Mary Castagnola, a twenty-one-year-old native of San Diego.

Ardizoia threw 24⅔ innings in nine games with Mission and had a remarkable first game. "We were in San Diego and they had [Jimmy] Reese and Ted Williams and a whole bunch of those old guys and Johnny Babich started and I relieved in the second inning and I pitched the next five innings of one-hit ball. That was my first game in professional ball. After that, look out!"

He fondly recalled those early days: "I had all these old guys around me and I was just a young guy and they all teased me and all that. We got along real good, though. That's one thing about the old days. There was [sic] no individuals. They were a team. . . . In those days, you pitched. You didn't count pitches. You didn't count innings. You just got it on. You got the guy out. I went as high as eighteen innings complete."

More than anyone else, some of the catchers he worked with taught the five-foot-eleven, 180-pound right-hander how to pitch. "I had a fastball. I had an overhand curve, a three-quarter curve, and a sidearmed curve — three different types — and some little sinker ball. Then later on when I started with Oakland I picked up a slider."

Ardizoia posted a 5.84 ERA in 1937 but did not record a decision. It was in 1938, pitching for the Bellingham (Washington) Chinooks in the Western International League, that he first got in a full season of work, 224 innings, with a 12-13 record and a 3.05 earned run average. During the off-season, he pitched in the San Francisco Winter League. He credited manager Ken Penner of Bellingham with teaching him how to hide his pitches better.[5]

In 1939 and 1940 Ardizoia pitched for the Hollywood Stars of the PCL. He first became associated with the New York Yankees in December 1939. The *New York World-Telegram* reported that the Yankees had acquired Ardizoia in exchange for pitchers Hiram Bithorn and Ivy Andrews. Ardizoia, described as the best pitching prospect in the Pacific Coast League, had finished the season 14-9 with a 3.98 ERA.

It was intended from the start that Rugger would spend 1940 with Hollywood. He won fourteen and lost twenty that year, and his 145 strikeouts were fifth highest in the league. In August 1940 the Yankees officially purchased his contract, and in the spring of 1941 he trained with the Major League club.

After spring training the Yankees sent him to the Newark Bears of the International League, but early in the season a problem cropped up. The International League included two clubs from Canada, Montreal and Toronto. Ardizoia was 0-1 with Newark before the Bears general manager realized Ardizoia was not a U.S. citizen. A trip to Ellis Island affirmed that he was legal in the United States, but Canada would not let him into the country. They were at war with Italy, and that made Rugger an enemy alien. "So I got sent to Kansas City. In those days, you had to wait two years and go before a judge and all that stuff. In the meantime, I got trapped in World War II and even though I wasn't a citizen, I accepted the induction [into the U.S. Army]," he said. Before being drafted, however, he got into twenty-seven games for the Kansas City Blues of the American Association, going 12-9. Back with the Blues in 1942, he won six and lost twelve.

Rugger served in the U.S. Army Air Force from May 1943 until he was discharged in November 1945. After eight months at McClellan Field, near Sacramento, he was transferred to Honolulu on June 1, 1944. Rugger joined the 7th Air Force's baseball team there, compiling, he recalled, a 12-0 record. In Hawaii he became a tow-target operator, flying over a firing range towing a target with a cable that was from 250 to 2,500 feet long. Baseball may have saved his life, he remembered with a bit of understatement: "One night that I was supposed to fly, I was relieved because we had a ballgame. The plane crashed. I was lucky."

Ardizoia joined a team that took him to some of the islands in the Pacific—Tinian, Saipan, and Iwo Jima. Playing baseball on volcanic and coral islands that had recently seen vicious fighting was not always the easiest of duty. There were still worries that a Japanese soldier would emerge from concealment and open fire. "There were so many zigzags there [in the tunnels], they didn't know if they got them all. They were hiding in the hills. We'd play every day or two. In the meantime, we had KP and cleanup jobs and stuff like that," Ardizoia recalled.[6]

When Corporal Ardizoia was discharged from the service at Camp Peale, California, he spoke up and said, "Hey, I want to become a citizen." The officer was a little stunned. "Aren't you a citizen? What the heck are you doing in the Army?" He replied, "I volunteered because this is my country." He was told, "OK, stick around for a couple of days." Ardizoia said, "'No way.' My son was

eighteen months old and I hadn't seen my wife for three years. So I came home and then went down to the Federal Building and went before the judge. He had me raise my right hand and he says, 'Do you solemnly swear to defend the United States . . . wait a minute, you just came out of the Army?' I said, 'Yessir.' He says, 'You're a citizen.'"[7]

In 1946 it was back to baseball, this time with the Oakland Oaks in the PCL. Rugger had an excellent year on an Oaks team that won 111 games for manager Casey Stengel. Rugger was 15-7 with a 2.83 ERA. The three seasons he lost during the war had not hindered him. His only home run in pro ball came in 1947, against Seattle.

In 1947 Ardizoia went to spring training with the Yankees again. He stuck with the big-league team for a while and finally had his opportunity to play in a Major League game. It was the last day of April. The Yanks had just arrived in St. Louis for a game against the Browns. When Ardizoia was brought on to pitch the bottom of the seventh, St. Louis had a 13–4 lead. He got through the seventh, but former Iwo Jima teammate Walt Judnich hit a homer in the eighth, one of two runs Rugger gave up.

As Ardizoia said in the 2006 interview, "The guy that hit the home run off me was one of my boyhood idols, Walter Judnich. I more or less slid it in for him because we were so far behind anyway." Johnny Lindell pinch-hit for Rugger in the ninth. It was Ardizoia's only Major League appearance, but by doing so, he became one of only seven natives of Italy to play in the Major Leagues.

After another week of throwing batting practice, Rugger was sold to Hollywood on May 8 and played the rest of the season for the Stars, going 11-10. His time in the Majors was over; the Yankees won the World Series that year, but Ardizoia never received either a ring or a World Series share.

In 1948 Rugger was with Hollywood again. In January 1949 he was traded to the Seattle Rainiers. He began the 1950 season with the Rainiers, but got into only two games, spending most of the year with the Dallas Stars in the Texas League, where he went 10-10. He pitched a second season for Dallas in 1951 and was 8-3 with a 2.88 earned run average.

After that season he retired from the game. He said he had a bone chip in his throwing arm and wanted to spend more time with his two children in San Francisco. Ardizoia finished baseball with just that one brief Major League appearance, with the 1947 Yankees. In the Minors he pitched for twelve seasons and won 123 games against 115 defeats, with a 3.63 ERA.

Ardizoia had worked during the off-seasons for Owl Drug Company, a retail chain. Owl had a baseball team, and he played winter ball for it in the Bay Area, but also put in eight-hour days. He worked for Owl until it went out of business and then took up work as a salesman for Galland Linen and then the National Linen Service. He worked at selling rental linen for about thirty years. Baseball helped. "A lot of accounts, people knew that I played ball and in those days they still remembered."

Rugger's wife, Mary, died in April 1983. The couple had two children, both born in San Francisco: Bill, in June 1944, and Janet, in April 1947. Janet died in April 2010.

The Yankees kept in touch, sending Ardizoia their alumni mailings, Christmas and birthday cards, and a big bouquet of flowers on his eighty-fifth birthday. After the 2009 World Series win, they sent him a medallion celebrating their twenty-seventh world championship. In 2009 a journalist in Italy wrote a story about him. Ardizoia helped start and remained a member of the Old Timers Baseball Association of San Francisco, a group mostly of semipro players, but open to anyone who played baseball.

Chapter 19. **Ken Silvestri**

Joseph M. Schuster

AGE	G	AB	R	H	2B	3B	HR	TB	RBI	BB	SO	BAV	OBP	SLG	SB	GDP	HBP
31	3	10	0	2	0	0	0	2	0	2	2	.200	.333	.200	0	0	0

Looking at Ken Silvestri's Major League statistics could leave the impression his baseball career was marginal at best. He played in 102 games in eight seasons spread over thirteen years, hit five home runs, and had a .217 batting average. However, by the time he died at seventy-five, in 1992, he had spent more than a half century in the game. In addition to playing for three teams that reached the World Series, he was a Minor League instructor, a Major League pitching coach, and a Major League manager (for 3 games). He was so beloved by the last organization for which he coached that the players wore an emblem in his honor on their uniform sleeves during the season after he died.

Kenneth Joseph Silvestri was born in Chicago on May 3, 1916, and as a young boy was adopted by Joseph and Florence Silvestri.[1] The details of Ken's birth parents are obscure; according to his son, Ken Silvestri Jr., Silvestri would never discuss his biological parents. "The one time I asked him about it, all he would say was, 'Joseph and Florence are your grandparents,'" Silvestri Jr. said.[2] Although the exact date of his adoption is apparently not available, Silvestri's name appears as the son of his adoptive parents in the 1930 U.S. Census.[3]

As a boy he attended Chicago's Carl Schurz School from the first grade to the eighth grade and then Carl Schurz High School until graduation in 1935.[4] Silvestri was a star athlete in high school, earning all-city and all-state honors in football as an end during two seasons, and he received a football scholarship to Purdue University.[5] However, Silvestri left Purdue after less than a year and played semipro baseball in Chicago for a season

Ken Silvestri was stuck behind catchers Aaron Robinson, Yogi Berra, Ralph Houk, and Sherman Lollar.

until a White Sox scout saw him and signed him as a catcher.[6]

The White Sox assigned the six-feet-one, two-hundred-pound switch hitter to a Class D affiliate, the Rayne (Louisiana) Rice Birds of the Evangeline League, for the 1936 season. Silvestri was the starting catcher, appearing in 128 games, with a .270 batting average, the second lowest on the team.

Silvestri was back in Rayne in 1937, where he boosted his batting average to .307 and led the league in home runs (23) and runs batted in (123), helping the team to a first-place finish.[7]

Silvestri's success convinced the White Sox to promote him in 1938 from their lowest-level Minor League team to their highest, the Class Double-A St. Paul Saints of the American Association. There, he impressed manager Babe Ganzel with his defense, throwing arm, and toughness. A press release from that season issued by the St. Paul team said, "It's a good thing that there are no weak hearts among St. Paul directors, for Silvestri lives dangerously. He had played with St. Paul three weeks before someone told him that base runners are entitled to score now and then on close plays at the plate. Enlightened now, he doesn't try to be the complete hockey goalie as runners bear down from third, but still manages to enjoy his share of spills."[8]

The next year Silvestri found himself with the inside track to the starting catcher's job with the White Sox, who were looking for youth behind the plate.[9] Manager Jimmy Dykes pointed to Silvestri as one of the keys to the team's improving on their sixth-place finish in 1938.[10]

Silvestri came out of spring training as the team's starting catcher and began the season with a rare cockiness for a twenty-two-year-old rookie, getting into trouble on opening day with plate umpire Bill McGowan because he complained about McGowan's calls on some of Johnny Rigney's pitches. Because Silvestri did his complaining quietly, McGowan did not eject him, but he let Dykes know "he wouldn't tolerate rookie aggressiveness after Opening Day."[11]

Silvestri kept the starting catcher's job for the first fifteen games of the season, despite hitting under .200 for most of the time with only one home run. His streak of starts ended on May 7,

when he developed the flu.[12] His replacement that day against the Yankees, Mike Tresh, went 2 for 4, then 1 for 3 the next day, and Dykes gave him the starting job thereafter. Silvestri was relegated to a handful of pinch-hit appearances and spot starts as catcher. Finally, on June 27, the White Sox sent him back to St. Paul, where he finished the season.[13]

Silvestri's abbreviated rookie season was a microcosm of his entire career as a player: high expectations followed by misfortune, bad timing, or losing a roster spot to another player who would have a hot streak.

Silvestri was back with the White Sox for the 1940 season, but Dykes used him in just twenty-eight games, almost exclusively as a pinch hitter. His season was highlighted by two ninth-inning pinch-hit home runs. The first was in a 7–5 White Sox loss to the Yankees on June 5; the second was a walk-off two-run shot in a 4–3 victory over the Philadelphia Athletics on September 12.

On December 31, 1940, the White Sox, who had a surplus of catchers, traded Silvestri to the Yankees for infielder Billy Knickerbocker.[14] Because the Yankees still had Bill Dickey, they saw Silvestri primarily as a pinch hitter who would double as a batting-practice and bullpen catcher.[15] As expected, Silvestri had limited playing time for the 1941 Yankees, appearing in only seventeen games. Part of the reason Silvestri saw so little action that year was that in May he underwent an emergency appendectomy.[16]

Although the Yankees reached the World Series, defeating the Brooklyn Dodgers in five games, Silvestri did not play in any of the games. In fact, Silvestri did not play a single professional game over the next four seasons: on December 3 he passed his physical and entered the army the next day, three days before the Japanese attack on Pearl Harbor.[17] Silvestri reportedly did not mind getting the call, telling a reporter, "I'm all set to be one of the $21 a month guys, but I'm not complaining."[18]

Silvestri spent more than four years in the army. After several postings in the United States, he was sent to the Pacific as part of the 577th Service Company and was based first in New Guinea and then Yokohama, Japan, not long after the Japanese surrendered.[19] On his discharge in November 1945 Silvestri was a first sergeant.[20]

In 1946 Silvestri was back with the Yankees, but appeared in only thirteen games. After the season, on November 16, he married Rose Markov.[21] The couple had one son, Kenneth Silvestri Jr., born in Chicago on April 10, 1952.[22] According to Ken Jr., his parents met during a game at Comiskey Park: "My grandfather Peter Markov was a big White Sox fan who lived a block from the ballpark.[23] He often took my mother [Rose] to a game and one day when they had good seats, she and my father started talking."[24]

The next year, 1947, was Silvestri's last in New York. The team's primary catcher was now Aaron Robinson, and behind him, and ahead of Silvestri, were Yogi Berra, Ralph Houk, and Sherm Lollar.[25] Silvestri got into just three games. Reportedly, the White Sox were interested in reacquiring him, but when he cleared waivers, New York sent him to their Class Triple-A club in Kansas City.[26]

Silvestri spent the balance of 1947 with Kansas City before the Yankees assigned him to their International League team, the Newark Bears, for 1948. Despite hitting just .218 with seventeen home runs and forty-four RBIs, he was named to the league's All-Star team.[27]

The Philadelphia Phillies chose Silvestri in the 1948 Rule 5 draft, because they saw him as someone who could help their pitching staff and defense. Phillies farm director Joe Reardon said, "This guy is the kind of a catcher who takes charge of the ballgame. He's aggressive, smart. . . . He's a catcher who runs his ballgames. He'll help us plenty."[28]

Silvestri spent the next three years with the Philadelphia team, but again saw limited playing time. From 1949 through 1951 he appeared in only nineteen games. However, he did have an impact on the team. In 1950, when the Phillies won the National League pennant, Silvestri was a steadying influence and unofficial coach for the team's young pitching staff.

A sportswriter called him "operating head of the bullpen," and described specifically his work with rookie starter Bubba Church: "[Church's] place, day after day, was in the bullpen, under Silvestri's psychological treatment."[29]

After the 1951 season, Silvestri's last as a Major League player, he spent the next forty years in baseball, as a scout, Minor League instructor, manager, player-manager, and Major League coach. During the off-seasons, he worked a variety of jobs; he was a store detective for Sears, a bartender, and an insurance salesman, among others.[30]

In the game he spent the bulk of the 1950s coaching and managing in the lowest levels of the Yankees' farm system. In 1959–60, he was the Phillies' bullpen coach, before moving to the Braves organization, first as a coach for their Class Triple-A team in Louisville in 1961–62 and then as bullpen coach for the Milwaukee and then the Atlanta Braves from 1963 to 1975.

In 1967 Silvestri spent three days—the final weekend of an abysmal season for the Braves—as interim manager, replacing Billy Hitchcock. The Braves went 0-3 during Silvestri's brief tenure, after which he returned to the bullpen as coach for the Braves through the end of the 1975 season. In that capacity he witnessed a historic moment in baseball history: Henry Aaron's record-breaking 715th career home run in the Braves' 1974 home opener. The event moved Silvestri: "Atlanta bullpen coach Ken Silvestri, a grizzled veteran, was sentimental," an Associated Press reporter wrote. "'It brought a few tears to my eyes. I was crying a bit and I felt like going up to Hank and saying, 'Now we both can retire.'"[31]

In 1976 Silvestri returned to his original base-ball home, the White Sox, when the team hired him as a combination bullpen and pitching coach.[32] After the White Sox finished the season in last place in the American League West, however, the team fired manager Paul Richards and either fired or reassigned the entire coaching staff; Silvestri ended up a Minor League instructor.[33]

Six years later, at the start of the 1982 season, the organization replaced him, and Silvestri, then sixty-five, went home to Tallahassee, Florida, and "presumably retired."[34] Midway through the season, the White Sox fired pitching coach Ron Schueler, and manager Tony LaRussa offered the job to Silvestri on an interim basis.[35]

Silvestri, however, did not attack the job as if he were just a placeholder for half a season. As the *Sporting News* put it roughly a month into his tenure, "No one expected a sixty-six-year-old career baseball man to do much with a struggling young staff. Silvestri surprised them all, coming in with a nothing-to-lose attitude. He told the pitchers exactly what was on his mind, which wasn't always fun to hear." His toughness paid off: in the first eighteen games after he took over, the White Sox went 15-3 with a 2.55 earned run average, more than a run lower than it had been under Schueler.[36]

When the season ended, however, he went back to being a scout and a Minor League instructor. He remained with the White Sox until his death in Tallahassee on March 31, 1992, from pancreatic cancer, a disease he learned he had only three months before.[37] His wife had died in 1984, also in Tallahassee.[38] Silvestri is buried in his home state at Mount Carmel Cemetery, Hillside, Illinois.

Chapter 20. **Mel Queen**

Marc Z Aaron

AGE	W	L	PCT.	ERA	G	GS	GF	CG	SHO	SV	IP	H	BB	SO	HBP	WP
29	0	0	000	9.45	5	0	2	0	0	0	6.2	9	4	2	1	0

Melvin Joseph Queen overcame frequent bouts of wildness to have a long baseball career. He was signed by the New York Yankees as a pitcher in 1938 and ended his playing career in 1955 as the property of the Pittsburgh Pirates. Queen appeared in a Yankees uniform in four different seasons. His only winning season at the Major League level was 1944, when he started ten games for the Yankees, winning six and losing three. In 1947 he relieved in five games for New York without getting a decision, and then was sold to the Pirates on July 10.

Queen was born in Maxwell, Pennsylvania, a coal mining town south of Pittsburgh, on March 4, 1918. The oldest of four children (three boys and a girl), he was of English, Scottish, and German descent. His father was killed in a mine explosion in 1926, when Mel was eight years old. His mother was not going to let fate repeat itself with any of her children, so she moved with them to Wellsburg, West Virginia, a factory town not far from the Pennsylvania state line. Mel attended high school there, and in 1934 he joined the Civilian Conservation Corps (CCC), a public works relief program established during the Depression. Assigned to a camp in Berkeley Springs, West Virginia, he spent thirty-six months building roads, constructing cabins, and clearing woods. On the weekends he played shortstop and third base in a baseball league made up of teams from CCC camps.

When Queen completed his three years of CCC service he returned home and landed a job at a power plant in Windsor, West Virginia, where he played first base for the plant's baseball team. Queen was slightly over six feet tall and weighed about two hundred pounds during his playing

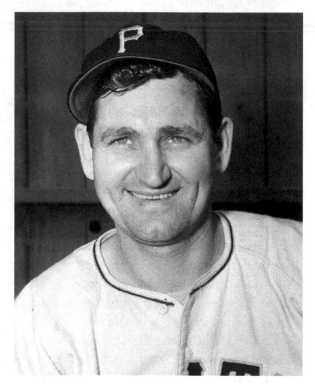

Mel Queen made five relief appearances for the Yankees in 1947 before they sold him to Pittsburgh in June.

days. He had tremendous wrists, large hands, and bulging biceps, perhaps as a result of his three years of labor for the CCC.

At the urging of his manager he became a pitcher. In August 1938, while pitching for the plant team, Queen was contacted by the Butler Yankees of the Class D Pennsylvania State Association. Apparently, a fan had recommended him to the team. Queen pitched in two games for Butler and in eight for the Dover (Delaware) Orioles of the Class D Eastern Shore League.

In 1939 the Yankees sent Queen to the Amsterdam (New York) Rugmakers of the Class C Canadian-American League. He pitched well enough (14-9, 3.15 earned run average) to be invited to 1940 spring training with the Binghamton (New York) Triplets of the Class A Eastern League. But Queen was not quite ready for Class A baseball and was sent to the Augusta (Georgia) Tigers of the Class B South Atlantic League. After three bad appearances he was sent down to the Akron (Ohio) Yankees of the Class C Middle Atlantic League. He hit his stride at Akron, with an 18-8 record, a 2.70 ERA, and 202 strikeouts in 210 innings that helped lead his team to the pennant.

Queen began the 1941 season with New York's top farm team, the International League Newark Bears. But after developing shoulder trouble, he was sent back to Binghamton, where he pitched a league-record eight shutouts. Late in the season he was sent to the Kansas City Blues of the American Association. In his only start for the Blues he pitched a one-hit shutout. Overall, he won sixteen games that season, which earned him an invitation to the Yankees' 1942 spring-training camp in St. Petersburg, Florida.

During the off-season Queen played winter ball in Cuba, where he developed an ingrown toenail. Sportswriter Will Wedge of the *New York Sun* claimed the affected toenail resulted "from a pair of 'gaudy' Cuban street shoes he had worn while gallivanting around Havana last month."[1] When the Yankees learned that Queen was playing in Cuba, they sent him an "admonitory" letter, ordering him to return to the United States.

Queen made his big-league debut on April 18, 1942. Facing the Boston Red Sox in relief, he pitched a scoreless inning in a 5–1 defeat. Five days later he pitched 1⅔ innings against the Philadelphia Athletics and got the victory when the Yankees rallied to win. Queen pitched twice more and was unscored upon, before being sent down. He spent the rest of the 1942 season with Newark, Kansas City, and Binghamton.

Queen spent all of the 1943 season with Kansas City, where he won seven and lost twelve. During the off-season he found work in a defense plant in Johnson City, New York, a small town near Binghamton. Mel's work and family commitments—he resided in Johnson City with his wife and children—resulted in his reporting to Newark only three days before the start of the 1944 season. His first five starts for the Bears served as his spring training. His arm was tight, and his muscles ached from the heavy labor. He lost all five starts.

Eventually, his arm got stronger, and Queen pitched twenty-eight consecutive scoreless innings during a four-start win streak. In mid-August he was recalled by the Yankees. Placed in the war-decimated rotation, Queen made ten starts and won six games while losing three. One of his victories was the first of his three Major League shutouts, over the Philadelphia Athletics in the second game of a Labor Day doubleheader. He also got three hits in the game, two of them doubles. Yankees manager Joe McCarthy called Queen's performance against the Athletics "wicked," adding, "The Athletics never had a chance. He was faster than any other hurler in this league."[2]

After the season Queen went to work in a defense plant in Wellsburg. In February 1945 he was inducted into the army at Huntington, West Virginia. He missed the entire 1945 season and was discharged in June 1946. Used sparingly for the rest of the '46 season by the Yankees, he pitched almost entirely in relief, winning one game and losing one. In 1947 Queen pitched in relief on April 30, did not pitch at all in May, and made four relief appearances in June before being sold to the Pirates. He made twelve starts for the last-place Pirates and compiled a 3-7 record.

Queen was 4-4 in 1948, and in 1949 the Pirates sent him to their Indianapolis affiliate in the Class Triple-A American Association. A 22-9 record earned him a return trip to Pittsburgh in 1950, where he went 5-14 for another last-place Pirates club. In 1951 the Pirates moved up one place, to seventh. Queen won seven games and lost nine. That season was the thirty-four-year-old right hander's busiest with the Pirates; he pitched 168⅓ innings, the most in his Major League career, making twenty-one starts and eighteen relief appearances. His 6.58 strikeouts per nine innings led all National League pitchers. He also walked 5.3 batters per nine innings. In his big-league career, Queen walked 329 batters, one more than he struck out.

On May 1, 1952, Queen started at home against the New York Giants; it was his last Major League appearance. He left after two innings, having given up six earned runs on four hits, three walks, and a wild pitch. The Pirates sent him to Hollywood in the Pacific Coast League, where he won fourteen games and lost nine as the Stars won the PCL pennant. He pitched for the Stars again in 1953 (when he was 8-7), 1954 (16-8), and briefly in 1955, the year he retired. After his playing career ended Queen worked as a plumber and pipe fitter for the aerospace manufacturer North American Aviation. He also did some scouting for the Cincinnati Reds in the early 1960s.

Queen was married three times. He and his first wife, Goldie Mae Bowersox, had two sons, Melvin and Gary, and a daughter, Valery. That marriage ended in divorce, and on September 3, 1969, Queen married Jewell Rebecca Smith. They resided in Bellflower, California. After Jewell died he married Wilma Mae Wynn on June 30, 1976. The newly married couple moved to Wilma Mae's home state of Arkansas. Queen went to work for Rockwell International in Van Buren, Arkansas. He died on April 4, 1982, after a long illness. He is buried at Gracelawn Memorial Park in Van Buren.

While Queen pitched for Hollywood, the family moved to San Luis Obispo, California. There, his son Melvin Douglas Queen excelled in high school sports and went on to play Major League Baseball with the Cincinnati Reds and California Angels from 1964 to 1972. He came to the Major Leagues as an outfielder but became a pitcher while with the Reds. He was the Toronto Blue Jays' farm director and later the pitching coach and then a senior adviser for player development. Melvin Douglas Queen died on May 11, 2011, at the age of sixty-nine. Valery died in 2003. Gary is still living.

Chapter 21. Timeline, May 23–June 12

Lyle Spatz

Friday, May 23, vs. Boston—Allie Reynolds pitched his third shutout of the season, downing the Red Sox, 9–0. Reynolds allowed only two singles, one a blooper and the other on a bad bounce. The Yankees had twelve hits against Harry Dorish and rookie Mel Parnell. Charlie Keller had a double, a home run, and two runs batted in. George McQuinn also had two hits, while George Stirnweiss had three. 14-14-1, Fourth (T), 3½ games behind.

Saturday, May 24, vs. Boston—Spud Chandler followed Allie Reynolds's two-hit shutout of the Red Sox with one of his own. Chandler also allowed two singles in winning, 5–0. The Yanks got all five runs off starter Dave Ferriss. George McQuinn and Joe DiMaggio each batted in two runs. 15-14-1, Fourth, 3½ games behind.

Sunday, May 25, vs. Boston—Bill Bevens just missed pitching the Yankees' third straight shutout in his 17–2 win against Boston. He held the Red Sox scoreless until the ninth inning, when Ted Williams hit his eleventh home run of the season with a man on. New York racked up seventeen hits against Tex Hughson and two relievers. George McQuinn batted in three runs and had three hits, including a home run; Joe DiMaggio had four hits and two runs batted in; Charlie Keller had a home run and three runs batted in; and Phil Rizzuto had two hits and four RBIS. 16-14-1, Third, 3 games behind.

Monday, May 26, vs. Boston—A crowd of 74,747, a record for a single game, saw the Yanks beat the

Red Sox, 9–3, under the lights. The four-game sweep of Boston was New York's fifth consecutive victory. Frank Shea started for the Yanks but had to be relieved for the first time this season. Joe Page came on in the third inning with the Yanks trailing, 3–0, the bases loaded and no one out. Page thrilled the crowd by not allowing any runs to score in that inning or for the rest of the game. Meanwhile, New York came back against Joe Dobson and three relievers, led by Joe DiMaggio with three hits, including a three-run homer, and four runs batted in. Billy Johnson also had four RBIS. The win moved the Yankees into second place behind the Detroit Tigers. 17-14-1, Second, 3 games behind.

Tuesday, May 27, at Washington—Leading 4–0 after three innings, the Yankees seemed on their way to a sixth consecutive win, but Washington scored two in the third, one in the fourth, and two in the eighth to pull out a 5–4 win. Walt Masterson was the winner and Allie Reynolds the loser. The Yanks managed only five singles and a double by George McQuinn. 17-15-1, Second, 4 games behind.

Wednesday, May 28, at Washington—Five scoreless innings of relief by Don Johnson helped the Yankees beat the Senators, 9–5. Tommy Byrne made his first start of the season but lasted only ⅓ of an inning. Randy Gumpert relieved Byrne and, though he was mostly ineffective in his 3⅔ innings, was credited with the win. After a review American League president Will Harridge awarded the win to Johnson. Starter Bobo Newsom was the

79

loser for Washington. Charlie Keller, Joe DiMaggio, and Billy Johnson each had three hits, and Johnson had five runs batted in. 18-15-1, Second, 3½ games behind.

Thursday, May 29, at Washington—All the runs by both sides in the Yankees' 5–2 win were scored in the sixth inning. The Yanks' scoring was highlighted by consecutive home runs from Billy Johnson and Yogi Berra. Johnson's came with two men on. Frank Shea won his fifth straight, but left after six innings because of the heat. Joe Page finished with three scoreless innings. Joe DiMaggio's single against starter and loser Early Wynn extended DiMaggio's hitting streak to eleven games. 19-15-1, Second, 2½ games behind.

Friday, May 30, at Philadelphia (2)—An overflow crowd at Shibe Park rejoiced as the hometown Athletics shut out the Yankees in both games of the Memorial Day doubleheader. Dick Fowler beat Spud Chandler, 1–0, in the opener, and rookie Joe Coleman beat Bill Bevens, 4–0, in the nightcap. Joe DiMaggio had a single in the first game and two singles in the second game, raising his consecutive-game hitting streak to thirteen. 19-17-1, Third, 3½ games behind.

Saturday, May 31, at Cleveland—Charlie Keller had three hits, including two home runs, and five RBIS as the Yankees battered Bob Feller and the Indians, 8–4. Karl Drews, making his first start of 1947, won his first big-league game. Joe Page pitched the final two innings, striking out four. Joe DiMaggio had a double, extending his hitting streak to fourteen games. DiMaggio had now hit safely in twenty-four of his last twenty-six games. 20-17-1, Second, 3½ games behind.

Sunday, June 1, at Cleveland—The Yankees defeated the Indians 11–9 in the first game of what was to be a doubleheader. But rain, which interrupted the game, caused the second game to be postponed and rescheduled as part of a doubleheader the following day. Joe DiMaggio led the Yankees' attack with four hits; two home runs, including a grand slam; and five runs batted in. DiMaggio's bases-loaded drive came in the eighth inning off Roger Wolff, the third of four Indians pitchers, and broke a 7–7 tie. Charlie Keller continued his hot hitting with his thirteenth home run and three RBIS. Keller led the league in both categories. George McQuinn, who was the league's leading hitter, also homered. Allie Reynolds started for New York, followed by Al Lyons, Randy Gumpert, and Joe Page. Lyons got the win, with Page again excelling in relief. Bob Lemon was the loser. 21-17-1, Second, 3 games behind.

Monday, June 2, at Cleveland (2)—Rained out. The Yankees purchased infielder Ted Sepkowski from the Indians. 21-17-1, Second, 3 games behind.

Tuesday, June 3, at Detroit—In a rematch of the May 21 game at Yankee Stadium, Frank Shea again shut out the first-place Tigers, defeating their ace, Hal Newhouser. Shea allowed five hits in his 3–0 win. Joe DiMaggio again led New York with four hits. During DiMaggio's hitting streak, which had now reached sixteen, he had gone 33 for 67, a .493 batting average. DiMaggio's overall average of .368 was now tops in the American League. 22-17-1, Second, 2 games behind.

Wednesday, June 4, at Detroit (2)—The Yankees and Tigers split a doubleheader, allowing Detroit to maintain their two-game lead over New York. Solo homers by Tommy Henrich and Aaron Robinson provided the Yanks with their only runs in a 6–2 loss to Dizzy Trout in the opener. Joe DiMaggio's consecutive-game hitting streak ended at sixteen. Starter Bill Bevens was the loser. In the second game the Yanks got three more home runs in a 17–8 victory. The Tigers scored four runs off Don Johnson in the first inning, but the Yanks tied it against Al Benton in the second. The big blow was a three-run homer by pinch hitter Frank Colman. New York also had a four-run fourth and a six-run ninth. Billy Johnson and Aaron Robinson had home runs, while Phil Rizzuto had two singles and two doubles. Butch Wensloff, making his first appearance of the season, pitched creditably in relief of Johnson. Joe Page pitched the final four innings and got the win. Al Benton took the loss. 23-18-1, Second, 2 games behind.

Thursday, June 5, at Detroit — The Yankees moved to within a game of first place behind Spud Chandler's 7–0, three-hit shutout of the league leaders. Tommy Henrich led the Yanks' attack with two home runs. 24-18-1, Second, 1 game behind.

Friday, June 6, at St. Louis — Fred Sanford made his first start of the season a winning one, downing the Yankees, 4–3. Sam Zoldak relieved Sanford in the ninth. Joe DiMaggio had three hits, including his seventh home run. Billy Johnson also homered, his third. For the Browns, Jeff Heath had two triples, and Vern Stephens had a home run and two RBIs. Allie Reynolds worked the first five innings for the Yanks and loser Joe Page the last three. 24-19-1, Second, 1½ games behind.

Saturday, June 7, at St. Louis — Rookie sensation Frank Shea won his seventh consecutive game, stopping the Browns, 3–1, on three hits. Shea also had a double off loser Nelson Potter and scored the Yanks' first run. Tommy Henrich had two runs batted in, and Joe DiMaggio slugged his eighth home run. 25-19-1, Second, 1 game behind.

Sunday, June 8, at St. Louis (2) — Four home runs propelled the Browns to a 9–2 win in the opener. Les Moss and Vern Stephens homered against starter and loser Karl Drews, and Walt Judnich

and Al Zarilla homered against Mel Queen. Jack Kramer went the distance for the win. New York won the second game, 5–4, with Joe Page getting the win in relief of starter Butch Wensloff. George McQuinn had two RBIs, and George Stirnweiss two runs scored. 26-20-1, Second, 1½ games behind.

Monday, June 9, at Chicago — The White Sox came back from an 8–2 deficit to defeat the Yankees in ten innings, 9–8. Allie Reynolds walked eight in five innings, and Bill Bevens, who walked three, allowed Luke Appling's two-run homer in the eighth that tied the game at 8–8. Joe Page took the loss. Chicago used five pitchers, with Joe Haynes getting the win. Johnny Lindell homered and scored two runs for New York. 26-21-1, Second, 1½ games behind.

Tuesday, June 10, at Chicago — Johnny Lindell, filling in for injured left fielder Charlie Keller, had three hits, including a triple and a home run, to lead the Yankees to a 5–3 victory. Spud Chandler went all the way to notch his fifth win. Ed Lopat was the loser. 27-21-1, Second, ½ game behind.

Wednesday, June 11, at Chicago — Frank Shea of the Yankees and Joe Haynes of the White Sox each went the distance in Chicago's eleven-inning, 3–2 win. Shea's loss ended his seven-game winning streak. The Yanks ended their eighteen-game road trip with ten wins and eight losses. Johnny Lindell continued his hot hitting with three more base hits. 27-22-1, Second, 1 game behind.

Thursday, June 12 — Not scheduled. 27-22-1, Second, 1 game behind.

Chapter 22. Al Lyons

Mike Richard

AGE	W	L	PCT.	ERA	G	GS	GF	CG	SHO	SV	IP	H	BB	SO	HBP	WP
28	1	0	1.000	9.00	6	0	1	0	0	0	11.0	18	9	7	0	1

Al Lyons was a pitcher during parts of four seasons in the Major Leagues, a slugging outfielder and ace pitcher in the Pacific Coast League and a Mets scout later in life. Albert Harold Lyons Jr. was born on July 18, 1918, in St. Joseph, Missouri, to Albert Harold Lyons and Irene V. (Sears) Lyons. The family, including Al's older brother, Jack, later relocated to California, where Al played baseball at Washington High School in Los Angeles. He was also an All-Southern California fullback on the football team, but Al's best sport was baseball, where he played for an American Legion team and a semipro squad in Los Angeles.

Lyons began his professional career in 1940, as an outfielder with the Joplin (Missouri) Miners, the New York Yankees affiliate in the Class C Western Association. The six-foot-two, 195-pound Lyons batted .299, with thirteen home runs and ninety-seven runs batted in. He returned to Joplin in 1941, batting .304 with ten home runs, eighty-three RBIs, and fifty-two extra-base hits. And in his first season as a pitcher, he posted a 5-1 record, with an impressive 1.26 ERA and forty-eight strikeouts in forty-three innings pitched.

Joplin battled the Springfield Cardinals much of the season before catching fire in August. The Miners went on a tear, winning thirty of forty-one games for the regular-season title. Lyons moved up to the Binghamton (New York) Triplets of the Class A Eastern League in 1942, where he again played the outfield. He had thirty-two assists and participated in eleven double plays, while hitting .249 with eight home runs and seventy-three RBIs.

Lyons was elevated to the Kansas City Blues of the American Association, one of the Yankees'

Al Lyons was 1-0 with four hits in six at bats in half a season but earned a half-share of the Yankees' World Series winnings.

two Class Triple-A (then called Double-A) teams in 1943. Lyons, who threw and batted right-handed, continued to showcase his talents as a pitcher and as an outfielder. Under manager Johnny Neun, he went 4-6 on the mound with a 3.49 ERA in eighty innings pitched, while batting .236 as a pitcher and in seventy-eight games as an outfielder.

As the 1944 season began, the draft called several Yankees pitchers into the military, including Butch Wensloff, Marius Russo, and Tommy Byrne. That opened up a pitching slot for Lyons, who appeared in eleven games that season. He made his Major League debut as a pinch hitter for Monk Dubiel at Boston's Fenway Park on April 19, 1944. Six days later Lyons made his pitching debut in relief of starter Tiny Bonham. He faced only nine batters in 1⅔ innings, but five of them had hits and three of them scored.

Lyons allowed twenty earned runs in 39⅔ innings for the third-place Yankees, without recording a decision. He averaged five walks per 9 innings, threw five wild pitches, committed two balks, and hit two batters. His season ended in early August when he had to report for duty with the U.S. Navy.

In late March 1945 Lyons participated in a spring-training three-game series against the New York Giants at the Bainbridge Naval Training Center in Maryland. On the twenty-fifth he held the Giants to a lone single over 4⅓ innings and also belted a home run to help the Bainbridge Commodores to an 8–4 victory. Other navy men with Major League experience in the Bainbridge lineup included Dick Sisler, Stan Musial, and Eddie Miksis.

Lyons spent the entire 1945 season in the navy, but he made the Yankees' opening-day roster in 1946. On April 24 he was optioned to Kansas City, where he pitched in twenty-four games with a 7-12 record and a 3.67 ERA. Lyons was recalled by the Yankees in September and appeared in two games, losing his only decision. On September 24 Lyons made his only Major League start, a losing effort in a meaningless game against the pennant-winning Red Sox at Fenway Park.

During the 1947 season Lyons pitched in six games for the Yankees, winning one, on June 1 against Cleveland. It was his first Major League victory and his only decision of the year for the Yankees. As a hitter he had four hits in six at bats, with a double and three runs batted in.

On August 3, 1947, the Pittsburgh Pirates purchased Lyons's contract from the Yankees for the waiver price. He appeared in thirteen games down the stretch for the Pirates, with a 1-2 record over 28⅓ innings. Lyons hit his only Major League home run on September 23, at Forbes Field, off St. Louis's Jim Hearn. Meanwhile, the Yankees went on to win the pennant, while the Pirates finished in last place. Nonetheless, after New York went on to beat Brooklyn in the World Series, the Yankees voted Lyons $2,915—half a Series share.

On November 18, 1947, the Pirates traded Lyons, outfielder Jim Russell, and catcher Bill Salkeld to the Boston Braves for outfielder–first baseman Johnny Hopp and infielder Danny Murtaugh. When the 1948 season began Lyons made only one appearance in the early going, April 24, pitching ⅔ of an inning and allowing three hits in a 16–9 home loss to the Giants. Three weeks later, on May 13, the Braves assigned Lyons to their Milwaukee farm team in the American Association, where he was 3-2 in eleven games.

The Braves recalled him on July 3, a move manager Billy Southworth felt would help energize his pitching staff. "Southworth thinks Lyons will become a 20-game winner," the game notes in the July 3, 1948, issue of the *Worcester Telegram* stated. "It is Southworth's opinion that Lyons was never allowed to concentrate on his pitching with the Yankees and Pirates."

Lyons appeared in only two games with the Braves in July. On the seventeenth he went 2⅓ innings, allowing two hits and two walks and striking out one in a 4–1 loss at Chicago. Three days later he surrendered three hits and a walk in ⅔ of an inning against Cincinnati. On July 24 outfielder Jim Russell was hospitalized, and the depleted Braves outfield needed some reserve help. Southworth used Lyons on occasion to fill one of the outfield spots and called upon him several times in pinch-hitting roles.

Lyons's last appearance in a Major League

game occurred during the pennant-winning Braves' final regular-season contest of 1948. Playing the Giants at the Polo Grounds, Southworth emptied his bench during an 11–1 rout of New York. Lyons played in center field and right field and was 0 for 2 with a walk. He rode the bench as the Braves bowed to the Cleveland Indians in the World Series, four games to two, but he did receive a half share of Series money, worth $2,285.

Overall Lyons wound up his career with a 3-3 record as a pitcher and as a .293 lifetime hitter in fifty-eight at bats. Shortly after the '48 World Series, Lyons was traded by the Braves to the Seattle Rainiers of the Pacific Coast League.

Lyons remained in the Pacific Coast League from 1949 until 1955, where he gained the reputation of being a power-hitting, strong-armed outfielder. He belted a total of seventy-six home runs with the Rainiers and had two stars painted on the center-field fence of Seals Stadium in San Francisco to signify two balls he hit over the 404-foot distant spot.

In 1949 Lyons led Seattle with twenty-three home runs. The following season he led the PCL in home runs with twenty-two, including one over the center-field fence, one of the longest blasts ever seen at Seattle's Sick's Stadium.

Lyons pitched in twelve games for Seattle in 1951, going 8-4 with a 2.78 ERA. The Rainiers won the Pacific Coast League championship under manager Rogers Hornsby, then captured the Governor's Cup over the Hollywood Stars, three games to two.

At the end of the 1951 season, Lyons was part of a contingent of PCL stars that joined Lefty O'Doul's entourage to play a series of exhibition games in Japan. The big leaguers in the group included Joe and Dom DiMaggio, Ferris Fain, Eddie Lopat, Bobby Shantz, Mel Parnell, and Billy Martin.

Playing in Shizuoka, Japan, on November 6, Lyons scattered seven hits against a Japanese team over eight innings and also hit a three-run homer to lead the U.S. All-Stars to a 6–1 victory.

Following another season with the Rainiers, Lyons was traded to the San Francisco Seals in December 1952. After playing the 1953 season and the start of the 1954 campaign with San Francisco, Lyons moved to the San Diego Padres. He returned to the mound for the 1954 season, appearing in twenty-one games with an 8-2 record and a 2.30 ERA.

Lyons began the 1955 season with San Diego, before moving on to play with Hollywood. He logged a combined 10-5 record, with a 5.81 ERA. That was his swan song in the PCL. Through his seven-year career in the league, from 1949 through 1955, he appeared in a total of 919 games, with a batting average of .263 and a pitching record of 26-12.

In 1956 Lyons became the player-manager of the Modesto Reds, a Yankees farm team in the Class C California League, but he was replaced as manager on July 26. Lyons ended the season batting .316 in sixty-three games and posted a 2-0 record in six pitching appearances.

Before the 1956 season ended, Lyons went on to play in the Man-Dak League, an independent league in Manitoba and North Dakota. Lyons's final season of organized baseball came at the age of thirty-eight in 1957, when he played for the Brandon (Manitoba) Greys in the Man-Dak League. Lyons later became a scout for the New York Mets, where he was credited with signing pitcher Dick Selma in 1963 and pitcher Don Shaw in 1965. Lyons remained a Mets scout until his early death of a heart attack at age forty-seven in Inglewood, California, on December 20, 1965. He is buried in Inglewood Park Cemetery. Lyons was survived by his wife, Margaret Louise (Runions) Lyons, and his son, Albert.

Chapter 23. **Tommy Henrich**

Rob Edelman

AGE	G	AB	R	H	2B	3B	HR	TB	RBI	BB	SO	BAV	OBP	SLG	SB	GDP	HBP
34	142	550	109	158	35	13	16	267	98	71	54	.287	.372	.485	3	9	3

"What do [you] think of Tommy Henrich?"

"I don't know, he's dependable, I guess."

This bit of repartee, from Philip Roth's novella *Goodbye, Columbus*, just about sums up Henrich's career with the New York Yankees during the late 1930s and 1940s. If Lou Gehrig, Joe DiMaggio, Joe Gordon, Bill Dickey, Phil Rizzuto, and Yogi Berra were the luminaries of the pre- and postwar Bronx Bombers, Henrich was a rock-solid supporting player. He was celebrated for his dedication to the game, his ability to deliver a timely hit, and his prowess on defense. It was for good reason that Henrich was nicknamed "Old Reliable," and he was sincere when he declared, "I get a thrill every time I put on my Yankee uniform. It sounds corny, but it's the gospel truth."[1]

Thomas David Henrich was born on February 20, 1913, in Massillon, Ohio. His parents were Edward M. Henrich, a plastering contractor, and Mary Elizabeth (Dressler) Henrich; he had four brothers and a sister. The Henriches were active in St. Mary's Catholic Church, and young Tommy attended the parish school.

Massillon was strictly football country, but Henrich's parents refused to allow him to play what they considered a violent sport. So instead the youngster became enamored of baseball. However, there were no baseball teams in Massillon; throughout his childhood and high school years — he graduated from St. John's Catholic High School in nearby Canton in 1933 — he could play only softball. In fact, for much of his big-league career, he claimed his birth year was 1916, to compensate for his lack of baseball playing in his youth.

Tommy Henrich's sixteen home runs were second highest on the Yankees in 1947, and he led the club with ten hits and a .323 batting average against Brooklyn in the World Series.

After graduation from high school, Henrich played baseball for the semipro Prince Horn and Acme Dairy teams and drew the attention of Billy Doyle, a Detroit Tigers scout. The Tigers offered him a contract, but he chose to continue playing semipro ball while earning a paycheck as a clerk in a steel mill.

Tommy Henrich is greeted by Johnny Lindell after his fifth-inning home run off Vic Lombardi in Game Two of the 1947 World Series. Babe Pinelli is the umpire.

In November 1933 Henrich was signed by the Cleveland Indians after catching the attention of scout Bill Bradley. He spent the following summer with the Monessen Indians in the Class D Pennsylvania State Association, where he hit .326 in 104 games; he also played in 4 games with the Zanesville (Ohio) Greys in the Class C Middle Atlantic League. He returned to Zanesville in 1935 and hit .337 in 115 games; he finished that campaign playing 17 games for the New Orleans Pelicans in the Class A Southern Association. Henrich, a left-handed batter and thrower, spent the entire 1936 campaign in New Orleans, and his progress as a ballplayer is reflected in the numbers he compiled: a .346 batting average with 15 home runs, 100 RBIS, and 117 runs scored.

The twenty-three-year-old Henrich believed his stellar Southern Association season would earn him a spring-training invite with the 1937 Indi-ans. Instead, he was ordered to report to the Minor League Milwaukee Brewers in the American Association. Henrich was baffled by this exclusion. Furthermore, as the Brewers had no Major League affiliation, he was unsure who exactly owned his contract. Instead of suffering quietly, he wrote a letter to Kenesaw Mountain Landis, the baseball commissioner, in which he wondered if he was being justly treated by the Indians. The commissioner responded by pronouncing that Cleveland was not offering Henrich a fair shot at making the big-league club. Furthermore, Landis declared Henrich a free agent who could sign with any Major League organization of his choosing. "I had a strong case [against the Indians]," Henrich recalled in 1971, "but I always had the feeling that Landis ruled in my favor because he disliked [Cleveland general manager Cy] Slapnicka so much."[2]

ROB EDELMAN

On April 14, 1937, Henrich was freed of his obligation to Cleveland. Though the Indians were the closest thing to a hometown big-league club, Henrich had long been a New York Yankees fan. He was won over in the early 1920s after the Yankees acquired Babe Ruth; Henrich readily admitted the Babe was his favorite ballplayer. After his liberation from Cleveland, more than half the big-league organizations expressed an interest in him. The New York Giants' Bill Terry told the press he would pay fifteen thousand dollars for Henrich's services. But less than a week after becoming a free agent, Henrich signed with the Yankees, earning a bonus that was reported to be in the range of twenty to twenty-five thousand dollars.[3]

"I still have a vivid memory of coming to town for the first time and checking into the Hotel New Yorker," he remembered. "The bellhop took my bag and discovered who I was before we even reached the room. 'So you're the new Yankee outfielder,' he said, sneering at me. 'How can you break in ahead of—let's see, who we've got—Joe DiMaggio, Jake Powell, Myril Hoag, George Selkirk, and Roy Johnson? Did you ever see them guys hit?' 'Not yet,' I said bravely, 'but they never saw me hit either.'"[4]

The Yankees assigned the six-foot, 180-pound Henrich to the International League Newark Bears, their top farm club. A week later Yankees manager Joe McCarthy overheard Roy Johnson rationalizing a defeat with a "you-can't-win-them-all" mind-set. McCarthy, who loathed losing, asked general manager Ed Barrow to replace the veteran outfielder with "the kid." Johnson was sold to the Boston Bees—and "the kid" had played his final Minor League game.

Henrich made his big-league debut on May 11, 1937. Batting seventh in the Yankees' lineup, he doubled in four at bats against Chicago White Sox hurler Monty Stratton. The Yanks then were mired in a slump, and McCarthy shuffled his batting order. With Henrich now hitting third, the Yanks scored a 4–2 victory on May 13 against the St. Louis Browns. The rookie—described in the *New York Times* as "our latest freshman sensation"—contributed two singles.[5] Then on May 16, playing against the Philadelphia Athletics, he belted his first home run, along with a triple and single. The four-bagger came in the sixth inning off A's starter George Caster.

Overall, Henrich appeared in sixty-seven games, completing the 1937 season with a .320 batting average, fourteen doubles, five triples, eight home runs, and forty-two RBIs. The only downside to his freshman campaign was an injury to his left knee. Before 1938 spring training, he included a note, addressed to Barrow, along with his signed Yankee contract, in which he declared, "I am feeling fine, have no complaints, and am prepared to give everybody a fight for an outfield berth. My knees have not troubled me lately and I intend to report with the first squad in St. Petersburg, Fla., to round into shape."[6]

Henrich did indeed stick with the Yankees in 1938. In fact, that spring and the next, he even worked out at first base. Rumor had it he might eventually replace Lou Gehrig as the team's first baseman. "For what is believed to be the first time in his fourteen year association with the Yankees, as a player under contract," reported James Dawson of the *New York Times* on March 23, 1939, "Lou Gehrig didn't play today when the world champions met their Kansas City farm club at Yale Field in Haines City, Florida."[7] Substituting for him was Henrich. When the Iron Horse finally benched himself during the regular season, ending his streak of 2,130 consecutive games, he was replaced by Babe Dahlgren, not Henrich. It was decided the "baby-faced guardian of right field" was too valuable to the Yankees as an outfielder.[8]

In his sophomore season and those that followed, Henrich occasionally lost playing time because of his knee injury, but his steady play won him respect among his teammates and coaches.

He also earned positive press. As the 1938 campaigned neared its conclusion, sportswriter John Kieran observed, "Tommy Henrich is a nice lad and a good ball player who should and probably will get better."[9]

In 1941 Henrich played a significant role in keeping alive Joe DiMaggio's fifty-six-game hitting streak. On June 26 the thirty-eighth game of the streak, the Yankee Clipper was still hitless as the team came to bat in the last of the eighth inning holding the lead against the St. Louis Browns. DiMaggio was due up fourth in the inning, with Henrich scheduled right before him. With one out and Red Rolfe on first, McCarthy ordered Henrich to bunt to avoid a possible ground-ball double play—and not allowing his teammate a final at bat. Henrich was thrown out, but Rolfe took second. DiMaggio slammed Elden Auker's first pitch for a double, and the streak remained intact.

Yankees broadcaster Mel Allen began calling Henrich "Old Reliable"—the name of a train that ran from Ohio to Alabama and was celebrated for always being on time—because of his propensity for hitting in the clutch. As Bobby Brown, who became his teammate in 1946, noted, "If we were ahead 10–1 or 10–2, he was just average. If we were behind 10–1 or 10–2, same thing. But get him in a big game and he was terrific."[10] Henrich, who practiced his fielding endlessly, once famously observed, "Catching a fly ball is a pleasure. But knowing what to do with it after you catch it is a business."[11] It was for good reason Joe DiMaggio called him "the smartest player in the big leagues."[12]

Upon the United States' entry into World War II, Henrich was one of the scores of big leaguers who went into the military. On August 30, 1942, the year in which he made his first American League All-Star team, he joined the U.S. Coast Guard. He was assigned the rating of specialist first class and spent the war years attached to a training station in Michigan, where he played baseball for military teams. He also volunteered to coach the girls' basketball team at Loretto Catholic High School in Sault Sainte Marie.

On September 29, 1945, Henrich completed his coast guard duty and rejoined the Yankees the following season. His batting average in 1946 sank to .251, but the slump was temporary, as he raised his average to .287 and .308 in 1947 and 1948. Additionally, he was an American League All-Star each season from 1947 to 1950. During this time, he displayed his versatility and athleticism by occasionally manning first base. By the end of the decade, he was a respected, hard-nosed veteran who readily criticized teammates who were not playing as hard as they could or were making thoughtless errors. By his standards such actions led to losing games and diminished opportunities for the Yankees to make the World Series.

Casey Stengel, who took over as the team's manager in 1949, complimented Henrich for his on-field prowess and added, "If he comes back to the hotel at three in the morning when we're on the road and says he's been sitting up with a sick friend, he's been sitting up with a sick friend."[13] *New York Times* columnist Arthur Daley observed, "Henrich has never been the captain of the Yankees. But the other players just gravitated to him as their natural leader. He was the captain in fact, if not in name."[14]

By the late 1940s, however, injuries were starting to debilitate Henrich. In 1949 he fractured the transverse vertebrae in his back, broke his toe, and played in just 115 games. In April 1950 he flew to Johns Hopkins Hospital in Baltimore to seek treatment for the left knee that had been bothering him since his rookie year. His physician, Dr. George Bennett, informed him he needed knee surgery, but could not promise the operation would allow him to continue playing ball. Henrich refused to have the surgery, and after playing in only 73 games in 1950, he announced his retirement as a player on December 18.

ROB EDELMAN

In the eleven seasons he spent with the Yankees, Henrich appeared in 1,284 games, compiling a .282 batting average and 183 home runs. His highest home run total was 31, in 1941, third best in the American League. In 1948 he tied a league record by belting 4 grand slams; led the league in triples, runs scored, and extra-base hits; and was second in doubles and total bases. In 1949 he was third in the American League in slugging percentage and tied for third in home runs. He finished sixth in the Most Valuable Player race in both 1948 and 1949. In January 1950 *Sport Magazine* honored him as its Athlete of the Year.

Henrich appeared in four World Series, in 1938, 1941, 1947, and 1949. On three occasions he played significant roles in deciding final scores. In each the Yankees were pitted against the Brooklyn Dodgers. In the fourth game of the 1941 fall classic, played at Ebbets Field—which the Dodgers needed to win to tie the series—Brooklyn's Hugh Casey nursed a one-run lead in the ninth inning. After retiring the first two Yankees, he faced Henrich. With the count at 3 and 2, Henrich swung and missed. The game would have been over, but Dodgers catcher Mickey Owen failed to catch the ball.

Henrich's baseball instincts had him heading toward first base as he watched the movement of the ball; when he realized that it had gotten past Owen, he began running at full speed and arrived safely at first base. "I saw that little white jackrabbit bouncing," Henrich recalled, "and I said, 'Let's go.' It rolled all the way to the fence. I could have walked down to first."[15] The Yankees rallied to win, 7–4, and then won the Series the next day. In the 1947 Series, another win against Brooklyn, Henrich paced the team with ten hits in thirty-one at bats.

Henrich was at his most clutch at the close of the 1949 regular season and in the first World Series game. On the final day of the campaign, he belted a home run and drove in two runs in the Yankees' 5–3 pennant-winning victory over the Boston Red Sox. Three days later, in Game One of the World Series against the Dodgers, he led off the bottom of the ninth with a home run off Don Newcombe to give Allie Reynolds and the Yankees a 1–0 victory. It was the first walk-off home run in World Series history.

After retiring as an active player, Henrich turned down an offer by George Weiss, the Yankees' general manager, to manage in the team's Minor League system. Stories circulated that he would join Mel Allen in the team broadcast booth, but instead he served as a Yankees coach during the 1951 season. His duties included mentoring nineteen-year-old rookie Mickey Mantle. Henrich also published a book that season: *The Way to Better Baseball: A Guide for Young Ball Players and Their Coaches*, written in collaboration with A. L. Plaut.

The Yankees dropped Henrich from their coaching staff after the 1951 campaign. He immediately signed a contract to broadcast sports reports on WJZ, ABC's flagship New York City television station; he also hosted sports programs on WJZ radio and appeared on other networks. In April 1953 he emceed and was the chief instructor on *Little League Baseball School*, broadcast by CBS-TV in New York.

In 1954 Henrich left broadcasting to become president of the Red Top Brewery in Cincinnati; by that time he also owned beer distributorships in two New Jersey counties. He resigned from Red Top in February 1956 and returned to the New York area. He was a commentator on New York (football) Giants broadcasts when, that November, he became the New York (baseball) Giants' third base coach. At the conclusion of the 1957 season, with the Giants moving to San Francisco, Henrich joined the Detroit Tigers as a batting instructor and first base coach. He spent the 1958 and 1959 seasons with the Tigers and then was released from his contract.

In 1968 Henrich had one last fling in professional baseball as the Kansas City Royals' Minor League hitting instructor; he also scouted for the team and worked in public relations for Deibold, an Ohio-based manufacturer of bank and security equipment. His outside business interests included his beer distributorships and the ownership of the Diamond Room, a Columbus, Ohio, nightclub.

In his retirement, Henrich enjoyed regaling listeners with stories about his time with the Yankees and, in particular, anecdotes relating to Joe DiMaggio, whom he regarded as the greatest player he had ever seen. He also was a regular presence at Yankees old-timers' games. In 1987 the team honored him with its annual Pride of the Yankees Award, handed out to a celebrated figure from the organization's history. In 1992 he published a second book, *Five O'Clock Lightning: Ruth, Gehrig, DiMaggio, Mantle, and the Glory Years of the NY Yankees*, written with Bill Gilbert.

Henrich played the piano, regularly attended church, and sang in his church choir. He was active in the Massillon chapter of the Society for the Preservation and Encouragement of Barber Shop Quartet Singing in America and in 1946 sang with Ohio's state championship barbershop foursome.

Henrich lived in Arizona during the 1980s and 1990s and then returned to his home state. In his later years he suffered a series of strokes. He died at the age of ninety-six on December 1, 2009, at his home in Beavercreek, Ohio, just outside Dayton; at the time he was the oldest living Yankee. Henrich's wife had died the previous March. She was the former Eileen Patricia O'Reilly, a nurse whom he met in September 1940 while hospitalized because of his knee injury; the pair were married on July 7, 1941. The Henrichs had five children—three daughters (Patricia, Ann, and Mary Louise) and two sons (Tom and Paul)—as well as three grandchildren and three great-grandchildren. He was eulogized in a private memorial service and was cremated, with his remains returned to his survivors.

Years before his passing, Henrich's career and love of baseball were summed up by *New York Times* columnist Red Smith, who observed. "[Henrich] got more pure joy out of baseball than any player I ever knew."[16] In his *Times* obituary he was described as "a timely hitter, an outstanding defensive player and a leader who epitomized the image of the classy Yankee who nearly always won."[17]

ROB EDELMAN

Chapter 24. **Frank Colman**

Tom Hawthorn

AGE	G	AB	R	H	2B	3B	HR	TB	RBI	BB	SO	BAV	OBP	SLG	SB	GDP	HBP
29	22	28	2	3	0	0	2	9	6	2	6	.107	.167	.321	0	0	0

In the opening game of the 1947 season, Frank Colman stepped to the plate at Yankee Stadium as a pinch hitter in the home half of the ninth inning. On the mound stood Phil Marchildon, a fellow Canadian also from the province of Ontario, who was attempting to close out an afternoon's stellar performance. The Philadelphia Athletics had a 6–1 lead over the Yankees, thus far spoiling the debut of Bucky Harris as Yankees manager and disappointing most of the 39,344 fans in attendance, among them the members of the United Nations Security Council, as well as former president Herbert Hoover.

On the mound stood a man who had endured more than nine months in German prisoner-of-war camps. At the plate stood a man who passed part of the war patrolling the outfield at Pittsburgh's Forbes Field but had spent most of the previous season with the Newark Bears, where he made a solid contribution at the plate. He was eager to stick with the parent Yankees.

In this opening-day showdown, the military veteran prevailed. Colman struck out. It was a suitable harbinger for a season of frustration for the twenty-nine-year-old batter.

Frank Lloyd Colman was born on March 2, 1918, in London, Ontario, to Frederick and Harriet Ann (Bartlett) Colman, both natives of England. He was the fifth of eight children in a farm family, though Frederick later owned a shoe-repair business. An older brother, Harold, pushed Frank onto the baseball diamond. Frank preferred hockey and won a scoring championship while skating for the London Technical and Commercial High School (renamed H. B. Beal High, after its founding principal, while Frank attended).

The Yankees chose Frank Colman over Allie Clark to open the season but reversed that decision in July. *Photo property of the Canadian Baseball Hall of Fame and Museum.*

By the time he was eighteen, Frank was wearing the uniform of the hometown London Majors of the Intercounty League, an amateur circuit based in Ontario. The left-handed Colman starred on the mound and at the plate, winning the batting crown and earning Most Valuable Player honors while leading his squad to the league championship in 1936.

After a couple more seasons on local sandlots, the five-foot-eleven, 186-pound hurler made his professional debut with the Batavia (New York)

Clippers in 1939, the inaugural season of the Pennsylvania-Ontario–New York (PONY) League. He went 8-7 in the Class D circuit and 0-1 in a two-game call-up to the Cornwall (Ontario) Maple Leafs of the Class C Canadian-American League.

In April 1940 the Wilmington (Delaware) Blue Rocks, a Philadelphia Athletics affiliate in the Class B Interstate League, had such a terrible exhibition season that manager Chief Bender released eleven players. Among those he acquired in restocking the team was Colman, who went 10-4 as a starter while also playing forty-one games in the outfield. His .361 average was second best on the team.

The solid numbers earned Colman a promotion to Philadelphia's top farm team, the Toronto Maple Leafs of the International League, the following year. The Leafs converted him into a full-time right fielder, and he responded with a steady performance, hitting .294 and .300 in his first two seasons with the club. In September 1942 the Pittsburgh Pirates, who were then Toronto's big-league affiliate, called him up, but his introduction to Major League pitching was a harsh one. He managed just five hits in thirty-seven at bats in ten games. Colman stuck with the Pirates for the first half of 1943, before being sent back to Toronto.

Meanwhile, Colman had married Anne Puchniak, whom he had met one off-season while working at General Steel Wares, a steel plant in London that produced housewares and appliances. She had asked a colleague for the time, and Frank, eager to make her acquaintance, butted in with a quick reply. They eventually married and had two sons: Frank, born in 1943, and Jerry, born in 1947.

Colman also had to deal with military obligations. Canada had declared war on Nazi Germany in 1939, twenty-seven months before the attack on Pearl Harbor, but he was originally rejected for service because of an old leg injury. During spring training in 1944, Colman stayed home after announcing he had been called for a draft reexam-ination. Rejected a second time, he then reported to the Pirates' spring-training camp in Muncie, Indiana.

After spending three months with the Pirates in 1943, Colman gained a regular spot in the lineup in 1944. He hit .270 in 252 at bats against war-depleted pitching rosters, knocking in fifty-three runs (including at least one RBI in eight consecutive games in August). In 1945, though, Colman played in only seventy-seven games, and his average plunged to an anemic .209.

A quiet man with a broad forehead and a lop-sided smile, Colman rarely spoke about his playing days. "My dad wasn't a talker," said his son, also named Frank Colman. "It was like digging for gold to get him to talk about his baseball career." One story that gained currency while he was still playing involved a long-running dispute with Pirates manager Frankie Frisch. The *Portland Oregonian* published a story, reprinted by the magazine *Baseball Digest*, about Colman demanding to be traded. In response an angry Frisch sent the left-handed batter to the plate as a pinch hitter to face Harry "the Cat" Brecheen, one of the league's top left-handers. Colman rapped out a double, called time, and retreated to the dugout, where he told the manager, "Get a substitute—I've had enough of this club. And trade me quick, for I'll never play for you again." "Nor did he," the story reported. Alas, whatever the tension between manager and platooned outfielder, the anecdote is apocryphal, as box scores do not show Colman getting a pinch-hit double off Brecheen in a regular-season game.

On June 17, 1946, the Pirates sold Colman to the Yankees. He spent the summer with the International League Newark Bears before making his Yankee debut as the right fielder in the second game of a doubleheader against Philadelphia on September 22. In his first at bat for his new team, Colman faced Marchildon, his compatriot from Ontario. The batter did better than the pitcher on this day. "Anyway, Frank enjoyed a perfect afternoon in the nightcap," wrote Louis Effrat the next day in the *New York Times*. "He slammed a two-run homer in the second, singled and scored in the fourth, and walked and scored in the fifth." The game was called because of darkness after 5½ innings, the Yankees prevailing 7–4 to complete a sweep.

Colman was penciled into the lineup for five games through the end of the 1946 season and then saw spot duty in left field in the early part of the 1947 season. Manager Bucky Harris opted for Colman to stay with the club over the promising Allie Clark. For part of the season, Colman wore uniform number 3, Babe Ruth's number, later retired, and a number also worn by George Selkirk, the Yankees' all-star outfielder during the 1930s who also hailed from Ontario. A back injury limited Colman's playing time, and then he found himself on the bench as Johnny Lindell, the subject of trade rumors during spring training, thrived at the plate.

On July 20 the Yankees arrived in Detroit for a doubleheader against the second-place Tigers, over whom they held a daunting 11½-game lead. A record crowd of 58,369 jammed every nook of Briggs Stadium. Between games about 120 fans from London made a presentation to their home-town hero. As it turned out, Colman did not play in either game, both of which the Yankees lost.

Two weeks later the Yankees shipped Colman back to Newark and brought up Clark. Colman had been unable to crack an outfield featuring Tommy Henrich in right and Joe DiMaggio in center. With Lindell hitting and catcher Yogi Berra available for outfield duty as well, Colman became expendable.

The transfer did not go smoothly. With Newark in Toronto for a series, Colman refused to sign a contract, instead retreating to his home in London, declaring that he was prepared "to sit tight and see what happens."[1] The outfielder said he had no beef with the Yankees calling up Clark, as they needed a right-handed pinch hitter, but said he did not deserve a cut in pay. "Some of the boys told me I should get more than I was asking for," he said. "In eight years in the big circuit this is the first time I've been what you might call a bad boy."[2]

Newark said Colman was "liable to suspension."[3] Colman demanded a guarantee of a full share of World Series proceeds due the Yankees players should they win the championship. An eleven-day holdout ended with Newark's management announcing it had refused the outfielder's salary demands.

In the end, after the Yankees won the World Series, the players voted Colman a three-quarters share, worth $4,372.52, a tidy sum for hitting .107 in twenty-two games. (He had smacked only three hits for the Yankees, but two of them were pinch-hit home runs.)

Colman played thirty-one games for Newark in '47 and twenty-nine in 1948, but he never again played in the Major Leagues. He batted .320 for Seattle of the Pacific Coast League in 1949 and enjoyed the finest season of his career in 1950, at the age of thirty-two, when he had eighteen home runs, ninety-seven runs batted in, and a batting average of .319.

Toronto signed Colman for 1951, along with first baseman Les Fleming, from San Francisco of the PCL. "Fleming and Colman give us the best one-two left-handed punch we've had in years in a league where a premium is placed on southpaw sluggers," said Toronto business manager Gord Walker. Colman, who also saw spot duty at first base, had three solid campaigns with the Leafs.

When Toronto traded the thirty-five-year-old veteran to the Charleston (West Virginia) Senators after the 1953 season, he instead placed himself on the voluntary retired list. He returned home to Ontario, where he became player-manager of his old Intercounty League team for 1954. By Dominion Day (July 1) he was hitting a paltry .250. A late-season surge by Colman left him in third place in the batting race at .360.

Before the start of the 1955 season, Colman and his brother Jack bought the London franchise. Frank was a player-manager, on occasion even pitching in relief. London won the league title in 1956. The Colman brothers sold the team in 1959.

Frank worked in a sporting-goods store for many years until it went out of business. He then joined the maintenance department at the University of Western Ontario. After hours he played cards, especially hearts, and was known to haunt the horse-racing tracks at Woodbine in Toronto and Fort Erie, Ontario. He died of cancer on February 19, 1983, aged sixty-four. He was buried at Woodland Cemetery in London. His wife, Anne, died in 1990 and is buried next to him.

In 1999 Colman was posthumously inducted into the Canadian Baseball Hall of Fame at St. Marys, about twenty-five miles north of his hometown. Yogi Berra sent a congratulatory letter for a late friend with whom he had roomed on the road. "I made a lot of friends in baseball through the years," he wrote, "but I'll also remember Frank as one of the most decent and genuine people that I ever met."

When he took over the amateur men's club, Colman also helped cofound a youth league with local sportsman Gordon Berryhill and longtime Pittsburgh Pirates catcher George (Moon) Gibson. The Eager Beaver Baseball Association has thrived ever since. After his death the association's annual all-star game was renamed Frank Colman Day. The budding stars play at Labatt Park, the same field on which a teenage Colman launched his own career in the Great Depression of the 1930s.

Chapter 25. **Tommy Byrne**

Jimmy Keenan

AGE	W	L	PCT.	ERA	G	GS	GF	CG	SHO	SV	IP	H	BB	SO	HBP	WP
27	0	0	.000	4.15	4	1	2	0	0	0	4.1	5	6	2	0	0

Tommy Byrne had three careers and was successful in all of them. A hard-throwing left-handed pitcher, he spent thirteen seasons in the Major Leagues. His ball-playing days over, Byrne turned to business, with considerable success. Then he devoted himself to politics and served two terms as mayor of his adopted hometown.

Thomas Joseph Byrne was born in Baltimore, Maryland, on December 31, 1919, one of three sons of Joseph Thomas Byrne and Grace C. (Phenice) Byrne. The youngster's favorite ballplayer was Babe Ruth, and he told friends he hoped someday to don the same pinstriped uniform of his hero.

Byrne first pitched for the Blessed Sacrament Elementary School team in the Baltimore Junior League. A neighbor, Philadelphia Athletics pitcher Eddie Rommel, mentored Tommy on the finer points of pitching and instilled baseball savvy in the youngster that would stay with him throughout his career.

In his first year at City College high school, Byrne failed to make the freshman baseball team. In his second year he made the junior-varsity squad and was called up to the varsity late in the season to pitch in an exhibition game against the Naval Academy's Plebe team. Tommy walked the first three batters and then settled down, leading his team to a 4–0 victory.

Finally installed on the varsity squad, Byrne dominated the Baltimore school baseball scene for the next two years. He helped guide City High to two undefeated seasons and a pair of Maryland Scholastic Association championships. During the summer months he hurled in the Baltimore ama-

Tommy Byrne had pitched only four innings for the 1947 Yankees when on June 14 they sent him to the Kansas City Blues of the American Association.

teur leagues with the Oriole Juniors and the Joe Cambria All Stars.

After graduating in 1937, Byrne had an opportunity to sign with the Detroit Tigers. He traveled with the club for part of the summer. The Tigers offered him a $4,000 signing bonus and a roster spot on their Texas League farm club in Beaumont. But Byrne, an excellent student, wanted to go to college and turned down the offer.

Duke University offered a scholarship that would have required him to work in the school cafeteria to defray some of his expenses. A friend in Baltimore, who had a connection with Wake Forest College, told Byrne he could get a scholarship there without having to work.

When Byrne got off the train in Wake Forest, North Carolina (the college had not yet moved to Winston-Salem and become a university), he was instantly smitten with the small-town atmosphere. He struck up an immediate friendship with baseball coach John Caddell. Byrne lived with the Caddell family during his stay at the school, and as their bond grew, he eventually came to know the coach and his wife as his adoptive parents.

Byrne was a mathematics major in the classroom and a standout pitcher on the Wake Forest baseball team for three seasons. He defeated Duke nine of the ten times he faced them. He also fanned seventeen in a game against Cornell. During the summers Byrne played in the semiprofessional Tobacco State League. He was scouted by Yankees regional scout Gene McCann and signed with New York on July 4, 1940. He received a $10,000 signing bonus and a $650 monthly salary. The Philadelphia Athletics had offered Byrne more money, but he was determined to play on the same team as his boyhood idol, Babe Ruth.

The Yankees started Byrne with their top farm club, the Newark Bears of the International League. He struggled in his first season, winning two games and losing five. He did better in 1941, as the Bears won the first of two consecutive pennants, winning ten games and losing seven.

In 1942 Byrne hit his stride. He won seventeen games while losing just four, and while he gave up only 160 hits in 209 innings, he walked 145 batters. But Bears manager Billy Meyer said, "Wild or not, he is the best prospect in the International League, as his record shows. There is no reason he can't get the ball over the plate in the majors." At the plate, the left-handed-hitting Byrne had ten

doubles, two triples, and two home runs while batting .328.

Byrne earned a spot on the Yankees' 1943 roster, making his Major League debut on April 27, against the Boston Red Sox. He pitched only a single inning, giving up no hits but a run on two walks. The rookie was with the Yankees for only a short time before enlisting in the navy. He won two games and lost one, but walked 35 batters in 31⅔ innings. Byrne's first Major League win came as a reliever in his second game, in Washington. To make the victory even sweeter, his mentor, Eddie Rommel, was umpiring at first base.

Byrne quickly grasped the Yankees tradition. "Part of the Yankee success lay in perpetuating the image," he recalled in later years.

From the moment you signed a contract with them they began instilling in you that Yankee tradition and they never stopped, not even when you were with the parent team. The attitude in those days was so great it was unreal. If we had a ballplayer on the Yankees who seemed to be doing things on his own, who didn't appear to have had bred in him what it meant to play and win as a team, he wasn't around too long. . . . They just wouldn't allow anyone, no matter how much ability he had, to tarnish that Yankee image. It meant too much, in ways that were as much practical as symbolic.

Because Byrne was a college graduate with a degree in mathematics, the Yankees' farm director, George Weiss, recommended him for Naval Officers' Training School. Byrne was accepted and was commissioned an ensign in November 1943.

His first assignment was to the Norfolk (Virginia) Naval Base, where, like many ballplayers in uniform, he mostly played baseball. In the spring of 1944, Byrne posted a 16-2 record for the powerful base team, while playing in the outfield on the days he did not pitch.

Later, Byrne was assigned to the destroyer USS

Ordronaux as the gunnery officer. In August 1944 he participated in the Allied invasion of the south coast of France and was in charge of the ship's guns as it shelled German shore defenses.

Discharged from the navy in January 1946, Byrne rejoined the Yankees. He made only four pitching appearances during the season, though he appeared in ten other games as a pinch hitter or pinch runner. Manager Joe McCarthy tried without success to get the six-foot-one, 182-pound Byrne to switch to first base. The highlight of the season for Byrne was probably Old-Timers Day at Yankee Stadium, when Babe Ruth asked to borrow his glove.

The emergence of rookie pitcher Frank Shea put Byrne's 1947 roster spot in jeopardy. Byrne had pitched only 4 innings when on June 14 the Yankees sent him to the Kansas City Blues of the American Association. With the Blues Byrne won twelve and lost six, but gave up 106 walks in 149 innings.

Byrne was back with the Yankees in 1948 and finally started to find his groove in the Majors, winning eight games and losing five. Still wild, he walked 101 in 133 innings and hit a league-leading 9 batsmen. Coach Bill Dickey, who had been his first Major League catcher, taught Byrne a cut fastball, which curtailed the natural rising movement of his fastball. But the wildness remained. He led the American League in walks three years in a row (1949–51) and hit batsmen in five seasons.

Even with his problems locating the strike zone, Byrne was considered a vital part of the Yankees squad and got a raise in salary in each of the three years he led the league in walks. "I never really believed in my own mind that I was so very wild," he said in later years. "I didn't think I was 'losing' wild, if you know what I mean. I used to feel that if they let me pitch I wasn't going to give more than three or four runs a game, and I would get a couple back with my own bat, because I could hit."

The Yankees had a new manager in 1949, Casey Stengel, and Byrne, with a 15-7 record, had his best season to date. The Yankees defeated the Brooklyn Dodgers in the World Series. Byrne started the third game but was lifted in the fourth inning after giving up a home run to Pee Wee Reese and loading the bases on a hit and two walks.

Byrne was a methodical worker on the mound, taking an inordinate amount of time between pitches. He was a sociable fellow on the mound, too. He talked to players in the opposing dugouts and also to opposing batters, all in an effort to shake their concentration.

Despite leading the American League in walks and hit batters in 1950, Byrne won fifteen games for the pennant-winning Yankees and was selected to the All-Star team. On July 5, 1950, he hit four batters in the five innings he pitched, which tied an American League record for most batters hit in a game. He did not pitch as New York swept the Philadelphia Phillies in the World Series.

When Byrne came to work at Yankee Stadium on June 15, 1951, he found left-handed pitcher Stubby Overmire occupying his locker. Byrne was summoned to Stengel's office and told he had been traded to the St. Louis Browns with twenty-five thousand dollars for Overmire.

Tommy did not fare well in St. Louis, winning eleven games while losing twenty-four during his year and a half with the club. "There was no greater tumble than going from the first-place Yankees to the last-place Browns," Byrne said. But he enjoyed playing for the colorful Bill Veeck, who gave him a raise despite his 4-10 record for the tailenders. Byrne tied another record for wildness on August 22, 1951, against Boston, when he walked sixteen batters in a game.

After Byrne posted a 7-14 record in 1952, the Browns traded him to the Chicago White Sox with shortstop Joe DeMaestri for outfielder Hank Edwards and shortstop Willie Miranda. His tenure with the White Sox was brief, but he did have one shining moment. On May 16 White Sox manager Paul Richards summoned him from the bull-pen to pinch-hit for infielder Vern Stephens with the bases loaded and two men out in the ninth inning. Right-handed pitcher Ewell Blackwell had just entered the game for New York. Byrne recalled, "Richards asked me, 'You ever hit this guy?' 'Yeah,' I said, 'about 11 years ago.' 'Well,' said Richards, 'how about going up and hitting one out of here?' So I go up there and, after getting the count to 2-2, I don't even remember swinging the bat, but I hit a line drive, 20 rows back in right field." The grand slam won the game. During his career Byrne batted .238 with fourteen home runs, ninety-eight RBIs, and a .378 slugging percentage.

Less than a month after the grand slam, Chicago sold Byrne to the Washington Senators. He appeared in six games for Washington in 1953, losing five, before being released on August 2 by owner Clark Griffith. "I had one day to go before becoming a 10-year man in the majors," Byrne recalled. That annoyed him, but not as much as the reason Griffith gave for the move—they could not understand what had happened to his hitting!

Byrne signed as a free agent with the White Sox, who sent him to the Charleston (West Virginia) Senators, their affiliate in the American Association. He was 1-6 with a 5.31 ERA for Charleston in the last two months of 1953. That December Chicago traded him to the Seattle Rainiers of the Pacific Coast League for first baseman Gordon Goldsberry.

During the winter Byrne played for a team in Pastora, Venezuela, where he began to experiment with changing speeds on his pitches. "I was determined to work on a slider down there, and it was amazing what I did in the short time there," he said.

When the Rainiers' newest addition joined the team in the spring of 1954, he picked up right where he left off in winter ball. The seasoned southpaw pitched great all year, keeping the Pacific Coast League hitters off balance with a variety

of off-speed offerings and his recently developed slider. "It turned out to be the perfect spot for me," Byrne said. "[Jerry] Priddy was a first-year manager and he needed a veteran pitcher who could give him innings. I was ready and willing. I needed starts on a regular basis to work on my contract."

When the season ended, Tommy had compiled a record of twenty wins and ten losses and a 3.15 ERA. His 199 strikeouts led the league and, for the first time, outnumbered his walks (118). He also played in fifty games as an outfielder, first baseman, or pinch hitter and hit for a .295 batting average, with seven home runs and thirty-nine RBIS.

Byrne's statistics impressed an opposing manager, Oakland's Charlie Dressen. When his old pal Casey Stengel sought his opinion on PCL players, Dressen told him, "The only guy here who can help you is Byrne. I suggest you get him. He's a different pitcher than when I saw him with the Yankees. He's learned what this is about." On September 3, 1954, the Yankees purchased Byrne's contract from Seattle. Byrne started five games for New York during the last month of the season, winning three and losing two.

By 1955 the Yankees' pitching staff had been revamped, and Stengel made Byrne his number-three starter behind Whitey Ford and Bob Turley.

At the age of thirty-five, Byrne set his career high for victories, finishing 16-5, with a 3.15 earned run average. His .762 winning percentage was the best in the league, and the Yankees won the pennant. "He beat the other first-division clubs, Cleveland, the White Sox, the Red Sox, when it was them or us," Stengel said. "Without him, we don't win."

Byrne started Game Two of the World Series against the Dodgers, in Yankee Stadium. He held them to five hits and two runs and rapped a two-run single as the Yankees won, 4–2.

Stengel had enough faith in his veteran pitcher to give him the start in Game Seven. Byrne pitched 5⅔ innings and gave up just two runs, but Johnny

Podres shut out the Yankees as the Dodgers won the game, and the World Series. After the Series Byrne was part of the Yankees squad that toured Japan.

In 1956 the starting rotation was retooled with the addition of youngsters Johnny Kucks and Tom Sturdivant. Byrne made only eight starts and posted a 7-3 record with six saves. He made one relief appearance in the World Series, giving up a home run to Duke Snider in Game Two.

The 1957 campaign was Byrne's last in the Major Leagues. He made four starts but did most of his work out of the bullpen. His last two mound appearances came in the World Series against the Milwaukee Braves. One of the outings was the occasion of a memorable incident.

The Yankees took a one-run lead in Game Four with a run in the top of the tenth inning. Byrne was summoned to save the game, and his first pitch to pinch hitter Nippy Jones skidded past catcher Yogi Berra and rolled back to the stands. Jones insisted the ball had hit him on the foot, proving his point by showing a shoe-polish scuff mark on the baseball. Home plate umpire Augie Donatelli awarded Jones first base. Byrne was replaced by Bob Grim, and the Braves won three batters later on a two-run homer by Eddie Mathews. Byrne said that if Berra had thrown the ball back to him instead of holding onto it for Donatelli, Byrne would have marked it up so that nobody could spot the shoe polish.

After appearing in a mop-up role in Game Seven, Byrne hung up his spikes for good. He was finding it harder to separate himself from the peaceful times and friendly people of Wake Forest. He had gotten into the oil business, owned a couple of farms, and even opened a clothing store in Algiers, near Wake Forest. "When I sent back my contract after the '57 season," Byrne said, "the Yankees called me and asked me to come to St. Petersburg for spring training anyway."

There, general manager George Weiss offered him a new contract and a raise of five thousand dollars, with a catch: it involved trading Byrne to the St. Louis Cardinals. "I told him, 'You don't understand, if I'm gonna pitch, the only place it's gonna ever be is for the New York Yankees.'"

The hard-throwing left-hander ended his career in the Majors with a lifetime record of eighty-five wins, sixty-nine losses, and a 4.11 earned run average. In eleven seasons with the Yankees he was 72-40 and had a 3.93 ERA. At the plate he finished with fourteen home runs and a very respectable .238 batting average.

A few years later Byrne became a scout for the New York Mets. In May 1963 he took over the manager's job with the Mets' Class A affiliate in Raleigh, North Carolina, and piloted the club for the remainder of the season.

Byrne retired from all baseball activities after the 1963 season. He had been living in Wake Forest during the off-season and would now make the college town his permanent home. His many business interests during this time included successful forays in real estate, a clothing store, farm equipment, and the oil industry. Byrne was also a dedicated civil servant: he served as a town commissioner, as Bureau of Recreation chairman, and two terms as mayor of Wake Forest, from 1973 to 1987.

Byrne's accomplishments on the ball field earned him induction into the North Carolina Sports Hall of Fame, Wake Forest College Hall of Fame, Maryland Sports Hall of Fame, and Baltimore City College Hall of Fame.

The town honored the former Yankee with two Tommy Byrne Days, in 1955 and 2007. He received numerous other accolades, including awards from the North Carolina governor and the Wake Forest Birthplace Society.

Byrne was a founding member of St. Catherine of Siena Catholic Church and a member of the Knights of Columbus. Beginning in 1957 the local high school gave an award in his name to the best athlete of the year.

Byrne died from congestive heart failure on December 20, 2007, at the age of eighty-seven. His wife of sixty-two years, Mary Susan (Nichols) Byrne, had died in 2002. Byrne was survived by three sons, Thomas, John, and Charles, and a daughter, Susan, along with numerous grandchildren and great-grandchildren. Byrne is buried in Wake Forest Cemetery.

Chapter 26. **Aaron Robinson**

Mark Stewart

AGE	G	AB	R	H	2B	3B	HR	TB	RBI	BB	SO	BAV	OBP	SLG	SB	GDP	HBP
32	82	252	23	68	11	5	5	104	36	40	26	.270	.370	.413	0	5	0

The leading member of the 1947 Yankees' catchers-by-committee group, Aaron Robinson was behind the plate in seventy-four games, more than any of his fellow backstops. But perhaps his most important role that season was helping groom his eventual successor, future Hall of Famer Yogi Berra.

Aaron Andrew Robinson was born on June 23, 1915, in Lancaster, South Carolina, a small town an hour or so south of Charlotte, North Carolina. Both his father, Charles Augustus "Gus" Robinson, and his mother, Jennie (McAteer) Robinson, were descendants of Scotch-Irish settlers. Gus died in 1953, at age 69, but Jennie lived to 104, outliving her son by a quarter century.

Aaron grew to be tall and powerfully built, at six foot two and 205 pounds. A left-handed batter, with a strong throwing arm and a good head for baseball, he played catcher and third base during his school days and sandlot career. Robinson began his professional career in 1937, after the New York Yankees signed him just before his twenty-second birthday. He reported to his first spring camp as a married man, having wed Myrtle McManus on February 6. The couple would produce six children: Sybil, (1938–2004), Joanne, Mary Ann (born and died 1941), Gerald (1946–2008), Charles, and David. They eventually divorced, and Robinson later married the former Eva Ransom.

Robinson's first stop on his way to the Major Leagues was with the Snow Hill (North Carolina) Billies of the Class D Coastal Plain League. He climbed up the Yankees' farm system, hitting above .300 at almost every stop. He played third

Aaron Robinson threw out both Eddie Stanky and Pee Wee Reese as they attempted to steal second base in the first inning of Game Seven of the 1947 World Series.

base in 1937 and 1938, after which the Yankees decided to move him to catcher. In 1942 he became the regular catcher for the International League Newark Bears, and in 1943 he got the call to the big leagues. He soon became known for shouting a resounding "Where *was* that ball?" when he felt an umpire had missed a call.

Robinson played his first game on May 6, 1943, and struck out in a pinch-hitting appearance.

He went into the U.S. Coast Guard before playing another game with the Yankees and did not return until 1945. After being discharged, Robinson rejoined the Yankees at the end of July and played in fifty games in 1945. He batted .281, with eight home runs, while sharing catching duties with Mike Garbark.

In 1946, with more players coming out of the service, the catching situation for the Yankees continued to evolve. Manager Joe McCarthy, unimpressed with his options in spring training, tabbed veteran star Bill Dickey as his starting backstop, at least to begin the year. The thirty-nine-year-old Dickey, back after two years in the navy, caught the bulk of the games in April and May. Robinson was picked to spell Dickey in the early going and hit .300 in this role. When McCarthy abruptly resigned in May, Dickey replaced him as manager and benched himself. Robinson became the starter.

Though injury prone, the thirty-one-year-old Robinson did the bulk of the catching the last four months of the '46 season. Gus Niarhos came up from Kansas City in June, and in late September twenty-one-year-old Yogi Berra joined the team from Newark. Robinson continued to hit with authority, finishing with sixteen home runs and sixty-four RBIs. He belted two of those homers in successive innings off Bob Feller on July 11 in New York. The second one was a grand slam — the only one of his career.

Robinson's .506 slugging percentage was the highest of his big-league career. He also became the answer to a trivia question that no doubt won countless bar bets over the years: On the third-place Yankees of 1946, a team that included Joe DiMaggio, Charlie Keller, Joe Gordon, Phil Rizzuto, Bill Dickey, and Tommy Henrich, who led the regulars in batting? The answer is Aaron Robinson, at .297.

Robinson garnered a handful of Most Valuable Player votes, finishing higher than any other catcher in the American League. He came to camp in 1947 solidly ensconced as the Yankees' number-one catcher. Bucky Harris had been hired to restore order to New York's managerial situation, while Dickey set about teaching young Berra the finer points of big-league backstopping.

Meanwhile, Robinson did a creditable job handling the improved Yankees pitching staff. He was named to the All-Star team, but spent the entire contest on the bench. In the season's second half, Bucky Harris and Bill Dickey felt Berra was ready to handle half the catching duties, so Robinson and Yogi split the job the rest of the way. Sherm Lollar, a prospect acquired from the Indians, also saw action down the stretch. Berra was clearly the superior offensive player. Robinson finished the year with a .270 average, but had only twenty-one extra-base hits and a mere thirty-six RBIs.

Robinson hit home runs in both games of a June 4 doubleheader against the Tigers in Detroit, and he had a three-hit, five-RBI game in the second game of an August 24 doubleheader against the White Sox at Chicago. He had a strong finish to the season, fashioning an eleven-game hitting streak in September.

During the World Series against the Dodgers, Harris used all three of his catchers. Robinson started twice — Game Five in Brooklyn and the Game Seven finale in the Bronx. The Yankees won both. In Game Five Robinson worked a two-out walk off Rex Barney and then came around to score the game's first run when pitcher Frank Shea singled to left. The Yankees went on to win, 2–1, behind rookie Shea's complete-game performance.

Robinson subbed for Lollar in Game Six, an 8–6 Dodgers victory. He entered the game in the top of the fourth inning and singled to center to lead off the bottom of the frame. Berra, in the game as an outfielder, subsequently singled him in to give New York a 5–4 lead. The Yankees failed to hold Brooklyn and found themselves trailing 8–5 with three outs to go. Robinson singled to load the bases with one out against reliever Hugh Casey. Pinch hitter Lonnie Frey hit into a force play, erasing Robinson at second as a run scored. Casey then got Snuffy Stirnweiss to hit a come-backer for the final out.

Game Seven found Robinson behind the plate and Shea on the mound again. The Yankees spotted Brooklyn two early runs, but it could have been much worse. In the first inning Eddie Stanky led off with a single. With Pee Wee Reese at the plate, Stanky took off for second. Robinson threw him out by so much that the umpire did not even bother to give an out signal. Shea ended up walking Reese, who tried to swipe second, too. Once again, Robinson fired the ball to Stirnweiss, who tagged Reese out.

Robinson contributed to New York's first run-scoring rally by drawing a second-inning walk off Hal Gregg. He struck out in the fourth, but New York scored twice to take a 3–2 lead. Joe Page came in to start the fifth inning and blanked the Dodgers the rest of the way. Robinson gave the Yankees an insurance run in the seventh inning when he followed Billy Johnson's triple with a long fly ball to left fielder Eddie Miksis. Johnson scored after the catch with New York's final run in a 5–2 victory.

Game Seven was Robinson's last in pinstripes. The following February New York packaged him with young left-hander Bill Wight and Minor League pitcher Fred Bradley in a trade that brought Eddie Lopat from the Chicago White Sox. Pitchers Wight and Bradley were coveted by Chicago, as was Robinson, whom it saw as an improvement over their catcher, Mike Tresh. Robinson played just one season in Chicago, a season in which the White Sox lost 101 games. He batted .252 and was second on the club with eight home runs.

At thirty-three Robinson, already one of the slowest players in the league, was beginning to slow down as a hitter, too. Apparently, this did not concern the Detroit Tigers, who traded pitcher

Billy Pierce for Robinson and kicked in an extra ten thousand dollars to seal the deal. Detroit was in a win-now mode and needed a catcher with championship experience to handle its veteran pitchers. New Tigers manager Red Rolfe, a former Yankee, probably liked Robinson's Yankee pedigree, too.

Pierce went on to win 211 Major League games (208 after leaving the Tigers), and Detroit fans would bemoan the Robinson-for-Pierce trade as one of the most lopsided in franchise history. Yet Robinson did everything the Tigers could have asked in 1949. He played in more than 100 games, threw out more than 40 percent of the runners who attempted to steal, batted .269, and regained his power stroke with thirteen homers and fifty-six RBIS. His on-base percentage was .402—a superb number for an aging catcher. Robinson worked well with the veteran pitchers and coaxed quality innings from youngsters Ted Gray and Art Houtteman. The Tigers fell short of a pennant, but finished 20 games over .500.

Although Robinson's offensive production fell off in 1950, the Tigers won 95 games and spent almost all of July and August in first place. A quartet of losses to Cleveland and St. Louis in late September doomed them to a second-place finish behind the Yankees.

When Tigers fans looked back on the season, many focused on Robinson's role in a loss to the Cleveland Indians on September 24. In the tenth inning of a 1–1 game, Cleveland's Luke Easter hit a ball to first base with the bases loaded. First baseman Don Kolloway touched the bag and fired home to Robinson. Because his view was blocked by Easter, Robinson did not see his teammate touch first and assumed a force was on at home. He did not bother to tag Bob Lemon as he slid across the plate with the deciding run.

All three Detroit catchers in 1950—Robinson, veteran Bob Swift, and rookie Joe Ginsberg—hit below .235. Robinson's main contribution on offense was his stellar discipline at the plate. He finished the year with sixty-four hits but seventy-five walks.

Enemy pitchers were not so kind in 1951. They challenged Robinson more, and he literally hit his weight—.205. The Tigers waived him in early August, and the Boston Red Sox claimed him. He finished the year as part of an ineffective catching jumble that included Buddy Rosar, Les Moss, Mike Guerra, Al Evans, Sammy White, and Matt Batts.

Robinson failed to catch on with a big-league club the following spring. He took a job with the Portland Beavers of the Pacific Coast League and played there for two years. In 1954 he headed across the country to play for the Charleston (West Virginia) Senators, a White Sox affiliate in the American Association. Later in the season he joined the Fayetteville (North Carolina) Highlanders of the Class B Carolina League, where he caught, coached, and managed. He returned to the Highlanders in a similar capacity in 1955 but was replaced before the season ended.

Robinson stayed in baseball as a Minor League coach. In his last season, 1961, he managed the Shelby (North Carolina) Colonels, who won the Western Carolina League title despite a losing record in the regular season.

Robinson earned a World Series ring, some good memories, and one of baseball's most inauspicious records. After his 2,189th and final plate appearance, for the Red Sox in 1951, Robinson had not stolen a base in the big leagues. It established a record that lasted until 1965, when fellow catcher Russ Nixon bumped him from the top spot. Robinson finished his career with a .260 batting mark—better than average for catchers of his day—with sixty-one homers and 272 RBIs.

Robinson died of cancer on March 9, 1966, at the age of fifty, in his hometown of Lancaster. He was survived by his wife, Eva; his mother, Jennie; his first wife, Myrtle; and his children, Sybil, Joanne, Gerald, Charles, and David.

Chapter 27. Timeline, June 13–June 30

Lyle Spatz

Friday, June 13, vs. St. Louis—The Yankees out-hit the Browns 13–8 in their return to the Stadium but still lost, 4–3, in ten innings. St. Louis got three runs in the first and the winner in the tenth against Bill Bevens. Fred Sanford was the complete-game winner. Ray Coleman's triple drove in Paul Lehner with the game-winning run. Johnny Lindell had three more hits for New York. Phil Rizzuto also had three hits. 27-23-1, Second, 1½ games behind.

Saturday, June 14, vs. St. Louis—Johnny Lindell had a double, triple, a home run, and three RBIS in the Yankees 12–4 win. Fortunately for New York, their recent attempts to trade Lindell were unsuccessful. Filling in while Charlie Keller recovered from his wrenched back, Lindell was 15 for 29, with three hits in each of his last four games. Allie Reynolds pitched a complete game for the Yankees. Little-used left-hander Tommy Byrne was optioned to Kansas City of the American Association. 28-23-1, Second, 1 game behind.

Sunday, June 15, vs. St. Louis (2)—More than fifty-five thousand fans saw the Yankees sweep a doubleheader from the Browns, 10–4 and 2–1, to move into first place. Spud Chandler pitched a complete game in the opener, and Randy Gumpert, in his first start of the season, followed suit in the nightcap. George McQuinn was the hitting star of the first game with a home run and three RBIS. Billy Johnson and Tommy Henrich each had three hits. McQuinn hit another homer in the second game. The Yankees backed Gumpert with four double plays, including an unassisted one at the

plate by catcher Yogi Berra in the ninth inning. 30-23-1, First, 1 game ahead.

Monday, June 16, vs. Chicago—Phil Rizzuto's ninth inning, bases-loaded squeeze bunt scored Joe DiMaggio with the winning run in the Yankees' 4–3 victory. A two-run rally in the eighth had allowed the Yanks to tie the score at 3–3. Joe Page, in relief of Frank Shea, was the winner, and Earl Caldwell, in relief of Joe Haynes, was the loser. 31-23-1, First, 1½ games ahead.

Tuesday, June 17—Not scheduled. 31-23-1, First, 1 game ahead.

Wednesday, June 18, vs. Chicago—Rained out. 31-23-1, First, ½ game ahead.

Thursday, June 19, vs. Chicago—The White Sox scored four runs in the fifth inning on their way to a 6–4 win, which dropped the Yankees to second place behind Boston. Dave Philley had four hits for Chicago, but Rudy York's two-run homer off Bill Bevens was the big blow. Bevens, the first of four Yankees pitchers, saw his record fall to 3-8. Gordon Maltzberger, in relief of starter Ed Lopat, was the winner. 31-24-1, Second, .005 percentage points behind.

Friday, June 20, vs. Detroit—Frank Shea won his eighth game of the season, beating the Tigers, 5–3. The win allowed the Yankees to move back into first place. Shea allowed only four hits—two were home runs by Eddie Mayo—and struck out nine in tossing his ninth complete game of the season. The loser was Hal Newhouser, who had now lost three consecutive outings to Shea. In beating Newhouser the Yanks evened their lifetime record against the great left-hander at 19-19. Tommy Henrich's two-run homer was the big blow for New York. 32-24-1, First, 1 game ahead.

Saturday, June 21, vs. Detroit (2) — Spud Chandler and Allie Reynolds pitched complete games as the Yankees swept the Tigers, 5–4 and 7–4. The Yanks scored the tying and winning runs against starter and loser Dizzy Trout in the opener. Tommy Henrich singled home pinch runner Ted Sepkowski with the game winner. Later that day, Sepkowski was released to the Newark Bears of the International League. Chandler's eleven strikeouts were the most by a Yankees pitcher so far that season. Billy Johnson's four hits and two runs batted in led the Yanks' offense in the second game. Phil Rizzuto and Joe DiMaggio also had two RBIs each. 34-24-1, First, 1½ games ahead.

Sunday, June 22, vs. Detroit — A five-run first inning, highlighted by Yogi Berra's grand slam, led the Yankees to a 6–5 win and a sweep of the four-game series with Detroit. The Tigers knocked out Randy Gumpert with three runs in the first. Gumpert was bailed out by Karl Drews, who held Detroit scoreless until the ninth. After yielding two runs, Bucky Harris called again on Joe Page to save the game, which he did by fanning Pat Mullin. 35-24-1, First, 2 games ahead.

Monday, June 23, vs. Cleveland — The Yankees scored four eighth-inning runs, three on a bases-loaded double by Tommy Henrich, to score an 8–5 comeback win over Cleveland. Bill Bevens, who had not won a game since May 25, was the starter but lasted only four innings. He was relieved by Butch Wensloff and then Joe Page, who pitched the final 3⅓ innings and got the win. Don Black started for the Indians, but reliever Bob Lemon

took the loss. Yogi Berra had three hits for New York, including a triple and a home run. 36-24-1, First, 2 games ahead.

Tuesday, June 24, vs. Cleveland — Rained out. 36-24-1, First, 2 games ahead.

Wednesday, June 25, vs. Cleveland — Frank Shea won his ninth game, shutting out the Indians, 3–0, on three hits. It was the rookie right-hander's third shutout of the season. The crowd of more than 60,000 pushed the Yankees' home attendance over the 1 million mark. Billy Johnson's two-run single in the first inning provided all the runs Shea would need. The Yanks purchased utility infielder Lonny Frey from the Chicago Cubs. 37-24-1, First, 2½ games ahead.

Thursday, June 26, at Philadelphia — Joe Coleman, who shut out the Yankees on Memorial Day, defeated them again. His 4–2 victory was only his second of the season against five losses, and it ended the Yanks' six-game winning streak. Allie Reynolds went the distance in losing. Pete Suder had two hits for Philadelphia, a double and a triple, while Johnny Lindell had three singles for New York. Sam Chapman of the A's and Joe DiMaggio hit home runs. 37-25-1, First, 2½ games ahead.

Friday, June 27, at Philadelphia — Spud Chandler disappointed the largest Shibe Park crowd of the season thus far (38,529), by downing the A's, 7–1. The win was the fifth straight for Chandler; the loss went to A's starter Carl Scheib. Tommy Henrich had two doubles and a home run, George Stirnweiss had two doubles, Joe DiMaggio had a single and a triple, and Phil Rizzuto had a double and two singles. Charlie Keller's continuing back problems forced him to check into New York Hospital for observation. 38-25-1, First, 3½ games ahead.

Saturday, June 28, at Philadelphia — George McQuinn's three-run homer off A's starter Jesse Flores in the first inning powered the Yankees to a 5–2 win. Tommy Henrich also had a home run, and Billy Johnson had two hits. Randy Gumpert pitched a complete game for his second win of the season. 39-25-1, First, 3½ games ahead.

Sunday, June 29, at Washington (2) — The Yankees split their doubleheader at Washington, but picked up a game on the second-place Red Sox who lost two one-run games at Philadelphia. Early Wynn beat the Yanks, 5–1, in the first game, besting Karl Drews. Twenty-year-old Don Johnson, with relief help from Allie Reynolds, defeated the Senators' Walt Masterson in the nightcap, 3–1. The Yanks managed only eleven hits on the day, with only Phil Rizzuto's triple in the opener and George McQuinn's and Aaron Robinson's doubles in the second game going for extra bases. 40-26-1, First, 4½ games ahead.

Monday, June 30, at Boston — Frank Shea's tenth win of the season, a 3–1 four-hitter at Fenway Park, allowed the Yanks to stretch their lead over the second-place Red Sox to 5½ games. Joe DiMaggio's first-inning triple off Joe Dobson drove in two runs, and Tommy Henrich's fifth-inning single accounted for the third run. Bobby Doerr's bases-loaded walk in the third accounted for Boston's only run. 41-26-1, First, 5½ games ahead.

Chapter 28. **Billy Johnson**

Cort Vitty

AGE	G	AB	R	H	2B	3B	HR	TB	RBI	BB	SO	BAV	OBP	SLG	SB	GDP	HBP
28	132	494	67	141	19	8	10	206	95	44	43	.285	.351	.417	1	21	6

Called "too small for a pitcher" by his high school coach, Billy Johnson switched to the outfield, and eventually to third base, where he played well enough to be given a "day" at Yankee Stadium. It took place before a crowd of 42,267 on July 25, 1948, between games of a doubleheader. The day was hot, and so was the pennant race: a game and a half separated the top four clubs in the American League. After being honored, the All-Star third baseman pleased family and friends in attendance by smashing a three-run homer in the nightcap, as the Yankees swept the White Sox, 5–3 and 7–3.

William Russell Johnson was born in Montclair, New Jersey, on August 30, 1918. His father, James, serviced trolley cars, while his mother, born Bebe Beulah Clark and nicknamed Bess, maintained the household. He had an older brother, Raymond, and a younger sister, Ann. Growing up in an Irish Catholic neighborhood during the Depression, Johnson attended Immaculate Conception grammar school and honed his early baseball skill on the spacious fields of Nishuane Park in Montclair.

While attending Montclair High and later Bloomfield Tech, Johnson set bowling pins and delivered groceries to earn spending money for baseball equipment. As a pitcher for the Montclair Pro Giants, the right-handed Johnson raised eyebrows after hurling a couple of impressive no-hitters. Appreciative teammates took up a collection and raised enough money to send him to a professional tryout in Binghamton, New York. Despite Johnson's effectiveness on the mound, Montclair High coach Carl Newman told him, "You're too small for a pitcher, Bill," and suggested he move

An injury to Bobby Brown in May 1947 allowed Billy Johnson to regain the third base position full-time.

to another position.[1] Heeding the advice of his former mentor, the powerfully built five-foot-ten youngster switched to the outfield.

In 1936, after a particularly impressive day against a neighboring semipro club, Johnson was tapped on the shoulder as he walked off the field. The tapper was Yankees scout Paul Krichell, who asked Billy if he would like to sign a contract with the New York club. Johnson's parents approved, and the youngster signed for a one-hundred-dollar signing bonus. The Yankees sent the seventeen-year-old Johnson to Butler in the Pennsylvania State Association, where he had a 1-0 record and batted .263 in five games.

Back in Butler as an outfielder in 1937, Johnson posted a .356 batting average, which earned him an end-of-the-season look (but no playing time) from the Newark Bears, the Yankees' top farm team. Johnson was still using his schoolboy spikes when he reported to Newark. He recalled Bears manager Ossie Vitt's reaction: "He took one look at the shoes and told me to throw 'em away before they killed my feet. He gave me a pair of his own shoes to wear in their place. They were manufactured of the softest black leather and fitted with gleaming steel spikes on the soles. I sure was proud to wear 'em."[2]

Johnson was batting a respectable .306 with the Augusta (Georgia) Tigers of the South Atlantic League in 1938, when the Yankees promoted him to the Norfolk (Virginia) Tars of the Piedmont League. An anemic .226 batting mark with Norfolk prompted Johnson to ask Yankees farm director George Weiss to send him back to Augusta. The puzzled Weiss was confused by a young ballplayer requesting a move down the ladder. He quizzed Johnson until he learned that Billy had a girlfriend named Louise Robinson back in Augusta, and he wanted to spend another season close to her home. The request was granted, and Johnson was sent back to Augusta, where he hit .328 in 1939 and became an All-Star center fielder.

Johnson not only enjoyed the company of Louise, but also had another fine season with Augusta in 1940, contributing a .346 average in 150 games as a third baseman. Bill and Louise were married on February 28, 1941. Moving up to the Binghamton (New York) Triplets of the Class A Eastern League in 1941, Johnson posted a .293 batting average with thirteen home runs. He was promoted to Newark for the 1942 season and moved to shortstop. He responded by hitting a solid .290 against International League pitching, though he committed forty errors at his new position. Johnson was also earning a reputation as an "iron man," having played every one of his team's games during the 1939, 1940, and 1942 seasons.

On March 15, 1943, the Yankees reported to their new spring-training facility at Asbury Park, New Jersey. (Wartime restrictions prohibited teams from traveling south to sunnier climates.) The oceanfront Albion Hotel served as team headquarters, and workouts took place on the adjacent high school field. The location was a few blocks from a gym, which provided ample room for workouts and calisthenics.

As a Minor League prospect, Johnson was invited to train with the parent club, but he was not expected to make the team. This lack of stature meant he was not listed for daily training assignments. One cold, damp day, Johnson sought out veteran shortstop Frank Crosetti and asked him to hit ground balls outside in the light snow. Johnson flawlessly fielded each sharp grounder hit in his direction. Manager Joe McCarthy walked out to the empty stands and silently watched the workout. McCarthy called the rookie over and asked, "Do you think you can play third base in the majors?" Johnson responded: "Give me a chance." McCarthy said: "You're getting one. Make the most of it. Starting today you're my third baseman."[3]

With Red Rolfe's retirement and several key players in the military, the Yankees, like most teams in 1943, had holes in their lineup. McCarthy, an infielder in his playing days, took it upon himself to teach Johnson the intricacies of third base. McCarthy also helped him as a hitter.

Johnson, a right-handed batter, stood even with the plate: "When I first came up, I hit everything to left, but Joe McCarthy told me that if I wanted to stay in the majors I would have to hit to all fields. So I learned to hit to right," Johnson once said. "I got my share of doubles and triples, but I would have hit a lot more homers if I didn't play in Yankee Stadium, where left field was so deep. I had power, which was why my teammates nicknamed me the bull."[4]

Johnson responded to McCarthy's tutoring by hitting .280 and driving in ninety-four runs for the Yankees in 1943. Among those he impressed was Connie Mack, the venerable manager of the Philadelphia Athletics, who called Johnson his unofficial "rookie of the year."

Johnson made his Major League debut on April 22, 1943, at home against Washington. Batting sixth, the third baseman went 0 for 3 but played errorless ball in the field. He collected his first Major League hit two days later off Senators lefthander Ewald Pyle. His first home run, a three-run blast, came at home on May 7 off Don Black of Philadelphia. Johnson played in all of the pennant-winning Yankees' 155 games and finished fourth in the voting for the American League's Most Valuable Player.

The significance of going to the World Series as a rookie was not lost on Johnson. "Some ballplayers spend their lives trying to get into a Series. And here I've done it in my first year in the big league! I'm going to play like hell against those Cardinals," he said.[5] And he did. Johnson's sixth-inning single helped the Yankees defeat St. Louis in the opener, and in Game Three he drove in the decisive runs with a bases-loaded triple off Al Brazle. Johnson's six hits led the Yankees as they won the World Series in five games.

Johnson missed the next two seasons, 1944 and 1945. He worked in a war plant during the winter of 1943–44. Then, although married with a child, he was drafted into the army on June 8, 1944. After basic training he was sent to Europe and served in a mortar crew. A corporal at war's end, Johnson returned home to Georgia in August 1945, where he played for the Infantry School All-Stars at Fort Benning.

The postwar Yankees were in serious disarray. In 1945 a group led by Dan Topping, Del Webb, and Larry MacPhail had purchased the club. The new ownership group immediately began making changes, and one of the first people to go was manager Joe McCarthy, who resigned early in the 1946 season. Veteran Bill Dickey succeeded McCarthy until he resigned in disgust late in the season and was replaced by coach Johnny Neun.

Johnson's discharge from the army was delayed; he did not resume his career until May 26 and did not make his first start until June 9. He hit .260 in eighty-five games and was one of many returning Yankees, including Joe DiMaggio, Tommy Henrich, Phil Rizzuto, and Joe Gordon, to have subpar seasons, as the club finished third.

Bucky Harris was named the Yankees' manager for 1947. Johnson thought Harris did a good job, despite being very quiet and lenient with players. There was a Yankees way of conduct on and off the field, and the veteran players simply knew what to do. Johnson had a quiet, businesslike demeanor in the clubhouse; he did not drink, swear, or chew tobacco. He generally headed straight home after a game, to enjoy a quiet family dinner and a good night's rest. Johnson enjoyed being recognized around the city, but never considered himself a celebrity. He thought Yankees fans were terrific and appreciated a winning team. In later years he told a sportswriter that he considered it an honor and a privilege to play for the Yankees.

At the start of spring training in 1947, Johnson did not have a job. Bobby Brown was the heir apparent at third base, after the Yankees signed the highly touted prospect for a bonus of fifty-two thousand dollars. Harris reportedly preferred having the veteran Johnson in the lineup, but the front office insisted that he platoon the players, with the left-handed-hitting Brown seeing the bulk of the playing time.

On May 23 a fastball thrown by Boston Red Sox pitcher Mel Parnell struck Brown on the hand, breaking a finger. Johnson regained the position full-time and blossomed into an All-Star. He replaced starting third baseman George Kell in the bottom of the seventh inning of the game at Wrigley Field; it was his only All-Star appearance. For the season he batted .285, with ninety-five runs batted in. Commenting on his ability to drive in runs, Johnson said, "To me, a man on base is like a red flag to the bull."[6]

In the 1947 World Series Johnson smacked three triples and led the team with eight runs scored, as the Yankees defeated the Brooklyn Dodgers in 7 games. The 1948 club won 94 games, but finished third in a close American League race. Johnson did his part in his usual workmanlike fashion, batting .294 with twelve home runs.

The Yankees' unimpressive performance cost manager Harris his job. His successor, Casey Stengel, reinstated the platoon system in 1949, with Johnson again sharing third base duties with Bobby Brown. Johnson and Brown were very good friends, but Billy did not mince words about not liking the Stengel system: "I never agreed with Casey about platooning. [But] I was a team player, so it was fine with me if Casey played Bobby Brown at third."[7] Johnson hit .249 in 113 games. Stengel's method resulted in a pennant for the Yankees and another World Series win against the Dodgers.

In 1950 the Yankees fought off the Red Sox and Tigers to win the pennant again. Johnson batted .260, although his playing time was reduced to 108 games. The Yankees swept the Philadelphia Phillies in the World Series. Although he appeared in all 4 games, Johnson was a starter only in Game Three.

The emergence of rookie Gil McDougald in 1951 made the thirty-two-year-old Johnson expendable. On May 14 he was traded to the Cardinals for first baseman Don Bollweg and cash. Initially apprehensive about the move, Johnson ended up adapting to his new team and became the regular third baseman. He posted a .262 average in 124 games with St. Louis and added a career-high fourteen home runs (all with the Cardinals).

In 1952 Johnson saw limited playing time, while giving way to the younger players manager Eddie Stanky preferred. "Under Eddie Stanky, I batted 200 fewer times in 1952 than in 1951 under Marty Marion," he noted.[8] The Cardinals had a new third baseman in 1953, Ray Jablonski, a power-hitting rookie. On May 18, after Johnson's six plate appearances in 11 games, St. Louis released the thirty-five-year-old to their Columbus (Ohio) farm team. Billy batted .233 in 113 games in the American Association and then retired. "I had no regrets," he said years later. "I lasted as long as I did because I had a winning attitude and worked and played hard."[9]

Johnson played a war-shortened nine Major League seasons, with a career batting average of .271. He made four trips to the World Series with the Yankees, each time winning a championship ring. "It was an honor and a privilege to play for those Yankee teams," Johnson told author Dom Forker in *The Men of Autumn*. "It was such a thrill to realize that I was good enough to wear the Yankee uniform and be a Yankee. Hey, I know a lot of players who were better than I was, and played in the majors for fifteen to twenty years, and never played in a World Series. I was one of the lucky ones."[10]

After retiring from the game, Johnson took a job as a shipping supervisor with the Graniteville Company in Augusta, Georgia. His second career lasted almost thirty years. He also served his community as a member of the volunteer fire department. His family attended Hill Baptist Church, where he actively participated in the men's Sunday-school classes. After a series of ailments, including open-heart surgery, a hip replacement, and bypass surgery, Johnson died on June 20, 2006, in Augusta. In addition to Louise, he was survived by a daughter, Brenda, and a son, William. He is buried in Westover Memorial Park in Augusta.

Chapter 29. **Randy Gumpert**

Steve Ferenchick

AGE	W	L	PCT.	ERA	G	GS	GF	CG	SHO	SV	IP	H	BB	SO	HBP	WP
29	4	1	.800	5.43	24	6	4	2	0	0	56.1	71	28	25	0	1

Randy Gumpert was feeling flush with confidence in the spring of 1947. After being out of the Major Leagues between the ages of twenty and twenty-eight, the six-foot-three, 185-pound right-hander had returned in 1946 with an excellent season. He had an 11-3 record for the third-place Yankees, with a 2.31 earned run average and a nearly two-to-one strikeout-to-walk ratio.

Gumpert started well again in 1947, allowing no runs in 2⅓ innings in his first three outings against the Philadelphia Athletics, the Washington Senators, and the St. Louis Browns. On June 15 manager Bucky Harris gave him his first start of the season in the second game of a doubleheader against the Browns. Gumpert came through with a complete-game 2–1 victory, scattering six hits and five walks. In his next start, however, he gave up three runs and lasted only ⅔ of an inning against the Detroit Tigers. Gumpert won his next two starts, both against the Athletics, but suffered an 8–0 loss to the Tigers on July 18, a loss that ended the Yankees' nineteen-game winning streak.

The purchase of Bobo Newsom from Washington, and the recall of Vic Raschi from the Minors, added depth to the Yankees' pitching staff and resulted in Gumpert making only one more start the rest of the season. In all he made six starts and eighteen relief appearances in 1947. He finished 4-1, with just 56⅓ innings pitched, a 5.43 earned run average, and more walks than strikeouts.

His performance was affected by an elbow injury that continued to worsen during the season. "They didn't do anything like they do now," he told author Victor Debs in 1998. "Ed Foley, the trainer, just put hot packs on my elbow. That

Randy Gumpert's 8–0 loss to the Tigers on July 18 ended the Yankees' nineteen-game winning streak.

didn't amount to anything. So I pitched with a bad arm the next five seasons. It used to take me twenty minutes into the game before my arm was warmed up and my elbow wasn't clicking."[1]

Gumpert was on the Yankees' World Series roster, and though he did not play, he did get a World Series ring and a $5,830 winner's share. As he told an interviewer late in his life, "Back then you could buy a few things for $5,200 [*sic*]."[2]

Randall Pennington Gumpert was born on January 23, 1918, to Abram Gumpert and Emma (Nolte) Gumpert on their family's seven-acre farm in Monocacy, Pennsylvania, a small town about fifty miles northwest of Philadelphia. Randy, who had an older brother, Albert, and an older sister, Winifred, attended Birdsboro High School, where he gained a reputation for his pitching. In 1934 his father wrote a letter to Philadelphia Athletics manager Connie Mack, suggesting the Athletics give his sixteen-year-old son a tryout. Mack liked what he saw and offered Randy a low-paying job throwing batting practice, which he did that year and the next after school had let out.

In 1936, two weeks after his high school graduation, Gumpert signed a contract for $300 a month with the Athletics and made his Major League debut on June 13. He pitched a perfect 1-2-3 eighth inning in a 19–1 loss to the Cleveland Indians. Gumpert made his first professional start at home against the Chicago White Sox on August 27, tossing a complete-game two-hitter for his first Major League win. "I never won another game until ten years later," he recalled many years later. "That's kind of a long gap, isn't it?"[3]

Gumpert made twenty-two appearances in that 1936 season, nineteen of them in relief, ending the season with a 1-2 record and a 4.76 ERA. On September 13 he faced Cleveland's Bob Feller in a much-hyped matchup between two teenagers literally just off the farm. (Feller would go back to the farm a couple weeks later, as he needed to return for his senior year of high school.) The teams shuffled their starting rotations specifically to get the matchup. The Indians topped the Athletics, 5–2; it would have been closer but for a throwing error by shortstop Rusty Peters of Philadelphia that let in two unearned runs. Feller set an American League record and tied the Major League record in the game by striking out his age in batters, seventeen.

In 1937 the Athletics tried to change Gumpert's pitching style from a three-quarters delivery to overhand, but he injured his arm in the process. He spent most of 1937 and 1938 recuperating in the Minors. He made just fourteen big-league appearances in those two seasons, pitching a combined 24⅓ innings.

Gumpert went 13-10 for the 1938 Williamsport (Pennsylvania) Grays, earning an "honorable mention" All-Star selection for the Eastern League. He began the 1939 season with the Class B Norfolk (Virginia) Tars, pitched well enough to jump up to the Class Double-A Baltimore Orioles, was then sent back down to Williamsport, and in July was sent to the Yankees system. The Yankees kept him in the Eastern League, assigning him to the Binghamton (New York) Triplets. He spent nearly all of 1940 in Binghamton, ending with a 15-8 record and a 3.24 ERA, before moving up to the Newark Bears for one game.

Gumpert continued to bounce around the Minor Leagues in 1941 and 1942, pitching for Newark, the Little Rock (Arkansas) Travelers, and the Kansas City Blues. But the war was on, and Gumpert enlisted in the coast guard. He was based in New London, Connecticut, during much of his enlistment and played baseball there along with other professional players to entertain his fellow coast guard members.

After the war ended Gumpert wrote to George Weiss, the director of the Yankees' farm system, to let him know he had kept up his strength during the war and gotten in some pitching. Weiss called to invite him to spring training. "The Yankees had two camps—one in St. Petersburg and another in Bradenton," Gumpert recalled in 1998. "Luckily I was placed in the St. Petersburg camp under [manager Joe] McCarthy while the coaches were running things in Bradenton. Evidently McCarthy took a liking to me."[4]

He had a strong spring training in 1946 and returned with the Yankees to New York to play a three-game exhibition series against Brooklyn.

In one of the games Gumpert shut out the Dodgers for seven innings. He later remarked, "If you asked me what my biggest thrill was, it wasn't on the field. It was in the manager's office at Ebbets Field after that game with Brooklyn when McCarthy called me in and said, 'Here's your contract.' It was the minimum salary—$4,000. They weren't taking any chances."[5]

After his disappointing 1947 season, made worse by the elbow injury, Gumpert went to training camp in 1948 with diminished expectations. He made the team and pitched well—a 2.88 ERA and a 1-0 record in fifteen relief appearances—but although he was big and strong, "he didn't have it," according to Harris.[6] On July 25, 1948, Gumpert was sold to the White Sox, where he was inserted into their starting rotation. He went just 2-6 for the eighth-place White Sox, with a 3.79 ERA.

The White Sox were counting on Gumpert in 1949, and he came through with a solid 3.81 ERA and career highs in wins (13), complete games (18), shutouts (3), innings (234), and strikeouts (78). He also lost sixteen games and led the league with twenty-two home runs allowed. He attributed his comeback to his ability to throw his screwball to left-handed hitters, something he had not done before.

Unfortunately, for Gumpert and the White Sox, he could not build on that solid season. Used more as a reliever than a starter in 1950, he added nearly a run to his previous year's ERA and could manage no better than a 5-12 record. The 1951 season brought the then thirty-three-year-old Gumpert's greatest individual honor and his greatest claim to fame, although the latter would reveal itself only as the years went by.

First, the individual honor: on the strength of his 7-2 record and 3.36 ERA at the midway point, Gumpert made the All-Star team for the only time in his career. He had also thrown five complete games, including a three-hit shutout. As with the 1947 World Series, however, he did not get into the game. "They were telling me something, I think," he joked years later.[7]

What happened on May 1, 1951, in Comiskey Park, linked Gumpert to all-time-great Mickey Mantle, and for the rest of his life, when signing autographs, he would be happy to add when requested the notation "Surrendered Mantle's 1st HR." As he said four decades later, "I threw Mantle a screwball. Evidently it didn't screw very well."[8] Mantle, swinging from the left side, launched the ball 440 feet into the Yankees' bullpen, just below the center-field grandstand.

In November 1951 the White Sox traded Gumpert to the Boston Red Sox. He appeared in only ten games for the Red Sox before being traded, on June 10, 1952, to the Senators. On August 24 Gumpert pitched two-hit shutout ball for the last 7⅔ innings of a 16-inning Senators victory over the Indians. He made his final start on September 3, shutting down the Red Sox on seven hits, two walks, and two runs, both unearned, while striking out six and winning his fifty-first and final game.

His combined record for 1952 was 5-9 with a 4.22 ERA in thirteen starts (all but one with the Senators) and seventeen relief appearances. Appropriately, Gumpert's last appearance was at Philadelphia's Shibe Park, where he pitched 2 innings in relief against the Athletics, now managed by Jimmy Dykes rather than Connie Mack.

The Senators did not re-sign Gumpert for the 1953 season, so he headed west, playing two seasons for the Los Angeles Angels of the Pacific Coast League. His pitching career ended in 1955 with the Charleston (West Virginia) Senators of the American Association, with whom he posted a 1-1 record and a 5.19 ERA in twenty relief appearances.

At the age of thirty-eight, with his playing career behind him, Gumpert became a Minor League manager. He split the 1956 season between the Bradford (Pennsylvania) Yankees of the Pennsylvania-Ontario–New York League and the

Kearney (Nebraska) Yankees of the newly formed Nebraska State League. He managed at Kearney again in 1957 and 1958 and served as a part-time manager for the St. Petersburg Saints of the Florida State League in 1960.

Gumpert had returned briefly to the Yankees in 1957, filling in for Coach Bill Dickey, who had to leave the club for health reasons. And in 1959 and other years, Casey Stengel invited Gumpert to be part of a pre-spring-training "instructional school" for the Yankees' top Minor League prospects. In 1961 he became a full-time scout for the Yankees.

One of his notable signings was George "Doc" Medich, who was drafted by the Yankees in 1970. Medich had planned a career in medicine and told Gumpert so. Gumpert put him in touch with Dr. Bobby Brown, the former Yankee infielder who became a cardiologist after baseball. Brown convinced Medich he could have both careers, and Medich went on to an eleven-year Major League career and a long medical career as well. Around 1974 Gumpert joined the newly formed Major League Scouting Bureau, a central scouting organization run by the Major League teams. He remained a member of the bureau until he retired in 1993.

Gumpert had married schoolteacher Ann Louise Boyer in 1952. The couple had three children, twin sons, Michael and Jeffrey, born in 1954, and a daughter, Cynthia, born in 1955. He enjoyed his retirement years and was honored in many local "halls of fame," including the Pennsylvania Sports Hall of Fame, Berks County Sports Hall of Fame, Reading Phillies Hall of Fame, Daniel Boone (successor to Birdsboro High) Hall of Fame, and Major League Scouting Hall of Fame.

He and Ann lived in the farmhouse where he had grown up (which he bought from his parents) and until his late eighties could be seen gardening, farming, and performing work around the house.

Gumpert regularly answered the autograph requests he received over the years and made appearances at banquets, charity events, and wherever else his presence was requested. Shortly after his ninetieth birthday, Gumpert moved from his Monocacy home to an assisted living center, where he died ten months later, on November 25, 2008.

Chapter 30. **Charlie Keller**

Chip Greene

AGE	G	AB	R	H	2B	3B	HR	TB	RBI	BB	SO	BAV	OBP	SLG	SB	GDP	HBP
30	45	151	36	36	6	1	13	83	36	41	18	.238	.404	.550	0	3	1

At the baseball field in Memorial Park in Middletown, Maryland, a rural community about fifty miles northwest of Washington DC, stands a monument that townspeople erected in honor of Charlie Keller. It is a bronze plaque affixed atop a waist-high, circular concrete pillar. Beneath a raised profile of Keller is a legend: "Charlie Keller . . . Middletown's own . . . Pride, Character and Sportsmanship." Below that are listed the highlights of Keller's career. The pillar stands in the deepest reaches of center field. In 1930, however, the baseball diamond at Memorial Park was reversed, and the spot on which the pillar was erected is the exact place where Charlie Keller stood at home plate and learned to hit a baseball.

Charles Ernest Keller Jr. was born on September 12, 1916, on a 140-acre farm about two and a half miles east of the park. He was the second child and eldest son of Charles Ernest and Naomi (Kefauver) Keller. In addition to his older sister, Ruth, Charlie had two younger brothers, John (known as Hugh) and Harold (known as Hal), who became a catcher for the Washington Senators.

All the children worked on the farm. "We all did," said Jack Remsberg, a cousin of the Kellers who grew up with them, in reference to all the Middletown farm families. Each morning Keller would arise at four and help with milking the cows and plowing before heading to school. Such activity developed in the young boy a solid and muscular physique. Remsberg said that after school let out for the day, Charlie would play ball at the field and then run two and a half miles to the farm, where he would change into his work clothes in the barn so his father would not know he had been playing.

Charlie Keller was leading the league in home runs and RBIS in June, but a slipped disk in his spine ended his season in July.

At Middletown High School, Charlie Keller, class of 1933, became a schoolboy legend. During the Depression, when he was seventeen, the Kellers lost their farm and moved into town. However bad that was for the family, it gave Charlie the opportunity to develop his athletic skills. In addition to playing baseball, he was a guard on the basketball team, the leading offensive threat on the soccer team, and a runner on the track team. Although primarily a sprinter in the 100-yard dash, Keller once ran a fifty-four-second quarter mile, which won a state meet.

It was in baseball, however, that he truly excelled. Starting as a catcher, Keller eventually played every position on the diamond, but alternated mostly between pitcher and catcher.[1] Keller also played in a weekly Frederick County league, and by the time his senior season arrived he was one of the leading batters in the county. Unfortunately, his senior season was cut short when he was stricken with appendicitis.

That summer, while recuperating, Keller obtained a scholarship to the University of Maryland. Keller was an outstanding student and earned a degree in agricultural economics. Keller worked hard outside the classroom as well. In 2006 his ninety-year-old widow, Martha, remembered Keller "dug ditches at the arts and science building," for which he was paid fifteen dollars a month for fifty hours of campus chores. He also became one of the best multisport athletes in the university's history.[2]

He played on the freshman baseball and basketball teams (freshmen could not play varsity sports), and by his sophomore year Keller played not only those two varsity sports but football as well.[3] Although Keller had not played the game in high school, given his build (five feet ten and 190 pounds, with broad shoulders and a thick chest), the athletic department was confident he could take to football as he had to other sports.

Accordingly, when the varsity opened its 1934 season against St. John's (Maryland) with a 13–0 victory, sophomore Keller made his football debut at left defensive end by "toss[ing] a passer for a 10-yard loss on [Keller's] first play." By midseason, though, an ankle injury had sidelined him indefinitely, and, fearing another injury might jeopardize his baseball chances, he decided to drop football.

Clearly, baseball was his future. He had proved to be a slugger from the moment he stepped on campus. In one of his earliest games with the freshman team, practicing against the varsity, Keller "cracked a triple over the center fielder's head," and he finished his two varsity seasons with batting averages of .500 and .495, the composite .497 average being at that time the best in school history. His head coach, Burton Shipley, who had managed Hack Wilson at Martinsburg in the Blue Ridge League in 1922, told the press that "Keller looks as good to me as Hack Wilson . . . in 1922." All Keller needed, opined Shipley, "is a little experience. He has a great arm, he's fast and he's a fighter."[4]

By the end of his junior season in the spring of 1936, Keller was one of the best college players in the country. Scouts had been coming to College Park for two years to watch him play. In the summer after both seasons, Keller traveled to Kinston, North Carolina, to play in the semiprofessional Coastal Plain League.[5] He posted a .385 average in 1935 and a .466 mark with twenty-five home runs in 1936. By the time he returned to College Park, he had accepted an offer from scout Gene McCann to play for the New York Yankees.[6]

The Yankees had agreed to let Keller finish his education. Once graduated, he was to report in June 1937 to the Newark Bears, the Yankees' entry in the International League. As it turned out, he arrived in Newark sooner than expected. "I read in the papers in March," Keller said, "that the Newark club had gone to spring training in Sebring, Florida, and I decided that I might just as well start playing ball and get my degree the next year. So I wired [Yankees' farm director] George Weiss I was on my way."[7]

Newark's manager, Ossie Vitt, was thrilled to have him. Keller was a left-handed hitter, a commodity Newark desperately needed. He arrived in Sebring on March 22 and took batting practice the next day. After watching the twenty-year-old slugger, Vitt decided Keller would be his starting right fielder, a position Keller had never played.

The Yankees were hoping Keller would be the left-handed pull hitter they had been seeking since the departure of Babe Ruth three years earlier, one who would hit home runs into the short porch in Yankee Stadium. Keller, though, was not that type of hitter. Rather than always trying to pull the ball, he usually hit it where it was pitched, hammering doubles and triples lined to left field and center field. Hall of Fame pitcher Herb Pennock, who scouted Keller for the Boston Red Sox, said Keller hit the ball harder to left than any left-handed hitter he had ever seen, except Ruth.[8]

In his exhibition debut, on March 25, pinch-hitting against the Cincinnati Reds, Keller tripled to left field at Sebring Park. A week later, against the Philadelphia Phillies, he hit a two-run inside-the-park homer over the center fielder's head, a hit, exclaimed Philadelphia's Chuck Klein, playing right field that day, that was "the longest drive [I] ever saw."[9] Still, if the Yankees wanted him to become a pull hitter, Keller, anxious to please, would try to accommodate them.

The experiment lasted for only a year. After trying throughout the 1937 season to please Yankees management by pulling the ball, by April 1938 Keller had returned to the style he favored. "They can save Babe Ruth's crown for someone else," he said. In 1937 Keller, who won the batting title with a .353 average and led the league in runs and hits, was named both the International League Rookie of the Year and the Minor League Player of the Year.

In August 1937 Weiss exclaimed, "What I'm looking forward to is the day when Charlie Keller puts on a Yankee uniform. . . . [He is] absolutely the best outfield prospect in the minor leagues . . . can go and get fly balls with nearly anybody and he has a great arm."[10] Still, Keller was disappointed when he was not invited to New York's 1938 training camp. "I'd have given any of (the current Yankee outfielders) a real battle," he said.[11] Instead, he grudgingly returned to Newark, where he batted .365 (second in the league) and finished third in league MVP voting.[12]

Keller had emerged as potentially the next great Yankees player. Rival clubs, a newspaper said in May 1938, were "shouting and bidding for Keller's services all winter and spring." Bob Quinn, president of the Boston Braves, remarked, "We'd gladly give $75,000 for Keller because he's a great ballplayer whose punch might even land us a pennant, but it's no sale. Instead, the Yanks keep him in hock at Newark."

On January 21, 1938, in Baltimore, Keller wed Martha Lee Williamson, an athletic instructor at a private school. Jack Remsberg remembered Martha, a Baltimore native, as a "beautiful tennis player and golfer." Keller and Martha had met three years previously when both were students at College Park. Their marriage lasted fifty-two years, until Keller's death in 1990, and produced three children.

On February 27, 1939, the three-time defending champion Yankees opened spring training in St. Petersburg, Florida. Manager Joe McCarthy had asked Keller to report a week ahead of the regulars so he could personally work with the twenty-two-year-old rookie who had played right field both years at Newark. Keller threw right-handed, explained McCarthy, a trait that "makes him conducive to left field," and Keller, the manager affirmed, "definitely [is] a left fielder."[13] He was expected to compete with veteran George Selkirk, another left-handed batter, for a starting spot at that position.

McCarthy also wanted Keller to again work on pulling the ball, but Keller was reluctant to do so. He said he did not want McCarthy to tinker with his swing. "I can hit well enough to make the grade even with a hitting team like the Yankees," the rookie said. "I hit with the pitch. I never will be one of those home-run sluggers. If a man cannot bat well, tinker with him. If he can hit, why not let him be?"[14] Nevertheless, Keller went to work once again, altering his hitting style.

If Keller initially disagreed with McCarthy, over time he came to idolize him. In the book *Sum-*

mer of '49, David Halberstam wrote that one night on the team train, broadcaster Curt Gowdy, sitting around the bridge table with some of the players, asked of the former Yankee manager, then with the Red Sox, "Wasn't he a bit of a drinker?" Afterward, Keller followed Gowdy to his train cabin and grabbed him, warning, "I never want you to make another remark about Joe McCarthy like that." In an interview in 1973 Keller said the Yankees "were just lucky to have the best manager that ever ran a ballclub." McCarthy, he said, "was a leader . . . who had no favorites" and "insisted that we act like men and it wasn't long before we were proud that we were acting the way we were."[15]

Throughout the spring of 1939, McCarthy mentored Keller. He calmed the rookie and settled him down as he struggled to adapt to the change in batting stroke and often became frustrated. Gradually, Keller's natural talent took over, and by April 1, when the team broke camp, McCarthy had named him the Yankees' starting left fielder. But when opening day arrived, Keller was not ready to play. A muscle tear he had suffered in his thigh while at Maryland flared up again at Newark and went without proper treatment. At St. Petersburg the problem returned, and the Yankees' trainer advised McCarthy that Keller's debut should be delayed. It was not until April 22 that he played in his first big-league game, as a pinch hitter against the Senators in Washington.

A week passed before Keller played again. He debuted before the home fans on April 29, against Washington. When Joe DiMaggio had to leave the game with an injured foot, McCarthy moved Jake Powell from left field to center field and inserted Keller in left. Keller had four at bats and collected his first hit, a single off Ken Chase. On May 2, in Detroit, the same day Lou Gehrig ended his legendary consecutive-games streak, Keller made his first start. Playing left field and batting fifth, he hit a triple and a home run and drove in six runs. By June 6 he had started thirty-four games and was

batting .319, with twenty-four runs batted in. Still, when DiMaggio returned to the lineup the next day, Keller returned to the bench.

According to Halberstam, when Keller arrived at the ballpark that afternoon and found he was not in the lineup, he cried. McCarthy attempted to console his young player. He told Keller someday he would be a great Yankee star, but he would have to work on pulling the ball more, particularly in Yankee Stadium. For the remainder of that season and, indeed, the rest of his career, Keller heeded McCarthy's advice.

Throughout most of June and July, Keller was largely forgotten. Then, on August 2, McCarthy put him in right field to replace the slumping Tommy Henrich. From then until the end of the 1946 season (minus 1944 and most of 1945, when he was in the military), Keller not only remained in the lineup, but also became one of the most feared sluggers in the American League.

Overall, in 111 games in 1939, he batted .334, fifth in the league, and was fourth with a .447 on-base percentage. In the World Series, as New York swept the Cincinnati Reds, Keller batted a team-high .438, with 3 home runs and 6 RBIs.[16] After a season of abrupt starts and stops, it appeared that Keller had finally arrived. In 1940, as Henrich reestablished himself in right field, Keller returned to left. Together with DiMaggio, the three formed arguably the premier outfield in the game during their time together.

At the University of Maryland, Keller was saddled with the nickname he never cared for, King Kong.[17] In 1948 writer Milton Gross visited the team in spring training and reminded readers why Keller had received the appellation. Keller, Gross wrote, "looked massive. His black, beetle-browed eyes, his muscled blacksmith arms, his thick neck and hogshead of a chest were of wrestler's proportions."[18] As Keller finally matured into the pull hitter the club had always desired, that impressive physique produced equally impressive results.

From 1940 through 1943, playing an average of 143 games a season, Keller batted .287 and had a .531 slugging percentage. He had 111 home runs, an average of 28 per season, and averaged 102 RBIS over the four years. For all his power, Keller displayed remarkable patience at the plate, averaging 107 bases on balls per year.

On January 20, 1944, Keller, now twenty-seven years old, at the peak of his skills and earning fifteen thousand dollars a year, was commissioned an ensign in the U.S. Maritime Service. For the next twenty months, he served as a purser, sailing the Pacific aboard merchant ships. "I didn't see or touch a ball the whole time I was away," he said in a 1973 interview.[19] Keller returned in August 1945 to play the final six weeks of the season. "I wasn't in shape to play," he admitted.

As it turned out, 1946 was the final full season of his career. At the beginning of 1947, the thirty-year-old Keller signed a contract for twenty-two thousand dollars. Coming off a season in which he had hit 30 home runs and driven in 101 runs, the Yankees deemed him worth every penny, and he picked up right where he had left off in '46. On June 5 Keller led the league in home runs, RBIS, and runs scored. That day, though, after walking and collecting a pair of base hits, he complained of soreness in his lower right back and left in the sixth inning. Afterward, Keller said he had first experienced pain the previous day; he thought it had come from swinging awkwardly. On June 27, with the pain now radiating down his leg, Keller checked into New York Hospital for observation.

He never played another game that season. On July 18 doctors removed a slipped disk from Keller's spine. The club said he might return in September. Instead, Keller's career was essentially finished. During the World Series against the Brooklyn Dodgers, he sat in uniform on the bench. A friend suggested that the slugger carry the lineup to home plate before the opening game. "Not for me," responded Keller. "The next time I go . . . on

to that playing field, I'm going out to play, not to try to get some sympathy. I'll try to be back out there next April. I'll know if I can make it. If I decide I can't I won't go out."[20]

For the next two years, the five-time All-Star made a valiant attempt to come back from his injury, but his efforts were largely futile. In 1948 and '49, although he played in 143 games, only 97 were as a fielder. Ironically, the surgery forced Keller to change his batting style. Instead of "murderously swinging" at each pitch, he favored his back; doing so forced him to cut down on his swing.[21] On occasion Keller could still deliver the long ball, but it was soon apparent that his power was gone. Finally, after two seasons of watching him struggle, the Yankees released him on December 6, 1949. "I had some marvelous years and I've no regrets," he graciously remarked.[22]

And with that, his Yankees playing career came to a close. On September 25, 1948, before 65,507 fans at Yankee Stadium, the team held Charlie Keller Day. With a Maryland delegation on hand, led by Senator Millard Tydings, Keller was presented with golf clubs, a watch, and a "pile of other gifts." With the money he received, the slugger began a University of Maryland scholarship.[23]

One has only to travel ten miles northeast of Keller's monument in Middletown to appreciate how he spent the rest of his life. Jack Remsberg said, "Charlie began his life on a farm and ended it that way too." Before Keller realized his dream, however, he gave baseball one last try.

On December 29, 1949, Keller signed with the Detroit Tigers for twenty thousand dollars to be the "the highest-paid pinch-hitter in the game." Over the next two seasons, in 104 games, he batted .283 and hit five home runs, before Detroit released him on November 9, 1951. The following September, after two evening workouts at Philadelphia's Shibe Park, Keller sufficiently impressed manager Casey Stengel for New York to re-sign the slugger as a pinch hitter. After only one at bat in 2 games (a strikeout), Keller was released by the Yankees on October 13, 1952. It was a testament to the Yankees' respect for him that although he had been with the team only two weeks in 1952, he was awarded a one-thousand-dollar World Series share.

Having grown up on a farm, Keller said in 1946, "I'll know what to do with a good piece of land. Baseball to me means the best farm in my part of the country." Sixty years later his widow remembered, "That's why he was playing ball. He wanted a farm someday." In retirement Keller bought four parcels of land in Frederick, ten miles from where he had been born, and eventually amassed three hundred acres. He lived there the remainder of his life.[24]

According to Jack Remsberg, Keller initially had standard farm animals, but when milking cows proved too demanding a lifestyle, "he got into the trotting horse business." In 1955 Yankeeland Farms was born. The former Yankee became a breeder, and over the next thirty-five years Yankeeland Farms became nationally renowned for its line of champion harness racers.

Each day Keller mucked stalls, repaired fences, and "savored the simplest of farming pleasures." His son, Donald, who worked beside him for thirty years, remembered that his father "liked feeding horses and liked just listening to them eat." Keller continued to work until he died of colon cancer in 1990 at the age of seventy-three.

Today Charlie Keller rests in the Christ Church Reformed Cemetery in Middletown, two miles from the site of his birth, just behind the high school and a very long home run's distance to right field from his monument, the place where it all began.

Chapter 31. **Ted Sepkowski**

Jack V. Morris

AGE	G	AB	R	H	2B	3B	HR	TB	RBI	BB	SO	BAV	OBP	SLG	SB	GDP	HBP
23	2	0	1	0	0	0	0	0	0	0	0	—	—	—	0	0	0

Ted Sepkowski was still a student in high school when he started a game at second base for the Cleveland Indians in 1942. Unfortunately for Ted, his Major League career would consist of only nineteen games, played over three seasons. Sepkowski was a speedy runner but a defensive liability, and by the time he got out of both the well-stocked Cleveland Indians and New York Yankees organizations, his skills had started to diminish.

Sepkowski was born Theodore Walter Szczepkowski on November 9, 1922, in Baltimore, Maryland, the youngest of fourteen children born to John and Leana Szczepkowski. His parents had emigrated from Poland in 1898 and had settled in Baltimore.[1] John, a laborer at an asphalt company, died shortly after Ted was born, and it was a struggle to keep food on the table for the family.[2] "We had it tough," Sepkowski told SABR historian David Paulson in 1999. His mother could not read or write English, so she stayed home to tend to the house. His older brothers supported the family with whatever income they could provide. Ted chipped in by shoveling coal, shining shoes, polishing cars, and cleaning yards.[3]

By the time he reached high school, his brothers had cobbled together enough money for the two-hundred-dollar tuition for Ted to attend Mount Saint Joseph High School in Baltimore. When he went out for baseball in his first year, the coach quickly moved him from junior varsity to varsity. He played so well that his tuition was waived for the following years.

John Donohue, the school's baseball coach, recommended Ted to Tommy Thomas, the manager of the Baltimore Orioles of the International

Ted Sepkowski's career with the Yankees consisted of two pinch-running assignments.

League. Thomas took the youngster under his wing. "Tommy was like a father to me," said Sepkowski. "He bought me a $50 pair of those kangaroo baseball shoes, the kind rich players wore, and a sport coat."[4]

No doubt it was Thomas who sent Sepkowski to Brattleboro, Vermont, to play in the semipro

Northern League in 1941. Using the name Sepko, he hit .231 while playing third base against some of the top collegiate and semipro players in the Northeast. Three big-league clubs tried to sign him, but Sepkowski was loyal to Thomas and signed with the Orioles for the following season.[5]

In the spring of 1942, Ted left his classes to attend spring training with the Orioles in Hollywood, Florida, but he took his books with him. He was not scheduled to graduate until June 1943. Before heading to spring training, Sepkowski had turned down a scholarship offer from Fordham University.[6]

Sportswriters covering the Orioles pestered Ted into changing the spelling of his last name. At some point before 1942, he had dropped one of the z's and spelled it Sczpkowski. *Cleveland Plain Dealer* sports editor Sam Otis wrote, "Baltimore sports writers have threatened Ted Szcepkowski that if he makes the ball club they will chop his name plenty."[7] However, Ted resisted efforts to change until 1946, when he shortened it to Sepkowski.

Sepkowski, who threw right-handed and batted left-handed, made the Orioles out of spring training in 1942, receiving a contract for two hundred dollars a month. Thomas's plan was to bring the eighteen-year-old along slowly, but when regular second baseman Sammy Bell went out with an injury, Sepkowski was inserted into the starting lineup. Bell never got his job back.[8]

After a slow start Ted soon was holding his own in the International League. In August he hit .363 in twenty-four games and was drawing rave reviews. One in particular directly led to his playing in the Major Leagues that season.[9]

International League president Frank J. Shaughnessy happened to see Sepkowski in a series. "That kid is the greatest 18-year-old player I have ever seen," Shaughnessy told the sportswriters. "He's a $50,000 prospect. He needs one or two more years, that's all." The tagline "$50,000 prospect" was added to Sepkowski's name whenever it was written by the International League sportswriters for the rest of the year.[10]

Shaughnessy was not the only one impressed with Sepkowski's play. Ty Cobb, Bill Terry, Montreal Royals manager Clyde Sukeforth, and, of course, Tommy Thomas all praised the youngster. Sepkowski had made an impression.[11]

At the time the Orioles had a working agreement with the Cleveland Indians. The Indians furnished the Orioles with players and were allowed to purchase two players from the Orioles' roster for ten thousand dollars each. Shaughnessy's remark forced the Orioles' hand. Originally, the Indians coveted first baseman Eddie Robinson and pitcher Ray Flanigan. Indians vice president Roger Peckinpaugh would rather have left Sepkowski in the Minors for another year or two but was forced to sign him to a contract to protect him from other clubs.[12] The Indians also purchased Robinson's contract. The players received a thousand dollars each for their sale. Hugh Trader Jr. in the *Sporting News* called Sepkowski and Robinson "two of the greatest major-league prospects ever developed by the Baltimore club."[13]

Sepkowski reported to Cleveland on September 9, 1942, and started that night's game against the Philadelphia Athletics. Batting seventh and playing second base, he went 1 for 5 (a single off starter Bob Harris) in a thirteen-inning loss.[14] Defensively, he committed two errors, one of which led to three runs being scored in the inning. Gordon Cobbledick of the *Cleveland Plain Dealer* put it succinctly: "[Sepkowski] failed to impress."[15] Sepkowski played four more games that season and was held hitless in them, finishing the season 1 for 10.

In 1943 Sepkowski was one of only thirty players the Indians invited to spring training at Purdue University in West Lafayette, Indiana. But he had no chance of making the team. If he did not go back to high school, he would be eligible for the draft. So on March 5 the Indians sent him back to Baltimore, where he could go to school and also play baseball. Sepkowski played in sixty-two games for the Orioles, hitting only .199, before Uncle Sam came calling in early August.

Sepkowski passed his army physical. "Then I heard from the Coast Guard and was told that Dick Porter, manager of the baseball team at Curtis Bay [Coast Guard Station in Baltimore], had arranged for me to go there," he said. "One day I'm going to the Army, the next day it's the Coast Guard."[16] Sepkowski played with several Major Leaguers for the Curtis Bay Station Cutters and turned in two excellent seasons. He also matured, filling out to a solid five-foot-eleven, 190-pound power hitter. One of the first things he did after his discharge from the coast guard was to change the spelling of his name.

Sepkowski, as he was now known, had begun playing the outfield while in the service. At spring training in Clearwater, Florida, Indians manager Lou Boudreau said Sepkowski had the inside track for right field. But in the end Hank Edwards won the position. Sepkowski was sent to the Oklahoma City Indians of the Texas League, where he batted .300 with 7 home runs and tied for the league lead in triples. After the 1946 Texas League season ended, the Indians recalled him, and he started both games of a doubleheader against the Athletics on September 15. They were the only two games he played for the Indians in 1946.

Late that year Sepkowski and his wife, Anna, with whom he had a son, were divorced. The following year he married Marguerite "Mimi" Golden. They were married for fifty-five years, until his death.[17]

Sepkowski made the opening-day roster in 1947, but he saw little playing time. In all he played in ten games, getting one hit in eight at bats. On June 2 the Indians sold him to the New York Yankees for the waiver price of ten thousand dollars. His career with the Yankees consisted of two pinch-running assignments. His final Major

League game was on June 21, 1947, against the Detroit Tigers. Sepkowski scored a run in the Yankees' 5–4 victory. New York sent him to the Newark Bears of the International League, where he batted .266 with 9 home runs.

In 1948, playing with Newark for the entire season, Sepkowski erupted as a power hitter, smashing 24 home runs with 91 RBIs. But he was still having trouble adjusting to playing the outfield. Newark center fielder Joe Collins, who played between Sepkowski and Lou Novikoff, said, "On every ball hit to the outfield, I'd hear them both yell, 'Take it Joe.' I made practically every catch."[18]

Sepkowski signed for the 1949 season with Newark, but after fifteen games, he was moved to the Yankees' other Class Triple-A farm team, the Kansas City Blues of the American Association. Playing in eighty games for the Blues, Sepkowski batted just .243, with 10 home runs and 48 RBIs. The Yankees gave up on him after the season, sending him to the Cubs' top farm team, the Springfield (Massachusetts) Cubs of the International League.

Sepkowski played a full season for Springfield in 1950, but after thirty games in 1951 he was traded to the Milwaukee Brewers of the American Association, a Boston Braves affiliate. Sepkowski struggled in Milwaukee and was sent down to the Atlanta Crackers of the Southern Association, where he continued to struggle. In 1952 the Brewers demoted him to the Hartford Blues of the Class A Eastern League. Sepkowski responded with a good season, batting .280, with 16 home runs, playing both the infield and the outfield.

In 1953 Sepkowski, now twenty-nine, was named player-manager for the Wellsville (New York) Braves, Boston's entrant in the Class D Pennsylvania-Ontario–New York League. He was not particularly successful as a manager in his two seasons with Wellsville, but he was very successful as a player. In 1953 he batted .339 and set PONY League single-season records for home runs (37) and RBIS (144). He broke his home run record the following year, with 45, while batting .377.

After being passed over for a coaching job with one of the higher-level teams in the Braves organization, he asked for his release. He was the player-manager for the Erie (Pennsylvania) Senators, a Washington Senators farm team, in 1955, but left after one season. In January 1956 Sepkowski placed an ad in the *Sporting News*, looking for employment as a playing manager.[19] Presumably, he got no feelers. At the age of thirty-two, his baseball career was over. He had hit 194 home runs in twelve Minor League seasons but none while in the Major Leagues.

After baseball Sepkowski drove a truck for a motor company. On the side he created and sold lamps made from baseball bats. He called his company Ted Sepkowski Enterprises. In 1966 he took a job with the *Baltimore Sun* as a suburban circulation sales manager. He remained there until his retirement in 1984. In 1976 he moved to Severna Park, a suburb of Baltimore, where he lived for the rest of his life.[20]

On March 8, 2002, Sepkowski died of a heart attack. He left behind his wife, Mimi; a son, Terry; a daughter, Sharyn; a stepson, Robert; and a stepdaughter, Melva. He was buried in Glen Haven Memorial Park in Glen Burnie, Maryland.[21]

Chapter 32. **Frank Shea**

Don Harrison

AGE	W	L	PCT.	ERA	G	GS	GF	CG	SHO	SV	IP	H	BB	SO	HBP	WP
26	14	5	.737	3.07	27	23	3	13	3	1	178.2	127	89	89	4	0

In the spring of 1947, *uncertain* may have been the word that best described the New York Yankees' prospects. The team that had dominated the American League throughout the late 1930s and the early 1940s was coming off an ignoble third-place finish in 1946, seventeen games behind—and seemingly light-years removed from—the champion Boston Red Sox.

The pitching, after twenty-game winner Spud Chandler, was suspect. Joe DiMaggio and short-stop Phil Rizzuto had returned from three years of military service and turned in subpar seasons. All-Star second baseman Joe Gordon batted .210 and was traded to Cleveland for right-handed pitcher Allie Reynolds, who lost as often as he won.

Would this group of Yankees be able to rebound to challenge the Red Sox? The answer was an emphatic "yes," with help.

Give a lion's share of the credit to Frank "Spec" Shea, a twenty-six-year-old rookie right-hander from Naugatuck, Connecticut, who threw hard and cracked wise. Shea assembled a 14-5 record with a 3.07 earned run average for the pennant-winning Bronx Bombers, leading the league in fewest hits allowed per nine innings (6.4) and winning percentage (.737). On July 8 he became the first rookie pitcher to receive credit for a victory in the All-Star Game, working the middle three innings of the American League's 2–1 win at Wrigley Field in Chicago.

Spec (so named as a youngster because of his freckles) capped his memorable first season by winning two decisions in the Yankees' seven-game World Series victory over the Brooklyn Dodgers.

If there had been separate Rookie of the Year

Frank Shea was the American League's top rookie in 1947, but he was never again as successful.

awards for each league, Shea would have been an overwhelming choice as the American League's best freshman. Instead, he placed third in the overall balloting behind two National Leaguers, Jackie Robinson of the Dodgers and pitcher Larry Jansen of the New York Giants. "Everything I touched turned to gold that year," Shea recalled. "Getting credit for the win in the All-Star Game. Two victories in the World Series. How fortunate I was. It was a year you dream about. The only thing I feel bad about was I hurt my arm that year. I had no problem winning in the big leagues."

Francis Joseph O'Shea was born in Naugatuck on October 2, 1920, to Frank Lawrence O'Shea and Helen (Morris) O'Shea. His only sibling, the future Eleanor Scheiber, had arrived two years earlier.

The senior O'Shea was an aspiring pitcher, too, but after a fine playing career at Naugatuck High School, he married young and limited his pitching to semipro ball. When Frank Jr. was born, his dad vowed that he would have a big-league career by proxy—the one he mapped out for his new-born son.

Young Frank was a whiz himself at Naugatuck High. In 1938 he pitched a four-hitter and hit a pair of home runs to propel the Greyhounds to a 7–0 verdict over Manchester High in Connecticut's first state championship game. As a senior the following season, he struck out twenty-one batters in eleven innings in the state title game against Torrington.

Paul Krichell, the Yankees scout credited with discovering Lou Gehrig, added Shea to his portfolio in the winter of 1940. A story goes with it.

En route to Naugatuck to sign Shea (he had by now dropped the O' in his name) to a Yankees contract, Krichell was stopped by a Connecticut state trooper in Westport. Asked to identify himself, he told the officer about his Yankees affiliation and said that he was heading to Naugatuck to sign a young pitcher named Frank Shea. "Hell's bells," the state trooper responded. "Why didn't you tell me that in the first place? Just follow me and I'll lead you to him. That Shea kid is a wow and I'm a Yankee fan."

Shea's progression through the Yankees' farm system was rapid—11-4 with Amsterdam, New York, of the Class C Canadian-American League in 1940; 16-10 with Norfolk, Virginia, of the Class B Piedmont League in 1941; and a luckless 5-8 (despite a 3.15 ERA and eighty-nine strikeouts

in one hundred innings) with Kansas City of the Class Double-A American Association in 1942. Then World War II intervened.

Shea spent three years in the U.S. Army Air Corps and was among the thousands of GIs who went ashore in Normandy just days after D-day. The oldest of his three children, also named Frank, recalled hearing a story from his dad about being injured in an explosion during the war. "He was carrying two cans of gasoline and a sniper's bullet hit one of the canisters," young Frank related. Scorched virtually from head to toe, Shea was a hospital case for months. "No Purple Heart, though," he said years later, "because it wasn't enemy action. I always wondered, though, if they called it friendly action."

Discharged from the army too late to return to organized ball in 1945, the former Sergeant Shea returned home to pitch for the semipro Waterbury Brasscos. Talk about timing. The Brasscos had an exhibition date scheduled with the Yankees, and Spec merely shut them out, 1–0.

That performance earned him an invitation to spring training with the Yankees in 1946. Alas, Shea required an emergency appendectomy during the team's trip to Panama, and he was sidelined for a couple of months. His pitching that summer, although outstanding, was with the Oakland Oaks of the Pacific Coast League under manager Casey Stengel.

Shea won fifteen of twenty decisions for the second-place Oaks, struck out 124, and compiled a brilliant 1.66 ERA, second in the league behind San Francisco's Larry Jansen, at 1.57.

The following spring in St. Petersburg, Florida, a healthy Shea impressed new Yankees manager Bucky Harris and, along with twenty-year-old prospect Don Johnson, was a candidate for a spot in the club's starting rotation.

Dan Parker, the *New York Mirror* sports columnist who had watched Shea's father pitch in high school, told Harris that if he liked Spec, he should have seen his dad. "I'll settle for him," said Bucky. "I wish I had a dozen like him. He's my type of pitcher. I don't see how he can miss."

The six-foot, 195-pound Shea made his Major League debut on April 19, 1947, pitching two innings of scoreless relief in a 4–2 loss at Griffith Stadium. He made his first start five days later, against the defending champion Red Sox at Yankee Stadium. He allowed just three singles in nine innings, but wound up on the short end of a 1–0 score. The lone Red Sox run crossed the plate in the fifth on a pair of walks (Shea walked seven in the game), a force out, and Sam Mele's scoring fly ball.

If a well-pitched defeat can be considered a portent, that was the case here. Mixing fastballs with curves and sliders, over his next eight starts Shea reeled off seven straight victories and a no-decision, including a pair of shutouts against Detroit Tigers ace Hal Newhouser. After a 3–2 loss to the Chicago White Sox in eleven innings, he won four more, highlighted by a three-hit 3–0 decision over the Cleveland Indians. Shea entered the All-Star break with a luminous 11-2 record, twelve complete games, and a 1.91 ERA.

Yankees announcer Mel Allen dubbed him the Naugatuck Nugget, a nickname that endured until the end. His Naugatuck neighbors and admirers, delighted by his early successes, turned out en masse to honor their native son on Frank "Spec" Shea Day at Yankee Stadium on June 22. Heading the delegation from his hometown was his dad, who, in his son's achievements, saw the fulfillment of his own aspirations.

The crowd of 53,765 included thousands from Connecticut who had purchased tickets weeks in advance in the hope of seeing Shea pitch. (He did not.) In pregame ceremonies the Borough of Naugatuck's warden, Harry L. Carter, presented Shea with a 1947 maroon Hudson, replete with the Connecticut license plate SPEC.

"I grew up as a Yankee fan," Shea said. "My father took me down to the Stadium when I was a kid, and this was when you could go on the field after the game. I used to run out to the mound and pretend I was pitching. 'Someday,' I'd say, 'I'm going to pitch here.'"

And so he did. But for the remainder of July and all of August, Shea pitched neither well nor often, due to a nagging neck injury that restricted him to a handful of appearances. He rebounded in September by winning three of four decisions, including a four-hit 3–1 triumph over the White Sox on September 18.

In the 1947 World Series, Shea proved more than a match for the Dodgers by winning two games. He captured the opener at Yankee Stadium by a 5–3 score, allowing just one run and two hits in five innings before departing for a pinch hitter.

In Game Five, two days after Shea celebrated his twenty-seventh birthday, the right-hander gave the Yankees a 3–2 Series lead by stopping the Dodgers, 2–1, on a four-hitter at Ebbets Field. At bat he contributed a double and single, the latter driving in New York's first run in the fourth inning. In a fitting coda Shea fired a third strike past the previous day's hero, Cookie Lavagetto, for the final out.

After the Dodgers won the sixth game, 8–6, to square the Series once again, the Yankees' mercurial president, Larry MacPhail, offered a one-thousand-dollar bonus to any Yankees pitcher who would start Game Seven.

Shea accepted the offer, but he departed in the second inning after allowing one run and three straight hits. And, "You know, I never got that thousand dollars," Frank Shea recalled his father telling him on several occasions. But the Yankees rallied to prevail, 5–2, to gain their eleventh world championship.

Likable and loquacious, the pitcher enjoyed a special friendship with DiMaggio, a man who could be aloof. "He used to buy me breakfast every day at the hotel. He'd never let me pay," Shea said. "I never treated DiMaggio like God. He was an everyday guy as far as I was concerned."

Shea provided frequent livery service for the Yankee Clipper during their years together in New York. He recalled one occasion when DiMaggio was opening his mail during their drive to Yankee Stadium. He opened an envelope. A check appeared. He opened another envelope. Another check. "By the time we got to the ballpark, he had $12,000 in endorsements," Spec said.

Never again did Shea approach his rookie accomplishments. He pitched reasonably well in 1948, but a lack of run support contributed to a 9-10 record despite his leading the American League a second time in the fewest hits allowed per nine innings. His ERA was a respectable 3.41.

The arm and neck maladies that kept Shea on the sidelines for several weeks late in the 1947 season forced his return to the Minor Leagues for a portion of 1949 and all of 1950. In '49 he was 1-1 with the parent club and 0-3 in five appearances with Newark of the International League. With Kansas City of the American Association in 1950, the results also were less than encouraging—6-11 with a 6.28 ERA.

Rejoining the Yankees in 1951 as a reliever and spot starter, Shea contributed a 5-5 record, a pair of shutouts, and a 4.33 ERA to the Bombers' drive to another American League pennant. But he was not called upon in the World Series when the Yankees bested the Giants in six games.

With an established Big Three of Reynolds, Vic Raschi, and Eddie Lopat, as well as Whitey Ford waiting in the wings, Shea was deemed expendable. On May 3, 1952, he accompanied outfielder Jackie Jensen to the Washington Senators in a six-player trade that brought outfielder Irv Noren to New York. Shea was not in the least disappointed. "Hey, that trade reunited me with Bucky Harris, and he gave me a chance to pitch," Shea said. "The owner, Clark Griffith, who was a grand guy, told me I wouldn't be making any World Series money here and he handed me a $2,500 check when I arrived to make me feel welcome."

With fifth-place Senators teams, Shea proved a solid number-two starter behind another former Yankee, Bob Porterfield, turning in records of 11-7 in 1952 and 12-7 in 1953. He contributed to the Yankees' pennant in 1953 by defeating runner-up Cleveland four times without a loss.

"He's still quite a funny guy, but he's more serious now than ever," Harris told the *Washington Star*'s Morris Siegel. "And Frank is a smarter pitcher now. He sets you up for a pitch. And what a battler he is. He'll fight you right down to the last pitch of the ballgame. And in those tough spots, he's always putting a little something extra on the pitch. I wish the Yankees or any other club would give up on a number of guys like him. I'll find a place for them."

When Shea's eight-year Major League career was nearing its end in 1955 (lifetime record: fifty-six wins, forty-six losses, 3.80 ERA), Clark Griffith asked him to be the Senators' pitching coach the following season. Shea was receptive. But Griffith died that fall, and his heirs had other plans.

So Spec and his wife, Genevieve (Martino) Shea, whom he had married in 1949, and their young sons, Frank and John, settled in Naugatuck. A third child, daughter Barbara, was born a decade later. Shea eventually became the borough's superintendent of parks and recreation, a position he held for twenty years until his retirement in 1989.

A gifted storyteller, he was a welcome guest on the banquet circuit, especially at the Connecticut Sports Writers' Alliance's annual Gold Key Dinner. He was among the three honorees at the group's 1962 banquet. He also returned to Yankee Stadium each summer to wear the pinstripes for the annual Old-Timers Day. (Writer to Shea: "Ready to go nine today?" Shea to writer: "Yeah, nine pitches.")

Accompanied by other retired Major Leaguers such as Ralph Branca, Willard Marshall, and Sal Yvars, Shea participated in charity golf tournaments throughout Connecticut and New York's

Westchester County, helping to raise funds for local nonprofits.

He also devoted considerable time to the Baseball Assistance Team, the organization founded by retired Major League catcher and broadcaster Joe Garagiola to help indigent former players and other baseball people in need.

In the early 1980s the Naugatuck Nugget had one additional brush with fame. The telephone rang in the Shea household one day, and Spec asked his daughter to answer it. "May I ask who's calling, please," said Barbara Shea, then nineteen years old. "It was Robert Redford. I think he said 'Bob Redford.'"

Indeed, Robert Redford was preparing for the role of Roy Hobbs in the acclaimed 1984 film *The Natural*, and he asked Spec Shea to teach him how to pitch and hit 1930s style. "I don't want to embarrass myself," Redford told the retired pitcher.

So, on at least one Sunday, perhaps on a few occasions (stories differ), Shea provided the rudiments of pitching and hitting to the Oscar-winning Hollywood actor and director at Breen Field in Naugatuck. "People were walking by, saying, 'Is that Robert Redford?'" Frank the son remembered. "It was supposed to be a big secret, but the word got out," Barbara said.

Shea "was just a big, happy guy," said Barry Lockwood, an officer in the Naugatuck Hall of Fame, which included the old pitcher among its original inductees in 1972. "Spec was one of the people this town was noted for. When he was on top of his game, no one was his equal."

John Hassenfeldt, a boyhood friend, remembered Shea as a guy who was "always willing to talk to everybody. And he did a lot to help the kids of this town."

Frank "Spec" Shea died on July 19, 2002, four weeks after heart-valve replacement surgery at Yale–New Haven Hospital. He was eighty-one years old.

Chapter 33. Johnny Lucadello

Richard Riis

AGE	G	AB	R	H	2B	3B	HR	TB	RBI	BB	SO	BAV	OBP	SLG	SB	GDP	HBP
28	12	12	0	1	0	0	0	1	0	1	5	.083	.154	.083	0	1	0

Johnny Lucadello was a hard-hitting and versatile infielder who, like many of his generation, saw a promising Major League career fizzle after he lost four prime years to military service.

John Lucadello was born on February 22, 1919, in Thurber, Texas.[1] At its peak, in the early 1900s, Thurber, situated between Fort Worth and Abilene, was the largest and most prosperous coal-mining town in Texas. The town's population of nearly ten thousand was made up predominantly of Italians, Poles, and Germans, most of them miners recruited overseas by the Texas and Pacific Coal Company.

One of those recruits was Domenico Lucadello, a native of San Zenone degli Ezzelini, Italy, a village near Venice. Domenico left Italy for Thurber in 1904 at the age of twenty-nine. There he married Maria Donesco, another Italian immigrant. John was the youngest of their seven children. By the time he was born, the conversion of America's railroads from coal to diesel fuel had caused a steep decline in the coal market. When Texas and Pacific began to close the mines and brickworks and sell its company housing, the Lucadellos moved to Chicago, where Domenico landed a job as a coal loader.

Growing up in the Little Italy section of Chicago's Roseland neighborhood, Johnny and his brother Tony developed a passion for baseball. Johnny taught himself how to hit from both sides of the plate and how to scoop ground balls off the rough, uneven surfaces of the Chicago sandlots, and he became a standout player on the Christian Fenger Academy High School baseball team. "I had always wanted to be a ballplayer," Luc

Johnny Lucadello saw little action with the Yankees, collecting one base hit in twelve at bats.

adello once told a reporter. "Nothing else had ever entered my mind."[2]

Tony, seven years older than Johnny, developed into a local semipro baseball star and in the spring of 1936 was signed by the Fostoria Redbirds of the Class D Ohio State League, a St. Louis Cardinals farm club.

Maria Lucadello, fearing that a fondness for billiards and dice could get her youngest child mixed up with the wrong crowd, sent seventeen-year-old Johnny to spend the summer with Tony in Fostoria. When the Redbirds' second baseman was sidelined with an injury, Tony recommended that manager George Silvey give Johnny a look. Johnny, at five feet eleven and 165 pounds, was four inches taller and twenty-five pounds heavier than Tony and already making a name for himself on Roseland's All-Nations semipro team.

Johnny's twenty-four games with Fostoria led Silvey to recommend him to the St. Louis front office. Cardinals general manager Branch Rickey was not sold enough on Lucadello's potential, though, to part with a two-hundred-dollar signing bonus, and Johnny returned to Chicago at the end of the season unsigned.[3]

A postseason charity game between Minor Leaguers living in the Chicago area and inmates of nearby Joliet State Prison proved to be Johnny's big break. The guest manager for the professional team was Rogers Hornsby, then managing the St. Louis Browns. Hornsby assigned Tony Lucadello the task of making out the lineup, and Tony made his brother the starting second baseman.

The professionals lost the game, but Johnny banged out three of his team's four hits. Upon learning the teenager was unsigned, Hornsby called the Browns' office to send a contract for Johnny and a two-hundred-dollar check for Tony.

The Browns placed eighteen-year-old Johnny with their Fairbury farm club in the Class D Nebraska League. Playing second base, Johnny batted .316 with eight home runs; he tied for the league lead in doubles and triples and was named to the league's all-star team. The following season he was promoted to the Johnstown (Pennsylvania) Johnnies of the Class C Middle Atlantic League. Splitting his time between second base and third base, Lucadello hit .318 with eleven home runs and again was selected to the all-star squad. Called

up to the Browns for a late-season look, he made his Major League debut on September 24, 1938, as a pinch hitter for second baseman Don Heffner. "I was scared to death when [manager] Gabby [Street] asked me to pinch-hit," recalled Lucadello, the youngest player in the American League that year. "Here he had all those good hitters sitting around and he picked me. If he had used the whole bench before me I would have understood it."[4]

With the Browns stuck in the cellar, Street was fired two days later. Late in the second game of a doubleheader against the Tigers on September 27, interim manager Ski Melillo used Lucadello as a replacement for third baseman Harlond Clift. Facing right-hander Slick Coffman, Johnny doubled to right field for his first Major League hit.

In 1939 Lucadello played second base for the San Antonio Missions of the Class A Texas League. His shaky fielding was helped by the June arrival of Sig Gryska, demoted to San Antonio after a brief stay with the Browns. Gryska worked closely with Lucadello on improving his defense. "Lucadello began to sprout wings on his feet," wrote San Antonio sports editor Harold Scherwitz. "Lucadello improved so fast he looked like a different ball player between home stands."[5]

Playing in 161 games and batting a team-high .298, Lucadello paced the league in hits, led the loop's second basemen in total chances and double plays, and was for the third time in three seasons voted a starter on his league's all-star team. All this earned him another late-season call-up.

Lucadello was now the brightest prospect in the Browns' system. A potential off-season trade with the Yankees was vetoed by St. Louis president Don Barnes when the Yankees asked for Lucadello as partial payment for center fielder Wally Judnich.

In 1940 Johnny was invited to the Browns' spring-training camp in San Antonio, where new manager Fred Haney described his swing as "one of the finest" he had seen.[6] Lucadello impressed the Browns with his natural talent and single-mindedness on and off the field "John is strictly business at all times," said one observer, "and his business is baseball."[7] But Haney and the Browns' management decided Lucadello would be better served by playing regularly in the Minor Leagues another year than by sitting on the bench in St. Louis, and he was optioned to the Toledo Mud Hens of the American Association.

For nearly half the 1940 season, Lucadello led the league in hitting, and although a late-season slump trimmed his average, he finished at .334 and was named to his fourth all-star team in four seasons. In September he once again got the call to the big leagues and took over second base and the second slot in the Browns' batting order.

On September 15, in St. Louis, the seventh-place Browns stunned the Yankees, who were in a three-way struggle for the league lead, by taking both games of a doubleheader. The next day proved to be Lucadello's finest in the Major Leagues. Batting right-handed against Yankees starter Marius Russo, he ignited a seven-run first-inning outburst with a home run into the left-field bleachers. In the fifth inning he drove in two runs with a bases-loaded single off reliever Bump Hadley, and in the seventh inning, batting left-handed now against the right-handed Steve Sundra, he launched a two-run home run onto Sportsman's Park's right-field pavilion roof. In pacing the Browns to a 16–4 rout of the Yankees, Lucadello became only the third Major Leaguer to hit home runs from both sides of the plate in a single game.[8]

The Browns broke training camp in 1941 with Lucadello installed at second base after a bad hop in a spring exhibition fractured the nose of regular Don Heffner. Lucadello went 4 for 5 in the season opener, but managed just one hit in his next nineteen at bats. When Heffner returned on April 26, he regained the starting position. For the rest of the season Lucadello shifted between second base, shortstop, and third base. He finished the season with a .279 batting average and only two

home runs in 107 games. United Press sportswriters voted him the second baseman on their all-star rookie team for 1941.[9]

America's entry into World War II put Lucadello's baseball career on hold. Having already begun war-related work in the off-season as a laborer in an ammunition plant in St. Louis, he enlisted in the navy in March 1942. He was sent to the Great Lakes Naval Training Center in North Chicago, where he was assigned to the physical training program and, not surprisingly, placed on the roster of the Great Lakes baseball team, managed by Lieutenant Mickey Cochrane.

The Great Lakes Bluejackets, featuring a current or future Major Leaguer at every position, compiled a 63-14 record in 1942 and a 52-10-1 mark in 1943. After a stint at the Bainbridge Naval Station in Maryland in 1943, Lucadello was reassigned to Aiea Barracks in Hawaii, where he played for the 14th Naval District All-Star team, and also played in the September–October 1944 Army versus Navy Service World Series, which raised funds for injured and disabled servicemen. Then he participated in a Navy All-Stars tour of the western Pacific. Finally, Lucadello was sent to Tinian and then the Marshall Islands, where his duties included overseeing sports activities. He was discharged on October 16, 1945.

It was a very different Browns team that assembled in Anaheim, California, for spring training in 1946 than the team Lucadello had played for before the war. Having risen to the first division in 1942, the Browns captured a surprise pennant in 1944, and although they dipped to third place in 1945, they were considered a pennant contender in 1946. Don Heffner and Don Gutteridge were gone, leaving the second base position up for grabs. Lucadello, perhaps owing to an extra fifteen pounds from his prewar playing weight, had an uncharacteristically sluggish spring, and the second base slot went to fellow returning vet (and Lucadello's close friend and roommate) Johnny Berardino.

Backing up at second and third bases, Lucadello appeared in eighty-seven games and batted .248, as the Browns slid to seventh place in 1946. When he held out at the start of training camp the following season, he was placed on waivers and, on March 1, 1947, was sold to the Yankees.

The Yankees expected that Lucadello would compete for the second base job with Snuffy Stirnweiss. Lucadello, trimmer by fifteen pounds, outperformed Stirnweiss in camp, but manager Bucky Harris opted to stick with the veteran Yankee. Lucadello saw little action with New York, spending most of the first two months on the bench, collecting one base hit in twelve at bats. On July 16 Lucadello, whose last appearance in a game had been as a pinch hitter on June 13, was optioned to the Kansas City Blues, the Yankees' Class Triple-A affiliate in the American Association.

After Lucadello batted a dismal .170 in thirty-four games for the Blues, the Yankees released him to Kansas City outright. His former Yankees teammates, meanwhile, voted him a half-share ($2,915) of their World Series championship money.

Lucadello never made it back to the Major Leagues, but he put together a journeyman's career in the Minors for nearly a decade. He regained much of his old form with the International League Newark Bears in 1948, hitting .275 with twelve home runs and 101 walks. A return to Kansas City in 1949 saw him boost his average to .286.

The Chicago Cubs purchased Lucadello's contract from Kansas City before the 1950 season and assigned him to the Los Angeles Angels of the Pacific Coast League. Lucadello struggled at bat and was traded to Sacramento. He split the 1951 season between the Minneapolis Millers and the Toledo Mud Hens of the American Association.

Lucadello rebounded in 1952 with Birmingham of the Class Double-A Southern Association, but was released when he refused to report after a trade to Augusta in midseason.[10] Signing with the Wichita Falls (Texas) Spudders of the Class B Big State League for 1953, Lucadello was named the league's all-star second baseman. That same year, having moved to San Antonio, he married Lena Gene "Lee" Granato, a twenty-five-year-old San Antonio native.

Now approaching thirty-five, Lucadello understood his playing days were nearing an end. "I realized I would have to get into another field, either the business end of baseball or something of that sort," Johnny told a San Antonio reporter. "The old bones are getting pretty tired."[11]

J. C. Stroud, an oilman and the owner of several Minor League teams, offered him the position of player-manager for the Decatur (Illinois) Commodores of the Class D Mississippi–Ohio Valley League. Lucadello repaid Stroud with an outstanding season, leading the team to a first-place finish while capturing the league's batting title with a .362 average. Exploiting his still-strong right arm, Johnny also made his professional debut on the mound, compiling a 4-1 record in five starts and five relief appearances.

In June 1955 Johnny and Lee welcomed their first child, Donna Marie. Considered for a managerial post at Albuquerque for 1955, Lucadello opted for a job closer to home, signing as a player-coach with another of J. C. Stroud's clubs, the Port Arthur (Texas) Sea Hawks of the Big State League, and proceeded to hit a robust .350, the third-highest average in the league. At the age of thirty-six, Johnny was selected as the third baseman on the league's all-star team.

After the season Lucadello hung up his spikes for the last time, closing out a sixteen-year professional career. He spent the ensuing years raising a family (Johnny and Lee welcomed a second child, Mark, in October 1962), appearing at baseball clinics and promotional events for the San Antonio Missions, and hunting in the rugged Texas hill country. In October 1972 Lucadello was inducted into the Roseland-Pullman Area Sports Hall of Fame in Chicago.

Tragedy struck the Lucadellos in 1989 when Johnny's brother Tony shot himself to death on a baseball diamond in Fostoria, Ohio. Tony had signed more than fifty future Major Leaguers in a fifty-year career as one of the game's most acclaimed scouts, but none made him more proud than his first signing, brother Johnny.

Johnny Lucadello died after a lengthy illness on October 30, 2001, in San Antonio at the age of eighty-two and was buried with military honors at Fort Sam Houston National Cemetery. He was survived by his wife, Lee, his two children, and four grandchildren.

Chapter 34. Timeline, July 1–July 21

Lyle Spatz

Tuesday, July 1 — Not scheduled. The Yankees played an exhibition game at Newark, losing to the Bears, 5–2, before a crowd of more than seventeen thousand. 41-26-1, First, 5½ games ahead.

Wednesday, July 2, vs. Washington — An 8–1 win over Washington raised the Yankees' lead over the Boston Red Sox and Detroit Tigers to 6½ games. Allie Reynolds pitched a complete game, while Joe DiMaggio hit his tenth home run. George Stirnweiss, Johnny Lindell, and Billy Johnson each had two hits. 42-26-1, First, 6½ games ahead.

Thursday, July 3 — Not scheduled. 42-26-1, First, 6 games ahead.

Friday, July 4, vs. Washington (2) — The Yanks swept the holiday doubleheader against Washington to raise their lead to 7½ games. Spud Chandler won the opener, 7–3, aided by his own three-run homer. George Stirnweiss also homered, his first of the season. The Yanks trailed Walt Masterson, 2–0, after six innings of the nightcap, but scored two in the seventh on Bobby Brown's pinch-hit single and two in the eighth to win, 4–2. Yogi Berra and Phil Rizzuto drove in the eighth-inning runs. Joe DiMaggio had three hits, including a triple. Joe Page was the winning pitcher in relief. 44-26-1, First, 7½ games ahead.

Saturday, July 5, vs. Philadelphia — Rookie Frank Shea continued his sensational pitching with a three-hit 5–1 win over the Athletics. The Yankees scored all their runs against Joe Coleman in the fourth inning after he had retired the first two bat-

ters. Joe DiMaggio started the rally with a double, and then after George McQuinn walked, the next five batters singled. 45-26-1, First, 8 games ahead.

Sunday, July 6, vs. Philadelphia (2) — New York raised its winning streak to eight by defeating Philadelphia in both ends of a doubleheader. The Yanks used a five-run first inning, highlighted by Joe DiMaggio's three-run homer, to romp in the opener, 8–2. Yogi Berra also had three RBIs, and Tommy Henrich and George McQuinn each contributed three hits. Starter Randy Gumpert was the winner, with Joe Page contributing 3⅔ scoreless innings in relief. Allie Reynolds (8-5) and Phil Marchildon were tied at 2–2 after 7½ innings of the second game, but the Yanks exploded for seven runs in the eighth to win, 9–2. New York entered the All-Star break with an eight-game lead. 47-26-1, First, 8 games ahead.

Monday, July 7 — Not scheduled. 47-26-1, First, 8 games ahead.

Tuesday, July 8 — All-Star Game. 47-26-1, First, 8 games ahead.

Wednesday, July 9 — Not scheduled. 47-26-1, First, 8 games ahead.

Thursday, July 10, at St. Louis — After Spud Chandler had allowed St. Louis to tie the score in the seventh inning, Joe Page came on and held the Browns scoreless over the final 2⅔ innings. The score was still tied at 3–3 with two outs in the top of the ninth when Page hit a game-winning home run off Nelson Potter. The 4–3 win was New York's ninth straight and raised its lead over Boston and Detroit to a season-high 8½ games. 48-26-1, First, 8½ games ahead.

Friday, July 11, at St. Louis—The Yankees managed only three hits against Ellis Kinder, but came away with a 3–1 victory, their tenth straight. Johnny Lindell's two-run double in the third inning was the big blow. Allie Reynolds allowed six hits and four walks, but went the distance for his ninth win. 49-26-1, First, 9 games ahead.

Saturday, July 12, at St. Louis (2)—Wins in both ends of the doubleheader gave the Yankees a sweep of the 5 games in St. Louis, raised their winning streak to 12, and marked their 24th win in their last 27 games. With half the season played, the Yankees' lead was 9½ games. The Yanks had seventeen hits in the first game's 12–2 win, including home runs by Billy Johnson and Joe DiMaggio, who batted in four runs. On the negative side, Frank Shea had to leave the game after retiring the Browns in order in the first inning. Butch Wensloff pitched the final eight innings to pick up his first win of the season. The Yanks overcame a 3–0 deficit to win the second game, 8–5. Starter Bill Bevens allowed the three runs. Karl Drews was the winning pitcher. Tommy Henrich, who had five hits in the doubleheader, had two home runs and Aaron Robinson one. 51-26-1, First, 9½ games ahead.

Sunday, July 13, at Chicago (2)—Another doubleheader sweep extended the Yankees' winning streak to 14 games. The 10–3 and 6–4 wins at Comiskey Park moved the club 10½ games ahead of the second-place Tigers. In the opener, Bobo Newsom, purchased from the Washington Senators two days earlier, made his Yankees debut with a complete-game win. New York had sixteen hits, including a grand slam by Phil Rizzuto and five hits by Billy Johnson. Vic Raschi, recently recalled

from Portland of the Pacific Coast League, won the nightcap, though he needed help from Joe Page and Allie Reynolds. Tommy Henrich, who had three hits in the opener, had three more in the second game. George Stirnweiss (two doubles), Rizzuto, and Raschi each had two hits. 53-26-1, First, 10½ games ahead.

Monday, July 14, at Chicago—Rained out. 53-26-1, First, 10½ games ahead.

Tuesday, July 15, at Cleveland (2)—Playing before a Municipal Stadium crowd of more than sixty-two thousand, the Yankees downed the Indians twice in sweeping their third consecutive doubleheader. The 9–4 and 2–1 victories raised the Yanks' winning streak to 16 games. Allie Reynolds won the opener, backed by home runs from George McQuinn and Joe DiMaggio and three runs batted in by Johnny Lindell. In the second game Bill Bevens defeated Bob Feller to win his first game since May 25. The Yankees scored the winning run in the ninth inning on Billy Johnson's triple that scored DiMaggio. 55-26-1, First, 11 games ahead.

Wednesday, July 16, at Cleveland—The Yankees set a franchise record with their seventeenth consecutive win. The 8–2 triumph over the Indians broke the mark established by the 1926 club. Cleveland starter Allen Gettel faced only four batters. George Stirnweiss singled, Tommy Henrich homered, Johnny Lindell singled, and Joe DiMaggio tripled. Each had two hits in the game, as did George McQuinn, Billy Johnson, and Yogi Berra. One of Berra's hits was a home run. Butch Wensloff was the starter and winner, but needed help from Karl Drews and Joe Page. 56-26-1, First, 11½ games ahead.

Thursday, July 17, at Cleveland (2)—Another doubleheader sweep raised the Yankees' consecutive-game winning streak to 19, tying the American League record set by the 1906 Chicago White Sox. The two newest Yankees, Bobo Newsom and Vic Raschi, each won his second consecutive start, and each pitched a complete game. Newsom's 3–1 win in the opener was the two hundredth of his career. George McQuinn had a home run and two runs batted in. Raschi allowed only six hits in the 7–2 win in the second game. Tommy Henrich had two hits, and Billy Johnson had three runs batted in. Cleveland's rookie outfielder Dale Mitchell had hits in each game to extend his consecutive-game hitting streak to 19. 58-26-1, First, 11½ games ahead.

Friday, July 18, at Detroit—Tigers pitcher Fred Hutchinson ended the Yankees' record-tying 19-game winning streak with a two-hit 8–0 shutout at Briggs Stadium. Hutchinson allowed a single to Joe DiMaggio in the second and a bunt single by George Stirnweiss in the seventh. Meanwhile, the Tigers reached Randy Gumpert and Karl Drews for eighteen hits. Dick Wakefield, Eddie Mayo, Hoot Evers, and Hutchinson each had three. Doctors removed a slipped disk from Charlie Keller's spine, an operation that would keep him sidelined for the rest of the season. 58-27-1, First, 10½ games ahead.

Saturday, July 19, at Detroit—Allie Reynolds's five-hit 2–1 win at Detroit got the Yankees back to their winning ways. New York's two first-inning runs were all Reynolds needed. Dizzy Trout was the loser. The win again moved the Yanks 11½ games ahead of the second-place Tigers. 59-27-1, First, 11½ games ahead.

Sunday, July 20, at Detroit (2)—The Tigers rewarded their record crowd (58,369) by winning both ends of the doubleheader, 4–1 and 12–11. The two wins reduced the Yanks' lead over Detroit to 9½ games. Hal Newhouser, who was

0-3 against the Yankees this season, beat Bill Bevens in the opener. Newhouser allowed triples to Joe DiMaggio and Billy Johnson and an infield single by George McQuinn, but faced only twenty-eight batters. In the second game, the Yankees had an 11–5 lead, but allowed the Tigers to tie it in the ninth inning and win it in the eleventh. Joe Page made a rare start for New York, but was ineffective, as were Randy Gumpert, Vic Raschi, and loser Allie Reynolds. DiMaggio, Yogi Berra, and Phil Rizzuto each had three hits, and Berra and Tommy Henrich hit home runs. 59-29-1, First, 9½ games ahead.

Monday, July 21—Not scheduled. 59-29-1, First, 9½ games ahead.

Chapter 35. **Vic Raschi**

Lawrence Baldassaro

AGE	W	L	PCT.	ERA	G	GS	GF	CG	SHO	SV	IP	H	BB	SO	HBP	WP
28	7	2	.778	3.87	15	14	0	6	1	0	104.2	89	38	51	1	2

In the Yankees' unprecedented streak of five straight World Series titles between 1949 and 1953, Vic Raschi's record was 92-40, an average of eighteen wins a season and a winning percentage of .697. From 1949, only his second full season in the Majors, through 1951, Raschi won twenty-one games each year.

Victor John Angelo Raschi was born in West Springfield, Massachusetts, on March 28, 1919. His nickname, "the Springfield Rifle," combined the speed of his fastball and the name of the neighboring city—the site of the U.S. Armory that had been producing army rifles since 1794. His parents, Massimino, a carpenter who worked for the railroad, and Egizia, had moved to Springfield when Raschi was still in diapers. Vic also had two older sisters and a younger brother.

A star in baseball, football, and basketball at Springfield Tech High School, Raschi attracted the attention of Yankees scout Gene McCann while still a freshman. In 1936 Raschi signed an agreement under which the Yankees would pay for his college education in return for getting the first chance to sign him when he graduated. He enrolled at the College of William and Mary, in Williamsburg, Virginia, in 1938, and by 1941 the Yankees decided it was time for Raschi to begin his professional career. After the '41 college baseball season, Raschi was sent to upstate New York to pitch for the Amsterdam Rugmakers in the Class C Canadian-American League. He continued to attend classes at William and Mary in the off-season.

A 10-6 season at Amsterdam earned Raschi a promotion in 1942 to the Norfolk (Virginia) Tars, the Yankees' affiliate in the Class B Piedmont

Vic Raschi posted a 7-2 record after coming up from the Portland Beavers in July.

League. His record at Norfolk was only 4-10, but he had an impressive 2.71 earned run average. World War II put both his career and his education on hold. After spending three years in the U.S. Army Air Corps as a physical-education instructor, he returned to school part-time while pitching for the Yankees, earning a degree in physical education in 1949. In the meantime he had married Sarah "Sally" Glenn, a fellow student at William and Mary.

The six-foot-one, two-hundred-pound right-hander resumed his professional career in 1946 with the Binghamton (New York) Triplets in the Class A Eastern League. The Yankees called him up in September, following his 10-10 season for the Triplets and 5 games with the Newark Bears, the Yankees' Class Triple-A affiliate.

On September 23, 1946, at the age of twenty-seven, Raschi made his Major League debut before a tiny turnout of 2,475 at the Yankees' home finale. Raschi, a "well-proportioned right-hander with burning speed," pitched a complete-game 9–6 win against the Philadelphia Athletics.[1] Six days later he won his second start, 2–1, over the A's in the season's final game.

Given that successful debut, Raschi was bitterly disappointed when the Yankees optioned him to the Portland Beavers of the Class Triple-A Pacific Coast League in May 1947. Initially, he refused to report but finally relented. In Portland he benefited from the tutelage of manager Jim Turner, a former Yankees reliever who in 1949 would become the Yankees' pitching coach and remain in that position for the rest of Raschi's career.

Raschi compiled an 8-2 record with Portland, including 9 complete games in 11 starts, and was called up to New York in July. The Yankees had won 9 straight games, but on July 10, with starter Spud Chandler injured and Mel Queen sold to Pittsburgh, manager Bucky Harris telephoned Turner. Late that night, after a doubleheader in San Diego, Turner approached Raschi, who had won his fourth straight in the second game, and asked if he could be ready to pitch on Sunday, three days later. When Raschi said yes, Turner told him he had been recalled by the Yankees. Raschi showered and caught a plane to Portland before flying on to Chicago to join the Yankees.

Raschi did pitch that Sunday, in the second game of a doubleheader in Chicago, giving up three runs in 6⅓ innings to earn a 6–4 win over the White Sox. It was the Yankees' fourteenth straight victory. Five days later Raschi gave up six hits in a complete-game 7–2 win over the Indians in Cleveland. It was the final win in the Yankees' 19-game streak, putting their record at 58-26 with an 11½-game lead over the Detroit Tigers.

By August 2 Raschi, a power pitcher who complemented his fastball with a slider and change-up, had won his first five starts. After a no-decision on August 8, he raised his record to 6-0 on August 13. (Wins two through five were all complete games.) After Raschi's fifth victory, a three-hit shutout of the Indians, J. G. Taylor Spink, in a front-page story in the August 13 issue of the *Sporting News*, described Raschi as "a quiet, very much reserved, hardly talkative man" and the "latest pitching 'remarkable' of the Yankees."

Raschi's first Major League loss was one of his best outings of the year. In an August 17 game at Yankee Stadium that according to the *New York Times* had "all the thrill and excitement of World Series combat," he shut out the defending American League champion Boston Red Sox on four hits for ten innings before giving up three runs in the eleventh. Five days later Raschi's record fell to 6-2 in a 4–3 loss to the Indians. His seventh and final victory of the season did not come until September 14, a 6–4 win over the last-place St. Louis Browns that clinched at least a tie for the pennant.

For the season Raschi compiled a 7-2 record with six complete games in fourteen starts and a 3.87 earned run average. In the Yankees' World Series victory over the Brooklyn Dodgers, Raschi made two relief appearances—in Games Three and Six—giving up one run on two hits in 1⅓ innings.

Though the Yankees finished in third place in 1948, Raschi won nineteen games and lost just eight. He was the winning pitcher in the All-Star Game and also drove in the winning run with a bases-loaded single. He finished eleventh in the

LAWRENCE BALDASSARO

Most Valuable Player voting after the season. Then followed three consecutive seasons with twenty-one wins (21-10, 21-8, 21-10); he averaged 263 innings and thirty-four starts, leading the league in starts in both 1949 and 1951. His winning percentage of .724 in 1950 led the American League. In 1952 his win total fell to sixteen (with six losses), but his 2.78 ERA was the lowest of his career.

In addition to his 92-40 record from 1949 to 1953, Raschi made 160 starts for the Yankees. What makes this stretch of endurance even more impressive is that a collision at home plate with Indians catcher Jim Hegan in August 1950 resulted in torn cartilage in Raschi's right knee. Playing in pain, he found it difficult to run or to put all his weight on his right leg when he pushed off the pitching rubber. Raschi and the Yankees kept the injury to themselves to prevent other teams from taking advantage by bunting on him. Not until November 1951 did he undergo surgery to remove the cartilage.

In 1952 Raschi signed for a reported forty thousand dollars, making him at that time the highest-paid pitcher in Yankees history. But the signing came with a stern warning from general manager George Weiss: "Don't you ever have a bad year."[2] Raschi's 13-6 record in 1953 apparently was a bad year, according to Weiss, who offered Raschi a contract calling for a 25 percent cut in 1954. Refusing to sign, Raschi held out until spring training, one of twelve Yankee holdouts. When he got to training camp in St. Petersburg, Florida, he was informed by newspaper reporters, not by Weiss, that he had been sold to the St. Louis Cardinals. Raschi's record in his eight years with the Yankees was 120-50, a .706 winning percentage.

Raschi spent his final two seasons with the Cardinals and the Kansas City Athletics, compiling a combined record of 12-16 before retiring in October 1955 at the age of thirty-six. In his ten-year career, he won 132 while losing only 66, with an earned run average of 3.72. As of 2012 his win-loss percentage of .667 was tied for twelfth best for any pitcher with at least one hundred decisions. He finished seventh and eighth in the Most Valuable Player voting in 1950 and 1951, respectively, and he pitched in four All-Star Games, starting in both 1950 and 1952.

As impressive as his overall won-lost record is, Raschi was at his best in the big games. Teammate Tommy Henrich said, "If there was only one game I had to win, the man I'd want out there on the mound for me would be Vic Raschi." Another teammate, Jerry Coleman, told the author, "He was our bread-and-butter guy. Reynolds had a better arm, but Raschi was a great competitor. Off the field he was shy and unassuming, nothing like he was on the mound. There he was a beast. Casey considered him our best starter." Stengel, who managed Raschi from 1949 through 1953, said, "I thought Raschi was the best pitcher I had on the team for nine innings. . . . Boy, he was the best on the club in the eighth and ninth inning."[3]

As Coleman said, Raschi was a beast on the mound, and not just because of his fastball. With his hazel eyes peering out from beneath his dark eyebrows, he stared down batters in an attempt to unsettle them and gain a psychological edge. "I figured if I could break their concentration when they came up to the plate I had them beat, or at least gained an advantage," he said. "Once you made them turn their eyes away you had a slight psychological edge." Yogi Berra, his batterymate, said, "He'd keep his eyes on their eyes, like a boxer before a fight."[4]

In eight World Series starts, Raschi won five games (against three losses), including a two-hit shutout of the Philadelphia Phillies in the 1950 opener and two wins over the Dodgers in the 1952 Series. His World Series ERA, including his two relief appearances in 1947, is 2.24. But perhaps his most memorable game came on the final day of the 1949 season when the Yankees hosted the

Red Sox with the pennant at stake. The Red Sox, who had trailed the Yankees by twelve games early in July but stormed back to take a one-game lead with two games left, needed to win only one of the two to take the flag. But the Yanks won the first game 5–4 to force the Red Sox into a do-or-die finale. Raschi, with a 20-10 record, was matched up against Ellis Kinder, who had won twenty-three (four against the Yankees) and lost five going into the game.

With 68,055 fans on hand, Raschi, given a 1–0 lead in the first, shut down the power-laden Red Sox on two hits over the first eight innings; the Yankees then took a 5–0 lead after scoring four in the eighth. But the Red Sox, who had been favored to win the pennant, would not go quietly, scoring three runs in the ninth with the tying run at the plate in Birdie Tebbetts. First baseman Tommy Henrich approached Raschi to offer some encouragement. But the glowering Raschi was in no mood for chitchat, and before Henrich could say a word he told him, "Give me the goddamned ball and get the hell out of here."[5] He then got Tebbetts to hit a foul pop that Henrich squeezed for the final out and the pennant.

After his retirement Raschi and his family settled in Groveland, his wife Sarah's hometown in upstate New York on the shores of Conesus Lake. Raschi owned and operated the Green Valley Liquor Store in nearby Conesus. He also coached baseball and basketball at Geneseo State Teachers College (now the State University of New York at Geneseo), where the baseball field was named in his honor. In 2001 he was posthumously inducted into the Geneseo Sports Hall of Fame. Beginning in 1969, at the age of fifty, he also taught elementary school. Raschi died of a heart attack on October 14, 1988, at the age of sixty-nine, survived by his wife; his son, William; his daughters, Victoria and Mitje; and two grandchildren.

Chapter 36. **Reynolds and Raschi, Building Blocks of a Dynasty**

Sol Gittleman

The 1947 season for the New York Yankees was expected to be another step down in the decline of the franchise. Joe DiMaggio and Joe Gordon had returned from the military in 1946, but both had subpar years. For the first time in his career, DiMaggio batted below .300 and failed to drive in one hundred runs. Gordon, the league's Most Valuable Player in 1942, batted an anemic .210. Ace pitcher Spud Chandler was a twenty-game winner in 1946, but he was now thirty-eight years old. New York finished seventeen games behind the Boston Red Sox, who were prohibitive favorites to repeat in 1947.

It never happened. In 1947 the Red Sox collapsed to a third-place finish, and the New York Yankees rode a midseason nineteen-game winning streak to capture the pennant by twelve games over Detroit, then beat Brooklyn in a tense seven-game World Series. After falling to third place in 1948, the Yankees went on to win an astounding five consecutive World Series championships from 1949 to 1953. Two pitchers emerged in that remarkable 1947 season who would lead the Yankees to this unprecedented success: Allie Reynolds and Vic Raschi.

Doubtless few saw it coming after the 1946 season. In October Yankees president Larry MacPhail traded Gordon to the Cleveland Indians for the underachieving twenty-nine-year-old Reynolds, who was coming off a disappointing 11-15 season. Reynolds, who was part Creek Indian, had been dubbed "the Vanishing American" in Cleveland because of his inability to pitch complete games.

In an effort to solve the Yankees' first base problems, MacPhail signed thirty-seven-year-old free agent George McQuinn in January. McQuinn was coming off a year in which he hit .225 for the last-place Philadelphia Athletics, who released him at the end of the 1946 season. Eyes rolled at the thought of a Yankees first baseman arriving after being released by a last-place team.

Manager Bucky Harris set his 1947 starting rotation with Reynolds third, behind Chandler and right-hander Bill Bevens. The fourth starter was an inconsistent, hard-throwing left-hander who enjoyed the nightlife a little too much: Joe Page. Soon rookie Spec Shea moved into the fourth spot, and Page was exiled to the bullpen, and in Harris's mind, as his patience ran out, would soon be pitching for the Class Triple-A Newark Bears.

When Boston came into Yankee Stadium on May 23 for a four-game series, New York seemed stuck at a mediocre 13-14. The Red Sox, at 17-12, were positioned to make a move on front-running Detroit, who, led by pitchers Hal Newhouser, Fred Hutchinson, and Dizzy Trout, had jumped out to a 17-8 record and the league lead.

In four Major League seasons with Cleveland, Reynolds never fulfilled the promise that management hoped for when they signed him off the Oklahoma A&M campus in 1939. His wife and two children afforded him an exemption from military service, and by 1942 Cleveland was looking for a replacement for their ace Bob Feller, who had enlisted soon after Pearl Harbor. In spite of stamina and control problems, Allie got the call to report to Cleveland for the end of the 1942 season. From then on it was a roller-coaster ride, resulting in a 51-47 record when the Indians finally gave up on him.[1]

Soon after the 1947 season began, a new Reynolds emerged. In the first of the four-game weekend series, he shut out the Red Sox, 9–0, on two hits. It was the kind of "big-game" performance that became the hallmark of Allie Reynolds in his New York Yankees incarnation. In the next three games, Chandler, Bevens, and Page handed Boston three more losses.

The Yankees had found their ace. Allie Reynolds became Harris's stopper. He faced the best of the Boston and Detroit staffs for the rest of the season, led the Yankees in starts (30) and complete games (17), and was the only starter with more than two hundred innings pitched (242). His record was 19-8 with an ERA of 3.20. He also showed Harris that he could work in between starts; Reynolds relieved four times and got the first two of his forty-one saves as a Yankee.

Vic Raschi, twenty-eight years old and languishing in the Pacific Coast League with the Portland Beavers in 1947, was ready to quit baseball. The Yankees had signed him in 1938 after the high school star turned down a football scholarship to Ohio State. Farm director George Weiss had promised Raschi's immigrant parents the club would pay for Vic's college education; the new Yankees recruit enrolled at the College of William and Mary in Williamsburg, Virginia, in the fall. After three seasons starring on the college baseball team, Raschi was ordered to report to the Amsterdam (New York) Rugmakers of the Class C Canadian-American League in 1941 after William and Mary's season was complete.

His professional career was under way. After the 1942 season with the Norfolk (Virginia) Tars of the Class B Piedmont League, Raschi enlisted in the U.S. Army Air Corps. For the next three years he moved all over the country as a physical-fitness trainer. He finally got back to Williamsburg in 1945 to marry his college sweetheart. When he was discharged he was twenty-seven years old, and time was running out. After a 1946 season with

the Class A Binghamton (New York) Triplets and Newark in the International League, Raschi got a September call-up to the big club; he was ready. He had two starts against the last-place Athletics and won both, going the distance each time.

When Raschi reported to spring training in 1947, he thought he had won a roster spot on the basis of his late-season performance. But Harris had turned the responsibility for pitchers over to coach Charlie Dressen, an old-time National League infielder and later manager of the Brooklyn Dodgers. Dressen thought he knew everything about pitchers and their makeup.[2] He used Raschi exclusively as a batting-practice pitcher during spring training, and before the season started, Vic was told to report to Portland of the Class Triple-A Pacific Coast League. The other two call-ups from Newark in September 1946, Yogi Berra and Bobby Brown, had made the team; Raschi, however, was going back to the Minors.

Instead of reporting, a bitter and discouraged Raschi returned to his wife, Sally, in upstate New York to tell her he was finished. The Yankees called him twice, threatening to ban him for life unless he reported. Raschi had the personality makeup of a stubborn bulldog, and he was not fazed by threats. Sally Raschi, who understood her husband, brought a calm, deliberate resolution to the crisis: "I've never seen Portland, so let's go." It was the most important decision of their lives.

After settling into an apartment, Raschi went over to the stadium, found the manager's office, knocked, entered, and saw a tall man walking toward him with an outstretched hand and a face he could trust. It was Jim Turner; this was to be a friendship for life. Turner, consummate mentor of pitchers, knew that this big, dour, hard-throwing pitcher had all the equipment: four-seam fastball, curve, slider, and change-up. Turner also noticed that at a critical moment, some .220 hitter would sit on Raschi's fastball and beat him. Vic needed to pitch inside, push the batter off the plate, but his brother Gene lost his sight after being beaned, and Raschi had a fear of hitting someone in the head. Turner worked on him. He knew that eventually any Major League hitter would catch up with any fastball; there was only one way to guarantee that the pitcher owned the plate, not the hitter: through intimidation, and that meant pitching "up and in."

It was through Turner's tutelage in this period at Portland that Raschi developed a terrifying scowl, a withering look that opposing teams, journalists, and even teammates came to appreciate—and fear. When they saw "the look" on Raschi's face, they stayed away. By the time Jim Turner was finished with his course of instruction, no one would come near Vic Raschi on the day that he pitched.[3]

In July Turner called Weiss and told him to get Raschi back to the Yankees. Weiss, who knew Turner was one of the most astute evaluators of pitching talent, did not waste any time. The Yankees were in the middle of their extraordinary win streak, but were running out of arms. Weiss recalled Raschi on the same day in July that he acquired thirty-nine-year-old veteran Bobo Newsom.

The two newcomers pitched in tandem, winning doubleheaders in games thirteen and fourteen of the streak, and again in eighteen and nineteen, the final two of the streak. When Raschi walked into the Yankees' clubhouse on that July day, he knew most of the faces from his brief stint at the end of the '46 season. But he looked for a new one in particular, that of Allie Reynolds, and a friendship was forged that lasted the rest of their lives.

Raschi started fifteen games in that half-season of 1947, completed six, and finished with a 7-2 record. Not even Charlie Dressen could stop his march to Yankees greatness. In his eight years with New York, his record was 120-50 for a win-loss percentage of .706, second only to Spud Chandler in Yankees history. After winning nineteen games in 1948, Raschi won twenty-one games in each of the 1949, 1950, and 1951 seasons. In World Series

competition he was 5-3; two of those losses were 1–0 and 3–2. His Series ERA is 2.24.

Like his friend Allie Reynolds, he would go on to become a big-game pitcher, winning the pennant clincher in the last game of the 1949 season and World Series final games in 1949 and 1951.

Neither Reynolds nor Raschi was the star of the 1947 World Series. That role was left to Joe Page. Reynolds went all the way in a second-game 10–3 victory for his only win. Raschi was used exclusively in relief, a role in which he never enjoyed success.

That season was prelude to one of the most unexpected runs in baseball history, and Allie Reynolds and Vic Raschi were on center stage for those five years between 1949 and 1953.

The unforeseen Yankees success of 1947 did not change the opinion of baseball writers who were convinced that the season had been an aberration. That sentiment seemed to be confirmed in 1948 when the Red Sox apparently regained their equilibrium, only to be deposed in a one-game playoff by the upstart Cleveland Indians. One historian wrote, "The Yankees showed every sign of having crumbled before the start of the [1949] season. The Bombers had fallen to third place, age was slowing up several key pinstripers, and both Cleveland and Boston seemed stronger on paper than their 1948 contending squads."[4]

In February 1948 George Weiss, by then the general manager, traded his starting catcher, Aaron Robinson, and two other players for Chicago White Sox left-hander Ed Lopat. Weiss fired manager Bucky Harris and hired Casey Stengel, and Weiss and Stengel agreed the best potential pitching coach in baseball was the manager of the Portland Beavers, Jim Turner. They also knew much depended on turning Yogi Berra into a respectable catcher.[5] That project was turned over to future Hall of Famer Bill Dickey and the three veteran pitchers who would lead the New York Yankees on to unprecedented glory: New York's

Big Three, a team within a team: Allie Reynolds, Vic Raschi, and Ed Lopat. In addition to Raschi's 120 victories, Reynolds was 131-60, with two no-hitters with the Yankees. In his eight years with New York, Ed Lopat produced a 113-59 record, a .657 winning percentage, and an ERA of 3.19. Collectively, they won sixteen of the twenty Yankees World Series victories between 1949 and 1953. Either Allie or Vic was the winning pitcher or got the save in each of the final games of those five World Series. But "In the Beginning" was the 1947 season that few saw coming.

Chapter 37. New York Yankees in the 1947 All-Star Game

Lyle Spatz

The 1947 All-Star Game was played at Chicago's Wrigley Field on July 8. The American League scored single runs in the sixth and seventh innings to eke out a 2–1 win. Baseball returned All-Star voting to the fans in 1947, and they selected two Yankees to the starting lineup: center fielder Joe DiMaggio and first baseman George McQuinn. Both played the entire game.

DiMaggio's second-inning leadoff single against Cincinnati's Ewell Blackwell was his one hit in four plate appearances. He grounded to third against the Cardinals' Harry Brecheen in the fourth inning and bounced into a double play against Brecheen in the sixth, with Luke Appling scoring on the play. In his last plate appearance, DiMaggio drew an eighth-inning walk against Boston's Warren Spahn. McQuinn went 0 for 4. He flied out against Blackwell, struck out against Brecheen, and grounded out against both the Braves' Johnny Sain and Spahn.

Two Yankees got into the game as late-inning substitutes. Tommy Henrich replaced Washington's Buddy Lewis in right field in the home half of the sixth. In his one at bat, he struck out against Spahn. Billy Johnson replaced Detroit's George Kell at third base in the home half of the seventh inning but did not bat. Catcher Aaron Robinson was selected to the team, but Buddy Rosar of the Philadelphia Athletics played the entire game.

Yankee pitchers Frank Shea and Joe Page made the biggest contributions to the American League victory. Shea, a rookie, replaced starter Hal Newhouser of Detroit in the fourth inning. Shea was the first rookie to make an American League All-Star team since Joe DiMaggio in 1936. He was also the first pitcher to do so, earning his spot with a league-leading eleven wins (11-2).

Shea got the first two batters he faced before surrendering a home run to Johnny Mize, the first ever All-Star home run by a member of the New York Giants. It was the only run Shea allowed in his three innings of work, and he emerged the winning pitcher, the first rookie in either league to get an All-Star win. Joe Page allowed one hit and one walk over the final inning and a third to earn the "save."

Chapter 38. **Bobo Newsom**

Ralph Berger

AGE	W	L	PCT.	ERA	G	GS	GF	CG	SHO	SV	IP	H	BB	SO	HBP	WP
39	7	5	.583	2.80	17	15	1	6	2	0	115.2	109	30	42	2	0

Few Major League players were traded as often as pitcher Louis Norman "Bobo" Newsom. The name Bobo came about because Newsom never could or would remember anybody's name, so he called everyone Bobo and thus earned that nickname for himself. Barrel-chested, standing six-foot-three and weighing more than two hundred pounds, the colorful right-hander was talkative and swelling with confidence. He would brag, "Ol' Bobo is on the mound today and you can put it in the win column." Yet for all his gruffness and posturing, Newsom was a sentimental and kind-hearted guy who just wanted to be loved by the fans and his teammates.

He was 211-222 in his twenty-year Major League career, one of only two pitchers who won more than 200 games but finished with a losing record.[1] Many of those losses came from pitching for poor teams like the Philadelphia Athletics, St. Louis Browns, and Washington Senators.[2] Newsom had five different stints with the Senators. He boasted that he had more terms in Washington than President Roosevelt.[3] The well-traveled Newsom also won 146 games and lost 112 in the Minor Leagues.

When Bobo started a game, he was determined to go the distance no matter what. On May 28, 1935, a third-inning line drive by Cleveland's Earl Averill broke his left kneecap. When Washington manager Bucky Harris reached the mound, Newsom said, "I think it's broke." Harris asked Bobo if he should take him out of the game. "You kidding me? I said it was broke, I didn't say I was dead." Bobo continued to pitch and after every inning would say, "It's broke." His teammates laughed at him, assuming it could not be broken because

Bobo Newsom won seven games with a 2.80 ERA for the Yankees, but they awarded him only a three-quarter share of the World Series money.

he would not be able to stand up if it was. Following the Senators' 5–4 loss, Newsom was hobbling around the lobby of the hotel, still insisting his kneecap was broken. Finally he went to get an X-ray, and it was indeed "broke."

Newsom was the starter in the 1936 home opener at Griffith Stadium. President Roosevelt was in attendance to throw out the first ball. In the fourth inning of the scoreless game, third baseman Ossie Bluege's throw struck Newsom's jaw. Bluege had made a sensational play, and Bobo was so transfixed he forgot to duck. In true Bobo fashion, he gritted his teeth and completed the game for a win. Newsom, who often spoke of himself in the third person, said, "When the president comes to see Ol' Bobo pitch he ain't gonna let him down."

Newsom always felt the need to express his feelings, often to his detriment. In 1943, when he was with the Brooklyn Dodgers, he had a run-in with manager Leo Durocher. The cause was a difference of opinion between the two over a pitch Newsom threw to Vince DiMaggio. Leo wanted the pitch high and inside. Newsom threw what he considered a high-and-inside pitch. Leo did not concur. After much debate about the merits of the pitch, Newsom finally said, "With two balls and one strike on the hitter and a man on first base you want me to throw a ball that isn't close to a strike. Why don't you just walk the guy and save time? If you want me to pitch that way, I don't know anything about the racket." Leo disagreed, and the arguing continued until Leo said, "You're suspended for the season." "What the hell for?" asked Newsom. "I haven't cussed you or gone against your orders. You know you can't suspend me for the season and make it stick."[4]

Newsom's teammates threatened to go on strike unless he was reinstated. The usually reserved and gentlemanly Arky Vaughan was so upset by the argument and subsequent suspension that he rolled up his uniform, handed it to Durocher, and told Leo to shove it up his ass. With the rest of the team ready to walk out in support of Newsom and Vaughan, Durocher relented and Newsom was reinstated.

But despite his bragging, Newsom was always ready to lend a helping hand. According to Hank Greenberg, Newsom was unfailingly kind to rookies, even treating them to dinner occasionally. Bobo, however, was shrewd in contract negotiations, at times gaining an outright release so he could bargain with other teams.

Like many baseball players, Newsom had his superstitions. On his way to the mound, he would scoop up a handful of dirt on the foul side of the first base line and another on the fair side. The rosin bag had to be one foot behind the mound. When he ended an inning, he would place his glove just five feet outside the foul line and forbid anyone to touch it. The mound had to be completely devoid of paper scraps; Bobo would meticulously pick up any that were there. Players on other teams picked up on that and would strew bits of paper on the mound.

When Newsom was slated to work, umpires had to be ready for frequent debates about pitch location. One night in Cleveland, Bobo had a 2–1 lead and was pitching to Lou Boudreau when he tossed up a blooper pitch. Umpire Bill Summers called it a ball, and Bobo, in a huff, arrived at home plate shortly after the pitch. Summers was not in the mood to debate with Bobo and said to him, "Scram," whereupon Newsom screamed, "Scram! I ain't even had time to unwrap a cuss word."[5]

Newsom was born in Hartsville, South Carolina, on August 11, 1907, to Quilline Bufkin Newsom, a farmer, and the former Lillian Holmes Hicks. (Bobo's mother was killed in a car accident in December 1924 when he was just seventeen. His father remarried shortly thereafter.) Buck, as young Louis was known in the family, had two sisters and two older brothers, one of whom died in childhood. Along with his siblings, Buck helped on the family farm in nearby Swift Creek, but his goal was to become a ballplayer. He played shortstop on the Hartsville High School team. As captain, Newsom decided one day he would relieve the pitcher, thus starting his pitching career. From Hartsville High, he went to Carlisle Prep School in Bamberg, South Carolina.[6]

Newsom began his professional career in 1928 with the Raleigh (North Carolina) Capitals of the Class C Piedmont League. After losing his only five decisions, he went to Greenville in the Class D East Carolina League, where he was 15-6. Newsom's 19-18 record and 3.87 ERA with the 1929 Macon (Georgia) Peaches in the Class B Southern Association led to a late-season call-up to the Brooklyn Dodgers. He made his big-league debut on September 11, 1929, going seven innings in a 4–2 loss at Cincinnati's Redland Field. Four days later, he lasted just two-thirds of an inning in a losing start at Wrigley Field against the pennant-bound Cubs. Newsom got one more opportunity to pitch for Brooklyn, losing in relief to the Philadelphia Phillies. His ERA for the Robins was a hefty 10.61 to go along with his three losses.

Over the next three seasons, Newsom appeared in two games for Brooklyn in 1930 and one game in 1932 with the Cubs. It all came together for him with the Los Angeles Angels of the Pacific Coast League in 1933, where he went 30-11 and posted a 3.18 ERA. Obtained by the St. Louis Browns in the Minor League draft, he was 16-20 with the sixth-place Brownies in 1934, while leading the league in losses and walks. On September 18 he pitched a nine-inning no-hitter against the Boston Red Sox, only to lose, 2–1, on a hit in the tenth inning.

In 1935 Newsom joined the Washington Senators for the first time. On May 7 Washington owner Clark Griffith paid forty thousand dollars for Newsom, despite his 0-6 record with the Browns. Buck had a 28-27 record with the 1935–36 Senators, and he was 3-4 in 1937 when he was traded to the Red Sox on June 11. Despite winning thirteen games for Boston in just over half a season, the Red Sox traded him to the Browns that winter.

Newsom won twenty and lost sixteen, with a 5.07 ERA for the 1938 Browns, while leading the league in innings pitched, games started, and complete games. He was only the second Major League pitcher to win twenty games with an ERA over 5.00.[7] Newsom repeated as a twenty-game winner in 1939. He was 3-1 for St. Louis and 17-10 fol-

lowing a May 13 trade to the Detroit Tigers. The following season the Tigers won the pennant by one game over the Cleveland Indians. Bobo had the best year of his career, going 21-5 with an ERA of 2.83.

But tragedy struck Newsom after he defeated Cincinnati, 7–2, in the first game of the 1940 World Series. His beloved father had a heart attack after watching his son pitch, reportedly for only the second time, and died the next morning in his Cincinnati hotel room.[8] While his family began the solemn trip back to Hartsville, Newsom remained behind and pitched Game Five, shutting out the Reds, 8–0, on just three hits. With the Series tied at 3–3, Bobo pitched the final game, on one day's rest, but lost, 2–1, to Paul Derringer.

In 1941 Bobo arrived at spring training at Lakeland, Florida, in a flashy new car that had a horn playing "Hold That Tiger" and a sign that flashed "Bobo." But the '41 season was not as good for the Tigers as the previous one. Hank Greenberg was in the army, and the offense scored two hundred fewer runs than they did in 1940. Bobo won only twelve while losing twenty.

Newsom's 1941 salary was $45,000, so he was very unhappy to receive a contract that called for a $22,500 cut in pay from Tigers general manager Jack Zeller. That same year, 1941, Commissioner Kenesaw M. Landis had freed ninety-one Minor Leaguers from the Tigers' farm system because of illegal dealings by the front office. Newsom said to the bald Zeller, "Hell, Curly, you lost ninety players and I don't see you taking no pay cut."[9] Zeller sold Bobo to the Senators before the 1942 season began, and in August Washington sold him to the Dodgers.

Dodger president Branch Rickey traded Newsom to the Browns after the Durocher fracas, and before the 1943 season ended, he was back with Washington again. Traded to Philadelphia in December, he went a combined 21-35 for the Athletics in 1944 and 1945. He was released in June

1946 and immediately went back to Washington. On July 11, 1947, the Yankees purchased Newsom's contract from the Senators; he won seven games with a 2.80 ERA for the pennant-bound New Yorkers.

Bobo started Game Three of the World Series against Brooklyn, but he lasted only 1⅔ innings and took the loss. Newsom made his last World Series appearance in Game Six, pitching ⅔ of an inning of scoreless relief. The winning Yankees awarded him only a three-quarter share of the World Series money. When he went to a jeweler to get his ring made, he said, "Just make it three-quarters size, that's all I'm worth in this city."

After the Yankees released him, Newsom signed with the New York Giants in April 1948. Released again in June, he played three years in the Class Double-A Southern Association, posting a 46-40 record in 102 games. Back in the Majors in 1951, at the age of forty-four, he made his final stop with the Senators, lasting 10 games before being traded to the Athletics. Retirement finally came in 1953 at the age of forty-six.

Newsom's marriage to Bessie Lucille (Arant) Newsom in Chesterfield, South Carolina, on February 17, 1927, ended in divorce. The couple had two children, Norma Jean and Alan. Newsom was married for a second time to Kay Griffiths. Kay was born Ruth Griffith. She had adopted the stage name Kay when Newsom met her singing at the Wardman Park Hotel in Washington DC.

In 1948 Newsom bought and ran a drive-in diner, complete with girl carhops on roller skates. He eventually retired to Winter Park, Florida. He died on December 7, 1962, from cirrhosis of the liver in an Orlando sanitarium. His wife, Kay, daughter, Norma Jean Nicolai, and son, Alan, survived him. Newsom was buried in Magnolia Cemetery in his hometown of Hartsville.[10]

Chapter 39. Bobo in New York

Mike Ross

"'What's the story, Scooter, what's the story?' This is how Bobo always greeted me," recalled the New York Yankees' star shortstop Phil Rizzuto, indicating that Newsom did not call *everybody* Bobo, as the legend has it.[1] As did almost all his legion of teammates over the years, the Yankees loved having Bobo Newsom on board. As a veteran who could still pitch effectively, and one appearing to be back at the top of his game, he brought new life and added wisdom to a team that was already pretty smart. "We really needed someone and everyone was really glad to see him, an established veteran," Rizzuto said.

Even Joe DiMaggio, noted for his aloofness among teammates, accepted Newsom. "I think Joe looked up to [Newsom] as an older and experienced guy," Rizzuto said.[2] A mutual respect may have been fostered during the 1933 season when Newsom beat out DiMaggio for the Pacific Coast League Most Valuable Player Award. Back then Bobo had spoken of young DiMaggio's potential for stardom.[3] Besides, it is likely Joe simply found him amusing and good company; for this reason Newsom was allowed into DiMaggio's well-protected domain in the back room of Toots Shor's high-end New York eatery.

"Bobo was a very warm person, always exuberant and smiling, and a great guy to have around, a true free spirit who loved life," Rizzuto said. "He had a rubber arm and he was a great competitor, a great pitcher. In fact, he was very hard for me to hit with that three-quarter, almost sidearm motion."[4]

Newsom and Vic Raschi joined the Yankees in midseason of 1947 and boosted a pitching staff struck suddenly, it seemed, by an epidemic of sore arms. By the time the two newcomers saw game action with the Yankees, New York had won twelve games of what was to become a nineteen-game winning streak. Bobo contributed wins thirteen and eighteen. (The latter was his two hundredth Major League victory.) He and Raschi combined to win nine straight. The two newcomers carried the Yankees through the first week in August until the team's ten-game lead appeared sufficient for New York to hold on and win the title. "I tell you, it was unbelievable!" Rizzuto said. "Those guys really saved us."[5]

In his first six appearances, Bobo gave up only ten runs in forty-three innings. He finished his Yankees half-season at seven wins and five losses, with an ERA of 2.80. After helping snap the Yankees' four-pennant string (1936–39) with a 21-5 record for Detroit in 1940, Newsom helped end the Yankees' three-year (1944–46) pennant drought in 1947.

When he joined the Yankees Bobo had promised there would be none of the high-profile clowning around universally associated with his persona. After all, the purpose of his deliverance from Washington was not for him to put on a show but to help preserve and extend the Yankees' eight-game lead in the American League pennant race. "Up until now, I've been with teams that needed box-office nonsense. It's all off now," Bobo reasoned. "New York doesn't need my shenanigans to draw the fans."[6] Joining the Yankees also guaranteed a respite from the mischief perpetrated upon him by their infield when he opposed New York. "He was very superstitious," recalled Phil Rizzuto, "so me and [second baseman] Joe Gordon, who was a joker anyway, and [third baseman] Red Rolfe used to sprinkle paper around the mound.

. . . Bobo wouldn't pitch until the umpire got the grounds crew to clear up every bit."[7]

Still, Newsom had changed uniforms but not his spots; he remained the Bobo that Larry MacPhail had bought in 1942 for Brooklyn and had again in 1947 with New York. After Newsom's debut pitching assignment in Chicago against the White Sox, one chauvinistic New York scribe presumed that simply being with the Yankees made Newsom greater: "Newsom was resplendent in his size 50 uniform. Convoyed by that irresistible Yankee force, he pitched a brilliant 5-hitter. But Newsom is still the clown. He just cannot suppress the impulse."[8]

Jimmy Dykes, the White Sox manager, was an unwitting accomplice to Newsom's comic relapse, no doubt taking advantage of the sweltering on-field temperatures and hoping to wear him down. After bouncing the ball back to pitcher Joe Haynes, Bobo headed to the dugout instead of running to first. Dykes shouted to his pitcher, "Make him run it out!" so a smiling Haynes held onto the ball. Then, as Haynes was getting ready to face Snuffy Stirnweiss, Newsom bolted from the dugout in a dash for the bag. Haynes got the ball to first baseman Rudy York just in time to retire Newsom.[9]

After the Yankees won the first two games of the 1947 World Series, Newsom was to start Game Three at Ebbets Field. A win would give the Yankees a three-games-to-none edge, a lead never overcome in the history of the World Series. It would also give Newsom some revenge for Brooklyn general manager Branch Rickey's shocking midseason sacking of him in 1943. The Dodgers would be on the verge of annihilation, but Newsom failed to carry the day, giving up five runs in 1⅔ innings. He seemed to sense his own defeat. Bobo's pregame behavior was uncharacteristic for the guy who was always smiling, always up. Pee Wee Reese spotted Bobo's delicate condition. "Things weren't right that day," Reese said later. "There was something unusual about him. Usually when he saw me he said, 'Hello Bobo,' but on that day he just said,

'Mornin' Pee Wee, how's the wife and kids?' He wasn't himself, not the cocksure character he usually was. He just said, 'Bobo is hoping, Bobo is hoping.'"[10] But Newsom was soundly bombed out of the game and took the loss.

One New York newsman wrote, "Newsom is still capable of helping a team to a pennant, but no longer can he command the great performance."[11] By contrast, another scribe wrote in 1949, after Newsom had returned to the Minor Leagues, "There was never a time in his career when Bobo could not win at the highest level of the game."[12]

Newsom's defeat notwithstanding, the Yankees beat the Dodgers in seven games. As the Yankees' victory celebration got into full swing at Manhattan's Biltmore Hotel, MacPhail, who had earlier that day told reporters he had offered his resignation, approached a concerned Bobo, who, amid rumors and the hullabaloo surrounding MacPhail's announcement, feared for his future as a Yankee. MacPhail put his arm around Bobo's shoulder and said, "Don't worry, my boy, I'm not going anywhere and as long as I'm here, you got a job with this club."[13]

But co-owners Dan Topping and Del Webb called MacPhail's bluff and accepted his resignation. MacPhail resigned from the Dodgers after the 1942 season, and one result was Bobo's departure from Brooklyn. MacPhail departed New York with similar results for Newsom. Perhaps the deepest cut for Bobo was that his teammates voted him only a three-quarters share of the players' World Series money.

Newsom, at the mercy of Topping and Webb, sealed his own doom. He bargained until February 1948 for a pay raise but failed to impress his new bosses. Phil Rizzuto expressed sympathy: "You can't blame him for wanting more money, he had a great season for us."[14] But as of February 6, 1948, Bobo was a free man again; any club could buy his contract for a dollar. HE'S 'ONE BUCK' NEWSOM NOW AS YANKEES RELEASE HIM, the headline in the *Detroit News* cruelly joked.

Chapter 40. The Yankees' Nineteen-Game Winning Streak

Brendan Bingham

Fans of the New York Yankees awoke on June 29, 1947, with their team in first place in the American League with a 39-25 record. Striving to return to the World Series for the first time in four seasons, the team, under the direction of manager Bucky Harris, held a 3½-game lead over the Boston Red Sox. The third-place Cleveland Indians were 6½ back; the Philadelphia Athletics and Detroit Tigers were each 7 games off the pace.

On the Yankees' schedule that Sunday afternoon was a doubleheader in Griffith Stadium against the Washington Senators. The Yankees sent rookie Karl Drews to the mound against the Senators' ace Early Wynn in the first game, and experience held to form. Wynn pitched like the 300-game winner he would become, allowing just one run on five hits. Drews pitched well in pursuit of what would have been just his third career victory, allowing one earned run in 7 innings, but he could not overcome two unearned runs that resulted from a Snuffy Stirnweiss error. Washington won the game 5–1.

At the time the loss seemed unremarkable. It appeared to be just another step in the 154-game journey from spring to fall, unremarkable except that it would be the team's last loss for nearly three weeks. The second game of the doubleheader began a streak that would not be snapped until the Yankees had set a team record and tied the forty-one-year-old American League mark for consecutive wins.

Game Two was a 3–1 win for the Yankees. Another rookie, Don Johnson, started for New York, but when he faltered in the sixth inning, Allie Reynolds, who had started in Philadelphia only three days earlier, came out of the bullpen to throw 3⅔ scoreless innings.

From Washington the Yankees traveled to Boston for a single game, a 3–1 win that came on the strength of a first-inning two-run triple by Joe DiMaggio. Spec Shea tossed a complete-game four-hitter, earning the rookie pitcher his tenth victory against only two defeats.

A six-game home stand followed in which the Yankees hosted the Senators and the Philadelphia Athletics. The New Yorkers swept Washington by scores of 8–1, 7–3, and 4–2. The last of those games was a tight one. New York trailed in the bottom of the seventh, but pinch hitter Bobby Brown delivered a two-run game-tying single, and an inning later the Yankees earned the win by scoring two runs on hits by DiMaggio, Yogi Berra, and Phil Rizzuto.

Completing the home stand, the Yankees swept the Athletics by scores of 5–1, 8–2, and 9–2, which brought New York to the All-Star break with a record of forty-seven wins and twenty-six losses and a lead of eight games over Detroit and Boston. It was at this point that the streak became newsworthy.[1] With eight straight wins, the Yankees had tied Boston for the longest winning streak of the season.

Reynolds, Shea, and Spud Chandler were a strong threesome of starting pitchers for the Yankees during the first half of the 1947 season. Johnson and Bill Bevens rounded out the rotation, with others on the staff occasionally contributing starts. Shea, Chandler, and reliever Joe Page were among the Yankees honored with selection to the All-Star team, with Shea earning the victory over the National Leaguers and Page collecting the retroactive save.

After the All-Star break, the New Yorkers embarked on an extended road trip. In the days before any city west of St. Louis had secured a Major League franchise, the so-called western swing took the Yankees to St. Louis, Chicago, Cleveland, and Detroit.

The opener in St. Louis was a narrow New York victory. Chandler, who had made a habit of pitching complete games, produced an uncharacteristically weak outing, giving up ten hits in 6⅓ innings. With the game tied, 3–3, Page came in and gave a doubly heroic performance. Not only did he complete the game by pitching 2⅔ scoreless innings, but in the top of the ninth he blasted a Nelson Potter pitch over the right-center-field fence for the game-winning home run. As it turned out, Chandler was injured. The eleven-year veteran would not start another game until September and would not return to the Major Leagues after off-season elbow surgery.[2]

The remaining 3 games in St. Louis were not as close. The Yankees won on a Reynolds six-hitter, 3–1, then swept a doubleheader by scores of 12–2 and 8–5. The offensive outbreak was well timed, as the Yankees' starting pitching struggled in both games of the twin bill. In the opener Shea could manage only one inning on the mound before withdrawing with arm stiffness. Butch Wensloff completed the game in relief. In the nightcap Bevens "staggered through four innings," as sportswriter James Dawson put it, before being lifted for a pinch hitter.[3] Drews and Page pitched well out of the bullpen, earning the win and save, respectively.

The performance by Bevens continued a trend that had seen him lose eight of nine decisions since May 3. The thirty-year-old Bevens had been, by contrast, a solid starter for New York the previous two seasons. Despite serious concerns about three of their starting pitchers, the Yankees ended the day with a winning streak that stood at 12 games and with a 9½-game lead.

A doubleheader in Chicago followed, and the Yankees sought to adjust to their starting-pitching woes by sending two newly acquired hurlers to the hill. Bobo Newsom pitched the opener only two days after having been purchased from the Senators. One month shy of his fortieth birthday, the well-traveled veteran came through with a five-hit complete game in the Yankees' 10–3 win.

Vic Raschi, also with the team only two days since being recalled from Portland of the Pacific Coast League, started the nightcap. Raschi pitched six strong innings before fading in the seventh; Page and Reynolds finished the Yankees' 6–4 win. Raschi's solid starting effort foreshadowed the role he would play for the team for some years to come. The twenty-eight-year-old had very little Major League experience to that point, but he would continue as a high-performing starter for the balance of the season and remain an anchor of the New York rotation through the 1953 season.

New York's hitting stars that Sunday in Chicago were Billy Johnson (five hits in the first game), Tommy Henrich (three hits in each game), and Rizzuto (four hits for the day, including a grand slam in the opener). The Yankees' pitching staff got a welcome rest the next day when their contest in Chicago was rained out.

While the Yankees' starting rotation was in a state of uncertainty, the position players Harris used were practically invariant. The infield starters for every game of the streak, and most games of the season, were George McQuinn at first base, Stirnweiss at second, Billy Johnson at third, and Rizzuto at shortstop. Similarly, Johnny Lindell, DiMaggio, and Henrich were steady starters in the outfield, although Lindell's opportunity came as a result of a back injury suffered by Charlie Keller earlier in the season.[4] Only the catcher's position changed regularly, as Berra and Aaron Robinson mostly shared the role, with an occasional start going to Ralph Houk.

With the Yankees having won fourteen in a

row, the team record sixteen-game winning streak was in sight, as was the league record of nineteen.[5] The opportunity to break one and equal the other came in a three-day five-game series in Cleveland.

Reynolds pitched the opener of the Tuesday twin bill and was not at his best. He allowed four runs on ten hits, but he went the distance for the fourth time during the streak. The outcome of the game was in little doubt, as the Yankees put up nine runs, including solo homers by McQuinn and DiMaggio.

The second game was a low-scoring affair that the Yankees won late. Bevens returned to winning form by outdueling future Hall of Famer Bob Feller. The decisive run in the Yankees' 2–1 win came in the top of the ninth when Billy Johnson's two-out triple scored DiMaggio.

The team record of sixteen straight wins had been matched, a noteworthy accomplishment given the long shadow cast by the Yankees greats of the 1920s who had forged that record. Louis Effrat put the feat in perspective:

Maybe the Yankees of 1947 are not quite as great as the Yankees of 1926. Maybe the current edition does not quite measure up to the Yankees of Ruth and Gehrig and Pennock and Shawkey. This is hardly the time to weigh their respective merits. Suffice to report that the New Yorkers tonight matched that 1926 aggregation's 16-game winning streak by defeating the Indians, 9–4 and 2–1, in a twilight-night double-header.

Nor can the men under Bucky Harris' command be accused of picking a soft one for their sixteenth straight victim. Rather, it was against one of the all-time greats, Bob Feller, that the New Yorkers, in a dramatic finish, achieved their latest success.[6]

The middle game of the Cleveland series was an 8–2 New York win. The team's first four batters produced hits, including a home run by Hen-rich, giving the Yankees a three-run lead before Cleveland could record an out. Wensloff pitched ably for five innings before relievers Drews and Page finished the game. With the win, Harris's Yankees had set the team record for consecutive wins. Again, recognition in the press came with a mix of celebration of the current accomplishment and deference to the team's history. John Drebinger wrote: "The Yankees of 1947 have just bettered the consecutive string of victories which those other Yanks of incredible deeds set a score of years ago. . . . However, when the Yanks of '47 surpassed the mark of their illustrious predecessors, it at least proved that what has been done once can be improved upon regardless of the fact that the first breathless record was written by such immortals as Babe Ruth, Lou Gehrig, Bob Meusel and Tony Lazzeri."[7]

The American League–record winning streak was held by the "Hitless Wonders," the 1906 Chicago White Sox who won the pennant and the World Series despite their .230 team batting average. A Yankees sweep of the July 17 doubleheader in Cleveland would equal the record. McQuinn was the hitting star in the opener, with a home run in the fourth inning providing two runs toward the Yankees' 3–1 victory. Newsom pitched the complete game, further proving his worth as a midseason acquisition. The victory was his second as a Yankee and the two hundredth of his career.

In the second game of the day, a barrage of singles in the early innings brought the Yankees a 5–0 lead. They cruised to the 7–2 victory behind Raschi's six-hit pitching. The streak that began in Washington in late June had grown to equal the 1906 White Sox' mark.

The Yankees' lead in the pennant race had widened to 11½ games. The second-place Tigers had played well since late June, and Detroit would be the setting for the New Yorkers' chance to break the league-record winning streak. A winning streak could not have met a more decisive end than the one that befell the Yankees' nineteen-game streak in the Motor City, however. Detroit starter Fred Hutchinson pitched one of the best games of his career, a two-hit, no-walk complete-game shutout. Meanwhile, the bats of George Kell, Vic Wertz, Eddie Mayo, and company pounded Randy Gumpert and Karl Drews for eight runs on eighteen hits. The streak was over, but New York's nineteen straight wins had all but ended the 1947 American League pennant race. The Yankees had stretched their slender late-June lead to an almost insurmountable mid-July margin. Not only would New York remain in first place for the remainder of the season, but its lead would only briefly drop below ten games.

Team accomplishments emerge from individual contributions. The Yankees batted .292 as a team during the streak. Not surprisingly, DiMaggio led the attack, but he was not alone in providing offensive firepower. None of New York's starters was slumping during the streak; only Lindell posted a batting average during the nineteen games that was substantially below his season and career marks.

The team ERA was a superb 2.00 for the streak, and no fewer than eleven pitchers earned victories, led by Reynolds with four complete-game wins and two critical relief outings. All Yankee pitchers outperformed their season and career ERA marks, except Chandler, who at 2.94 was only slightly above.

Viewed from the distance of more than six decades, the 1947 Yankees' winning streak remains a monumental accomplishment. Of note, the streak was achieved mostly on the road and included six sweeps of doubleheaders. The American League record for consecutive wins would not fall until the Oakland Athletics won twenty straight in 2002, and meanwhile no team has approached the Major League mark of twenty-six straight set by the New York Giants in 1916. Nonetheless, any baseball team in any era would be thrilled to put together the kind of run that the Yankees did in June and July 1947, when they combined consistent hitting, superb pitching, and timely roster moves to amass nineteen consecutive victories.

Chapter 41. Timeline, July 22–August 7

Lyle Spatz

Tuesday, July 22, vs. St. Louis — Bobo Newsom shut out the Browns, 6–0, in his home debut. Newsom allowed just three hits and walked one. Tommy Henrich had three hits, and Phil Rizzuto had two doubles for the Yankees. Second baseman Hank Thompson and right fielder Willard Brown were in the Browns' lineup, becoming the first African Americans to play in an American League game at Yankee Stadium. Detroit's loss to Washington raised the Yankees' lead to a season-high 10½ games. 60-29-1, First, 10½ games ahead.

Wednesday, July 23, vs. St. Louis — The pitching of Ellis Kinder, a first-inning two-run homer by Jeff Heath, and four singles and three runs batted in by Willard Brown highlighted the Browns' 8–2 win. Yankees starter Frank Shea had to leave in the third inning with a sore arm. Joe DiMaggio had a triple to extend his hitting streak to 11 games. The Yankees got the news that Charlie Keller's return to action this season was doubtful. 60-30-1, First, 10½ games ahead.

Thursday, July 24, vs. St. Louis — A seven-run second inning helped New York to a 14–5 win over St. Louis. The Yankees, who were making a shambles of the American League pennant race, had twenty hits, including home runs by Tommy Henrich, Johnny Lindell, and George McQuinn. Henrich, Joe DiMaggio, Yogi Berra, and Lindell each had three hits. Vic Raschi went all the way for his third consecutive victory. Jeff Heath hit two home runs for the Browns, raising his season's total to nineteen and tying him with Ted Williams for the American League lead. 61-30-1, First, 11½ games ahead.

Friday, July 25, vs. Chicago — The Yankees scored three runs in the first inning and led 9–0 after six on their way to a 12–4 win over the White Sox. Yogi Berra, recently moved into the third spot in the batting order, had a two-run home run in the first inning. George McQuinn had three hits, and Joe DiMaggio's third-inning single extended his hitting streak to 13 games. Though he weakened some in the late innings, Allie Reynolds pitched a complete game for the win. 62-30-1, First, 11½ games ahead.

Saturday, July 26, vs. Chicago — Eddie Lopat pitched a three-hitter and singled in the tying run, as Chicago edged Bill Bevens and the Yankees, 2–1. The Yankees' only run came on Tommy Henrich's fourth-inning home run. Joe DiMaggio went hitless, ending his consecutive-game hitting streak at thirteen. 62-31-1, First, 10½ games ahead.

Sunday, July 27, vs. Chicago (2) — The Yankees pounded Red Ruffing in his return to Yankee Stadium, defeating their old teammate 7–4 in the opener. Bobo Newsom won for the Yanks with 3⅔ innings of relief help from Joe Page. Phil Rizzuto had a triple and three runs batted in. Chicago took the second game, 5–4, scoring the winning run off Page in the ninth inning. Joe DiMaggio, Johnny Lindell, and Yogi Berra homered in the loss. The split, combined with Boston's sweep of the Browns, dropped New York's lead over the Red Sox to 9½ games. 63-32-1, First, 9½ games ahead.

Monday, July 28, vs. Detroit — For the fourth time this season the Yankees defeated Detroit's ace

158

left-hander Hal Newhouser. Vic Raschi allowed the Tigers just six hits and an eighth-inning run in New York's 5–1 victory. Tommy Henrich had three hits and two runs scored, and Johnny Lindell hit a home run for the winners. 64-32-1, First, 10 games ahead.

Tuesday, July 29 — Not scheduled. 64-32-1, First, 10½ games ahead.

Wednesday, July 30, vs. Detroit — Yogi Berra's grand slam off Dizzy Trout powered the Yankees to an 8–5 win over the Tigers. Berra's blast came in a five-run third inning after Detroit had taken an early 3–0 lead against Allie Reynolds. Joe Page pitched 5⅓ innings in relief of Reynolds to gain the win. Phil Rizzuto had three hits, including a home run. Boston's loss to Cleveland raised the Yankees' lead to 11½ games. 65-32-1, First, 11½ games ahead.

Thursday, July 31, vs. Detroit — Rained out. 65-32-1, First, 12 games ahead.

Friday, August 1, vs. Cleveland — The Indians scored a ninth-inning run to defeat the Yankees, 4–3, ending a streak of nine straight losses to New York. The Yanks loaded the bases with one out in the last of the ninth but could not score against Bryan Stephens. Red Embree, the second of four Cleveland pitchers, was the winner. Joe Page, in relief of starter Bill Bevens, was the loser. George McQuinn led New York with three hits. 65-33-1, First, 12 games ahead.

Saturday, August 2, vs. Cleveland (2) — The biggest daytime crowd of the season at Yankee Stadium (62,537) saw the home team sweep a doubleheader from Cleveland. The Yanks won the opener, 3–2, in fourteen innings, and the nightcap, 3–0, in a game called after eight innings because of darkness. Bob Feller pitched twelve

innings and Bobo Newsom nine in the first game. The win went to Karl Drews and the loss to Steve Gromek. George Stirnweiss, Tommy Henrich, and Joe DiMaggio had two hits for New York, while George Metkovich had three for the Indians. Vic Raschi pitched the game-two shutout. His three-hitter raised his record to 5-0 since being recalled in mid-July. Billy Johnson had two hits, including a home run. 67-33-1, First, 12½ games ahead.

Sunday, August 3, vs. Cleveland — After New York scored four runs in the first inning off Don Black, the Indians, with home runs by Joe Gordon and George Metkovich, rallied to tie the score at 4–4 after seven. Bryan Stephens, who replaced Black in the first inning, held the Yankees scoreless until the ninth, when he was replaced by Ed Klieman with the bases loaded and one out. Yogi Berra's fly ball to center fielder Bob Lemon was deep enough to score Bobby Brown and give the Yanks a 5–4 win. Allie Reynolds pitched a complete game for his thirteenth win. After the game the Yankees announced they were bringing Allie Clark up from Newark and sending Frank Colman to the Bears. 68-33-1, First, 13½ games ahead.

Monday, August 4, vs. Philadelphia — The Athletics got fourteen hits in pounding the Yankees, 9–5. New York used Randy Gumpert, Don Johnson, Karl Drews, and Joe Page, with Johnson taking the loss. Carl Sheib, in relief of Bill Dietrich, was the winner. Sam Chapman had three hits and three runs batted in for Philadelphia. George Stirnweiss had three hits for New York. The Yankees announced they had sold pitcher Al Lyons to the Pittsburgh Pirates. 68-34-1, First, 13 games ahead.

Tuesday, August 5, at Philadelphia — The Yankees rallied for four runs in the top of the ninth inning to beat the A's, 8–5. New York's lead was now fourteen games over the second-place Red Sox, their largest lead of the season. The Yanks had fourteen hits, including three more by George Stirnweiss. Allie Clark, making his debut filling in for the injured Joe DiMaggio, had a single during the ninth-inning rally. Bill Bevens started for the Yanks, but Allie Reynolds got the win. Bob Savage, in relief of starter Joe Coleman, was the loser. 69-34-1, First, 14 games ahead.

Wednesday, August 6, at Philadelphia — After winning four straight, Bobo Newsom suffered his first defeat as a Yankee. Newsom went seven innings in New York's 5–3 loss at Philadelphia. Rookie Bill McCahan went the distance for the A's. Billy Johnson and Allie Clark homered for the Yankees, Clark's first Major League home run. 69-35-1, First, 13 games ahead.

Thursday, August 7 — Not scheduled. 69-35-1, First, 13 games ahead.

Chapter 42. **Johnny Lindell**

Rob Neyer

AGE	G	AB	R	H	2B	3B	HR	TB	RBI	BB	SO	BAV	OBP	SLG	SB	GDP	HBP
30	127	476	66	131	18	7	11	196	67	32	70	.275	.322	.412	1	15	1

John Harlan Lindell Jr., who reinvented himself as a pitcher after a decade as a Major League outfielder, was born in Greeley, Colorado, on August 30, 1916. He was the only child of John Harlan Oliver Lindell and Laura Lucille (Evans) Lindell. The family moved to Southern California in 1925, and John attended high school there. He reportedly spent five months at the University of Southern California on a track and football scholarship, before being discovered and signed by New York Yankees scout Bill Essick.[1]

Lindell began his professional career in 1936 as a pitcher with the Yankees' Joplin, Missouri, farm club in the Class C Western Association, where he went 17-8. Two years later Lindell was in the high Minors and over the course of four seasons pitched in the Pacific Coast League with Oakland, the International League with Newark, and the American Association with Kansas City. In 1940, his second season in Kansas City, he went 18-7 with a 2.70 ERA.

Lindell broke camp with the Yankees the next spring but appeared in just one regular-season game — pinch-hitting on April 18 — before getting sent to Newark. In 1941, his only full season with the Bears, the Yankees' top farm club, he went 23-4 with a league-leading 2.05 earned run average, plus three more victories in the playoffs. For those feats, the *Sporting News* named Lindell Minor League Player of the Year.[2]

When he reported to spring training in 1942, Lindell was widely expected to win a job on the big-league staff, particularly with the military draft beginning to take its toll on the Yankees' roster. Shortly after signing his 1942 contract, Lin-

Johnny Lindell went 9 for 18 in the World Series and led the Yankees with seven runs batted in.

dell said, "Last spring when I was here I had only a fair curve and my natural sinker have improved all around, especially on control. And I have picked up a slider."[3] A few weeks later Yankees manager Joe McCarthy announced that Lindell would indeed make the opening-day roster.[4]

What Lindell would not do is crack the Yankees' rotation. He lost that job to (among others)

Johnny Lindell is out on a fifth-inning ground ball to Pee Wee Reese in Game Five of the 1947 World Series at Brooklyn. Jackie Robinson is the first baseman, and Babe Pinelli is the umpire.

Hank Borowy, one of his Newark teammates in 1941. Lindell instead pitched most often in games already decided and did not pick up his first decision until the second game of a doubleheader on the last day of June, when he pitched 2⅔ innings of shutout relief and knocked in the winning run in the top of the ninth inning to beat the Philadelphia Athletics, 4–3.

A month later sportswriter Dan Daniel reviewed the spring's top pitching prospects and found Lindell a serious disappointment: "Lindell came up from the Newark farm team last spring with the flamboyant and promising label, 'No. 1 player of all the minor leagues.' For the Bears he had piled up the majestic total of 26 [sic] victories. From a lofty pinnacle Lindell looked down on Hank Borowy, Virgil Trucks and Hal White, fellow products of the International League. . . . But the Lindell fastball no longer is in evidence, the Lindell curve hangs high temptation before the batters and they're getting ready to engrave 'John Harlan Lindell' on that pewter mug."[5]

Lindell finished the 1942 season with two wins, one loss, and a 3.76 ERA in 52⅔ innings; he did not appear in the Yankees' World Series loss to the St. Louis Cardinals that fall.

ROB NEYER

With so many Yankees going into the service in 1943, Lindell might have expected another shot at breaking into the rotation that spring. But McCarthy apparently had already given up on him as a pitcher. According to columnist Joe Williams, Lindell's "small, stubby fingers" limited his speed, leaving him to get by with "tricky stuff, sliders and such. That's what Lindell was winning with in the minors; it wasn't good enough in the majors."[6]

Lindell had not hit much with the Yankees in his limited 1942 opportunities, but apparently he had looked better than his .250 batting average would indicate. After the season he had worked out at first base, and in the spring of 1943 McCarthy said, "I know he can hit, but I don't know if he can hit playing every day."[7]

Nevertheless, with 1942 regulars Joe DiMaggio and Tommy Henrich in the service, McCarthy made Lindell an outfielder. It was a successful transition, as Lindell got off to a fast start, made the All-Star team, and led the American League with a dozen triples.

The 1943 World Series was a rematch of 1942, and this time Lindell played a key role, despite collecting just one hit in four games. In Game Three, with the Yankees down 2–1 in the eighth inning, Lindell led off with a single and moved to second on the center fielder's error. Snuffy Stirnweiss laid down a bunt, and St. Louis first baseman Ray Sanders threw to third trying to nab Lindell. Standing six feet four and weighing around 220 pounds, Lindell barreled into third baseman Whitey Kurowski, knocking Kurowski down and the ball from his glove. The Yankees now had two on and nobody out and eventually scored five runs in the inning on their way to a 6–2 victory. They also won Games Four and Five, and the Series.

In 1944 the Yankees' roster—like every other Major League roster—was further depleted by the draft. Lindell remained and not coincidentally enjoyed the best season of his career. He led the American League in total bases and triples; was third in home runs, RBIS, and slugging percentage; and was fourth in hits.

Regarding the draft, Lindell had been classified 2-B because of his off-season job as a shipyard worker back in California. Later there was some suggestion that an old head injury—the result of a beaning, or perhaps high school football action—might keep him from passing the physical. But after a postseason 1944 USO tour that took him and four other baseball personalities to the South Pacific, Lindell was classified 1-A. And after playing in forty-one games for the Yankees in the spring of 1945, he was ordered to report for induction on June 8. He spent the rest of the year in the army.

Of course, everything changed in 1946. With DiMaggio, Henrich, and Charlie Keller all back from the service, the outfield was exceptionally well stocked. Lindell's other position, first base, was manned by Nick Etten, who had knocked in 111 runs in 1945. Etten got off to a slow start, and there was talk about replacing him with Lindell. Though Etten never really did hit much in 1946 (or afterward), most of Lindell's action came in the outfield, spelling the three regulars.

Lindell played much more in 1947, mainly because of Keller's chronic back problems. He went 9 for 18 in the World Series and led the Yankees with seven runs batted in as the Bronx Bombers defeated the Brooklyn Dodgers in seven games.

According to David Halberstam in *Summer of '49*, by the late 1940s "Lindell was the team rogue. He was exuberant, generous, and crude, and his humor seemed to dominate the locker room. . . . Even DiMaggio was vulnerable."

His teasing was generally good-natured, however, and he was generous with the younger players. When the team arrived in New York, he would take them to his favorite hangouts near the Stadium, including one where the specialty of the house was something called "The Lindell Bomber." "Try one, you're going to love it," he told the young Charlie Silvera. . . . It turned out to be the biggest martini anyone had ever seen—as big as a birdbath. He was the bane of management because his off-field activities were so outrageous. He liked to boast about how much money [Yankees general manager] George Weiss had spent putting private detectives on him.

With Keller healthier in 1948 and the Yankees adding Yogi Berra to the outfield mix, Lindell was just a part-timer for the third-place Yankees. Yet he hit well when he did play. His playing time fell still further in 1949, and this time his numbers fell as well. Late in the season, though, Lindell enjoyed his single biggest moment as a Yankee.

On the last Saturday of the season, the Boston Red Sox arrived in the Bronx for a two-game series that would decide the pennant. Boston led New York by one game in the standings, so there would be no tie; if the Yanks did not win both games, they were out.

The Red Sox jumped to an early lead, but the Yankees bounced back and the score was 4–4 into the bottom of the eighth inning. With Red Sox right-hander Joe Dobson on the mound, Casey Stengel sent two left-handed pinch hitters to face Dobson, who retired them both. The right-handed-hitting Lindell, who was in the starting lineup only because the Red Sox started left-hander Mel Parnell, was due next; he had collected two hits in the game already, and Stengel did not make a move, even though the lefty-hitting Charlie Keller was available on the bench. Lindell rewarded his manager's confidence by driving a high fastball into the left-field seats to give the Yankees a 5–4 lead they would not relinquish; it was just his sixth home run of the season and his first since July.

Lindell started again in the season finale, which would decide the pennant. His single in the eighth started a two-out rally that proved deci-

sive. Though the Red Sox scored three runs in the ninth, the Yankees won 5–3.

Ever since 1946, with so many of the Yankees' prewar stars returning from the service, there had been rumors and suggestions regarding Lindell's relative worth to the Yankees and to other clubs; surely, the arguments went, the Yankees' fourth outfielder could be a starter for a lot of teams. Though there was interest in Lindell, the Yankees had the luxury of hanging on to him as long as he could hit.

In the spring of 1950, Lindell did not hit. Keller was gone and Henrich was old, but now the Yankees had Gene Woodling, Hank Bauer, and Cliff Mapes fighting for time in the outfield. When the thirty-three-year-old Lindell went 4 for 25 in his first seven games, management finally deemed him expendable, selling him to the Cardinals in the middle of May. Lindell sounded thrilled at the trade in his comments to the newspapers. "Every day I'd hear new rumors about which club I was going to be sent to soon," he said. "The way I look at it, I got a swell break being sent to a first division club like the Cardinals. Why, I might have been sent to the White Sox, Browns, or Senators!"[8]

But Lindell fared no better in the National League, batting .186 in thirty-six games with St. Louis, and wound up being sent to the Minor Leagues, where he also failed to hit, first with Columbus in the International League, then later in the summer with the Pacific Coast League's Hollywood Stars. In 1951 Lindell bounced back to hit .292 with the Stars . . . but he and his manager actually had something else entirely in mind.

While still playing for the Yankees late in the 1948 season, Lindell had started pitching again. Only on the sidelines, but this time he worked on developing a dependable knuckle ball.[9] So while he did play outfield and first base with Hollywood in 1951, he also pitched in twenty-six games. Relying largely on his knuckle ball, Lindell went 12-9 with a 3.03 ERA.

ROB NEYER

Lindell returned to Hollywood in 1952, this time primarily as a pitcher. He was a sensation, going 24-9 with a 2.52 ERA and earning Most Valuable Player honors in the Pacific Coast League. Shortly after the Stars captured the PCL championship, Lindell's contract was purchased by the Pittsburgh Pirates.

In training camp with the Pirates in the spring of 1953, the thirty-six-year-old Lindell gave a great deal of credit for his comeback to Hollywood manager Fred Haney and Stars catcher Mike Sandlock, both of whom had also joined the Pirates. "He helped me greatly," Lindell said of Sandlock. "It was he who nursed me along, gave me encouragement and acted as my tutor and counselor. My luckiest break, next to coming back to the big leagues, was when Haney and Sandlock were brought up to the Pirates with me."[10]

About his pitching style, Lindell observed, "I'm no great shucks as a pitcher, really. About all I possess is a knuckleball, I have a dinky slider and a straight ball. No curve whatsoever. I throw the knuckleball about 85 percent of the time. It's a pretty difficult pitch to hit except that half the time I can't get it over the plate."[11]

Lindell's assessment was accurate. Hurling for Haney's Pirates and (later) Steve O'Neill's Philadelphia Phillies, Lindell led the National League with 139 walks and 11 wild pitches while going 6-17 with a 4.66 earned run average. He fared little better the next spring with the Phillies, who released him on May 10.

That summer Lindell tried to find work in the Pacific Coast League again, but his "dead arm" just would not come around. The previous winter he had been a guest instructor at 7-Up's baseball clinic, held at Hollywood's Gilmore Field. After admitting he would not pitch again, Lindell took a position as athletic director of the 7-Up Foundation, attending dinners and luncheons, traveling all over Southern California, and generally playing the part of the local hero and former Major League star.[12]

Lindell held that position for the rest of the 1950s. He joined the expansion Los Angeles Angels in 1961, serving for most of the decade as head of the franchise's speakers' bureau.

In 1985 Lindell died of lung cancer in a Long Beach, California, hospital, three days before his sixty-ninth birthday. He left behind his wife, the former Esther Kent, whom he had married in 1938, and two children, Teresa and John Harlan Lindell III.

Chapter 43. **Karl Drews**

Peter Mancuso

AGE	W	L	PCT.	ERA	G	GS	GF	CG	SHO	SV	IP	H	BB	SO	HBP	WP
27	6	6	.500	4.91	30	10	9	0	0	1	91.2	92	55	45	5	1

One day in the mid-1930s, in the New York City borough of Staten Island, teenager Karl Drews anxiously watched as older boys of his small community of Eltingville climbed into a truck to go to a baseball team tryout. As the truck was about to depart, Drews pleaded with the older boys to take him along. Showing some compassion for their younger friend, they squeezed him in and headed off to the tryout. When the teenagers returned, the only kid to make the team was the youngest in the bunch, Karl Drews.[1] This was despite not having played structured baseball until he was fifteen years old.[2]

Drews eventually became a Major League pitcher for the New York Yankees, St. Louis Browns, Philadelphia Phillies, and Cincinnati Reds. The six-foot-four, 192-pound right-hander played professional baseball for twenty-one seasons, eight of which were in the Major Leagues.

Karl August Drews was born on Staten Island on February 22, 1920, to Karl and Anna (Theil) Drews. Both parents were born in Germany and had arrived in the United States around the turn of the twentieth century. They were married in January 1918. The father was a dock foreman for a shipping line. By 1925 Karl and Anna had three more children: Walter, Hortense, and Roy. Karl's brothers followed him into professional baseball. Walter, a left-handed pitcher, and Roy, a catcher, both played in the Minor Leagues.

While he was a teenager, Karl's principal weapon was his fastball; then, while catching batting practice before a grammar school alumni game, he broke a finger on his throwing hand and changed his grip on the ball, giving him a potent

Karl Drews was 6-6 with a 4.91 earned run average in 1947, his first full Major League season.

second pitch, a very effective sinker.[3] More than sixty years after they played together as rookies, Yankees catcher Yogi Berra still recalled Drews and that very effective pitch.[4]

Veteran baseball scout George Genovese, who played with and against Drews on Staten Island, said he could throw as hard in his late teens as any top prospect of similar age and in modern times would easily command a signing bonus in the high six figures or more.[5]

At New Dorp High School, Drews played baseball, football, and basketball, but he was best known in the New York City Public Schools Athletic League for his pitching.[6] He starred on his high school team, amateur teams, and the semipro Gulf Oilers. He led Staten Island's team entry to the New York City championship in the *New York Daily Mirror*'s Borough League Tournament.

In the fall of 1938 Drews attended a Yankees tryout camp on Staten Island. Yankee coaches Bill Skiff and Benny Bengough were impressed with Drews and soon offered the high school senior a contract.[7] He signed and headed off that spring to Butler, Pennsylvania, where the Yankees had a farm team in the Class D Pennsylvania State Association. The nineteen-year-old had no trouble in Butler, going 16-5, with a 3.66 ERA in thirty-one games. After the season Drews returned to New Dorp High School to make up the school time he had lost when he was bedridden after a bout with rheumatic fever.

He received his diploma in January 1940 and began a steady climb through the Yankees' Minor League system. From 1940 through 1942 Drews saw duty in Akron, Ohio; Amsterdam, New York; Augusta, Georgia; Evansville, Indiana; and Norfolk, Virginia. In 1943, with the country at war, he attempted to enlist in the military but was medically rejected for a heart murmur that was a result of his rheumatic fever. He spent the year playing on Staten Island and working on the docks with his father.

Drews returned to the Minors in 1944, where he went 14-8 for the Binghamton (New York) Triplets in the Class A Eastern League and 1-3 in five games with the Newark Bears in the International League. In 1945 he finally spent a complete season with one team, Newark, compiling a 19-9 record with a 2.70 earned run average. On June 3 of that year, Drews and Nancy Lindboe, who had

known each other growing up in Eltingville, were married.[8]

After the 1945 season Drews was among thirty-two members of the Yankees' organization who flew to Panama to play for American troops stationed there.[9] Drews went to spring training with the Yankees in 1946, but was sent to the Kansas City Blues of the American Association, where he won fourteen games and lost nine. Called up by the Yankees in September, Drews made his big-league debut on September 8, starting against the Washington Senators. He lasted just two-thirds of an inning, giving up six runs on two hits and four walks. He later made two scoreless appearances, both in relief.

In 1947 Drews went to spring training with the Yankees again. He was now the father of a daughter, Geraldine, born the previous summer. Shortly before spring training ended, he broke a finger in a pepper game.[10] Drews stayed behind when the Yankees headed north, but he was cleared to return to action by team doctors and arrived in Washington for a game against the Senators on April 19. He was one of four pitchers who followed starter Joe Page in the 5–2 loss. Drews gave up a hit and a walk in his brief relief appearance.[11]

In his first full Major League season, Drews had a 6-6 record with a 4.91 earned run average. Four of his six wins were in a relief role, but his best effort of the season was in a start against the Boston Red Sox on August 10 at Fenway Park. Drews pitched 8⅔ innings, allowing only five hits and one run, and striking out nine before being removed because of a finger blister.

Drews pitched in two games of the 1947 World Series, and shortly before the first of those two appearances, he became a father for the second time. About five hours prior to his taking the mound at Brooklyn's Ebbets Field in the third inning of Game Three, Ronald Karl Drews came into the world. After spending a sleepless night, Karl was en route to Brooklyn at 9:10 a.m. when his son was born. By the time he got to the visitors' clubhouse, his teammates were already "whooping it up," as they had already gotten the news by telephone.[12]

The Yankees had won the opening pair of Series games at Yankee Stadium. Now, in Game Three, the Dodgers jumped out in the second inning, scoring six runs off Bobo Newsom and Vic Raschi. After New York got two runs in the top of the third, Drews came in to start the bottom of the inning. Nervous, and tired from lack of sleep, he hit the first batter, Gene Hermanski, who eventually scored. That was it for Drews; Spud Chandler came in for the Yankees to start the fourth.[13]

Drews pitched again in Game Six, at Yankee Stadium. At that point the Yankees led three games to two. He replaced Allie Reynolds with one out in the third and pitched two scoreless innings before being replaced by Joe Page.[14]

In 1948 Drews pitched in nineteen games for the Yankees, only two of which were starts. He won two, lost three, and had a 3.79 ERA. In early August the Yankees sold him to the lowly St. Louis Browns for the waiver fee of ten thousand dollars; he won three, lost two, and posted an 8.05 ERA with St. Louis.

Drews, who preferred to start, got his wish in 1949, with twenty-three starts in thirty-one appearances. He faltered badly, though, with a 4-12 record, the worst in his career, and a dismal 6.64 ERA. After the season the Browns sold his contract to the Baltimore Orioles of the International League for ten thousand dollars. On Memorial Day 1950, pitching against the Syracuse (New York) Chiefs, Drews raced to cover first base on a dribbler to the right side. Second baseman Eddie Pellagrini's off-balance throw was low and wide, forcing Drews to stretch into the baseline, where batter Dutch Mele's knee struck him in the temple.

The bloody gash was thought to have been a spike wound and was stitched. Drews attempted to fight off the dizziness and severe head pain for nearly a week, but eventually was taken to a hospital, where it was discovered that he had suffered a fractured skull. Twelve hours of surgery were needed to remove three bone splinters from his brain and install a silver plate in his head. Drews later recalled:

I lay in that hospital and wondered what was going to happen to me. I figured the accident would finish me as a pitcher, and frankly I didn't care much one way or the other. I wasn't going anywhere or getting any younger. All the time I'd been in the Yankee chain I was a strange kind of guy; I worried about a heart murmur I was supposed to have. I got mean and morose. I was losing my taste for the game.

Then a funny thing happened after the accident. I developed some sort of personality change. . . . I became a different guy off the field and a different one on it.

By late August, nearly three months after his injury, Drews was pitching again, winning six in a row before the season ended. "When I came back to pitch, I found that I couldn't hurry myself," Drews said. "I used to be the type of pitcher who threw to the plate as soon as the catcher got the ball back to me. Because of the operation I couldn't do it; I had to save my strength. Everything I did I had to do slower. . . . When I pitched before and was wild, I'd just keep throwing faster and faster and getting wilder and wilder. Now I took my time. The ball started going where I wanted it to go. It got to be so much fun I even stopped worrying about my heart."[15]

The Orioles' 1951 change in Major League affiliation from the Browns to the reigning National League champion Philadelphia Phillies was a fortuitous one for Drews. Phillies manager Eddie Sawyer had managed Drews in Norfolk eight years earlier. Impressed by the improvement in Drews's control, Sawyer got the Phillies to purchase his contract just before the end of the season.[16] Drews arrived in time to post one win in five appearances. Things got much better in 1952, when he started thirty games, winning fourteen (including two shutouts of the Dodgers) and losing fifteen with a 2.72 earned run average. In 1953, Drews had a 10-11 record, though his earned run average rose to 4.52.

Karl and Nancy Drews had left Staten Island in 1951 and moved their young family to Hollywood, Florida. The family had made a number of trips to Florida for spring training, and Nancy Drews loved the climate. She was a swimming enthusiast and instructor.[17]

The thirty-four-year-old Drews was back in the bullpen in 1954. He made eight appearances for Philadelphia before his contract was sold to the Cincinnati Reds on June 15. With the Reds he got nine starts in twenty-two appearances, going 4-4 with a 6.00 ERA. Drews pitched in his last Major League game on September 20, as the Reds released him at the end of the 1954 season.

Drews threw hard enough and was just wild enough to keep batters on their toes. *New York Post* sportswriter Milton Gross had written in 1953 that teammates did not like it when Drews threw batting practice because they were afraid of his wildness.[18] Earlier, in 1947, Ben Epstein of the *Post* wrote that when Drews had absolute control of his sinker, his teammates could not hit it and grew frustrated in batting practice. Even DiMaggio would not face him, Epstein wrote.

After four middling years in the high Minors, Drews began the 1959 season with the Miami Marlins of the International League but was released after two appearances. Drews, now thirty-nine, landed a spot in the Mexican League with the Mexico City Diablos. He returned to the Diablos in 1960, his final season as a player. His daughter, Geraldine, recalled how her father would write her from the road, making each letter in part a bit of a geography lesson by encouraging her to follow his travels on a map of the United States and Mexico.[19]

After moving to Florida, Drews had a variety of off-season jobs, among them selling cars and working as a lifeguard. Now, with baseball behind him, he could take a more permanent job and had more time for his family, particularly lending support to his children's athletic endeavors. He worked as a regional sales representative in the sporting goods industry.

Three years after Drews settled into his new life, tragedy struck. On August 15, 1963, he was killed by a drunken driver while attempting to wave down passing vehicles for assistance after his car became disabled in Dania, Florida, a short distance from his Hollywood home. Drews had started out in the early morning to drive his daughter, Geraldine, to a swimming meet in Jacksonville.[20]

Drews was just forty-three years old. He left behind his wife of eighteen years, his daughter, Geraldine; and three sons, Ronald, John (born in 1952), and Michael (born in 1954). Drews's widow, Nancy, died in 2010.

Dave Williams

AGE	G	AB	R	H	2B	3B	HR	TB	RBI	BB	SO	BAV	OBP	SLG	SB	GDP	HBP
22	83	293	41	82	15	3	11	136	54	13	12	.280	.310	.464	0	7	0

Many images come to mind when one hears the name Yogi Berra. One of the more obvious is that of a winner. Berra won three American League Most Valuable Player Awards and appeared in fourteen World Series as a player and another five as a manager or a coach. He won thirteen championship rings and holds several Series records. Berra met with numerous roadblocks on his journey to fame, but he overcame them with grit and dedication and went on to become one of the more beloved figures in American sports history.

Berra's father, Pietro, arrived in New York on October 18, 1909, at the age of twenty-three. He had left Robecchetto, Italy, a town about twenty-five miles south of Milan, where he was a tenant farmer. Pietro left behind Paolina Lingori, a young girl whom he planned to marry after earning enough money to pay her way to the United States. Paolina (subsequently, Paulina) arrived on March 10, 1912, aged eighteen. Peter and Paulina married nine days later and settled in a largely Italian section of St. Louis called "the Hill."

Their first child, Anthony, was born in 1914. The second child, Mario, was born in Malvaglio, Italy, as Paulina, pregnant and homesick, went back to her hometown in 1915 for a visit. While she was there, World War I escalated, and mother and child did not return to the United States until September 3, 1919. The Berras had a third son, John, in 1922, and on May 12, 1925, Lorenzo Pietro came into the world. His parents' desire to assimilate in their new homeland led them to the English translation of Lawrence Peter, which, due to their accent, they pronounced Lawdie.

Lawdie Berra and his family lived on 5447 Eliz-

Yogi Berra hit the first pinch-hit home run in World Series history in Game Three of the 1947 Series.

abeth Avenue, across the street from Giovanni Garagiola and his family; they had a boy named Joe who was Lawdie's age. The two youngsters spent most of their time playing games with the other neighborhood boys, and their favorite sport was baseball. Besides sports, the boys loved to go to the movies. One day they watched a feature that had a Hindu fakir, a snake charmer who sat with his legs crossed and wore a turban on his head. When the yogi got up, he waddled, and one of the

Catcher Yogi Berra is flanked by winner Frank Shea and relief ace Joe Page after the Yankees' triumph in Game One of the 1947 World Series.

boys joked that he walked like Lawdie. From then on Berra was known as Yogi. Even his parents called him by his nickname.

As a youngster Berra displayed the stubbornness and determination that carried over to his playing days. This was no more in evidence than when he decided he was going to quit school after the eighth grade. Yogi had never been a very good student, and he felt he was wasting his time in school. Pietro disapproved and enlisted the aid of the school's principal and the local parish priest to help keep his son in school. Yogi held firm, and eventually his father relented and Yogi went to work in a coal yard. He lost the job because he often left work early to play ball with his friends after they got out of school. Pietro, furious his son would lose a job that paid $25 a week, was able to get Yogi a job working on a Pepsi-Cola truck that paid $27 a week. He was fired from that job as well. After much arguing, it was decided Yogi

would find a job that would allow him to play ball in the afternoon.

Yogi and Joe Garagiola were stars on an American Legion team that made the playoffs two consecutive years. Garagiola was six feet tall, athletic, and handsome. By contrast Berra, at five feet seven and 185 pounds, was short and dumpy and had an awkward swing in which he chopped at the ball. He would also swing at anything near the plate. The man who ran the team, Leo Browne, arranged a tryout with the St. Louis Cardinals for his star players. Garagiola did well and was offered a contract with a $500 bonus with the order to keep quiet about it until he turned sixteen (the boys were fifteen at the time).

Despite not having a particularly good tryout, Berra was offered a contract but no bonus. Berra knew he could not go home without the same bonus as Garagiola, so he refused the offer. Cardinals general manager Branch Rickey offered a

$250 bonus, and again Berra refused. Yogi later had a tryout with the St. Louis Browns and once more was offered a contract without a bonus; once more he turned it down.

Browne wrote to his old friend George Weiss, who was in charge of the New York Yankees' farm system. He said all Yogi wanted was a $500 bonus and whatever he made a month was fine. Berra signed with the Yankees in October 1942 for the $500 bonus he so adamantly desired, plus a monthly salary of $90. Rickey, now with the Dodgers, sent Berra a telegram offering him a chance to sign with Brooklyn, but Yogi never responded because he was the property of the Yankees. So Yogi Berra was off to Norfolk, Virginia, to begin his professional baseball career.

Berra batted .253 in 111 games for the Norfolk (Virginia) Tars in 1943, with seven home runs and fifty-six runs batted in. After the season Berra enlisted in the navy. He became a machine gunner and saw action on D-day aboard a rocket boat deployed just off the Normandy coast before the soldiers assaulted the beach. Berra spent ten days on the thirty-six-foot boat before he finally returned to his ship, the USS *Bayfield*, an attack transport.

Before he was discharged Berra was shipped to the submarine base at Groton, Connecticut. He played for the base's baseball team, managed by Lieutenant Commander James Gleeson, a former big-league outfielder. Gleeson had a difficult time believing the squat, awkward-looking seaman was a professional ballplayer, much less property of the Yankees. But in a game between the sailors and the New York Giants, Berra went 3 for 4 and impressed Giants manager Mel Ott so much he called the Yankees and offered $50,000 for Berra. Yankees president Larry MacPhail turned Ott down. Years later MacPhail confessed he had never heard of Yogi, but if Ott thought he was worth that kind of money, then the Yankees should keep him.

In 1946 the Yankees assigned Berra to the Newark Bears of the Class Triple-A International League, managed by former Yankees All-Star George Selkirk. Like Gleeson before him, Selkirk was skeptical that this squat young man was a ballplayer or a Yankee. He forced Yogi to show him the telegram from MacPhail ordering him to report to Newark.

Berra played in 77 games and batted .314 with 15 home runs and 59 RBIs but displayed an erratic arm behind the plate. In the regular-season finale, Berra tied the game with a ninth-inning homer, a game that Newark eventually won. The victory put Newark in the playoffs for the fourteenth consecutive season, though the Bears lost to a Montreal Royals squad that included Jackie Robinson.

After the loss to Montreal, Berra was called up to the Yankees and made his Major League debut on September 22, 1946, against the Philadelphia Athletics. He went 2 for 4, with a home run off Jesse Flores in his second at bat. His second home run came the next day.

At spring training in 1947, Berra played mostly in right field, where he showed little skill. He was, however, earning a reputation as a hitter, although one who would often hit pitches well out of the strike zone. Because of Berra's erratic outfield play, he saw more time at catcher once the season began; this seemed to be the safest place for him to play.

On June 15 he made an unassisted double play in a game against St. Louis. A week later he hit his first grand slam in a win over Detroit, and when he homered again the next day, he had registered 6 RBIs in 2 games. On August 26 a group from "the Hill" organized Yogi Berra Night in St. Louis to honor their native son. Before the series in St. Louis, Berra had contracted strep throat in Cleveland and had to be hospitalized. When he arrived in town for his night, Yogi was very nervous about making an acceptance speech. That was the night he uttered the famous line, "I want to thank everyone for making this night necessary."

Berra batted .280 in his rookie campaign, with 11 home runs and 54 RBIs in 83 games. The Yankees faced Brooklyn in the World Series, the first fall classic to be televised. Yogi went 0 for 7 in the first 2 games, but came off the bench in Game Three to hit the first pinch-hit home run in Series history. Overall, he was 3 for 19, as New York won in 7 games.

Berra spent the off-season in St. Louis, where he met a pretty waitress named Carmen Short working at a restaurant co-owned by Stan Musial. Yogi and Carmen hit it off and six months later were engaged. They were married on January 26, 1949, and old pal Joe Garagiola served as best man.

In 1948 Berra had a strong year at the plate, batting .305 with 14 home runs and 98 RBIs while appearing in 125 games (71 as a catcher). The All-Star Game was played in St. Louis that year; Berra made the squad but did not play. The Yanks finished third behind Cleveland and Boston and entered the off-season in the market for a better defensive catcher. This changed when the Yankees surprised the baseball world by picking fifty-eight-year-old Casey Stengel as their manager; Stengel nixed any thought of replacing Berra behind the plate.

Casey took an immediate liking to Berra, calling him "my assistant manager." Stengel had an idea Yogi was much more sensitive than he let on and decided to act as a buffer against those who criticized or just made fun of his young catcher. He also assigned future Hall of Famer Bill Dickey to act as Berra's personal tutor. Dickey spent hours working with his student to improve his mechanics behind the plate and teaching him to think ahead during games.

Despite the improvement in his defensive play, Berra had some trouble with Yankee pitchers, especially Vic Raschi and Allie Reynolds, who thought he smothered curve balls and stabbed at fastballs, and thus made it difficult to get close calls from umpires. For his part, Stengel did not yet com-

pletely trust Berra, either. In some critical situations the manager would call the pitches from the dugout, infuriating the veteran pitchers. Finally, one day in a game against the Athletics, Reynolds had enough. Stengel began waving to Yogi to get his attention so he could call a pitch. Meanwhile, Allie warned his young catcher if he looked into the dugout he would cross him up intentionally.

Berra knew this was not an idle threat and ignored his manager at the risk of being fined. The incident proved to be a turning point in his relationship with the pitching staff; they now felt that they could trust Berra. The season ended with the Yankees sweeping a two-game series against the Red Sox to claim the pennant. Yogi was a disappointing 1 for 16 in the World Series, though the Yanks beat Brooklyn in five games.

By the next season Berra had established himself not only as a legitimate big-league catcher but also as a rising star in the American League. He had a stellar season in 1950, batting .322 with 28 home runs and 124 RBIs, as the Yanks swept the Philadelphia Phillies to win their second straight world championship. After finishing third in the 1950 AL MVP voting, Berra won his first Most Valuable Player Award in 1951, when he led New York to yet another World Series title, this time at the expense of the New York Giants.

The next two seasons were more of the same, as the Yanks won their fourth and fifth consecutive titles with wins over Brooklyn. Berra continued to develop his reputation as a clutch hitter, driving home 98 runs in '52 and 108 in '53. He batted a robust .429 in the Yankees' six-game World Series victory in '53. A second MVP came in 1954, despite the Cleveland Indians' temporarily interrupting the Yankees' dynasty. That year Berra batted .307 with 22 homers and 125 RBIs.

Berra entered the 1955 season as the highest-paid Yankee, and he earned his forty-eight thousand dollars by winning his second consecutive MVP award and third overall. The season ended in disappointment, however, as the Dodgers were finally able to take a Series from the Yankees. Jackie Robinson stole home in Game One, and Berra argued the call vociferously while jumping up and down. He never stopped insisting Robinson was out, and he even signed photos of the play, "He was out." In the decisive seventh game, Yogi came to the plate in the sixth inning with two men aboard and hit a fly ball toward the left-field corner, but left fielder Sandy Amoros raced over, made a spectacular catch, and turned it into a double play.

The Yankees regained the world championship in 1956—against the Dodgers—and Berra had a big Series, with 3 home runs, including 2 off Don Newcombe in the decisive seventh game. Berra batted in 10 runs, yet the highlight of the Series for him was catching Don Larsen's perfect game in Game Five. Larsen said he did not shake off Berra once during his masterpiece.

Berra slumped to a .251 average in 1957 but was still productive, with 24 home runs and 82 RBIs. He followed that with a similarly productive 1958 with a .266 batting average, 22 homers, and 90 RBIs. In those two seasons the Yankees and Milwaukee Braves split the World Series; Milwaukee won in 1957, and New York won in 1958.

The thirty-three-year-old Berra reached some milestones in 1959, including his 300th career home run. He also set records (since broken) for the most consecutive chances by a catcher without an error and the most consecutive games without an error. The erratic catcher of the early years was now a distant memory.

Though the Yankees did not win the pennant in 1959, they did win in 1960, the tenth and final flag under Casey Stengel. Yogi played more in the outfield, appearing in only 63 of 120 games as a catcher. In the thrilling Game Seven against Pittsburgh, he hit a three-run homer in the sixth inning that only served as backdrop to Bill Mazeroski's Series-ending home run in the ninth inning. That fabled shot sailed over left fielder Berra's head.

Yogi played three more seasons before retiring after the 1963 World Series. He batted just once in the Series, a sweep at the hands of the Los Angeles Dodgers. Even with that loss, he finished with a 10-4 record in Series play. He was named an All-Star eighteen times between 1948 and 1962 (including four years when two All-Star Games were played each summer). He started behind the plate for the American League eleven times.

Berra had a career batting average of .285, with 358 home runs. At the time of his retirement, his 306 homers as a catcher were the most ever at the position. He still holds several World Series records, including the most games played (75). In his eighteen-year career, he drew 704 walks against just 414 strikeouts—proof that this legendary bad-ball hitter indeed hit what he chased.

On October 24, 1963, Berra was named the Yankees' manager to replace Ralph Houk after Houk became general manager. The Yankees offered Berra a two-year contract, but he insisted on a one-year deal, as he was not sure he could manage. He would later regret that decision. Berra had intended to keep pitching coach Johnny Sain on his staff, but Sain could not agree on a contract and Berra turned to old friend Whitey Ford to be a player-coach. He always believed Ford was one of the more intelligent pitchers and thought he would be outstanding in handling young pitchers.

The 1964 Yankees were not an easy bunch to manage. Veterans Mantle and Ford were famous for their off-the-field drinking and carousing, and the young players wanted to follow along. Players like Jim Bouton and Joe Pepitone were brash, and the clubhouse was out of control.

The Yankees came out of the gate sluggish, but by early August, Berra somehow had them in first place. Yet they spent the rest of the month playing uninspired and inconsistent ball. The nadir came in mid-August with a 4-game sweep at the hands of the Chicago White Sox that dropped them 4½ games behind the first-place White Sox. After the series concluded, the team bus was stuck in traffic on the way to the airport and everyone was feeling impatient.

It was then that one of the more memorable incidents of Berra's stewardship took place. Infielder Phil Linz pulled out his harmonica and began to play "Mary Had a Little Lamb." Berra angrily yelled from the front of the bus for him to stop. There are different accounts of what happened next.

According to Mantle, Linz asked him what Berra had said. Mantle reportedly responded, "Play louder." Linz obliged. When Yogi heard the harmonica again, he stormed to the back of the bus and smacked the instrument away, and a heated argument ensued. When news of the confrontation came out, Houk told reporters he had no intention of speaking to Berra about the incident. With Berra's job security already in danger, this appeared to make his firing a fait accompli.

The Yankees lost the next two games to Boston to fall six games behind, but then came on with a rush. They finished August strongly and went 22-6 in September before clinching the pennant on October 3. Their opponent in the World Series was the St. Louis Cardinals, who had also rallied to claim a thrilling National League race.

It was a back-and-forth Series that came down to a seventh-game matchup between Cardinals ace Bob Gibson and twenty-two-year-old Mel Stottlemyre. St. Louis broke through for three runs in the fourth inning with the aid of some sloppy New York defense, and Gibson held on to clinch the Series.

Overall, Berra had done a good job with an aging team. Ford had a sore arm, and Mantle's bad legs were making it increasingly difficult for him to cover center field. It was Berra who pushed for Stottlemyre to be called up in mid-August, and the rookie came through with a 9-3 record. It is unlikely the Yankees would have won the pennant without the young right-hander. They had

responded well after the Linz episode, and Yogi had every intention of asking for a two-year extension. Instead, he was fired and offered a job as a scout.

Across town, the New York Mets had finished their third season of play, and two former Yankees were running the show, general manager George Weiss and manager Casey Stengel. With wife Carmen advocating he break with the Yankees after their shabby treatment of him, Berra took Weiss's offer and joined Stengel's staff as a player-coach. He caught only two games and batted .222, playing his final game three days before his fortieth birthday in May.

Berra stayed with the Mets even though he was passed over for manager on three occasions. The first was when Stengel retired after breaking his hip in August 1965 and the Mets—with Stengel's input—chose Wes Westrum as his replacement. Salty Parker was tabbed as Westrum's interim replacement when he resigned in the final week of the 1967 season. In October 1967 the Mets dealt for Senators manager Gil Hodges to replace Parker. Berra knew and respected Hodges and was not upset at being passed over in favor of his old Dodger rival.

So Berra stayed on to coach under Hodges and won his eleventh World Series ring in 1969 when the Miracle Mets upset the Baltimore Orioles. Berra's opportunity to finally manage the Mets came under tragic circumstances. He replaced Hodges when the Mets manager died of a heart attack on April 2, 1972, after playing golf.

Although Berra had coached under Hodges for four years, he was a different type of manager. Hodges was a disciplinarian who took a more hands-on approach with his players. By contrast, Berra treated his players as adults and left the responsibility of being in shape to them, figuring that just being a ballplayer should be motivation enough to take your job seriously and be prepared. Unlike his predecessor, Berra did not platoon and kept the same lineup, a change the veterans found to their liking.

The Mets were 30-11 on June 1, but beset by injuries they staggered to a third-place finish. On a brighter note for Berra, that summer marked his induction into the Hall of Fame in Cooperstown.

In 1973 injuries slowed the Mets again, and there were rumors that Yogi might not make it through the summer. The team was in fifth place at the end of August, but as players regained their health, the Mets closed the gap in the tightly bunched National League East.

On September 21 the Mets reached .500 and first place at the same time. With a victory over the Cubs on October 1, the Mets completed their remarkable comeback, winning the division title with just eighty-two victories. They defeated the highly favored Cincinnati Reds in the National League Championship Series, making Berra only the second manager to win a pennant in each league (Joe McCarthy was the first). In the World Series the Mets lost to the Oakland A's in seven games.

The Mets fell to fifth place in 1974 with a 71-91 record, the club's worst mark since 1966. Simmering trouble between Berra and left fielder Cleon Jones deepened in 1975, and when Jones refused to enter a game as a pinch hitter, matters came to a head. Yogi refused to let Jones back on the team and demanded he be released. Chairman of the board M. Donald Grant did not want to cut Jones, but Berra remained firm and soon thereafter Jones was waived. The team was struggling, and when it suffered a five-game losing streak in early August—culminating with a doubleheader shutout at home at the hands of the last-place Expos—Yogi was fired. Coach Roy McMillan was picked to replace him.

After a twelve-year absence, Yogi returned to the Yankees when old friend and teammate Billy Martin picked him to be on his staff in 1976. With Berra on board at the reopened Yankee Stadium in 1976, the Yanks won their first pennant since 1964. Though they were swept in the Series by the Reds, Berra added two more World Series rings with back-to-back titles in 1977 and 1978. Berra was a constant on the Yankees' coaching staff through the 1983 season, despite several managerial changes. He got one more chance to manage when he was named Yankees manager for 1984.

New York struggled early in the season, and there was no catching the Detroit Tigers, who cruised to the division title. Prior to the '85 season, rumors swirled that owner George M. Steinbrenner wanted to fire his manager, but as spring training came around, he declared Berra safe for the year. This was a season Yogi looked forward to because the Yankees had acquired his son Dale from Pittsburgh. Not only did Berra not survive the season, but he was fired before the end of April, with a record of 6-10. Upset that Steinbrenner broke his promise to let him manage the entire year, Berra stayed away from Yankee Stadium until reconciliation in 1999.

Although his managing days were now over, his coaching career was not. Houston Astros owner John McMullen offered Berra the Astros' manager position just three days after he was fired, but he turned it down. At the end of the season, he did accept a coaching job with Houston under rookie manager Hal Lanier. Yogi stayed with the Astros through the 1989 season, ending his long and illustrious career in uniform. He had spent seventeen years as a player, two years as a player-coach, eighteen years as a coach, and seven years as a manager.

Berra remained not only a Yankees legend but an American icon as well. A museum dedicated to him opened in Montclair, New Jersey, his and Carmen's home for more than a half century. There they raised their three sons: Larry, a former Minor League catcher; Tim, who played in the National Football League (NFL) for the Baltimore Colts in 1974; and Dale, who spent the last couple of

DAVE WILLIAMS

months of his eleven-year career with his dad on the 1987 Astros.

Yogi promoted numerous products — most famously Yoo-Hoo, the chocolate soft drink, and even had a cartoon bear named after him. The former catcher's Yogi-isms are known worldwide. As one of the oldest and most recognizable Hall of Famers, Yogi Berra maintained a connection back to what many consider the golden era of baseball.

Chapter 45. **Johnny Schulte**

James Lincoln Ray

A backup catcher in all of his five years in the Major Leagues, Johnny Schulte found greater success as a coach under manager Joe McCarthy. Schulte was a Yankees coach during almost all of McCarthy's tenure with the team. After McCarthy left the Yankees in the middle of the 1946 season, Schulte stayed on with the Yankees until the end of the 1948 season, coaching under managers Bill Dickey, Johnny Neun, and Bucky Harris. In 1949 he rejoined McCarthy, who was then managing the Boston Red Sox. When McCarthy retired in 1950, Schulte also left the game. A year later he turned up in Cleveland, where he worked as a scout for more than a decade before retiring for good in 1963.

John Clement Schulte was born on September 8, 1896, in Fredericktown, Missouri, a town in the foothills of the Ozarks about seventy-five miles south of St. Louis. Schulte's parents were Michael Charles Schulte, a bank clerk, and the former Amelia Rosar. John was one of seven children, three girls and four boys. He was the third child and the second son.

Schulte began playing baseball in grade school and competed in the citywide *St. Louis Post-Dispatch* tournament in 1912, at the age of fifteen. He signed his first professional baseball contract in 1915, with the Oklahoma City Senators of the Class D Western Association. Schulte, an eighteen-year-old outfielder, batted .167 in 28 games. In 1916 he played for three teams, Newport News of the Class C Virginia League and Wheeling (West Virginia) and Terre Haute (Indiana) of the Class B Central League. Overall he batted .202 in 82 games.

Johnny Schulte was the lone full-time holdover from the Joe McCarthy era on manager Bucky Harris's coaching staff.

Schulte served in the navy during World War I, playing baseball at the Great Lakes Naval Training Station. He missed the 1917 and 1918 seasons, but when he returned to baseball in 1919, he seemed to have found his batting eye. With the Terre Haute Browns of the Three-I League, Schulte hit .304 in 102 games, mostly as an outfielder.

With Terre Haute again the next season,

Schulte played in 131 games and batted .278. In 1921 he moved up to the Mobile (Alabama) Bears of the Class A Southern Association, where he was switched from the outfield to catcher, his position for the rest of his baseball career. Schulte had the best season of his career in 1922, leading the Southern Association in batting (.357), home runs (12), and slugging (.597) for the pennant-winning Bears.

After the season the St. Louis Browns purchased Schulte's contract. He made his Major League debut on opening day 1923, as a late-inning substitute at first base. The next day he pinch-hit, drew a walk, and scored. After a month, in which he appeared in 7 games, Schulte was sent to the San Antonio Bears of the Class A Texas League, where he stayed the rest of the season, hitting .269 in 59 games and showing none of the power he had displayed the year before in Mobile.

The five-foot-eleven, 190-pound Schulte spent the next three seasons (1924 through 1926) at the Class Double-A level, at the time the Minor League's highest classification. Playing in the American Association in 1924–25, and in the International League in 1926, he regained his batting ability and played strong defense. He began the 1927 season in the International League, but made it back to the Majors, with the St. Louis Cardinals, on May 29. Schulte was 3 for 5 in his National League debut, with four runs batted in as the Cardinals defeated Cincinnati, 11–3. The next day he was 2 for 3 with a walk. Just over a week later, on June 8, Schulte smacked his first Major League home run, a two-run shot off Hal Goldsmith of the Boston Braves.

Schulte remained with the Cardinals for the rest of the 1927 season. He hit .288 in 208 plate appearances, with an impressive on-base percentage of .456. He hit nine home runs and had thirty-two RBIS. However, the Cardinals had a surplus of catchers and traded Schulte after the season to the Philadelphia Phillies. He appeared in 65 games for the Phillies in 1928, many of them as a pinch hitter, and batted .248.

On January 17, 1928, Schulte married twenty-year-old Gladys Moran of St. Louis, a professional singer. The marriage lasted until Schulte's death more than fifty years later.

The Phillies sold Schulte to the Columbus (Ohio) Senators of the American Association in January 1929, but before he could play for Columbus, the Chicago Cubs purchased his contract. As a reserve catcher and pinch hitter on the pennant-winning team managed by Joe McCarthy, Schulte hit .261 in 31 games. He had no appearances in the World Series, which the Cubs lost to the Philadelphia Athletics in 5 games.

Schulte did not play in the 1930 season but returned to baseball in 1931 with the Los Angeles Angels of the Pacific Coast League, where he served as a catcher and pinch hitter, appearing in 101 games and hitting .283. The Browns picked him up in the off-season, but he was released in early August after playing in just 15 games. A few days later he signed with the Boston Braves, but played in just 10 games for them. Schulte was one of a select group of players that hit a home run in his last Major League at bat; it came off Freddie Fitzsimmons of the New York Giants on September 20, 1932, in the Polo Grounds. He finished with a career Major League batting average of .262 in 374 at bats.

Schulte caught on as a coach on Charlie Grimm's Cubs staff in 1933. In 1934 Joe McCarthy, in his fourth year as manager of the Yankees, recalled how well Schulte handled the pitchers on the 1929 Cubs and hired Schulte as the Yankees' bullpen coach and pitching instructor. Schulte spent the next fifteen seasons in the Bronx, coaching on seven pennant winners, six of which won the World Series.

In addition to his coaching duties, Schulte occasionally worked as a scout for the Yankees. In 1936 he persuaded Yankees chief scout Paul Krichell to sign a skinny young shortstop who had been passed over by the Brooklyn Dodgers and the New York Giants. The kid was Phil Rizzuto, and though Krichell originally was not impressed, he agreed to send him to the Yankees' lowest Minor League club if Schulte would pay Rizzuto's twenty-dollar train fare from New York City to Bassett, Virginia.

Six years later, in 1942, Schulte spotted an awk-ward-looking, wild-swinging seventeen-year-old catcher playing in an American Legion game in St. Louis. The catcher, Yogi Berra, blasted two home runs, and Schulte got the Yankees to sign him, for five hundred dollars.

When Whitey Ford first tried out for the Yan-kees in 1946, he did so as a potential first baseman. As with Rizzuto, the head scout was not impressed and was ready to send the eighteen-year-old home. But when Ford told Schulte that he could pitch, Schulte grabbed his catcher's mitt and said, in clas-sic Missouri fashion, "Show me." Ford showed him, and the Yankees signed the left-hander, who went on to win more games than any other Yan-kee pitcher.

Schulte died on June 28, 1978, in St. Louis at the age of eighty-one, and was survived by his wife and his son, John Jr. He is buried in St. Louis's Calvary Cemetery.

Chapter 46. **Allie Clark**

Rick Malwitz

AGE	G	AB	R	H	2B	3B	HR	TB	RBI	BB	SO	BAV	OBP	SLG	SB	GDP	HBP
24	24	67	9	25	5	0	1	33	14	5	2	.373	.417	.493	0	5	0

What was Yankees manager Bucky Harris thinking? With his team leading the Brooklyn Dodgers, 3–2, with two outs in the sixth inning of Game Seven of the 1947 World Series, he sent rookie Allie Clark up to pinch-hit for rookie Yogi Berra. Out of context, given Berra's Hall of Fame career, the move might seem puzzling. Allie Clark, called up from the Newark Bears in August, would never be a regular in his seven seasons with four different teams. But on this day Harris deemed him a better choice than Berra, and the move worked. Clark, who hit .373 (25 for 67) in the regular season, singled home Phil Rizzuto with the Yankees' fourth run in a 5–2 victory. He replaced Berra in right field and was there when the Dodgers were retired in the ninth inning.

Clark would later meet one of Berra's sons at the Yogi Berra Museum in Montclair, New Jersey, and would tell the unbelieving young man that he once pinch-hit for his father. "He said, 'No one ever hit for my father,' but then he found out it was true. The box scores don't lie," said Clark. "It was the biggest thrill I had in baseball. The seventh game, there was a lot on our shoulders. We had to win, it was scary."[1]

The crowd in Yankee Stadium that day was 71,528, though Clark's wife, Frances, who had been his high school sweetheart, was not among them. Allie had assumed she did not want to attend the game and gave away the free passes he was allowed. Soon after the game ended, Clark called Frances at their home in South Amboy, New Jersey, and told her to meet him at a victory celebration that night at the Biltmore Hotel in Manhattan. "The one thing I remember most was Joe

After making his big-league debut on August 5, 1947, Allie Clark batted .373 in twenty-four games for New York.

DiMaggio walking in with two girls under each arm," she said in a 1999 interview.[2]

Clark's pinch-hit single came in the last at bat he had as a Yankee. That winter the Yankees traded the six-foot, 185-pound outfielder to the Cleveland Indians for pitcher Red Embree. Because no one from the Yankees called Clark, he heard about the trade on the radio. More than six decades later, he still bristled at the memory. Though Clark lamented the trade to Cleveland, when the Indians won the 1948 World Series he became the first player to win back-to-back World Series titles with different teams.

To get to the World Series in 1948, Cleveland had to win a one-game playoff at Boston's Fenway Park. When Clark arrived at the park that day, he noticed a first baseman's glove had been placed in his locker. There had to be a mistake, he thought, as he had never played first base in his professional career. "I asked [manager Lou] Boudreau, 'What the hell's this for? He said, 'You're playing first base.'"[3] Boudreau told the right-handed-hitting Clark he wanted him in the lineup to take aim at Fenway Park's left-field wall.

The experiment lasted only three innings. After the Indians took a 5–1 lead in the top of the fourth, Boudreau replaced Clark with Eddie Robinson. Clark, hitless in two at bats, had handled five chances flawlessly. When the move to Robinson was made, Clark recalled, "I was the happiest guy in the ballpark."[4] He earned faint praise from Rud Rennie of the *New York Herald Tribune*: "Clark played the position as one might expect it to be played by a man who never played it before. He did not drop any ball, but he always looked as if he might."[5]

The Indians defeated the Red Sox, 8–3, and remained in Boston, where they opened the World Series two days later against the Boston Braves. Clark played only in the second game, batting second and playing right field. His fifth-inning sacrifice against Warren Spahn led to a run in a 4–1 Indians victory. Frances Clark, who attended the games in Cleveland, said her biggest thrill as the wife of a baseball player was riding in an open car on Euclid Avenue in the victory parade.

Alfred Aloysius "Allie" Clark was born in South Amboy on June 16, 1923, the oldest child of Alfred and Helen Clark. Aside from the time he served in World War II and the summers he was playing professional baseball, he never left South Amboy, a small town at the mouth of the Raritan River, linked to New York by commuter trains and ferryboats. He attended Saint Mary's High School, whose former students had five World Series rings as of 2011: two for Clark; two for Tom Kelly, who managed the Minnesota Twins to titles in 1987 and 1991; and one for Jack McKeon, who managed the Florida Marlins in 2003. "South Amboy was a baseball-crazy town," said South Amboy native Johnny O'Brien, who played six seasons in the National League in the 1950s. "Every park where we went to play, people would point to spots way beyond the outfield fences and say things like 'Allie Clark hit one way out there.' That's all you ever heard, things like 'Allie hit a home run here.' 'Allie made a great play over there.' You couldn't help but want to become the next Allie Clark."[6]

"We all have Allie to thank," said McKeon. "He set the stage for all of us who followed. We all wanted to make it because he made it, so we ate, drank and slept baseball every day of our lives. No girls, no cars, just baseball."[7]

"All we wanted to do was play ball. We made baseballs out of golf balls, wrapping them in black tape. If someone had white tape we were in hog heaven," said Johnny O'Brien.[8] The youth sports complex in South Amboy is named for Allie Clark, and until his health declined in 2011 he was present when the baseball season opened every spring. He lamented, however, that the number of players has declined, and when it is hot in the summer, boys are apt to be indoors playing computer games. "Kids aren't playing ball every day like we did back then," he said in 1999. "That's why you see so many players from Latin America. They play ball like we did, growing up."[9]

Clark was signed by the Yankees in 1941, receiving a bonus of $250. He split that year with farm teams in Amsterdam, New York, and Easton, Maryland, hitting a combined 334. In 1942 he batted .328 in 129 games for the Norfolk (Virginia) Tars of the Class B Piedmont League. One game that did not count in his official statistics was an exhibition against a team stationed at the U.S.

Navy base in Norfolk, where he faced Bob Feller. "I think he struck about eighteen of us out. He got me once."[10]

Clark began the 1943 season with the International League Newark Bears, the Yankees' top farm team. But midway in the season, he recalled, "Uncle Sam took care of me." He was drafted into the army and served as a combat medic for three years before being discharged before the 1946 season. "I was lucky I came out without a scratch," he said.[11]

Two weeks after Clark was discharged the Yankees sent him a letter telling him to report to a Minor League camp in Sebring, Florida, where he was joined by future teammates Bobby Brown and Yogi Berra. "They still had [Charlie] Keller and [Tommy] Henrich and DiMaggio in the outfield, so they sent me down," he remembered. "They kept Bobby Brown and Yogi. Then [in 1947] DiMaggio got hurt a little with the heel and they called me up."[12]

Clark had proved he could hit at the highest level of the Minors. In 1946 he hit .344 in ninety-seven games at Newark, with fourteen home runs and seventy runs batted in. He was batting .334 with twenty-three home runs and eighty-six RBIS in 1947 before his August call-up.

His first game was on August 5 against the Athletics in Philadelphia. He batted cleanup and played left field, while the regular left fielder, Johnny Lindell, replaced Joe DiMaggio in center field. With the bases loaded, two outs in the top of the ninth, and the scored tied 5–5, Clark had an infield hit to drive in the eventual winning run. The single, his first big-league hit, came off Russ Christopher. The next day, hitting cleanup again, Clark hit his first Major League home run off the Athletics' Bill McCahan.

Clark lived at home that summer, commuting first to Newark and then the Bronx. Bobby Brown, who was living at the Jersey Shore, routinely drove Clark to Yankee Stadium. He said his Yankees teammates treated him well during the less than three months he spent on the team. One teammate, DiMaggio, remained aloof. "He never associated too much with the ballplayers. But he was a great ballplayer," Clark said.[13]

Cleveland drew a league-leading 2,620,627 fans to Municipal Stadium in 1948, a record for the team at the time. "That town was wild about the Indians that year," Clark said.[14] Moreover, his roommate was second baseman Joe Gordon, his boyhood idol who had starred for the Yankees while Clark was in high school.

The 298 plate appearances in 1948 were the most Clark had in a season in a Major League career that also included stints with the Athletics (1951–53) and the Chicago White Sox (1953). After the White Sox released him in June 1953, Clark signed with the St. Louis Cardinals organization. For five seasons he was a regular with the Cardinals' International League affiliate, the Rochester (New York) Red Wings. As of 2011 he was seventh on Rochester's all-time RBI list and tenth in base hits. "Rochester was a great baseball town," said Clark, who was inducted into the Red Wings Hall of Fame in 1998.[15] In 1958, after splitting the season with Minor League teams in New Orleans, San Antonio, and Indianapolis, he retired.

The player who once pinch-hit for Yogi Berra allowed that his game had one weakness. "I didn't have a great arm," he said, pointing to a scar on the inside of his right arm, the result of an operation he had at Johns Hopkins Hospital in Baltimore after the 1946 season. "They loosened up some tissue. I never should have had it done. That's why I was never a regular [in the Major Leagues]. I didn't throw very well."[16]

While Clark was playing professional baseball, he spent his off-seasons working with Local 373 of the Iron Workers Union in Perth Amboy, New Jersey. "I had to make money outside [of baseball] or we couldn't get by. You ask any old-time ballplayer and they had jobs, working in stores, driving trucks, stocking stuff in warehouses, anything to support their families," said Clark, whose peak salary in baseball was eleven thousand dollars.[17]

Clark proudly wore his 1947 World Series ring at social occasions and on the job as an ironworker. Over time the diamond was dislodged, and the words on the ring were worn so much that it was hard to read the inscription. It was hard to impress Little Leaguers when the words were blurred, but the city of South Amboy came to the rescue. The police department helped raise twenty-five hundred dollars to have the ring replaced. They contacted the Balfour Company, which made the ring, and with permission from the Yankees, Balfour replicated the 1947 World Series ring for Clark.

What Clark did not have in his possession were any game-used number-3 Yankees jerseys. At the end of the season players were required to turn in their uniforms. After Clark left the Yankees, outfielder Cliff Mapes wore the iconic number 3. The number was retired at a 1948 ceremony that honored the original wearer of number 3, the dying Babe Ruth.

Clark said taking a jersey at the end of a season was simply not done during his playing career. In the 1990s he attended an old-timers game, and the Yankees gave him a uniform with the number 2, which he was allowed to keep. Times had changed. "When I played we had to buy our own gloves and spikes."[18]

After he retired from baseball, Clark returned to South Amboy to work full time as an ironworker. He said he was proud of his work, having helped erect scores of buildings in central New Jersey. "It was good steady work, outdoors, and I always enjoyed it. I was a strong guy and it didn't bother me," he said.[19] Decades later he would feel the effects of heavy lifting with arthritis in his joints. He also survived bypass heart surgery and cancer.

In the spring of 2011 he said he knew of only three other members of the 1947 Yankees who were still alive: Bobby Brown, Yogi Berra, and pitcher Don Johnson. (Contrary to Clark's recollection, Rugger Ardizoia and Dick Starr were also still alive.) Allie Clark died in South Amboy on April 1, 2012. His wife, Frances, whose memory was robbed by Alzheimer's disease, is living in a nearby assisted living facility.

Chapter 47. Joe DiMaggio

Lawrence Baldassaro

AGE	G	AB	R	H	2B	3B	HR	TB	RBI	BB	SO	BAV	OBP	SLG	SB	GDP	HBP
32	141	534	97	168	31	10	20	279	97	64	32	.315	.391	.522	3	14	3

Baseball isn't statistics; it's Joe DiMaggio rounding second.

— *attributed to Jimmy Breslin by Herb Caen*, San Francisco Chronicle, *June 3, 1975*

Joe DiMaggio was one of the most recognizable and popular men in mid-twentieth-century America. He was celebrated in song and literature as an iconic hero, and he was married, briefly, to the nation's number-one glamour girl. On March 16, 1999, the House of Representatives passed a resolution honoring him "for his storied baseball career; for his many contributions to the nation throughout his lifetime; and for transcending baseball and becoming a symbol for the ages of talent, commitment and achievement."[1]

But first and foremost Joe DiMaggio was a ballplayer. Known as the Yankee Clipper, he was the undisputed leader of New York Yankees teams that won nine World Series titles in his thirteen-year career that ran from 1936 to 1951, with three years lost to duty in World War II. He was three times the American League's Most Valuable Player, and he holds what many consider to be the most remarkable baseball record of all, a fifty-six-game hitting streak in 1941. As the son of immigrants, he was the embodiment of the American Dream, a rags-to-riches story played out in pinstripes.

Joseph Paul DiMaggio was born Giuseppe Paolo DiMaggio on November 25, 1914, in Martinez, California, twenty-five miles northeast of San Francisco. His parents, Giuseppe and Rosalia (Mercurio) DiMaggio, had settled there after emigrating from Sicily. After Joe was born they moved

Joe DiMaggio's statistics were below his prewar levels, but combined with his inspirational leadership they earned him his third Most Valuable Player Award.

the family to San Francisco, where Giuseppe continued to work as a fisherman. Joe was the eighth of their nine children, one of five sons. Two of his brothers, Vince and Dominic, would also play in the Major Leagues.

Unlike two of his older brothers, Joe had no interest in joining his father on the fishing boat. Instead, he played for several amateur and semipro teams in baseball-rich San Francisco. It was nineteen-year-old Vince, who was then playing for the

Joe DiMaggio scores the Yankees' first run in Game One of the 1947 World Series. George McQuinn scores behind him as Phil Rizzuto looks on. Ralph Branca is the Dodgers' pitcher and Bruce Edwards the catcher.

San Francisco Seals of the Pacific Coast League, who got Joe into professional ball. When the Seals found themselves in need of a shortstop near the end of the 1932 season, Vince convinced Seals manager Ike Caveney to give his seventeen-year-old brother a chance. Joe played in the final three games of the season and then was signed to a contract in 1933 for $225 a month.

Moved to the outfield because of his erratic arm, DiMaggio hit .340 and set a PCL record by hitting in sixty-one straight games. In 1934 he hit .341, but a knee injury that sidelined him in August made Major League teams leery of signing him. The Yankees offered to buy his contract for $25,000 and five players, but with the contingency that he remain with the Seals in 1935 to prove he was healthy. DiMaggio made a convincing case by hitting .398, with 34 homers and 154 runs batted in.

In 1936, only two years after the departure of Babe Ruth, the heralded rookie came to spring training facing big expectations. Writing in the

Sporting News on March 26, Dan Daniel noted, "Yankee fans regard him as the Moses who is to lead their club out of the second-place wilderness." It didn't take long for the rookie to make his mark. Halfway through the season, when he was hitting around .350 and had started in right field in the All-Star Game, his photo was on the cover of *Time*. For the year he hit .323 with 29 homers and drove in 125 runs.

DiMaggio was the classic five-tool player: in addition to hitting for average and power, he could run, throw, and field. Joe McCarthy, the Yankees' manager from 1931 to 1946, called him the best base runner he ever saw. His all-around play led the 1936 Yankees to the first of four straight World Series titles. The twenty-one-year-old sensation had established himself as the successor to Babe Ruth. After the Series he received a hero's welcome in his hometown of San Francisco, where Mayor Angelo Rossi gave him the key to the city.

DiMaggio finished second in the MVP vote in 1937, despite leading the American League in

LAWRENCE BALDASSARO

home runs, slugging percentage, runs, and total bases. He won the first of his three MVP Awards in 1939, when he led the league with a career-best .381 average. Following that season, he married twenty-one-year-old Dorothy Arnold, a singer, dancer, and actress he met while filming a bit part in the movie *Manhattan Merry-Go-Round*.

By then the six-foot-two, 190-pound outfielder was acknowledged as the best player in baseball, but to some his ethnic background was still ripe for stereotypical portrayal. In a cover story in the May 1, 1939, issue of *Life*, Noel Busch identified DiMaggio as a "tall, thin Italian youth equipped with slick black hair" and "squirrel teeth." But the young ballplayer apparently confounded Busch's general perception of Italian Americans. "Although he learned Italian first, Joe, now twenty-four, speaks English without an accent and is otherwise well adapted to most U.S. mores. Instead of olive oil or smelly bear grease he keeps his hair slick with water. He never reeks of garlic and prefers chicken chow mein to spaghetti."

After winning a second consecutive batting title in 1940, DiMaggio reached a new level of fame in 1941. He set one of the most enduring records in sports by hitting in fifty-six consecutive games. On May 15, the day the streak began, the Yankees were in fourth place, and DiMaggio had batted a lowly .194 over the previous twenty games. On June 17 DiMaggio broke the Yankee hitting-streak record of twenty-nine games, set by Roger Peckinpaugh in 1919 and equaled by Earle Combs in 1931.

As DiMaggio's streak continued to grow, it gradually became a national obsession. Day after day, across the country, the question was, "Did he get one today?" In its July 14 issue, *Time* wrote, "Ever since it became apparent that the big Italian from San Francisco's Fisherman's Wharf was approaching a record that had eluded Ty Cobb, Babe Ruth, Lou Gehrig and other great batsmen, Big Joe's hits have been the biggest news in

U.S. sport. Radio programs were interrupted for DiMaggio bulletins."

On June 29, in the seventh inning of the second game of a doubleheader in Washington, DiMaggio hit a single to pass George Sisler's forty-one-game streak set in 1922, commonly referred to as the "modern record" to distinguish it from Wee Willie Keeler's forty-four-game streak, the "all-time record" set in 1897. The *New York Times* reported on June 30 that the fans "roared thunderous acclaim" to "one of the greatest players baseball has ever known," while his teammates 'to a man,' were as excited as schoolboys over the feat." On July 2 DiMaggio broke Keeler's record with a fifth-inning home run off Red Sox pitcher Dick Newsome.

Fifteen days later, on July 17, the streak ended in Cleveland's Municipal Stadium in front of 67,468 fans—at that time the largest crowd ever to see a night game—when Indians third baseman Ken Keltner robbed DiMaggio of hits with two spectacular plays. Over the course of the streak the Yankees moved from fourth place, 5½ games back, to first, 7 games ahead of Cleveland. DiMaggio went on to hit safely in his next 16 games, and the Yankees went on to win the pennant and then beat the Brooklyn Dodgers in the World Series.

One of the fascinating sidelights of the streak is that in his 223 times at bat, DiMaggio struck out only five times. In fact, he struck out only thirteen times in the entire season. The late Harvard paleontologist and essayist Stephen Jay Gould, noting the streak, called it "the most extraordinary thing that ever happened in American sports."[2]

DiMaggio batted .357 for the 1941 season and led the league in runs batted in and total bases. He won his second MVP Award, receiving fifteen first-place votes, while Ted Williams, who hit .406 and led the league in home runs, slugging percentage, on-base percentage, and runs, received eight.

DiMaggio batted just .305 in 1942, the lowest average of his seven years in the Majors, and he also compiled the lowest number of home runs and runs batted in. The Yankees won the pennant, but they lost the World Series to the Cardinals, marking the team's only loss in ten trips to the Series during DiMaggio's career.

On February 17, 1943, DiMaggio enlisted in the U.S. Army Air Corps. Like many other Major Leaguers, he never saw combat, serving instead in a morale-boosting role by playing on service baseball squads. In June 1944 he was sent to Hawaii, where he continued to play ball but also spent several weeks in a Honolulu hospital suffering from stomach ulcers. After being sent back to the mainland, he was granted a medical discharge in September 1945. In the meantime, his wife had been granted a divorce and custody of their son, Joe Jr.

DiMaggio's first season following the war was a disappointment for the thirty-one-year-old returning veteran, dubbed "America's No. 1 athletic hero" by the *New York Daily News*.[3] While his slugging percentage was fourth best in the AL, his batting average (.290) and RBIs (95) were lower than in any previous season and his home run total (25) the second lowest. As the 1947 season neared, the outlook for improvement was not good. The first news about DiMaggio that year was the announcement of his upcoming surgery to remove a bone spur from his left heel. On January 7 a three-inch spur was removed. Then when skin-graft surgery was needed two months later to close the wound from the first operation, John Drebinger of the *New York Times* wrote that DiMaggio "seems to be giving more prominence to the human heel than it has received since the days of Achilles."[4]

The injury kept him out of the lineup until April 19, when he appeared as a pinch hitter. He made his first start the next day, hitting a three-run homer in a 6–2 win over the Athletics, but by the end of April he was hitting a paltry .143. A 4 for 5 performance against the Red Sox on May 25 put him over the .300 mark for the first time.

On May 26, before 74,747 fans, the Yankees won their fourth straight over Boston and fifth straight overall. In the 9–3 win DiMaggio went 3 for 4 and raised his average to .323. On June 3, in a 3–0 win over the first-place Detroit Tigers, DiMaggio got four hits to raise his average to a league-leading .368. He had hit safely in 16 straight games since May 18, hitting .493 over that stretch.

The Yankees moved into first place on June 15 with a doubleheader sweep of the St. Louis Browns. A 19-game winning streak, between June 29 and July 17, put them 11½ games ahead of Detroit, and they finished the season with a 12-game lead over the Tigers.

By the end of the season, DiMaggio's statistics were again below his prewar levels. His average had fallen to .315, seventh best in the AL, with twenty home runs (his lowest total to date) and ninety-seven RBIs, third in the league but his second lowest total. Although surpassed in virtually every offensive category by Ted Williams, who won his second Triple Crown, DiMaggio was awarded his third MVP Award on the basis of his all-around play in leading the Yankees to their first pennant since 1943. Receiving eight first-place votes compared to three for the Red Sox slugger, the Yankee Clipper edged his perennial rival by a single point, 202–201.

In the memorable World Series against the Dodgers, DiMaggio hit only .231, but he did hit two home runs, one of which gave the Yanks a 2–1 win in Game Five. In this Series, however, he is best remembered for his reaction to Al Gionfriddo's spectacular catch in Game Six. In the sixth inning the Yankees, trailing 8–5, put two men on with two out, bringing DiMaggio to the plate as the tying run. Gionfriddo, a seldom-used outfielder, had entered the game that inning as a defensive replacement. The Yankee slugger launched a long drive toward the visitors' bullpen in deep left, but Gionfriddo was able to track it down and make a lunging catch just short of the bullpen before crashing into the waist-high gate near the 415-foot sign. No less memorable than the catch was DiMaggio's reaction. In a rare display of emotion, the famously stoic star kicked at the dirt near second base when he saw that Gionfriddo had caught the ball.

The year 1948 proved to be DiMaggio's last great season, at least in terms of statistics. Playing in 153 games, in spite of a bone spur in his right heel, he led the league in home runs, RBIs, and total bases and finished second to Lou Boudreau in the MVP vote. The 1949 season proved to be one of the worst of his career; however, his heroic midseason return from injury helped cement his reputation as an inspirational team leader.

The lingering bone spur injury caused DiMaggio to miss the first 65 games of the '49 season. With the press speculating that the Yankee Clipper might be nearing the end of the road, a sullen DiMaggio isolated himself in his hotel room. Then, in mid-June, the pain suddenly disappeared. Two weeks later he made his debut in a crucial series against the Red Sox at Fenway. In the opener, on June 28, he drove in two runs and scored two in a 5–4 win. The next day he hit two homers and drove in four, then wrapped up his first regular-season series since the previous September with his fourth homer in 3 games and 3 RBIs. The sweep put the Yankees 8 games ahead of the Red Sox.

Boston bounced back with a late-season surge that gave them a 1-game lead over New York with 2 games at Yankee Stadium remaining. DiMaggio, meanwhile, had been hospitalized in September with pneumonia, but was in the starting lineup when the final series began.

The day of the opener, October 1, was also "Joe DiMaggio Day." Before 69,551 fans, the Yankee Clipper, with his mother and brother Dom by his side, was lauded in several speeches and received what the *New York Times* described as "a small mountain of gifts." At the conclusion of the hour-

long ceremony, DiMaggio spoke to the crowd, ending his speech by saying, "I want to thank the good Lord for making me a Yankee."[5]

DiMaggio, described as looking "wan and weak after his recent siege," had told manager Casey Stengel that he hoped to play three innings. Instead, he played the entire game. With the Yankees trailing, 4–0, he doubled in the fourth and scored their first run in the 5–4 win that brought the two teams to a tie with one game left.

In the finale Vic Raschi held the Sox scoreless through eight innings, but in the ninth two runs scored when DiMaggio's tired legs were not able to catch up to a drive by Bobby Doerr that went for a triple. Drained of energy and realizing that he was a detriment to his team, DiMaggio ran in from center field, taking himself out of the game. The Yankees held on to win the game, 5–3, and the pennant. Limited to 76 games, he hit .346 with 67 RBIs. The Associated Press gave him its award for sports' greatest comeback of 1949, with second place going to the Yankees, a team that had been plagued by injuries for much of the season.

DiMaggio was able to play in 139 games in 1950, hitting .301 with 32 home runs, 122 RBIs, and a league-leading .585 slugging percentage. But age and injury limited him to 116 games in 1951, when he hit only 12 homers and compiled the lowest average of his career at .263. On December 11, 1951, the thirty-six-year-old veteran announced his retirement, saying, "If I can't do it right, I don't want to play any longer."[6]

In the six years he played after the war, DiMaggio remained the leader of a Yankees team that won the World Series in each of his final three seasons. But while he won the MVP Award in 1947, and 1948 was one of his best seasons, overall his postwar performance was not at the same level as it had been before the war. "Baseball wasn't much fun for Joe from 1949 until he quit," said teammate Phil Rizzuto. "He was getting older and he was hurt a lot." His postwar batting average was

.304, with an average of 24 home runs per year, compared to .339 and 31 homers per year between 1936 and 1942.

In his career DiMaggio, hit .325 with 361 home runs, 1,537 RBIS, and a .579 slugging average. He was an All-Star in each of his thirteen seasons, and in addition to winning three MVP Awards, he finished in the top nine seven other times. Perhaps more impressive than any other statistic is the fact that in 6,821 times at bat, he struck out 369 times — only 8 more than his total number of home runs — for an average of once every 18.5 times at bat.

Given the relative brevity of his career, DiMaggio's totals do not measure up to those of many other major stars. But he was admired not only for what he did on the field but for how he looked doing it. Columnist Jim Murray wrote, "Joe DiMaggio played the game at least at a couple of levels higher than the rest of baseball. A lot of guys, all you had to see to know they were great was a stat sheet. DiMaggio, you had to see. It wasn't only numbers on a page — although they were there too — it was a question of command, style, grace."[7]

In the eyes of his contemporaries, Joe DiMaggio was universally considered the best player they had ever seen. Even his arch rival, Ted Williams, said, "I have always felt I was a better hitter than Joe, but I have to say that he was the greatest baseball player of our time. He could do it all." Stan Musial, the often overlooked third member of the great triad of the 1940s and 1950s, said: "There was never a day when I was as good as Joe DiMaggio at his best. Joe was the best, the very best I ever saw." Pulitzer Prize-winning columnist Red Smith called DiMaggio "indisputably the finest ballplayer of his time."[8]

Rico Petrocelli, a New York native who played for the Red Sox between 1965 and 1976, recalled going to Yankee Stadium as a youngster: "We were in the bleachers, and Joe DiMaggio was still playing. I looked around and noticed nobody was watching the pitcher throw the ball. Everyone was looking at DiMaggio. When he'd catch a ball, he'd lope after it. It was just beautiful to watch. I'll never forget it."[9]

An unsigned column in the *Washington Post* on July 2, 1941, the day after DiMaggio surpassed George Sisler's consecutive-game hit streak, placed the Yankee star alongside the other "Olympians" of baseball, such as Cobb, Ruth, and Speaker, and said of his style, "there is something about it, at bat and in the field, that suggests some of the great sculptures of the Italian Renaissance: Donatello's, for example."[10]

In the batter's box, DiMaggio was the picture of understated calm. He stood there motionless, hands and head still, feet wide apart. Only at the last moment, when he whipped the bat around in his trademark long swing, did he unleash the force that he had kept under tight control.

DiMaggio was no less adept at keeping his emotions under tight control, at least in public. DiMaggio embodied *sprezzatura*, the Italian term for the ability to make the difficult look easy. Teammate Jerry Coleman called him "the only professional athlete I've ever seen who had an imperial presence."[11] But DiMaggio's calm exterior masqueraded the inner turmoil that drove him to always be at his best. Whatever emotions he stuffed inside and hid from the paying customers manifested themselves in the ulcers that earned him a discharge from the service in 1945.

DiMaggio understood his role as a public figure, and he did his best to live up to his image as the greatest player in the game and the leader of its best team. His grace and style on the field were matched by his appearance off of it. In his elegant tailored suits, he was the model of quiet elegance.

For all that DiMaggio was an intensely private man who never felt completely comfortable in his role as hero. Before he became a national icon, he bore the additional, and unwanted, burden of being the great hero of Americans of Italian descent. Yankee pitcher Lefty Gomez, a close friend, said, "All the Italians in America adopted him. Just about every day at home and on the road there would be an invitation from some Italian-American club."[12]

For former New York governor Mario Cuomo, DiMaggio's life "demonstrated to all the strivers and seekers—like me—that America would make a place for true excellence whatever its color or accent or origin." *New York Daily News* columnist Mike Lupica acknowledged DiMaggio's significance for his father and grandfather: "There was only one ballplayer for them, an Italian American ballplayer of such talent and fierce pride it made them fiercely proud, fiercely biased toward their man even after he had left the playing field for good." Hall of Fame manager Tommy Lasorda summed it up this way: "I knew every big leaguer when I was growing up, but Joe DiMaggio was my hero. He was our hero; he was everything we wanted to be."[13]

DiMaggio's appeal to the general public was due, in part, to the stylish way he displayed his all-around ability as a ballplayer. But beyond that his colorless but dependable performance was right for the times. This sober, serious young man who went about his work without bravado or flamboyance was the ideal hero for a nation that was struggling, first to survive the Great Depression and then to win a war. The refrain of "Joe, Joe DiMaggio, we want you on our side," from Les Brown's 1941 hit song was a timely reflection of how the public identified with the young star.

The 1941 hitting streak, followed by his military service in World War II, helped DiMaggio become a national hero whose ethnic background, often noted by the prewar press, became increasingly irrelevant. His fame and popularity were celebrated in song and literature as he became a touchstone of popular culture. In the 1949 Rodgers and Hammerstein musical *South Pacific*, sailors sing of the character named Bloody Mary that "her skin is tender as DiMaggio's glove." Santiago, the indomitable protagonist of Ernest Hemingway's 1952 novella *The Old Man and the Sea* says that he must be worthy of his idol, the great DiMaggio. Paul Simon's 1968 hit song "Mrs. Robinson" expressed nostalgia for a simpler, more innocent time by asking, "Where have you gone, Joe DiMaggio, a nation turns its lonely eyes to you."

Unlike most professional athletes, Joe DiMaggio enjoyed a resurgence of fame and adulation in his postbaseball life. His legend was enhanced when, in January 1954, he once again made headlines by marrying Marilyn Monroe. But the ill-fated union of two of America's most celebrated personalities lasted only nine months. DiMaggio had naively expected the film star to become a devoted housewife. According to Joe's brother Dom, "Her career was first. Joe could not condone the things that Marilyn had to do. Joe wanted a wife he could raise children with. She could not do that." But DiMaggio, who remained devoted to Monroe, held out hope that they would remarry. "Joe had wanted that relationship to work," said Dom. "He held on to it for the rest of his life."[14] When Monroe died in 1962 Joe took charge of her funeral and ordered that roses be placed at her crypt twice a week.

DiMaggio spent several years in relative obscurity before appearing, incongruously, in the green-and-white uniform of the Oakland A's, serving as a coach and vice president for Charlie Finley's newly transplanted franchise in 1968–69. Then, in the 1970s, he reemerged as a national celebrity when, overcoming the shyness that had inhibited him during his playing days, he became a television spokesman for New York's Bowery Savings Bank and the "Mr. Coffee" coffee maker. For much of his life thereafter, DiMaggio remained in the public eye by carefully orchestrating appearances at celebrity golf outings, card shows, and Old-Timers Day, where he was introduced as "baseball's greatest living player," a title bestowed upon him in a 1969 poll. By limiting his personal appearances and rigidly protecting his privacy, he was able to sustain the mystique that made him one of the most admired men in America, even when his career was long over.

On October 12, 1998, DiMaggio was admitted to Regional Memorial Hospital in Hollywood, Florida, where he had been living for many years. (It was the same hospital where the Joe DiMaggio Children's Hospital had been established.) Two days later he underwent surgery for lung cancer and never fully recovered. He died at his home on March 8, 1999, at the age of eighty-four.

One of those rare athletes—like Babe Ruth and Muhammad Ali—who transcended the world of sport, DiMaggio has been called by more than one writer the last American hero. Revisionist historians later offered a more nuanced view, portraying him as a flawed hero who became increasingly reclusive and suspicious of others. Nevertheless, when he died his enduring status as a cultural icon was confirmed by an outpouring of adulation that few public figures, in any walk of life, could evoke. His death was front-page news in every major newspaper, was covered extensively on television newscasts and specials, and was the cover story in *Newsweek*. Referring to the frequent bulletins on DiMaggio's health that had been issued in the months prior to his death, Frank Deford wrote that it was "as if he were some great head of state." As one Brooklyn native put it, DiMaggio "epitomized an era when, for a lot of us, baseball was the most important thing in life."[15]

The answer to Paul Simon's question—"Where has Joe DiMaggio gone?"—remains the same: nowhere. He remains firmly lodged in the American consciousness as a stylish symbol of a time when baseball was the undisputed national pastime and America was enjoying unprecedented prosperity. On April 25, 1999, two months after

his death, DiMaggio's monument was unveiled in Yankee Stadium's Monument Park, joining those honoring Miller Huggins, Lou Gehrig, Babe Ruth, and Mickey Mantle. The inscription reads, in part, "A Baseball Legend and An American Icon."

Chapter 48. Timeline, August 8–August 28

Lyle Spatz

Friday, August 8, at Boston — The Red Sox reached Joe Page for four runs in the bottom of the eighth to down the Yankees, 9–6. Page had successfully rescued starter Vic Raschi in the sixth but gave up four hits, including home runs by Jake Jones and Sam Mele in Boston's winning rally. The largest night-game crowd ever in Fenway Park saw Mickey Harris win in relief of Harry Dorish. New York, led by Yogi Berra and George McQuinn, outhit Boston 14–10. Bobby Doerr had a double, a home run, and four runs batted in for the Red Sox. Joe DiMaggio's injured neck continued to keep him out of the Yankees' lineup. 69-36-1, First, 12½ games ahead.

Saturday, August 9, at Boston — Bobby Doerr continued pounding the Yankees, blasting two homeruns and driving in four as the Red Sox won, 6–4. Dave Ferris was the winner, and Frank Shea, who relieved Allie Reynolds in the eighth inning and yielded Doerr's second home run, took the loss. It was Shea's first appearance since July 23. Aaron Robinson had three hits, including two triples. Robinson caught, while Yogi Berra played left field. The Yankees' lead was reduced to 11½ games over Boston, and manager Bucky Harris cautioned that the race was not yet over. 69-37-1, First, 11½ games ahead.

Sunday, August 10, at Boston — One of the best pitching duels of the season ended with a 2–1 Yankees victory that ended their three-game losing streak. After eight scoreless innings, New York scored two in the ninth and Boston just one. The Yankees' Karl Drews had to leave with two outs

in the ninth and the potential tying run on second because of a blister on his pitching hand. Joe Page came in and got pinch hitter Roy Partee for the final out. Joe Dobson went all the way for the Red Sox. George Stirnweiss's two-run single accounted for the two Yankees runs. 70-37-1, First, 12½ games ahead.

Monday, August 11, vs. Philadelphia — In their second matchup in five days, A's rookie Bill McCahan again got the best of Yankees veteran Bobo Newsom. Sam Chapman had a home run, and Pete Suder had a two-run triple to account for all of Philadelphia's runs in their 3–2 victory. Barney McCosky added four hits for the A's. Yogi Berra and Johnny Lindell drove in New York's runs, and Joe DiMaggio had a triple in his return to the lineup. 70-38-1, First, 11½ games ahead.

Tuesday, August 12 — Not scheduled. 70-38-1, First, 11 games ahead.

Wednesday, August 13, vs. Philadelphia — Vic Raschi raised his record to 6-0 with a complete-game 8–2 triumph over the Athletics. Allie Clark had four runs batted in, and Phil Rizzuto, Yogi Berra, and Johnny Lindell each had two hits. Joe DiMaggio missed the game with a heel injury. 71-38-1, First, 11 games ahead.

Thursday, August 14, vs. Philadelphia — Joe DiMaggio and Tommy Henrich missed their second consecutive games, but Allie Reynolds won his league-leading fifteenth game, with final-inning help from Frank Shea. Phil Rizzuto had three hits, and Allie Clark had two doubles in the Yankees' 8–5 win. Clark and George McQuinn each had three runs batted in. 72-38-1, First, 11½ games ahead.

Friday, August 15, vs. Boston—The Yankees used a six-run second inning to power them past the Red Sox, 10–6, in a game that featured the return to action of Joe DiMaggio and Tommy Henrich. Joe Page came on in the second inning after the Red Sox scored four runs in the inning off starter Karl Drews. Page pitched the rest of the way for his ninth win. Mickey Harris, the first of five Boston pitchers, was the loser. George Stirnweiss had a triple and a home run, and Yogi Berra had three runs batted in. Ted Williams had four hits, including two doubles, for the Red Sox. 73-38-1, First, 12½ games ahead.

Saturday, August 16, vs. Boston—A ninth-inning run allowed Bobo Newsom and the Yankees to edge Earl Johnson and the Red Sox, 1–0. Allie Clark opened the ninth with his fourth single and eventually came around to score on a single by Johnny Lindell. He also robbed Boston of a run with a sensational catch of a Bobby Doerr liner. Ted Williams walked twice to raise his season total to 123. 74-38-1, First, 13½ games ahead.

Sunday, August 17, vs. Boston—The sensational pitching continued at Yankee Stadium, with the Red Sox winning 3–0 in eleven innings. Denny Galehouse shut out the Yankees on six hits, giving Vic Raschi his first big-league loss. Both pitchers went the distance. Sam Mele drove in the first two runs in the eleventh inning and Johnny Pesky the third. George Stirnweiss, Joe DiMaggio, and Johnny Lindell had all the Yankees' hits, each getting two. 74-39-1, First, 12½ games ahead.

Monday, August 18—Not scheduled. 74-39-1, First, 12½ games ahead.

Tuesday, August 19, at Detroit—Stubby Overmire of the Tigers outpitched Allie Reynolds, as the Yankees began their final western trip with a 2–1 loss to the Tigers. Hoot Evers's sixth-inning home run was the deciding blow. The loss dropped Reynolds's record to 15-7. The Yanks managed only seven singles against Overmire, with two each by Billy Johnson and Ralph Houk. 74-40-1, First, 11½ games ahead.

Wednesday, August 20, at Detroit—After a three-hour-and-eighteen-minute marathon, the Yankees came away with a 14–13 win in eleven innings. The Tigers scored nine runs in the seventh inning to take a 13–5 lead, but the Yankees came back with three in the eighth and five in the ninth to send the game into extra innings. The Yankees had nineteen hits, including a double and a home run by Yogi Berra and triples by George Stirnweiss and Johnny Lindell. The Tigers had four doubles among their twenty-two hits, two by Vic Wertz, and one each by Virgil Trucks and Hoot Evers. Karl Drews, who followed Bobo Newsom, Frank Shea, Joe Page, and Randy Gumpert to the mound, got the win; Hal White took the loss. 75-40-1, First, 12 games ahead.

Thursday, August 21, at Cleveland—Billy Johnson had a home run, a triple, and two singles to lead New York to a 9–3 win over the Indians. The win, combined with Boston's loss at Chicago, increased the Yankees' lead to 13 games. Bill Bevens went all the way for his fifth win. 76-40-1, First, 13 games ahead.

Friday, August 22, at Cleveland (2)—After eight straight wins at Municipal Stadium this season, the Yanks dropped both ends of a doubleheader. Cleveland won the opener, 4–3 behind Bob Lemon and Ed Klieman. Vic Raschi, who surrendered home runs to Joe Gordon and Eddie Robinson, was the loser. The Yanks had twelve hits to Cleveland's six, but doubles by Billy Johnson and Joe DiMaggio were the their only extra-base blows. Bob Feller's four-hit, 6–1 victory in the second game secured the sweep. Karl Drews, the first of three Yankee pitchers, took the loss. Jack Phillips made his Major League debut when he struck out as a pinch hitter for Randy Gumpert in the ninth. 76-42-1, First, 12 games ahead.

Saturday, August 23, at Cleveland—An eight-run second inning powered the Yankees to a 13–6 win in their final game in Cleveland this season. New York had seventeen hits against starter and loser Red Embree and Les Willis, a thirty-nine-year-old rookie making his final big-league appearance. Allie Reynolds picked up his league-leading sixteenth victory, but injured his shoulder in the ninth inning, making it necessary for Joe Page to get the final out. Tommy Henrich had three hits for New York, and Johnny Lindell had his eighth home run. 77-42-1, First, 12½ games ahead.

Sunday, August 24, at Chicago (2)—Chicago's Joe Haynes edged Bobo Newsom, 3–2 in the first game, but the Yankees pounded out sixteen hits to win the nightcap, 16–6, in a game called after seven innings. Frank Shea started the second game, but Joe Page, who came on in the fifth, got the win. Red Ruffing and Orval Grove were the victims of the Yankees' attack. Tommy Henrich, Joe DiMaggio, Billy Johnson, and Aaron Robinson each had three hits. DiMaggio and Robinson had home runs. DiMaggio, who drove in four runs, also scored four times, while Phil Rizzuto, who had four hits in the opener, scored three runs in the nightcap. 78-43-1, First, 12½ games ahead.

Monday, August 25, at Chicago—Chicago defeated the Yankees, 4–3, on a muddy, rain-soaked field. The Yanks had only six hits off winner Frank Papish, who pitched the first five innings, and Pete Gebrian, who pitched the final

four. George Stirnweiss had three of the hits. Loser Bill Bevens allowed all the runs in his two innings of work, while Butch Wensloff held the White Sox scoreless for six innings. 78-44-1, First, 12½ games ahead.

Tuesday, August 26, at St. Louis—A 4–3 loss to the last-place St. Louis Browns gave the Yankees their third one-run loss in their last four games. Trailing 3–1, the Yanks tied it on George Stirnweiss's two-run double in the top of the ninth, but Paul Lehner singled home Bob Dillinger in the home half to win it for St. Louis. Bill Bevens, who came on to pitch the ninth, suffered his second loss in two days. Nelson Potter, in relief of Bob Muncrief, was the winner. 78-45-1, First, 12 games ahead.

Wednesday, August 27, at St. Louis—Three hits by George Stirnweiss, including two home runs, helped lead the Yankees to a ten-inning 7–6 win in St. Louis. Stirnweiss homered off Jack Kramer on the first pitch of the game and broke a 6–6 tie with a home run off Nelson Potter with two outs in the tenth. Karl Drews started for New York, but Joe Page, with five innings of scoreless relief, got the win. 79-45-1, First, 12½ games ahead.

Thursday, August 28—Not scheduled. 79-45-1, First, 12 games ahead.

Chapter 49. Ralph Houk

John Vorperian

AGE	G	AB	R	H	2B	3B	HR	TB	RBI	BB	SO	BAV	OBP	SLG	SB	GDP	HBP
27	41	92	7	25	3	1	0	30	12	11	5	.272	.356	.326	0	2	1

Ralph Houk was the first manager to have two World Series championships in his first two seasons, piloting the 1961 and 1962 New York Yankees to triumphs over the Cincinnati Reds and San Francisco Giants. His Yankees won a third consecutive pennant in 1963 but lost the World Series to the Los Angeles Dodgers.

A backup catcher throughout his playing career, Houk sought to build the morale and confidence of his players and seldom criticized them publicly. "I don't think you can humiliate a player and expect him to perform," he once said.[1]

Ralph George Houk was born on August 9, 1919, in Lawrence, Kansas. His father, George J. Houk, raised cattle and farmed 160 acres of land in Kanwaka, Kansas, about eight miles east of Lawrence. Ralph's mother was Emma A. (Schael) Houk. He had two older brothers, Harold M. and Russell V.; an older sister, Hazel; and a younger brother, Clifford.

Houk's baseball education began at the tender age of eleven. His uncles Harvey, Albert, Rudy, and Charlie Houk played weekend baseball on a semipro club, the Belvoirs. Charlie, the manager, took Ralph to a tryout with the Lawrence Twilight League, a circuit sponsored by fraternal orders and small businesses for boys eleven to seventeen. Young Ralph, who had a sturdy frame and strong throwing arm, was selected by the Fraternal Order of Eagles and played left field his first season.

The following year Houk filled in at catcher, became the regular, and found his niche in baseball. He later remarked, "I liked catching. I had the whole game in front of me. I was in on every pitch. At fifteen I was solid as a rock, 170 pounds

Ralph Houk made his Major League debut on April 26, 1947, by going 3 for 3 against the Washington Senators.

of hard-muscled flesh. I could block onrushing base runners at home plate. In fact blocking was easy for me."

Houk was also drawn to football. At Lawrence High, he played quarterback and defensive back.

"I seldom passed from my post behind center," he remembered.[2] In the 1937 state title game against Emporia, Houk ran for three touchdowns, one for sixty-seven yards. He earned all-state honors, and the Universities of Kansas and Oklahoma, and several smaller colleges, offered him football scholarships. Yet as much as the teenager desired a college education, he wanted a career in baseball.

At sixteen Houk moved up from the Eagles to the Belvoirs and also played for a Lawrence team in the Ban Johnson League, a regional circuit for teenagers. Houk later recalled that in 1938, he batted .411 as Lawrence raced into the league tournament at Kansas City, Kansas. He caught the first game of a tourney doubleheader, slugged three hits, threw out a base stealer, and twice blocked runners at the plate as Lawrence prevailed, 5–4.

Yankees scouts Bill Essick and Bill Skiff, who attended the game, later went into the clubhouse. While Skiff guarded the door to keep other scouts out, Essick signed the nineteen-year-old Houk to a contract with a two-hundred-dollar bonus.

In March 1939 Houk went to spring training with Joplin (Missouri) Miners of the Class C Western Association. Later in the season he was assigned to the Neosho (Missouri) Yankees in the Class D Arkansas-Missouri League. There, for a monthly salary of seventy-five dollars, he caught 109 games and batted .286, with fifty-six RBIS, playing well enough to be honored with a "day" at the Neosho ballpark.

Houk was promoted back to Joplin in 1940, but his contract called for the same seventy-five-dollar salary. Believing he should not be paid Class D wages in a Class C league, he sent a letter to the Yankees. When he got no response, Houk went to Joplin to plead his case with the manager, Red O'Malley, who offered him another fifteen dollars. Houk accepted the ninety-dollar monthly salary and played in 110 games, batted .313, drove in sixty-three runs, and led the league's catchers in assists.

Houk credited O'Malley, a former Pacific Coast League catcher, with improving his defensive skills and understanding of the game. Under O'Malley, he learned to position his fielders and memorize the batters' habits. Most important, he made a habit of knowing his pitchers. He knew which hurlers had fortitude and who had fragile egos. "I knew their best pitches and their worst, and when to call for speed and when to use their slower stuff," he said later.[3]

After opening the 1941 season with the Binghamton (New York) Triplets of the Class A Eastern League, Houk was demoted to the Augusta (Georgia) Tigers of the Class B South Atlantic League. There he batted .271 in 97 games, and caught a no-hitter by future New York Yankees relief ace Joe Page.

In February 1942 both Ralph and his brother Harold joined the army and were sent to Fort Leavenworth, Kansas. Twenty-two-year-old Ralph was made the manager of the camp baseball team. When the weather was too cold for baseball, he was placed in charge of a barracks for recruits. It was good experience for a future big-league manager. "I learned fast how to keep all kinds of men in line, from weepy homesick boys to neurotics who pulled knives on each other," he said.[4] Ralph and Harold applied for Officers' Candidate School and were accepted. Ralph was sent to the armored warfare school at Fort Knox, Kentucky. Upon graduation he was commissioned a second lieutenant and in July 1944 was sent overseas with the 89th Cavalry Reconnaissance Squadron of the Ninth Armored Division.

A few days after D-day Houk landed on Omaha Beach in Normandy, where his helmet was pierced by a bullet that narrowly missed his skull. As the GIs pushed through Europe, Houk and his troops found themselves in the Ardennes Forest, where the Germans launched the counterattack we now call the Battle of the Bulge. "Suddenly all hell broke loose," Houk wrote. "They opened the attack with a furious barrage; followed by wave after wave of Hitler's battle-tested troopers. . . . Panzer divisions . . . were turned loose on us."[5] His unit was pushed back to the town of Waldbillig. When two other lieutenants were killed, Houk was left as the senior officer. As the Germans pushed forward he found a tank destroyer, rode it back to Waldbillig, and held the town.

Houk was awarded the Silver Star. Later he was given a battlefield promotion to first lieutenant, and just before the war's end he was promoted to captain and was awarded a Bronze Star and Purple Heart. Before being discharged he was automatically lifted one grade to major, which accounted for his postwar nickname, "the Major."

In 1946 the Yankees assigned the twenty-six-year-old Houk, four years removed from his last Minor League season, to the Class Triple-A Kansas City Blues. After eight games he was sent down to the Class Double-A Beaumont (Texas) Exporters. In eighty-seven games with Beaumont, he handled catching and outfield duties and batted .294 with ninety RBIs. Houk went to spring training with the Yankees in 1947, where he competed for the receiver position with veterans Aaron Robinson, Ken Silvestri, and Gus Niarhos and rookie Yogi Berra.

On an exhibition tour of Latin America, manager Bucky Harris started Houk in the opening game, in San Juan, Puerto Rico, because all the other catchers had sore arms. Houk had a good series in San Juan and started the opener in Caracas, Venezuela. The pitcher was a rookie left-hander who was wild. Several times coach Charlie Dressen directed Houk to go into a lower stance. At one point the five-foot-eleven, 193-pound Houk called time, ran toward Dressen, and said, "Where the hell do you want me to go? Under the plate?"[6]

Houk caught no more in Venezuela or the next stop, Havana. The exhibition tour over, Houk was sent from the Yankees' main camp at St. Petersburg, Florida, to their Minor League camp in Bra-

denton. But when the Yankees headed north, he was with the team.

On April 26, 1947, Houk made his Major League debut in a 3–1 victory over the Washington Senators at Yankee Stadium. Catching fellow rookie Don Johnson, Houk batted in the eighth slot and went 3 for 3 with a double. Manager Harris, impressed with the performance, kept Houk as the team's third-string catcher. He spent the season catching in the bullpen and subbing for Aaron Robinson or Yogi Berra in late innings of lopsided contests or second games of doubleheaders. Houk played in forty-one games and batted .272. In his only World Series appearance that year, he had a pinch-hit single off the Brooklyn Dodgers' Joe Hatten in Game Six.

At spring training the next March, Houk was irate when Yankees traveling secretary Red Patterson handed him a plane ticket for Kansas City. General manager George Weiss believed Houk would get more seasoning playing in Kansas City rather than spending another year in the Yankees' bullpen. Houk felt he had been with the team an entire year and should be retained. He refused to go to Kansas City. In his book, *Ballplayers Are Human, Too*, Houk wrote that someone persuaded him to go. That someone appeared to be New York sportswriter Dan Daniel. In Jerome Holtzman's *No Cheering in the Press Box*, Daniel was quoted as saying, "Houk was sitting in the Serena Hotel . . . refusing to join the Kansas City club. Houk told me he was returning home. . . . I told him, 'Do you like baseball? . . . Would you like a career in baseball?' Houk responded in the affirmative."[7] Daniel told him go to Kansas City and even bet him he would be back in the big leagues.

Although disappointed with the move to Kansas City, Houk took advantage of his club's location and often returned to Lawrence. On June 3, 1948, he married Lawrence resident Bette Jean Porter. Bette had two children from a previous marriage, Donna and Richard, and the couple later had a son, Robert. Houk's first wife, Lela Belle Slover, had died in September 1944.

Houk played in 103 games behind the plate and at third base for the Blues. He batted .302 and got a late-August call-up to the Yankees and appeared in 14 games. After a brief stint with New York in 1949, Houk was back with the Blues, where he batted .275 in 95 games. He was recalled and caught a hotly contested loss to the Boston Red Sox at Yankee Stadium that helped cement his hard-nosed image.

The Yankees and Red Sox were battling for the pennant. The Red Sox scored the eventual game-winning run on a squeeze play on which Houk put the tag on Johnny Pesky. Umpire Bill Grieve called Pesky safe, ruling that he had slid under the tag. An infuriated Houk had to be restrained from going after the umpire. Baseball historian Leonard Koppett later wrote, "For the next few years Houk's identity in the minds of Yankee fans was encompassed in that one wild game."[8]

Houk had impressed manager Casey Stengel with his assertive manner and baseball smarts. Although he was primarily a bullpen catcher under Stengel, to his teammates he was "the answer man." "Newcomers turned to me for information about life, love, and baseball" said Houk. "Veterans on the decline asked me what was wrong with their form."[9]

From 1949 through 1954 Houk played in only 36 games as a Yankee. His final game was on May 1, 1954, against Cleveland at Yankee Stadium, when he grounded out as a pinch hitter. Later that season, Yankees' farm director Lee MacPhail talked with Houk about his interest in managing. In 1955, at the age of thirty-five, Houk became manager of the Yankees' new American Association farm club in Denver. The team went 83-71 in his first year and improved the next two seasons. In 1957 the Bears won the Junior World Series over the Buffalo Bisons.

Houk had coached for the Yankees in 1953–54, and in 1958 the Yankees brought him back as a coach to replace Bill Dickey. The Yanks won the pennant that year and defeated the Milwaukee Braves in the World Series, but the 1959 club slipped to third place, only 4 games above .500. Speculation centered on Houk as a possible replacement for Stengel.

In 1960 the Yankees won the pennant but lost the World Series to the Pittsburgh Pirates on Bill Mazeroski's Game Seven home run. After the Series Stengel was fired, and Houk was named to replace him. He inherited a team that included Mickey Mantle, Roger Maris, Yogi Berra, Whitey Ford, Elston Howard, Tony Kubek, Bill Skowron, and Bobby Richardson.

Richardson recalled that one of Houk's first steps was to tell Whitey Ford, "You're gonna pitch every three days."[10] In 1961 Ford was 25-4 with a 3.21 ERA, worked a league-best 283 innings, and won the Cy Young Award. Houk moved Roger Maris into the number-three slot and Mickey Mantle into the cleanup position. The pair battled each other all season in an attempt to eclipse Babe Ruth's home run record. Houk later said watching that race was a highlight of his career. The Yankees won 109 games and defeated the Cincinnati Reds in the World Series.

When Houk again led the Yankees to pennants in 1962 and 1963, he became the first manager since Hughie Jennings of the 1907–9 Detroit Tigers to win pennants in each of his first three seasons.

In 1964 the New York hierarchy moved Houk up to the general manager's post and named Yogi Berra the new manager. The Yankees made a late-September surge to win the pennant, but lost to the St. Louis Cardinals in a seven-game World Series. Houk fired Berra and hired Cardinals manager Johnny Keane to replace him.

The Yankees finished sixth in 1965 and were in last place with a 4-16 record in 1966 when Houk flew to California and fired Keane. Houk returned as manager, but the team was plagued with injuries and aging players. The Yankees finished in last place, the first time they finished at the bottom of the American League since 1912.

From 1967 to 1972 Houk's Yankees were not contenders. Their closest finish was second place in 1970, but they were fifteen games behind first-place Baltimore. The 1973 Yankees finished in fourth place in the American League East Division with an 80-82 record. Houk resigned on the final day of the season.

He was not unemployed for long. Two weeks after resigning he was hired by the Detroit Tigers, who had released manager Billy Martin. From 1974 to 1978 under Houk, the Tigers finished at or near the bottom of the six-team division.

After the 1978 season Houk retired to Florida. Three years later he returned to baseball as the manager of the 1981 Boston Red Sox. He became one of only four men to have directed the Yankees and the Red Sox. (The others, all Hall of Famers, were Frank Chance, Bucky Harris, and Joe McCarthy.) Houk left Boston after the 1984 season. Under his leadership the Red Sox contended for the playoffs in only the second half of the strike-shortened 1981 season. At the age of sixty-four he retired from managing. In twenty years at the helm for three different clubs, he amassed 1,619 victories and 1,531 defeats.

In November 1986 Houk became a vice president of the Minnesota Twins. Working with manager Tom Kelly and general manager Andy MacPhail, he helped assemble the Twins' 1987 world championship team. He retired again in 1989. On July 21, 2010, at age ninety, Ralph Houk passed away at his Winter Haven, Florida, home. His wife, Bette, had died in 2006. Houk was buried in Rolling Hills Cemetery in Winter Haven.

Chapter 50. **Dan Topping**

Dan Levitt and Mark Armour

Dan Topping enjoyed a "sportsman" lifestyle we seldom see anymore in America, one founded on inherited wealth, some athletic ability, and active involvement in professional or other sports. The life also often entailed a playboy youth and multiple attractive socialite wives. Topping fit the mold perfectly. Unlike many who lived this lifestyle, however, Topping was highly successful in his final sports endeavor as co-owner of the New York Yankees from 1945 to 1964. He had help, of course, in the front office: general manager George Weiss was one of baseball's best and co-owner Del Webb was a brilliant businessman, but Topping deserves his share of the credit. Under his oversight the team remained a dynasty in America's largest market for two decades.

Daniel Reid Topping was born on June 11, 1912, in Greenwich, Connecticut, to Henry Junkins Topping and Rhea (Reid) Topping. Rhea's father, Daniel G. Reid, amassed a fortune in the tinplate business, started the American Can Company, and had interests in railroads, tobacco, and banks. He left virtually his entire fortune of forty to fifty million dollars to Rhea. Henry's father, industrialist John A. Topping, was a longtime president of the Republic Iron and Steel Company.

Dan Topping's parents gave him the education befitting a young aristocrat. He attended the Hun School, an expensive boarding school in New Jersey, where he starred in football, baseball, and hockey. He next attended the University of Pennsylvania and played both baseball and football. Topping took up golf and became a top-notch amateur, winning several tournaments. After finishing school Topping spent three years working at

Dan Topping fired Larry MacPhail as team president and bought him out following the Yankees' 1947 World Series victory.

a bank, but quickly realized that the life of toiling for a dollar was not for him.

In 1934 the twenty-two-year-old Topping purchased a partial interest in the Brooklyn Dodgers of the fledgling National Football League. Topping soon acquired a majority ownership and spent some money to improve his club. By 1940 he had assembled a decent squad, but with the coming of World War II, most of the Dodgers' best players entered the military, and the team fell back in the standings. Topping joined the marines and served for forty-two months, twenty-six of them out of the country.

Because Topping's Dodgers played in Brooklyn's Ebbets Field, he became friendly with Larry MacPhail, president of the baseball Dodgers in the late 1930s and early 1940s. When Topping ran into MacPhail in California during the war, MacPhail told him of his interest in buying the New York Yankees and invited Topping to join his syndicate.

The Yankees were owned by the Jacob Ruppert estate, which needed money to pay estate taxes. Team president Ed Barrow despised MacPhail, whom he considered a showboat. But Barrow had to sell, and by late 1944 the partnership Topping had formed with MacPhail and construction tycoon Del Webb was the only available option. Topping eased Barrow's concerns enough that he bowed to the inevitable.

In late January 1945, in one of the greatest sports business deals ever, MacPhail, Webb, and Topping purchased 96.88 percent of the Yankees for just $2.8 million. They purchased the final 3.12 percent in March, giving them complete ownership of the team. Topping and Webb supplied the bulk of the capital, lending MacPhail much of his share so he could become an equal one-third partner. MacPhail also received a ten-year contract as team president.

With his partial interest in the Yankees, Topping hoped to move his football Dodgers to Yankee Stadium. New York football Giants owner Tim Mara, holder of the NFL's rights to New York, vetoed the move. The Giants played their home games at the Polo Grounds; nevertheless, Mara argued that "New York is too small to support professional football eleven Sundays each year."[1] At the end of 1945 a new rival football league, the All America Football Conference (AAFC), had just

formed and was scheduled to begin play in 1946. The league's owners offered Topping $100,000 to switch his franchise to the new league and play his games in Yankee Stadium. Topping jumped to the AAFC, renaming his football team the New York Yankees. After four years of competing with the NFL, in 1950 the AAFC reached a peace settlement with the NFL. Topping, by this time concentrating on baseball, happily accepted a settlement offer and rented Yankee Stadium to the NFL's New York Bulldogs for Sundays in the fall.

After three years running the baseball Yankees, the pressure and constant limelight began to tell on Larry MacPhail, who was becoming increasingly agitated and erratic. His maniacal behavior culminated with a drunken breakdown at the celebration dinner in the Biltmore Hotel after the Yankees won the 1947 World Series (see chapter 1). After firing MacPhail as team president and buying him out for $2 million, Topping and Webb now owned the Yankees equally. Both were independent, wealthy men who were not used to sharing authority. Furthermore, they were an original odd couple: Topping, educated in an East Coast boarding school and expensive college, had little in common with Webb, a Californian who grew up in the construction business, playing semipro ball. Nevertheless, the two arranged a surprisingly smooth working relationship. Topping oversaw the operations of the ball club, while Webb assumed a more active role in league affairs.

The Yankees could not repeat in 1948, and Weiss, elevated to general manager after the buyout of MacPhail, jettisoned manager Bucky Harris, with the blessing of Webb and Topping. Weiss wanted to hire Casey Stengel, a somewhat quixotic choice, and Topping had some misgivings. Webb, however, had known Stengel for many years and vouched for him. Topping acquiesced, and Stengel became one of baseball's most successful managers.

Topping generally let Weiss run the show, but he

occasionally interfered on personnel matters and often in player disciplinary issues. When Weiss wanted slugging first baseman Johnny Mize from the Giants in 1949, he asked Topping to negotiate with Giants owner Horace Stoneham, a friend of Topping's. In 1951 Topping tired of pitcher Tommy Byrne's wildness on the mound and directed Weiss to trade him. In 1954 Topping tried to bring Joe DiMaggio back as a coach, with the expectation he would take over as manager when Stengel retired, but DiMaggio declined.

On the disciplinary front Topping occasionally sided with a player, once interceding on behalf of Whitey Ford, who believed he was about to be unfairly fined. But he could also be arbitrary when he felt the aura of the Yankees had been tarnished. After an incident between several players and patrons at the Copacabana nightclub in 1957, Topping fined several players based on initial press reports before the full story came out.

Topping also continually fine-tuned his front office. In 1954 when Roy Hamey, Weiss's top assistant, was hired by the Phillies as general manager, Topping brought in Bill DeWitt, onetime co-owner of the St. Louis Browns and a notorious peddler of players for cash. DeWitt was a surprisingly senior baseball executive to take an assistant general manager position, and Topping considered him a worthy successor to Weiss. "If George were hit by a truck, Bill would take over," Topping stated.[2] After the 1955 season Topping gave Weiss a new five-year contract. DeWitt realized his chances at the top job were slim without the truck and moved on to a job in the commissioner's office. To fill the vacancy, Topping brought in Lee MacPhail, Larry's son and a future general manager and American League president.

When the team fell to 79-75 in 1959, stories raged about what was wrong with the Yankees. It turned out to be just a one-year blip, and the Yankees returned to the top the following year. Nevertheless, the difficulties of 1959 caused Topping and

Webb to reconsider their commitments to Weiss and Stengel.

In the aftermath of the seven-game loss to the underdog Pittsburgh Pirates in the 1960 World Series, Topping eased both Stengel and Weiss out of their positions. "A contract with Casey didn't mean anything," Topping complained. "Casey was always talking about quitting. For a couple of months there [late in the 1958 season] we didn't know whether we had a manager or not. We decided right then that we would never be put in that position again."[3]

Topping and Webb were also concerned about losing manager-in-waiting Ralph Houk to another opportunity. "He's been leading men all his life," Topping said of Houk. "That war record, which was a hell of war record, had us thinking about him from the time he came back. And then during the Denver period, he showed he was a good organization man. He not only developed the players, he kept the New York office informed. He sent back the best reports I've ever seen."[4] Another factor was that Topping wanted to get more directly involved in the operation of the franchise, something that would have been much trickier with the imperial Weiss still in charge.

To fill their spots Topping elevated Roy Hamey, who had returned as Weiss's assistant, to Weiss's spot and Houk to manager. Hamey had much less authority than Weiss, leaving Topping with some of the higher-level functions. Topping quickly took to his activist role. When the Yankees won the World Series in 1961 after a two-year drought, the *Sporting News* named Topping its Executive of the Year for making "a radical change in the leadership of the Yankee club." The *Sporting News* further touted his "courage" and emphasized that he had become the key man running the franchise. "Had this bold move failed," opined the paper, "Topping's own position could conceivably have become untenable."[5]

Over the next several years the Yankees continued their winning ways. In 1962 Topping hired his son, twenty-four-year-old Dan Jr., to be the general manager at a Yankees Class D farm team. The next season Topping promoted him to assistant general manager with the Yankees, right below Hamey. Hamey retired after the 1963 season, and Topping and Webb promoted Houk to general manager and named Yogi Berra manager. The players generally liked and respected Houk, and his transfer to the front office frustrated the players. It also put Houk in a position for which he had little experience or training. Webb was not in favor of the shuffle, but Topping talked him into it.

The Yankees were behind their usual pace for much of the 1964 season, and Topping and Webb resolved to let Berra go when it ended. Berra's club rallied in September, however, to win the pennant, putting the owners in an awkward position. Nevertheless, after the Yankees lost the World Series they fired Berra and hired Johnny Keane, the manager of the St. Louis Cardinals, their Series opponent. Berra may have been in over his head as manager—he had no managerial experience and was criticized for his handling of pitchers—but he had just won the pennant and was a long-venerated and beloved Yankee.

This public-relations disaster was overshadowed by the sale of the Yankees to CBS, announced in August 1964, but dragged out by additional revelations and commentary throughout the off-season. Webb and Topping first seriously considered selling the team a couple of years earlier when Topping went through some health problems. Topping felt he could no longer run the team and sounded out Webb about buying him out. Topping eventually rebounded but needed the money a sale could bring, and the two owners agreed to explore selling the team. With his many ex-wives and children to support, the proceeds from the sale of the team would ease Topping's financial burdens.

The two initially reached an agreement with Lehman Brothers, then a large investment house,

to purchase the team. The sale was dependent on some complex tax angles, and while the lawyers and accountants were working them out, CBS chairman William Paley called his friend Topping to see if the team was available for sale. Topping told him they were already committed in another direction, but that if something changed, he would get back to him. When the sale fell through, Topping called Paley on July 1, 1964, to see if he was still interested. Paley was, and the two began negotiations. On August 14 Topping and Webb agreed to the final deal, selling 80 percent of the Yankees to CBS for $11.2 million. Additionally, Topping would stay on as the operating partner. Topping later testified that he had received offers as high as $16 million, "but they wanted to run the whole show, and I preferred a deal where I could remain active."[6]

It is hard to overestimate the outcry generated by the sale of the Yankees. Up to this point baseball teams rarely had true corporate ownership. More important, in 1964 television was rightly seen as a large and growing phenomenon in American life, and its ultimate impact was not yet fully understood. The sale of America's number-one baseball team to its number-one television network foreshadowed all sorts of grave consequences.

Many criticized the process as much as the substance. Fearing just this sort of reaction, Webb and Topping persuaded American League president Joe Cronin to get league approval by telephoning the league owners rather than calling a meeting. The owners approved the sale 8–2, but the two dissidents, Charles Finley of the Kansas City Athletics and Arthur Allyn of the Chicago White Sox, went public with their opposition. Eventually, Cronin felt compelled to call a league meeting to confirm the sale, but the vote remained the same, and the sale was finalized on November 2, 1964. Webb had little desire to remain in a ceremonial position; in March he sold his remaining share for $1.4 million. Topping stayed on as team president.

Topping was soon overmatched without a strong baseball executive as general manager. Houk knew baseball but had spent the bulk of his career on the field as a manager and coach. On the field Keane could not continue the run of pennants, and the Yankees fell to sixth place in 1965. After a slow start in 1966, with encouragement from CBS, Topping jettisoned Keane, reinstated Houk as manager, and made Dan Jr. the interim general manager. "Houk is the best manager we ever had in the years I've been with the Yankees," Topping said when he made the switch.[7] Unfortunately, not even Houk could help in 1966, as the team finished last. Topping resigned on September 19, selling his remaining 10 percent share to CBS. Topping publicly stated that he had resigned for personal reasons, but there can be little doubt that CBS wanted little to do with the men who had sold them a now struggling club for a record price.

Topping did his best to uphold the playboy image of a sportsman. He was married six times: in 1932 to Theodora Boettger, in 1937 to actress Arline Judge (the mother of Dan Jr.), in 1940 to Norwegian Olympic gold-medal figure skater Sonja Henie, in 1946 to actress Kay Sutton, in 1952 to New York model Alice Meade Lowthers, and in 1957 to Charlotte Ann Lillard. After his last marriage, Topping seemed to settle down, and the marriage with Lillard lasted until his death seventeen years later. After Topping's death, Lillard married Rankin Smith, owner of the NFL's Atlanta Falcons. Topping's brother Harry J. (Bob) Topping, a sportsman in his own right, also married Arline Judge several years after she and Dan divorced. Among his marriages Bob Topping was also wed for several years to actress Lana Turner. Dan Topping was survived by nine children, including five from his marriage to Lillard.

In addition to the Yankees' stellar on-field record, the team that Topping and his partners purchased in 1945 for $2.8 million was resold nineteen years later based on a valuation of $14 million. And along the way the Yankees were consistently baseball's most profitable franchise. As the operating partner during the dynasty, Topping deserves his fair share of the credit. He smartly sided with Weiss after MacPhail's meltdown and acquiesced to the unorthodox decision to bring in Stengel as manager. In partnership with Del Webb, Dan Topping presided over one of the greatest runs ever in professional team sports.

Chapter 51. **Del Webb**

Dan Levitt and Mark Armour

Del Webb's father was a native-born Californian who spent his youth playing baseball before becoming a construction executive. Del followed a similar path. After washing out as a ballplayer, Webb spent several years as a carpenter before starting his own construction company. By landing a number of large government contracts during the Depression and World War II, Webb built his construction company into one of the largest and most profitable in the country.

As the war dragged on, Webb began considering additional business challenges. Always a ballplayer at heart, owning a baseball team intrigued him, and he informally scouted for opportunities to acquire one. He was lucky in that one of the most profitable and successful teams in America was available because of estate-tax issues, and on the heels of the Depression, in the middle of the war, very few had any money to spend buying a baseball team. In January 1945 Webb purchased an interest in the New York Yankees, America's preeminent sports franchise, for a war-depressed, bargain-basement price.

Three years later Webb and Dan Topping acquired full ownership of the team as equal partners. Webb's force of personality and good business sense quickly made him one of baseball's most powerful owners. Webb dominated the most important baseball issues of the 1950s and early 1960s, particularly the franchise shifts and expansion. He and Topping also continued the tradition of Yankee excellence: under their seventeen years of direct control, the Yankees won fourteen pennants and nine World Series.

On May 17, 1899, in Fresno, California Del-

Del Webb, who got wealthy in the construction business, joined with Larry MacPhail and Dan Topping to buy the Yankees in 1945.

bert Eugene became the first of three sons born to Ernest and Henrietta (Forthcamp) Webb. Webb's paternal grandfather spent time in the state legislature, and his mother's family later left her a sizable inheritance. During Del's youth his father ran a profitable sand and gravel operation.

By the time he was thirteen Webb stood six foot three but weighed only 130 pounds. He was regarded as a standout first baseman and occasionally played semiprofessionally. Unfortunately, in 1913 economic disaster struck the family, and Webb was forced to quit school and go to work as a carpenter's apprentice. After America's entry into World War I, Webb went to work in the Oakland shipyards for $8 a day and played on the shipyard baseball team.

When the war ended Webb married his childhood sweetheart, Hazel Church, then an operating-room nurse. Webb continued to believe he had a future in baseball, and for a few years he wandered around the western United States, playing semipro ball and working carpentry jobs. As a player he had developed into a powerful pitcher, now standing six feet four and weighing around 200 pounds. But he never got the break he longed for. Webb believed that by 1921 his heavy pitching workload had wrecked his arm.

In 1928, after playing a game in San Quentin against the prisoners, Webb missed the return boat carrying his teammates because of a hangover. Thirsty, he asked one of the inmates for a glass of water and caught a later boat. The inmate turned out to be sick and highly contagious; Webb contracted typhoid fever, a life-threatening disease at the time. Webb's weight fell to just 99 pounds, and on a couple of occasions it appeared as if he might not survive. He was hospitalized for eleven weeks and incapable of working for a year. After Webb finally recovered the doctor advised him to move to a dry climate. Webb and Hazel took their $100 in savings and moved to Phoenix, Arizona.

In Phoenix Webb was hired by grocery store developer A. J. Bayless to build his stores. When the Depression came, he managed to secure large government projects to keep his company afloat and even thrive. By the mid-1930s Webb's annual gross sales were in the neighborhood of $3 million. Webb's contacts eventually included President Franklin Roosevelt, oil millionaire Ed Pauley, and Democratic power broker Robert Hannegan. The government contracts Webb landed during World War II made his company one of the country's largest contractors.

He also became a teetotaler. When he went to a doctor complaining of a minor illness, the doctor took a routine medical history. "When I told him I drank 10 to 20 bourbons a day," Webb recalled, "he damn near dropped his teeth. He said I should cut down, but I told him I would quit. And I did."[1]

When the Oakland Oaks, a franchise in the Pacific Coast League, became available for $60,000 during World War II, Webb considered buying it. But while contemplating the purchase, Webb encountered Larry MacPhail, whom Webb knew from his frequent visits to Washington to negotiate war-related construction work. MacPhail, then working as an assistant to Undersecretary of War Robert Patterson, was working to purchase the New York Yankees and trying to put together a moneyed syndicate. MacPhail told Webb to quit fooling around with a Minor League team and come in with him to buy baseball's most storied franchise. Webb knew a good deal when he saw one. "Count me in," he told MacPhail.[2]

As MacPhail tried to assemble his investment group, Webb returned to his government construction contracts. While building the El Toro marine base Webb ran into Dan Topping, a marine captain and wealthy sportsman. Topping mentioned that he was also hoping to purchase the Yankees, with or without MacPhail. Yankees president Ed Barrow loved running the Yankees and did not want to sell, particularly to MacPhail, a longtime antagonist. The Ruppert family trust that owned the team, however, had a large estate-tax liability and little choice but to sell. Finally, Barrow agreed to sell to a three-headed partnership of Webb, Topping, and MacPhail, and in January 1945 the threesome purchased the Yankees for $2.8 million.

For the first three years of their Yankees ownership, Webb and Topping let MacPhail run the team more or less autonomously. But after an infamous altercation in New York's Biltmore Hotel in 1947, Webb and Topping had to make a change (see chapter 1).

After this incident the two were no longer willing to keep their baseball investment in the hands of the mercurial MacPhail. They immediately called their lawyers and drew up papers to buy MacPhail's third. "We sent word that we would give him $2 million [a huge profit on his original investment] and he'd damned well better take it," Webb recalled. "We gave him until 6 o'clock that night. I was in the back room that afternoon. ... [T]hey came in and told me that MacPhail had signed and wanted to see me. I went outside and MacPhail was standing there smiling and he put out his hand and said, 'Del, you've been a good partner to me.' I said, 'I don't want to shake your hand,' and told him what I thought of him and walked away."[3]

Webb and Topping now owned the Yankees equally. Both were wealthy and independent, and neither liked or had experience with equal partners. Moreover, their personalities were diametrically opposed: "Webb is the far westerner who looks as though he just shucked off his cowboy stuff," wrote Harold Rosenthal. "Topping is an Easterner in the yachts-polo-anyone-for-tennis mold. Unless Webb has known you a long time, you'll get a 'yes,' 'no' or 'maybe' from him. Topping is the open, friendly type, the kind the headmaster tells you your boy will turn out to be when you enroll him in one of the more fashionable Eastern prep schools."[4] Nevertheless, the duo made a surprisingly long-lasting and effective team. In general Webb took the lead in league matters, while Topping oversaw the operational side.

The Yankees could not repeat in 1948, and recently promoted general manager George Weiss,

with the blessing of Webb and Topping, jettisoned manager Bucky Harris. "The main reason was that Bucky believed it wasn't necessary to work with a club much beyond the time it took to play a game," Webb explained. "He didn't think it was his job to develop young players."[5] Weiss wanted to hire Casey Stengel, a somewhat quixotic choice, and Topping had some misgivings. Webb, however, had known Stengel for many years and vouched for him to Topping, who acquiesced.

Webb's next high-profile baseball involvement came in December 1950 when the owners were considering extending the contract of baseball commissioner Happy Chandler. Webb detested Chandler and considered him rather a prude and prone to offer opinions and decisions without all the facts. Webb also had a more personal reason to dislike the commissioner. "His construction company built the Flamingo Hotel in Las Vegas and I investigated to make sure that Webb's involvement with the gambling center ended there," Chandler recalled. "This seemed a sensible and understandable precaution, but Webb was furious."[6]

Webb and Topping proved adept at working the back rooms of baseball ownership. Despite initial support for Chandler among many of the owners, the Yankees duo, supported by St. Louis Cardinals owner Fred Saigh, maneuvered the vote away from Chandler. Webb was not reticent about his involvement: "If I've never done anything else for baseball, I did it when I got rid of Chandler."[7]

During the 1950s the owners spent considerable time and energy mulling over the geographic future of their sport. After fifty years of franchise stability, many of baseball's owners began to salivate over the potential huge payday in untapped metropolitan areas. Webb believed in realignment as opposed to expansion, as there were still plenty of struggling two-team cities that could no longer support two teams.

St. Louis Browns owner Bill Veeck, after an abortive attempt to move his franchise to Baltimore early in 1953, tried again at the end of the season. He believed he had effectively lobbied the other owners and expected approval. Webb, however, wanted Veeck, who was barely in front of his creditors, out of baseball and maneuvered him into selling to a more stable Baltimore group. Veeck received a nice price for the team, and the franchise moved to Baltimore.

The next year the league had to deal with another two-city team going bankrupt. The Philadelphia Athletics were on the verge of receivership. One of the most aggressive and persistent suitors for the Athletics was Arnold Johnson, a Chicago-based businessman and business associate of Webb and Topping who also owned the Minor League Kansas City Blues stadium and planned to move the A's there. After some financial maneuvering that benefited Messrs. Johnson, Topping, and Webb, the Athletics moved to Kansas City.

By the end of the 1950s it was clear to most observers there were more Major League–ready cities than there were franchises to go around. Business interests and politicians in those cities were pressing baseball for expansion. The inherently conservative baseball owners, however, continued to resist growing beyond sixteen franchises. Ironically, the greatest pressure came in New York. To rectify the situation, well-connected New York lawyer Bill Shea, with the support of New York politicians and the possibility of a new stadium in Queens, began canvassing the country for potential investors and cities in a new third major league, named the Continental League.

After fighting a cagey rearguard action for a roughly a year, Webb eventually realized he had little choice but to accept a National League expansion team in Queens as the least-bad option. He was also the driving force in directing American League expansion into Los Angeles. Although other cites appeared to have more support, Webb wanted an American League team in California, and if the National League was going to force a

second team on his city, he could do the same in Los Angeles.

In the aftermath of the 1960 World Series, the Yankees duo eased both Stengel and Weiss out of their positions. "We had been bringing Houk [subsequent manager Ralph] along in our organization," Webb defended the substance if not the staging of the managerial change. "And we couldn't hold Houk any longer because other clubs had been making managerial offers. . . . I still think this was good organizational thinking to make the change when we did. I think one of the big mistakes that baseball commits is to hang on to a star for sentimental reasons without having a capable replacement ready. The same thing applies to Stengel."[8]

The two owners botched another managerial firing four years later when they jettisoned Yogi Berra after winning the 1964 pennant. Webb had never been in favor of hiring Berra in the first place but had been talked into it by Topping. "I never thought it wise to select a manager from the player ranks," Webb justified later, "particularly to handle a group of men with whom he has played. I also have thought that managing in the minors is by far the best method of developing a major league manager."[9]

This public relations disaster was generally overshadowed by the sale of the Yankees to CBS, announced in August 1964 and dragged out by additional revelations and commentary throughout the off-season. "I didn't want to sell," Webb claimed. "It was Dan's doing. He wanted to get out and I couldn't run it by myself because I'm too busy with my other things, so we talked it over and decided it was best this way. Dan has ten kids to think of. He has to take care of them and now's the time to start thinking about it."[10]

CBS now owned 80 percent of the Yankees, and Webb and Topping split $11.2 million. CBS agreed to keep Webb and Topping on as executives, but Webb had little desire to remain in a generally ceremonial position; in March he sold his remaining share for $1.4 million.

Del Webb owned the Yankees during one of the greatest runs in professional team sports. The team that he and his partners had purchased in 1945 for $2.89 million sold twenty years later based on a valuation of $14 million, and along the way the Yankees were consistently baseball's most profitable franchise. And although he did not initially intend to play an active ownership role, once he and Topping took full control, Webb, the consummate backroom politician, became the most influential power broker in the American League.

When *Time* put Webb on its August 3, 1962, cover, the accompanying article devoted only one paragraph to his ownership in the Yankees. The publicly traded Del E. Webb Corporation built and owned hotels in Las Vegas, shopping malls and office buildings in Phoenix and Tucson, large housing communities throughout the Southwest, military bases and missile-silo complexes all over the country, and large high-profile construction projects all over the world.

Maybe most significantly, though, Webb created and introduced the giant retirement communities that now seem ubiquitous all across America. In the late 1950s Webb bought ten thousand acres in Arizona on the distant edge of the Phoenix metropolitan area to build a community for active seniors. The concept proved a huge and immediate hit. Webb delivered a "complete and functioning town," for people who "loved their grandchildren, but didn't want to 'raise somebody else's children.'"[11] Named "Sun City," the community became the blueprint for many similar developments throughout the southern United States, built by Webb and later imitators.

As his empire grew, Webb began living a much faster-paced life, although he remained a teetotaler and antismoking fanatic. He split his time between three first-class permanent hotel suites: the Beverly Hilton in Beverly Hills, California, which he built; the Mountain Shadows resort in Phoenix, which he also built; and the Waldorf-Astoria in New York. Each was kept fully furnished, including a complete set of clothes, with an ample staff. In 1953, after thirty-four years of marriage, Hazel divorced him, although the two remained close. In August 1961 Webb remarried the much-younger Toni Ince after meeting her on a blind date on the previous Halloween. Webb had no children from either marriage.

Not surprisingly for someone building casinos in Las Vegas in the 1950s and 1960s, Webb worked with suspected mobsters. Accusations later surfaced that some of these business relationships might be less than fully aboveboard. A March 19, 1977, story featured Webb and accused him of being "an active business partner with organized crime figures for three decades."[12] The article claimed that Webb was more intimately involved in the ownership of the casinos than previously believed. Surprisingly, given the widespread distribution the series received and the other high-profile public personalities referenced in the articles, few repercussions ever came out of the enormous investigative effort.

After the 1964 sale of the Yankees, Webb remained active in running his construction company. Most significantly, he expanded internationally into the leisure business. In March 1973, at age seventy-three, Webb became chairman of the board and made Bob Johnson the new chief executive officer. Since his bout with typhoid fever and giving up drinking, Webb had generally been in good health. This changed about a year later when Webb needed a tumor removed from his right lung. The surgery was apparently successful, but shortly thereafter Webb was diagnosed with prostate cancer. Following additional exploratory surgery, Webb died on July 4, 1974. At Webb's request no funeral was held. His body was cremated and his ashes scattered over Arizona.

Chapter 52. **George Stirnweiss**

Rob Edelman

AGE	G	AB	R	H	2B	3B	HR	TB	RBI	BB	SO	BAV	OBP	SLG	SB	GDP	HBP
28	148	571	102	146	18	8	5	195	41	89	47	.256	.358	.342	5	13	2

On the morning of September 15, 1958, Central Railroad of New Jersey commuter train number 3314 was nearing Bayonne when it ran through several signals and plunged off an open drawbridge into Newark Bay. Forty-eight people lost their lives. One of the victims was George "Snuffy" Stirnweiss, a second baseman who played for the New York Yankees between 1943 and 1950. During his second and third seasons, he earned accolades as one of the top players in the American League. Most notably, he was the 1945 American League batting champion.

Of the eight Yankees that have won batting titles, Stirnweiss is the least remembered, the most obscure. Two weeks after his death, Arthur Daley wrote in the *New York Times*, "Many fans already had forgotten that the stocky little Yankee second baseman of yesteryear had won a hitting crown until that fact was cited in the stories of his tragic death recently in the New Jersey train disaster."[1]

George Henry "Snuffy" Stirnweiss was born on October 26, 1918, in New York City. His parents were Sophie (née Daly) and Andrew P. "Andy" Stirnweiss, a city policeman. George also had a younger brother, Andrew P. Stirnweiss Jr., who was a career U.S. Navy pilot, serving in World War II, Korea, and Vietnam.

George starred in baseball, football, and basketball at Fordham Prep in the Bronx. In 1935 he led his team to the New York City Catholic High Schools Athletic Association baseball championship. In the title game, which Fordham won, 5–2, the *New York Times* reported, "Stirnweiss . . . was the batter who did the most damage. . . . After clouting a long triple into deep right field in the

George Stirnweiss returned to second base full-time in 1947 after Joe Gordon was traded to Cleveland.

first inning . . . [he] came through with a home run in the seventh, a prodigious drive to right centre. . . . In the other two trips to the plate Stirnweiss was passed."[2]

It was no different on the gridiron. "Stirnweiss Smashes through for Touchdown . . ." began the subhead of an October 20, 1935, *Times* article reporting on a 6–6 tie between Fordham Prep and Brooklyn Prep. It also was noted that "superb punting by Captain Stirnweiss aided the Fordham cause." In basketball he helped lead Fordham to

George Stirnweiss tries to avoid a sliding Pee Wee Reese at second base during the 1947 World Series.

the Bronx-Westchester Catholic High Schools Athletic Association basketball crown.

Stirnweiss was graduated from Fordham Prep in 1936 and eventually inducted into the school's Hall of Honor. At the University of North Carolina, he became the first Tar Heel to captain the football and baseball teams. He was heralded primarily for his gridiron exploits at UNC, where he was a quadruple threat as halfback-quarterback-punter–punt returner. Fordham University's coach Sleepy Jim Crowley observed, "I regard George Stirnweiss as the most dangerous back we have to face. . . . He is likely to score every time he gets his hands on a punt or a pass." On another occasion, Crowley remarked, "[Stirnweiss] can kick sixty yards under pressure and he's a jackrabbit with that ball. In our game, I got the creeps every time we had to punt to him."[3]

Stirnweiss was the first-team quarterback on the 1938 Associated Press All-Southern Conference team. He averaged 6.2 yards per carry at North Carolina and in his senior year was the nation's sixth-best punter. In 1940 he was awarded the Patterson Medal, presented to the Tar Heels' most outstanding senior athlete.

Stirnweiss's baseball accomplishments in college did not match his football heroics, but he did hit .390 as a senior, and Paul Krichell, the Yankees' top scout, was determined to sign him. Upon his graduation in 1940, the five-foot-eight, 175-pounder was drafted in the second round by the National Football League Chicago Cardinals. But Stirnweiss felt that baseball allowed him the best chance for an extended pro career. What is more, he was an ardent Yankees fan. And so, on the day of his graduation, he signed with his hometown team.

ROB EDELMAN

The Yankees assigned Stirnweiss to the Nor-folk (Virginia) Tars in the Piedmont League. He appeared in eighty-six games and batted .307, earning him an end-of-the-season promotion to the International League Newark Bears. Accord-ing to the *Sporting News*, it was here that Stirn-weiss was first dubbed Snuffy. The paper reported that upon arriving in Newark, he produced an array of tobacco products. After watching him stuff his mouth with chewing tobacco and light up a stogie, teammate Hank Majeski quipped, "What, no snuff?" "Since then," the paper noted, "he has been 'Snuffy the Bear.'"

That fall Stirnweiss remained in Virginia and coached and played for the Norfolk Shamrocks, a pro football team competing in the Dixie League. He spent future off-seasons working as an ath-letic director at the College of William and Mary in Williamsburg, Virginia; coaching football and basketball at Connecticut's Canterbury Prep School; coaching football and baseball at his alma mater; and operating a baseball school in Bartow, Florida.

Stirnweiss spent the 1941 season at Newark, batting an unimpressive .264. He returned to the Bears in 1942, and it was then he really began to flourish, as he honed his skills as a base stealer under the tutelage of new manager Billy Meyer. His .270 batting average was unexceptional, but his speed electrified fans—and he set an Inter-national League record with seventy-three sto-len bases. Stirnweiss "steals bases like no one else since the days of Ty Cobb," gushed Michael F. Gaven in the *Sporting News*. Gaven further described Stirnweiss as "a player and gentleman of the old school" and "just about the best prospect in the minors today."[4]

During the 1942 season, Stirnweiss smashed a triple and two singles in the first-ever Interna-tional League All-Star Game. That summer, he also almost landed in Brooklyn. On August 20 the *Sporting News* reported that Ed Barrow, the Yan-kees' general manager, had been discussing such a trade, but nixed the deal after he began feuding with Dodgers president Larry MacPhail.

Ten days later the Bears clinched the Interna-tional League pennant. Between games of a dou-bleheader, Stirnweiss put on quite a show, first running a seventy-five-yard dash in 8.2 seconds and then circling the bases in 14 seconds. It was while playing for the Bears that Stirnweiss began dating Jayne Powers, an ardent baseball fan whom he later married.

On March 21, 1943, the *New York Times* reported, "George Stirnweiss breezed into town, the first infielder on the grounds [of the team's Asbury Park, New Jersey, training camp]. . . . Interest centered on the arrival of Stirnweiss a day early. . . . He will be something of a novelty if he carries [his] speed with him to the Stadium." Joe Gordon was entrenched at second base, but Stirn-weiss also worked out at shortstop, a position that had been vacated when Phil Rizzuto entered the navy. The rookie impressed manager Joe McCar-thy, who declared that he expected Stirnweiss to develop into a top shortstop.

A severe stomach ulcer—some accounts note that he also suffered from an acute case of hay fever—was expected to keep Stirnweiss out of the military. But there was confusion regarding his draft status, as his registration was in the process of being transferred from Norfolk, Virginia, to Connecticut. (Stirnweiss then was residing in Kent, Connecticut.) Then he was inexplicably classified 1-A and was advised at the end of March that he would be called into the military within a month.

McCarthy nonetheless named Stirnweiss his starting shortstop and leadoff man prior to the team's initial exhibition game. He held down both positions for the season opener, on April 22, against the Washington Senators. On April 28 Stirnweiss took a train from New York to Hart-ford, Connecticut, to take an army physical. It was here that he was rejected for military service.

Stirnweiss was relegated to a utility role in his rookie season. He appeared in 83 games, mostly at shortstop, with a .219 batting average. But after Joe Gordon entered the army, Stirnweiss began the 1944 season as the Yankees' second baseman and leadoff hitter. In the eighth inning of the home opener against Washington, he displayed his speed by beating out an infield hit, stealing second, going to third on a wild pitch, and scoring on a balk. "The art of base stealing may have passed out with the horse-and-buggy age," wrote John Drebinger in the *New York Times*. "But, just as the horse has come back in this gas-restricted era, so has the stolen base. Its modern trail blazer is a stockily built athlete named George Stirnweiss, better known as Snuffy."[5]

Stirnweiss played in 154 games in 1944, and his .319 batting average was fourth best in the American League. Additionally, he led the league in runs, hits, triples, and stolen bases. His sixteen triples tied teammate Johnny Lindell for the lead, and his 296 total bases were one behind Lindell, the league leader. He was fourth in the league's Most Valuable Player voting. That September *Time* described Stirnweiss as "the apple of [Joe] McCarthy's managerial eye." In media reports, Stirnweiss was not merely the Yankees second baseman; he had become their *star* player. In June 1945 Arthur Daley wrote, "The youngster has improved so amazingly in little more than a season that even as astounding a performer as Joe Gordon may have trouble in winning back his job."[6]

Stirnweiss was named to the American League All-Star squad (though no game was played in 1945) and was feted for his accomplishments in a late-September game at Yankee Stadium. On the final day of the season, he was second to Chicago White Sox third baseman Tony Cuccinello in the American League batting race. Stirnweiss was at .306, while Cuccinello was at .308 — or, more specifically, .308457. Cuccinello's number remained frozen, as a rainout ended his season, but Stirn-

weiss came to bat five times and totaled three hits; two were solid, and he was credited with the third when the official scorer changed his ruling from an error to a hit. Thus, he emerged with an average of .308544 — which was rounded off to .309 — and the AL batting championship.

It was the lowest figure to win the crown in either league since Cleveland's Elmer Flick hit exactly .308 in 1905; as of 2012 only Carl Yastrzemski's .301 has been lower. Additionally, Stirnweiss won the title without ever having led the race during the season. He appeared in 152 games and topped the league in plate appearances (717), at bats (632), runs (107), hits (195), triples (22), extra-base hits (64), total bases (301), stolen bases (33), and slugging average (.476). He finished third in the MVP race behind pitcher Hal Newhouser and second baseman Eddie Mayo of the pennant-winning Detroit Tigers. That off-season Stirnweiss won the Sid Mercer Memorial Plaque, given to the player of the year as voted on by the New York chapter of the Baseball Writers' Association of America.

Nevertheless, Stirnweiss was uncertain of his status when he reported to the Yankees' training camp in the Panama Canal Zone in 1946. Among the veterans returning from military service were Joe Gordon and Phil Rizzuto, who were expected to be reunited as the team's double-play combination, with Stirnweiss moving to third base. Furthermore, the batting champ would relinquish to Rizzuto his leadoff spot in the batting order.

Stirnweiss was also displeased with the fifteen-thousand-dollar contract offered him by the Yankees, which he initially returned unsigned. The *Sporting News* observed that he was "in a position to ask for a fine contract and is not likely to be sucker enough to weaken." However, Arthur Daley sardonically quipped, "Free-Advice Department: George Stirnweiss is hereby warned to watch his step. If the holdout Yankee star continues his wage battle with Larry MacPhail [now the

ROB EDELMAN

top man with the Yankees], the rambunctious red-head probably will sell him to the Chicago Cubs . . . for $100,000 and a couple of used bottle tops."

By the beginning of March Stirnweiss had signed and reported to the team. Before the season began, Dan Daniel, writing in the *Sporting News*, described him as "one of the American League's up-and-coming young stars, whose versatility and high skills would make him a worthy rival for prewar stars returning from the service."[7]

But Stirnweiss's 1946 numbers were way down, and though he earned a spot on the American League All-Star squad, the honor was primarily for past achievements. In July St. Louis Browns skipper Luke Sewell observed, "How can anyone account for a fine ball player like George Stirnweiss . . . poking along this year at a .240 pace? From all I've seen there is absolutely nothing the matter with him. He is the same player who more than once raised hob with my pitchers in the past. But he just isn't clicking."

Overall, Stirnweiss appeared in 46 games at second base and 79 at third. He returned to second full-time in 1947 and 1948, after Gordon was traded to Cleveland, but his batting average and stolen-base totals were well below his 1945 peak. He did, however, set Major League records in 1948 for the best fielding average (.9930) and the fewest errors (5) at second base, records that stood until 1964 and 1988 respectively. "He was called a war-time freak," wrote Charles Dexter in *Baseball Digest*, "but last summer [1947] as the Bombers regained their peace-time stature, little George worked fielding wonders around second base, clicking off double plays with his partner, Scooter Rizzuto, like a mechanical man."[8]

Stirnweiss opened the 1949 season as the starter, but he was spiked in the hand on opening day. Jerry Coleman, a rookie whom he had tutored during spring training, replaced him and won the position. Stirnweiss played in just 51 games at second base, mostly as a nonstarter.

That winter Stirnweiss was frequently mentioned in trade rumors. He began the 1950 campaign a Yankee, but was strictly a bench warmer. At the June 15 deadline, after having appeared in just 7 games, Stirnweiss was shipped to the St. Louis Browns in a seven-player deal that brought pitchers Tom Ferrick and Joe Ostrowski to New York. He made it into 93 games for the Browns, hitting .218. "There can be no denying the fact that Snuffy had become a Yankee expendable," wrote Arthur Daley.[9] One reason was Coleman's emergence. Another was that Casey Stengel, the Yankees' skipper since 1949, "had fiery Billy Martin up his sleeve as the Yankee second baseman of the future."[10]

In April 1951 the Browns traded Stirnweiss to the Cleveland Indians. As the deal was announced, St. Louis skipper Zack Taylor noted, "Stirnweiss has slowed considerably, and I'm going with our new boy, Bob Young, at second base." Cleveland manager Al Lopez declared, "Stirnweiss is an experienced man and a great competitor, but I hope nothing happens to [Ray] Boone or any of our other youngsters on the infield. I'd prefer just to have Snuffy around when we need him on account of an injury."[11]

Stirnweiss played in 50 games for the Tribe, hitting .216. After appearing in 1 game for Cleveland in 1952, he was released. In his decade in the majors, he appeared in 1,028 games and compiled a .268 batting average and had 134 stolen bases.

Stirnweiss appeared in three World Series. In 1943 he made it into a game as a pinch hitter and went hitless. He played in all 7 games of the 1947 Series, getting seven hits and eight walks and making several excellent defensive plays, most significantly in Game Four—the one in which Bill Bevens tossed his almost-no-hitter. Brooklyn's Pee Wee Reese hit a ground ball up the middle in the first inning that appeared to be a hit, but Stirnweiss darted to his left, snagged the ball, and threw Reese out. He appeared in 1 game of the 1949 Series, without coming to bat.

Following his release by Cleveland, Stirnweiss completed the 1952 season with the American Association Indianapolis Indians. Two years later he signed to manage the Schenectady (New York) Blue Jays, the Philadelphia Phillies' Eastern League affiliate. On July 16 the Phillies made him a roving batting instructor for several of their lower-level farm teams.

In 1955 Stirnweiss was a manager again, leading the Eastern League Binghamton (New York) Triplets, a Yankees affiliate. After the season he met with officials of the International League Richmond Virginians. "I'd like to get the [manager's] job here," he declared, but he was not offered the slot.[12]

The responsibilities of providing for his growing family led Stirnweiss to abandon baseball at the professional level. But his desire to impart his knowledge to youngsters made him an ideal choice to run the *New York Journal-American* sandlot baseball program. He accepted this job in April 1956. That same year he was hired as a solicitor of new accounts for the Federation Bank and Trust Company. On the morning of June 24, 1957, he collapsed while working at the bank's Columbus Circle office and was rushed to Manhattan's Roosevelt Hospital. The nature of his illness remains unclear—according to some reports, he suffered a heart attack—but what is certain is that the episode ended Stirnweiss's career with the bank.

Upon his death the media reported that Stirnweiss was employed as a "foreign freight agent" at Caldwell and Company, located at 50 Broad Street in Manhattan. He resided with his family at 140 Maple Street in Red Bank, New Jersey. On September 15, 1958, he was scheduled to represent his company at a luncheon meeting in Manhattan. That morning, he was observed boarding Central Railroad of New Jersey train number 3314 just before it left the Red Bank station. Had he lived, he would have celebrated his fortieth birthday six weeks later.

A month before the accident, on August 10, Stirnweiss played in the Yankees' annual Old-Timers Day, which pitted players from the 1946 Boston Red Sox against the 1947 Bronx Bombers. The *New York Times* reported that "the nifty fielding of [Phil] Rizzuto, Stirnweiss and [Bobby] Doerr drew whoops and hollers from the fascinated fans."[13]

Stirnweiss's funeral was held on September 19 at Red Bank's St. James Roman Catholic Church. Among those attending were present and former Yankees Rizzuto, Coleman, Joe Collins, and Frank Shea. Stirnweiss was buried in Mount Olivet Cemetery in Middletown, New Jersey. At his death he was the father of six children—two boys (George Jr. and Edward) and four girls (Susan, Barbara, Cathy, and Mary Ellen)—ranging in age from seventeen months to fifteen years.

Back in August 1956, when the Yankees involuntarily retired Phil Rizzuto as an active player, the Scooter was irate. Stirnweiss advised him to "cool off" and "take a few days' vacation with Cora and the kids." "It was great advice," Rizzuto recalled in 1994, "because when I came back I was offered a broadcasting job. If I had popped off, I would have made people mad and I'd never have gotten it."[14] It was no surprise, then, that Rizzuto occasionally uttered "George Stirnweiss" instead of "George Steinbrenner" during Yankees broadcasts.

Chapter 53. **Jack Phillips**

Charles F. Faber

AGE	G	AB	R	H	2B	3B	HR	TB	RBI	BB	SO	BAV	OBP	SLG	SB	GDP	HBP
25	16	36	5	10	0	1	1	15	2	3	5	.278	.333	.417	0	0	0

Jack Phillips spent almost a decade on Major League rosters and never got into more than seventy games in a season. But that less-than-stellar playing career was followed by an all-star second act: twenty-four seasons as a baseball coach and athletic administrator at his alma mater, Clarkson University.

Jack Dorn Phillips, the second son of Howard and Emma (Struwe) Phillips, was born at Clarence, New York, near Buffalo, on September 6, 1921. On his father's side he was of English ancestry, on his mother's side German. He grew up in nearby Marilla, New York, where his father owned a meat market. Jack started playing baseball with the men of Marilla when he was only thirteen. At Lancaster High School he lettered in baseball, basketball, football, and track. In 1939 Jack enrolled at Clarkson College (now Clarkson University) in Potsdam, New York, where he majored in business administration and became one of the top all-around student athletes the school has ever produced.

Phillips's six-foot-four frame enabled him to carry his nearly two hundred pounds with ease and earned him the nickname Stretch. His size helped him lead the basketball team in scoring each of his three years on the varsity squad. He was the starting center on the 1942–43 Clarkson team that went 14-1, losing only to national powerhouse St. John's of Brooklyn. However, it was on the baseball diamond that Jack was most dominant. During his three seasons he led the Clarkson Golden Knights to wins in 85 percent of their games, including a 19-1 mark in 1943.

Phillips was a pitcher and first baseman on the

The Yankees brought rookie first baseman Jack Phillips to New York in August to give the aging George McQuinn an occasional day off.

1943 club. In the summers he played for the semi-pro Watertown Collegians. Professional scouts rated him among the best right-handed-hitting prospects in the nation and flocked to see him play. Since childhood he had been a fan of the New York Yankees, so he was thrilled when legendary Yankees scout Paul Krichell signed him to a contract. Phillips left Clarkson before graduating to play in the Yankees' farm system, but continued his studies during the off-seasons and received a bachelor of business administration degree on February 22, 1948.

Phillips made his professional debut with the 1943 Norfolk (Virginia) Tars of the Class B Piedmont League. There he met eighteen-year-old Yogi Berra. "Yogi and I broke in together," said Phillips. "I remember I made $150 a month and he made $90. He'd always give me half his paycheck, because he was always borrowing money from me."[1] It was the start of a lifelong friendship between the two men. Phillips led the Piedmont League with eight home runs and hit well enough (.284) to earn a trip to Atlantic City, New Jersey, for spring training with the Yankees in 1944. He was assigned to the Newark Bears of the International League, one of the Yankees' top-two farm clubs, for the 1944 season, but played only seven games before the Selective Service Board beckoned.

Phillips was sworn into the U.S. Navy on May 4, 1944, and assigned to the Naval Training Center at Sampson, New York. He joined the base's powerful baseball squad, the Sampson Bluejackets, which won twenty-six of twenty-seven games that summer. The lone loss was to the National League's Boston Braves.

Phillips spent most of the 1944 and 1945 seasons in the navy. He was stationed at Treasure Island in San Francisco Bay, and later in Hawaii and Japan. While at Treasure Island he met Helene McBride, a member of the WAVES, the navy's female component. They were married on October 15, 1946, at St. Rita's Church in Detroit.

After the war Phillips returned to Newark, where he spent most of the 1946 and 1947 campaigns. In 1947 he was hitting .298 for the Bears when he was called up to New York. He made his Major League debut on August 22 at Cleveland, striking out as a pinch hitter for pitcher Randy Gumpert. Phillips's first big-league hit, a single off Pete Gebrian of the White Sox, came in his first start, on August 25, at Chicago's Comiskey Park. He hit his first home run on September 21 at Shibe Park in Philadelphia, a fifth-inning solo shot off the A's Joe Coleman.

Phillips played only sixteen games for the Yankees that summer, mainly as a replacement for aging first baseman George McQuinn. In the World Series against the Brooklyn Dodgers, Jack appeared in two games as a pinch hitter, going hitless in two at bats. The Yankees won the Series, and Jack's teammates voted him a quarter share of the winners' take.

During 1948 spring training the Yankees considered trying Phillips at shortstop, but abandoned the idea before the season started. If they had gone through with the experiment, he would have become perhaps the tallest shortstop in Major League history up to that time. As it was, Phillips played in only one game for New York (at first base) and split the rest of the season between Yankees farm teams in Newark and Kansas City.

He was back in New York in 1949 and was hitting .308 in forty-five games, but on August 6 the Yankees sold him to the Pittsburgh Pirates. His former teammates voted Jack a half-share of their 1949 World Series victor's money.

On July 8, 1950, Phillips earned a place in the record books. He became the first Major Leaguer to pinch-hit a home run with the bases loaded and the home team trailing by three runs.[2] The Pirates were trailing the St. Louis Cardinals, 6–3, in the ninth inning. With one out and the bases loaded, manager Billy Meyer sent Phillips to the plate to bat for pitcher Murry Dickson. Jack drove Harry Brecheen's second pitch over the left-field fence for a 7–6 victory. At first there was some doubt whether it was a home run. The Cardinals' Stan Musial appeared to have caught the ball. The runners held their bases. Then one of the players in the Pirates bullpen held up the ball. Apparently, Musial had tipped the ball over the fence into the bullpen.

Phillips also did mop-up duty as a pitcher in 1950, appearing in a 14–2 blowout loss to the Bos-

CHARLES F. FABER

ton Braves on June 1. While position players taking the mound in such games usually work only an inning or two, Phillips hurled five innings. After driving in a run with a fly ball as a pinch hitter in the fourth inning, he stayed in the game, allowing seven hits and four runs in his five innings. The year 1950 was Phillips's best in the Major Leagues. He hit .293 with seven doubles, six triples, five home runs, and thirty-four runs batted in.

In 1951 Pittsburgh's general manager, Branch Rickey, tried to make a first baseman out of outfielder Ralph Kiner. "I taught him how to play first base," joked Phillips. "I was a reserve infielder and he had led the league in home runs for several years. I called the first-base job a $75,000 job; he got $70,000 and I got $5,000."[3]

Phillips played a career-high 70 games for the Pirates in 1951, but hit only .237. After playing in one game in 1952, he was sold to the Hollywood Stars, the Pirates' farm club in the Pacific Coast League. He was a regular with the Stars for the next three seasons. In both 1952 and 1954 he hit .300 (he hit .270 in 1953) and was named to the PCL all-star team both years. He was named the league's Most Valuable Player in 1954, earning him another Major League opportunity. In September the Stars traded him to the Chicago White Sox for Jim Baumer and cash. Three months later the White Sox traded him, along with Leo Cristante and Ferris Fain, to the Detroit Tigers for Walt Dropo, Ted Gray, and Bob Nieman.

Phillips never became a full-time player for the Tigers. In April 1957 Detroit traded him to the Boston Red Sox for Karl Olson. Boston promptly sent him to San Francisco in the PCL, and Jack's Major League career was over. In nine seasons he had played in 343 games and compiled a .283 batting average.

After one year in San Francisco, Phillips closed his playing career with Buffalo of the International League in 1958 and 1959. In eleven seasons in the Minors, he appeared in 1,212 games and hit for a

.278 average. Although he had never played shortstop in the Majors, he did play 278 games at the position in the Minors.

From 1960 to 1964 Phillips was a manager in the Phillies' and Tigers' farm systems, for such clubs as Elmira (New York) and Jamestown (New York) in the New York–Pennsylvania League, Magic Valley (Idaho) in the Class C Pioneer League, and Chattanooga of the Class Double-A South Atlantic League.

Leaving professional baseball, Phillips returned to Clarkson University as baseball coach from 1965 through 1988. He also helped administer the athletic department, worked in the sports information office, assisted with basketball, and coached cross-country. When he retired in 1988 he was named a professor emeritus.

Phillips was active in promoting Potsdam's youth through the Elks Lodge. He also was involved with golf tournaments, both locally and nationally. For many years he refereed high school basketball games in northern New York.

In 1992 Jack became one of the first fifteen inductees into the Clarkson University Athletic Hall of Fame. Even after "retiring" he served as assistant coach of the golf team until 2001. As a coach he was a tough taskmaster, but inspired his players with his enthusiasm, jokes, and funny stories. His daughter Sharon wrote, "Throughout his life my dad loved to tell jokes and was quite the comedian with his funny stories and antics."[4] In 2008 the school renamed its baseball facility Jack Phillips Stadium at Snell Field. In remarks accompanying various ceremonies, Clarkson officials frequently referred to Phillips as a local icon. Jack and Helene had five children, all of whom were inducted into the Potsdam Central High School Hall of Fame.

Jack Phillips died at the Chelsea Retirement Center in Chelsea, Michigan, on August 30, 2009, at the age of eighty-seven. In failing health, he had gone to Michigan to be near his daughter Patty

Roberts. He was buried in St. Mary Cemetery in Potsdam, near the campus of his beloved Clarkson University. He was survived by his wife, Helene; three daughters, Susan, Sharon, and Patty; thirteen grandchildren; and five great-grandchildren. His sons, Jack Jr. and Michael, predeceased him.

Chapter 54. **Phil Rizzuto**

Lawrence Baldassaro

AGE	G	AB	R	H	2B	3B	HR	TB	RBI	BB	SO	BAV	OBP	SLG	SB	GDP	HBP
29	153	549	78	150	26	9	2	200	60	57	31	.273	.350	.364	11	6	8

When Phil Rizzuto went to his first Major League tryout, a New York Giants coach told him he was too small to play in the big leagues and suggested he should make a living by shining shoes.[1] But in a later tryout with the Yankees, Rizzuto impressed scout Paul Krichell, who recommended they sign the Brooklyn native. The five-foot-six, 150-pound shortstop went on to become the anchor of the infield for Yankee teams that won nine pennants and seven World Series in his twelve full seasons. He also won a Most Valuable Player Award, was enshrined in the Hall of Fame, and spent forty years as the voice of the Yankees on radio and television.

Philip Francis Rizzuto was born in Brooklyn on September 25, 1917, to Fiore and Rose (Angotti) Rizzuto. (His mother was born in Italy, his father in the United States.) In a 1993 interview Rizzuto spoke animatedly of his family and his childhood in Brooklyn. "They were laborers," he said. "They built homes, they built sidewalks, they built garages, in New York City and out in Long Island. They all moved into these three-family houses that were connected to each other with a little alleyway and a backyard. It was one of the greatest times of my life because they all played musical instruments; they'd sing, they'd tell stories in Italian, they'd make wine. As long as there was food on the table, everyone was happy."[2] Eventually, his father got a job as a motorman on a trolley car and later as a watchman on the docks.

The Rizzutos baptized their son as Fiero, but Rizzuto chose to call himself Phil, same as his father. "I just took Phil because it sounded more American," he once said. "A ballplayer has to be

Phil Rizzuto's three singles were instrumental in the Yankees' seventh-game World Series win against Brooklyn.

as American as the Statue of Liberty, is the way I figure."[3]

Even as a kid, Rizzuto had to overcome the perception that he was not big enough to be a ballplayer. "More than 50 percent of the time nobody would pick me because I was so small," he said. He began to prove himself in earnest while playing for Richmond Hill High School in Queens. By the summer before his senior year he was good enough to play for a semipro team (under an assumed name). "That was better than any Minor League

A partially hidden Phil Rizzuto tags out Jackie Robinson in a first-inning rundown in Game One of the 1947 World Series. George Stirnweiss at second base, Billy Johnson at third base, pitcher Frank Shea, Brooklyn base runner Pete Reiser, and umpire Eddie Rommel are also pictured.

experience," he said. "I batted against Satchel Paige, the House of David, the Black Yankees. These guys, they knew how to play the game. So many of them could have been in the big leagues, but because of the color line, you know . . ."

Like so many Italian fathers, Fiore Rizzuto thought baseball was a waste of time and never wanted his son to play. "He wanted me to get a job, to follow in his footsteps," recalled Rizzuto. "He said, 'You can't make a living playing baseball.'" When Mrs. Rizzuto supported her son's desire to play ball, his father finally relented. Signed by the Yankees in 1937, Rizzuto was assigned to the Bassett (Virginia) Furnituremakers, in the Class D Bi-State League.

When he first arrived in Virginia, the nineteen-year-old city-reared Rizzuto felt out of place. "I get off the train and there's nothing there. I said, 'Where the hell is the town?' Then the train pulled away and there was the town. There was a drugstore, a post office, and a diner. They had only thirteen hundred people in the whole town. The people were so nice, but they couldn't understand me with my Brooklyn accent, and I couldn't understand them with their Southern accent."

Once acclimated, Rizzuto moved quickly through the Yankees' farm system. After hitting .336 at Norfolk in the Piedmont League in 1938, he was sent to Kansas City of the American Association. (It was while he was playing for Kansas City that teammate Billy Hitchcock gave the quick-footed shortstop his trademark nickname of Scooter.) Rizzuto continued to excel in his two years at Kansas City; in 1940, after getting 201 hits for a .347 batting average, he was the MVP of the American Association and was named Minor League Player of the Year by the *Sporting News*.

Rizzuto was slated to be the Yankees starting shortstop in 1941 after Frank Crosetti, the starter since 1932, hit only .194 in 1940. But in spite of Rizzuto's credentials, the Yankees' veterans resented the rookie who threatened to replace the popular Crosetti. Players tried to keep him out of the batting cage until Joe DiMaggio intervened and told them to let the kid hit. "I had a rough time," Rizzuto recalled. "Crosetti was one of their

LAWRENCE BALDASSARO

big favorites and a great guy, and here I was a fresh rookie trying to take his job."

The twenty-three-year-old rookie did replace Crosetti in the starting lineup when the 1941 season began. Crosetti himself was more supportive of his replacement than his teammates had been initially. Rizzuto recalled how the veteran helped position him in his very first game, against the Washington Senators. "If it hadn't been for Crosetti, I'd have looked like a bum. He made me look great." Given the chance, Rizzuto showed that he belonged; he hit .307, second only to DiMaggio's .357 among Yankees players. Then, in 1942, he hit .284, was named to the All-Star team, and led American League shortstops in double plays and putouts. He hit .381 in the Yankees' five-game World Series loss to the St. Louis Cardinals.

Like so many other Major Leaguers, Rizzuto then spent the next three years in the service, initially playing baseball at the Naval Training Station in Norfolk, Virginia. It was there that, in June 1943, he married Cora Esselborn. He recalled the first time he met her, at her parents' home in Newark during his rookie year. "I saw this vision of loveliness come down the stairs, and you know how they say in the movies, it was love at first sight. I'd never dated a girl. Holy cow, I was struck." In 1944 he was sent to New Guinea and assigned to lead a gun crew on a ship, but his naval combat duty was hampered by malaria and chronic seasickness. He was then mercifully assigned to organize sports programs in Australia and the Philippines.

Upon returning from the war, Rizzuto was recruited by the Mexican League, which was making a strong attempt to lure ballplayers away from the Major Leagues. Early in May 1946, Jorge Pasquel, a wealthy industrialist who was president of the league, offered Rizzuto twelve thousand dollars a year for a five-year contract, plus a signing bonus of fifteen thousand dollars.[4] "Right after the war," said Rizzuto, "you couldn't get a car, you couldn't get tires, you couldn't get butter, you couldn't get anything. They had *everything*. I was ready to go, and so was George [Stirnweiss]." The Yankees, however, filed a lawsuit to enjoin the Mexican League from inducing their players to jump their contracts.

After a disappointing season in 1946, both for the Yankees (who finished third) and for Rizzuto (whose average dropped to .257), the Scooter bounced back in 1947, hitting .273 and driving in sixty runs. He led the Yankees in games played and stolen bases and led the league in being hit by pitches.

In the memorable World Series with the Dodgers—the first of six "Subway Series" matching the interborough rivals between 1947 and 1956—Rizzuto went 5 for 22 in the first six games, scoring one run and driving in another. (According to the *New York Times*, the diminutive shortstop had trouble getting into Ebbets Field for Game Three. A police officer reportedly told him, "Go on, beat it. You can't even play first for a midget team.")[5]

But in the deciding seventh game, Rizzuto played a key role. With the Yankees trailing, 2–0, he drove in their first run in the bottom of the second with a two-out single. In the fourth, with a man on first, he again hit a two-out single, sending the runner to second. He went to third when Bobby Brown hit a game-tying double, then scored what proved to be the winning run on a single by Tommy Henrich. In the sixth, he led off with a bunt single, stole second, and then scored on a single to make the score 4–2. The Yankees went on to clinch the Series with a 5–2 win. Of the Yankee starters, only Johnny Lindell (.500) and Henrich (.323) hit for a higher average than Rizzuto (.308).

After a solid but unspectacular 1948 season, Rizzuto had the two best years of his career. In 1949 he hit .275, scored 110 runs, and finished second to Ted Williams in the MVP vote. He followed that performance with his single best season, with career highs in hits, average, slugging percentage, runs, doubles, and walks. At one point he handled 238 consecutive chances at shortstop without an error, a Major League record at that time.

Rizzuto was named the American League's MVP in 1950, winning 16 of 23 first-place votes and easily outdistancing Billy Goodman of the Boston Red Sox, 284 points to 180. In its story the *New York Times* referred to Rizzuto as "the dashing little shortstop, widely hailed as the 'indispensable man' of the world champion Bombers."[6] He also won the first S. Rae Hickock Award as the Professional Athlete of the Year. In December Rizzuto signed a one-year contract for fifty thousand dollars, making him the third-highest-paid player in Yankees history, behind Ruth and DiMaggio.

Beginning in 1950 Rizzuto was named to four consecutive All-Star teams, starting at shortstop in 1950 and 1952. He finished eleventh in the MVP vote in 1951, fourteenth in 1952, and sixth in 1953. But in 1954 he hit only .195, and the following year, now thirty-seven years old, he played only seventy-nine games at shortstop. On August 25, 1956, Rizzuto, who had appeared in only thirty-one games with fifteen starts, was told by general manager George Weiss that he was being released to make room on the roster for Enos "Country" Slaughter, one of the many veteran players the Yankees bought in those years to patch a hole in their lineup. It was an abrupt and unceremonious end to the thirteen-year career of a player who had become synonymous with the Yankees. The news came as a shock to Rizzuto, the consummate company man. "I couldn't believe it," he told me. "The pinstripes meant so much then. It was something to live up to and live for."

The man who had been dismissed as being too small had become one of the best shortstops of his era and played in five All-Star games and nine World Series for one of the greatest teams of all time. But now, his playing days suddenly over, the thirty-nine-year-old Scooter began a new career as a Yankees broadcaster, initially teaming up with two other legends, Mel Allen and Red Barber. With his rambling, stream-of-consciousness style, featuring his trademark call of "holy cow," he entertained Yankee fans for forty years and endeared himself to a new generation. In 1993 his on-air musings were transcribed into free verse in *O Holy Cow! The Selected Verse of Phil Rizzuto*. In a review of the book, poet Robert Pinsky, alluding to the equally idiosyncratic linguistic stylings of Yogi Berra and Yankee manager Casey Stengel, wrote: "Mr. Rizzuto now joins Mr. Berra and the creator of Stengelese in a New York School of diamond-oriented language manipulators."[7]

The 1984 selection of Pee Wee Reese to the Hall of Fame by the Veterans Committee led some to argue that Rizzuto was no less deserving than his Dodger counterpart. Finally, on February 25, 1994, Rizzuto got the call from Yogi Berra, a member of the Veterans Committee, telling him he was in. Rizzuto's response? "Holy cow!"

Questions about Rizzuto's Hall of Fame qualifications always centered on his modest hitting statistics. Meanwhile, supporters pointed to his intangible value as the spark plug of teams that won nine pennants and seven World Series in his twelve full seasons and his remarkable defensive skills. He had great range, was exceptionally skillful at going back on pop-ups, and was a fearless and agile pivotman on double plays.

Jerry Coleman, who played alongside Rizzuto for parts of eight seasons, said of his double-play partner: "He didn't have a great arm, but he had a great pair of hands and he never made a mistake. . . . The only other shortstops I'd put in his class were Ozzie Smith and Luis Aparicio."[8]

Casey Stengel, with whom Rizzuto had an increasingly uneasy relationship because of what he perceived as the manager's preference for younger players, called him "the greatest shortstop I ever saw. He can't hit with Honus Wagner, but I've seen him make plays that old Dutchman couldn't."[9] On teams that featured DiMaggio,

LAWRENCE BALDASSARO

Berra, and, later, Mantle, the little guy at short never threatened to steal the spotlight, but he was, according to *New York Times* columnist Arthur Daley, "a key man in every Yankee pennant drive since 1941."[10]

Phil Rizzuto was one of the most popular players of his era, with both fans and teammates. Initially shunned at the start of his rookie year, Rizzuto soon won over his teammates with his boyish enthusiasm and willingness to be the butt of their pranks. As scrappy as he was on the field, Rizzuto had an almost manic fear of creepy, crawly things, which only served to make him a more inviting target. "They were always playing tricks on him," said Coleman. "Once [outfielder] Johnny Lindell put a dead mouse in his glove (when infielders still left their gloves on the outfield grass between innings). He put the glove on, then threw it in the air and ran into center field screaming."[11] According to Daley, the Yankees "may never have had a more popular player than this little guy, admired and beloved even by those pranksters who used to put snakes in his glove."[12]

By the time he retired from broadcasting in 1996, the seventy-nine-year-old Rizzuto had logged fifty-three years of service to the Yankees, more than anyone else in the history of the franchise. In 1985 the Yankees retired his number, 10, and added his plaque to those in Yankee Stadium's Monument Park. In his characteristically rambling but hilarious Hall of Fame acceptance speech in 1994, Rizzuto said, "I've had the most wonderful lifetime that one man could possibly have." He died on August 13, 2007, survived by his widow, Cora (since deceased), and their four children.

Lyle Spatz

Friday, August 29, vs. Washington—The Yankees came away with a ten-inning, 4–3 victory, greatly aided by two unearned runs in the seventh that allowed them to tie the score. Joe Page, who made his forty-fourth appearance of the season when he relieved Bobo Newsom in the eighth, was the winner. Early Wynn, the hard-luck loser, went the distance for Washington. Stan Spence drove in the Senators' three runs with two home runs off Newsom. George McQuinn's long fly in the tenth scored Tommy Henrich with the winning run. 80-45-1, First, 12 games ahead.

Saturday, August 30, vs. Washington—After dissipating a 5–1 lead, the Yankees scored in the bottom of the ninth to edge Washington, 6–5. Joe Page, in relief of Frank Shea, picked up his second win in two days and raised his record to 13-6. Johnny Lindell had three RBIs, and Joe DiMaggio had a home run and two RBIs. 81-45-1, First, 12 games ahead.

Sunday, August 31, vs. Washington (2)—The Yankees completed a four-game sweep of the Senators by taking both ends of a doubleheader, 6–5 and 5–1. Randy Gumpert was the first-game winner, though he pitched just two-thirds of an inning in relief of Vic Raschi. Joe Page came on yet again to hold Washington scoreless in the final two innings. George Stirnweiss had a home run and three runs batted in for New York. A bases-loaded triple by catcher Sherman Lollar, recently recalled from the Newark Bears, was the key blow for the Yanks in the second game. Butch Wensloff's distance-going

performance was New York's first complete game in its last 12. 83-45-1, First, 12½ games ahead.

Monday, September 1, at Boston (2)—The largest crowd of the season at Fenway Park saw the Red Sox win both ends of doubleheader, raising their winning streak to seven and keeping their fading pennant hope alive. Boston's 6–3 and 4–1 wins chopped 2 games off the Yankees' lead to bring it down to 10½ games. Denny Galehouse stifled the Yanks on seven hits in the opener. Karl Drews was the starter and loser for New York. Spud Chandler worked an ineffective third of an inning in his return to action after seven weeks. Manager Bucky Harris was tossed out of the game in the sixth inning, Harris's first ejection of the season. Bill Bevens and Boston's Earl Johnson both pitched complete games in the nightcap. First baseman Jake Jones homered and drove in all four Red Sox runs. The Yankees' lone run came on an eighth-inning home run by Joe DiMaggio. 83-47-1, First, 10½ games ahead.

Tuesday, September 2, at Boston—Rained out. 83-47-1, First, 10½ games ahead.

Wednesday, September 3, at Boston (2)—Following the previous day's rainout, the Yankees and Red Sox played another doubleheader at Fenway Park. This time the Yankees won both ends, reducing their magic number to 12. The Yanks won the opener, 11–2, behind Bobo Newsom. They had eighteen hits, all singles, off Tex Hughson and three successors. The only extra-base hits in the game were doubles by Ted Williams and Bobby

Doerr and home runs by Dom DiMaggio and Sam Mele. Tommy Henrich and Joe DiMaggio each had four hits, and Billy Johnson had three runs batted in. The Yankees had sixteen more hits in their 9–6 win in the second game. George McQuinn and Johnny Lindell had three hits. Lindell also had a home run and three runs batted in. Frank Shea was the winner, but had to be rescued in the eighth inning by Joe Page. The Yanks recalled pitcher Dick Starr from Newark. 85-47-1, First, 12½ games ahead.

Thursday, September 4, at Washington — The Yanks fought back from a 4–0 deficit with a four-run seventh inning to tie the score at 4–4. But a dropped pop fly by third baseman Billy Johnson in the home seventh led to a Senators run and a 5–4 win. Starter Vic Raschi went six innings and gave up Washington's first four runs, but Joe Page, victimized by Johnson's error, took the loss. Walt Masterson was the winner. Joe DiMaggio hit his eighteenth home run of the season. Stan Spence had three runs batted in, including the game winner. 85-48-1, First, 12 games ahead.

Friday, September 5, at Washington — Left-handed knuckleballer Micky Haefner dealt the Yankees another one-run defeat, as the seventh-place Senators edged the Yankees, 3–2. First baseman Mickey Vernon had two runs batted in for Washington. New York's two runs came in the ninth inning. Joe DiMaggio's single scored the first one, and Billy Johnson's fly ball scored Tommy Henrich with the second. Butch Wensloff allowed two runs and five hits in seven innings but was the loser. Dick Starr, making his big-league debut, allowed the final run. 85-49-1, First, 12 games ahead.

Saturday, September 6, at Washington — Despite outhitting the Senators, 14–12, the Yankees dropped their third straight game at Griffith Stadium. The Senators raced off to a 9–1 lead, then

held on to win, 9–6. Early Wynn, with late-inning help from Milo Candini, got the win. Starter Karl Drews, the first of five Yankees pitchers, did not survive the third inning and took the loss. Sherry Robertson had three hits and Mickey Vernon three runs batted in for the Senators. Johnny Lindell's double was the only extra-base hit for the Yankees. Lindell, Joe DiMaggio, and Billy Johnson each had two hits, while Phil Rizzuto had three. 85-50-1, First, 11 games ahead.

Sunday, September 7, at Washington — The Yankees ended their three-game losing streak, all to Washington, by downing the Senators, 7–1. Allie Reynolds won his seventeenth game of the season, aided by an inning and two-thirds of relief from Joe Page. Ray Scarborough was the starter and loser for Washington. George Stirnweiss, Tommy Henrich, and Joe DiMaggio each had two hits. The win, combined with Boston's doubleheader loss to Philadelphia, raised the Yankees' lead to 12½ games with 18 games remaining. 86-50-1, First, 12½ games ahead.

Monday, September 8, vs. Cleveland — Bob Feller turned in a sensational relief effort as Cleveland topped the Yankees, 4–3. Feller relieved Bob Lemon in the ninth inning with no outs, Joe DiMaggio, the tying run on third, and pinch runner Lonny Frey, the potential winning run, on first. But Feller kept DiMaggio at third, as he retired Billy Johnson, Aaron Robinson, and Phil Rizzuto. Bobo Newsom was the loser. George McQuinn had three hits off Lemon, including two home runs. The more than fifty-three thousand who witnessed the final night game of the season at Yankee Stadium raised the Yanks' home attendance past the two million mark. 86-51-1, First, 12 games ahead.

Tuesday, September 9 — Not scheduled. 86-51-1, First, 11½ games ahead.

Wednesday, September 10, vs. Cleveland—Joe Page, in relief of Vic Raschi, picked up his fourteenth win of the season in the Yankees' 7–4 victory. Bob Feller started for the Indians, but the loss went to Bryan Stephens. Feller lasted only four innings before he was pinch-hit for by Hal Peck. Indians rookie Al Rosen made his Major League debut as a pinch hitter. Billy Johnson had a triple, a home run, and two runs batted in. 87-51-1, First, 12½ games ahead.

Thursday, September 11, vs. Detroit (2)—Hal Newhouser's six-hitter and two home runs by Roy Cullenbine led the Tigers to a 7–2 triumph in the first game. Frank Shea, who had beaten Newhouser three times previously, was the loser. New York won the nightcap, 11–5, with a sixteen-hit attack against Stubby Overmire, Al Benton, and Dizzy Trout. Detroit jumped off to a 4–0 lead off Butch Wensloff in the first inning, but Bill Bevens held them to one run the rest of the way to gain the win. The one run Bevens allowed was a seventh-inning home run by Roy Cullenbine, his third home run of the day. Joe DiMaggio had a single, double, home run, and three runs batted in to take over the team lead. 88-52-1, First, 12½ games ahead.

Friday, September 12, vs. Detroit—Twenty-year-old rookie right-hander Art Houtteman pitched the Tigers into second place by downing the Yankees, 7–2. The win allowed Detroit to pass the Boston Red Sox. Houtteman was aided by Vic Wertz, who had three hits, and Roy Cullenbine and Hoot Evers, who drove in two runs each. Cullenbine had his fourth home run in three games. Allie Reynolds was New York's starter and loser. 88-53-1, First, 12 games ahead.

Saturday, September 13, vs. Detroit—The Yankees reduced their magic number to 2 with a 5–2 win over the Tigers. The loss dropped the Tigers

to third place, as the Red Sox regained second. Starter Bobo Newsom pitched seven innings for the win, with Joe Page adding two innings of scoreless relief. Virgil Trucks was the loser. George McQuinn had a home run and a single for New York; Billy Johnson had two runs batted in. 89-53-1, First, 12½ games ahead.

Sunday, September 14, vs. St. Louis—By beating the Browns, 6–4, the Yankees clinched at least a tie for the pennant. Vic Raschi was the winner, but Joe Page was magnificent again, allowing just one hit in 3⅔ innings of relief. Johnny Lindell and Tommy Henrich had home runs, and Henrich had three runs batted in. Ellis Kinder was the loser, as the Browns' six-game winning streak came to an end. 90-53-1, First, 12½ games ahead.

Monday, September 15, vs. St. Louis—Rained out. The game between the Yankees and Browns was called in the top of the first inning after only four batters had come to the plate. Meanwhile, the Red Sox lost the first game of their doubleheader against the White Sox, 6–3, clinching the pennant for the Yankees. 90-53-1, First, 12 games ahead.

Tuesday, September 16, vs. St. Louis (2)—The new American League champions split a doubleheader with St. Louis, winning, 8–3, and losing, 8–2. Dick Starr went all the way to notch his first big-league win in the opener. Fred Sanford was the loser. Sam Zoldak won the second game, with Yankees starter Karl Drews taking the loss. Bobby Brown and Sherman Lollar homered, and Tommy Henrich had four hits in the first game. George Stirnweiss had three hits in the nightcap. Yogi Berra appeared in both games after missing more than three weeks with a throat ailment. Manager Bucky Harris rested his regulars in one game or the other. 91-54-1, First, 12½ games ahead.

Wednesday, September 17, vs. Chicago — The smallest home crowd of the season, 5,804, saw Allie Reynolds shut out the White Sox, 5–0, for his eighteenth win of the season. The Yankees, using mostly second-stringers, had only seven hits against loser Thornton Lee and two relievers. Shortstop Bobby Brown was the only Yankee with two hits. 92-54-1, First, 13½ games ahead.

Thursday, September 18, vs. Chicago — Frank Shea pitched his first complete game since injuring his arm on July 5. Shea allowed only four hits and struck out eight in beating the White Sox, 4–1. Chicago's lone run came on a home run by Rudy York with one out in the ninth inning. Loser Ed Lopat also pitched a complete game. Shea also had two hits, as did George Stirnweiss and Sherman Lollar. The Yanks recalled left-hander Bill Wight from the Kansas City Blues. 93-54-1, First, 13½ games ahead.

Friday, September 19 — Not scheduled. 93-54-1, First, 13½ games ahead.

Chapter 56. **Sherman Lollar**

John McMurray

AGE	G	AB	R	H	2B	3B	HR	TB	RBI	BB	SO	BAV	OBP	SLG	SB	GDP	HBP
22	11	32	4	7	0	1	1	12	6	1	5	.219	.242	.375	0	3	0

Soft-spoken and self-effacing, Sherman Lollar provided a strong defensive presence behind the plate during his eighteen-year Major League career. Lollar spent twelve seasons with the Chicago White Sox, after spending all or parts of six seasons with three other American League teams. An All-Star catcher seven times, Lollar won American League Gold Glove awards from 1957 through 1959, the first three years it was given.

Though Lollar played well and received awards during the 1950s, he did not receive as much national recognition as did fellow catcher Yogi Berra, who won three Most Valuable Player Awards. As Red Gleason wrote in the *Saturday Evening Post* in 1957, "It is the fate of some illustrious men to spend a career in the shadow of a contemporary. Adlai Stevenson had his Dwight Eisenhower. Lou Gehrig had his Babe Ruth. Bob Hope had his Bing Crosby. And Sherman Lollar has his Yogi Berra."

John Sherman Lollar Jr. was born on August 23, 1924, in Durham, Arkansas, to John and Ruby (Springfield) Lollar. When Lollar Jr. was three years old, he moved with his family to Fayetteville, Arkansas, where his parents opened a grocery store.

Lollar's interest in baseball began at an early age, and he remembered playing catch with his father outside the store as a six-year-old.[1] When John Jr. was eight, his father died unexpectedly during surgery. At that early age, Lollar, who was the oldest of four children, including two girls (Bonnie and Pat) and a boy (Jerry, who was born after his father's death), had to take on additional responsibilities at home.

Sherm Lollar spent most of the 1947 season with the Newark Bears, caught in a catching logjam that included Ralph Houk, Charlie Silvera, Aaron Robinson, Gus Niarhos, and Yogi Berra.

His mother sold the grocery store and began working in a nursing home for the Veterans Administration. She told Gleason, "Sherman took a large share of the responsibility of looking after the younger children. He was both a big brother and father. Our being left alone so soon created a sense of oneness in all of us that remains even now."

Despite his additional responsibilities, Lollar's interest in baseball never waned. In 1936, shortly before he turned twelve, Lollar became a batboy for the Fayetteville Bears in the Arkansas-Missouri League. After graduating from Fayetteville High School, a school that had no baseball team, the sixteen-year-old Lollar took a job with J. C. Penney in Pittsburg, Kansas. He played with a team affiliated with the Chamber of Commerce in the Ban Johnson League while also studying at Pittsburg State Teachers College (now Pittsburgh State University). Two years later, after the Ban Johnson League folded, Lollar both played for and managed the semipro Baxter Springs (Kansas) Miners, working as a brakeman in a local mine when he was not playing baseball.

The Baltimore Orioles of the International League signed Lollar in 1943, when he was eighteen. His pay was twenty dollars a month. He batted just .118 in twelve games, but improved to .250 with fifteen home runs in 1944. He also drove in seventy-two runs, one of the highest totals for any catcher in organized baseball that year.

Lollar won the International League's Most Valuable Player Award in 1945, tearing up the league with thirty-four home runs, 111 runs batted in, and a league-leading batting average of .364. Baltimore had a working agreement with the Cleveland Indians and was forced to sell its top slugger to the Major League team for ten thousand dollars.

After making his big-league debut on April 20, 1946, Lollar played infrequently behind veteran catchers Frankie Hayes and Jim Hegan. He asked to go back to Baltimore so he could play regularly. Back in the International League, Lollar was unable to duplicate his previous year's batting success. He batted just .234, but he did hit twenty home runs in only 222 at bats for the Orioles. His biggest plus that year was meeting his future wife, Connie Mattard, whom he married in 1949.

In December 1946 Cleveland included Lollar in a five-player deal with the New York Yankees. The Indians had been willing to trade Lollar because of concerns about his attitude. According to writer Bill Roeder, "The Cleveland complaint was that Lollar displayed insufficient dash and spirit. He had the ability all right, but no inclination to exploit it. Within a month, he was homesick for Baltimore, and [Cleveland manager Lou] Boudreau sent him back. Now Sherman belongs to the Yankees, and they hope he will react favorably to the fresh start."

In New York he was caught in a catching logjam that included Ralph Houk, Charlie Silvera, Aaron Robinson, Gus Niarhos, and Yogi Berra. As a consequence, Lollar spent most of the 1947 season with the Newark Bears, the Yankees' farm club in the International League.

Lollar appeared in only eleven regular-season games for the Yankees in 1947, but he did play in the World Series against the Brooklyn Dodgers, getting three hits, including two doubles, in four at bats. About Game Three, sportswriter Dan Daniel wrote, "A secondary standout was Sherman Lollar, who started the game as a surprise entry. [Manager Bucky] Harris benched Berra in favor of the right-handed Lollar against the southpaw [Joe] Hatten. Lollar got a single which became a run in the third, and in the fourth drove in a run with a double."

A contemporaneous article called Lollar "a Charley Gehringer type," adding, "He appears a colorless, dispassionate individual, on and off the field, but he gets his job done effectively. If Lollar hits as well as Gehringer did, no one will care if he doesn't say a word all season."

In parts of two seasons with the Yankees, Lollar saw action in only thirty-three games. Yogi Berra was on his way to becoming a star, and Lollar's playing time was further reduced by a hand injury caused by a foul tip, requiring him to get stitches on two fingers of his throwing hand. In August 1948 Dan Daniel wrote, "Sherman Lollar, right-handed hitting catcher, is another who has possibly had his last big opportunity with the Bombers. Now that Yogi Berra is available again, Gus Niarhos will handle all the receiving duties against left-handed pitching."

Not surprisingly, Lollar was soon traded, this time to the St. Louis Browns on December 13, 1948, with pitchers Red Embree and Dick Starr and one hundred thousand dollars in return for catcher Roy Partee and pitcher Fred Sanford. In St. Louis Lollar took over for Les Moss as the team's regular catcher and batted .261 in 1949 with eight home runs. For three seasons Lollar stabilized the catching position for the second-division Browns while earning All-Star honors for the first time in 1950.

After the 1951 season the Chicago White Sox were looking for a replacement for incumbent catcher Phil Masi, and on November 27 they received Lollar from the Browns in an eight-player deal. According to his son, Lollar's salary was increased to about twelve thousand dollars when he was traded.

Arriving in Chicago was the break Sherm Lollar needed. Unlike the Browns, who had won only fifty-two games in 1951, the White Sox had finished eight games over .500 and were considered a potential World Series contender. But the 1952 season was a disappointment for Lollar, who endured additional stress when his wife fell ill after childbirth. While he batted only .240, his work with manager Paul Richards helped turn the young catcher's career around. As Gleason recounted in the *Saturday Evening Post*, Lollar later said:

When I was having that terrible year in 1952, Richards called me into his office late in the season. He told me that my natural style of catching lacked appeal and I would have to be more of a holler guy. Paul said he understood my problem because he had been the same kind of catcher that I was. I feel that I've always hustled in baseball, but until Paul talked to me I probably had a misconception of what "hustle" meant. I hustled to first base on a batted ball, and I hustled when the ball was around me. Richards made me see that something more was expected.

Paul told me to show a little more animation. He wanted me to be a little more agile in receiving, and to show more zip in returning the ball to the pitcher. He recommended that I run to and from the catcher's box between innings, instead of just strolling out there.

Gleason wrote that Richards recommended Lollar's distinctive style of catching, with his left knee on the ground, because, according to Richards, "This moved him up — closer to the plate — and down — closer to the ground."

Lollar caught one hundred or more games in each of his twelve seasons with the White Sox, and he was an American League All-Star six times (1954–56 and 1958–60). As evidenced by his Gold Gloves, he developed into perhaps the best defensive catcher in the game. In 1957 he played without making an error in his first eighty-nine games before throwing wildly to second base on September 14.

Years after trading for Lollar, White Sox general manager Frank Lane said, "It was one of the best trades I ever made. Sherm turned out to be one of the best catchers in the American League, behind only Yogi Berra and maybe Jim Hegan." Paul Richards told Gleason that Lollar was a better handler of pitchers than Berra.

Throughout his time in the American League, Lollar was compared to Berra, whose offensive numbers and championships outshined Lollar's. Wrote Gleason in the *Saturday Evening Post*, "Where Berra is distinctive looking, to put it mildly, the brown-haired Lollar is a sad-faced, sad-eyed individual. In most of his pictures, he looks as though someone has stolen his favorite catcher's mitt. In his 'smiling' pictures, the smile seems forced. Berra is celebrated for malapropisms. Lollar is seldom quoted. An unobtrusive workman, he is obscured on his own club by crowd-pleasers such as Nellie Fox, Minnie Minoso, Jim Rivera, and Luis Aparicio."

On April 23, 1955, against Kansas City during a 29–6 rout, Lollar accomplished the rare feat of getting two hits in an inning twice in the same game. He had his finest offensive season for Chicago's 1959 pennant winners, batting .265 with twenty-two home runs and eighty-four RBIs. In both 1958 and 1959 he finished ninth in the American League's Most Valuable Player voting.

Perhaps most important, Lollar was instrumental in handling the team's pitching staff in 1959. Although he batted only .227 in the World Series, he hit a three-run homer in Game Four off the Dodgers' Roger Craig with two outs in the seventh inning to tie the game at 4–4. Other than the three home runs hit by Ted Kluszewski, Lollar's home run was the only one hit by a White Sox player in that Series. However, a key point of the Series came in Game Two, when the slow-footed Lollar was thrown out at the plate while trying to score from first base on Al Smith's eighth-inning double, which helped ensure a 4–3 Chicago loss.

Lollar's overall offensive performance began to decline in 1960, and the White Sox released him on October 4, 1963. Although he was not known as a power hitter, the six-foot-one, 185-pounder had 155 career home runs among his 1,415 hits. Lollar committed only 62 errors in 1,571 games behind the plate in his Major League career, finishing with a .992 fielding percentage.

In his 2001 *Historical Baseball Abstract*, historian Bill James rates Lollar as the thirty-first best catcher ever. James wrote, "[Lollar] led his league in fielding percentage five times, in double plays three times, also has the lowest career passed ball rate of any catcher listed here."[2]

After his playing career ended, Lollar sought a Minor League manager's job. Al Lopez remarked, "[Lollar] had tremendous ability with young pitchers. I think he shows great ability at handling men, which is the most important part of managing in the game."

Lollar coached with the Baltimore Orioles from 1964 through 1967 and with the Oakland Athletics in 1968. He managed two Oakland farm teams: the Iowa Oaks of the American Association from 1970 through 1972 and the Tucson Toros of the Pacific Coast League in 1973 and 1974. He left the Toros after the 1974 season, reportedly because of a dispute with Athletics owner Charley Finley.

Lollar barely escaped serious injury while managing in Iowa in 1970. He was sitting in his car at a red light after a game when a nearby building suddenly collapsed. "I was just sitting there listening to the radio when—wham! It was like the sky falling," he recalled. "What made it worse was that I had no idea what was happening. I couldn't see a thing because of the dust and debris." Luckily, he was unhurt.

In the last few years of his life, Lollar operated a bowling alley in Springfield, Missouri, and refereed high school basketball games. After a long battle with cancer, he died in Springfield on September 24, 1977. He was fifty-three years old. Lollar was survived by his wife, Connie, and a son, Sherman III. He is buried in Rivermonte Memorial Gardens in Springfield.

Chapter 57. **Butch Wensloff**

Christine L. Putnam

AGE	W	L	PCT.	ERA	G	GS	GF	CG	SHO	SV	IP	H	BB	SO	HBP	WP
31	3	1	.750	2.61	11	5	3	1	0	0	51.2	41	22	18	0	0

He played in only forty-one games in his Major League career, but took home two World Series rings. During his ten years playing professional baseball, he earned such nicknames as Iron Man, Buster, and Butch. No matter what they called Charley Wensloff, one thing was certain: he knew how to pitch. His fastball, curve ball, and knuckle ball baffled some of the best hitters in the game. He pitched through illnesses and injuries from the scorching Texas heat of his first professional season to the high pressure of taking the mound at Yankee Stadium.

Wensloff broke into the Majors under the critical eye of manager Joe McCarthy. After World War II he returned from military service to play for Bucky Harris on a team destined for the fall classic. On the Yankees he was surrounded by players destined for the Hall of Fame. Yet Wensloff never felt intimidated.

Charles William Wensloff was born on December 3, 1915, in Sausalito, California. He was the first child of Charles William Wensloff Sr. and his wife, Lucy (Machado) Wensloff. Although the family grew to include two more sons, the elder Charles did not stick around long. By the time his namesake was six years old, Charles Sr. left the family and soon lost touch with his sons. His mother remarried, but Wensloff quit school after his freshman year of high school and took various jobs to help his family. He pitched for local semipro teams, where he developed a good fastball and a knuckle ball.

In 1937 Wensloff was twenty-two years old, married, and starting his first season in professional baseball. The five-foot-eleven, 185-pound

Butch Wensloff's sore pitching arm never healed after he injured it in a 1947 spring-training game in Havana.

right-hander joined the El Paso Texans of the Class D Arizona-Texas League, where he found the intense heat of a Texas summer much different from the cool coastal climate of his native San Francisco Bay Area. Most of his teammates were young and unmarried. Local sportswriters took a liking to the quiet youngster, who compiled a 17-10 record with a 4.67 ERA in 233 innings. Wensloff returned to Sausalito and continued to pitch on local teams through the winter.

In 1938 Wensloff moved up to the Joplin (Missouri) Miners in the Class C Western Association. The move was a fortuitous one, as Joplin was part of the New York Yankees' farm system. Despite the opportunity Wensloff began his career with the Yankees organization on a sour note. He wanted more money. For a while it seemed that his career would be derailed before it began. Eventually, he signed a contract without a pay raise.

Wensloff joined the Joplin starting rotation and faced greater challenges than anything he had seen in the local semipros or Texas. He finished the 1938 season with only a 13-13 record, but a respectable 3.48 earned run average. He suffered through heat stroke and tonsillitis that caused him to miss several starts, yet he still made a few headlines. One, in the *Joplin Globe* of May 28, 1938, read, "Wensloff Pitches Route for Miners." In that game he struck out eleven Hutchinson, Kansas, batters on his way to the victory. He also earned a reputation as an ambitious, disciplined player. Despite his illnesses he always returned to the mound stronger and better.

Wensloff remained with Joplin for the 1939 season, where he finished the season with a spectacular 26-4 record. During the off-season he returned to Sausalito with his wife, the former Helen Swearingen, and their newborn son, Charles Glenn Wensloff, where he worked on a survey crew.

Wensloff's work at Joplin earned him a promotion to the Kansas City Blues of the American Association, one of the Yankees' two top farm teams, for 1940. He was now closer than ever to achieving his dream of playing for a big-league club.

When he reported for spring training, Blues coaches criticized the follow-through on his delivery to the plate. Wensloff did not say a word, but a sportswriter back in Joplin, Porter Wittick of the *Joplin Globe*, who continued to follow Wensloff's career, wrote that the Blues "forgot that Charley's forearm looks like a barrel, and his chest and shoulders are as solid as rock. And if they want to know more, Charley isn't afraid of anything."[1]

By the time he made his first start for Kansas City, in April 1940, he had solved the problems with his pitching mechanics and took everyone by surprise with a dominating debut. "Charley Wensloff, pitching his first game in any sort of fast company, won for Kansas City Sunday and gave Columbus only two hits," wrote a sportswriter for the *Toledo Blade*.[2]

Wensloff spent three seasons with Kansas City, from 1940 through 1942. He compiled a 49-26 record and demonstrated he had the ability and control to pitch in the big leagues. In 1942 he had a 21-10 record with twenty-five complete games. His fearlessness on the mound and readiness to pitch whenever he was needed earned him the nickname Iron Man.

The New York Yankees called him up for the 1943 season. Wensloff, spending his winter in Sausalito working at the docks in San Francisco Bay, wasted no time returning his signed contract to New York. At spring training manager Joe McCarthy was quickly impressed with Wensloff. He told the press, "Wensloff has everything, including a well-controlled knuckler."[3] With so many star players in the military or doing war work, McCarthy figured that the rookie pitcher had a good chance to do well in 1943.

Wensloff made his Major League debut on May 2, 1943, against the Washington Senators at Washington. He pitched a complete game and gave up only seven hits but lost, 4–1. He started again on May 7, against the Philadelphia Athletics, and won, 6–2, allowing just six hits without a walk.

By the end of June, Wensloff had a 4-4 record despite a .248 ERA. "Wensloff is definitely a contender for the majors' 'hard luck' championship this year," wrote the *Sporting News*.[4] His four losses were by scores of 4–1, 3–0, 3–2, and 5–3.

Despite his unlucky start he earned a reputation as one of the best rookie pitchers in the American

League. "Wensloff has more stuff than any other new pitcher in the major leagues," wrote Dan Daniel in the *Sporting News*. "He is fast, has control, boasts a fine curve and mixes in a tough knuckler." J. G. Taylor Spink, editor of the *Sporting News,* agreed: "American Leaguers say Wensloff of the Yankees is the best new pitcher in the majors."[5]

Wensloff also made a few rookie mistakes. In the sixth inning of a game on June 20, he disagreed with umpire Ernie Stewart's strike zone. Wensloff threw his glove down on the mound and was ejected. On July 31 his third-inning balk allowed the tying run to score in a game the Yankees would eventually lose, 7–6. Nevertheless, McCarthy relied on the rookie as his third starter in the rotation through the season and considered him as a potential starter for the World Series.

Wensloff pitched his first Major League shutout on September 29 against Chicago. By the end of the season, he had a 13-11 record and ranked third behind Spud Chandler and Hank Borowy in strikeouts by Yankees pitchers. But McCarthy reconsidered placing the rookie in his World Series rotation and decided to use him in relief. Wensloff spent the entire 1943 World Series warming up in the bullpen. He received his World Series share and ring, but he never threw a single pitch in the Yankees' five-game Series victory over the St. Louis Cardinals. McCarthy later suggested that if the Series had gone to a sixth game, Wensloff would have started.

Wensloff was unhappy with the Yankees' contract offer in 1944 and chose to hold out. Unable to come to terms, the Yankees and Wensloff agreed he should be placed on the voluntarily retired list. He spent the remainder of the war away from New York, but not baseball. In April 1945 the Yankees optioned the twenty-nine-year-old to the San Diego Padres of the Pacific Coast League so that he could play baseball and perform civilian war work. He pitched well in his limited appearances for the Padres, but the military draft ended his season. On July 2 he was inducted into the U.S. Army.

In 1946 World War II was over, but Wensloff was one of seven Yankees still in the military. He was not discharged until mid-August, and though the Yankees wanted him to report immediately, Wensloff felt that he was not in shape for big-league competition. Instead, he pitched for the San Francisco area Moffatt Mantecas through September.

Despite Wensloff's refusal to join the team in 1946, new Yankees manager Bucky Harris told the press that he wanted the tough right-hander on his pitching staff in 1947. "Those who saw Charley before he went into the Army know that he is top-flight big league," Harris said.[6] On December 31, 1946, Wensloff was placed on the Yankees' active players list. He signed and returned his contract. Three years after the rookie watched the World Series from the bullpen, he returned for his sophomore season in the Bronx.

Wensloff was one of thirty-three Yankees chosen by Harris to take part in a 1947 series of fourteen spring-training games in Puerto Rico, Venezuela, and Cuba. He started the spring in good form, but something happened to his arm when he threw a curve ball in a game in Havana. A year later a doctor said Wensloff told him that "he felt a sharp, tearing pain in the back of his right arm just above the elbow. . . . He continued to have aching pain in this region for the remainder of the 1947 season."[7] The pain in his arm kept him sidelined for the remainder of spring training and through the start of the season.

Wensloff finally made his 1947 debut on June 4, forty-five months after the end of his rookie season. Pitching in relief against the Detroit Tigers, he gave up three runs in four innings. His sore pitching arm limited his appearances, though there were occasional moments of brilliance. He earned his first two victories in July, during the Yankees' nineteen-game winning streak from June 29 to

July 17. On July 12 he beat the St. Louis Browns, 12–2, for his first victory of the season. He added another win four days later against Cleveland, 8–2. Wensloff's win gave the Yankees their seventeenth straight victory and broke the club's record of consecutive wins set by Miller Huggins's Yankees in 1926.

Wensloff ended the season with a 3-1 record and a 2.61 ERA. But he pitched only 51⅔ innings and had just one complete game. He did finally make a World Series appearance. He pitched the eighth and ninth innings of Game Six, allowing no hits or runs as the Yankees lost to the Dodgers, 8–6.

After a long winter, Wensloff felt his arm was healed enough for him to deserve a better contract from the Yankees for the 1948 season. He joined several teammates who held out for more money. As the other players signed their contracts and made their way to spring training in Florida, Wensloff remained unsigned at his home in California. When the Yankees continued to refuse his salary demands, he asked to be traded.

Few could understand why any player would give up the opportunity to be a Yankee. "There must be 50 or 60 hurlers in the league eager to be traded to the Bombers," Dan Daniel wrote in the Sporting News, "but Wensloff wanted it the other way. Man bites dog."[8] The Yankees offered him to the New York Giants, but they were not interested. The Philadelphia Phillies agreed to take him in a conditional deal, but Wensloff refused to report, forcing the Phillies to return him. Finally, the Cleveland Indians picked him up for a sum just over the waiver price of ten thousand dollars.

Wensloff made his Cleveland Indians debut on May 4, 1948, in relief. He gave up a two-run home run in the tenth inning that gave the Philadelphia Athletics a victory over the Indians. It was the last time he took the mound as a Major Leaguer. The sore arm never healed. He could not pitch without pain. The Indians tried to return him to the Yankees, but it was too late. They sent him to the Mayo Clinic, but doctors advised him against surgery. "They said, 'Go home,' which he did."

Helen Wensloff said years later that Dr. James Dickson of the Cleveland Clinic informed the Indians in a letter dated May 15, 1948, "I feel confident that he is never going to be able to do strenuous pitching." Wensloff returned to his home in Sausalito. His Major League career was over, but he continued to pitch for local teams.

In 1949 local newspapers speculated that he might get that sore arm back in shape and return to the Major Leagues. But the arm never healed. The former big-league pitcher worked at a variety of occupations, including roofing and commercial fishing. He continued to play and manage local baseball teams. In 1969 he was inducted into the Marin County Athletic Hall of Fame for his work in establishing a Little League team near his Mill Valley home. Wensloff died in San Rafael, California, on February 18, 2001, at the age of eighty-five.

James Lincoln Ray

AGE	W	L	PCT.	ERA	G	GS	GF	CG	SHO	SV	IP	H	BB	SO	HBP	WP
26	1	0	1.000	1.46	4	1	2	1	0	0	12.1	12	8	1	0	0

Right-handed pitcher Dick Starr, a September call-up from the Newark Bears, recorded a complete-game victory in his only start with the 1947 New York Yankees. He was back with Newark for most of the 1948 season and then traded to the St. Louis Browns in 1949.

Dick was born Richard Eugene Starr to John and Emma Starr in Kittanning, Pennsylvania, on March 2, 1921. Tall and slender, at six feet three and 190 pounds, he was a natural athlete who became a local standout throughout his teenage years. While playing local semipro ball, Starr drew the attention of professional scouts. The Yankees signed him before the 1941 season and assigned him to a Class D affiliate, the Butler Yankees of the Pennsylvania State Association. Starr spent most of the season with Butler before being moved to another Class D team, the Findlay Browns of the Ohio State League. The twenty-year-old youngster proved he was a competent starter with both teams, posting a combined record of 15-9 with an ERA of 3.40.

Starr's excellent season did not earn him a promotion. The Yankees kept him at Class D Butler in 1942, where he was even better than the previous year, winning eighteen games and losing five.

After this promising start to his professional career, Starr enlisted in the army on October 19, 1942. Stateside, he was assigned to camps in Alabama, California, and Arizona, and he later served in Hawaii, Guadalcanal, Palau Island, New Caledonia, the Philippines, and Japan. Starr earned three Bronze Stars in addition to the Good Conduct Medal and numerous campaign ribbons. He attained the rank of sergeant and was discharged on December 11, 1945.

Dick Starr's complete-game victory over the St. Louis Browns on September 16, 1947, was his only win as a member of the Yankees.

After three years away from professional baseball, Starr returned to the Yankees organization in 1946. The Yanks sent him to the Augusta (Georgia) Tigers of the Class A South Atlantic League, where he led the league in wins (19), strikeouts (233), and earned run average (2.07).

In 1947 the Yankees promoted Starr to their top farm team, the Newark Bears of the Class Triple-A International League. He proved capable of competing at the highest Minor League level, going 9-6 with a 4.01 ERA. When the Bears' season ended, the Yankees called him to the Majors. Starr made his debut on September 5, 1947, against the Washington Senators, at Griffith Stadium. He entered the game in the bottom of the eighth inning with the Yankees trailing, 2–0. He pitched one inning, gave up two hits and a walk, and allowed one earned run.

After two more relief appearances, Starr made his first start on September 16, in the first game of a doubleheader at Yankee Stadium against the St. Louis Browns. The season was winding down, the Yankees had clinched the American League pennant the day before, and the Browns were in the cellar, thirty-five games behind the Yankees. Starr struggled throughout the game, giving up eight hits (seven singles and a home run to Walt Judnich) and walking seven, but managed to hold the Browns to three runs (one earned) in a complete-game victory. It was his last game of the season. He finished with a 1-0 record and a 1.46 ERA. Starr did not appear in the World Series against Brooklyn, but the Yankees voted him $750 of their Series winnings.

Starr was back with Newark for the 1948 season. He won fourteen games, lost nine, and posted a 4.21 ERA. He again was called up to the Yankees late in the season and appeared in one game, a two-inning relief effort against the Boston Red Sox in which he surrendered one earned run in two innings.

On December 13, 1948, the Yankees traded Starr, along with pitcher Red Embree, catcher Sherm Lollar, and $100,000, to the St. Louis Browns for catcher Roy Partee and pitcher Fred Sanford. Starr began the 1949 season as a starter for the Browns, but he lost his first five starts and was sent to the bullpen, where he mostly remained for the rest of the season. He was 1-6 with an ERA of 4.98 in eight starts and 0-1 with a 4.05 ERA in twenty-two relief appearances. Starr's only win of the season came on June 9, when he pitched the first of his two Major League shutouts, an 11–0 win over the Red Sox.

On October 2, 1949, Starr was part of a pitch-

ing stunt concocted by the Browns. In the first game of a doubleheader on the last day of the season, the Browns used nine pitchers, one per inning, setting a Major League record for most pitchers used by one team. Starr pitched the ninth in the 4–3 loss to the White Sox at Sportsman's Park.

Starr's 1950 season began with great promise. In the second game of the season, he pitched a complete game and defeated the White Sox, 6–1. He did not fare so well in his next few starts and again was relegated to the bullpen. Starr spent the rest of the season rotating between starting and relieving. Of his thirty-two appearances, sixteen were starts and sixteen were in relief. Overall he was 7-5 with a 5.02 ERA. On September 7 he pitched his second and last career shutout, 6–0 over the White Sox.

Starr spent the first four months of the 1951 season with the Browns. After compiling a 2-5 record and a 7.40 ERA, he was traded to the Senators. Again, he was traded for Fred Sanford, who had been the key player in his 1948 trade to the Browns. Washington turned out to be no better for Starr than St. Louis had been. In eleven games, all starts, he was 1-7 with an ERA of 5.58. His final Major League appearance came on September 29, a loss to the Philadelphia Athletics. His overall record for the season was 3-12 with a 6.49 ERA.

Starr spent the rest of his professional career in Class Triple-A. In 1952 and 1953 he pitched for the Baltimore Orioles of the International League, a Philadelphia Phillies farm team. In two seasons Starr was 21-21. At the conclusion of both seasons he pitched in the Venezuelan Winter League with the Caracas Lions and Magellan's Navigators; in 1953 he appeared with the Navigators in the Caribbean Series.

From 1954 through 1956 Starr worked as a starter and reliever for the Richmond Virginians of the International League, where over the three seasons he was 12-12. After the 1956 season, Starr retired from professional baseball.

In his Minor League career Starr had a 108-72 record with a 3.57 ERA. In the Major Leagues he posted a 12-24 record and a 5.25 ERA in ninety-three appearances.

After baseball Starr lived with his wife, Bonnie (the former Bonnie Leach), whom he married in 1942, in his hometown of Kittanning and worked for the Allegheny Ludlum Steel Corporation until he retired. The Starrs had three children, Carol, Richard Jr., and William. As of early 2012, Dick and Bonnie Starr are still living in Kittanning.

Chapter 59. **Lonny Frey**

James Forr

AGE	G	AB	R	H	2B	3B	HR	TB	RBI	BB	SO	BAV	OBP	SLG	SB	GDP	HBP
36	24	28	10	5	2	0	0	7	2	10	1	.179	.410	.250	3	1	1

The Cincinnati Reds of the 1930s were the National League's weakest team, logging five last-place finishes from 1931 to 1937. That futility ended when Bill McKechnie took over as the Reds' manager in 1938. McKechnie led Cincinnati to back-to-back pennants in 1939 and 1940 and a world championship in 1940.

Although several key players were in place when McKechnie arrived, including Frank McCormick, Paul Derringer, and Ernie Lombardi, it was the 1938 additions of pitcher Bucky Walters and second baseman Lonny Frey that turned the Reds from also-rans into champions. Walters was the league's best pitcher in 1939 and 1940, while Frey helped to anchor one of the best defensive infields ever.

Linus Reinhard Frey (pronounced Fry) was born on August 23, 1910, in St. Louis, Missouri, the second of Frank and Louise (Scherer) Frey's three sons. They named him for Saint Linus (considered Saint Peter's successor as pope), though hardly anyone called him Linus. To his mother he was Liney, friends knew him as Lonny or Lonnie, and newspapers sometimes called him Junior, a named he disliked.

The Freys were a close-knit, solidly middle-class German Catholic family. Frank drove a truck for the Great Atlantic and Pacific Tea Company, while Louise stayed home and looked after the children in the modest brick house they owned in the northwestern part of the city. Although Frey was bright and curious, his formal education lasted only through grammar school. Later he attended a business school to learn stenography, but for the most part he was his own teacher. He became a

Lonny Frey appeared in twenty-four games for the 1947 Yankees, mostly as a pinch runner or pinch hitter.

voracious reader; when he could not find a book or magazine that held his interest, he read the dictionary. "There was not a word he couldn't spell," his son Thomas marveled.[1]

Initially, soccer was his sport. He enjoyed baseball and grew up a rabid St. Louis Cardinals fan, but never thought very seriously about making a living at the game. As Frey entered his twenties, he secured a job as a secretary at a meatpacking plant. He played sandlot baseball in the evenings and on weekends, but that was as far as it went.

Then one day in 1931, he arrived at work to find a layoff notice. In the throes of the Great Depression, Frey and the other junior staffers were out of a job. After weeks of searching for work unsuccessfully, he decided to attend an open tryout with the Cardinals. Frey needed a job, and baseball was one of his few marketable skills.

Within a few years Cardinals general manager Branch Rickey would accumulate more prospects than he knew what to do with. But Rickey's scouts judged Frey too scrawny and passed on signing him. (Frey eventually filled out to five feet ten and 160 pounds.) Harvey Albrecht, Frey's sandlot coach and a former Minor League player, believed his young shortstop deserved another look. Albrecht asked his onetime manager Jimmy Hamilton, who was now a scout for Nashville of the Southern Association, to take a look at Frey. Hamilton did and signed him to a contract, complete with an invitation to spring training in 1932. Albrecht matched Frey not only with a job, but also with a bride. His sister Mary Ann became Frey's wife of forty-seven years and mother to his four sons.

Frey batted a combined .288 in 1932, splitting the season between two Class B leagues: York (Pennsylvania) of the New York–Pennsylvania League, and Montgomery (Alabama) of the Southeastern League. In August 1933 the twenty-three-year-old Frey was hitting a solid .294 for Nashville of the Class A Southern Association, when he was summoned to join the lowly Brooklyn Dodgers, who were desperate for infield help after a string of injuries.

With his wiry frame and boyish face he could have passed for a high school student. Max Carey, Brooklyn's manager, gave Frey the once-over and exclaimed, "You're just a kid! You're no bigger than a minute."[2] But Frey's matter-of-fact confidence belied his callow appearance and unassuming demeanor. "I didn't come up here to go back," he declared to a reporter.[3]

He immediately became Brooklyn's starting shortstop and maintained a grip on the position for the next three-plus seasons. Frey hit well for a shortstop, flashing occasional power and demonstrating a good eye. In 1935 he ranked in the top ten in the National League in extra-base hits and walks. He did not steal many bases—few in that era did—but he was a fast, aggressive runner, unafraid to take an extra base or crash into a pivotman. His quiet, professional approach earned him the post of team captain prior to the 1936 season.

On the downside, Frey was a dreadful defender. "Shortstop was not my position as far as pro ball was concerned," he admitted. He led the Majors in errors in both 1935 and 1936, and his range was adequate at best. Frey lacked the arm strength required of a big-league shortstop, so he was always in a rush to scoop up the ball and get it away as quickly as possible. The result was an endless mess of misplayed grounders and off-target throws.

Dodgers fans turned on Frey in 1936, after he committed fourteen errors in the Dodgers' first twenty-seven games. "You couldn't believe the booin' I'd get in Brooklyn. I couldn't get the ball to first base."[4] His misadventures turned him into a punch line. Author Roger Kahn related one quip about Frey that made the rounds: "There's an infielder with only one weakness. Batted balls."[5]

People made Frey sound like a man teetering on the edge of an emotional breakdown. In May manager Casey Stengel publicly questioned his shortstop's guts, saying, "Lonny is sensitive about the way those fans in Brooklyn holler and when they jumped on him he went to pieces."[6] Headlines read, "Dodgers' Defeat Breaks Frey's Spirit" and "Dodgers' Captain Unable to Stand Riding from Fans."[7] A teammate questioned how much more Frey could take: "When they roast a ballplayer like that a fellow might just as well root to be traded."[8]

It is possible Frey had thicker skin than he got

credit for. Although some writers claimed he hit better on the road than in Ebbets Field in front of his critics, the opposite actually was true. As for his defense, that was just as wretched in Brooklyn as it was anywhere else. Frey insisted the remnants of a springtime bout with tonsillitis bothered him more than the loudmouths in the bleachers. "It wasn't the Brooklyn fans booing me that affected my play," he said. "I've seen that written but it was just because my health was so bad. I never felt right all year. I felt like lying down and taking a week off. It was that poison in my system from the throat infection I had."[9]

In December 1936 the Dodgers dealt Frey to the Chicago Cubs for infielder Woody English and pitcher Roy Henshaw. Frey was happy to get away from Stengel. "I could never understand what Stengel was saying," he said years later. "I had him long enough. All he thought of was himself. All he did was tell stories to reporters. He didn't know what he was doing."[10]

On the other hand, he was fond of Brooklyn, despite the abuse. "When he got traded he kind of thought that was the end of the world," according to Thomas Frey. He was comfortable in the neighborhood he lived in and appreciated the enthusiasm of the fans, even though he was not their favorite. "What a place that will be to play ball if those directors ever straighten the club's affairs out or if someone can buy the whole outfit," he mused.[11]

Frey played in seventy-eight games for Chicago in 1937, filling in admirably at four positions. In February 1938 the Cubs sold him to Cincinnati. He could not have landed in a more perfect spot. For Frey, Bill McKechnie was everything Stengel was not. "He could look at a fellow and pick out his flaws and correct them."[12]

McKechnie's solution for Frey's defensive troubles was to shift him to second base, a position he had played in only forty-seven Major League games. Within two years Frey had transformed himself into the league's preeminent defensive second baseman. His newfound success surprised everyone but him. "I thought I could play regular anywhere," he said. "That's the confidence I had in myself."[13]

Frey's best offensive day of the 1938 season came in a June 26 doubleheader against the Phillies in the Baker Bowl. After going 3 for 5 with a double in the first game, he went 5 for 5 with two triples and three RBIs in the nightcap.

Frey and his infield mates were a colorful bunch. Third baseman Bill Werber came over in 1939 and decided the group needed a nickname because, as he put it, "The ballclub was a little deadass."[14] They became the Jungle Club. Frey had birthmarks all over him, so Werber took to calling him Leopard. Shortstop Billy Myers was Jaguar, first baseman Frank McCormick became Wildcat, while Werber tagged himself with Tiger.

Werber and Frey grew particularly close. Both were thoughtful and intelligent men, homebodies at heart; boozing and chasing women held no appeal. They killed time at the movies and even attended mass together, with Werber tagging along even though he was not Catholic. The two friends exchanged cards and phone calls into their nineties.

The 1939 season was Frey's best as he helped lead the Reds to the National League pennant. At the start of the season, McKechnie persuaded him to forget switch-hitting and bat exclusively left-handed. He also suggested that Frey try to pull the ball more. Frey responded by hitting .291 with eleven home runs, a league-leading twenty-five sacrifice hits. He made the first of his three appearances in the All-Star Game, where he knocked in the National League's only run. Arthur Patterson of the *New York Herald Tribune* was floored. "Anyone predicting this spring that Linus Frey not only would play a full game at second base in the All-Star Game but also avert a shutout for the National League . . . would have been gently led away to the nearest psychopathic ward and barred from the press box for life," he wrote.[15] However, the year ended with a thud for Frey—an 0-for-17 collar in the World Series, which the New York Yankees swept in four games.

Frey led the league with twenty-two stolen bases in 1940, and he was fourth in runs scored (102) and sixth in walks (80). Defensively, he led all National League second basemen in games played, assists, chances, put-outs, double plays, and fielding percentage.

The Reds made it back to the World Series in 1940 and defeated the Detroit Tigers in seven games to capture their first title since 1919. "We were so confident," boasted Frey. "It was almost ridiculous to say we were going to get beat."[16] Frey sat out most of the Series with a toe injury; he batted twice as a pinch hitter and made one late-game appearance at second base.

Frey remained a steady, reliable presence in the Reds' lineup through 1943, when Uncle Sam beckoned. Private Frey spent two years stationed at Fort Riley, Kansas, where he batted .450, as his Fort Riley Centaurs took the Western Victory League championship. However, when he returned to Cincinnati at the age of thirty-four in 1946, something was missing. "I just didn't have it anymore. Two years in the service and you lose it. . . . I was just too old, I guess," he said.[17]

With his skills declining, Frey bounced from the Reds back to the Cubs briefly and then in June 1947 to the Yankees. As the story goes, he arrived early in the morning at the Yankees' hotel in Philadelphia, immediately phoned manager Bucky Harris, and announced, "I'm here." Harris grumbled, "I am delighted," hung up, and went back to bed. Frey appeared in just twenty-four games for New York that season, mostly as a pinch runner or pinch hitter, and drove in a run in Game Six of the Yanks' World Series victory over Brooklyn.

Frey made one pinch-running appearance for the Yankees in 1948 and then was released in May.

He signed with the New York Giants, spent half the season with their Minneapolis farm team, and was released after the season. He played for Buffalo in 1949 and Seattle in 1950 and retired after the 1950 season. He finished his fourteen-year big-league career with 1,482 hits and a .269 batting average in 1,535 games.

Frey discovered that life in the Northwest suited his family perfectly. "We rented a house on Lake Washington. [My sons] learned how to swim, they learned how to fish, [and] they learned how to drive a motorboat."[18] The Freys sold their home in suburban St. Louis and relocated to Washington.

Neither coaching nor scouting interested him in the least. "I had enough traveling. I wanted to get out of it," he said. He spent a number of years at a large Seattle sporting-goods store, sold luggage for a while, and then retired, content to toil part-time as a handyman at his church.

As an old man Frey relished the constant stream of autograph requests that came his way and enjoyed attending both college and professional ball games. On Frey's ninetieth birthday the Seattle Mariners invited him to throw out the opening pitch at a game at Safeco Field. "He was a warm, very down-to-earth guy," said Pacific Coast League historian Dave Eskenazi. "He shared a number of entertaining baseball anecdotes, mainly about his old teams and teammates. I remember him telling me that Ernie Lombardi hit the ball harder than anyone else he'd seen, and he'd seen them all."[19]

Frey was ever the athlete—walking, biking, ice skating, and bow hunting. After Mary's death in 1982, he moved to a small house in Hayden, Idaho, to be closer to his children. There, at the age of seventy-two, he took up skiing for the first time. And no one could get him off that bicycle. Even when he was ninety-five, after two knee replacements and quadruple-bypass surgery, he pedaled all over town.

A stroke finally slowed Frey down and forced

him into an assisted living facility. When he died, in Coeur d'Alene, Idaho, on September 13, 2009, at the age of ninety-nine, he was the second oldest living Major Leaguer; the oldest was his good friend Billy Werber. Frey and his wife are buried in Bellevue, Washington. Asked a few years before his death to name the one highlight of his career, he could not do it. "Every day was a highlight."[20]

Chapter 60. Timeline, September 20–September 28

Lyle Spatz

Saturday, September 20, at Philadelphia — On a chilly, drizzly day in Philadelphia, the Yankees lost to the Athletics, 3–2. Winner Dick Fowler and loser Bobo Newsom each went the distance. Yogi Berra, batting third and catching, had two hits, including a triple. For the A's, Hank Majeski had three hits, and Sam Chapman had a home run. 93-55-1, First, 13 games ahead.

Sunday, September 21, at Philadelphia — Bill Bevens made strong case to be a World Series starter, with a three-hit, 6–0 shutout of the Athletics. Although Bucky Harris continued to rest a portion of his regulars in each game, every Yankee hit safely against Joe Coleman and Russ Christopher except Joe DiMaggio. Yogi Berra, Bobby Brown, Jack Phillips, and Aaron Robinson each had two hits. Both Berra's hits were doubles, while Robinson had a triple and Phillips a home run. 94-55-1, First, 14 games ahead.

Monday, September 22, vs. Washington — Rained out. 94-55-1, First, 14 games ahead.

Tuesday, September 23, vs. Washington (2) — Allie Reynolds and Frank Shea tuned up for the World Series with excellent outings, as the Yankees swept the Senators, 2–0 and 3–1. Each man pitched eight innings, and in each game Joe Page indicated he too was ready for the World Series with a scoreless ninth. Reynolds won his nineteenth game after a brilliant duel with Walt Masterson, who allowed only five hits. The Yanks scored their two runs in the eighth inning. Joe DiMaggio, with his club-leading twentieth, and Billy Johnson homered in

Final 1947 American League Standings

TEAM	G	W	L	T	PCT	GB
New York Yankees	155	97	57	1	.630	—
Detroit Tigers	158	85	69	4	.552	12.0
Boston Red Sox	157	83	71	3	.539	14.0
Cleveland Indians	157	80	74	3	.519	17.0
Philadelphia Athletics	156	78	76	2	.506	19.0
Chicago White Sox	155	70	84	1	.455	27.0
Washington Senators	154	64	90	0	.416	33.0
St. Louis Browns	154	59	95	0	.383	38.0

the second game off loser Micky Haefner. 96-55-1, First, 14½ games ahead.

Wednesday, September 24 — Not scheduled. 96-55-1, First, 14 games ahead.

Thursday, September 25, vs. Boston — Rained out. 96-55-1, First, 14 games ahead.

Friday, September 26, vs. Boston — The Red Sox got three runs off Spud Chandler in the first inning and held on to beat the Yankees, 3–2, behind Denny Galehouse. Bobo Newsom and Karl Drews also pitched for New York. 96-56-1, First, 13 games ahead.

Saturday, September 27, vs. Philadelphia — Joe Page pitched the final four innings of a ten-inning 2–1 loss on "Joe Page Day" at Yankee Stadium. Page's fifty-sixth appearance of the season broke the club record set by Jack Chesbro in 1904. Bill Bevens pitched the first six innings for the Yankees. Philadelphia's Phil Marchildon went the dis-

tance to win his nineteenth game. 96-57-1, First,
12 games ahead.

Sunday, September 28, vs. Philadelphia — Bill
Wight, recently recalled from Kansas City, went
the distance, as the Yankees ended the regular season with a 5–3 win over the Athletics. Rookie left-
hander Lou Brissie, making his big-league debut,
was the loser. The Yankees finished the season 12
games ahead of the second-place Detroit Tigers.
97-57-1, First, 12 games ahead.

Chapter 61. **Bill Wight**

Bill Nowlin

AGE	W	L	PCT.	ERA	G	GS	GF	CG	SHO	SV	IP	H	BB	SO	HBP	WP
25	1	0	1.000	1.00	1	1	0	1	0	0	9.0	8	2	3	0	0

Left-handed pitcher Bill Wight spent twelve seasons in the Major Leagues with eight different clubs. He appeared in 347 games, compiling a mediocre 77-99 won-lost record and a 3.95 earned run average. Wight does hold one record; however, it is for batting, and it is one he never took pride in. Pitching for the Chicago White Sox in 1950, Wight was hitless in sixty-one at bats, the most at bats by an American Leaguer in a season without getting a hit.

Bill was born William Robert Wight on April 12, 1922, in Rio Vista, California, inland about sixty miles from San Francisco. His father, Bert, worked on the water as a launch operator and later as a shipping captain. Bert Wight was a California native. His wife, Laura (Quinn) Wight, was from Oregon. The couple had two sons, Charles, born in 1914, and then Bill eight years later.

Bill attended Lafayette elementary school and Lowell Junior High in Oakland and was graduated from McClymonds High School in Oakland in 1940. The six-foot-one, 180-pound teenager was signed by legendary New York Yankees scout Joe Devine and played his first season as a professional in 1941 for the Idaho Falls Russets in the Class C Pioneer League.

"In California, a kid can play all year around. I used to haunt Bay View Park in Oakland," Wight told sportswriter Will Wedge.

That must have been where Joe Devine saw me first. He's the Yanks' scout and a great organizer of kid teams. He got together the Yankee rookies along about 1938, and fitted us out in uniforms that were practically the same as

Bill Wight's one appearance with the Yankees in 1947 was a win in the final game of the regular season.

those of the real Yanks. The only kid on the team over 18 was Russ Christopher. I was only 16, and maybe I wasn't excited the day Devine went home with me and had my father sign an agreement that I wouldn't sign up with any professional team but the big Yankees. I got $1,000 for that, and it seemed like all the dough in the world. A couple of years later, after I had turned 18, the Yankees sent my father and me a contract and I stepped out with Idaho Falls.[1]

Bill later admitted that he was more interested in sketching than playing ball.[2]

There was a benefit to growing up when he did. "All the playgrounds were free and during the Depression, they'd give you equipment if you wanted. Sign out for it. You could play every day and it helped you develop faster."[3] Wight played outfield at first, but had a strong arm and soon turned to pitching. It was not in high school that he got any real help; he learned the most playing semipro baseball, often against veteran ballplayers. "We were all in high school, 16 to 18, and we'd get the hell kicked out of us in some of those games by those old semi-pros, you know, but that's who you played against. You learn when you hang a curve against a good hitter. In high school, a guy takes it for strike three. There's a big difference. You learn quicker. And they'd tell you about your mistakes."

The University of California made Wight an offer, but he had not been on a college track and said he did not think he had the grades. "I was an art major," he said, and got straight As, but it was purely by taking art classes and no others. He met his future wife, Janice, in high school art class.

Yankees scout Devine had an edge, however. He would take a number of prospects on a bus down to Modesto on weekends and work them out, giving them experience, getting to know them and letting them and their families to get to know him.

Wight was 8-12 with Idaho Falls, in his debut 1941 season. He moved up to the Class A Binghamton (New York) Triplets in 1942, but the weather in upstate New York was too cold for him. He was shifted to the Class B Norfolk Tars in Virginia, where he went 7-5, with a 2.43 ERA. He was slated to pitch for the Kansas City Blues, one of the Yankees' top farm teams, at the end of the year, but shoulder trouble ended his season a few weeks early. Wight took advantage of the extra free time and married Janice Irene Carlson on September 8.

In November 1942 Wight joined the U.S. Navy and served until his discharge in December 1945.

The navy took over Oakland's St. Mary's College and made it into a preflight school, bringing in many pro athletes to help build a program. Wight's primary duty was being the base mailman and helping with physical training. There was, naturally, a baseball team organized. "Me and Charlie Gehringer managed the club and Bill Rigney was on shortstop," he said.[4] His overall record pitching for the St. Mary's Pre-Flighters was 33-5.[5]

With the end of the war, the Yankees were unsure of what they had in terms of players available for the 1946 season, so they scheduled an early spring training in Panama. Bill was on the Newark Bears' roster but had asked if he could train with the big-league team. Manager Joe McCarthy agreed on a bit of a hunch and was impressed by what he saw of Wight. "The southpaw operated with all the poise of a veteran, had plenty of stuff and made even the customarily wary and cautious McCarthy grow exuberant."[6]

The *New York World-Telegram*'s Bill Roeder's February 28 dispatch was headlined "Bill Wight Looks Like He Might Be That Southpaw Pitcher Yankees Need." The *New York Sun*'s Will Wedge featured his pickoff move in a March 30 column headed "Rookie Wight Perfects Pickoff." The opposition protested balk, but Wight was charged with only seven in all his time in the Majors. He had developed the move himself. "I used to watch Walter Mails in San Francisco," he explained. "Mails was one of the best ever nipping guys off first. I studied the way he stood and how he glanced out of the tail of his eye and then swiveled his neck around. He was nifty. Once Mails picked five guys off first."[7]

Despite so many players contending for spots on the club, Wight remembered everyone just being happy to be there. The Yanks purchased his contract from Newark four days before opening day, and Bill made his first appearance in Philadelphia on April 17, the second game of the 1946 season. He relieved starter Randy Gumpert in the bottom of the seventh after Bobo Newsom had executed the second successful squeeze bunt of the inning. McCarthy instructed Wight to pick Newsom off first base, which he did. But he failed to retire any of the three batters he faced and threw wildly on another pickoff attempt for an error.

Wight's first of four starts that season was on April 20, against Washington at Yankee Stadium. He lasted 6⅓ innings and was charged with the 7–3 loss. Wight stayed with the Yankees all season. Appearing in fourteen games, he had a 2-2 record and a 4.46 earned run average.

Wight spent 1947 with the Class Triple-A Kansas City Blues of the American Association. He won sixteen games with a 2.85 ERA as the Blues cruised to a first-place finish. The Yankees recalled him on September 19, and he appeared in one game, a complete-game win in the final game of the year, against Philadelphia, at Yankee Stadium.

Wight's connection with the Yankees ended in 1948 when he was packaged as part of a late-February trade with the White Sox that brought left-hander Eddie Lopat to New York. Unaware of the trade, Wight was driving from his home in Healdsburg, California, to the Yankees' camp in St. Petersburg, Florida. The White Sox trained in Pasadena, California. "We're just hoping Bill picks up a paper somewhere along the way before he gets too far," said New York public relations man Red Patterson. "Otherwise, it's going to be a long trip back."[8] The *Chicago Tribune* printed a helpful headline: "NOTE TO BILL WIGHT: GET IN REVERSE AND HEAD FOR CALIFORNIA."[9] It did not work. On February 29 Wight and his wife and son, Larry (born in 1943), arrived in St. Petersburg after driving eight days cross-country. He learned of the trade from a gas station attendant in Clearwater, less than twenty miles from camp.

Wight was 9-20 with a 4.80 ERA in 223⅓ innings for the last-place White Sox in 1948. He also led the league in walks with 135. His best game was a three-hit shutout of the Yankees on May 21. His first big-league RBI came on his game-winning single, breaking a scoreless tie in the bottom of the fifth.

There was an amusing sidelight: Jerry Coleman had known Wight since childhood and knew about his pickoff move, so when Wight was with the White Sox and Coleman with the Yanks, Jerry kept warning his teammates to be careful. The only Yankee Wight picked off that year was Jerry Coleman.[10]

Wight enjoyed a much better year in 1949, winning fifteen games and losing thirteen with a greatly improved 3.31 earned run average. Cleveland manager Lou Boudreau later told him he had just missed making the All-Star team.

He started well in 1950, but he missed almost three weeks due to hemorrhoids, followed by an ailing elbow that developed in a loss to New York on July 28. He did manage to pitch at least two hundred innings for the third consecutive season, but his record slipped to 10-16 despite a decent 3.58 ERA. This was the year Wight batted sixty-one times without getting a hit.

In October and November Wight took part in a thirty-three-game postseason exhibition tour pitting the American League All-Stars versus the National League All-Stars and visiting twelve states and Canada. On December 10 Boston moved to bolster its pitching staff by trading for Wight and Ray Scarborough. Strangely, before the season began, Wight was named president of the New York Yankees Alumni Association. The association was the sole creation of Yankees scout Joe Devine, who named its presidents.[11]

After Wight was knocked out in his first five starts for Boston, he was pulled from the rotation and used as a reliever and spot starter from that point on. Also, opposing managers ratcheted up their complaints about Wight's pickoff move to first base, claiming that he balked every time. By season's end he was 7-7 with a 5.10 earned run average.

Red Sox pitching coach Bill McKechnie was pleased with Wight's attitude at spring training in 1952, but when it came time for a trade, Wight was made available. He was sent to the Tigers as part of a nine-player deal on June 3; his first start with his new club was a losing effort against the Red Sox on June 8. However, by July 5 he'd already registered two shutouts. Wight was stingier with runs for both teams that season, finishing 1952 with a combined ERA of 3.75 and a 7-10 record.

Wight was the first Tiger to sign his 1953 contract. Pitching coach Ted Lyons was hopeful that a little work on his defense could help him: "Wight got himself in a jam four times last year by not covering first base. We'll work on that this spring," Lyons said.[12] Bill was sharp in spring training, but he faltered badly when the season started. His ERA for Detroit was 8.88 in thirteen appearances. Just a little over a year after the trade to Detroit, Wight was sent to Cleveland in an eight-player trade in June. He pitched just fifty-two innings for the season, split almost evenly between the two teams.

Wight missed the Indians' trip to the World Series in 1954, though he did get a one-thousand-dollar Series share. He had trained with Cleveland in Tucson, but was sold to San Diego and spent all of 1954 pitching for Lefty O'Doul in the Pacific Coast League. He excelled against PCL batters, posting a 17-5 record with a 1.93 earned run average for the pennant-winning Padres. Wight led the league in both winning percentage and ERA and was one of three pitchers named to the league's All-Star team.

His work in the PCL propelled him back to the Majors in 1955, where the Indians used him in seventeen games. Though Wight had pitched well in limited action, he was placed on waivers in mid-July and claimed by the Baltimore Orioles. For the year he had only a 6-8 record, but his ERA was a sparkling 2.48.

Seen from the start as part of manager Paul Richards's four-man rotation, Wight was the Ori-oles' opening-day starter in 1956, but was hit for four runs in one-third of an inning and then hammered for another four runs without getting a man out just four days later. He recovered from that abysmal beginning with his first of nine wins that season, a 5–1 seven-hitter against the Yanks on May 13. By December 1957 Wight found himself in the National League, after being sold to the Cincinnati Reds.

Bill Wight was a man who had a few different talents. He enjoyed playing chess on the road, when he could find a suitable opponent, and he was a very good sketch artist. The January 1, 1958, *San Francisco Examiner* shows Bill with a sketch he had done of Ted Williams. While in Cleveland he had supplied sketches to accompany a column Early Wynn wrote for a newspaper there. In 1952, thanks to a friend of Red Sox owner Tom Yawkey, Bill had received a scholarship for a mail-order course from the Famous Artists School of Westport, Connecticut.

Cincinnati planned to use Wight in the bullpen in 1958, but after he appeared in seven games, the Reds released him on May 20. The St. Louis Cardinals picked him up as a free agent the next day so they could have at least one lefty reliever on the staff. Wight won three games without a loss for St. Louis, but his earned run average was 5.02.

During the off-season he toured East Asia with the Cardinals, traveling to the Philippines, Korea, and Japan. After beating the Hawaiian All-Stars on October 12, 3–1, he was released by the Cardinals but welcomed to continue on the tour. He loved it, he told the *Sporting News*. "Wonderful, just wonderful. In fact, (the Japanese) want me to pitch in their league. I'm seriously considering that offer, too. It sounds very good, except for being so far away from home." Wight went on to talk about his hopes for a career in sports cartooning or commercial art. "Baseball put me in a position to return to my art work when I no longer can get anybody out."[13]

In 1959 Wight worked briefly in one final season, pitching in four games for the PCL Seattle Rainiers, and then retired. He worked for a while as a liquor salesman, but also enjoyed time at his ranch in Mount Shasta, California. From 1962 to 1966 he was a scout in Northern California for the National League's new Houston club, where he signed future Hall of Famer Joe Morgan. Wight was an area scout for the Atlanta Braves from 1967 to 1994 and signed more than a dozen players, including Dusty Baker, Dale Murphy, Bob Horner, and David Justice. He then served as a Major League scout for the Braves from 1995 through 1998. Bill and Janice Wight were at Mount Shasta when Bill died of a heart attack on May 17, 2007.

Chapter 62. **Frank Crosetti**

Tara Krieger

AGE	G	AB	R	H	2B	3B	HR	TB	RBI	BB	SO	BAV	OBP	SLG	SB	GDP	HBP
36	3	1	0	0	0	0	0	0	0	0	0	—	—	—	0	0	0

In thirty-seven seasons as an infielder and third base coach for the Yankees, Frank Crosetti was on the field for twenty-three Fall Classics, of which New York won seventeen. After a while "the Crow" had collected so many rings that the Yankees started giving him engraved shotguns instead.

Frank Crosetti may not have been the most talented player in pinstripes, but he was often the glue that held everyone together. He was a consummate professional, a sure-handed fielder, and, as one writer put it, "one of the most annoying .245 batters that baseball ever had."[1]

"Crosetti is the sparkplug of the Yankees," Rogers Hornsby once said. "Without him they wouldn't have a chance. He is a great player and he is about the only one on the club who does any hollering."[2]

Crow's reputation as the Yankees' "holler guy" gave secondary meaning to a moniker that superficially seemed like a shortened version of his last name. Players grew accustomed to hearing his high-pitched voice cawing from all corners of the field.

It may have come about incidentally. During a frustratingly sluggish stretch of Crosetti's rookie year, manager Joe McCarthy told the kid that Lou Gehrig looked too lackadaisical at first base. "When you get the ball in infield practice," McCarthy said, "fire it back hard at Gehrig. Holler at him. See if you can't wake him up."

Obligingly, Crosetti obeyed. Years later McCarthy related that Gehrig was never the problem at all—it was Crosetti who had needed the extra motivation. Apparently, it worked—his animated style on the field stuck.[3] Off the field Crosetti had

Veteran shortstop Frank Crosetti had been with the Yankees since 1932, but he had only one at bat in 1947.

"the same approximate loquacity as the Sphinx," as *New York Times* columnist Arthur Daley once described him.[4]

The younger son of Domenico Crosetti, who emigrated from near Genoa, Italy, around the turn of the century, and Rachele Monteverde Crosetti, a California native whose parents were from the same region, Frank Peter Joseph Crosetti was born in San Francisco on October 4, 1910.

Because he suffered from poor health as a toddler, the family relocated to the more rural Los Gatos, and Domenico Crosetti started a vegetable farm. Frank's first baseball experiences were playing one-a-cat (a baseball-cricket hybrid) with his brother, John, using a board and a dried corncob.

An unimpressive student, Crosetti, whose family moved to Santa Clara, then to the North Beach area of San Francisco, left school at sixteen. After playing semipro ball in Montana, he played winter ball in San Francisco, where Sam Fugazy, an informal Seals scout, invited him for a tryout with the professional club. The Seals appreciated Crosetti's talent but deemed him too small to be a regular, so team secretary George Putnam had bottles of milk delivered to his house every morning, and Crosetti put on ten pounds.[5] He wasted little time in grabbing his first headlines, hitting a grand slam off Joe Dawson of the Pittsburgh Pirates in a March 21, 1928, exhibition game against the reigning National League champions.

Crosetti batted a modest .248 in 96 games in 1928, mainly playing third base. The following year he was moved to shortstop. Playing nearly the entire grueling 180-plus-game schedule, Crosetti improved to .314 in 1929 and to .334 in 1930. In the latter season he hit twenty-seven home runs, stole eighteen bases, and led the league with 171 runs scored.

The slick-fielding leadoff hitter attracted the attention of Major League scouts, including Bill Essick of the New York Yankees. Convinced that he had just seen the greatest shortstop in the game, Essick persuaded Yankees owner Jacob Ruppert to open his wallet.[6] On August 23, 1930, Crosetti became the property of the Yankees for what eventually amounted to three marginal players and seventy-five thousand dollars in cash.

Still barely twenty years old, Crosetti remained with the Seals in 1931 for more seasoning. He batted cleanup for the only time in his career and hit .343.

Crosetti headed to spring training in St. Petersburg in 1932 as the Yankees' leading shortstop can-

didate.[7] There, he impressed manager Joe McCarthy as "one of the fastest infielders around [with] a fine, sure pair of hands."[8] Double-play partner and fellow San Franciscan Tony Lazzeri took him under his wing.

Ultimately, McCarthy went with the veteran Lyn Lary at short and started Crosetti at third. Crosetti went 0 for 5 on opening day against Philadelphia (his first big-league hit, a triple, came in the Yankees' next game) and was benched after batting .228 in his first twenty-nine games. He won the shortstop job later that summer when Lary stopped hitting.

Crosetti endured relatively unremarkable seasons in 1933 and 1934 and was often in danger of losing his job. Before the 1935 season he worked out with University of Southern California track coach Brutus Hamilton to become bigger, faster, and stronger[9] and was assured by McCarthy he was the only shortstop candidate in the running.[10] And he thrived, particularly defensively, making just sixteen errors after hovering around forty in each of the prior two years.

Then on August 4, 1935, Crosetti blew out his left knee untying his shoes. He had strained it three weeks earlier, but when he pulled his leg up to get undressed in his Pullman berth that night, some cartilage tore loose. The diagnosis: season-ending knee surgery.

Team president Ed Barrow invited Crosetti to spring training the next year on a provisional one-dollar contract. Crosetti not only disposed of any doubt surrounding the status of his knee, but also put together the best offensive season of his career and was selected to the American League All-Star team.

He did strike out quite a bit—the most in the AL in 1937 and '38. Conversely, Crosetti took tremendous pride in consistently leading the league in hit-by-pitched balls, which Yankees coach Art Fletcher taught him how to execute without getting seriously injured. Crosetti's career on-base percentage was .341—typically some 90 to 100 points higher than his season batting averages—and he set a then-record of 757 plate appearance in 1938. He also fooled many a base runner by pulling off the hidden-ball trick.

Crosetti's shining moment (and greatest thrill) as a player came in the Yankees' sweep of the Cubs in the 1938 World Series. His defense, which included nailing a runner at the plate from the foul line in short left field, as well as coming "from nowhere" to field a "certain single" up the middle for an out, saved three runs in the Yanks' 3–1 victory in the opener.[11] His eighth-inning home run off Dizzy Dean in Game Two proved the deciding blast in the 6–3 victory. Add a two-run double and a two-run triple in Game Four, and Crosetti tallied six RBIS for the Series.

His sparkling Series topped off a season in which he had led the league in stolen bases, hit thirty-five doubles, and set a record for shortstops by turning 120 double plays.[12] Much of his defensive success in 1938 could be attributed to the arrival of Joe Gordon at second base to replace Lazzeri.

After the Series, on October 22, 1938, Crosetti and Norma Devincenzi—a San Francisco girl whose family owned the apartment building where his brother, John, lived—quietly eloped at the Church of the Transfiguration in downtown Manhattan. Their union lasted until his death, sixty-three years later, along the way producing a daughter, Ellen Rachel, and a son, John Dominic.[13]

Crosetti staged a much-publicized holdout in the early days of spring training 1939, refusing to sign for less than fifteen thousand dollars. By mid-March he had settled for fourteen thousand. In the rush to catch up in his conditioning, Crosetti developed a sore arm and got off to a slow start. Eventually, he came around and was selected to the AL All-Star team. He received a nice raise for 1940—signing for eighteen thousand dollars.

Then, abruptly, the honeymoon ended. Despite Yankees president Ed Barrow's new mandate that all players stay in shape during the off-season, Crosetti, determined to condition himself "slowly" so he would not develop another sore arm, passed up that advice.[14] By mid-March the sore arm returned; he could not hit, and he bobbled balls on plays he would normally make. After the Yankees lost seven straight in May, McCarthy benched him for a week in favor of Bill Knickerbocker. In August, Crosetti was dropped to eighth in the batting order. The Yankees finished third, and Crosetti hit .194.

Phil Rizzuto, a young shortstop, had been tearing up the Yanks' Kansas City farm club in 1940. Only the looming possibility that young, unmarried players like Rizzuto might be sent to war probably saved Crosetti from being traded that off-season.[15]

Determined to keep his job, Crosetti had worked furiously to stay in shape. He even experimented batting left-handed in spring training, hoping it would increase his average.[16] Yet as many of Crosetti's teammates initially gave the usurper Rizzuto the cold shoulder, Crosetti actively helped the diminutive youngster. "He made me look good—and here I am trying to take his job away," Rizzuto recalled years later.[17]

Rizzuto won the starting spot, but when he was not hitting by May, the Crow reclaimed the position. Then, on June 16, Crosetti was spiked in the throwing hand, and Rizzuto took over again, for good. Crosetti found playing time later in the season at third base when Red Rolfe was hospitalized with chronic ulcerative colitis—but overall, his role was limited to fifty games. Crosetti rode the bench all five games of the Yankees' World Series victory over the Dodgers.

The reportedly "aging" Crosetti (he was only thirty-one, but he was losing his hair) started the 1942 season as a utility infielder. He worked some with young Jerry Priddy, who was being groomed for third base to replace the ailing Rolfe, but Priddy's bat stayed cold, and Crosetti became the regular third baseman. He played well enough that he narrowly missed another All-Star selection.[18] Rolfe displaced Crosetti when he returned later that summer.

Crosetti did get into Game Three of the World Series, which the Yankees lost to the Cardinals. Playing third base, he shoved umpire Bill Summers over what he considered a bad call. Commissioner Kenesaw Mountain Landis fined Crosetti $250 and suspended him for the first thirty days of the 1943 season.

In February 1943 Crosetti's father, Domenico, was struck by a car and killed. Barrow gave Crosetti permission to report to camp late, so he could spend more time with his family. Crosetti would be needed to help fill the void at short left when Rizzuto joined the navy. A bout with the flu days before his suspension ended left him weak and out of shape, however, and rookies Snuffy Stirnweiss and Billy Johnson had the left side of the infield covered. Crosetti's return on May 21 went with a whimper.

Still, Barrow and McCarthy recognized Crosetti's value on the bench. Despite continued interest from other teams over the years, Barrow refused to sell him. "I don't care how much they offer," Barrow said. "Nobody can buy Crosetti. He stays with the Yankees as long as I have anything to do with running them."[19] The feeling was mutual: for Crosetti, it was "the Yankees—or nothing."[20]

When Stirnweiss stopped hitting, Crosetti was back at short—and the Yankees cruised to another pennant and a successful World Series rematch with the Cardinals. Crosetti reached base in each of the five games, started the winning rally in the sixth inning of Game One, and made game-saving defensive plays in Games Four and Five.

Working in a shipyard in Stockton, California, in the off-season gave Crosetti an occupational draft deferment as a defense worker but tied him to his job. All he could do was wait patiently, play-

ing semipro ball once or twice a week. When the draft board eased restrictions on men over thirty in July 1944, Crosetti rejoined the Yankees.

The war's sapping baseball of talent gave Crosetti leverage; he was again a late holdout in 1945, signing for fifteen thousand dollars two weeks before opening day. He did not have the greatest of seasons, but he was better than the alternative—Joe Buzas, who had iron hands.[21]

By 1946 Rizzuto had returned, and Crosetti, now thirty-five, batted .288 in twenty-eight games off the bench. The Yankees had started traveling out west by airplane, and Crosetti was afraid to fly. He was granted permission to follow the team around by train.

In 1947 Crosetti signed as a player-coach alongside new manager Bucky Harris and got into three games, going hitless in his only at bat. He went on the inactive list late that summer and was making calls to the bullpen on Harris's behalf when the Yankees beat the Dodgers in the World Series.

At his request Crosetti reported to spring training in 1948 as a player, not as a coach, though he spent much of the spring helping teammates. He played in seventeen games, in the last of which, on October 3 in Boston, he appeared as a defensive replacement at second base. After that season—and for the next two decades—Crosetti coached full-time.

Crosetti lived somewhat old-fashionedly—rising at six, the first one in the clubhouse and the last one out, retiring no later than nine thirty or ten (unless there was a night game). Baseball was all that mattered. He would not hesitate to call players out for making mistakes if he thought they were not giving their all. When infielder Phil Linz's harmonica playing amid a losing streak started a fracas on the team bus in 1964, Crosetti had little sense of humor about it, calling it the worst thing he had ever witnessed in all his years with the club.

And he hardly hid his disdain for the media or anything involving spectacle—pitcher Jim Bouton, who skewered him in his baseball exposé *Ball Four*, wrote that Crosetti's "twin fortes" were "saving baseballs . . . to the point of jumping into the stands after them, and chasing photographers off the field."[22]

Even after the Yankees would win the World Series, Crosetti would not stick around to celebrate, preferring instead to jump into a car the next day and begin the drive back to Stockton to be with his family. In the off-season he enjoyed fishing and hunting, biding his time until he could head to Florida for spring training.

When the Yankees needed a guide for young players first joining the team, they had Crosetti pen the twelve-page pamphlet. It covered such topics as staying in peak physical condition, eating and sleeping well, hustling ("Do not let the fans walk out . . . feeling like they have watched a listless group of ballplayers"), keeping one's temper, and obligations as a teammate and as a public figure—which included choosing one's friends wisely and avoiding the temptations of drinking, carousing, gambling, and loose women. In 1966 Crosetti (and not a ghostwriter) published a book, a youth instructional titled *Frank Crosetti's Secrets of Baserunning and Infield Play*.

Crosetti was the ringleader in a 1962 suit filed on behalf of a couple of hundred contemporaries against the owners' pension committee. The Major League Baseball Players' Association, propelled by lucrative television and marketing deals, had met secretly the previous fall to raise the per-month pension rate to $250; players already retired more than ten years, however, like Crosetti, were frozen at $175. The players lost the suit and eventually settled for $750,000. Decades later Crosetti was also one of a handful of old-time ballplayers unsuccessfully bringing what they hoped would be a class-action suit against Major League Baseball for using their names and images in promotional materials.[23]

Not that Crosetti was ever in dire straits finan-

cially. His World Series checks alone totaled a reported $142,989—a stunning amount in an era when season salaries were still in the low five figures. He had also made a small fortune from shrewd real-estate investments—something he began doing while with the Seals when a banker friend advised him to acquire all the local real estate he could find in Depression-era San Francisco.[24]

By 1968, though, the Yankees' World Series bounty had dried up, and Crosetti longed to spend more time with his mother, children, and grandchildren on the West Coast. On October 4, his fifty-eighth birthday, he submitted a six-page handwritten letter of resignation. It concluded: "Once a Yankee, always a Yankee!"[25]

Yet Crosetti signed to coach the expansion Seattle Pilots in 1969—thousands of miles closer to home than New York—and planned on eventually transitioning into a scout with the organization. But Seattle finished last, and general manager Marvin Milkes did not renew his contract.[26] Crosetti felt betrayed, but before Christmas he had been recruited by the Minnesota Twins.

Crosetti was in the coach's box along third to shake hands with Harmon Killebrew for the slugger's five hundredth home run in 1971. He rarely ever shook hands after a player hit a round-tripper—Mickey Mantle's walk-off home run in the 1964 World Series and Roger Maris's sixtieth and sixty-first homers in 1961 being three other notable exceptions.

But after two seasons, he had truly had enough. He retired and coached high school ball at St. Mary's in Stockton.

Although he never attended a Yankees Old-Timers Day after he retired, Crosetti avidly followed the team from his home in Stockton and was a frequent visitor when the Yankees came to Oakland each year, even appearing in the broadcast booth on occasion. Until a broken hip from a fall incapacitated him in January 2002, he went fishing regularly, and he rarely shied away from an opportunity to talk baseball or reminisce about his years in pinstripes with those who would listen. "He was Yankee all the way around," his wife, Norma, said after he died at the age of ninety-one on February 11, 2002. "He had no other team."

Chapter 63. **Joe Page**

Mark Stewart

AGE	W	L	PCT.	ERA	G	GS	GF	CG	SHO	SV	IP	H	BB	SO	HBP	WP
29	14	8	.636	2.48	56	2	44	0	0	17	141.1	105	72	116	1	1

Among the men who set the early standard for today's closers was left-hander Joe Page of the New York Yankees. Page used his physical presence—he was six feet three and two hundred pounds—along with an excellent fastball and an occasional spitball to dominate batters in the late 1940s.

Joseph Francis Page was born on October 28, 1917, in Cherry Valley, Pennsylvania, to Joseph and Lorena (Couch) Page. He grew up in Springdale, a coal-mining area near Pittsburgh. Page was the eldest of seven children—four girls and three boys. As soon as he was able, Joe worked in the mines. He would rise before dawn, take a ferry with his father over to a mine in the community of Barking, and work there as a breaker boy. Breaker boys worked with elderly and incapacitated miners, removing by hand impurities from hunks of coal that ascended from the depths.

Page's ticket out of coal mining was his powerful left arm, but his budding career almost ended when he nearly lost a leg in a 1936 car accident. He suffered a compound fracture of his left fibula that required surgery and a five-month hospital stay. Between the ages of eighteen and twenty he was discouraged from competing in any sports.

Page had not attracted much attention from scouts as a teenager, and he went completely off the radar during his convalescence. A couple of years working in the mines added muscle to his body and a few miles per hour to his fastball, however.

After some semipro experience, Page pitched in Pittsburgh's amateur league. Several teams instructed their scouts to report on him, but no one was overly impressed. In 1939 the home-

Joe Page went from being one pitch away from the Minors to the savior of the Yankees' pitching staff.

town Pirates gave Page a tryout but did not sign him. The following year Yankees scout Bill Haddock, swayed by the twenty-two-year-old's towering presence, advised the team's head scout, Paul Krichell, to take a closer look. The Yankees eventually signed Page in 1940. He broke in with the Butler (Pennsylvania) Yankees in the Class D

Catcher Yogi Berra and first baseman George McQuinn congratulate Joe Page after Page recorded the final out in the Yankees' Game One win in the 1947 World Series.

Pennsylvania State Association, going 11-3 with a 3.67 earned run average.

In the off-seasons Page kept in shape working for a local aluminum company, loading sixty-pound blocks of metal into boxcars. Before his departure for spring training in 1941, Joe married Catherine "Kay" Carrigan, whom he had met while playing semipro ball in Springdale.

That summer Page pitched for the Class B Augusta (Georgia) Tigers in the South Atlantic League. Page appeared in forty games while splitting twenty-four decisions. His ability to pitch both as a starter and as a reliever—and a no-hitter he threw against Savannah—made the Yankees' brass take notice.

Page's career took a major step forward in 1942 when he moved up to the Newark Bears, the Yankees' top farm team. He went 7-6 with a 4.19 ERA in twenty appearances, including thirteen starts.

The Bears won the International League regular season by ten games but lost in the first round of the league's playoffs.

Newark finished second to the Toronto Maple Leafs in 1943, as Page made twenty-three starts and five relief appearances, logging 186 innings. He won fourteen and lost five, had three shutouts, and led the team with 140 strikeouts and 119 walks.

Page was not drafted for military service after being classified as 4-F. His leg injury had not mended particularly well. In fact, he sometimes picked tiny slivers of bone out of his leg that had worked their way up as high as his hip. Page also suffered from a stomach ulcer.

In 1944 Page was promoted to the Yankees, a team that was a far cry from the pennant-winning clubs of 1941, '42, and '43. Gone from the lineup were high-profile stars like Joe DiMaggio, Joe

Gordon, Charlie Keller, and Spud Chandler. Sadly, three members of his immediate family would not be around to enjoy his big-league career. During the 1943 season Page's mother died. Between the 1943 and 1944 seasons his oldest sister died after being hit by a car. In the summer of 1944 his father suffered a heart attack and died while in the hospital for a minor procedure. Everyone in Page's family now depended on him.

Page got into his first Major League game on April 19, 1944, pitching two perfect innings in a loss to the Boston Red Sox in the second game of the season. He made his first start and earned his first victory eleven days later, pitching into the seventh inning against the Washington Senators.

Manager Joe McCarthy added Page to the rotation, where he pitched well enough to be named to the American League All-Star squad. He had won five of his first six decisions, but his record later fell to 5–7, and his ERA ballooned by nearly two full runs. In Page's final two starts, he gave up eleven runs in 1⅔ innings and was banished to the bullpen. After getting shelled in a July relief outing against the Detroit Tigers, McCarthy sent him to Newark for the rest of the season.

In a sport full of tough guys and hard drinkers, Joe Page stood out among his peers when it came to after-hours activities. He may have been drinking milk to calm his ulcers between breakfast and lunch and between lunch and dinner. But between dinner and breakfast it was mostly the hard stuff. Page's carousing concerned McCarthy early in the 1944 season, but winning helped the team look the other way for a while. Once the Yankees began to fade from pennant contention, McCarthy had no hesitation in sending Page to Newark.

In terms of his toughness, Page was strong physically, but as a rookie he had a hard time tuning out the bench jockeys. Al Simmons, then coaching for Connie Mack's Philadelphia Athletics, especially seemed to have Page's number. This would soon change.

Page missed the first two months of the 1945 season with a sore arm. When he returned he pitched primarily out of the bullpen until September, when McCarthy put him back in the rotation. Page won five of his six September starts and finished the year 6-3 with a 2.82 ERA for the fourth-place Yankees, the best mark among hurlers with at least 100 innings. Yet wildness continued to be an issue: Page walked almost as many batters as he struck out.

Because of postwar housing shortages at their spring-training base in St. Petersburg, Florida, the Yankees had to get creative with their rooming situation in 1946. They often had to split their squads and keep one group on the road. One day Page found himself assigned to a team populated almost exclusively with Yankees farmhands. He packed his bags and stormed out of the team's hotel in nearby Bradenton. Page ran into traveling secretary Red Patterson in the lobby and informed him that he could make more money pitching semipro ball around Pittsburgh than toiling for Newark again. Patterson eventually convinced Joe that he would be with the Yankees when the season opened.

Page's touchiness may have had something to do with the attention he was drawing from McCarthy. Again and again during the spring of 1946, the manager tried to hammer home to him that he had to turn the corner on his career and start thinking of the team before he disappeared on one of his nocturnal jaunts.

When the season began Page was a member of the rotation. But McCarthy, suffering from a touchy gallbladder and exasperated by the team's play, took out his frustrations on Page, berating him in front of the team during a flight out of Detroit. McCarthy quit two days later, after only thirty-five games.

In mid-July Page's record stood at a lackluster 5-4. The team stashed him in the bullpen for most of the second half. In August the Yankees asked waivers on Page, presumably to farm him out. The Senators put in a claim, forcing New York to pull him back and keep him on the big-league roster. Page made a few spot starts, pitched fairly well, and finished 9-8 with a 3.57 ERA. The Yankees, a non–pennant winner for the third year in a row, went shopping for a new manager.

The man they chose was Bucky Harris. Dubbed the Boy Wonder in 1924, when he led the Senators to a World Series victory at the age of twenty-seven, he had later managed the Tigers, Red Sox, and Phillies. With baseball fully recovered from its wartime talent drain, Harris had a lot of quality pitchers in camp when it came time to set his starting staff. He had heard the stories of Page's drinking and was skeptical about the high-living left-hander being a consistent contributor.

The 1947 season started slowly for the Yankees. On May 26, having taken the first three games of the series, they faced the Red Sox at Yankee Stadium in front of a packed house. Rookie Frank Shea was getting cuffed around, and Harris sent for Page with no one out in the third inning and two men on. Page had been in six games to that point, and the Yankees had been losers in each.

The first batter Page faced was Ted Williams, who reached on an error to load the bases. Page then threw three straight balls to Rudy York. Harris later admitted that at this moment Page was literally one pitch away from the Minors. York was taking all the way on the next two deliveries, so Page fired a pair of fastballs across the plate. The payoff pitch was a perfect curve, which caught York by surprise. He waved helplessly at it for the first out. Page fanned the next batter, Bobby Doerr, and got Eddie Pellagrini on a fly ball to right field to end the inning. Page later learned that as he strutted off the field to the adoring roar of seventy-five thousand fans, the paperwork for his demotion was being prepared by the team's front-office staff. Harris called owner Larry MacPhail and told him to hang on to it.

The Yankees came back to tie the score and ultimately scored nine runs. Page went the rest of the way, allowing Boston two hits and three walks while striking out eight. It was a transformational moment both for Page and the Yankees and for Harris. He sent Page to the mound forty-nine more times in 1947, all but one of those appearances coming in relief.

The night of the Red Sox game, Page had been sitting about ten feet away from his teammates in the bullpen. When he returned to the pen the next day, he plunked himself down in the same spot. He would maintain that approximate distance for the rest of the season—and the balance of his career.

The Yankees moved into first place in June and opened up a double-digit lead over the Tigers and Red Sox a week after the All-Star break during a magnificent 19–0 run. Page, who appeared in only six games during the streak, figured directly in five of those victories, with two wins and three saves (though the save statistic was not being tabulated at that time). His looming presence in the bullpen no doubt played a part in other Yankee triumphs, as it forced enemy managers into early game-altering decisions. One sportswriter summed it up as follows: "If you're going to beat the Yankees you have to get your runs before the seventh inning . . . or you get Page."

Page's new role was recognized that July when he pitched the final inning and a third of the All-Star Game to earn a save in the 2–1 American League win. Soon everyone was calling New York's new relief ace Fireman Page.

The nickname fit because he was the man who rushed to the scene to extinguish fires. However, the story behind the Fireman Page moniker was a bit more complicated. During World War II thousands of New York apartments were occupied by workers lured to the city by war-industry jobs. When the veterans returned from overseas in 1945 and 1946, the few remaining apartments disappeared quickly. Page and Kay rented a room from a retired firefighter named Dan Malkin, who lived with his wife in a Bronx building. Malkin gave Page a red FDNY shirt that he often wore to the ballpark.

Page's newfound success did little to dampen his postgame club hopping. He became fast friends with the team's more famous Joe—DiMaggio—who was also a night owl. The two spent so much time together that the other players starting teasing Page. DiMaggio's nickname for his happy-go-lucky, blue-eyed friend was the Gay Reliever (when the word *gay* meant "carefree"). The Yankee Clipper drew the line, however, when it came to heavy drinking. He often chided Page about how his carousing might hurt the team one day.

That day certainly did not come in 1947. Page finished the year with a 14-8 record, a 2.48 ERA, and 116 strikeouts in 141⅓ innings. He retroactively qualified for a league-best seventeen saves. Page finished fourth in the MVP voting, won by DiMaggio. He received seven first-place votes—one less than DiMaggio and four more than runner-up Ted Williams.

Page's relief appearances ranged in length from ⅓ of an inning to 7⅔, but down the stretch Harris typically limited him to just an inning or two. The Yankees finished the year 97-57, twelve games ahead of Detroit.

The Page story got even better in a wild World Series against the Brooklyn Dodgers. Page saw action in four games. He saved the opener for Shea, pitching the final four innings of a 5–3 victory. In Game Three Page entered in the sixth inning with the Dodgers up, 9–7. He threw three scoreless innings, but the Yankees lost, 9–8.

Page's next appearance was in Game Six. He allowed four runs in one inning of relief and was the losing pitcher in Brooklyn's 8–6 victory.

Harris started Shea on one day's rest in Game Seven, and the Dodgers quickly tagged him for two runs. Bill Bevens relieved Shea in the second but was pulled for a pinch hitter during a fourth-inning rally that saw New York take a 3–2 lead.

Harris now had to make his biggest decision of the season. He stood by as coach Frank Crosetti phoned bullpen coach Johnny Schulte. MacPhail was in the dugout, too. "Schulte says the Indian is knocking the glove off his hand," reported Crosetti, referring to Allie Reynolds. "Page hasn't got a thing."

Despite Schulte's advice, Harris decided to go with his ace reliever one more time. Page retired the Dodgers in order in the fifth, sixth, seventh, and eighth. With the score 5–2, Miksis singled for Brooklyn with one out in the ninth, but Page got Edwards to ground the ball to Phil Rizzuto, who started a Series-ending double play. Page was credited with the victory. A few months later *Sportfolio*, an influential magazine of the era covering all sports, named Page its Professional Athlete of the Year for 1947.

Page and the Yankees could not repeat the magic of '47 the following season. The team finished third in an exciting three-team tussle with Cleveland and Boston. Page led the league in appearances and games finished and had sixteen saves, but his ERA climbed to 4.26 and his record was a mediocre 7-8. He had been sharp during the season's first three months, but lost some of his stuff after the All-Star break. His ERA was over 8.00 during July and August, during which the Yankees fell from second place to fourth.

Page regained his bearings in 1949 under new manager Casey Stengel. Stengel was a master when it came to getting the matchups he wanted, and late in games the matchup he wanted most was Joe Page versus anyone carrying a bat. Stengel ran Page out to the mound a league-high sixty times, and he responded with thirteen wins, a 2.59 ERA, and ninety-nine strikeouts in 135⅓ innings. His twenty-seven saves were seventeen more than runner-up Al Benton and at least eight more than any other American League *team*. At season's end, Page finished third in the MVP tally behind Williams and teammate Rizzuto.

The Yankees and Red Sox went down to the wire, with Boston owning a one-game lead with two to play—both against the Yankees in Yankee Stadium. In the first game the Red Sox opened an early 2–0 lead. Stengel pulled an ineffective Allie Reynolds in the third inning and sent in Page. Joe walked the first two batters, forcing in two runs to make the score 4–0. Stengel strolled out to the mound to see if there was a problem. "I'll get us out of this," Joe assured his manager.

True to his word, he went the rest of the way, hurling 6⅔ innings of one-hit ball. The Yankees tied the score in the fifth and won the game, 5–4, on a Johnny Lindell homer in the eighth inning. Page's thirteenth win of the year is still considered one of the great clutch pitching performances in history. That Joe McCarthy was Boston's skipper made this moment extra sweet for Page. The following day Vic Raschi outpitched Ellis Kinder to win 5–3 and nail down the pennant.

The Dodgers and Yankees tangled again in the World Series. After the teams split a pair of 1–0 pitching duels, the Yankees swept the remaining three games. Page got the win in pivotal Game Three with one of his patented multi-inning relief jobs after relieving Tommy Byrne in the fourth inning with one out and the bases loaded. He got Luis Olmo to pop out and retired Duke Snider on a grounder to second. The Yankees broke a 1–1 tie with three runs in the top of the ninth to make the score 4–1. Page allowed a pair of Brooklyn home runs in the home ninth, but Stengel stuck with him and he got Bruce Edwards looking to end the game.

Page made one more appearance, in Game Five in relief of Vic Raschi. He took the mound in the seventh inning and preserved a 10–6 New York lead. Page allowed two base runners in the ninth inning, but struck out Snider, Jackie Robinson, and Gil Hodges to preserve the victory. He received the inaugural Babe Ruth Award as the World Series MVP.

That winter, the Yankees raised Page's salary to thirty-five thousand dollars. It was the biggest contract ever given to a relief pitcher. Joe Page was not the game's first ace reliever, but with that salary he certainly helped glamorize the role of the closer.

Page's career took a turn for the worse in 1950. He relieved twice in a May doubleheader against the Athletics and felt something pop in his hip. He lost the "rise" on his fastball and the sharp break on his curve, and he could only get by on his swagger for so long. By mid-September his ERA was over 5.00, and he was not on the roster when the Yankees defended their world championship against the Phillies that October.

Page injured his arm during spring training in 1951 and split the year between the team's farm clubs in Kansas City and San Francisco. His now-aching left arm could manage only thirty-six innings. The thirty-four-year-old Page caught on with the International League Syracuse (New York) Chiefs in 1952 but quit after three appearances. He went home to Pennsylvania and reinvented himself as a sinker-ball pitcher. He still threw a spitball—something he did not admit until 1955, when his playing days were done—but he no longer had that overpowering fastball.

Page was back in the big leagues in 1954 with the Pirates, where he was used in a mop-up role during the early days of the season. He was effective in his first five appearances, but then allowed seven runs (two earned) to the Cardinals in a third of an inning on May 20. After he was touched for seven runs by the Giants in an inning of work, the Pirates released him.

Page operated two bars in his retirement years, the Bullpen in Irwin, Pennsylvania, and Page's Rocky Lodge near Laughlintown. Divorced from Kay in 1955, he later married Mildred Brown. The pair had three sons, Charles, Joseph Jr., and Jon. Page was a regular at the Yankees' Old-Timers Day in the 1960s. In 1970, while in New York for the event, he suffered a heart attack. His life was saved by open-heart surgery at Lenox Hill Hospital, but a few years later he developed throat cancer.

Page was a victim of identity theft in the early 1970s, when sportswriter Dick Schaap interviewed a man in a bar who claimed to be Joe Page. Schaap ran a story in the magazine *Sport*, which painted Page as a degenerate drunk. Joe sued the publication for $1.5 million and later settled for $25,000.

In the spring of 1980, Page, sixty-two, entered a Latrobe, Pennsylvania, hospital after suffering a heart attack. Three weeks later, on April 21, while still in the hospital, he died of heart failure. Joe Page was survived by Mildred and their three sons; he is buried at Greenwood Memorial Park in Lower Burrell, Pennsylvania.

Chapter 64. **Mel Allen**

Warren Corbett

Mel Allen was the Voice:

his boom box of a voice
   — *Curt Smith*

that wonderful, unmistakable voice
   — *Dick Young*

the venerable Voice of Summer
   — *Sports Illustrated*

He was the voice of the Yankees from 1939 through 1964 and became the most prominent sports broadcaster in America. His credits include twenty World Series, twenty-four All-Star Games, fourteen Rose Bowls, five Orange Bowls, and two Sugar Bowls. During his prime years it seemed that Allen was on the air for every major sports event; the presence of the Voice signified that the game was a major event.

He was born Melvin Israel in Birmingham, Alabama, on St. Valentine's Day, 1913, the first of three children of Russian immigrants Julius and Anna (Leibowitz) Israel. (The family was living in Johns, Alabama, but the nearest hospital was in Birmingham.) Julius sold dry goods in several small southern towns before settling his family in Tuscaloosa, Alabama.

Allen told broadcast historian Curt Smith he got his first exposure to baseball while sitting in an outhouse looking at pictures of bats and gloves in catalogs from Sears or Montgomery Ward. He saw his first Major League games when he visited an aunt in Detroit; Babe Ruth hit a home run in one of them.

Melvin advanced quickly through small-town

Yankees announcer Mel Allen's style was exuberant; his rich voice conveyed excitement.

schools and entered the University of Alabama at the age of fifteen. He tried out for football but did not make the team; instead, he became an equipment manager.

He also served as public-address announcer for the Crimson Tide's home games. When a Birmingham radio station asked Coach Frank Thomas to recommend a play-by-play announcer, Thomas — apparently figuring play-by-play was just like PA announcing — named Melvin Israel. His radio career began on station WBRC in 1935.

In addition to doing play-by-play for the Tide, Israel received both an undergraduate degree and a law degree from Alabama and passed the bar exam.

On vacation in New York in 1937, he auditioned for the CBS radio network. In later years he made it seem like a lark, as if he had just wandered in off the street. In fact, his Alabama football broadcasts had been noticed by Ted Husing, CBS's top sports announcer, and by the entertainment newspaper *Variety*. Whether it was lark or design, he was offered a job at forty-five dollars a week.

Mel's father was not pleased, thinking his son was wasting a good education. He was even less pleased when Melvin explained that CBS wanted to change his "Jewish" surname. Trying to placate his father, Mel took Julius's middle name as his new last name. At CBS Allen announced variety shows starring Perry Como, Jo Stafford, and Harry James. He interrupted Kate Smith's afternoon program with a news bulletin reporting the crash of the airship Hindenburg. He worked some college football games.

Allen particularly impressed his bosses with a long ad-lib description of the Vanderbilt Cup yacht race, broadcasting from an airplane overhead. That led to his first baseball assignment, as a color commentator on the 1938 World Series. (In those days there was no exclusive Series broadcast; all the major networks carried the games.)

When Allen arrived in New York, the Yankees, Giants, and Dodgers were the last holdouts against radio. Since all the other teams were broadcasting some of their games, the fear that radio would hurt attendance had been buried. But at least one of the New York clubs was always at home, so the teams agreed to a blackout to avoid competing with each other. Opening-day games were broadcast, along with an occasional important series. Local stations re-created highlights of some afternoon games in the evenings, and the Yankees permitted a New York station to carry the night games of their farm team in nearby Newark, New Jersey.

In 1938 the pioneering executive Larry MacPhail became general manager at Brooklyn. He notified the other teams that the Dodgers were going on the air in 1939, and he brought Red Barber from Cincinnati to handle the broadcasts. The Yankees and Giants decided to broadcast their home games, since they never played at home on the same day. Arch McDonald, an established play-by-play man in Washington, was hired as the principal announcer for both teams.

Wheaties, baseball's primary sponsor, chose Allen to replace McDonald on the Washington Senators' broadcasts. But Washington owner Clark Griffith signed his former pitcher, the Hall of Famer Walter Johnson, to go behind the mike, so Allen never became the voice of the Senators.

McDonald's assistant, Garnett Marks, did not last long. He was not fired when he delivered a commercial for Ivory Soap, and the words came out "Ovary Soap." But when he did it again, he was gone. Allen replaced him in June.

Arch McDonald did not last long, either. His down-home style—low-key, with long pauses between pitches—did not play in New York. After one season he returned to Washington.

In 1940 Allen began his reign as Voice of the Yankees. He continued doing only home games of the Yanks and Giants. Allen often told of an encounter with Lou Gehrig during that season, when Gehrig was dying of the disease that now bears his name. On a rare visit to the Stadium, the Yankee legend said, "Mel, I never got a chance to listen to your games before because I was playing every day. But I want you to know they're the only thing that keeps me going." Allen said he left the dugout in tears.

The Yankees and Giants could not find a sponsor for their broadcasts in 1941, so the teams were off the air. Accordingly, Allen never got a chance to chronicle Joe DiMaggio's fifty-six-game hitting streak, although he later recorded a re-creation of the end of the streak.

Allen entered the army in 1943 and was stationed at Fort Benning, Georgia. According to the Library of American Broadcasting at the University of Maryland, Sergeant Allen kept his hand in by calling a few Alabama football games while in the service.

When Allen was discharged early in 1946, both the Giants and the Yankees wanted him, but the Yankees had an edge. MacPhail had taken over the Yankees by then, with co-owners Dan Topping and Del Webb. He announced another innovation: Yankee broadcasters would travel with the team. Until then road games were re-created in a studio from a telegraphed play-by-play summary. Allen went with the Yankees. (Barber said MacPhail had offered him the Yankees' job, but he chose to stay in Brooklyn, where he was a civic institution.)

It was a marriage of the Voice and the Dynasty. Beginning in 1947 the Yanks played in fifteen of the next eighteen World Series. Broadcasters from the two league champions customarily handled network coverage of the Series, so Allen claimed the Fall Classic as his own stage.

His signature phrases entered the American language: A home run was "going, going, gone!" He punctuated any remarkable play with "How about that?" Although he is often credited with coining Joe DiMaggio's nickname, the Yankee Clipper, David Halberstam says Arch McDonald deserves credit for that. Allen was the first to call DiMag Joltin' Joe. He labeled Tommy Henrich Ol' Reliable.

Allen's style was exuberant; his rich voice conveyed excitement. He was constantly compared with Red Barber — inevitably, they became the first broadcasters honored by the Baseball Hall of Fame in 1978. Curt Smith described them this way: "The Ol' Redhead was white wine, crêpes suzette and bluegrass music; Mel, beer, hot dogs, and the U.S. Marine Band." Jim Woods, who worked with both men, said, "One was a machine gun, the other a violin." Nobody who heard them would have any difficulty discerning which was which.

In radio days a team's principal broadcaster — usually hired by the sponsors — ruled the booth. He assigned innings to his assistants, decided who would read the commercials, and parceled out pregame and postgame duties. Several of Allen's assistants agreed with Curt Gowdy's assessment: "It wasn't very easy to work for him, but when it was all over, you were glad you did." Gowdy and Jim Woods said they learned from his polish and professionalism but chafed under his high-handedness. As Woods put it, "Whatever Allen wanted, Allen got."

Red Barber joined the Yankees' broadcast team in 1954, after leaving Brooklyn over a dispute with owner Walter O'Malley. It was quite a comedown for a man who had commanded his own booth as principal broadcaster for twenty seasons. At first Barber worked only televised home games, handling pregame and postgame shows and two and one-half innings of play-by-play on TV.

Barber insisted in his autobiography that there was no friction between this pair of giant egos — "Mel accepted me as an equal" — but others said their relationship was cool. They were opposites: Barber was married, a homebody who disliked traveling, and a devout Christian; Allen, single, gregarious, a man about town, and a Jew. Barber's career was going downhill; Allen was king of the hill. According to Jim Woods, who was dumped from the Yankees" broadcasts in 1957 to make room for former shortstop Phil Rizzuto, Allen and Barber were united in their mutual loathing of the jock in the booth. Allen and Barber resolved their differences enough that Allen, nearly eighty years old, traveled from New York to Florida in 1992 to attend Barber's funeral.

Allen's fame grew as television replaced radio as the primary mass entertainment. He switched to TV coverage of the World Series in 1951, the first time the Series was televised coast-to-coast.

Like most radio broadcasters who attempted that transition, Allen never fully mastered the new medium. Echoing a common complaint, Ben Gross of the *New York Daily News* wrote in 1954 that Mel "has frequently been castigated for talking too much during his baseball telecasts. Like so many others, he often seems unwilling to permit the camera to tell the story and, at times, attempts to gild the picture on the tube with excessive verbiage."

Some accounts say Allen was the first to suggest the center-field camera shot that is now standard on baseball telecasts. Yankees general manager George Weiss limited the use of the shot for fear that opposing teams, watching TV, would steal the catcher's signs.

Since Allen was the Voice of the Yankees, he was accused of partisanship on the Series broadcasts. Allen acknowledged he was partisan, but also declared, "I never rooted."

He was renowned, too, as a skillful pitchman for the sponsors. A home run was "a Ballantine blast," after the beer sponsor, or "a White Owl wallop," after the cigar sponsor. In addition to his work on network college-football broadcasts, Allen was the sports voice of Movietone newsreels and hosted boxing matches.

Allen moved his parents, brother, and sister to the New York area and continued living with his sister after their parents died. His brother, Larry, who also adopted the name Allen, became his statistician and assistant.

Allen was six foot one, slim, and dark haired in his youth, but began balding at an early age. By the 1950s he usually wore a hat during his TV broadcasts. He never married, but was often seen in the company of beautiful Broadway showgirls. Red Barber wrote in *The Broadcasters*, "His job was his life . . . the wife and children he never had."

"I never saw anyone love his work more than he did," said Lindsey Nelson, a prominent football broadcaster of the 1950s and later the voice of the New York Mets.

In the fourth game of the 1963 World Series, the Dodgers were on their way to an unprecedented sweep of the Yankees. In midgame Allen was suddenly unable to speak. He blamed a flare-up of a "nasal condition," but many commentators said he was struck speechless by the Yanks' humiliation. Sportswriter Dick Young called it "psychosomatic laryngitis."

As the 1964 season ended, Allen's world came crashing down. The Yankees' president, Dan Topping, summarily fired him. Rizzuto represented the team on World Series telecasts. Joe Garagiola replaced Allen on the 1965 broadcasts.

The Yankees never explained his dismissal, so the rumor mill percolated. "They said I was a lush or that I beat my relatives or that I'd had a breakdown or that I was taking so many medicines for my voice that I turned numb," he told Curt Smith years later. None of the rumors appeared in print, so Allen never publicly denied them. He said Topping gave him no explanation, saying only, "It wasn't anything you did, Mel, and it wasn't CBS." CBS had just bought the team; as soon as Allen was gone, the network brought in one of its executives to supervise the Yankees' broadcasts. There would be no more principal broadcaster. Allen believed the Yankees' primary sponsor, Ballantine Beer, wanted to shed his high salary.

Topping told Red Barber, "I'm tired of him popping off." But Allen said, "If they had objected to my talking a lot, I'd have been fired long ago." Larger issues were at play; Ballantine Beer was losing market share, and the Yankees, despite winning the 1964 pennant, had drawn fewer fans than the last-place Mets. CBS wanted to promote a new, friendlier image for the regal Bronx Bombers.

The true story of Allen's sudden fall from the pinnacle remains a mystery. "He gave the Yankees his life," Barber said, "and they broke his heart." Adding insult to injury, NBC dropped him from its college-football telecasts.

Only fifty-one years old, he was not out of work

for long. The Braves played their final season in Milwaukee in 1965, held hostage by a court order, although they had already announced that they intended to move to Atlanta. An Atlanta TV station hired Mel to broadcast some of the team's games to their soon-to-be home.

Allen and Atlanta seemed a natural match: the biggest of big-league voices for the new big-league city and a southerner to boot. But he did not join the Braves in Atlanta. In 1968 he went to Cleveland to televise Indians' games. During one dull evening in a losing season, he stunned his broadcast partner—and, no doubt, the audience—by reciting Longfellow's "Song of Hiawatha." He turned down an offer to broadcast the Athletics' games when they moved to Oakland. Allen said his business interests, including a Canada Dry soft-drink dealership, kept him on the East Coast, but his sister, Esther Kaufman, told biographer Stephen Borelli he would not leave New York because that would be admitting defeat.

Allen made public appearances for Canada Dry, broadcast University of Miami football, and hosted local and network radio sports shows. One of his few baseball assignments was the 1966 Little League World Series for a Sacramento radio station. While other broadcasters routinely jumped from team to team, Allen vanished from big-time sports for eight years. "It was as if he had leprosy," *Sports Illustrated*'s William Taafe wrote in a 1985 profile.

Allen returned to Yankee Stadium on June 8, 1969, to serve as master of ceremonies on Mickey Mantle Day. In 1976 WPIX, the Yankees' flagship TV station, hired him to narrate a special program celebrating the opening of the refurbished Yankee Stadium.

By then CBS and Dan Topping were long gone; George Steinbrenner owned the franchise. When Steinbrenner was a young assistant football coach, he had sought Allen's advice about getting into broadcasting, and Allen spent forty-five minutes

with him. Steinbrenner never forgot that kindness. On opening day in the new-old stadium, the Yankees recognized Allen's place in their history. He stood on the field during pregame ceremonies alongside other symbols of the Yankee legacy: Bob Shawkey, who had thrown the first pitch in the stadium in 1923; Pete Sheehy, the clubhouse manager since 1927; restaurant owner Toots Shor; and former postmaster general James Farley, who was said to be "the longest-running season-ticket holder."

The next year Allen was back on Yankee broadcasts, calling a few dozen games for the SportsChannel cable network. He continued in that role until 1985. Beginning in 1977 Allen said, "How about that?" to a new generation of fans across the country as narrator of Major League Baseball's weekly highlight show, *This Week in Baseball* (known as TWIB). Joe Reichler, a former sportswriter working in the commissioner's office, gave him the job. He was the program's signature voice even after his death: TWIB created an animated figure, complete with microphone and fedora, to introduce each week's show with his trademark greeting, "Hello, everybody. This is Mel Allen."

In 1978 the Baseball Hall of Fame established the Ford C. Frick Award to honor broadcasters for "major contributions to baseball." Allen and Barber were the first to be recognized. (Broadcasters are not considered members of the Hall of Fame; there is no "broadcasters' wing," either. The winners are honored in an exhibit near the hall's library.)

Marty Appel, a former Yankees publicist who was producing the team's broadcasts on WPIX, brought Allen back one last time in 1990 so he could be the answer to a trivia question: the first man to broadcast a Major League game in seven decades. His Yankee career stretched from Lou Gehrig to Don Mattingly.

Allen died on June 16, 1996, at his home in Greenwich, Connecticut. He had suffered from heart trouble for years. He was buried in Temple Beth El Cemetery in Stamford, Connecticut. His grave stone reads, "Mel Allen Beloved son brother—uncle." More than a thousand people attended a memorial service in New York's St. Patrick's Cathedral sponsored by the Committee for Christian-Jewish Understanding. On July 25, 1998, a plaque commemorating his career was unveiled in Monument Park at Yankee Stadium.

Only two sports broadcasters have equaled Mel Allen's fame: the pioneer radio announcer Graham McNamee and Howard Cosell, the man so many fans loved to hate. Like Allen, both dominated the big events of their time. In Allen's time more than half of the television sets in the United States would be tuned in to the World Series. There were just three national TV networks—ABC, CBS, and NBC—and no regional sports networks.

With fewer games on television and fewer sports competing for attention, the leading broadcasters—Allen on baseball, Lindsey Nelson on college football—were the voices and faces of American sports. As Allen acknowledged, his renown was partly an accident of time and place: in New York, when the Yankees were giants. His success was also a product of his unique, vibrant voice and the craftsmanship and showmanship that he achieved by hard work.

Later generations of broadcasters—Gowdy, Brent Musberger, and Joe Buck—enjoyed similar wide exposure on showcase events. None was ever called *the Voice*.

Chapter 65. **Russ Hodges**

Curt Smith

People of a certain age know where they were when the Japanese attacked Pearl Harbor, Franklin Roosevelt died, and Bobby Thomson swung. "The most famous sports moment of all time," Jon Miller termed Thomson's October 3, 1951, pennant-winning blast. We still recall the Shot Heard 'Round the World.

One reason is announcer Russ Hodges's legendary call on the radio broadcast of the game. Another: the New York Giants–Brooklyn Dodgers nonpareil rivalry. The two teams faced each other twenty-two times yearly, with radio and television broadcasts of the games coursing through New York City. On August 11, 1951, the Giants trailed the first-place Dodgers by thirteen games. On Friday, September 28, they were tied for first. The next day each won.

After Sunday's regular-season finale, a 3–2 victory in Boston, the Giants rode back to New York by train. As Hodges wrote in his 1963 memoir, *My Giants*, he used the train telephone to call the Giants' office and monitored Brooklyn's fourteen-inning 9–8 victory in Philadelphia. In the noisy train, Russ, developing a cold, was forced to shout to relay play-by-play to players. A day later the best-of-three National League playoff series began: "A world focused on our rivalry," said the Giants' Voice.

New York won the opener at Ebbets Field, 3–1. On Tuesday they changed place (the Polo Grounds) and outcome (Dodgers, 10–0). That night Hodges stayed awake gargling. Worse, "To test my voice, I kept talking into an imaginary microphone at home," which hurt his throat. "I had trouble breathing, my nose was running, and I was sure I had a fever."

Mel Allen called Russ Hodges his "all-time favorite partner."

CBS-TV was televising the playoff series. It was the first coast-to-coast network sports telecast. Hodges and Ernie Harwell were alternating game to game as play-by-play men on TV and the Giants' flagship radio station, WMCA. Harwell had Game Three on TV, "feeling a little sorry for [Hodges]," he said later. "Ole' Russ [was] going to be stuck on the radio, there were five radio broadcasts [Mutual, Liberty, Giants, Dodgers, and re-created Brooklyn Dodgers Network] and I was gonna' be on . . . TV, and I thought that I had the plum assignment."

At 3:58 p.m., the Giants behind, 4–2, Thomson hit a ninth-inning two-on, one-out home run off Ralph Branca. "Branca throws. There's a long drive!" Hodges cried on WMCA. "It's going to be, I believe . . . The Giants win the pennant! The Giants win the pennant! The Giants win the pennant! The Giants win the pennant! Bobby Thomson hits into the lower deck of the left-field stands. . . . The Giants win the pennant and they're going crazy! They are going crazy! Oh, oh!" Confetti flew. Brooklyn staggered to its clubhouse. "I don't believe it! I don't believe it! I do not believe it!" Russ continued. "Bobby Thomson hit a line drive into the lower deck of the left-field stands, and the whole place is going crazy! The Giants . . . won it by a score of 5 to 4, and they're picking Bobby Thomson up and carrying him off the field!"

Before videotape, to record a television program, a camera had to photograph a TV screen or monitor, a process called kinescope. "Kinescopes were bulky," said Harwell. "So CBS didn't save my call." Few even had a radio reel-to-reel recorder. In Brooklyn Lawrence Goldberg, who did, had to leave for work, asking his mother, Sylvia, to hit *record* in the bottom of the ninth. Urban legend dubbed him a Dodgers fan, wanting to preserve their victory. In fact, Goldberg liked the Giants, and Russ used his borrowed copy to record a Christmas gift for friends.

That fall, Giants' sponsor Chesterfield cigarettes released a record of "the most exciting moment in baseball history," some later calling it revisionist, not real. One writer claimed Hodges stood on his chair for two minutes screaming, "The Giants win the pennant!" Dodgers broadcaster Red Barber dubbed him "unprofessional," to which Russ's partner, Lon Simmons (1958–70), said, "He was dramatic, but gave the essentials: score, meaning, who won." Russ lived off the Shot until his death, the call gracing TV's *M*A*S*H* and film's *The Godfather*.

In 1980 Hodges received posthumously the Ford C. Frick Award for broadcast excellence from the National Baseball Hall of Fame, five years after being inducted into the National Association of Sportscasters and Sportswriters Hall of Fame. "I know darned well I don't have a good radio voice," he had said. On the other hand, "I know sports well." A voting member ascribed Russ's choice to "the committee's New York tilt." Also helping: likability, the Miracle of Coogan's Bluff, and a full life before and after Thomson swung. TV rules today's culture. Radio ruled 1951's. "What did I get from being on TV?" Harwell laughed. *Anonymity.* "What did Russ get from radio? *Immortality*!"

Russell Pleasant Hodges was the second son born to Rufus and Maud (Dodd) Hodges on June 18, 1910, in Dayton, Tennessee. His dad was a Southern Railroad telegrapher, who moved his family almost every year. In 1929 Russ, a University of Kentucky sophomore, broke an ankle playing football. He became a spotter and said a "few words on air. I got the bug bad." After law school at the University of Cincinnati, Russ passed the bar but never practiced. "In those days, lawyers were jumping out of windows."

In 1932 Hodges got a job as a Covington, Kentucky, hillbilly disc jockey. Soon he asked for a five-dollar raise. "Hodges," station manager L. B. Wilson said, "I can go down any alley, fire a shotgun, and hit thirty guys who are better than you." Russ then aired the Reds, the Cubs and White Sox, boxing, and Big Ten football, then Class-B Charlotte, using Morse code received in studio— "B1O" ball one outside; "S2C" strike two called—to re-create what he never saw.

In 1942 Hodges joined Washington's Arch McDonald in broadcasting the Senators: "No flag, but finally I did games in person." By 1946 the Yankees' Mel Allen needed a number-two man. "I knew of Russ's law degree," Allen, a lawyer, said, "and Arch said he'd be great. Soon Russ and I almost read each other's mind." In 1946 the

Yankees began broadcasting *live* each of their 154 games, and soon began home coverage on the DuMont Television Network—both a big-league first. "We had one staff, not today's three," said Allen. "Russ and I'd go down a ladder, do several TV innings, then breathe."

The partners tended to finish each other's thoughts. Their ad agency took advantage. "At inning's end I'd ask something," said Allen. "When next inning started, Russ'd answer. Love those spontaneous ad-libs." Mel changed one question, Hodges giving a scripted answer, "which made no sense, which was the idea," Allen said. The agency did not know what to do with us." Wisely, it did nothing.

The two men also roomed together, Hodges finding Mel a mix of Oscar Madison and Felix Unger. Allen ate at odd hours, put pajamas on at ten o'clock, and could be, Russ said, "a bundle of nerves." Hodges was less intense, venerating, if not grasping, Mel. George Stirnweiss once popped up a 3-1 ninth-inning pitch, stranding the tying run. At four thirty in the morning, Russ awoke to groans in the next bed. "Mel, should I get a doctor? What's the matter?" he said. "I just can't forget about that 3-1 pitch to Stirnweiss," Allen said. "Don't you think he made a mistake swinging?"

In late 1948 Russ—Allen's "all-time favorite partner"—left the Yankees for the Giants. Hodges soon contacted Bell's palsy, paralyzing a side of his face. Recovering, he did NBC college football, the Kentucky Derby, CBS's *Pabst Blue Ribbon Bouts*, and other fights, saying, "I'm rather dull, not imaginative. I don't believe in keeping the listeners on the edge of their seats." "While Barber gave his listeners corn-fed philosophy and humor," Wells Twombly wrote, "and Allen told you more about baseball than you cared to know, Hodges of the Giants told it the way it was."

Russ swelled New York's southern colony of Barber, from Mississippi, Allen, from near Birmingham, and Georgia's Harwell, the latter leav-ing the Dodgers in 1950 to join the Giants. Hodges was gradually escaping Allen's shadow, the *Sporting News* naming him 1950 Announcer of the Year. He had much more to announce in 1951.

For the 1951 World Series NBC-TV "put together a network [sixty-four stations, including one in Mexico]," said Russ. The Giants won two of the first three games. "We had 'em till Game Four was called," resting the Yankees' tired staff, which then won the Series. In 1954 the pennant-winning Giants drew 1,155,067 at home, but more people were watching the games on television. "The Polo Grounds was fraying. People around it were getting mugged," said Hodges. Still, the Giants swept the World Series over the heavily favored Cleveland Indians. Hodges witnessed another Miracle of Coogan's Bluff: Willie Mays's iconic catch of Vic Wertz's blast to deep center field.

In 1956 Russ hired Jim Woods, recently fired by the Yankees. "At a time like that, you need someone to reach down and save you," Woods said. "Russ did. No one will ever know the money he gave to charities and guys down on their luck."

Few could imagine the Giants or Dodgers leaving New York, especially Hodges, happy in his adopted city. The Giants needed only a new park to stay. Brooklyn had drawn a million people each year since 1945. Yet on May 28, 1957, the league approved the move of both teams to California. In August Giants owner Horace Stoneham said, "We're sorry to disappoint the kids of New York, but we didn't see many of their parents out there at the Polo Grounds in recent years." Bayed the *New York World-Telegram*: "It's Official: Giants to Frisco." (The Dodgers moved to Los Angeles on October 8.) On September 29 11,606 mourners braved a dreary adieu. "Giants Bow to Bucs in Polo Grounds Finale," said the *Daily News*. For Hodges, moving day had truly come.

On April 15, 1958, baseball's transplanted tag team opened at the Giants' temporary twenty-two-thousand-seat home, Russ wrongly calling it "the

Polo Grounds, I mean Seals Stadium." Jim Woods had hoped to relocate with Hodges. Instead, the Giants chose Lon Simmons, a local who aired them through 1973, then returned in 1976–78 and 1996–2002.

In 1958 the Giants finished over .500 for the first of fourteen straight years. By the next year the Bay Area had bought more than six hundred thousand transistor radios. "A restaurant—they'd have baseball on," said KSFO's Stu Smith. "With most games in the afternoon, it flooded offices, bars, cable cars." Russ and Lon quickly bonded, like two veins from a common mine. Simmons called Hodges "'The Fabulous Fat Man,' more fabulous than fat." Hodges did NBC Radio's second All-Star Game in 1959, and the first of two in 1961, played at the Giants' new home, Candlestick Park.

The Giants played by day, and "then Russ'd recreate the Dodgers at night on KSFO," later Giants broadcaster Jon Miller said. On September 30, 1962, Mays's last-day home run edged Houston, 2–1: "Mays hits one a long way! Tell it bye-bye baby! Mays put one into orbit!" Hodges then did Dodgers-Cardinals play-by-play for the crowd. St. Louis won, 1–0: "[Jim Gilliam] pops up to [Julian] Javier! We have a playoff!" The football 49ers played at Kezar Stadium, "the crowd going nuts hearing baseball on transistors," said Miller. "The football guys wonder what's going on." Ahead: another best-of-three playoff series.

After the teams split the first two games, four ninth-inning runs in Game Three gave the Giants a 6–4 pennant-winning victory. The 1962 Giants-Yankees World Series featured Russ on NBC-TV—his final appearance on network television.

In New York Stoneham had televised his entire home schedule. Out west he banned home TV: to see the Giants, fans had to pay. "Everything was fine," said Russ, "then it wasn't." The 1968 A's moved to Oakland, dividing the area. A football makeover destroyed Candlestick's baseball feel. Attendance fell to 519,987. Finally, in 2000

the team opened the grand Pacific Bell Park, near China Basin. In 2010 the Giants won their first world title since 1954. Miller emceed a city-hall salute to "the whole panorama" of the post-1957 team history, crying, "Bye-bye baby!"

Hodges had retired after the 1970 season. "Next season Russ agreed to do Giants PR and baseball for me when I did the 49ers, but it wasn't the same," said Simmons. The chain-smoking Hodges died on April 19, 1971, at sixty, of a heart attack. He was survived by wife, Gay, whom he married in 1962; son, Pat; and daughter, Judy. Mays wept, "Russ was like my big brother. I turned to him for everything." Autograph seekers crashed the funeral, infuriating Jim Woods: "What a horrible thing for a man like Russ. He was the greatest human being I ever knew."

Hodges never equaled October 3, 1951, but no one else has, either. "Hartung down the line at third base, not taking any chances. Lockman with not too big of a lead at second, but he'll be running like the wind if Thomson hits one." Fate threw. Thomson hit one. The Giants won the pennant.

Chapter 66. **The 1947 World Series**

Tom Hawthorn

As the New York Yankees and Brooklyn Dodgers took to the grass of Yankee Stadium for the opening game of the 1947 World Series, a snowy image flickered on the small screens of that newfangled invention, the television. For the first time the World Series would be witnessed by spectators not actually in attendance, who did not purchase tickets, or peanuts, or Cracker Jack. An estimated audience of 3.9 million saw the spectacle, an astounding number but only a hint of the massive appeal of televised baseball.

They watched as, for the first time, an African American player took part in the Fall Classic. His presence, too, hinted at the changes to come, as professional baseball abandoned nineteenth-century racial attitudes on the way to becoming a global sport.

Other changes were afoot in the postwar world. On Long Island delegates to the fledgling United Nations received a pamphlet explaining the homegrown passion for the game. "Americans would rather use a bat for sport than a gun for keeps," it stated. "They would rather fly a pennant than an airplane."

The on-field matchups held great promise. Would the Yankees' pitchers and catcher Yogi Berra be able to prevent the larcenous intentions of Jackie Robinson, who led his league with twenty-nine stolen bases? Would Joe DiMaggio rediscover his power stroke after a campaign in which he hit a career-low (until then) twenty home runs?

Game One (September 30): Yankees 5, Dodgers 3

The opening game at Yankee Stadium attracted stars from both Hollywood and Washington. The

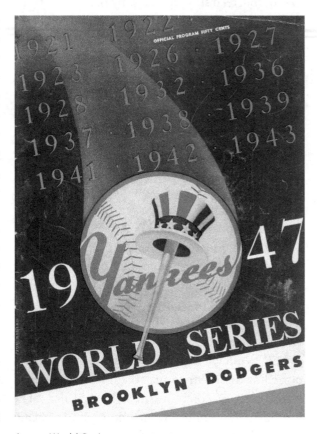

A 1947 World Series program.

Tinseltown contingent included the actress Laraine Day, known as "the first lady of baseball" for her marriage earlier in the year to Leo Durocher, the Dodgers' manager, who had been suspended that season for various indiscretions, named and unnamed. The newlyweds were accompanied by the comedian Danny Kaye. Durocher was photographed shaking hands with baseball commissioner Happy Chandler, who had issued the controversial banishment.

Less glamorous was a gathering of political dignitaries, including former president Herbert Hoover, Secretary of State George C. Marshall, and New York governor Thomas Dewey, who would be the unsuccessful Republican nominee for president the following year. He was joined in the box seats by the governors of four other states — New Jersey, Rhode Island, Connecticut, and Pennsylvania — as well as by more than fifty disabled war veterans.

The promising Series also lured four dozen retired diamond stars, including Babe Ruth, Ty Cobb, Tris Speaker, and Cy Young. Young, eighty, had pitched in the inaugural World Series forty-four years earlier.

Al Schacht, the player-comedian known as the "Clown Prince of Baseball," performed pantomimes and impersonations to the amusement of the crowd, which included among its number Joe DiMaggio's mother, who sat with her son Dominic, an outfielder with the rival Boston Red Sox.

Helen Jepson, a soprano with the Metropolitan Opera, sang "The Star-Spangled Banner" before New York mayor William O'Dwyer threw out the ceremonial first pitch from a box seat near the Dodgers' dugout. In the opinion of the *New York Times*, it was "a typical New York gathering."

Yankee manager Bucky Harris picked righthander Spec Shea to open the Series after the twenty-six-year-old rookie (he was two days shy of his twenty-seventh birthday) went 14-5 during the season. His start was not auspicious, as he walked Robinson, the game's second batter, who promptly stole second. Shea then snagged a comebacker to the mound, catching Robinson between second and third, though the daring runner managing to stay alive long enough for Pete Reiser to get as far as second. Reiser scored on Dixie Walker's single.

The Yankees were stymied by Brooklyn's Ralph Branca (21-12) for the first four innings, failing to produce a single base runner. Branca had five

A four-dollar standing-room ticket in the grandstand to Game One.

strikeouts, four ground outs, three fly outs. Twelve up, twelve down.

The Yankees' bats finally came alive in the home half of the fifth. Joe DiMaggio legged out an infield hit to shortstop. A base on balls and a hit batsman loaded the bases for Johnny Lindell, who drove in a pair with a double to left. Another walk loaded the bases again. Bobby Brown then stepped to the plate as a pinch hitter for Shea, who

The Yankees celebrate winning the 1947 World Series.

was being yanked after just five innings' work. The wily move seemed to unnerve Branca, whose first two pitches were nowhere near the strike zone. That led Dodger manager Burt Shotton to yank his starter in favor of Hank Behrman. Brown walked, forcing in a run. Two more scored on Tommy Henrich's single. The inning ended when DiMaggio, up for a second time in the stanza, flied out. The Dodgers nibbled away for a couple of runs off lefty reliever Joe Page, but the five runs in the fifth stood up for the Yankees.

Game Two (October 1): Yankees 10, Dodgers 3

The Yankees opened the scoring in the bottom of the first off Brooklyn lefty Vic Lombardi. Snuffy Stirnweiss singled and advanced to third on Henrich's single, then scored when Lindell grounded into a double play.

The Dodgers tied the score in the top half of the third, Robinson knocking in the run with a single. The Yankees replied in the bottom half with triples by Stirnweiss and Lindell to go ahead 2–1. The Dodgers tied the score again the next inning

on Dixie Walker's home run off right-hander Allie Reynolds. The Yankees again replied with extra-base hits, as Billy Johnson's triple (the Yankees' third in the game, tying a World Series record) was followed by Phil Rizzuto's double. Johnny Lindell's double following Henrich's solo shot to open the fifth finally chased Lombardi, who had been touched for seven extra-base hits.

The Yankees settled matters with a four-run seventh, an easy victory helped by shoddy Brooklyn fielding, as Pete Reiser misplayed balls in center and a trio of Dodgers watched another catchable ball fall for a double. The official scorer was kind in only pronouncing two errors on the day, because the sloppy visitors stunk up the joint. "It just wasn't the Dodgers' day," the *Sporting News* proclaimed.

Game Three (October 2): Dodgers 9, Yankees 8

The Series shifted to Ebbets Field, where the Dodgers chased Yankees starter Bobo Newsom in the second inning. The home side scored six runs on six hits, a walk, and a passed ball by Sherm Lollar. The score was 7–2 by the end of the third, 9–4 after four.

The Yankees kept nibbling at that comfortable lead. DiMaggio smacked a two-run homer off Brooklyn starter Joe Hatten in the fifth for his first RBIs in the Series. The Yanks added another in the sixth on doubles by Brown (pinch-hitting for pitcher Spud Chandler) and Henrich. Yogi Berra's smash over the scoreboard in right — the first pinch-hit homer in World Series history — narrowed the score to 9–8.

To open the eighth, Henrich walked and Lindell singled to center, but the threat was stymied when DiMaggio grounded into a double play. The next four Yankees batters went quietly.

Game Four (October 3): Dodgers 3, Yankees 2

The Yankees chased Harry Taylor before the Brooklyn starter recorded an out. DiMaggio walked after two singles and an error by Pee Wee Reese had loaded the bases. Reliever Hal Gregg induced a pop-out and a double play to snuff the threat of a big inning.

For the Yankees pitcher Floyd "Bill" Bevens gave up two walks in the bottom of the first, though he managed to get out of trouble without surrendering a hit. The six-foot-three, 210-pound right-hander from a small Oregon farming community issued another walk in the second, a walk and a wild pitch in the third, and another two walks in the fifth, with Spider Jorgensen scoring on a fielder's choice preceded by a sacrifice bunt. Bevens gave up more bases on balls in the sixth and seventh. But through eight innings, he had yet to be touched for a hit, thanks to some spectacular fielding.

Going into the ninth, the Yankees nursed a 2–1 lead. (Back in the fourth a Billy Johnson triple had been followed by a Lindell double.) The Yankees loaded the bases, with Henrich coming to the plate. Hugh Casey came on in relief to replace Hank Behrman. On the first pitch the outfielder

known as Old Reliable grounded a one-hopper back to Casey, who started an inning-ending pitcher-to-catcher-to-first double play.

The drama of that confrontation had barely abated when attention returned to Bevens's bid for the first no-hitter in World Series history. Bruce Edwards flied out to left. One down. Carl Furillo walked. Jorgensen fouled out on a pop to first. Two down. Reiser came on to hit for the pitcher, while Al Gionfriddo ran for Furillo. After Gionfriddo stole second, Reiser was walked intentionally. Eddie Miksis took his place as a runner.

Now, Harry Lavagetto stepped to the plate as a pinch hitter. Cookie, as he was known, swung and missed on Bevens's first pitch. But he sent the second offering clattering off the right-field fence for a double, as both runners raced home. In that instant, Bevens lost his no-hitter and the game, as Brooklyn won, 3–2, and tied the Series.

Delirious fans poured onto the field. Jubilant teammates pounded Lavagetto on the back, while supporters surrounded the celebrating players. One fan snatched Cookie's baseball cap. Police escorted him to the dugout. Later, in the outfield, Brooklynites gathered beneath the point on the wall where Lavagetto's drive had struck. In the bedlam Bevens walked in glum silence to the Yankees' clubhouse. On the radio Red Barber said, "Well, I'll be a suck-egg mule!"

Life called the ninth-inning confrontation the "most exciting two minutes in history of World Series." (It was an odd headline for a sport played without a clock.) "It was an inning that will never be forgotten," the *Sporting News* judged correctly.

Casey got the win, his second, though he had made but a single pitch. He became the first pitcher to be credited with victory in consecutive World Series games.

Game Five (October 4): Yankees 2, Dodgers 1

Spec Shea returned to the mound for the Yankees, retiring the first ten batters he faced. Meanwhile, his own single in the fourth drove in Aaron Robinson from second base for the game's first run. In the fifth, DiMaggio homered off Brooklyn starter Rex Barney, who was soon replaced. The two runs would be all the Yankees needed.

Shea frustrated the Dodgers, who could only scratch out a run in the sixth after Gionfriddo and Reese walked and Jackie Robinson singled. In the ninth, Bruce Edwards singled, to be replaced by pinch runner Vic Lombardi. With two outs Lavagetto came to the plate again as a pinch hitter with the game on the line. The Dodgers had managed just five hits in the previous 17⅔ innings, and here again was a chance for Lavagetto to snatch victory from defeat. This time, however, he struck out, as Shea gained his second Series victory. "A hero one day—a bum the next," Lavagetto said afterward in the clubhouse. "The toast of the world one afternoon—forgotten the next."

Game Six (October 5): Dodgers 8, Yankees 6

After two games of pitching dominance, the batters came to the fore on a return to Yankee Stadium. Neither starter—Vic Lombardi for the Dodgers, Allie Reynolds for the Yankees—lasted through the third inning.

The first three Dodger batters hit singles, and Brooklyn managed two runs—one scoring during a shortstop-to-first double play and the other on a passed ball by catcher Sherm Lollar.

The Dodgers jumped to a 4–0 lead before the Yankees got on the board, but a leadoff double by Lollar in the third followed by an error by Spider Jorgensen and five singles tied the game.

The home side went ahead by a run in the fourth when right fielder Yogi Berra's single scored Aaron Robinson.

The Dodgers responded with four runs of their own in the sixth with a pair of doubles and a trio of singles for an 8–5 lead. In the home half of the inning, Al Gionfriddo came in as a replacement in left field, the first time he had ever played the field

at Yankee Stadium. With two outs, Snuffy Stirnweiss on second and Berra on first, Joe DiMaggio stepped to the plate. He took a mighty swing at a Joe Hatten offering.

The left fielder raced back "like a miscreant into the deepening shadows," according to one account, before reaching over to snag the drive at the 415-foot marker. "I put my head down and ran," Gionfriddo recalled later. "I looked over my shoulder once and knew I was going in the right direction. When I got close to the fence, I looked over my left shoulder and then jumped practically at the same time and caught the ball over my shoulder. I turned in the air coming down and hit the fence with my butt. I caught it in the webbing."

DiMaggio, not known for showing emotion on the field of play, kicked at the base-path dirt in frustration. "Taking his position in center field with the start of the next inning," wrote John Drebinger of the *New York Times,* "he was still walking inconsolably in circles, doubtless wondering whether he could believe his senses." The catch preserved a three-run lead that lasted until the bottom of the ninth.

The Yanks loaded the bases on a walk and two singles. With one out and Casey on the mound, the Yankees scored a run on a fielder's choice. With the tying run on first and representing the Series-winning run, Stirnweiss grounded to the pitcher for an easy out at first. The Yanks had left thirteen men on base.

A messy Sunday game featuring fourteen runs, twenty-seven hits, and three errors led to a final showdown the following day.

Game Seven (October 6): Yankees 5, Dodgers 2

The Dodgers sent Hal Gregg to the mound at Yankee Stadium for the deciding game. Three days earlier, the right-hander had kept the Dodgers close in a long relief stint opposite Bevens's no-hit bid. The Yankees' Bucky Harris countered with Spec Shea, who had won Games One and Five.

Eddie Stanky singled and Reese walked in the Dodgers' first, but both men were thrown out on steal attempts by Yankee catcher Aaron Robinson.

The Dodgers got on the scoreboard in the second, when Gene Hermanski's triple to right was followed by a single by Bruce Edwards. When the next batter, Carl Furillo, also singled, Shea was replaced by Bevens, the almost hero of Game Four. The first batter he faced, Spider Jorgensen, rapped a double, scoring Edwards. More damage was limited when shortstop Phil Rizzuto fielded a grounder by Gregg and gunned down Furillo at the plate.

The Yankees got a run back in the bottom of the inning when a pair of walks were followed by a Rizzuto single, bringing home George McQuinn.

The home side chased Gregg in the fourth, scoring two runs on two walks, two singles, and a double.

In the sixth Rizzuto got on base with a bunt single, stole second, and scored on pinch hitter Allie Clark's single.

The Yankees added yet another insurance run in the seventh when Billy Johnson tripled and scored on a fly ball to left by Aaron Robinson.

Lefty Joe Page, who had come on in relief in the fifth, kept the Dodgers scoreless. In the ninth Eddie Miksis singled with one out to give Brooklyn a faint hope, but Edwards hit a grounder to Rizzuto, who tossed to Stirnweiss to start a game-ending, Series-ending, season-ending double play. The Yankees had their eleventh World Series title, while the Dodgers would continue to pursue their first.

Chapter 67. **Bill Bevens**

Peter M. Gordon

AGE	W	L	PCT.	ERA	G	GS	GF	CG	SHO	SV	IP	H	BB	SO	HBP	WP
30	7	13	.350	3.82	28	23	3	11	1	0	165.0	167	77	77	1	0

On October 3, 1947, Bill Bevens stood on the mound at Ebbets Field one out away from baseball immortality. He had pitched the first 8⅔ innings of the fourth game of the World Series without giving up a hit. All he had to do was retire Brooklyn Dodgers pinch-hitter Cookie Lavagetto, and he would become the first man to pitch a World Series no-hitter.

Bill stood six-feet-three and weighed 215 pounds in his prime. In 1946 he was a key member of the Yankees' rotation, second only to Spud Chandler. A season later he was manager Bucky Harris's starter in Game Four. A win would give the Yankees a commanding 3–1 lead in the Series, which was as important to Bill as the no-hitter. What no one else in the ballpark knew was that at this point, Bevens was pitching largely on guts and guile. He had hurt his arm earlier in the game and had lost some speed off his fastball. Still, he thought he could get one more out. It was not to be.

Floyd Clifford Bevens was born on October 21, 1916, in Hubbard, Oregon, a small farming town about twenty-five miles south of Portland.[1] Floyd was born to John Ezra and Edna Elizabeth (Jones) Bevens. He had three older brothers (Roy, Ray, and Henry) and an older sister, Ruby. Two other siblings had died before he was born. His family grew hops and berries and kept some animals. They needed Floyd, his three brothers, and his sister to do chores and help run the farm. Reminiscing about his childhood to a reporter in 1947, Bevens called his part of Oregon "a grand country to live in. What with the chores, my schoolboy life was a busy one."[2]

Bill Bevens's 2⅔ scoreless innings of relief in the seventh and deciding game of the 1947 World Series are often forgotten.

Bevens described how he started pitching. "I went to grade school and then high school in Hubbard. I was a ballplayer in high school. Third base. Our coach was a man named Silkie. He needed pitching badly. He saw that I could throw hard. Well, the inevitable happened."[3]

After high school Bevens went to work at a garage and then at a cannery. He also played junior American Legion ball for two years with the Woodburn, Oregon, post. His team reached the national semifinals before losing to a team from Chicago, whose star pitcher was future Chicago Cubs first baseman Phil Cavarretta. After Legion ball Bevens pitched for semipro teams in Oregon while working at a warehouse. He also courted and married Mildred Louise Hartman.

Bevens's success as a semipro attracted the attention of professional scouts, like the Yankees' Joe Devine, who signed him in 1936. The Yankees sent the twenty-year-old right-hander to El Paso in the Class D Arizona-Texas League. In his first year in the minors, Bevens won sixteen games and struck out 179 men in 242 innings. (Sixteen was the most games Bevens ever won in a season, in the Majors or the Minors.)

Bevens progressed steadily through the Yankees' farm system during the late 1930s and early 1940s. He won fourteen games for the Class B Wenatchee (Washington) Chiefs in 1938 and 1939, pitching a no-hitter each year. In 1940 he won fourteen for the Binghamton (New York) Triplets, the Yankees' entrant in the Class A Eastern League. Bevens appeared ready to advance further, but his career stalled.

In 1947 he told an interviewer, "In 1941 I just couldn't get going and was demoted to Augusta (Georgia) in the Sally League."[4] Bevens was 6-5 with Augusta after starting the season 0-7 with the Triplets. When the United States entered World War II, the Yankees transferred Bevens to the higher-level Pacific Coast League so he would be closer to home if he got drafted. He won four and lost eleven for Seattle and Hollywood in 1942, then went 7-8 for Kansas City of the American Association in 1943.

At age twenty-six and married, Bevens did not get drafted. The Yankees brought him to spring training in 1944 and then promoted him to their top Minor League affiliate, the Newark Bears, where, he said, "I began to get somewhere. I won 12 and lost 6. I was asked to report to the Yankees about midseason, and won 4 and lost 1 in

the American League. Once with the Yankees I decided that it was a far superior life to working in the minors and decided to stick."[5]

Bevens's first Major League victory was against the Boston Red Sox in the heat of a pennant race. He also won a key game at the end of the '44 season that put the Yankees in position to take the pennant if they could only win the last four games against the St. Louis Browns. The Yankees lost the first game and were eliminated, as the Browns captured their only twentieth-century flag.

Bevens attributed his success in the Majors to his control. "I began to get somewhere in 1945 because I developed my control to the point at which I was able to keep my passes down."[6] He went 13-9 in 1945 and then 16-13 with a 2.23 ERA in 1946, walking only seventy-eight men in 249⅔ innings. Eight of Bevens's thirteen losses in 1946 were by one run, including two 1–0 defeats.

Bevens prided himself on staying in shape by working out during the off-season. He refereed high school and college basketball games to keep his legs strong. His off-season job in the cannery also built up muscle. He threw a fastball, curve ball, and change-up but stayed away from more exotic pitches like the knuckle ball. Bevens told a reporter during the 1947 season, "I never have suffered from a sore arm. I throw hard every day. You cannot expect your arm to be strong if you do not exercise it."[7] Even though Bevens was in good shape, he suffered from poor run support and lost almost twice as many games as he won in 1947, finishing with a 7-13 record and a 3.82 ERA.

The Yankees went into Game Four of the 1947 World Series up two games to one, with a chance to take a commanding lead. While he had allowed no hits when he faced Lavagetto with two outs in the ninth inning, his ten walks broke a Series record set by the Philadelphia Athletics' Jack Coombs thirty-seven years earlier. Brooklyn scored a run in the fifth inning on two walks, a sacrifice, and a ground out. Meanwhile, the Yankees managed two runs, which looked like enough for the win.

In the ninth inning the Dodgers came up for their last chance. Bevens got Bruce Edwards to ground out to start the inning. One down. Then he walked Carl Furillo. Spider Jorgensen popped up in foul territory for the second out. Al Gionfriddo, running for Furillo, stole second. Pete Reiser, unable to play in the field because of a leg injury, hobbled up to the plate to pinch-hit. With first base open, Bevens pitched the dangerous Reiser carefully. When the count reached 3-1, Harris ordered an intentional walk to Reiser, violating the fundamental precept of putting the potential winning run on base. Eddie Miksis ran for Reiser. Dodgers manager Burt Shotton sent the right-handed-hitting Lavagetto up to bat for Eddie Stanky, also a right-handed hitter. "The book said Lavagetto couldn't handle hard stuff away," Bevens said many years later. "That's what I gave him." The first pitch was on the corner for strike one. As it turned out, the book the Yankees had on Lavagetto was wrong. "Fast and tight was the way to handle me," Lavagetto said.[8]

Bevens's next pitch was in the same place, and Lavagetto lined it over Tommy Henrich's head off the right-field wall. With two outs the runners were off at the crack of the bat, and Miksis scored all the way from first with the winning run. Bevens said the next day that after Lavagetto's hit, he "felt like a guy who had dropped ten stories in an elevator. My heart and my brains and everything was right down by my spikes."[9]

While the Dodgers celebrated at home plate, Bevens turned and walked slowly to the clubhouse. The Yankees kept the door closed after the game for more than a half hour while they tried to regroup. Afterward, they put the best face on it they could, praising Bill's effort and vowing to win the World Series anyway.

Win it they did, and Bevens made a significant contribution in the seventh and deciding game. After Frank Shea gave up two runs to Brooklyn in

the second inning, Bevens relieved him and pitched 2⅔ scoreless innings before leaving for a pinch hitter. Joe Page pitched the last five innings and got the win. Bevens was able to pitch only because his wife, Mildred, stayed up the night before the game massaging his right arm.

Nothing could restore Bevens's arm for the 1948 season. At the time it was reported that his struggles were caused by a leg injury he suffered while refereeing a basketball game during the off-season. However, some years later, Bevens told reporter Tom Meany that his arm went dead during the World Series.

Bevens and the Yankees tried everything and anything to get his arm to come back. He even suffered a quack doctor injecting his arm with saline solution, but nothing worked. Bevens was sold to the White Sox on a conditional basis in January 1949 and then returned by the White Sox on March 28. He reported to Minor League spring training and then was released by the Yankees on April 18.

For several years after that, Bevens tried to pitch professionally. In 1950 he pitched for Sacramento in the Pacific Coast League but was released and went to San Diego. His arm had improved, but his pitching had not. Bevens said, "Although I couldn't pitch winning ball, my arm no longer gave me any trouble."[10]

In 1951 he pitched for the Salem (Oregon) Senators in the Western International League, going 20-12 with a 3.08 earned run average in this Class B Minor League. He took comfort from pitching in his hometown, where Mildred and his three sons, Larry, Danny, and Bobbie, could watch him. As a former Major League pitcher, and only four years removed from his "almost" no-hitter, Bevens was a celebrity in the league and attracted reporters after every game.

Bevens's success in Salem earned a trip to San Francisco in the PCL in 1952, where he was 6-12 with a 4.47 ERA in 155 innings. He tried again with Salem the next year, but the thirty-six-year-old Oregonian's baseball career was at an end. He returned home to Salem to raise his family. Eventually, he stopped working at the local cannery and worked his way up to manager of a trucking company.

Baseball fans remembered Bevens. Almost to the day he died, people would regularly ask Bevens about the almost no-hitter, said his son Larry. Bevens was never angry or regretful. "I don't think he ever had any sense of 'Gee whiz, what if,'" Larry said. "He didn't toss or turn, or end up bemoaning Lavagetto's hit."[11]

Bevens died on October 26, 1991, from lymphoma, at the age of seventy-five. Every obituary led with mention of the fourth game of the 1947 World Series. So in the end Bevens did achieve baseball immortality, even if it was the "close-but-didn't-quite-make-it" kind. He did make a significant contribution to a world championship team.

Bevens was survived by his wife, Mildred, whom he married in 1936, three sons, eight grandchildren, and six great-grandchildren. No doubt Bevens considered his marriage of more than a half century, and the size of his extended family, more than enough compensation for losing his no-hitter.

In a piece on Bevens for *Collier's* in 1951, author Tom Meany wrote that a reporter asked Bevens, "How do you feel about being one out away from glory? When you think back about that game and realize that Lavagetto's hit cheated you of something nobody else had ever done, what are your reactions?"

"Well," answered Bevens, "I figure I was lucky to be up there in the first place."[12]

Chapter 68. Bill Bevens's Almost World Series No-Hitter

Joe Dittmar

Despite Pete Reiser's injured leg, manager Bucky Harris chose to walk him in the ninth inning of Game Three. Reiser is shown here sliding into Yankees shortstop Phil Rizzuto.

With the Yankees leading the 1947 World Series two games to one over the Dodgers, the two clubs met for Game Four in Brooklyn's Ebbets Field. New York started Bill Bevens, a mediocre right-hander who was a few weeks shy of his thirty-first birthday. Bevens had been 16-13 for the Yankees in 1946 but slipped to 7-13 in the pennant year, the result of some bad luck and his seventy-seven walks in 165 innings pitched. For the Dodgers, rookie Harry Taylor, whose promising season had been curtailed by an elbow problem that sidelined him for five weeks in August and September, got the call.

The Yankees wasted no time getting to Taylor. The first two batters, Snuffy Stirnweiss and Tommy Henrich, singled, and Yogi Berra reached first on an error by shortstop Pee Wee Reese. A walk to Joe DiMaggio forced in a run and sent Taylor to an early shower. Hal Gregg assumed the pitching duties for Brooklyn and extinguished the rally on a pop-up and a double-play grounder. In the home half of the first the Dodgers worked Bevens for two walks, but both runners were left stranded.

In the third, after DiMaggio walked, George McQuinn tapped a ball near the plate that catcher Bruce Edwards threw wildly to first. DiMaggio, on a sign from third base coach Chuck Dressen, tried to score on the errant throw but was cut down easily at the plate. Dressen's decision to send DiMaggio home on the play provided the second-guessers with ample grist during the following few days.

In the bottom of the third the Dodgers' Eddie Stanky led off with a walk and advanced to second on a Bevens wild pitch. But Johnny Lindell helped the Yankees escape damage with a tumbling catch of Jackie Robinson's foul fly. New York added an insurance run in the fourth when Billy Johnson tripled and Lindell doubled him home. It was 2–0, Yankees.

The Dodgers finally took advantage of Bevens's wildness in the fifth. The first two batters, Spider Jorgensen and Hal Gregg, walked. Although the Dodgers had yet to hit safely, they now had six free passes from the big right-hander. Stanky sacrificed both runners into scoring position. Pee Wee Reese then sent a ground ball to shortstop Phil Rizzuto, who tossed out Gregg running to third. But Jorgensen scored. It was now 2–1, Yankees.

Hank Behrman replaced Gregg on the mound for Brooklyn in the eighth. Behrman withstood an error by Jorgensen in that inning, but ran into serious trouble in the ninth. With Rizzuto on first, Bevens sacrificed, but both he and Rizzuto were safe when the throw to second was late. When Stirnweiss singled to center, the Yankees had the bases loaded and a golden opportunity to put the game out of reach.

Brooklyn called in its ace reliever, Hugh Casey, to face the always dangerous Henrich. On Casey's first pitch, Henrich grounded sharply back to the hurler, who started a snappy pitcher-to-catcher-to-first double play, pulling the Dodgers out of potential disaster. They still had no hits but were only one run down entering the do-or-die bottom of the ninth.

Bevens's high-wire act finally caught up with him in the strategy-filled, fatal ninth. After Bruce Edwards flied out, Carl Furillo collected the Dodgers' ninth walk. When Jorgensen fouled out, Bevens was one out away from the first World Series no-hitter. Al Gionfriddo, running for Furillo, stole second. This changed the Yankees' thinking about pitching to Pete Reiser, who was batting for Casey. Although the talented outfielder was injured and could not run well, New York decided to walk him. It was the tenth walk for Brooklyn and a disaster-inviting strategy—putting the winning run on base. Eddie Miksis ran for Reiser.

The cat-and-mouse game reached another level when, for only the second time this season, right-handed-hitting Eddie Stanky was lifted for a pinch hitter. Cookie Lavagetto, who also batted from the right side, was an aging veteran who had seen limited action during the season. He swung at the first pitch and missed, leaving Bevens only two strikes away from victory and fame. But Lavagetto drilled the next offering off the right-field wall. The ball bounced around long enough for Gionfriddo to score the tying run and Miksis to tally the game winner.

As his near fame turned into an unforgettable loss, Bevens's locker-room quote never rang truer: "Those bases on balls sure kill you." Bevens came back to pitch 2⅔ scoreless relief innings in the Yankees' triumphant Game Seven. That was the final game of his four-year Major League career. It was also the final game of Lavagetto's career.

Chapter 69. Larry MacPhail

Ralph Berger

Flamboyant, *visionary*, *ego-* or *monomaniacal*, *tempestuous*, *alcoholic*, and *self-destructive*—the words approach but do not satisfactorily explain Larry MacPhail. His innovative approach to the game brought about night baseball and baseball on the radio. He was a mover and shaker in the world of Major League Baseball until in a fury he catapulted himself right into retirement.

MacPhail was a baseball genius. In addition to his pioneering work with baseball and the broadcast media, he had incredible foresight in many other disparate aspects of the game, including pension plans, airplane travel, and batting helmets. He had a particular talent for bailing out poor teams in desperate financial straits. With his ability to wheel and deal, he saw opportunities way ahead of other baseball executives. But just when his clubs were making money and winning, he self-destructed. While alienating almost everyone around him, MacPhail was an oracle who saw how baseball could survive, and even flourish, in a changing world.

Larry MacPhail got in people's faces. He wore flashy clothes and drank heavily. His swiftly changing moods made him difficult if not impossible to comprehend. He would fire Leo Durocher, his manager in Brooklyn, one day, only to rehire him the next. Many thought he verged on insanity.

Leland Stanford MacPhail was born in Cass City, Michigan, on February 3, 1890. His father, William Curtis McPhail, a Scottish immigrant, was a prosperous storekeeper and banker. MacPhail, who later changed the spelling of his surname to emphasize his Scottish heritage, got his first name because his mother, Catherine Ann

Larry MacPhail's tumultuous 1947 season began in spring training with his involvement in the Leo Durocher suspension and ended with his ouster after the 1947 World Series.

(MacMurtrie) McPhail, was a close friend of Mrs. Jane Lathrop Stanford, the wife of Leland Stanford, the famous railroad builder, governor and senator from California and founder of Stanford University.

At the age of sixteen and recently graduated from Staunton Military Academy, MacPhail was accepted at the U.S. Naval Academy but instead went to Beloit College in Wisconsin. At Beloit he played baseball and was a halfback on the football team. Later he attended the University of Michigan and George Washington University in Washington DC, emerging with a law degree at age twenty. He practiced law in Chicago and later headed up a department store in Nashville, Tennessee.

MacPhail married Inez Thompson of Oak Park, Illinois, on October 19, 1910, and had three children with her: Leland Jr., William, and Marian. William was a television executive, Marian was the head of research at *Time*, and Lee MacPhail became a baseball executive who was elected to the Baseball Hall of Fame in 1998, twenty years after his father's election. For Inez, life as the wife of a baseball executive and the 1938 move of the family from Columbus to Larchmont, New York, left her feeling alone and deprived of her Ohio friends. They separated in 1939 and were divorced in May 1945.

When America entered World War I, in 1917, MacPhail enlisted in the army as a private, rose to the rank of captain, and was wounded fighting in France. At the end of the war MacPhail, his commanding officer, Colonel Luke Lea, a former U.S. senator from Tennessee, and several others tried to kidnap the former German emperor, Kaiser Wilhelm II, who was living in exile in Holland. They almost were imprisoned themselves, as they were unsuccessful in the attempt and barely got out with their lives.

After being discharged from the army, MacPhail refereed Big Ten football games and toyed with various ventures, most of which were unsuccessful. In 1930 he acquired an option to buy the Columbus (Ohio) Red Birds baseball team, which was failing financially. MacPhail brokered the sale of the club to Branch Rickey, and Columbus became part of the St. Louis Cardinals' farm system, with MacPhail as president of the club.

Through his entrepreneurial farsightedness and boldness, MacPhail brought the ailing Columbus team back to financial stability. He had a new stadium built and introduced three-dollar Ladies Day season tickets. He organized a knothole gang and also had lights installed. In 1932 the Columbus team outdrew the parent Cardinals 310,000 to 279,000. But MacPhail's insistence on putting the welfare of the Columbus team ahead of the parent team caused the first of his many rifts with Rickey, as they argued over the makeup of the Columbus and St. Louis rosters.

The personalities and lifestyles of MacPhail and Rickey made it highly unlikely they would ever get along. Rickey was an abstemious, churchgoing person; MacPhail was a drinker, a flashy dresser, and a loudmouth. Cincinnati offered MacPhail a way out from under Rickey. Sidney Weil, president and director of the Reds, retired in 1933 and turned his stock over to the Central Trust Company in Cincinnati. In 1934 Powel Crosley Jr., the owner of radio manufacturing plants and radio stations, bought the team and wanted Rickey to run it. Rickey did not want to leave St. Louis, but suggested MacPhail.

As vice president and general manager of the Reds, MacPhail soon brought winning baseball back to Cincinnati. He put in lights at Crosley Field and set about building a team that helped pave the way for pennant winners in 1939 and 1940 and a World Series championship in 1940.

Nocturnal baseball in the Major Leagues (the Minor Leagues had been playing under lights for some time) began on May 24, 1935. At 8:30 p.m. President Franklin D. Roosevelt pushed a button in the White House, signaling MacPhail to turn on the lights at Crosley Field. The ballplayers' reaction to night baseball was positive. There had been some speculation that under lights, only the top side of the ball would be visible; this was not the case, and most everyone was quite satisfied with the game, which was viewed by more than 25,000 fans. The Reds defeated the Phillies, 2–1.

Embroiled in controversy, however, MacPhail left at the end of the 1937 season before the Reds had success. Crosley was displeased with

MacPhail's altercations with the police, fueled by his heavy drinking. MacPhail departed and spent the rest of 1937 in the banking business in Michigan. In 1938 MacPhail received a call from the Brooklyn Trust Company to come to Brooklyn and bail out the team that was in dire financial straits. MacPhail answered the call and put the Dodgers back into contention.

MacPhail realized that average workingmen and -women could rarely go to a ball game in the afternoon. He began night baseball at Ebbets Field as a means of increasing attendance and profits at the box office. Also, at Brooklyn in his first year he hired Babe Ruth as a coach and tried out a lemon-yellow ball; neither of these experiments helped much.

However, it was his clever trading ability that really counted. In March 1938 he got slugging first baseman Dolph Camilli from the Phillies and in October secured pitcher Hugh Casey in the Rule 5 draft. In 1939 he hired Leo Durocher as manager, claimed Dixie Walker on waivers, and brought in Red Barber to call the games on radio. Barber, whom MacPhail had first hired in Cincinnati, had a soothing southern voice that taught many a housewife and young boys and girls the intricacies of baseball. At first many club owners were leery of broadcasting games, but they soon found that it brought more fans to the ballpark. The Dodgers' attendance soared in 1939; they outdrew the mighty Yankees by almost 100,000 and the Giants by more than 250,000.

In 1940 MacPhail added rookie Pee Wee Reese at shortstop and acquired outfielder Joe Medwick and pitcher Curt Davis in a trade with St. Louis. Pete Reiser, plucked out of the St. Louis farm system in 1938, also made his big-league debut. Rickey had asked MacPhail to sign Reiser and keep him out of sight in the low Minors until 1940, when he could be traded back to the Cardinals. But Reiser sparkled in spring training with the Dodgers in 1940, and Durocher, unaware of

the deal with Rickey, started playing him in exhibition games. MacPhail sent a wire to Durocher, "DO NOT PLAY REISER AGAIN." When Durocher inserted Reiser into the lineup in a game in Macon, Georgia, MacPhail called him to his hotel room, cursed him, and fired him. The angry Durocher shoved MacPhail, who fell over the bed in a somersault, got up, and, as if by magic, had a change of heart. He put his arm around Leo and told him he was still the manager and then calmly went on to say that Reiser should be optioned to Elmira so that he could further develop his talent.

On June 18 Medwick was struck on the temple by a pitch thrown by the Cardinals' Bob Bowman and suffered a severe concussion. MacPhail demanded that National League president Ford Frick bar Bowman from baseball, but cooled down as Medwick missed only three games. In the aftermath of the incident, MacPhail and Dr. George Eli Bennett, a professor of orthopedic surgery at the Johns Hopkins School of Medicine in Baltimore, devised one of the earliest protective helmets for players.

In 1941 the Dodgers won their first pennant since 1920. After the team clinched the flag in Boston, MacPhail tried to meet their return train at New York's 125th Street Station so that he would be aboard when they triumphantly reached a throng of fans at Grand Central Terminal in midtown Manhattan. Upon hearing that some players were going to disembark at 125th Street, Durocher decided to skip the stop to ensure the entire team would disembark at Grand Central. Eagerly awaiting the train, MacPhail was left standing as the train rushed by him in a whirl of dust. Finally catching up with the team, MacPhail was livid and again fired Durocher, only to rehire him a short time later. As Durocher said, "There is a thin line between genius and insanity, and in Larry's case it was sometimes so thin you could see him drifting back and forth."[1]

MacPhail was back in the army during World

RALPH BERGER

War II, doing public-relations work for the War Department. His old mentor and sometime foe Branch Rickey replaced him at Brooklyn.

Commissioner Landis died in November 1944. MacPhail attended meetings in February 1945 to elect a new commissioner and promoted Albert "Happy" Chandler, a U.S. senator from Kentucky, to succeed Landis. Chandler was elected commissioner in April.

In 1943, after Jacob Ruppert, owner of the Yankees, died, the team was put up for sale. MacPhail had assembled a syndicate to bid on the team, but Judge Landis squelched any deal because one of the members of the syndicate owned racehorses. The pressure to sell the team to pay estate taxes grew, and MacPhail stepped up again. With two other members of his original syndicate, Dan Topping, a wealthy sportsman who owned the Brooklyn Dodgers of the National Football League, and Del Webb, an Arizonan who ran construction and real-estate ventures, MacPhail proffered a successful bid in January 1945. MacPhail took over as the team's president after he was discharged from the army in February 1945. Also in 1945, a week after his divorce from Inez, MacPhail married Brooklyn-born Jean Bennett Wanamaker, who had been his secretary when he was with the Dodgers. As with Durocher, he had fired and rehired her several times. The couple had one daughter, Jean, born in 1950.

Almost immediately, the Yankees' businesslike operation took a reverse course. MacPhail's tempestuous side was in such full swing that three managers quit on him in 1946: Joe McCarthy, Bill Dickey, and Johnny Neun. Major League Baseball had to deal with some labor problems in 1946. Chandler banned several ballplayers who had signed contracts to play with the Mexican League. Also, Robert Murphy, a labor lawyer, tried to organize a players union. MacPhail headed an owners committee that agreed to set a minimum salary of five thousand dollars, institute a mod-est pension plan, give players a weekly allowance of twenty-five dollars during spring training (still called Murphy money), and give the players formal representation on a council with the owners and the league presidents. These were small concessions; the ballplayers would have to wait many years before free agency and greater bargaining power came their way.

MacPhail's and Durocher's brashness embroiled them in an uproar during spring training in 1947 that had serious consequences. Durocher, still managing the Dodgers and under heavy criticism for fighting with fans and umpires, was also under attack for his life away from the ball field. At a spring-training game in Havana he pointed to some well-known gamblers who appeared to be in a box seat with MacPhail and said, "If that was my box I'd be barred from baseball."

Actually, the gamblers were not sitting in the same box as MacPhail; they were in a box behind him. Hearing of Durocher's remark, MacPhail demanded that Commissioner Chandler do something about it. Chandler held two hearings, and on April 9, just before the season was to open, he suspended Durocher from baseball for one year—for actions other than the Havana incident. This suspension resulted in outcries from fans, and even some owners, who felt Durocher had been unfairly punished. Many felt that this harsh treatment was a political payback to MacPhail for his aid in getting the commissioner's job for Chandler.

The Yankees won the pennant and the World Series in 1947. MacPhail was ecstatic. As Branch Rickey left the field, MacPhail caught up with the disconsolate Rickey, putting his arm around his shoulder, offering his hand, and starting to congratulate him on the fine job he had done with the Dodgers. Rickey cut him short. "I am taking your hand only because people are watching us," he said. Rickey launched into reasons for his disappointment in MacPhail as a man and ended their relationship once and for all: "Don't you ever speak to me again." MacPhail's elation turned to deep anger as he entered the Yankees' clubhouse.

As the Yankees were whooping it up, MacPhail entered and turned the clubhouse celebration on its head when, in a drunken stupor, he unleashed a barrage of insults, punched a writer, and announced his resignation. His behavior continued at the Biltmore Hotel, where MacPhail tearfully announced his retirement again. Del Webb and Dan Topping bought out the fifty-seven-year-old MacPhail the next day for two million dollars (see chapter 1).

Following the "Battle of the Biltmore," MacPhail and baseball were finished with each other. Possibly seeking a more placid life, he bought a farm near the Bowie Racetrack in Maryland that he called Glenangus and where he raised Black Angus cattle and bred racehorses. He became president of the racetrack during his retirement, but sold the farm when it ran into financial troubles.

MacPhail had his first battle with cancer in 1952. Informed that he might have cancer of the throat, he asked the opinions of several doctors; some affirmed the diagnosis, while others rejected it. But MacPhail was not satisfied with the answers and sought the opinion of his daughter Marian's husband, Dr. Walsh McDermott, who confirmed the diagnosis as cancer of the larynx and suggested immediate surgery. The operation was a success, but MacPhail was diagnosed with cancer of the intestines in 1957, and again had lifesaving surgery.

MacPhail's last years were sad. The ravages of alcohol and the onset of what is now presumed to be Alzheimer's disease were affecting his once great entrepreneurial mind. He was failing psychologically and physically. His children wanted to put him into a private institution, but he insisted on going to a veterans hospital, as if he wanted to recapture the past when he was an officer in both world wars. He was obstreperous with the staff and to the very end true to his nature as the Roaring Redhead.

MacPhail died on October 1, 1975, at the age of eighty-five, in the Jackson Manor Nursing home in Miami, Florida. Surviving were his wife, Jean; sons, Bill and Lee; and daughters, Jean MacPhail and Marian McDermott. He is buried in Cass City.

Whatever his shortcomings, MacPhail was a major contributor to baseball. For seventeen years his almost manic energy and farsightedness carried him far beyond the innate conservatism of Major League Baseball in his time. He was a baseball maverick at a time when his fellow executives were satisfied with the status quo. He played a vital role in baseball's enduring the difficult times in which he operated. MacPhail's contributions to the game earned him election to the Hall of Fame in 1978, three years after his death.

Three generations of MacPhails became baseball executives. Son Lee was instrumental in continuing the Yankee dynasty into the 1950s, building the great Baltimore Orioles teams of the 1960s, and he also served as president of the American League; he was elected to the Hall of Fame in 1998. Grandson Andy was general manager of the 1987 world champion Minnesota Twins and later was president and general manager of the Chicago Cubs and Baltimore Orioles. None inherited Larry's instability.

RALPH BERGER

Chapter 70. **George Weiss**

Dan Levitt

George Weiss presided over the greatest sustained run of excellence in baseball history. Under Weiss's leadership, from 1948 through 1960, the New York Yankees won ten pennants and seven World Series. After the team slipped to third place in 1959, Weiss retooled his squad and returned to the top the following season. For this accomplishment the *Sporting News* named him Executive the Year, the fourth time Weiss had been so honored, more than anyone else in the history of the award.

Weiss understood the importance of creating a strong organization and was not afraid to have strong, intelligent men in subordinate roles. "The entire organization bears down all the time. Every day, 12 months a year," Weiss remarked. In today's world of twenty-four-hour sports channels and football coaches sleeping in their office, this may seem unremarkable. But in the 1950s, with family ownership and sportsmen owners, Weiss's professional approach was groundbreaking.

George Martin Weiss was born on June 23, 1894, in New Haven, Connecticut, the first child of Anna and Conrad Weiss. Conrad, a German immigrant, owned a grocery store. The Weisses later added a daughter, Florence, and another son, Edwin.

While still in his teens Weiss began his career in baseball promotion. At Hillhouse High School he became the business manager for the school's baseball team. After graduation Weiss held much of the high school baseball team together, brought in a couple of new players, and promoted his squad as a semipro team. Weiss also enrolled at Yale. When his father died Weiss quit college to help run the family grocery business and concentrate

When George Weiss was named general manager of the Yankees, in October 1947, they were already established as baseball's preeminent organization.

on his baseball ventures. For a venue he leased the grounds at Lighthouse Point, an amusement park just outside the New Haven city limits. By guaranteeing a purse, Weiss brought in stars such as Ty Cobb and Walter Johnson to play in Sunday exhibitions — then prohibited by the blue laws in New York, Massachusetts, and New Haven proper—with his semipro team.

Weiss's promotional skills made his semipro team so popular that it began siphoning off interest from New Haven's organized baseball team in the Eastern League. Rather than continue to struggle for the same fans, the league approached Weiss in 1919 and offered him an opportunity to buy the team for $5,000. Weiss borrowed the money and purchased the franchise. He quickly turned around the team's on-field fortunes, and New Haven won the Eastern League pennant in 1920.

In December 1923 disaster struck Weiss and New Haven manager Wild Bill Donovan, traveling to the winter meetings in Chicago aboard the Twentieth Century Limited. Outside of Forsyth, New York, the train crashed, killing Donovan and eight other passengers. Badly injured with lacerations to his back, Weiss spent the next month hospitalized in Erie, Pennsylvania, followed by a long convalescence at home.

As a Minor League operator, Weiss learned quickly that financial survival depended on player sales to Major League and higher-classification Minor League teams. He easily transferred his promotional skills to negotiating player sales, and during his tenure with New Haven he sold twenty-six players for about $300,000. Weiss's club was also highly competitive on the field. From 1920 through 1928 New Haven won three Eastern League pennants and had only two losing seasons.

In late 1928 Jack Dunn, the principal owner of the International League's Baltimore Orioles, died. The remaining stockholders concluded they needed an experienced baseball executive to run the franchise and turned to Weiss. Ready for a new challenge at a higher level, Weiss accepted the Baltimore offer, sold the New Haven team, and took over the Orioles. Over the next three seasons Weiss rebuilt the struggling Baltimore franchise and earned another $242,000 on player sales.[1] Under his leadership the Orioles won at least ninety games each season for the next four years.

As the Depression deepened in the early 1930s, organized baseball relaxed the roster rules to make it advantageous for Major League teams to invest in the Minors. New York Yankees owner Jacob Ruppert was one of the first to grasp the true impact of this change, which suddenly made establishing a farm system worthwhile. Late in 1931 the Yankees purchased the International League's Newark franchise and soon thereafter announced that they intended to own or control four Minor League franchises in different classifications.[2] With their commitment to a Minor League farm system, the Yankees needed someone to run it. Ruppert chose Weiss, who was only thirty-seven years old, but had already spent nearly twenty years in baseball.

Over the next several years Weiss's farm system began graduating players like Red Rolfe, Joe Gordon, Charlie Keller, and Phil Rizzuto, who would become mainstays for the Yankees' dynasty from 1936 through 1943. While the Yankees were dominating the American League, their expanding farm system further testified to the excellence of the Yankees' player-procurement and -development organization. In 1937 Newark won the International League by a record twenty-five and a half games as one of the greatest Minor League teams ever. Later that year the Yankees brought another top Minor League team, the Kansas City Blues of the American Association, into the fold with a working agreement. The Yankees now possessed a ten-team farm system: four by outright ownership and six by working agreement.

In 1937 Weiss ended his long bachelorhood, marrying Hazel Wood. Hazel was a flying enthusiast, one of relatively few women who learned how to fly a plane, and a multitalented artist.

After the 1942 season Brooklyn Dodgers president Larry MacPhail resigned to join the war effort. As finalists to replace MacPhail, the Dodgers identified Bill Terry, New York Giants manager and de facto general manager during the 1930s; Branch Rickey, legendary builder of the St. Louis Cardinals' farm system; and Weiss. MacPhail later recalled that when Yankees president Ed Barrow learned the Dodgers were considering Weiss, Barrow demanding that he either affirm his interest in the Yankees or quit to pursue the Dodgers job. Fortunately for the Yankees, Weiss chose to stay in New York. He recognized that Barrow was nearing the end of his active role and naturally expected to succeed him. With Weiss no longer a candidate, the Dodgers opted for Rickey.[3]

Jacob Ruppert had died in January 1939, muddying the Yankees' ownership and financial situation. In January 1945, no longer able to defer payment of the estate tax, the trustees of Ruppert's trust sold the team to a triumvirate of Dan Topping, Del Webb, and Larry MacPhail. The mercurial MacPhail ran the team, but had little patience or tolerance for administrative structure; he was an outgoing, boisterous genius — exactly the antithesis of Ruppert and Barrow. After thirteen years building the organization and waiting his turn, Weiss found himself working for a man with whom he had no connection and who had little interest in administrative excellence.

After three uneasy years running the Yankees, the pressure and constant limelight began to affect MacPhail. MacPhail's deteriorating behavior culminated with his breakdown at the celebration dinner in the Biltmore Hotel after the Yankees won the 1947 World Series. A drunken MacPhail lurched over to Weiss's table, where he was dining with Hazel, Barrow, and several others. MacPhail started cursing Weiss and berating his work. Weiss remained as calm as possible and suggested, "We have all been drinking. I would like to wait until tomorrow and discuss this with you." MacPhail, in no condition to be mollified, responded by firing Weiss on the spot. Reason, however, won out. Webb and Topping bought out MacPhail and pro-

moted Weiss to general manager, with Topping becoming team president.[4]

Taking over as the Yankees' GM at the age of fifty-three, after sixteen years as farm director, Weiss dressed and acted like a corporate executive. He was often cold and unemotional to those outside his closest circle, partly out of a conscious effort to keep his distance from players and subordinates and partly out of extreme shyness.[5]

When Weiss was named general manager of the Yankees, they were already established as baseball's preeminent organization. Yet the team Weiss inherited, like all the immediate postwar teams, was one in transition. From 1944 to 1948 five different American League teams had won the pennant. The Yankees had struggled in 1946, finishing a distant third, but had come back to win in 1947 under new manager Bucky Harris. When the Yankees slumped back to third in 1948, Weiss dumped Harris, who Weiss felt was "an old-style, 'book' manager."[6] Additionally, Harris was a MacPhail hire, and Weiss wanted his own man in charge on the field.

Weiss surprised the baseball community by hiring Casey Stengel, who had just won the Pacific Coast League pennant in Oakland. Weiss and Stengel had been friends for many years, dating back to Stengel's brief managing stint in the Eastern League.

The team Weiss built won a record five consecutive World Series from 1949 through 1953. The next season the Yankees won 103 games, the highwater mark of Weiss's tenure, but fell to second behind Cleveland, which won a then American League record 111.

One of the keys to the Yankees' success was their remarkable farm system. All-time greats Mickey Mantle and Whitey Ford graduated to the Yankees early in Weiss's tenure as general manager. Yogi Berra was called up just prior to Weiss's promotion while he still ran the farm system.

Weiss believed his scouts could outhustle their

competitors and dig up amateurs others might miss or whose potential they might not fully recognize. They proved him right: Mantle, Berra, Ford, and future stars such as Bill Skowron, Gil McDougald, Hank Bauer, Bobby Richardson, and Tony Kubek all cost less than seven thousand dollars to sign.[7]

The Yankees' farm system proved much more successful at developing position players than pitchers. Other than Ford and Vic Raschi, most of the Yankees' top pitching during Weiss's tenure—men like Allie Reynolds, Ed Lopat, and Bob Turley—came through trades. Weiss trusted his scouts to be able to recognize pitchers of ability often struggling with poor win-loss records on second-division teams. He would then acquire these hurlers by surrendering prospects and occasionally cash.

The first of these turned out to be the worst. After the 1948 season Weiss sent three players and one hundred thousand dollars to the St. Louis Browns for pitcher Fred Sanford and a throw-in catcher, Roy Partee. Sanford never performed the way the Yankees hoped he would. Weiss remembered the trade with dismay for the rest of his career. He later blamed the deal on his succumbing to pressure from the press and co-owner Dan Topping.

Weiss became a master of the midseason trade, often using his cash and prospects to add a valuable veteran for the stretch drive. He described his thinking on trades: "Our trading philosophy has been one of trying to get a man to fill a needed gap, often short-term, without helping the opposition too much and without trading away a star."[8] Late in the 1949 season Weiss purchased aging veteran Johnny Mize, who still had a couple of good years left, for forty thousand dollars. At the 1950 trading deadline he picked up pitchers Tom Ferrick and Joe Ostrowski for several players and forty thousand dollars. "They weren't stars," Weiss explained, "but they helped us considerably." The next year Weiss made another poor trade—sending pitcher Tommy Byrne and twenty-five thou-

sand dollars to the St. Louis Browns for Stubby Overmire—which he again blamed on Topping's influence. A couple of years later, after Byrne had been sent back to the Minors, Weiss reacquired him, and Byrne turned in several good seasons for the Yankees. Other midseason acquisitions included Johnny Sain, Johnny Hopp, Ewell Blackwell, Harry Simpson, and Ryne Duren.[9]

Weiss found another source of talent in the Kansas City Athletics. The Athletics franchise had been purchased by Dan Topping's close pal Arnold Johnson after the 1953 season and moved from Philadelphia. Johnson had little interest in building a winner. Throughout his tenure the Athletics were consistently woeful on the field. Weiss made numerous trades with Johnson and Kansas City general manager Parke Carroll, who had once worked for the Yankees. Yet other than the deal that brought Roger Maris to New York, the trades were not nearly as one-sided as is often remembered. Weiss summarized Johnson's typical response to the criticism, which was to argue that he was "out to improve the A's whether it helps the Yanks or not."[10]

Weiss and the Yankees have been criticized for their slow reaction to bringing in black players. The team's first black player, Elston Howard, did not appear with the Yankees until 1955, eight years after Jackie Robinson broke the color barrier in Brooklyn. Weiss, however, was certainly not alone in either baseball or American society in being slow to integrate. Ten of the sixteen teams still had no black players as late as September 1953. Moreover, most teams integrated not simply out of some moral imperative, but because once the door was opened, integration was the quickest and cheapest way to grab top talent. The Yankees, however, alone among the Major League teams, continued to win without aggressively acquiring black stars.

While the Yankees continued to shy away from black players for the first couple of years after Robinson signed with organized baseball, by the late 1940s they were actively scouting the Negro Leagues. In addition to Howard, the Yankees made a couple of notable acquisitions, including Vic Power and Luis Marquez. Weiss was later criticized for trading Power before he appeared in the Majors with the Yankees. On the other hand, Weiss was livid when Commissioner Happy Chandler awarded Marquez to Cleveland because of a dispute over which Negro League club held his rights. "This decision soured George Weiss on Chandler," Lee MacPhail wrote. "Del Webb was already against him and the Yankees then took the lead in putting together enough votes to eventually unseat Chandler as commissioner."[11]

Weiss had a reputation as a rough negotiator with his players, which in fact made him little different from most other front-office executives. In this era before free agency, a player was effectively bound to his team for life, or until the team wanted to trade or release him.

In December 1958, with the impending retirement of American League president Will Harridge, a group of owners approached Weiss. They informally offered him first shot at taking over from Harridge. After bouncing the opportunity off Webb and Topping, Weiss decided to stay with the Yankees. "It was a nice honor to receive after a long run," Weiss acknowledged, "but the aspirin bills would have been terrific."[12] His wife, Hazel, later revealed he had turned the job down because of his morbid fear of public speaking. "You have to go all over and talk," Hazel remembered her husband complaining. "He wouldn't do it."[13]

After four more consecutive pennants, from 1955 to 1958, the Yankees fell to third in 1959. "Injuries ruined the team," Weiss explained, but he also thought that his players maybe were not hungry enough. The team rebounded in 1960 to capture the pennant before losing a heartbreaking seven-game World Series to the Pittsburgh Pirates.[14]

In the aftermath of the 1960 Series, Topping eased both Stengel and Weiss out of their positions. At Topping's request both the seventy-year-old manager and the sixty-six-year-old general manager announced at their press conferences that they had decided to retire. Stengel managed to convey that he was not quitting voluntarily. Weiss was a little less transparent, but he "did not sound altogether happy, despite his protestations to the contrary."[15]

Exactly why the Yankee owners fired Weiss and Stengel remains murky. The stated reason of looking to get younger—the Yankees instituted a mandatory sixty-five-year-old retirement age—probably had a grain of truth. Topping wanted to get more directly involved in the operation of the franchise, something that would have been much trickier with the imperial Weiss still nominally in charge.

Weiss still had one act remaining in his baseball career. On March 1, 1961, he drove to Florida to meet with Joan Whitney Payson, principal owner of the expansion New York Mets, who would begin play in 1962. Payson needed a baseball man to run the franchise and after the meeting offered the team presidency to Weiss. Weiss eagerly jumped into all the challenges and headaches of building a baseball organization from scratch. He hired his old friend Casey Stengel to manage and quickly assembled an excellent team of scouts and a solid organization. He also negotiated radio and TV contracts and involved himself in all aspects of the design of Shea Stadium, the new ballpark being built in Queens.[16]

The problem of landing good players turned out to be much more difficult than Weiss ever imagined. The lack of talent quickly became apparent, and for their first several years the Mets were the laughingstock of baseball.

In September 1964 the club hired Bing Devine as a special assistant to Weiss. Devine had just been unceremoniously dumped as general manager of the St. Louis Cardinals. With Weiss on the last year of his contract, the Mets wanted to put a succession plan in place and jumped at the now available Devine. Once on board, Devine assumed most of the general manager's day-to-day duties. Weiss, however, was not quite ready to retire and exercised an option in his contract to run the operation for one more season. In his six years running the franchise, Weiss assembled the front-office infrastructure that would create the "miracle" 1969 World Series champion.

After the 1966 season the seventy-two-year-old Weiss finally retired. At his retirement party Weiss joked about his well-known fear of public speaking: "Now that I have the time to take a course in public speaking, I'll probably never have another opportunity to speak." In retirement honors continued to come Weiss's way, culminating with election to the Baseball Hall of Fame in 1971. Weiss died one year later, on August 13, 1972, at a nursing home in Greenwich, Connecticut.

For someone not supposed to be emotional, Weiss was surprisingly sentimental about his baseball career. In his stately old home in Greenwich, Weiss had what he called his "Baseball Room." It was filled with all sorts of memorabilia, including original player contracts and personalized mementos from baseball greats Ty Cobb and Walter Johnson through Joe DiMaggio and Mickey Mantle. Visitors to the sanctum were "never disappointed."[17] The room reflected Weiss's life. He had spent his entire adult life in baseball with few hobbies. The mementos and memories were well earned.

Chapter 71. **American League Most Valuable Player Award**

Lyle Spatz

The twenty-four baseball writers—three in each American League city—split their first-place votes among six players, including three Yankees, on their American League Most Valuable Player Award ballots. At the top of the list was Joe DiMaggio, who edged Ted Williams 202–201 to win his third MVP award. DiMaggio batted .315, with twenty home runs and 97 runs batted in. Williams topped DiMaggio in every offensive category. He led the league with a .343 batting average, thirty-two home runs, and 114 runs batted, to earn his second Triple Crown. He also led the AL in runs scored, walks, on-base percentage, and slugging percentage. Voters evidently placed great emphasis on DiMaggio's all-around play and leadership qualities in awarding him eight first-place votes compared to three for Williams. The result was controversial at the time and remains so to this day.

Third-place finisher Lou Boudreau, the man-ager-shortstop of the Cleveland Indians, had one first-place vote; Yankees relief pitcher Joe Page had seven; Yankees first baseman George McQuinn had three; and Philadelphia Athletics shortstop Eddie Joost had two.

Page, who finished fourth, one point behind Boudreau, had a 14-8 record and a 2.48 earned run average. He appeared in fifty-six games for New York, with a league-leading forty-four games finished and a league-leading seventeen saves (retroactively computed).

Thirty-seven-year-old McQuinn, who finished sixth, batted .304 with thirty home runs and 80 RBIs in his first year as a Yankee. Other Yankees receiving votes were outfielder Tommy Henrich (thirteenth place), rookie pitcher Frank Shea (fourteenth place), catcher-outfielder Yogi Berra and pitcher Allie Reynolds (tied for fifteenth place), and third baseman Billy Johnson (tied for nineteenth place).

Chapter 72. American League Rookie of the Year Award

Lyle Spatz

The Baseball Writers' Association of America's Rookie of the Year Award in 1947 went to Jackie Robinson in a contest that included first-year players from both leagues. The Brooklyn first baseman batted .297, scored 125 runs, and had a league-leading twenty-nine stolen bases. Larry Jansen of the New York Giants, who won twenty-one games and had a league-leading .808 winning percentage, was second.

New York Yankees pitcher Frank Shea was third, meaning that had there been Rookie of the Year Awards in both leagues in 1947, Shea would have been the American League winner. Shea had a 14-5 record and a league-leading .737 winning percentage. The only other American Leaguer to receive votes was Philadelphia Athletics first baseman Ferris Fain, who batted .291 and finished fourth. Cincinnati Reds outfielder Frank Baumholtz, a .283 hitter, finished just behind Fain.

Chapter 73. American League Cy Young Award

Lyle Spatz

Official recognition of baseball's best pitcher did not begin until 1956, when Brooklyn's Don Newcombe won the first Cy Young Award. Starting in 1967 two awards were given, one to the best pitcher in each league. Although there was no official vote in 1947, two retrospective attempts have been made to determine the likely pre-1956 Cy Young winners for each league. The two, one by the Society for American Baseball Research and one by awards historian Bill Deane, agree that the 1947 winner in the American League would have been Cleveland's Bob Feller.

Feller (20-11) was the American League's only twenty-game winner. He also led in games started (37), innings pitched (299), shutouts (5), and strikeouts (196) while finishing second in earned run average (2.68).

Because there was no separate award for them, pitchers were always well represented in the voting for the league's Most Valuable Player. In just the previous five years, Mort Cooper of the Cardinals was the National League winner in 1942, while Spud Chandler of the Yankees had won the AL award in 1943, followed by Hal Newhouser of the Detroit Tigers, who won in both 1944 and 1945.

In the majority of cases, the pitcher with the highest MVP vote total was the winner of the retroactive Cy Young Award. But that was not the case in 1947. Feller, the presumed Cy Young winner, finished eighth in the MVP voting, while Joe Page of the Yankees finished fourth. The left-handed relief ace had a 14-8 record, finished a league-leading forty-four games, and led the league with a retroactively determined seventeen saves. Among pitchers, Phil Marchildon of the Philadelphia Athletics was the next highest vote getter after Feller, followed by two Yankees, rookie Frank Shea (14-5) and Allie Reynolds, 19-8 in his first year with the club.

Chapter 74. Yankees Attendance in 1947

Gary Gillette

Some of the more than 2 million fans who saw the Yankees play in 1947 line up for tickets.

The New York Yankees drew 2,178,937 fans in 1947, then the second-highest total of all time. In almost a half century of modern (i.e., post-1900) baseball history, no team had ever drawn 2 million paying customers until the Yankees shattered that mark in 1946, with 2,265,512. Powered by Babe Ruth and his game-changing circuit clouts, the Yankees had also been the first team to draw 1 million, in 1920, more than doubling their attendance from the previous year. (In 1920 the Yankees were still tenants of the New York Giants at the Polo Grounds.)

The Yankees' 1947 total was a modest 3.8 percent drop from '46, the first postwar season, while the rest of the American League was down less than 1 percent. Considering that New York won the 1947 American League pennant by twelve games over Detroit, it was an impressive feat, as the Yankees held onto first place from June 20 onward and boasted a double-digit lead from July 28 to the end of the season.

Moreover, though New York had led the American League in offense in 1947, pacing the loop with 115 home runs and 72 triples, it definitely did not feature a Murderers' Row. Joe DiMaggio led the club in home runs with twenty.

The summer of 1947 was notable for two other reasons. It was the last year of the gargantuan Yankee Stadium with its 70,000-plus seating, achieved when the second and third decks in right field were extended into fair territory in 1937. Starting in 1948 New York reduced capacity to about 67,000 and kept it close to that number until the 1970s.

The 1947 season was also the first full season for night baseball at the corner of River Avenue and 161st Street, with lights having been added in late May 1946. Only fourteen night games were scheduled at the start of the season, with none on Saturdays or Sundays.

New York's newfound drawing power came as part of a huge postwar boom in baseball that—at the time—seemed as though it might last forever. In 1948 *two* teams surpassed 2 million, as the American and National Leagues combined to draw more than 20 million fans for the first time.

In '46 the Yankees had drawn 2,265,512 paying customers, more than two and a half times their 1945 total, as the American League enjoyed a 72 percent jump in attendance in the first full season after World War II. Surprisingly, the record was set by the Yankees without the benefit of a hot pennant race. New York settled into a comfortable second place in mid-July 1946, more than ten games off the pace set by Boston. The Yanks gradually drifted downward as the season wore on, finishing third, a distant seventeen games behind the Red Sox.

So the record attendance in 1946 was really much more a function of the pent-up demand for the national pastime than the exploits of the New York club. The 1947 *Sporting News Guide* ran an article, "Record Attendance for Majors and Minors," that contained the breakdown of 1946 attendance by leagues (and, for the Major Leagues, by teams), but made no mention specifically of any club, although the *Guide*'s year-end essay does note the Yankees' playing before more than 2 million fans at home.

In the 1948 season, 2,373,901 fans came out to the Bronx, setting a club record that lasted for more than three decades. Cleveland also drew more than 2 million paying customers in 1948 and 1949. Aided by a classic three-way pennant race that produced the first playoff game in American League history, the Indians' attendance of 2,620,627 in '48 set a high-water mark for the big leagues that would last until 1962. The Yankees drew more than 2 million in '49 and '50, but no other American League club cracked the 2 million mark until the 1968 Detroit Tigers.

New York drew more than 2 million fans each summer from 1946 to 1950. In the National League, the transplanted Braves were the only other club that would reach that lofty mark (1954–57). Milwaukee was followed by the transplanted Dodgers, who were the next senior-circuit club to poll 2 million, attaining it in 1959 and 1960. Los Angeles then established a new record with more than 2.75 million in 1962 when Dodger Stadium opened.

After 1948 the Yankees saw year-to-year attendance declines for the next six seasons (1949–54) despite their remarkable on-field success. Even with the size and wealth of their enormous market, the Bronx Bombers did not draw 2 million fans again from 1951 through 1976. In fact, in the slightly truncated 1972 season (a players strike from April 1 to April 13 reduced the schedule by up to nine games), the Yanks actually dipped slightly below the 1 million mark—hard to imagine today, given the near-capacity throngs at Yankee Stadium (both new and old) for most games in the past decade.

Among the many differences in the way fans consumed their baseball in the 1940s was the diminished importance of opening day. Clubs back then expected a good crowd for their home opener, but sellouts for the first home game were by no means guaranteed. The 1947 Yankees opened the season at home with a day game on Tuesday, April 15, in front of a crowd of "only" 39,344—more than 30,000 below capacity. Two days later, only

8,350 came out to watch, the smallest crowd of the season until the final month.

Another difference between the postwar game and the twenty-first-century version was the steep decline in attendance after Labor Day, even for first-place teams. In 1947 that manifested itself in the Bronx in five consecutive openings with sub-10,000 crowds. The season's nadir in terms of attendance occurred on Friday, September 26, when barely 5,000 showed up to watch the Yankees tune up for the World Series.

Attendance in 1947 was built primarily on big walk-up gates and not on season-ticket sales or advance-ticket orders placed during the off-season. A big part of that pattern was the frequency of doubleheaders; in 1947 New York played 11 twin bills at home. Only 2 (May 17 and July 4) were originally scheduled, however; the rest were makeup doubleheaders forced by postponements.

A year earlier New York had 7 doubleheaders on its original home schedule: 5 on Sundays, the other 2 on Memorial Day and Labor Day. So the record crowds of 1946 definitely caused the New York brain trust to rethink the desirability of offering two-for-one dates. (In 1946 there were an average of 9.3 scheduled doubleheaders per Major League team; in 1947, 7.7.)

The eventual world champions benefited from several premier gates in 1947, the biggest being an amazing 74,747 for a Monday-night game against Boston on May 26. The *Los Angeles Times* reported, "Actually 75,887 tickets were sold tonight, but 1140 people refused to buck the mob, asked for a refund, and got it."[1] That "mob" broke the record for single-game attendance at a Major League game and would remain the record at the original Yankee Stadium (that is, before the 1974–75 rebuilding). Three other 1947 openings pulled in 60,000 or more; at least seven more crowds of 50,000–60,000 were recorded.

The first huge crowd of the '47 season came on Sunday, April 27, when the Yankees celebrated Babe Ruth Day in front of 58,339. All other games in organized baseball that day also featured tributes to the ailing Bambino, who spoke to fans all over the country via a national radio hookup—as did Commissioner Happy Chandler, American League president Will Harridge, and National League president Ford Frick. Francis Cardinal Spellman, former Fordham University second baseman, gave the invocation. The fourth featured speaker that day was Larry Cutler, a teenage American Legion ballplayer: the *New York Times*'s coverage explained that "Ruth's main interest now is the American Legion baseball program, for which he has been signed as a consultant."[2]

Ruth's remarks were "piped direct into most of the ball parks in the nation," according to the Associated Press, which also reported that Ruth was honored in Japan that day.[3] The Sultan of Swat may not have been as eloquent as his former teammate Lou Gehrig eight years earlier, but the final words of Ruth's simple good-bye were gracious and touching: "There has been so many lovely things said about me, and I'm glad that I've had the opportunity to thank everybody. Thank you."[4]

The first scheduled twin bill of the year, on Saturday, May 17, was one of twenty-one "Yankee Junior" days on the schedule. The crowd of 66,666 included more than 12,000 youngsters "from twenty-six different child welfare organizations" admitted free.[5] They saw their hometown heroes sweep the White Sox.

Two dates against Cleveland pulled in crowds of 60,000-plus. On Wednesday night, June 25, 60,090 fans at the stadium witnessed a whitewash of the Indians. On August 2, a Saturday, 62,537 flocked to the Bronx for a doubleheader sweep of Cleveland. The first game lasted fourteen innings and almost four hours, but the nightcap, ended by darkness after seven and a half innings, was played in a scant ninety-four minutes.

In mid-August more than 148,000 faithful—including 67,803 on Friday night, the fifteenth—came out to see a three-game week-end series against the second-place Red Sox, even though the Yankees were eleven and a half games up at the time.

On Monday, September 8, 53,101 turned out to watch the home team lose to the Indians by 4-3, with Bob Feller coming on in the ninth for the save. Another future Cooperstown inductee, Bob Lemon, started for the Indians, opposing New York's midseason acquisition Bobo Newsom.

The '47 season finale, on September 28, was viewed by a quite modest gathering of 25,084, especially in light of the staging of the first old-timers game as a fund-raiser for the Babe Ruth Foundation. (The original Yankees' Old-Timers Day in 1939 did not include an exhibition game.) On hand to honor Babe Ruth were many illustrious guests and baseball titans, including Ty Cobb, Jimmie Foxx, Tris Speaker, and Cy Young. All save Ruth suited up and played! A team of former Yankees, headed by future Hall of Fame manager Joe McCarthy (who had resigned his duties in the Yankees' dugout during the 1946 season), faced off in a two-inning scrimmage against an American League all-star squad skippered by Connie Mack. Ruth would succumb to throat cancer the following August.

The first "Subway Series" of the postwar era packed Gotham fans into Yankee Stadium, with Game One setting a new attendance record for a World Series game, 73,365. The peak attendance of 74,065 in the Series was reached in Game Six, played on Sunday with the potential for the Yankees to win it all. The Yankees' rooters may have been disappointed by the final score that day (8–6 Dodgers), but they could console themselves that they were eyewitnesses to one of the most famous catches in the history of the fall classic when Al Gionfriddo robbed Joe DiMaggio of a home run to left-center in the sixth inning. The Yankees' victory over the Brooklyn Dodgers in Game Seven the next day was savored in person by 71,548.

Epilogue

Lyle Spatz

Pitchers

RUGGER ARDIZOIA, April 30, 1947: Pitched for Yankees in his final Major League game

MEL QUEEN, July 10, 1947: Sold to the Pittsburgh Pirates

AL LYONS, August 3, 1947: Sold to the Pittsburgh Pirates

SPUD CHANDLER, September 26, 1947: Pitched for the Yankees in his final regular-season Major League game

BILL BEVENS, September 27, 1947: Pitched for the Yankees in his final regular-season Major League game

BOBO NEWSOM, February 6, 1948: Released by the Yankees

BILL WIGHT, February 24, 1948: Traded to the Chicago White Sox with pitcher Fred Bradley and catcher Aaron Robinson for pitcher Ed Lopat

BUTCH WENSLOFF, April 12, 1948: Sold to the Cleveland Indians

RANDY GUMPERT, July 25, 1948: Sold to the Chicago White Sox

KARL DREWS, August 9, 1948: Sold to the St. Louis Browns

DICK STARR, December 13, 1948: Traded to the St. Louis Browns with pitcher Red Embree, catcher Sherm Lollar, and one hundred thousand dollars for pitcher Fred Sanford and catcher Roy Partee

DON JOHNSON, June 15, 1950: Traded to the St. Louis Browns with second baseman George Stirnweiss, outfielder Jim Delsing, pitcher Duane Pillette, and fifty thousand dollars for pitcher Tom Ferrick, pitcher Joe Ostrowski, and third baseman Leo Thomas

JOE PAGE, May 16, 1951: Released by the Yankees

TOMMY BYRNE, June 15, 1951: Traded to the St. Louis Browns with twenty-five thousand dollars for pitcher Stubby Overmire

FRANK SHEA, May 3, 1952: Traded to the Washington Senators with outfielder Jackie Jensen, infielder Jerry Snyder, and infielder Archie Wilson for outfielder Irv Noren and shortstop Tom Upton

VIC RASCHI, February 23, 1954: Sold to the St. Louis Cardinals

ALLIE REYNOLDS, September, 25, 1954: Pitched for the Yankees in his final Major League game

Catchers

AARON ROBINSON, February 24, 1948: Traded to the Chicago White Sox with pitcher Bill Wight and pitcher Fred Bradley for pitcher Ed Lopat

KEN SILVESTRI, November 10, 1948: Drafted by the Philadelphia Phillies in the Rule 5 draft

SHERM LOLLAR, December 13, 1948: Traded to the St. Louis Browns with pitcher Red Embree, pitcher Dick Starr, and one hundred thousand dollars for pitcher Fred Sanford and catcher Roy Partee

RALPH HOUK, May 1, 1954: Played for the Yankees in his final Major League game

YOGI BERRA, October 29, 1963: Released by the Yankees

Infielders

JOHNNY LUCADELLO, June 13, 1947: Played for the Yankees in his final Major League game

TED SEPKOWSKI, June 21, 1947: Played for the Yankees in his final Major League game

RAY MACK, September 7, 1947: Sold to the Chicago Cubs

LONNY FREY, May 17, 1948: Released by the Yankees

GEORGE MCQUINN, October 2, 1948: Played for the Yankees in his final Major League game

FRANK CROSETTI: October 3, 1948: Played for the Yankees in his final Major League game

JACK PHILLIPS, August 6, 1949: Sold to the Pittsburgh Pirates

GEORGE STIRNWEISS, June 15, 1950: Traded to the St. Louis Browns with outfielder Jim Delsing, pitcher Don Johnson, pitcher Duane Pillette, and fifty thousand dollars for pitcher Tom Ferrick, pitcher Joe Ostrowski, and third baseman Leo Thomas

BILLY JOHNSON, May 14, 1951: Traded to the St. Louis Cardinals for first baseman Don Bollweg and fifteen thousand dollars

BOBBY BROWN, June 30, 1954: Played for the Yankees in his final Major League game

PHIL RIZZUTO, August 16, 1956: Played for the Yankees in his final Major League game

Outfielders

FRANK COLMAN, August 3, 1947: Played for the Yankees in his final Major League game

ALLIE CLARK, December 11, 1947: Traded to the Cleveland Indians for pitcher Red Embree

CHARLIE KELLER, December 6, 1949: Released by the Yankees

JOHNNY LINDELL, May 15, 1950: Sold to the St. Louis Cardinals

TOMMY HENRICH, October 1, 1950: Played for the Yankees in his final Major League game

JOE DIMAGGIO, September 30, 1951: Played for the Yankees in his final regular-season Major League game

Notes and References

This section first lists a number of key sources that were consulted repeatedly while researching this book, followed by chapter-by-chapter notes and bibliographies.

General References

Baseball. The Biographical Encyclopedia. Kingston, New York: Total/Sports Illustrated, 2000.
The Sporting News Baseball Guide
The Sporting News Baseball Register

New York Times
Sporting News

The ProQuest newspaper archive.
U.S. Census Bureau. 1920 census (*Fourteenth Census of the United States*).
U.S. Census Bureau. 1930 census (*Fifteenth Census of the United States*).

Ancestry.com
Baseball-Almanac.com
Baseball Hall of Fame
Baseballinwartime.com
BaseballLibrary.com
Baseball-Reference.com
DeadballEra.com
Findagrave.com
Genealogybank.com
Retrosheet.com
SABR.org

National Baseball Hall of Fame and Library, Cooperstown NY
ProQuest newspaper archive

1. The Yankees' Ownership

1. Levitt, *Ed Barrow*.
2. Many years later, a plausible explanation surfaced for the Yankees' seemingly inexplicable sale of Borowy to the Cubs. It was, the theory went, Larry MacPhail's repayment to Chicago general manager Jim Gallagher for the 1941 deal that brought Billy Herman to Brooklyn.
3. McKelvey, *The MacPhails*, 75.
4. McKelvey, *The MacPhails*, 79–80.
5. Spink, "Battle of the Biltmore," 1, 4.
6. Spink, "Battle of the Biltmore."
7. Spink, "Battle of the Biltmore."
8. Spink, "Battle of the Biltmore."
9. Daniel, "Bombers to Ban Ballyhoo."

Levitt, Daniel R. *Ed Barrow: The Bulldog Who Built the Yankees' First Dynasty*. Lincoln: University of Nebraska Press, 2008.
McKelvey, G. Richard. *The MacPhails*. Jefferson NC: McFarland, 2000.

Daniel, Dan. "Bombers to Ban Ballyhoo in New Regime." *Sporting News*, October 15, 1947.
Spink, J. G. Taylor. "Battle of the Biltmore — Victory Brawl." *Sporting News*, October 15, 1947.

3. The Hiring of Bucky Harris

1. Drebinger, "Harris Signs Two-Year Contract."
2. McGowen, "Yanks Sign Harris as M'Phail Aide."
3. McGowen, "Yanks Sign Harris as M'Phail Aide."
4. Kritzer, "Harris Managed 'for Last Time.'"
5. Kritzer, "Harris Managed 'for Last Time.'"
6. McGowen, "Yanks Sign Harris as M'Phail Aide."
7. Drebinger, "Yanks Not Ready to Name New Pilot."
8. "Johnny Neun Installed as Yankee Pilot."
9. "Lippy Tells of Yanks Offer."
10. Hand, "Yanks Claim Assist on Leo's Deal."
11. Hand, "Yanks Claim Assist on Leo's Deal."
12. "Lippy Tells of Yank Offer."
13. Because he was still under contract to the Dodgers when he signed with the Yankees, Dressen was fined and suspended for thirty days.

14. Hand, "Yanks Claim Assist on Leo's Deal."

15. Daley, "Harris Is Elected."

16. Dawson, "Harris Will Stay with Yanks."

17. Drebinger, "Sometimes the 'Nice Guys' Also Win."

Daley, Arthur. "Harris Is Elected." *New York Times*, November 6, 1946.

Dawson, James P. "Harris Will Stay with Yanks Despite Tigers' Offer of General Management." *New York Times*, December 11, 1946.

Drebinger, John. "Harris Signs Two-Year Contract to Manage Yankees for $35,000 Annually." *New York Times*, November 6, 1946.

———. "Sometimes the 'Nice Guys' Also Win." *New York Times*, July 20, 1947.

———. "Yanks Not Ready to Name New Pilot." *New York Times*, September 13, 1946.

Hand, Jack (Associated Press). "Yanks Claim Assist on Leo's Deal." *Washington Post*, November 27, 1946.

"Johnny Neun Installed as Yankee Pilot." *Washington Post*, September 14, 1946.

Kritzer, Cy. "Harris Managed 'for Last Time' with Bisons." *Sporting News*, November 13, 1946.

"Lippy Tells of Yanks Offer." *Washington Post*, November 17, 1946.

McGowen, Roscoe. "Yanks Sign Harris as M'Phail Aide." *New York Times*, September 10, 1946.

5. Suspension of Leo Durocher

The author gratefully acknowledges the assistance of Freddy Berowski, National Baseball Hall of Fame Library, Cooperstown NY; JOE Emmick; Patrick Hayes; and Lyle Spatz.

1. Durocher, *Nice Guys Finish Last*, 257.

2. Quoted in Durocher, *Nice Guys Finish Last*, 22.

3. Mann, *Baseball Confidential*, 43–47; Parrott, *The Lords of Baseball*, 252; Lowenfish, *Branch Rickey*, 424.

4. Daley, "The Lip Talked Too Much," 21; Durocher, *Nice Guys Finish Last*, 247–48.

5. Lowenfish, *Branch Rickey*, 425; Mann, *Baseball Confidential*, 100–121 (quoted on 113); Durocher, *Nice Guys Finish Last*, 252–56.

6. Barber, *1947*, 19. See also Eskenazi, *The Lip*, 199–200.

7. See Kahn, *The Boys of Summer*, 110–12, for Dressen's background; and Tygiel, *Past Time*, 163, for Dressen and Durocher's shared managerial style.

8. Warfield, *Roaring Redhead*, 68 (quoted), 180–81 (Harris), 169–70 (Chandler).

9. Durocher, *Nice Guys Finish Last*, 259, 263.

10. Both quoted in Schumach, "Tempers Flare from Greenpoint to Canarsie," 31.

11. Daley, "Chandler Flexes His Muscles."

12. Fisher, *On the Irish Waterfront*, 174.

13. Durocher, *Nice Guys Finish Last*, 242.

14. Mann, *Baseball Confidential*, 114; Durocher, *Nice Guys Finish Last*, 262.

15. Parrott, *The Lords of Baseball*, 253–54.

16. Fine, *Frank Murphy*.

17. Fine, *Frank Murphy*, 3:10–12, 199–200.

18. Durocher, *Nice Guys Finish Last*, 261–62. The only evidence Chandler actually possessed correspondence from Murphy himself appears in Marshall's *Baseball's Pivotal Era*, 453n65.

19. Smith, "Open a Window, Albert," 33.

20. Smith, "Open a Window, Albert," 34.

21. Daley, "Chandler Flexes His Muscles."

22. Marshall, *Baseball's Pivotal Era*, 115 (effigy and sportswriters), 116 (Yankee Stadium).

23. Murray, "Whose Deal?," 1, 7.

24. Golenbock, *Bums*, 25–26, 55–61.

25. Kahn, *Era*, 141–43.

26. Vecsey, "The Lion Roars a Little"; Durocher, *Nice Guys Finish Last*, 263–68.

27. Durocher, *Nice Guys Finish Last*, 119.

28. Parrott, *Lords of Baseball*, 196.

Barber, Red. *1947: When All Hell Broke Loose in Baseball*. New York: Da Capo, 1982.

Durocher, Leo, with Ed Linn. *Nice Guys Finish Last*. New York: Simon and Schuster, 1975.

Eskenazi, Gerald. *The Lip: A Biography of Leo Durocher*. New York: William Morrow, 1993.

Fine, Sidney. *Frank Murphy*. 3 vols. Ann Arbor: University of Michigan Press, 1975, 1979, 1984.

Fisher, James T. *On the Irish Waterfront: The Crusader, the Movie, and the Soul of the Port of New York*. Ithaca NY: Cornell University Press, 2010.

Golenbock, Peter. *Bums: An Oral History of the Brooklyn Dodgers*. New York: Contemporary Books, 2000.

Kahn, Roger. *The Boys of Summer*. New York: Perennial Classics, 2000.

———. *The Era: 1947–1957, When the Yankees, the Giants, and the Dodgers Ruled the World*. Lincoln: University of Nebraska Press, 2002.

Lowenfish, Lee. *Branch Rickey: Baseball's Ferocious Gentleman*. Lincoln: University of Nebraska Press, 2007.

Mann, Arthur. *Baseball Confidential: Secret History of the War among Chandler, Durocher, MacPhail, and Rickey*. New York: David McKay, 1951.

Marshall, William. *Baseball's Pivotal Era, 1945–1951*. Lexington: University Press of Kentucky, 1999.

Parrott, Harold. *The Lords of Baseball*. 2nd ed. Atlanta: Longstreet Press, 2001.

Smith, Red. "Open a Window, Albert." In *Red Smith on Baseball*. Chicago: Ivan R. Dee, 2000.

Tygiel, Jules. *Past Time: Baseball as History*. New York: Oxford University Press, 2000.

Warfield, Don. *The Roaring Redhead: Larry MacPhail, Baseball's Great Innovator*. South Bend IN: Diamond Communications, 1987.

Daley, Arthur. "Chandler Flexes His Muscles." *New York Times*, April 10, 1947.

———. "The Lip Talked Too Much." *New York Times*, April 11, 1947.

Murray, Jim. "Whose Deal?" *Los Angeles Times*, September 9, 1964.

Schumach, Murray. "Tempers Flare from Greenpoint to Canarsie by Ban on Durocher." *New York Times*, April 10, 1947.

Vecsey, George. "Sports of the Times: The Lion Roars a Little." *New York Times*, May 24, 1987.

6. Bucky Harris

1. Harris, *Playing the Game*, 98.
2. Harris, *Playing the Game*, 105–6.
3. Harris, *Playing the Game*, 180.
4. Harris obituary; DiMaggio quote from http://www.baseball-reference.com; Goslin quote from "How Stuff Works," http://entertainment.howstuffworks.com.

Harris, Stanley. *Playing the Game*. New York: Grosset and Dunlap, 1925.

Kashatus, William C. *Diamonds in the Coalfields: 21 Remarkable Baseball Players, Managers, and Umpires from Northeast Pennsylvania*. Jefferson NC: McFarland, 2002.

Barbieri, Richard. *Hardball Times*, November 11, 2010.

Markusen, Bruce, and Ron Visco. "Bucky and the Big Train." *Elysian Fields Quarterly* 17 (2000).

Sullivan, Paul. "The Young Owner Who May Have Saved the Phillies." *Hardball Times*, May 31, 2011.

"Alien Property Custodian." *New York Times*, September 12, 1926.

"Bucky Harris to Wed Elizabeth Sutherland, Daughter of the Alien Property Custodian." *New York Times*, September 12, 1926.

Harris, Bucky. Obituary. *New York Times*, November 10, 1977.

Harris, Thomas. Obituary. *New York Times*, September 27, 1943.

Armour, Mark. "Firpo Marberry." SABR Baseball Biography Project, http://bioproj.sabr.org/bioproj.cfm?a=v&v=l&bid=369&pid=8804.

http://alt.nntp2http.com/obituaries/2006/11/12a51be1364ddd72239c9a059329281f.html.

http://www.baseball-almanac.com/players/player.php?p=harribu01.

http://thebaseballpage.com/players/harribu01.

http://www.baseball-reference.com/players/h/harribu01-field.shtml.

http://captnsblog.wordpress.com/2010/10/29/the-curious-case-of-curly-ogden-or-how-bucky-harris-tricked-john-mcgraw-in-the-1924-world-series.

http://www.efqreview.com/NewFiles/v17n3/onhistoricalground.html.

http://entertainment.howstuffworks.com/bucky-harris-hof.htm.

http://www.hardballtimes.com/main/article/this-annotated-week-in-baseball-history-nov.-6-nov.-13-1896.

http://www.hardballtimes.com/main/printarticle/the-young-owner-who-may-have-saved-the-Phillies.

http://www.lahabrahighschool.net/ourpages/auto/2009/11/18/41264327/Cilld%20Labor%20Coal%20Mines.pdf.

7. Charlie Dressen

1. Dressen's birth date is often mistakenly given as

September 28, 1898. Throughout his baseball career, he was actually four years older than he claimed to be.

2. Dressen's father, Phillip, had immigrated from Germany in 1882; his mother, the former Kate Driscoll, had immigrated from England in 1880. The family spelled the name "Dresen," which is how Charles signed his World War I draft card.

Barra, Allen. *Yogi Berra: Eternal Yankee*. New York: W. W. Norton, 2009.

Frommer, Harvey. *Baseball's Greatest Managers*. New York: Franklin Watts, 1985.

Henrich, Tommy, with Bill Gilbert. *Five O'Clock Lightning*. New York: Birch Lane Press, 1992.

Rosenthal, Harold. *Baseball's Best Managers*. New York: Bartholomew House, 1961.

Baseball Digest
Look
Sport
Sport Life Complete Baseball
Sports Illustrated
True Baseball Yearbook

Brooklyn Eagle
Detroit Free Press
New York Daily News

8. Red Corriden

1. Epstein, "Corriden Is Good Will and Good Humor Man."

2. Brown telephone interview.

3. References to the "Iron Man Infield" neglect the fact that Jay Kirke joined the Colonels that year in June in a trade from Milwaukee of the American Association. Corriden, McCarthy, and Roach did play every inning of every game, and thus Kirke must have done the same once he joined the team.

4. Of course, as all Cubs fans know, the team failed to win the World Series all three pennant-winning years in the 1930s.

5. Brown telephone interview.

6. Robinson telephone interview.

7. Epstein, "Corriden Is Good Will and Good Humor Man."

Alexander, Charles C. *Ty Cobb*. New York: Oxford University Press, 1984.

Bak, Richard. *Peach: Ty Cobb in His Time and Ours*. Ann Arbor: Sports Media Group, 2005.

Bartell, Dick, with Norman L. Macht. *Rowdy Richard*. Berkeley CA: North Atlantic Books, 1987.

Golenbock, Peter. *The Spirit of St. Louis: A History of the St. Louis Cardinals and Browns*. New York: Avon Books, 2000.

Grimm, Charlie, with Ed Prell. *Jolly Cholly's Story: Baseball, I Love You!* Chicago: Henry Regnery, 1968.

Gutteridge, Don, with Ronnie Joyner and Bill Bozman. *From the Gas House Gang to the Go-Go Sox: My 50-Plus Years in Big League Baseball*. Dunkirk MD: Pepperpot Productions, 2007.

Higbe, Kirby, with Martin Quigley. *The High Hard One*. New York: Viking Press, 1967.

Johnson, Lloyd, and Miles Wolff, eds. *The Encyclopedia of Minor League Baseball*. 2nd ed. Durham NC: Baseball America, 1997.

Jones, David, ed. *Deadball Stars of the American League*. Dulles VA: Potomac Books, 2006.

Levy, Alan. *Joe McCarthy: Architect of the Yankee Dynasty*. Jefferson NC: McFarland, 2005.

Lieb, Frederick C. *The Detroit Tigers*. New York: G. P. Putnam and Sons, 1946.

Reed, Ted. *Carl Furillo: Brooklyn Dodger All-Star*. Jefferson NC: McFarland, 2011.

Robinson, Eddie, and C. Paul Rogers III. *Lucky Me: My Sixty-Five Years in Baseball*. Dallas: SMU Press, 2011.

Skipper, John C. *A Biographical Dictionary of Major League Managers*. Jefferson NC: McFarland, 2003.

Spatz, Lyle. *Dixie Walker: A Life in Baseball*. Jefferson NC: McFarland, 2011.

Stump, Al. *Cobb: A Biography*. Chapel Hill NC: Algonquin Books of Chapel Hill, 1994.

Baseball Register (Sporting News) 1941.

Murphy, J. M. "Napoleon Lajoie: Modern Baseball's First Superstar." *National Pastime*, no. 1 (1988).

Corriden, Red. Obituary. *New York Times*, September 30, 1959, 29.

Epstein, Ben. "Corriden Is Good Will and Good Humor Man." Undated clipping from Red Corriden file, National Baseball Library, Cooperstown NY.

Brown, Dr. Bobby. Telephone interview by the author. June 23, 2011.

Robinson, Eddie. Telephone interview by the author. June 23, 2011.

10. Yankee Stadium

1. Robinson and Jennison, *Yankee Stadium*.
2. Vancil and Santasiere, *Yankee Stadium*.
3. Robinson and Jennison, *Yankee Stadium*.
4. White, *Creating the National Pastime*.
5. Frommer, *A Yankee Century*.
6. Robinson and Jennison, *Yankee Stadium*.
7. Frommer, *A Yankee Century*.
8. Robinson and Jennison, *Yankee Stadium*.

Buchanan, Andy. *#1 Guide to Yankee Stadium*. Chicago: Wise Guides, 2007.

Frommer, Harvey. *A Yankee Century*. New York: Berkley Publishing Group, 2002.

Robinson, Ray, and Christopher Jennison. *Yankee Stadium: 75 Years of Drama, Glamor, and Glory*. New York: Penguin Group, 1998.

Vancil, Mark, and Alfred Santasiere III. *Yankee Stadium: The Official Retrospective*. New York: Pocket Books, 2008.

White, Edward. *Creating the National Pastime*. Princeton NJ: Princeton University Press, 1996.

11. Spud Chandler

Freese, Mel R. *Charmed Circle*. Jefferson NC: McFarland, 1997.

Gentile, Derek, ed. *The Complete New York Yankees*. New York: Black Dog and Leventhal, 2001.

Honig, Donald. *Baseball: When the Grass Was Real*. New York: Coward, McCann, and Geoghegan, 1975.

James, Bill, and Rob Neyer. *The Neyer/James Guide to Pitchers*. New York: Simon and Schuster, 2004.

Mead, William B. *Baseball Goes to War*. Washington DC: Farragut, 1985.

Peary, Danny, ed. *Cult Baseball Players*. New York: Simon and Schuster, 1990.

Smith, Loran, ed. *Between the Hedges: 100 Years of Georgia Football*. Atlanta: Longstreet Press, 1992.

Westcott, Rich. *Diamond Greats*. Westport CT: Meckler Books, 1988.

Baseball Digest
Baseball Magazine
Saturday Evening Post

http://www.newgeorgiaencyclopedia.com

12. Don Johnson

1. Unless indicated otherwise, all quotations are from a telephone interview conducted by the author with Don Johnson on April 20, 2011.
2. LaPointe, "60 Years of Adventures."
3. Hand, "Yankees Casting about for Pitching," 2:1.
4. "Nats Obtain Don Johnson," 23.
5. "Leafs, Chisox in Ball Trade," 20.
6. "Leaf Pitcher Tops League," 19.
7. The White Sox won ninety-four games in 1954.
8. "Don Johnson Fails to Show and Faces Suspension," 16.
9. "Disappearing Act Costly to Pitcher," 30.

"Disappearing Act Costly to Pitcher." *St. Joseph (MO) News-Press*, July 6, 1958.

"Don Johnson Fails to Show and Faces Suspension." *Modesto (CA) Bee*, August 23, 1955.

Hand, Jack (Associated Press). "Yankees Casting about for Pitching to Bolster Outfit." *Prescott (AZ) Evening Courier*, June 12, 1950.

LaPointe, Joe. "60 Years of Adventures on Way Back to the Bronx." *New York Times*, July 18, 2010.

"Leaf Pitcher Tops League." *Regina (Saskatchewan) Leader Post*, December 8, 1953.

"Leafs, Chisox in Ball Trade." *Saskatoon (Saskatchewan) Star-Phoenix*, October 10, 1953.

"Nats Obtain Don Johnson." *Youngstown (OH) Vindicator*, May 31, 1951.

Johnson, Don. Interview with Thomas Bourke. October 21, 2011.

13. George McQuinn

1. Gross, "The Man Nobody Wanted," 98.
2. Gross, "The Man Nobody Wanted," 97.
3. Gaven, "McQuinn Getting His Chance with Browns."
4. Gross, "The Man Nobody Wanted," 98.
5. Mead, *Even the Browns*, 41.

Borst, Bill. *The Best of Seasons: The 1944 St. Louis Cardinals and St. Louis Browns.* Jefferson NC: McFarland, 1995.

———. *Still Last in the American League.* West Bloomfield MI: Altwerger and Mandel, 1992.

Dahlgren, Matt. *Rumor in Town.* Ashland OH: Woodlyn Lane, 2007.

Goldstein, Richard. *Spartan Seasons: How Baseball Survived the Second World War.* New York: Macmillan, 1980.

Golenbock, Peter. *The Spirit of St. Louis: A History of the St. Louis Cardinals and Browns.* New York: Avon Books, 2000.

Gross, Milton. "The Man Nobody Wanted." In *Yankee Doodles.* Boston: House of Kent, 1948.

Heidenry, John, and Brett Topel. *The Boys Who Were Left Behind.* Lincoln: University of Nebraska Press, 2006.

Heller, David Allan. *As Good as It Got: The 1944 St. Louis Browns.* Charleston SC: Arcadia, 2003.

Johnson, Lloyd, and Miles Wolff, eds. *The Encyclopedia of Minor League Baseball.* 2nd ed. Durham NC: Baseball America, 1997.

Karst, Gene, and Martin Jones, eds. *Who's Who in Professional Baseball.* New Rochelle NY: Arlington House, 1973.

Mayer, Ronald A. *The Newark Bears: A Baseball Legend.* East Hanover NJ: Vintage Press, 1980.

Mead, William B. *Even the Browns: The Zany, True Story of Baseball in the Early Forties.* Chicago: Contemporary Books, 1978.

Porter, David L. *Biographical Dictionary of American Sports: Baseball, Revised and Expanded Edition, G–P.* Westport CT: Greenwood Press, 2000.

Shatzkin, Mike, ed. *The Ballplayers.* New York: Arbor House, 1990.

Van Lindt, Carson. *One Championship Season: The Story of the 1944 St. Louis Browns.* New York: Marabou, 1994.

Vincent, David, Lyle Spatz, and David Smith. *The Midsummer Classic: The Complete History of the All-Star Game.* Lincoln: University of Nebraska Press, 2001.

Gaven, Michael F. "George McQuinn, Kept Off Yankees for Eight Seasons by Gehrig, Getting His Chance with Browns via Draft." *Sporting News,* February 28, 1938.

Brown, Dr. Bobby. Telephone interview by the author. June 23, 2011.

14. Allie Reynolds

Bischoff, John Paul. *Mr. Iba: Basketball's Aggie Iron Duke.* Oklahoma City: Western Heritage Books, 1980.

Bucek, Jeanine. *The Baseball Encyclopedia.* 10th ed. New York: Macmillan, 1996.

Burke, Bob, Kenny A. Franks, and Royse Parr. *Glory Days of Summer: The History of Baseball in Oklahoma.* Oklahoma City: Oklahoma Heritage Association, 1999.

Golenboch, Peter. *Dynasty: The New York Yankees, 1949–1964.* Englewood Cliffs NJ: Prentice-Hall, 1975.

Halberstam, David. *Summer of '49.* New York: William Morrow, 1989.

Kahn, Roger. *The Head Game: Baseball Seen from the Pitcher's Mound.* New York: Harcourt, 2000.

Parr, Royse, and Bob Burke. *Allie Reynolds: Super Chief.* Oklahoma City: Oklahoma Heritage Association, 2002.

Bourke, Thomas. Telephone conversation with Allie Reynolds's daughter, Bobbye Kay Ferguson. February 12, 2011.

http://www.okstate.com/trads/hall-of-honor.html

16. Ray Mack

1. *Cleveland Plain Dealer,* April 18, 1940.

2. *Cleveland Plain Dealer,* April 18, 1940.

3. National Baseball Hall of Fame Archives, Player's File.

4. National Baseball Hall of Fame Archives, Player's File.

5. National Baseball Hall of Fame Archives, Player's File.

6. National Baseball Hall of Fame Archives, Player's File.

7. National Baseball Hall of Fame Archives, Player's File.

8. National Baseball Hall of Fame Archives, Player's File.

9. *Sporting News*, February 19, 1947.

10. *Cleveland Press*, May 8, 1969.

Boudreau, Lou, Russell Schneider, and Rich Schneider. *Covering All the Bases*. Oregon IL: Quality Books, 1993.

Sullivan, Brad, ed. *Batting Four Thousand: Baseball in the Western Reserve*. Lincoln: University of Nebraska Press, 2008.

Baseball Digest
Cleveland Plain Dealer
Cleveland Press
Sporting News

http://minors.sabrwebs.com/cgi-bin/index.php
http://www.chicagobears.com/index.html
http://www.ohiostatebuckeyes.com
http://www.profootballhof.com/default.aspx

17. Bobby Brown

The author expresses his sincere appreciation to Fr. Gabriel Costa, U.S. Military Academy, and Dr. John Saccoman, Seton Hall University, for their support in this project. Gabe and J. T. (both longtime SABR members) were instrumental in introducing the author to Dr. Brown and in offering advice with the biography.

1. Brown interview, January 2007.

2. Brown file, National Baseball Hall of Fame.

3. Brown interview, January 2007.

4. Freeze, "Kingfisher Crash Off San Francisco."

5. Oates, "Calling Dr. Brown!"

6. Oates, "Calling Dr. Brown!"

7. Brown interview, June 2007.

8. Brown interview, June 2007.

9. *Sporting News*, June 8, 1949.

Porter, David L., ed. *Biographical Dictionary of American Sports: Baseball, Revised and Expanded Edition*. Westport CT: Greenwood Press, 2000.

Los Angeles Times
New York Times
Sporting News

Oates, Bob. "Calling Dr. Brown!" *Los Angeles Times*, May 9, 1974.

Freeze, Ken. "Kingfisher Crash Off San Francisco." Check-Six.com, http://www.check-six.com/Coast_Guard/9_May_1943_OS2U_crash.htm.

Brown, Dr. Robert. Interviews with the author, January 2007 through June 2007.

Brown, Bobby. Various undated articles and newspaper clippings (including contract cards) in Robert W. Brown's file at the A. Bartlett Giamatti Research Center, National Baseball Hall of Fame and Museum, Cooperstown NY (accessed May 2007).

18. Rugger Ardizoia

1. Ardizoia interview, February 6, 2010. Rugger said the double *z* in *Ardizzoia* reflected in census and steamship records was a simple error.

2. Ardizoia interview, February 6, 2010. Asked about his mother being recorded in the census as a tailor, he said, "She was very, very good. She worked at a place where they made clothes and repaired them."

3. *Los Angeles Times*, June 3, 1939.

4. Attanasio oral history. All quotations from Ardizoia are from this 2006 oral history unless otherwise noted.

5. *Los Angeles Times*, June 3, 1939.

6. Ardizoia interview, December 10, 2008.

7. It is not possible to verify this story. He appears to have applied for citizenship as early as 1941 and was granted it about five and a half years later.

Goldstein, Richard. *Spartan Seasons: How Baseball Survived the Second World War*. New York: Macmillan, 1980.

Ardizoia, Rugger. Interviews by the author. December 10, 2008, February 6, 2010. Correspondence from February 17, 2010.

——. Oral history by Ed Attanasio, November 21, 2006, transcribed by Tom Hetrick in February 2007.

19. Ken Silvestri

1. Florence (Horn) Daley Silvestri was Ken's biological mother. Ken's father was John Daley, born in Chicago

about 1881. Florence, apparently divorced, married Joseph Silvestri about 1927. It was Joseph who adopted Kenneth (whether officially or not) and, evidently, changed his middle name to Joseph. He was born Kenneth L. Daley.

2. Silvestri interview.

3. U.S. Census Bureau, *Fifteenth Census of the United States: 1930*, census place: Chicago, Cook, Illinois; roll 474; page 2B; Enumeration District 1376.

4. Silvestri player questionnaire.

5. Heise, "Ken Silvestri."

6. Silvestri player questionnaire.

7. Johnson and Wolff, *Encyclopedia of Minor League Baseball*.

8. St. Paul Saints press release.

9. Vaughn, "Dykes Has Mind Made Up."

10. Vaughn, "Sox End Camp Labor Today."

11. Vaughan, "Mud Is Too Deep."

12. Vaughan, "Yankees Blast Out 19 Hits."

13. "Sox Assign Lee to Face Browns and Harris Today."

14. "Yankees Trade Knickerbocker."

15. Rennie, "Silvestri Valued by Yankees."

16. "Silvestri Rests Well after Appendectomy."

17. "From Army Front."

18. "Ken Silvestri Enters Army."

19. "Where Have You Been."

20. "Silvestri Again Civilian."

21. Silvestri player questionnaire.

22. Silvestri interview.

23. It was actually five blocks.

24. Silvestri interview.

25. "Dressen, Ban Lifted, Aids Harris."

26. "Dressen, Ban Lifted, Aids Harris."

27. Selko, *Minor League All Star Teams*.

28. "Silvestri Big Factor in '49 Phillies Plans."

29. Yeutter, "Church—Answer to Phil's Prayer," 15.

30. Silvestri interview.

31. "Pressure? Aaron Stopped It Quickly."

32. Holtzman, "White Sox Tap Silvestri."

33. "Doby, Knoop, Williams New ChiSox Coaches."

34. Holtzman, "Sox Recycle Ken Silvestri."

35. Holtzman, "Sox Recycle Ken Silvestri."

36. "Hatch's Plan Talk Sharpens Pitching," 37.

37. Silvestri interview.

38. Silvestri interview.

Johnson, Lloyd, and Miles Wolff. *The Encyclopedia of Minor League Baseball*. Durham NC: Baseball America, 1993.

Selko, James. *Minor League All Star Teams, 1922–1962*. Jefferson NC: McFarland, 2007.

Yeutter, Frank. "Church—Answer to Phil's Prayer: Silvestri's Bullpen Sermons Pay Off." *Baseball Digest*, August 1951.

"Doby, Knoop, Williams New ChiSox Coaches." *Sporting News*, December 11, 1976.

"Dressen, Ban Lifted, Aids Harris." *New York World-Telegram*, May 15, 1947.

"From Army Front." *Sporting News*, December 11, 1941.

"Hatch's Plan Talk Sharpens Pitching." *Sporting News*, August 30, 1982.

Heise, Kenan. "Ken Silvestri, Ex-Catcher, White Sox Pitching Coach." *Chicago Tribune*, April 4, 1992.

Holtzman, Jerome. "Sox Recycle Ken Silvestri as Pitching Coach." *Chicago Tribune*, July 14, 1982.

———. "White Sox Tap Silvestri to Complete Coaching Staff." *Sporting News*, February 14, 1976.

"Ken Silvestri Enters Army." *New York World-Telegram*, December 4, 1941.

"Pressure? Aaron Stopped It Quickly." *Long Beach (CA) Press-Telegram*, April 5, 1974.

Rennie, Rud. "Silvestri Valued by Yankees for His Pinch-Hitting Power." *New York Herald Tribune*, March 29, 1941.

"Silvestri Again Civilian." *New York Times*, November 20, 1945.

"Silvestri Big Factor in '49 Phillies Plans." *Bradford (PA) Era*, February 24, 1949.

"Silvestri Rests Well after Appendectomy." *New York World-Telegram*, May 19, 1941.

"Sox Assign Lee to Face Browns and Harris Today." *Chicago Daily Tribune*, June 28, 1939.

Vaughn, Irving. "Dykes Has Mind Made Up on His Staf [sic] of Hurlers." *Chicago Daily Tribune*, March 9, 1939.

———. "Mud Is Too Deep, So Sox, Tigers Have Day's Rest." *Chicago Daily Tribune*, April 20, 1939.

———. "Sox End Camp Labor Today; It's 'Play Ball' from Now On." *Chicago Daily Tribune*, March 16, 1939.

———. "Yankees Blast Out 19 Hits Off 3 Sox Pitchers." *Chicago Daily Tribune*, May 8, 1939.

"Where Have You Been: Silvestri Was on Leyte under Gen. Eichelberger." *New York World-Telegram*, May 18, 1946.

"Yankees Trade Knickerbocker." *New York World-Tele-gram*, December 31, 1940.

Silvestri, Kenneth, Jr. Interview by the author. March 28, 2011.

20. Mel Queen

1. Will Wedge, *New York Sun*, February 25, 1942.
2. Dan Daniel, *New York World-Telegram*, September 14, 1944.

Bourke, Thomas. Conversation with Gail Queen, widow of Melvin Douglas Queen, on July 12, 2011.

Queen, Melvin Douglas. Interview by the author. February 25, 2011.

22. Al Lyons

Milwaukee Brewers Media Guide, 1948.

Phillips, John. *The Story of Al Lyons.* Kathleen GA: Capital, 2006.

Worcester Telegram. Game coverage for 1948 season.

23. Tommy Henrich

1. Golenbock, *Dynasty.*
2. Daley, "Rediscovery of Henrich."
3. Smith, "Tommy Henrich Gives His View."
4. Daley, "Rediscovery of Henrich."
5. Drebinger, "Revised Line-Up Shakes Slump."
6. "Yankees Report Henrich in Fold."
7. Dawson, "Henrich in Game at Gehrig's Post."
8. Dawson, "Henrich Set to Try New Yankee Post."
9. Kieran, "Best Ever in Baseball."
10. "Tommy Henrich Dies at 96."
11. Will, *Men at Work.*
12. Daley, "Rediscovery of Henrich."
13. Goldstein, "Tommy Henrich, Yankees Clutch Hitter."
14. Daley, "End of a Career."
15. Goldstein, "Tommy Henrich, Yankees Clutch Hitter."

16. Gallagher, *The Yankee Encyclopedia.*
17. Goldstein, "Tommy Henrich, Yankees Clutch Hitter."

Gallagher, Mark. *The Yankee Encyclopedia.* Champaign IL: Sagamore, 1996.

Golenbock, Peter. *Dynasty: The New York Yankees, 1949–1964.* Englewood Cliffs NJ: Prentice-Hall, 1975.

Henrich, Tommy, with Bill Gilbert. *Five O'Clock Lightning: Ruth, Gehrig, DiMaggio, Mantle, and the Glory Years of the NY Yankees.* New York: Birch Lane Press, 1992.

Okrent, Daniel, and Harris Lewine, eds. *The Ultimate Baseball Book.* Boston: Houghton Mifflin, 1979.

Pietrusza, David. *Judge and Jury: The Life and Times of Judge Kenesaw Mountain Landis.* South Bend IN: Diamond Communications, 1998.

Roth, Philip. *Goodbye, Columbus, and Five Short Stories.* Boston: Houghton Mifflin, 1959.

Schiffer, Don, ed. *World Series Encyclopedia.* New York: Thomas Nelson and Sons, 1961.

Thorn, John, Pete Palmer, Michael Gershman, and David Pietrusza. *Total Baseball.* 6th ed. New York: Total Sports, 1999.

Vincent, Fay. *The Only Game in Town: Baseball Stars of the 1930s and 1940s Talk about the Game They Loved.* New York: Simon and Schuster, 2006.

Waldman, Frank. *Eleventh Series of Famous American Athletes of Today.* Boston: L. C. Page, 1949.

Will, George. *Men at Work: The Craft of Baseball.* New York: Macmillan, 1990.

Henrich, Tommy. "Hot to Hit." *Boys' Life,* July 1946.

Henrich, Tommy, as told to George Vass. "The Game I'll Never Forget." *Baseball Digest,* January 1972.

Steadman, John F. "Value of a Yankee Uniform." *Baseball Digest,* March 1962.

Wade, Dick. "Humor of the Game Recalled by Henrich." *Baseball Digest,* July 1970.

Briordy, William J. "Henrich to Do TV Sports Show with Russ Hodges on Channel 7." *New York Times,* December 18, 1951.

Daley, Arthur. "The Rediscovery of Tommy Henrich." *New York Times,* November 3, 1971.

———. "Sports of the Times: End of a Career." *New York Times,* December 20, 1950.

———. "Sports of the Times: Two Tough Guys." *New York Times*, September 29, 1953.

Dawson, James P. "Henrich, Shifted to Class 1 by Draft Board, May Be Lost to Yanks This Year." *New York Times*, January 28, 1942.

———. "Henrich in Game at Gehrig's Post; Barrow Observes Work Closely." *New York Times*, March 23, 1939.

———. "Henrich Retires as an Active Player to Take Yankee Coaching Post." *New York Times*, December 19, 1950.

———. "Henrich's Batting Helps Yanks Score." *New York Times*, May 17, 1937.

———. "Henrich Set to Try New Yankee Post." *New York Times*, March 3, 1941.

———. "Rolfe Drives Two as Yanks Win, 9–4." *New York Times*, April 25, 1940.

———. "Yankees Again Grooming Henrich as Understudy for Dahlgren at First Base." *New York Times*, March 8, 1940.

———. "Yanks Try Henrich as Infielder Again." *New York Times*, March 9, 1939.

"Dodger Pilot Decision Is Expected This Week." *New York Times*, November 17, 1953.

Drebinger, John. "Henrich of Yankees Signs for $45,000." *New York Times*, January 19, 1950.

———. "Revised Line-Up Shakes Slump and Yankees Down Browns, 4–2." *New York Times*, May 14, 1937.

———. "White Sox Victors over Yankees, 7–2." *New York Times*, May 12, 1937.

———. "Yankees' Henrich Sent to Hospital." *New York Times*, April 11, 1950.

"Financial and Business Sidelights of the Day." *New York Times*, May 21, 1954.

Goldstein, Richard. "Tommy Henrich, Yankees Clutch Hitter, Dies at 96." *New York Times*, December 2, 2009.

"Henrich Gets Royals Post." *New York Times*, July 6, 1968.

"Henrich Resigns Post as Coach with Giants." *New York Times*, September 30, 1957.

"Henrich to Resume TV Work." *New York Times*, February 5, 1956.

Kieran, John. "Sports of the Times: The Yankees; The Best Ever in Baseball." *New York Times*, September 20, 1938.

"Landis Will Air Deal for Henrich." *New York Times*, March 31, 1937.

Lohman, Sidney. "News of TV and Radio." *New York Times*, April 26, 1953.

"Magazine Honors 49's Top Athletes." *New York Times*, January 20, 1950.

McGowen, Roscoe. "Henrich, Former Yankee Star, Signs Contract to Join Giants' Coaching Staff." *New York Times*, November 1, 1956.

———. "Henrich, Seen through as Yank Regular, Rejects Minor League Job." *New York Times*, November 10, 1950.

"Radio-TV Notes." *New York Times*, April 30, 1954.

Schudel, Matt. "Yankees 'Old Reliable' Delivered When It Counted." *Washington Post*, December 3, 2009.

Smith, Red. "The Glory of Their Times: T. Henrich." *New York Times*, May 31, 1972.

———. "Sports of the Times: Tommy Henrich, Very Patient Man." *New York Times*, January 3, 1982.

———. "Sports of the Times: Tommy Henrich Gives His View." *New York Times*, February 18, 1981.

"Tigers, Aiming for Lively Attack, Sign Henrich as Batting Coach." *New York Times*, November 1, 1957.

"Tommy Henrich Dies at 96; New York Yankees Star." *Los Angeles Times*, December 2, 2009.

"Yankees Report Henrich in Fold." *New York Times*, February 22, 1938.

Baseball Necrology. http://thebbnlive.com.

"Former Massillon, Yankees Star Tommy Henrich Dies at 96." http://www.cantonrep.com.

24. Frank Colman

1. "Yank Castoff Refuses to Join Bears."
2. "Yank Castoff Refuses to Join Bears."
3. "Yank Castoff Refuses to Join Bears."

Baseball Digest, September 1948.

"Baseball Leafs Buy First-Sacker Fleming." *Toronto Globe and Mail*, October 17, 1950.

"Colman Is Daddy." *Toronto Globe and Mail*, August 3, 1943.

"Colman Signs with Bears; No Series Share Promised." *Sporting News*, August 20, 1947.

Drebinger, John. "Marchildon Wins from Bomber, 6–1." *New York Times*, April 16, 1947.

Effrat, Louis. "Tigers Halt Bombers, 4–1, 12–11, before 58,369, a Detroit Record." *New York Times*, July 21, 1947.

———. "Yanks Defeat Athletics, 4–3, 7–4, Chandler Gaining 19th of Season." *New York Times*, September 23, 1946.

"Reject Frank Colman." *Toronto Globe and Mail*, March 20, 1944.

"Wilmington Drops 11 Players, and Acquires Five in Shakeup." *Sporting News*, April 18, 1940.

"Yank Castoff Refuses to Join Bears." *St. Petersburg (FL) Times*, August 10, 1947.

Canadian Baseball Hall of Fame. http://baseballhalloffame.ca.

Eager Beaver Baseball Association. http://www.ebba.ca.

Intercounty League material in the 1950s. http://www.attheplate.com.

Bourke, Thomas. Two telephone conversations with Mrs. Joan Fraser Frank (Frank Colman's sister), November 15, 2011.

Colman, Frank D. [Frank Colman's sign]. Interview by the author.

25. Tommy Byrne

All quotes are from Madden, *Pride of October*.

Forker, Dom. *The Men of Autumn: An Oral History of the 1949–53 World Champion New York Yankees*. Dallas: Taylor, 1989.

Frommer, Harvey. *New York City Baseball*. New York: Macmillan, 1980.

Golenbock, Peter. *Dynasty: The New York Yankees, 1949–1964*. Englewood Cliffs NJ: Prentice-Hall, 1975.

Halberstam, David. *Summer of '49*. New York: Morrow, 1989.

Honig, Donald. *The October Heroes*. New York: Simon and Schuster, 1979.

Kahn, Roger. *The Era: 1947–1957, When the Yankees, the Giants, and the Dodgers Ruled the World*. New York: Houghton Mifflin, 1993.

Lally, Richard. *Bombers: An Oral History of the New York Yankees*. New York: Three Rivers Press, 2002.

Madden, Bill. *Pride of October: To Be Young and a Yankee*. New York: Warner Books, 2003.

Rizzuto, Phil, and Tom Horton. *The October Twelve: The Years of Yankee Glory, 1949–1953*. New York: Forge, 1994.

Strauss, Frank. *Dawn of a Dynasty*. Lincoln: University of Nebraska Press, 2008.

Byrne, Tommy. Obituary. *Baltimore Sun*, December 23, 2007.

Hoch, Bryan. Tommy Byrne obituary. http://www.thedeadballera.com.

Benesch, John (information on Byrne's 1953–54 season in Venezuela). Interview by the author.

Bourke, Thomas. Telephone conversations with Susan B. Gantt (Byrne's daughter). July 11, July 21, and August 15, 2011.

Kardash, Mike [former professional baseball player]. Telephone interview by the author. February 5, 2010.

Nemec, Ray (information on Byrne's semipro career in North Carolina). Interview by the author.

Russo, Frank (information about Byrne playing in old-timers games at Yankee Stadium). Interview by the author.

Salazar, Anthony, former chairman of SABR's Latino Committee. Interview by the author.

26. Aaron Robinson

A special thank-you to Gary Harris, genealogy assistant, Lancaster County Library, Lancaster SC.

Barber, Red. *1947: When All Hell Broke Loose in Baseball*. New York: Da Capo Press, 1982.

Barra, Allen. *Yogi Berra: Eternal Yankee*. New York: W. W. Norton, 2009.

Gallagher, Mark. *The Yankee Encyclopedia*. Champaign IL: Sagamore, 1996.

Gentile, Derek. *The Complete New York Yankees*. New York: Black Dog and Leventhal, 2001.

Madden, Bill. *Pride of October: What It Was to Be Young and a Yankee*. New York: Warner Books, 2003.

Spatz, Lyle. *Yankees Coming, Yankees Going*. Jefferson NC: McFarland, 2000.

Chicago Sun-Times

28. Billy Johnson

Special thanks to Brenda Johnson Prince for helping me contact her mother, Louise Robinson Johnson. In telephone interviews conducted on October 28 and December 9, 2010, Mrs. Johnson was an incredible source of colorful information about her husband and his career. She died on December 27, 2010.

1. Harold Burr, *Sporting News*, October 14, 1943.
2. Burr, *Sporting News*.
3. Forker, *Men of Autumn*.
4. Peary, *We Played the Game*.
5. Forker, *Men of Autumn*.
6. Burr, *Sporting News*.
7. Peary, *We Played the Game*.
8. Peary, *We Played the Game*.
9. Forker, *Men of Autumn*.
10. Forker, *Men of Autumn*.

Forker, Dom. *The Men of Autumn: An Oral History of the 1949–53 World Champion New York Yankees.* Dallas: Taylor, 1989.
Peary, Danny. *We Played the Game: 65 Players Remember Baseball's Greatest Era, 1947–1964.* New York: Hyperion Books, 1994.

New York Times
Sporting News
Titusville (PA) Herald

29. Randy Gumpert

1. Fehler, *Baseball's Golden Age*, 76.
2. Debs, "Randy Gumpert," 92.
3. Debs, "Randy Gumpert," 92.
4. Debs, "Randy Gumpert," 92.
5. Debs, "Randy Gumpert," 92.
6. *New York Sun*, July 16, 1949.
7. Fehler, *Baseball's Golden Age*, 78.
8. Debs, "Randy Gumpert," 94.

Barthel, Thomas. *Baseball Barnstorming and Exhibition Games, 1901–1962: A History of Offseason Major League Play.* Jefferson NC: McFarland, 2007.
Fehler, Gene. *More Tales from Baseball's Golden Age.* Champaign IL: Sports Publishing, 2002.
Greenberg, Robert A. *"Swish" Nicholson: A Biography of Wartime Baseball's Leading Slugger.* Jefferson NC: McFarland, 2008.
James, Bill, and Rob Neyer. *The Neyer/James Guide to Pitchers: An Historical Compendium of Pitching, Pitchers, and Pitches.* New York: Fireside, 2004.
Vincent, David, Lyle Spatz, and David W. Smith. *The Midsummer Classic: The Complete History of Baseball's All-Star Game.* Lincoln: University of Nebraska Press, 2001.

Allen, Phil. "Cubs Pace Majors in Brisk Midyear Player Turnover." *Baseball Digest*, July 1957, 94.
Debs, Victor, Jr. "Randy Gumpert." *National Pastime* 19 (1999): 91–94.
O'Brien, Jim. "Doc Medich: He's Good Medicine for the Yankees." *Baseball Digest*, February 1975, 72.

Gumpert, Randy, and Ann Gumpert. Interview by the author, June 11, 2007.

Ceresi, Frank, and Carol McMains. "Mickey Charles Mantle: May 1, 1951: A Career Begins . . ." FC Associates, http://www.fcassociates.com/ntmantle.htm (accessed March 28, 2011).

30. Charlie Keller

1. When Keller was later at Newark, in May 1938, the press observed that the soon-to-be Yankee superstar was "one of the few young fellows who wanted to be a catcher." Also, as detailed by author David Halberstam in his book *Summer of '49*, when Yankees power pitcher Tommy Byrne, who led the American League in walks for three consecutive years, struggled to harness his wildness, "everyone tried to help with his control problem. Even Charlie Keller," Halberstam wrote, who was then physically a shell of what he had been, "would put on a catcher's mitt hoping to help [Byrne] develop a better sense of the target" (216).

2. Keller was elected to the University of Maryland Athletics Hall of Fame in 1982.

3. About Keller the basketball player, Maryland coach Burton Shipley, who coached him in both basketball and baseball for two varsity seasons, said Keller "played basketball with a gorilla's abandon" and "would do almost anything to get hold of the ball." Shipley said Keller "wanted the ball more than anyone I ever coached." As

a junior in 1936, Keller was named All-Southern Conference as a guard and also served as team captain.

4. *Frederick (MD) News*, March 31, 1935.

5. In 1983 Keller was elected to the initial class of the Kinston Professional Baseball Hall of Fame.

6. Writers have suggested Keller was paid a bonus of twenty-five hundred to seventy-five hundred dollars, but in a *Frederick (MD) Post* article from January 12, 1938, Keller claimed McCann gave him "just a couple of hundred dollars."

7. *Frederick (MD) News-Post*, June 3, 1939.

8. *Frederick (MD) News-Post*, March 5, 1939.

9. *Frederick (MD) News-Post*, April 19, 1938.

10. *Frederick (MD) News-Post*, August 23, 1937.

11. *Frederick (MD) News-Post*, May 24, 1938.

12. In 1947 Keller was named to the inaugural class of the International League Hall of Fame.

13. *Sporting News*, March 16, 1939.

14. *Sporting News*, March 9, 1939.

15. SABR Oral History Committee interview of Keller by Crissey.

16. In four World Series, totaling nineteen games, Keller batted a combined .306, with five home runs, eighteen RBIs, a .367 OBP, and a .611 slugging percentage.

17. When Keller left the University of Maryland to sign with the Yankees, the Associated Press described him as "Charlie (King Kong) Keller, ace slugger of the University of Maryland's baseball team" (see, for instance, *Reading (PA) Eagle*, March 21, 1937). In *Summer of '49*, author David Halberstam related that although Keller was one of the quietest Yankees, he was also "intimidating physically." When Phil Rizzuto once dared to call Keller King Kong, Keller picked up Rizzuto "with one massive arm" and stuffed the shortstop in an empty locker.

18. Gross, "Charlie Keller's Comeback."

19. SABR Oral History Committee interview of Keller by Crissey.

20. Gross, "Charlie Keller's Comeback."

21. In a February 1946 article in *Baseball Digest*, it was written of Keller that "chances are he will never hit .300 consistently; he swings too hard at too many bad pitches." In a July 1948 issue of *Baseball Magazine*, Keller was listed with, among others, Jeff Heath and Hal Trosky as "consistent first-ball hitters," and in his 1973 oral interview, when asked if he preferred to hit a fastball, Keller responded, "I would rather they threw it straight, yeah."

22. Actually, according to Halberstam, Keller admitted to just one career regret: he "regretted being made a pull-hitter. He and his teammates were sure it had cost him 30 points in average."

23. In both 1957 and '59, Keller returned to the Yankees as a coach.

24. Keller's two sons, Charlie Jr. and Donald, were also ballplayers, and Keller managed their Little League teams. Both went on to careers in the Yankees' Minor League system before back injuries similar to their father's ended their careers. Charlie played four seasons, and Donald played three seasons.

Cramer, Richard Ben. *Joe DiMaggio: The Hero's Life.* New York: Simon and Schuster, 2000.

Creamer, Robert W. *Stengel: His Life and Times.* New York: Simon and Schuster, 1984.

Greenberg, Hank. *The Story of My Life.* Edited by Ira Berkow. Chicago: Times Books, 1989.

Halberstam, David. *Summer of '49.* New York: William Morrow, 1989.

Ungrady, David. *Tales from the Maryland Terrapins: A Collection of the Greatest Stories Ever Told.* Champaign IL: Sports Publishing, 2003.

Frank, Stanley. "Muscles in His Sweat." *Baseball Digest*, February 1946.

Gross, Milton. "Charlie Keller's Comeback." *Sportfolio*, September 1948.

Rumill, Ed. "Hitting the First Pitch." *Baseball Magazine*, July 1948.

Baltimore Sun
Burlington (NC) Daily Times-News
Cumberland (MD) Evening Times
Frederick (MD) News-Post
Hagerstown (MD) Daily Mail
Hagerstown (MD) Morning Herald
Kingsport (TN) Times
Lowell (MA) Sun
Middletown (MD) Times Herald
Monessen (PA) Daily Independent

http://en.wikipedia.org/wiki/List_of_Kinston_base
ball_people#Kinston_Professional_Baseball_Hall_
of_Fame

http://www.oddsonracing.com/docs/
YankeelandFarmClosesMay1506

http://www.tomdunkel.com/portfolio/article

http://www.umterps.com/trads/md-wall-of-fame.html

Keller, Charlie. Interview by Kit Crissey, SABR Oral History Committee. February 10, 1973.

Remsberg, Jack [Charlie Keller's cousin]. Interview by the author. July 2, 2009.

31. Ted Sepkowski

1. The 1922 date for Sepkowski's date of birth is not certain. The Hall of Fame questionnaire he filled out says 1923. However, the Social Security Death Index lists a date of 1922. His obituary in the *Baltimore Sun*, his former employer, said he was seventy-nine at his time of death, which implied that he was born in 1922. 1920 U.S. Census.

2. *Baltimore Sun*, June 28, 1999.

3. Sepkowski interview; *Sporting News*, July 30, 1942; *Baltimore Sun*, June 28, 1999; Williams, *So Many Summer Fields*, 75.

4. Sepkowski interview; *Baltimore Sun*, February 9, 1997.

5. *Glens Falls (NY) Post-Star*, August 5, 1942; *Sporting News*, July 30, 1942; *Syracuse (NY) Herald-Journal*, June 24, 1942.

6. *Sporting News*, July 30, 1942; *Baltimore Sun*, February 9, 1997; *Cleveland Plain Dealer*, February 23, 1946.

7. Sam Otis, *Cleveland Plain Dealer*, April 2, 1942.

8. *Baltimore Sun*, June 28, 1999; *Sporting News*, July 30, August 20, 1942.

9. *Sporting News*, August 20, 1942.

10. *Cleveland Plain Dealer*, July 20, 1942; *Sporting News*, July 30, 1942.

11. *Glens Falls (NY) Post-Star*, August 5, 1942; *Dallas Morning News*, August 2, 1942; *Sporting News*, July 30, 1942.

12. *Syracuse (NY) Herald-Journal*, June 24, 1942; *Sporting News*, September 17, 1942.

13. *Sporting News*, August 20, 1942.

14. *Titusville (PA) Herald*, September 10, 1942.

15. *Cleveland Plain Dealer*, September 21, 1944.

16. *Baltimore Sun*, February 9, 1997.

17. *Sporting News*, December 18, 1946.

18. *Daily Sitka (AK) Sentinel and Arrowhead Press*, March 26, 1955; Forker, *Men of Autumn*, 168.

19. *Sporting News*, January 11, 1956.

20. Sepkowski interview; *Sporting News*, January 11, 1956; *Baltimore Sun*, March 14, 2002; *Annapolis (MD) Capital*, March 11, 2002; Williams, *So Many Summer Fields*, 76.

21. *Baltimore Sun*, March 14, 2002; *Annapolis (MD) Capital*, March 11, 2002.

Forker, Don. *The Men of Autumn: An Oral History of the 1949–53 World Champion New York Yankees.* Dallas: Taylor, 1989.

Williams, Douglas. *So Many Summer Fields.* Bloomington IN: Author House, 2005.

Annapolis (MD) Capital
Baltimore Sun
Cleveland Plain Dealer
Daily Sitka (AK) Sentinel and Arrowhead Press
Dallas Morning News
Glens Falls (NY) Post-Star
Sporting News
Syracuse (NY) Herald-Journal
Titusville (PA) Herald

Sepkowski, Ted. Interview by David Paulson. March 29, 1999.

32. Frank Shea

Special thanks to Frank Shea and Joe Palladino.

Cramer, Richard Ben. *Joe DiMaggio: The Hero's Life.* New York: Simon and Schuster, 2000.

Daniel, Dan. "Hats Off . . . !" *Sporting News*, June 18, 1947.

———. "Shea Seeks 20-Game Circle with New Fadeaway Pitch." *New York World-Telegram*, March 5, 1948.

Goldstein, Richard. "Frank Shea, 81, Yankee Pitcher in '47 Series." *New York Times*, July 23, 2002.

Harrison, Don. "Growing Up with a Naugatuck Legend." *Naugatuck (CT) Patch*, July 28, 2011.

———. "Loquacious Shea Was a Wit." *Fairfield (CT) Citizen-News*, July 26, 2002.

———. "Memories of a Memorable Yankee Year." *New York Times*, October 23, 1995.

———. "Shea: Page Was the Best." *Waterbury (CT) Republican*, April 27, 1980.

———. "Spec's Era Tamer." *Waterbury (CT) Republican*, May 23, 1976.

Heinz, W. C. "Harris Grooms Shea for the Series." *New York Sun*, September 17, 1947.

Palladino, Joe. "'Spec' Shea, Yanks' Naugatuck Nugget, Dies." *Waterbury (CT) Republican-American*, July 20, 2002.

Parker, Dan. "Shea of Yanks Making Dad's Dream Come True." *New York Mirror*, March 24, 1947.

———. "Timing Made Shea Day Anti-Climax." *New York Mirror*, June 23, 1947.

Povich, Shirley. "Shea of Nats Is Newsom Character with Class." *Washington Post*, May 25, 1952.

———. "This Morning." *Washington Post*, June 30, 1947.

Scannell, Ed. "Connecticut Yankee." *Worcester (MA) Telegram and Gazette*, 1948 (no month or day indicated).

Siegel, Morris. "Shea as Senator Back in Freshman Form." *Sporting News*, July 30, 1952.

Wedge, Will. "Shea to Rest Damaged Elbow." *New York Sun*, July 24, 1947.

Bourke, Thomas. Telephone conversation with Frank Shea's son, Frank. December 13, 2011.

33. Johnny Lucadello

1. Lucadello often gave the year of his birth as 1920, and that is the year that appears on his headstone. However, the 1920 U.S. Census shows him already one year old. Although local birth records confirm his birth as taking place in 1919, Lucadello himself was never sure of his birth year and played it safe by registering for the draft as a twenty-one-year-old in 1940.

2. Trowbridge, "Johnny Lucadello Achieved Ambition," 59.

3. Hanneman, *Diamonds in the Rough*, 12.

4. Trowbridge, "Johnny Lucadello Achieved Ambition," 59.

5. Scherwitz, "Fences Rattle for This Baby," 2:1.

6. Burris, "Browns Out of Last Place," 3.

7. Scherwitz, "Fences Rattle for This Baby," 2:2.

8. The other two were the Philadelphia Athletics' Wally Schang in 1916 and the Chicago Cubs' Augie Galan in 1937.

9. Kirksey, "Rookie Crop Is below Par," 11.

10. "Conyers to Barons," 31.

11. Trowbridge, "Johnny Lucadello Achieved Ambition," 59.

Hanneman, David V. *Diamonds in the Rough: The Legend and Legacy of Tony Lucadello*. Austin TX: Diamond Books, 1989.

Burris, Ward. "Browns Out of Last Place in Team Spirit." *Sporting News*, March 14, 1940.

"Conyers to Barons." *Berkshire Evening Eagle* (Pittsfield MA), June 20, 1952.

Kirksey, George. "Rookie Crop Is below Par for Major Leagues." *Rockford (IL) Morning Star*, August 12, 1941.

Scherwitz, Harold. "Fences Rattle for This Baby." *San Antonio Light*, July 30, 1939.

Trowbridge, John. "Johnny Lucadello Achieved Ambition." *San Antonio Light*, February 14, 1954.

35. Vic Raschi

1. *New York Times*, September 24, 1946.

2. Honig, *Baseball between the Lines*, 179.

3. Tommy Henrich, quoted in *New York Times*, February 23, 1954, 31; Coleman interview; Creamer, *Stengel*, 327.

4. Honig, *Baseball between the Lines*, 175; Berra, *Ten Rings*, 115.

5. Honig, *Baseball between the Lines*, 173.

Berra, Yogi, with Dave Kaplan. *Ten Rings: My Championship Seasons*. New York: Morrow, 2003.

Creamer, Robert. *Stengel: His Life and Times*. 1984. Reprint, Lincoln: University of Nebraska Press, 1996.

Gittleman, Sol. *Reynolds, Raschi, and Lopat: New York's Big Three and the Great Yankee Dynasty of 1949–1953*. Jefferson NC: McFarland, 2007.

Honig, Donald, ed. *Baseball between the Lines: Baseball in the Forties and Fifties as Told by the Men Who Played It*. 1976. Reprint, Lincoln: University of Nebraska Press, 1993.

Kahn, Roger. *The Era: 1947–1957, When the Yankees, the Giants, and the Dodgers Ruled the World.* New York: Ticknor and Fields, 1993.

New York Times
Springfield (MA) Republican

Coleman, Jerry. Interview by the author. September 1, 2005.

36. Reynolds and Raschi, Building Blocks of a Dynasty

1. Reynolds was eventually diagnosed with diabetes, and large doses of orange juice in 1947 solved his stamina problems.

2. Charlie Silvera, backup catcher to Berra during the great Yankees years, came up in 1949 and knew Dressen from the Pacific Coast League. His comment on Dressen as a pitching coach: "Dressen thought he knew everything about pitching, and he knew nothing. He would stop and tell the pitchers what they were doing wrong. He almost ruined Reynolds" (interview). Reynolds also had no use for Dressen: "Dressen would make himself look good by making you look bad" (Rizzuto, *The October Twelve*, 168). Ralph Branca, who pitched for Brooklyn when Dressen managed there in 1951, referred to him as "that piece of dreck Dressen," using a very unflattering Yiddish expression. Branca was not Jewish, but he found the right word (Kahn, *Era*, 107).

3. Raschi's "look" actually took the place of his pitching "up and in." Of the three Yankee greats of those teams, Vic hit the fewest batsmen in his career, a total of 25, far fewer than Allie Reynolds's 57 and even control pitcher Ed Lopat's 43. Reynolds would terrify opposing hitters with a fastball under the chin; Raschi would terrify them with his "look." Lopat would plunk any hitter who thought he was getting too smart for his own good. None of them approached the numbers of someone like Don Drysdale, who delighted in hitting 154 batters in his career.

4. Neft and Cohen, *Baseball*, 278.

5. At the start of the 1949 season, there was still uncertainty about Berra. The opening-day catcher was Gus Niarhos, and Berra was on the bench.

Frommer, Harvey. *New York City Baseball: The Last Golden Age, 1947–1957.* New York: Macmillan, 1980.

Gittleman, Sol. *Reynolds, Raschi, and Lopat: New York's Big Three and the Great Yankee Dynasty of 1949–1953.* Jefferson NC: McFarland, 2007.

Golenbock, Peter. *Dynasty: The New York Yankees, 1949–1964.* Englewood Cliffs NJ: Prentice-Hall, 1975.

Halberstam, David. *Summer of '49.* New York: William Morrow, 1989.

Kahn, Roger. *The Era: 1947–1957, When the Yankees, the Giants, and the Dodgers Ruled the World.* New York: Ticknor and Fields, 1993.

Lanctot, Neil. *Campy.* New York: Simon and Schuster, 2011.

Neft, David S., and Richard M. Cohen. *Baseball.* 14th ed. Sports Encyclopedia Series. New York: St. Martin's, 1994.

Rizzuto, Phil, with Tom Horton. *The October Twelve.* New York: Tom Doherty Associates, 1994.

Spatz, Lyle. *Yankees Coming, Yankees Going.* Jefferson NC: McFarland, 2000.

Brown, Dr. Bobby. Interview by the author. June 21, 2004.

Raschi, Sally. Interview by the author. June 27, 2004.

Silvera, Charlie. Interview by the author. August 19, 2004.

38. Bobo Newsom

The author is indebted to Tallulah Williams, cousin of Bobo Newsom, for e-mails and printed material about Newsom.

1. Jack Powell (245-254), who pitched for five teams between 1897 and 1912, was the other.

2. Newsom lost sixty-six games with Washington, his most with any team, but he had his lowest winning percentage with Philadelphia (.397).

3. Light, *Cultural Encyclopedia of Baseball*, 517.

4. Light, *Cultural Encyclopedia of Baseball*, 748.

5. Light, *Cultural Encyclopedia of Baseball*, 712.

6. E-mails from Tallulah Williams, cousin of Bobo Newsom.

7. Ray Kremer of the 1930 Pittsburgh Pirates was the first.

8. "Newsom's Father Taken by Death."

9. John Holway, *Baseball Gurus*, online.

10. Obituary, *New York Times*, December 8, 1962.

Coffin, Tristram P. *The Old Ball Game: Baseball in Folklore and Fiction.* New York: Herder and Herder, 1971.

Light, Jonathan Fraser. *The Cultural Encyclopedia of Baseball.* Jefferson NC: McFarland, 1997.

Neft, David S., Richard M. Cohen, and Michael L. Neft. *The Sports Encyclopedia: Baseball.* New York: St. Martin's, 2000.

Shatzkin, Mike, and Jim Charlton, eds. *The Ball Players.* New York: William Morrow, 1990.

Smith, Red. *Red Smith on Baseball.* Chicago: Ivan R. Dee, 2000.

Ross, Mike. "Hank Greenberg & Bobo." *National Pastime: A Review of Baseball History* 22 (2002): 124–28.

Addie, Bob. "Bobo Newsom, 55, Succumbs in Orlando." *Washington Post*, December 8, 1962.

"Bobo Newsom, Colorful Pitcher for 24 Years, Dies in Florida." *New York Times*, December 8, 1962.

"Newsom's Father Taken by Death after Seeing Son Defeat Reds." *Hartford (CT) Courant*, October 4, 1940.

Idea Logical Company. BaseballLibrary.com. http://www.baseballlibrary.com/homepage/ (accessed May 20, 2011).

39. Bobo in New York

1. Rizzuto interviews.

2. Rizzuto interviews.

3. Bobo Newsom, personal archive/scrapbook clipping, uncredited fragment: "DiMaggio is *a natural type to me, I see no reason why he should drop off*" (re: DiMaggio's sixty-two-game hitting streak), PCL, Los Angeles newspaper interview, August 15, 1933.

4. Rizzuto interviews.

5. Rizzuto interviews.

6. Morrow, "Rounding the Bases with Bobo."

7. Rizzuto interviews.

8. Morrow, "Rounding the Bases with Bobo."

9. Morrow, "Rounding the Bases with Bobo."

10. Lee Allen "Bobo" Newsom archives, Chattanooga.

11. Newsom archives.

12. Newsom archives, 1950, fragment, no additional citation.

13. Newsom interview.

14. Rizzuto interviews.

Morrow, Art. "Rounding the Bases with Bobo: Life & Times." Pt. 3 of 3. *Sporting News*, January 27, 1954.

Newsom, Mrs. Kay. Interview by the author.

Rizzuto, Phil. Two interviews by the author. Yankee Stadium, June 1987, 1988.

40. The Yankees' Nineteen-Game Winning Streak

1. Effrat, "Bombers' Two Big Innings."

2. Drebinger, "'Fully Recovered' Chandler Reports."

3. Dawson, "Yankees Vanquish Browns."

4. Effrat, "Shea and Yankees Stop Athletics."

5. Dawson, "Rain Halts Yanks at Comiskey Park."

6. Effrat, "Bombers Trip Indians."

7. Drebinger, "Parade Always Moves Forward."

James P. Dawson, "Rain Halts Yanks at Comiskey Park." *New York Times*, July 15, 1947.

———. "Yankees Vanquish Browns by 12–2, 8–5." *New York Times*, July 13, 1947.

Drebinger, John. "'Fully Recovered' Chandler Reports." *New York Times*, January 21, 1948.

———. "The Parade Always Moves Forward." *New York Times*, July 17, 1947.

Effrat, Louis. "Bombers Trip Indians by 9–4, 2–1, with Reynolds and Bevens in Box." *New York Times*, July 16, 1947.

———. "Bombers' Two Big Innings Conquer Athletics, 8–2, 9–2, before 51,957." *New York Times*, July 7, 1947.

———. "Shea and Yankees Stop Athletics, 5–1." *New York Times*, July 6, 1947.

42. Johnny Lindell

1. Johnny Lindell, personal letter, n.d.

2. "Barrow, Southworth, Williams."

3. Daniel, "Lindell Says He's on Yanks to Stay."

4. Daniel, "Lindell Gets McCarthy OK."

5. Daniel, "Lindell Again Fails in Big Test."

6. Williams, "Etten Deal Spotlights Yankee Problem."

7. Rud Rennie, *New York Herald Tribune*, June 8, 1943.

8. "Lindell Glad to Be Card."

9. King, "Veeck Gives Yank Arm Another Twist."
10. Associated Press, February 20, 1953.
11. Associated Press, February 20, 1953.
12. Lindell, "Los Angeles Boys Learn Baseball."

Lindell, Johnny. "Los Angeles Boys Learn Baseball from Big Leaguers." *Baseball Magazine*, August 1954.

Daniel, Dan. "Lindell Again Fails in Big Test." *New York World-Telegram*, August 5, 1942.
———. "Lindell Gets McCarthy OK for Yank Job." *New York World-Telegram*, March 26, 1942.
———. "Lindell Says He's on Yanks to Stay." *New York World-Telegram*, February 25, 1942.
"Barrow, Southworth, Williams Ranked as Outstanding in '41." *Sporting News*, January 1, 1942.
King, Joe. "Veeck Gives Yank Arm Another Twist." *New York World-Telegram*, February 23, 1949.
"Lindell Glad to Be Card; Hopes to Share Left Field." *New York World-Telegram*, May 16, 1950.
Williams, Joe. "Etten Deal Spotlights Yankee Problem." *New York World-Telegram*, March 18, 1943.

Associated Press
New York Herald Tribune

Bourke, Thomas. Telephone conversation with John Harlan Lindell III. August 6, 2011.

43. Karl Drews

1. Geraldine Garrison (daughter of Karl Drews), personal communication, March 2010.
2. Yuetter, "Karl Drews Fooled 'Em All," 41.
3. Yuetter, "Karl Drews Fooled 'Em All," 40.
4. David Kaplan (director, Yogi Berra Museum and Learning Center), e-mail, June 11, 2010; Yogi Berra, personal communication.
5. George Genovese, personal communication, December 7, 2010.
6. Garrison, personal communication.
7. Yuetter, "Karl Drews Fooled 'Em All," 41.
8. Garrison, personal communication.
9. *Sporting News*, February 7, 1946, 10.
10. *Dixon (IL) Evening Journal*, March 29, 1947.
11. *Sporting News*, April 20, 1947, 18.
12. "Karl Drews Gets a Son on Series Debut Day."
13. Squier, "Sport Trail."
14. Squier, "With Karl Drews in Game Six," 17.
15. Gross, "Operation for Victory," 30.
16. Yuetter, "Karl Drews Fooled 'Em All," 15, 40.
17. Garrison, e-mail, June 23, 2010.
18. Gross, "Operation for Victory," 29–31.
19. Karl Drews, letter to daughter, May 11, 1960.
20. Squier, "Karl Drews' Death Shocks Sports World"; obituary, *Staten Island Advance*, August 17, 1963.

Gross, Milton. "Operation for Victory: Skull Fracture Turned Drews into Winner" (condensed from *New York Post*). *Baseball Digest*, May 1953.
Yuetter, Frank. "Karl Drews Fooled 'Em All: He Went the Distance." *Baseball Magazine*, September 1953.

"Karl Drews Gets a Son on Series Debut Day." *Staten Island Advance*, October 3, 1947.
Squier, Hal J. "Karl Drews' Death Shocks Sports World." *Staten Island Advance*, August 16, 1963.
———. "Sport Trail." *Staten Island Advance*, October 3, 1947.
———. "With Karl Drews in Game Six." *Staten Island Advance*, October 6, 1947.

Dixon (IL) Evening Journal
Staten Island Advance

44. Yogi Berra

DeVito, Carlo. *Yogi: The Life and Times of an American Original*. Chicago: Triumph Books, 2008.
Hernandez, Keith, and Matthew Silverman. *Shea Goodbye: The Untold Story of the Historic 2008 Season*. Chicago: Triumph Books, 2009.
Lang, Jack, and Peter Simon. *The New York Mets: Twenty-Five Years of Baseball Magic*. New York: Henry Holt, 1986.
Palmer, Pete, and Gary Gillette, eds. *The 2005 ESPN Baseball Encyclopedia*. New York: Sterling, 2005.

http://www.achievement.org/autodoc/page/beroint-3

Koosman, Jerry. Interview by the author. December 16, 2008.

45. Johnny Schulte

Broeg, Bob. "Schulte: One of Baseball's Top Scouts." *St. Louis Post-Dispatch*, July 1, 1978.

Burns, Robert L. "Eagle Eye Johnny Schulte." *St. Louis Globe-Democrat*, July 4, 1978.

"Cubs Get Ed Baecht for 7 Players, Cash." *New York Times*, November 7, 1930.

Orthwein, Walter E. "Whatever Happened to Johnny Schulte." *St. Louis Post-Dispatch*, January 1978.

"Phils Release Ring Outright, Sell J. Schulte to Columbus." *New York Times*, January 6, 1929.

Russo, Neil. "John Schulte Recalls Happy Years as Scout." *St. Louis Post-Dispatch*, January 15, 1961.

Newyorkyankees.com
Wikipedia.com

46. Allie Clark

1. *Home News Tribune* (East Brunswick NJ), October 15, 1999.
2. *Home News Tribune* (East Brunswick NJ), October 15, 1999.
3. *Home News Tribune* (East Brunswick NJ), October 15, 1999.
4. Clark interview.
5. *New York Herald Tribune*, October 5, 1948.
6. *New York Times*, October 11, 2010.
7. *New York Times*, October 11, 2010.
8. *Home News Tribune* (East Brunswick NJ), February 2, 2003.
9. *Home News Tribune* (East Brunswick NJ), October 15, 1999.
10. Clark interview.
11. Clark interview.
12. Clark interview.
13. Clark interview.
14. Clark interview.
15. Clark interview.
16. Clark interview.
17. Allen, *Yankees*, 106–7.
18. Allen, *Yankees*, 106–7.
19. Clark interview.

Allen, Maury. *Yankees: Where Have You Gone?* Champaign IL: Sports Publishing, 2004.

Home News Tribune (East Brunswick NJ)
New York Herald Tribune
New York Times

Clark, Allie. Interview by the author. South Amboy NJ, May 17, 2011.

47. Joe DiMaggio

1. H RES 105 EH, 106th Congress, March 16, 1999.
2. Gould, "Streak of Streaks," 591.
3. *New York Daily News*, April 28, 1946.
4. *New York Times*, February 26, 1947.
5. *New York Times*, October 2, 1949.
6. *New York Daily News*, December 12, 1951.
7. *New York Times*, December 12, 1951; Jim Murray, *Los Angeles Times*, July 7, 1994.
8. Williams, *My Turn at Bat*, 209–10; Stan Musial, quoted in http://www.baseball-almanac.com; Red Smith, *New York Herald Tribune*, August 13, 1950.
9. Petrocelli interview.
10. "The Great DiMagg'."
11. Coleman interview.
12. Quoted in Allen, *Where Have You Gone*, 29.
13. Mario Cuomo and Mike Lupica quoted in *New York Daily News*, March 9, 1999; Lasorda interview.
14. Bamberger, "Dom DiMaggio," 110.
15. http://www.cnnsi.com, March 8, 1999; *New York Daily News*, March 9, 1999.

Allen, Maury. *Where Have You Gone, Joe DiMaggio? The Story of America's Last Hero.* New York: Dutton, 1975.

Baldassaro, Lawrence. *Beyond DiMaggio: Italian Americans in Baseball.* Lincoln: University of Nebraska Press, 2011.

Cramer, Richard Ben. *Joe DiMaggio: The Hero's Life.* New York: Simon and Schuster, 2000.

DiMaggio, Dom, with Bill Gilbert. *Real Grass, Real Heroes: Baseball's Historic 1941 Season.* 1990. Reprint, New York: Zebra Books, 1991.

Gould, Stephen Jay. "Streak of Streaks." In *Baseball: A Literary Anthology*, edited by Nicholas Dawidoff. New York: Library of America, 2002.

Johnson, Richard A., and Glenn Stout. *DiMaggio: An Illustrated Life.* New York: Walker, 1995.

Kahn, Roger. *The Era: 1947–1957, When the Yankees, the Giants, and the Dodgers Ruled the World.* New York: Ticknor and Fields, 1993.

Moore, Jack B. *Joe DiMaggio: Baseball's Yankee Clipper.* New York: Praeger, 1987.

Seidel, Michael. *Streak: Joe DiMaggio and the Summer of '41.* New York: McGraw-Hill, 1988.

Williams, Ted, as told to John Underwood. *My Turn at Bat: The Story of My Life.* 1969. Reprint, New York: Pocket Book, 1970.

Bamberger, Michael. "Dom DiMaggio." *Sports Illustrated*, July 2, 2001.

"The Great DiMagg'." *Washington Post*, July 2, 1941.

Los Angeles Times
New York Daily News
New York Herald Tribune
New York Times
Washington Post

http://www.baseball-almanac.com
http://www.cnnsi.com

Coleman, Jerry. Interview by the author. September 1, 2005.

Lasorda, Tommy. Interview by the author. January 19, 2001.

Petrocelli, Rico. Interview by the author. February 12, 2004.

49. Ralph Houk

1. "Ralph Houk, Yankees Manager Dies at 90," *New York Times*, July 21, 2010.
2. Houk and Dexter, *Ballplayers Are Human Too*, 28.
3. Houk and Dexter, *Ballplayers Are Human Too*, 32.
4. Houk and Dexter, *Ballplayers Are Human Too*, 34.
5. Houk and Dexter, *Ballplayers Are Human Too*, 39.
6. Houk and Dexter, *Ballplayers Are Human Too*, 45.
7. Holtzman, *No Cheering in the Press Box*, 11.
8. Koppett, *Man in the Dugout*, 191.
9. Houk and Dexter, *Ballplayers Are Human Too*, 50.
10. *Sporting News Magazine*, July 4, 2011, 31.

Allen, Kevin. *The People's Champion.* Wayne MI: Immortal Investments, 2004.

Billington, Ray A. *American History after 1865.* Lanham MD: Littlefield Adams, 1981.

Holtzman, Jerome, ed. *No Cheering in the Press Box.* New York: Henry Holt, 1995.

Houk, Ralph, and Robert W. Creamer. *Season of Glory.* New York: Pocket Books, 1989.

Houk, Ralph, and Charles Dexter. *Ballplayers Are Human Too.* New York: G. P. Putnam's Sons, 1962.

Karst, Gene, and Martin J. Jones Jr. *Who's Who in Professional Baseball.* New Rochelle NY: Arlington House, 1973.

Koppett, Leonard. *The Man in the Dugout.* Philadelphia: Temple University Press, 2000.

Miller, Jon, with Mark Hyman. *Confessions of a Baseball Purist.* Baltimore: Johns Hopkins University Press, 2000.

Pietrusza, David, Matthew Silverman, and Michael Gershman. *Baseball: The Biographical Encyclopedia.* New York: Total / Sports Illustrated, 2000.

The Sporting News Baseball Trivia Book. St. Louis: Sporting News, 1983.

Amore, Dom. blog.courant.com, July 23, 2010.

Bourke, Thomas. Telephone conversation with Robert Houk. August 21, 2011.

———. Telephone conversation with Donna Houk Slaboden. November 3, 2011.

50. Dan Topping

1. Coenen, *From Sandlots to the Super Bowl*, 120.
2. Daniel, "DeWitt in Line for the 'Big Job.'"
3. Linn, "Man in the Pin-Striped Suit."
4. Linn, "Man in the Pin-Striped Suit."
5. C. Spink, "Yanks Cop Trio of 'Bible' Prizes."
6. Koppett, "CBS Was Outbid."
7. Burns, "'Houk Best Pilot.'"

Armour, Mark. *Joe Cronin: A Life in Baseball.* Lincoln: University of Nebraska Press, 2010.

Bashe, Philip. *Dog Days: The New York Yankees' Fall from Grace and Return to Glory, 1964–1976.* San Jose CA: Authors Choice Press, 2000.

Coenen, Craig C. *From Sandlots to the Super Bowl.* Knoxville: University of Tennessee Press, 2005.

Creamer, Robert W. *Stengel: His Life and Times.* New York: Fireside, 1990.

Golenbock, Peter. *Dynasty: The New York Yankees, 1949–1964.* Englewood Cliffs NJ: Prentice-Hall, 1975.

Levitt, Daniel R. *Ed Barrow: The Bulldog Who Built the Yankees' First Dynasty.* Lincoln: University of Nebraska Press, 2008.

Meany, Tom. *The Yankee Story*. New York: E. P. Dutton, 1960.

Peterson, Robert W. *Pigskin: The Early Years of Pro Football*. Oxford: Oxford University Press, 1997.

Surdam, David G. *The Postwar Yankees: Baseball's Golden Age Revisited*. Lincoln: University of Nebraska Press, 2008.

Veeck, Bill, with Ed Linn. *The Hustlers Handbook*. New York: Fireside, 1989.

———. *Veeck as in Wreck*. New York: Fireside, 1989.

Burns, Jimmy. "'Houk Best Pilot Yanks Have Had in My Years with Club'—Topping." *Sporting News*, May 21, 1966.

Carroll, Bob. "How to Get from Dayton to Indianapolis by Way of Brooklyn, Boston, New York, Dallas, Hershey, and Baltimore." *Coffin Corner* [Professional Football Researchers Association] 17, no. 5 (1995).

Daniel, Dan. "DeWitt, as Aid to Weiss, in Line for the 'Big Job.'" *Sporting News*, May 5, 1954.

"Dan Topping Dead at 61; Yankee Owner 22 Years." *New York Times*, May 20, 1974.

"Experienced Youth Yankees' Key to Success, Says Lopat." *Sporting News*, October 3, 1963.

Gross, Milton. "Why Yanks Fired Bucky Harris." *Baseball Digest*, August 1951.

Grosshandler, Stan. "The Brooklyn Dodgers." *Coffin Corner* (Professional Football Researchers Association) 12, no. 3 (1990).

"Harry J. (Bob) Topping Dies; Was Heir to Tin Plate Fortune." *New York Times*, April 24, 1968.

Koppett, Leonard. "CBS Was Outbid, Topping Reveals." *New York Times*, February 19, 1965.

Linn, Ed. "The Man in the Pin-Striped Suit: Ralph Houk." *Saturday Evening Post*, September 28, 1963.

Lipsyte, Robert. "Yankees' Most Promising Rookie." *New York Times*, May 19, 1963.

Ray, Ralph. "Bomber Sale Stirs Bees' Nest of Boos." *Sporting News*, August 29, 1964.

Spink, C. C. Johnson. "Yanks Cop Trio of 'Bible' Prizes." *Sporting News*, January 3, 1962.

Spink, J. G. Taylor. "Battle of Biltmore: Victory Brawl." *Sporting News*, October 15, 1947.

Susskind, Arthur, Jr. "Topping, the Tycoon Who Makes Yankees Tick." *Sporting News*, January 3, 1962.

Williams, Roger. "Goodby, Casey, Goodby!" *Sports Illustrated*, October 31, 1960.

AAFC Chronology. http://www.profootballresearchers.org/AAFC/AAFC_Chronology.pdf.

51. Del Webb

1. Hopkins, "Del Webb."
2. Finnerty, *Del Webb*, 48.
3. Brown, "The Webb of Mystery."
4. Rosenthal, draft article, 1.
5. Dyer, "Del Tells Story," 13.
6. Chandler, "Gunned Down by the Heavies."
7. Brown, "The Webb of Mystery."
8. Dyer, "Del Tells Story," 20.
9. Dyer, "Del Webb," 20.
10. Young, unidentified clipping.
11. Finnerty, *Del Webb*, 84.
12. "Del Webb, Long an Associate of Organized Crime."

Armour, Mark. *Joe Cronin: A Life in Baseball*. Lincoln: University of Nebraska Press, 2010.

Creamer, Robert W. *Stengel: His Life and Times*. New York: Fireside, 1990.

Finnerty, Margaret. *Del Webb: A Man, a Company*. Flagstaff AZ: Heritage, 1991.

Golenbock, Peter. *Dynasty: The New York Yankees, 1949–1964*. Englewood Cliffs NJ: Prentice-Hall, 1975.

Katz, Jeff. *The Kansas City A's and the Wrong Half of the Yankees*. Hingham MA: Maple Street Press, 2007.

Levitt, Daniel R. *Ed Barrow: The Bulldog Who Built the Yankees' First Dynasty*. Lincoln: University of Nebraska Press, 2008.

Lieb, Frederick G. *The Baltimore Orioles*. Carbondale: Southern Illinois University Press, 2001.

Peterson, John E. *The Kansas City A's: A Baseball History, 1954–1967*. Jefferson NC: McFarland, 2003.

Shapiro, Michael. *Bottom of the Ninth*. New York: Times Books, Henry Holt, 2009.

Surdam, David G. *The Postwar Yankees: Baseball's Golden Age Revisited*. Lincoln: University of Nebraska Press, 2008.

Veeck, Bill, with Ed Linn. *The Hustlers Handbook*. New York: Fireside, 1989.

———. *Veeck as in Wreck*. New York: Fireside, 1989.

Brown, Joe David. "The Webb of Mystery." *Sports Illustrated*, February 29, 1960.

Chandler, A. B., with John Underwood. "Gunned Down by the Heavies." *Sports Illustrated*, May 3, 1971.

"Modern Living: Man on the Cover: Del Webb." *Time*, August 3, 1964.

Addie, Bob. *Washington Post*, October 21, 1954.

"Del Webb: Long an Associate of Organized Crime." *Elyria (OH) Chronicle-Telegram*, March 19, 1977.

Dyer, Braven. "Del Tells Story behind Yank Pilot Shifts." *Sporting News*, April 17, 1965.

———. "Del Webb: Strong Man behind the Throne." *Sporting News*, April 10, 1965.

Hopkins, A. D. "Del Webb: Man of the Years." *Las Vegas Review-Journal*. http://www.1st100.com/part2/webb.

Ray, Ralph. "Bomber Sale Stirs Bees' Nest of Boos." *Sporting News*, August 29, 1964.

Vazquez, Lauren. "A Look Back at the Arizona Project." *Arizona Republic* (Phoenix), May 28, 2006. http://www.azcentral.com.

Drachman, Roy, Sr. *Just Memories: This Is Not a Book.* http://parentseyes.arizona.edu/drachman.

Rosenthal, Harold. Draft article for *Milwaukee Journal* on the 1957 World Series. Del Webb Baseball Hall of Fame file, Cooperstown NY.

Young, Dick. Unidentified clipping in the Del Webb Baseball Hall of Fame File, Cooperstown NY, October 24, 1964.

52. George Stirnweiss

1. Daley, "List of Distinction."
2. "City Title Is Won by Fordham Prep."
3. Kieran, "Heard in the Huddle."
4. Gaven, "Stirnweiss, Newarks' Nimble-Limbed Keystoner."
5. Drebinger, "The Man Who Never Walks."
6. Daley, "Local Boy Makes Good."
7. Daniel, "Yankees' Lineup Looks Formidable."
8. Dexter, "Bronx Express: Snuffy Stirnweiss."
9. Daley, "The Big Trade."
10. Daley, "The Big Trade."
11. "Snuffy Serves Notice He's after Regular Tribe Birth."
12. "Devine Gives Triple-A Tips to New Richmond Owners."
13. Tuckner, "Sox of '46 Top '47 Yankees."
14. Berkow, "Too Small to Play, Right Size for Hall."

Graham, Frank. *The New York Yankees: An Informal History.* New York: G. P. Putnam's Sons, 1943.

Spatz, Lyle, ed. *The SABR Baseball List and Record Book.* New York: Scribner, 2007.

Thorn, John, Pete Palmer, Michael Gershman, and David Pietrusza. *TotalBaseball.* 6th ed. New York: Total Sports, 1999.

Brady, James. "Brady's Bunch." *Advertising Age*, March 28, 1988.

Dexter, Charles. "Bronx Express: Snuffy Stirnweiss." *Baseball Digest*, January 1948.

"Sport: Pennant Parade." *Time*, September 11, 1944.

"Bears Break Even to Clinch Pennant." *New York Times*, August 31, 1942.

Berkow, Ira. "Too Small to Play, Right Size for Hall." *New York Times*, July 31, 1994.

"Biographical Sketches of Dead and Missing Passengers in Bayonne Wreck." *New York Times*, September 16, 1958.

Brands, Edgar G. "Jobs Open—4 of Them—on Brownies' Infield." *Sporting News*, February 15, 1950.

Brennan, John. "Sustained Drive for Touchdown Gives Brooklyn Prep Draw with Fordham Prep." *New York Times*, October 20, 1935.

"City Title Is Won by Fordham Prep." *New York Times*, June 16, 1935.

Daley, Arthur. "On College Gridirons." *New York Times*, November 16, 1939.

———. "Sports of the Times: List of Distinction." *New York Times*, September 29, 1958.

———. "Sports of the Times: Local Boy Makes Good." *New York Times*, June 2, 1945.

———. "Sports of the Times: Please Omit Flowers." *New York Times*, March 31, 1944.

———. "Sports of the Times: The Big Trade." *New York Times*, June 21, 1950.

———. "Trick Play Helps Fordham Beat North Carolina, 14–0." *New York Times*, October 31, 1937.

Daniel, Dan. "Champion Yankees to Stand or Fall on Legs of Their Vets." *Sporting News*, February 15, 1950.

———. "Ed Barrow One Up on Larry in Feud." *Sporting News*, August 20, 1942.

———. "High Cost of Living Hikes Salary Ideas of Yankees." *Sporting News*, February 15, 1945.

———. "No Razzberry by Yankees on Asbury Return." *Sporting News*, October 28, 1943.

———. "Snuffy, Fourth in Scribes' Poll, No. 1 in Yank Lineup." *Sporting News*, November 30, 1944.

———. "Snuffy's Winning Bat Drive No. 1 Individual Feat." *Sporting News*, November 29, 1945.

———. "Yankees' Lineup Looks Formidable, but Draft Calls Make It Vulnerable." *Sporting News*, March 29, 1945.

———. "Yanks Color Calls Open Race to All." *Sporting News*, March 23, 1944.

———. "Yank Tradition Upheld by Etten, Stirnweiss." *Sporting News*, September 27, 1945.

Danzig, Allison. "Veteran NYU Array Hopes to Put North Carolina Jinx to Rout on Saturday." *New York Times*, October 12, 1938.

Dawson, James P. "Bauer Helps Sain Beat Indians, 5–3." *New York Times*, May 15, 1952.

———. "Bonham Shuts Out Red Sox by 5 to 0." *New York Times*, April 29, 1943.

———. "Cronin of Red Sox Chats with Weiss." *New York Times*, January 17, 1950.

———. "Garbark's Single Caps Rally as Yankees Beat Dodgers in Eleventh." *New York Times*, April 3, 1944.

———. "Rally in the 7th." *New York Times*, April 23, 1944.

———. "Stirnweiss Choice of Yanks' Manager as Second Baseman." *New York Times*, March 19, 1944.

———. "Stirnweiss Named Lead-Off Man in Yanks' Batting Order." *New York Times*, April 1, 1943.

———. "Stirnweiss' Triple Enables Yankees to Halt Phils, 5–4." *New York Times*, April 2, 1944.

———. "Yankees Retain Title to Etten; Phillies to Get 2 Other Players." *New York Times*, March 26, 1943.

———. "Yankees Start Pennant Defense at Stadium by Beating Senators in Ninth." *New York Times*, April 23, 1943.

———. "Yankees Triumph over Red Sox, 12–2." *New York Times*, October 1, 1945.

———. "Yanks Welcome Trio of Rookies." *New York Times*, March 21, 1943.

Dean, Clarence. "40 Feared Dead as Train Dives Off Open Newark Bay Bridge; Sunken Cars Trap Commuters." *New York Times*, September 16, 1958.

"Devine Gives Triple-A Tips to New Richmond Owners." *Sporting News*, November 30, 1955.

Drebinger, John. "Rizzuto Named Player of Year by Writers; Giants Buy Hughson." *New York Times*, December 16, 1949.

———. "Schultz in Service on Capital Review." *New York Times*, March 8, 1945.

———. "Sports of the Times: The Man Who Never Walks." *New York Times*, August 4, 1944.

———. "Yanks Always Well Fortified behind Plate." *New York Times*, February, 21, 1959.

———. "Yanks Release Keller and Weigh Two Offers for Newark Franchise." *New York Times*, December 7, 1949.

———. "Yanks' Stirnweiss Voted 1945 Award in Writers' Poll." *New York Times*, January 20, 1946.

Flynn, Art. "Hal Edges Staff-Mate Paul Trout." *Sporting News*, November 30, 1944.

"Fordham Prep Victor." *New York Times*, February 2, 1936.

"Former Orphan Takes the Name Stirnweiss." *Red Bank (NJ) Daily Register*, October 7, 1968.

Gaven, Michael F. "Stirnweiss, Newarks' Nimble-Limbed Keystoner." *Sporting News*, August 20, 1942.

Goldberg, Hy. "Bears Hitting in True Embryo Yankee Style." *Sporting News*, March 27, 1941.

"International Loop Announces All-Stars." *New York Times*, July 2, 1942.

Kieran, John. "Sports of the Times: Heard in the Huddle." *New York Times*, November 15, 1938.

"MacPhail Plans Players' Bonus from Last Six Games of Yankees." *New York Times*, September 22, 1945.

Madden, Bill. "Generally Speaking, Boss Barrage Motivates Tino." *New York Daily News*, October 19, 1998.

"M'Burncy Routed by Fordham Prep." *New York Times*, November 2, 1935.

Murphy, Ken. "Sports Mill: Thanksgiving Day." *Fayetteville (NC) Observer*, November 29, 1939.

"North Carolina Wins on Passes." *New York Times*, October 23, 1938.

"Rejoins Yankees Today." *New York Times*, April 30, 1943.

Rokeach, Morrey. "Stirnweiss New Director of J-A Sand-
lot Activity." *Sporting News*, April 11, 1956.
Sills, JoAnne. "A Day Bayonne Can't Forget." *Newark
(NJ Star-Ledger*, September 14, 2008.
"Snuffy Fills in for Barillari." *Sporting News*, August
4, 1954.
"Snuffy Serves Notice He's after Regular Tribe Birth."
Sporting News, April 18, 1951.
"South Tops North in International." *New York Times*,
July 9, 1942.
"Stirnweiss, Ex-AL Hitting King, Killed in Rail Tragedy."
Sporting News, September 24, 1958.
"Stirnweiss and Combs Are Traded to Cleveland for
Marsh and $35,000." *Sporting News*, April 11, 1951.
"Stirnweiss Coaching Aide." *New York Times*, Decem-
ber 6, 1945.
"Stirnweiss Exam Put Off." *New York Times*, March
30, 1943.
"Stirnweiss Gets Pilot Job." *New York Times*, January
19, 1954.
"Stirnweiss Is Buried." *New York Times*, September 20,
1958.
"Stirnweiss Is Stricken." *New York Times*, June 25, 1957.
"Tar Heel Gridmen among Best." *Fayetteville (NC)
Observer*, November 1, 1939.
Tuckner, Howard M. "Sox of '46 Top '47 Yankees in Not-
So-Old-Timers' Contest." *New York Times*, August
10, 1958.
Verducci, Tom. "Value Judgment." *Sporting News*, Sep-
tember 30, 2002.
Williams, Joe. "Gordon, Stirnweiss Are Question Marks
in Yankees' Lineup." *Toledo (OH) Blade*, February
20, 1946.
"Yanks Buy 9 Players." *New York Times*, September
27, 1942.
"Yanks Get Ferrick in 8-Player Deal." *New York Times*,
June 16, 1950.
Young, Charley. "Stirnweiss Fired, Krausse Named Sche-
nectady Pilot." *Sporting News*, July 28, 1954.

Find a Grave. http://www.findagrave.com.
Fordham Preparatory School. http://www.fordhamprep
.org.
Hardball Times. http://www.hardballtimes.com.

53. Jack Phillips

1. *Syracuse (NY) Herald American*, June 12, 1988.
2. Brooks Conrad of the Atlanta Braves duplicated
the feat on May 20, 2010.
3. *Syracuse (NY) Herald American*, June 12, 1988.
4. Sharon Mohns, e-mail to Charles Faber, April 6, 2010.

Johnson, W. Lloyd, and Miles Wolff, eds. *Encyclopedia of Minor League Baseball*. Durham NC: Baseball America, 1993.
Palmer, Pete, and Gary Gillette, eds. *The Baseball Encyclopedia*. New York: Barnes and Noble, 2004.
Spatz, Lyle, ed. *The SABR Baseball List and Record
Book*. New York: Scribner, 2007.

E-mail correspondence with Sharon Mohns, Patty Roberts, and Tommy Szarka.

http://www.clarksonathletics.com

54. Phil Rizzuto

1. In a personal interview with the author on June 12,
1993, Rizzuto attributed the comment to Dodgers manager Casey Stengel, but Stengel was not in New York
when the incident occurred. In a *Sporting News* interview (May 1, 1941), Rizzuto cited a Giants coach as the
source of the comment. In his biography of Rizzuto, Gene
Schoor identified the coach as Pancho Snyder (*Scooter*, 7).
2. Rizzuto interview. Unless otherwise noted, all quotations by Rizzuto are from this interview.
3. *Sporting News*, May 1, 1941, 4.
4. According to testimony by Bernardo Pasquel, *New
York Times*, June 9, 1946.
5. *New York Times*, October 4, 1947.
6. *New York Times*, October 27, 1950.
7. *New York Times Book Review*, April 4, 1993, 26.
8. Coleman interview.
9. Creamer, *Stengel*, 237.
10. *New York Times*, September 19, 1955.
11. Coleman interview.
12. *New York Times*, September 19, 1955.

Creamer, Robert. *Stengel: His Life and Times*. 1984.
Reprint, Lincoln: University of Nebraska Press, 1996.
DeVito, Carlo. *Scooter: The Biography of Phil Rizzuto*.
Chicago: Triumph Books, 2010.

Hirshberg, Dan. *Phil Rizzuto: A Yankee Tradition.* Champaign IL: Sagamore Publishing, 1993.

Peyer, Tom, and Seely Hart, eds. *O Holy Cow! The Selected Verse of Phil Rizzuto.* Hopewell NJ: Ecco Press, 1993.

Schoor, Gene. *The Scooter: The Phil Rizzuto Story.* New York: Scribner, 1982.

New York Times
New York Times Book Review
Sporting News

Coleman, Jerry. Interview by the author. September 1, 2005.

Rizzuto, Phil. Interview by the author. June 12, 1993.

56. Sherman Lollar

1. From an unattributed clipping without a title, author, or date in Lollar's player file at the Baseball Hall of Fame, Cooperstown NY.

2. James, *Historical Baseball Abstract*, 394.

James, Bill. *The New Bill James Historical Baseball Abstract.* New York: Free Press, 2001.

"Dad Just Felt Lucky to Play the Game for a Living." *Fort Myers (FL) News-Press,* August 26, 2002. http://www.news-press.com/sports/today/p_020826lollar.html.

Daniel, Dan. "Experience Will Swing Flag for Us: Bucky." *New York Times,* August 4, 1948.

———. "Sherry's Series Hero on Stingy 0.75 ERA." *New York Times,* October 9, 1959.

———. "Winning Pitcher? Who Else but Casey?" *New York Times,* date illegible.

"Fleeing Finley." Publication unidentified, December 23, 1974.

Gleason, William "Red." "Is Lollar Better than Berra?" *Saturday Evening Post,* June 16, 1957, 36.

"Lollar's Bad Peg to Second His First Bobble of the Season." Publication unidentified, September 25, 1957.

"Lollar Sidelined as Injury Jinx Stays with Yanks." Publication and date unidentified.

Musburger, Brent. "Lollar Seeking Minor League Manager's Job." *Chicago American,* September 30, 1963.

"Narrow Escape for Lollar." Publication unidentified, June 20, 1970.

"Record Ejection." Publication unidentified, June 3, 1972.

Roeder, Bill. "Yankees Hope Lollar Will Catch Fire." Publication and exact date illegible, but from 1947.

"Sherman Lollar, an Ex-Catcher for White Sox, Is Dead at 53." *New York Times,* September 26, 1977.

Traber, Hugh, Jr. "When Orioles Are Perched on Bases, Baltimore Rooters Holler for Lollar." Publication unidentified, May 10, 1945.

57. Butch Wensloff

1. Wittick, "The Globe Trotter."

2. "Pitchers Show Dazzling Power."

3. Daniel, "Joe McCarthy Rings Welkin on Flinging."

4. "Wensloff Gets Off in Lead for 'Hard Luck' Crown."

5. Daniel, "Yankees Hippity-Hop Back East in Top Spot"; Spink, "Looping the Loops."

6. Daniel, "Harris High on Yankees' Incoming Mound Brigade."

7. Letter from Dr. James A. Dickson to Rudy Schafer, Cleveland Indians, May 15, 1948, from personal collection of Peter Wensloff.

8. Daniel, "15 Hurlers Scrambling for 10 Jobs."

Gallagher, Mark. *The Yankee Encyclopedia.* 6th ed. Champaign IL: Sports Publishing, 2003.

Gillette, Gary, Pete Palmer, and Greg Spira, eds. *The Ultimate Yankees Companion.* Dulles VA: Potomac Books, 2007.

Daniel, Dan. "15 Hurlers Scrambling for 10 Jobs on Yank Staff." *Sporting News,* April 7, 1948.

———. "Harris High on Yankees' Incoming Mound Brigade." *Sporting News,* November 27, 1946.

———. "Joe McCarthy Rings Welkin on Flinging." *Sporting News,* March 25, 1943.

———. "Yankees Hippity-Hop Back East in Top Spot." *Sporting News,* July 15, 1943.

"Pitchers Show Dazzling Power." *Toledo (OH) Blade,* April 20, 1940.

Spink, J. G. T. "Looping the Loops." *Sporting News,* July 29, 1943.

"Wensloff Gets Off in Lead for 'Hard Luck' Crown." *Sporting News,* July 1, 1943.

Wittick, Porter. "The Globe Trotter." *Joplin (MO) Globe,* March 22, 1940.

Chicago Daily Tribune
Daily Mail
El Paso (TX) Herald Post
Fresno Bee
Joplin (MO) Globe
Joplin (MO) News Herald
Lima (OH) News
Los Angeles Times
Marin (CA) Independent Journal
Milwaukee Journal
Oakland Tribune
Prescott (AZ) Evening Courier
Reno (NV) Evening Gazette
San Rafael (CA) Daily Independent Journal
St. Petersburg Times
Syracuse (NY) Herald Journal
Toledo (OH) Blade

58. Dick Starr

Young American Patriots: The Youth of Pennsylvania in World War II. Richmond VA: National Publishing, 1947.

Drebinger, John. "Bombers Beaten by Senators, 3–2." *New York Times,* September 6, 1947.
———. "Yankees Turn Back Browns, 8–3. Then Drop 8–2 Contest to Zoldak." *New York Times,* September 17, 1947.
McGowen, Roscoe. "Yanks Sign Shea for $16,000." *New York Times,* February 27, 1948.
"Senators Trade Sanford." *New York Times,* July 13, 1951.
"Starr Hurls His 2nd Shutout in Beating White Sox." *New York Times,* September 8, 1950.
"Starr's 7-Hitter Trips Boston." *New York Times,* August 11, 1951.

Bourke, Thomas. Telephone conversation with Dick Starr. July 16, 2011.

59. Lonny Frey

1. T. Frey interview.
2. L. Frey oral history interview.
3. *New York World-Telegram,* August 30, 1933.
4. *St. Louis Post-Dispatch,* August 23, 2005.
5. Kahn, *The Boys of Summer,* xiii.
6. *New York Sun,* May 27, 1936.
7. *New York Sun,* June 9, 1936; *Brooklyn Times-Union,* May 25, 1936.
8. Lonny Frey, National Baseball Hall of Fame and Museum player file, undated article, Cooperstown NY.
9. Frey, player file, undated article.
10. Frey, player file, undated article.
11. Frey, player file, undated article.
12. Frey oral history interview.
13. Frey oral history interview.
14. *Sports Collectors' Digest,* June 17, 1994, quoted in Mulligan, *The 1940 Cincinnati Reds,* 36.
15. Frey, player file, undated article.
16. Frey oral history interview.
17. Frey oral history interview.
18. Frey oral history interview.
19. "Former Major-Leaguer Lonnie Frey Dies."
20. *St. Louis Post-Dispatch,* August 23, 2005.

Kahn, Roger. *The Boys of Summer.* 1972. Reprint, New York: HarperCollins, 2006.
Mulligan, Brian. *The 1940 Cincinnati Reds.* Jefferson NC: McFarland, 2005.
Vitti, Jim. *Chicago Cubs: Baseball on Catalina Island.* Mount Pleasant SC: Arcadia, 2010.
Werber, Bill, and C. Paul Rogers III. *Memories of a Ballplayer: Bill Werber and Baseball in the 1930s.* Cleveland: Society for American Baseball Research, 2001.

"Former Major-Leaguer Lonnie Frey Dies." *Seattle Times,* September 16, 2009.

Brooklyn Eagle
Brooklyn Times-Union
Charlotte (NC) Magazine
Cincinnati Enquirer
New York Sun
New York World-Telegram
St. Louis Post-Dispatch

Ancestry.com. *1930 United States Federal Census* [online database]. Provo UT: Ancestry.com Operations, 2002.

Bedington, Gary. "Lonny Frey." In *Gary Bedington's Baseball in Wartime*. 2008. Accessed August 26, 2011.

Bourke, Thomas. Telephone conversations with Thomas Frey. September 20 and September 27, 2011.

Frey, Lonny. Oral history interview. August 27, 1991. Society for American Baseball Research Oral History Collection, Cleveland.

Frey, Thomas. Telephone interview by the author. August 29, 2011.

61. Bill Wight

Thanks to Jim Sandoval for scouting information. Thanks to Eileen Canepari.

1. Unattributed column by Will Wedge, March 31, 1946 in Wight's player file at the National Baseball Hall of Fame, Cooperstown NY.

2. *Sporting News*, December 17, 1958.

3. B. Wight interview. All quotations attributed to Wight are from this interview unless otherwise indicated.

4. Interview on July 14, 2005, available through the online American Association Almanac at http://www.americanassociationalmanac.com/billwight.php.

5. *New York World-Telegram*, March 1, 1946.

6. *Sporting News*, March 14, 1946.

7. Wedge clipping in the Wight's Hall of Fame player file. Mails was a left-handed pitcher with the Brooklyn Robins, Cleveland Indians, and St. Louis Cardinals in the teens and '20s and a longtime coach and scout afterward.

8. *New York Times*, February 26, 1948.

9. *Chicago Tribune*, February 26, 1948.

10. Online American Association Almanac.

11. *Sporting News*, February 7, 1951. Devine died in late September.

12. *Sporting News*, January 14, 1953.

13. *Sporting News*, December 17, 1958. One of Wight's cartoons, commissioned by the *Sporting News*, illustrates the feature on Wight and his art.

Chicago Tribune
New York Times
New York World-Telegram
Sporting News

Wight, Bill. Interview by Ed Attanasio. September 11, 2003.

Wight, Janice. Interview by Bill Nowlin. February 18, 2010.

62. Frank Crosetti

Special thanks to the Baseball Hall of Fame for providing me a copy of Crosetti's file, to Lawrence Baldassaro for sharing his research, and to Crosetti's grandson Michael McCoy for tracking down relatives to answer questions about his grandparents' history. All statistics, unless otherwise noted, are from http://www.baseball-reference.com.

1. Daley, "End of the Trail."

2. Daniel, "A Shoestring, a Slip, and an Injured Right Knee."

3. Crosetti, "I Coach the Hot Corner."

4. Daley, "End of the Trail."

5. Hughes, "Frisco to Fatten Up Gaunt Young Pitcher."

6. Daniel, "Lou Gehrig, on Hitting Spree."

7. Meany, "Crosetti Leading Candidate."

8. Meany, "Crosetti Leading Candidate."

9. Daniel, "Lou to Stay at No. 4 in New Lineup."

10. Daniel, "Yank Midway Combination May Rank Best in League."

11. "Crosetti New Hero of Yankees."

12. He also led AL shortstops in chances (905) and putouts (352); then again, he tied with Senators third baseman Buddy Lewis for the league lead in errors (47).

13. Several newspapers reported that the owner and operator of the PCL Oakland Oaks at the time, Victor "Cookie" Devincenzi, was Mrs. Crosetti's brother. However, when Crosetti's grandson Michael McCoy addressed the matter with his grandmother (in her late nineties in the fall of 2011), she told him that none of her brothers ever worked in baseball.

14. Daniel, "Crosetti Sees Good Season."

15. Daniel, "Daniel's Dope."

16. Apparently, Crosetti had originally batted lefty in semipro, until his brother informed him there was a demand for right-handed hitters. "Crosetti Switches at Bat."

17. Trachtenberg, "Mr. Yankee, Frank Crosetti."

18. Daniel, "Yanks Favor Crosetti for All-Star Berth."

19. Williams, "Barrow Rates an Assist for Keeping Crosetti."

20. Daniel, "Johnson Earns Yank Spurs."

21. Buzas started the first twelve games of the 1945 season at short, made six errors, and never put on a glove in a Major League game again.

22. Bouton, *Ball Four*, 22.

23. The suit, *Gionfriddo v. Major League Baseball* (2001), was filed in California by Al Gionfriddo, Pete Coscarart, Dolph Camilli, and Crosetti—four high-profile ballplayers active before 1947, when a clause was inserted into all players' contracts to allow their image to be used for commercial purposes. They lost because the court concluded that "the public interest favoring the free dissemination of information regarding baseball's history far outweighs any proprietary interests at stake."

24. Daniel, "Frisco Product Proven Maestro." The friend was Amadeo Giannini, who founded what is now Bank of America.

25. Ogle, "Crosetti Ends 37 Years in Yankee Uniform." Ogle was one of a handful of writers who suggested that the Yankees actually retire Crosetti's number, 2, which he had worn since 1945. "Ahh, that's a lot of bull," Crosetti told *New York Newsday*'s Stan Isaacs. "When I leave, they oughta give my number to somebody right away. I don't think any number should be retired. Maybe Ruth's—that's all because he was special—but the other numbers should be passed on to young players" (Isaacs, "The 37 Seasons of Frank Crosetti"). Fitting that the number would eventually end up on the back of another great Yankees shortstop, Derek Jeter.

26. It was probably just as well, seeing as the team would move to Milwaukee a few months later.

Bouton, Jim. *Ball Four*. 1st ed. New York: Dell, 1971.

Trachtenberg, Leo. "Mr. Yankee, Frank Crosetti." *Yankees Magazine*, October 16, 1986.

Crosetti, Frank, as told to Al Hirshberg. "I Coach the Hot Corner." *Saturday Evening Post*, August 8, 1959.
"Crosetti New Hero of Yankees." UPI report in *New York World-Telegram*, October 6, 1938.
"Crosetti Switches at Bat." *New York World-Telegram*, March 13, 1941.

Daley, Arthur. "Sports of the Times: End of the Trail." *New York Times*, January 20, 1947.
Daniel, Daniel M. "Crosetti Sees Good Season." *New York World-Telegram*, March 2, 1940.
———. "Daniel's Dope." *New York World-Telegram*, November 27, 1940.
———. "Frisco Product Proven Maestro." *New York World-Telegram and Sun*, March 9, 1957.
———. "Johnson Earns Yank Spurs." *New York World-Telegram*, June 22, 1943.
———. "Lou Gehrig, on Hitting Spree, Sets Flag Pace for Yankees." *New York World-Telegram*, June 18, 1935.
———. "Lou to Stay at No. 4 in New Lineup." *New York World-Telegram*, March 12, 1935.
———. "A Shoestring, a Slip, and an Injured Right Knee Made Crosetti Yanks' Musketeer Number Three." *New York World-Telegram*, May 21, 1936.
———. "Yank Midway Combination May Rank Best in League." *New York World-Telegram*, April 6, 1935.
———. "Yanks Favor Crosetti for All-Star Berth." *New York World-Telegram*, June 26, 1942.
Hughes, Ed R. "Frisco to Fatten Up Gaunt Young Pitcher." *Sporting News*, February 14, 1929.
Isaacs, Stan. "The 37 Seasons of Frank Crosetti." In "Out of Left Field . . ." *New York Newsday*, April 9, 1968.
Meany, Tom. "Crosetti Leading Candidate for Yankee Shortstop Berth." *New York World-Telegram*, March 9, 1932.
Ogle, Jim. "Crosetti Ends 37 Years in Yankee Uniform." *Newark (NJ) Star-Ledger*, April 19, 1968.
Williams, Joe. "Barrow Rates an Assist for Keeping Crosetti." *New York World-Telegram*, October 14, 1943.

Bourke, Thomas. Telephone conversation with Ellen Biggs, Frank Crosetti's daughter. November 20, 2011.

63. Joe Page

Frommer, Harvey. *Five O'Clock Lightning*. Hoboken NJ: John Wiley and Sons, 2007.
Gentile, Derek. *The Complete New York Yankees*. New York: Black Dog and Leventhal, 2001.
Heiman, Lee, Dave Weiner, and Bill Gutman. *When the Cheering Stops*. New York: Macmillan, 1990.
James, Bill, and Rob Neyer. *The Neyer/James Guide to Pitchers*. New York: Simon and Schuster, 2004.

Madden, Bill, *Pride of October*. New York: Grand Central, 2004.

Spatz, Lyle. *Yankees Coming, Yankees Going*. Jefferson NC: McFarland, 2000.

Baseball Digest
Binghamton (NY) Sunday Press
New York Daily News
New York Mirror
New York Post
New York Sun
New York World-Telegram
Pittsburgh Post-Gazette
Saturday Evening Post
Sportfolio
Sport Magazine
Yankees Magazine

Bourke, Thomas. Telephone conversation with Page's grandson Joseph Page. July 2, 2011.

64. Mel Allen

Appel, Marty. *Now Pitching for the Yankees*. Toronto: Sport Classic Books, 2001.

Barber, Red. *The Broadcasters*. New York: Dial Press, 1970.

Barber, Red, and Robert Creamer. *Rhubarb in the Catbird Seat*. Garden City NY: Doubleday, 1968.

Borelli, Stephen. *How about That! The Life of Mel Allen*. Champaign IL: Sports Publishing, 2005.

Gross, Ben. *I Looked and I Listened*. New York: Random House, 1954.

Halberstam, David J. *Sports on New York Radio: A Play-by-Play History*. Lincolnwood IL: Masters Press, 1999.

———. *Summer of '49*. New York: William Morrow, 1989.

Patterson, Ted. *The Golden Voices of Baseball*. Champaign IL: Sports Publishing, 2002.

Smith, Curt. *The Storytellers*. New York: Macmillan, 1995.

———. *Voices of the Game*. South Bend IN: Diamond Communications, 1987.

Associated Press. Obituary of Mel Allen. June 16, 1996.

Hoffman, Roy. "The Late Mel Allen: Alabama's Voice of the Yankees." *Mobile (AL) Register*, July 6, 2003.

Smith, Curt. "Buck Known for Effortless Style, Class." June 21, 2002. http://espn.go.com/classic/obit/s/2002/0603/1390037.html.

http://www.americansportscasters.com
http://www.anecdotage.com
http://www.espn.com

65. Russ Hodges

Material on Russ Hodges's October 3, 1951, illness and Lawrence Goldberg's role in preserving Thomson's homer is found in Tim Wiles's "A Paper Trail to History," in the Hall of Fame's opening-day 2011 *Memories and Dreams* issue. Other material, including quotes, is derived from Curt Smith's books *Voices of the Game*, *Storied Stadiums*, *Voices of Summer*, *The Voice*, *Pull Up a Chair*, and *A Talk in the Park*.

Smith, Curt. *Pull Up a Chair*. Washington DC: Potomac Books, 2009.

———. *Storied Stadiums*. New York: Carroll and Graf, 2001.

———. *A Talk in the Park*. Washington DC: Potomac Books, 2011.

———. *The Voice*. Guilford CT: Lyons Press, 2007.

———. *Voices of Summer*. New York: Carroll and Graf, 2005.

———. *Voices of the Game*. New York: Simon and Schuster, 1992.

66. The 1947 World Series

Drebinger, John. "Dodgers' Only Hit Beats Yankees, 3–2, with 2 Out in Ninth." *New York Times*, October 4, 1947, 1.

———. "Dodgers Set Back Yankees by 8 to 6 for 3–3 Series Tie." *New York Times*, October 6, 1947, 1.

———. "Shea Wins in Box." *New York Times*, October 5, 1947, 1.

———. "Yanks' 5 in Fifth Beat Dodgers, 5–3, in Series Opener." *New York Times*, October 1, 1947.

http://www.ieeeghn.org/wiki/index.php/Televised_sports (estimated 3.9 million viewers).

67. Bill Bevens

1. There are several unconfirmed version of how Bevens acquired the name Bill.

2. Daniel, "Bevens, Big Modest," 227.

3. Daniel, "Bevens, Big Modest," 227.

4. Daniel, "Bevens, Big Modest," 227–28.

5. Daniel, "Bevens, Big Modest," 228.

6. Daniel, "Bevens, Big Modest," 228.

7. Daniel, "Bevens, Big Modest," 228.

8. Daniel, "Bevens, Big Modest," 229.

9. Bill Bevens, as told to Jack Cuddy in New York, published in the *Detroit News*, October 4, 1947.

10. Meany, "Hard Luck Keeps Bill Pitching."

11. Kirst, "Almost Immortality."

12. Meany, "Hard Luck Keeps Bill Pitching."

Daniel, Daniel M. "Bevens, Big Modest, Reticent Hombre Heads for Hurling Heights with Yanks." *Baseball Magazine*, June 7, 1947.

Meany, Tom. "Hard Luck Keeps Bill Pitching." *Collier's*, July 28, 1951.

Kirst, Sean. "Almost Immortality: The Baseball Heartbreak of Bill Bevens." *Syracuse (NY) Post-Standard*, October 14, 2010.

Bevens, Larry. E-mail to Thomas Bourke. June 17, 2011.

Bourke, Thomas. Telephone conversation with Bill Bevens's son Larry Bevens. June 15, 2011.

69. Larry MacPhail

1. Fimrite, "The Play That Beat the Bums."

Barber, Red. *1947—When All Hell Broke Loose in Baseball*. New York: Doubleday, 1982.

James, Bill. *The New Bill James Historical Baseball Abstract*. New York: Free Press, 2001.

Karst, Gene. "MacPhail, Leland Stanford, Sr. 'Larry.'" In *Biographical Dictionary of American Sports—Baseball*, edited by David L. Porter. New York: Greenwood Press, 1987.

Koppett, Leonard. *Koppett's Concise History of Major League Baseball*. New York: Carroll and Graf, 2004.

Light, Jonathan Fraser. *The Cultural Encyclopedia of Baseball*. Jefferson NC: McFarland, 1997.

McKelvey, G. Richard. "Larry MacPhail." In *Scribner Encyclopedia of American Lives, Thematic Series: The 1960s*, edited by William L. O'Neill and Kenneth T. Jackson. New York: Charles Scribner's Sons, 2002.

———. *The MacPhails, Baseball's First Family of the Front Office*. Jefferson NC: McFarland, 2000.

Rader, Benjamin G. *Baseball: A History of America's Game*. Urbana: University of Illinois Press, 1992.

Smith, Red. *Red Smith on Baseball*. Chicago: Ivan R. Dee, 2000.

Warfield, Don. *The Roaring Redhead*. South Bend IN: Diamond Communications, 1987.

White, G. Edward. *The National Pastime*. Princeton NJ: Princeton University Press, 1996.

Fimrite, Ron. "The Play That Beat the Bums." *Sports Illustrated*, October 20, 1997.

Holland, Gerald. "The Great MacPhail." *Sports Illustrated*, August 17–31, 1958, 62–68.

Durso, Joseph. "Baseball's Larry MacPhail Dies; Started Night Games, Led Yanks." *New York Times*, October 2, 1975.

"Landis, Kenesaw Mountain." Obituary. *New York Times*, November 26, 1944.

"Powel Crosley Jr. Is Dead at 74; Owner of the Cincinnati Reds." *New York Times*, March 29, 1961.

Bourke, Thomas. Telephone conversations with Mrs. Jean Duncan, Larry MacPhail's daughter. October 22 and 23, 2011.

70. George Weiss

1. Frank, "Yankee Kingmaker," 110.

2. *New York Times*, February 13, 1932; Levitt, *Ed Barrow*, 277.

3. Levitt, *Ed Barrow*, 351.

4. *Sporting News*, October 15, 1947.

5. Meany, *The Yankee Story*, 145.

6. Shaplen, "The Yankees' Real Boss," 37.

7. *Newsweek*, July 15, 1957, 62.

8. Weiss, "The Best Decision I Ever Made," 32.

9. *Sporting News*, July 19, 1961

10. Weiss, "The Man of Silence Speaks," 48.

11. MacPhail, *My Nine Innings*, 49; *Sporting News*, November 25, 1949.

12. Frank, "Boss of the Yankees," 113.

13. Golenbock, *Amazin'*, 96.

14. Frank, "Boss of the Yankees," 111.

15. *New York Times*, November 3, 1960.

16. Shaplen, "How to Build a Ballclub," 38.

17. *Nutmegger*, June 1971, 34.

Golenbock, Peter. *Amazin'*. New York: St. Martin's Press, 2002.

Levitt, Daniel R. *Ed Barrow: The Bulldog Who Built the Yankees' First Dynasty*. Lincoln: University of Nebraska Press, 2008.

MacPhail, Lee. *My Nine Innings*. Westport CT: Meckler, 1989.

Meany, Tom. *The Yankee Story*. New York: E. P. Dutton, 1960.

Frank, Stanley. "Boss of the Yankees." *Saturday Evening Post*, April 16, 1960.

———. "Yankee Kingmaker." *Saturday Evening Post*, May 24, 1948.

Shaplen, Robert. "How to Build a Ballclub." *Sports Illustrated*, March 5, 1962.

———. "The Yankees' Real Boss." *Sports Illustrated*, September 20, 1954.

Weiss, George M., with Robert Shaplen. "The Best Decision I Ever Made." *Sports Illustrated*, March 13, 1961.

———. "The Man of Silence Speaks." *Sports Illustrated*, March 6, 1961.

74. Yankees Attendance in 1947

1. "Record Crowd Sees Yanks Beat Bosox."

2. Effrat, "58,339 Acclaim Babe Ruth."

3. "Baseball Pays Highest Tribute to Babe Ruth."

4. Effrat, "58,339 Acclaim Babe Ruth."

5. Dawson, "DiMaggio Is Hero."

"Baseball Pays Highest Tribute to Babe Ruth." *Los Angeles Times*, April 28, 1947.

Dawson, James P. "DiMaggio Is Hero." *New York Times*, May 18, 1947.

Effrat, Louis. "58,339 Acclaim Babe Ruth in Rare Tribute at Stadium." *New York Times*, April 28, 1947.

"Record Crowd Sees Yanks Beat Bosox, 9–3." *Los Angeles Times*, May 27, 1947.

Contributors

MARC Z AARON is a certified public accountant and certified valuation analyst with a tax practice in Randolph, Vermont. He is also an adjunct professor of economics at Vermont Technical College and the Anglo-American University in Prague and an adjunct professor of accounting at Norwich University and the University of New York in Prague. A born and bred Yankees fan, Marc has four sons, coached Little League for six seasons, and, like Tony LaRussa, retired after his team (sadly named Red Sox) won the league championship. Marc, a tournament tennis player, has been a ranked singles player by the New England U.S. Tennis Association and has captained several USTA league teams.

MARTY APPEL, former public relations director of the Yankees and then executive producer of their telecasts, is the author of *Pinstripe Empire: The New York Yankees from before the Babe to after the Boss.*

MARK ARMOUR is the founder and chair of the Baseball Biography Project and the author or editor of five books on baseball, including *Pitching, Defense, and Three Run Homers: The 1970 Baltimore Orioles* (University of Nebraska Press, 2012). He researches and writes from his home in the Pacific Northwest.

LAWRENCE BALDASSARO is professor emeritus of Italian and former director of the Honors College at the University of Wisconsin–Milwaukee. He has written for several baseball journals and is a regular contributor to *GameDay*, the Milwaukee Brewers magazine. He is the editor of *Ted Williams: Reflections on a Splendid Life* and coeditor, with Richard Johnson, of *The American Game: Baseball and Ethnicity*. His latest book is *Beyond DiMaggio: Italian Americans in Baseball* (University of Nebraska Press, 2011).

RALPH BERGER is a graduate of the University of Pennsylvania. He lives in Huntingdon Valley, Pennsylvania, with his wife, Reina. They collect art and love to travel. He has been writing articles for SABR for ten years.

BRENDAN BINGHAM has been a SABR member since 2009 and is an occasional contributor to the website Baseball: Past and Present. Brendan currently works in the medical-device industry. During a twenty-five-year career as a research scientist, he has published original work in genetics, endocrinology, and neuroscience.

MAURICE BOUCHARD, a SABR member since 1999, spends more time in front of his computer trying to find the maiden names of obscure players' mothers than he should admit. He has worked as an author, editor, or fact-checker on nine SABR team books, starting in 2005 with *'75: The Red Sox Team That Saved Baseball.* An academic cicada, Bouchard recently completed a second master's degree (this one from Simmons College's Graduate School of Library and Information Science) fourteen years after his first one, which in turn was fourteen years after his undergraduate degree. The discipline for the 2025 degree is anyone's guess. At the time of publication, Bouchard and his painfully beautiful wife, Kim, are living with their two pooches, Spencer and Abby, in Westford, New York, just ten minutes' drive from 25 Main Street, Cooperstown.

THOMAS A. BOURKE has been a member of the Society for American Baseball Research since 1984. Born in New York City in 1945, he grew up near Yankee Stadium and the old Polo Grounds where the New York Giants used to play. He holds an MA in French from Fordham University and an MS in library science from Columbia University. He was a librarian for almost forty years, first at the New York Public Library and later at the Gulfport Public Library near St. Petersburg, Florida, where the Yankees did spring training in 1947 and where he currently resides. His research specialties are bibliography, biography, genealogy, and newspaper history.

JOHN CONTOIS works in the clinical diagnostics industry and lives in Maine with his wife and two daughters. John is a lifelong Red Sox fan and longtime SABR member who grew up in the Boston area and has fond memories of skipping school with friends for opening day at Fenway Park.

WARREN CORBETT is a contributor to SABR's Baseball Biography Project and the author of *The Wizard of Waxahachie: Paul Richards and the End of Baseball as We Knew It*. He lives in Bethesda, Maryland.

JOE DITTMAR, a SABR member since 1988, has written numerous articles for SABR publications as well as three books on baseball records. For nearly twenty years Joe served as the vice chairman for SABR's Baseball Records Committee as well as one of the leaders of Philadelphia's Connie Mack Chapter. With roots in, and a love for, teaching, Joe has also delivered an occasional baseball history class at his local community college.

NICHOLAS DIUNTE is a high school teacher and coach in New York City. A former collegiate baseball player, he joined SABR to merge his love for baseball and scholarship by chronicling baseball's history through oral interviews with those who played during baseball's golden era of the 1940s and 1950s.

ROB EDELMAN teaches film history courses at the University at Albany. He is the author of *Great Baseball Films* and *Baseball on the Web* and is coauthor (with his wife, Audrey Kupferberg) of *Meet the Mertzes*, a double biography of *I Love Lucy*'s Vivian Vance and fabled baseball fan William Frawley, and *Matthau: A Life*. He is a film commentator on WAMC (Northeast) Public Radio and a contributing editor of *Leonard Maltin's Movie Guide*. He is a frequent contributor to *Base Ball: A Journal of the Early Game* and has written for *Baseball and American Culture: Across the Diamond*, *Total Baseball*, *Baseball in the Classroom*, *Memories and Dreams*, and *NINE: A Journal of Baseball History and Culture*. His essay on early baseball films appears on the DVD *Reel Baseball: Baseball Films from the Silent Era, 1899–1926*, and he is an interviewee on the director's cut DVD of *The Natural*.

CHARLES F. FABER, a retired university professor and administrator, has written several books on baseball. Included are *Baseball Ratings: The All-Time Best Players at Each Position* (3rd ed., 2008), *Baseball Pioneers: Ratings of Nineteenth Century Players* (1997), *Spitballers: The Last Legal Hurlers of the Wet One* (with Richard B. Faber, 2006), and *Major League Careers Cut Short: Leading Players Gone by 30* (2011). He has also written several other books in other fields, such as history, law, and education. He lives in Lexington, Kentucky.

STEVE FERENCHICK, like Randy Gumpert, is a native of Berks County, Pennsylvania (West Reading, in Steve's case), and considers himself fortunate to have spent a couple hours at the Gumpert home in the summer of 2007, enjoying both Randy's stories and Ann's homemade cookies and iced tea. Although not exactly a Yankees fan, Steve has also had the pleasure of meeting 1947 Yankees Joe DiMaggio, Tommy Henrich, and Yogi Berra and chatting up Phil Rizzuto and his lovely wife, Cora, in a New Jersey Macy's while Scooter was shopping for a new belt. Steve has been an attorney since 1998 and a member of SABR for four years longer than that. He lives with his wife, two daughters, and son in Wynnewood, Pennsylvania.

JAMES FORR'S book *Pie Traynor: A Baseball Biography* (coauthored with David Proctor) was a finalist for the 2010 CASEY Award. In 2005 he was named winner of the SABR-McFarland Baseball Research Award. He lives in Columbia, Missouri.

GARY GILLETTE is editor of SABR's annual *Emerald Guide* as well as coeditor of the ESPN *Baseball Encyclopedia* and executive editor of the ESPN *Pro Football Encyclopedia*. He has written, edited, or contributed to dozens of baseball books, including six editions of *Total Baseball*. His most recent trade book is *Big League Ballparks*, a complete history of Major League parks, coauthored with SABR members Stuart Shea and Matt Silverman. Gillette has been a member of SABR's board of directors since 2009 and is cochair of the Ballparks Committee and past cochair of the Business of Baseball Committee. As a director of the Tiger Stadium Conservancy, he continues the fight to save the historic field at Michigan and Trumbull. As a member of the Mayor's Committee to save Hamtramck Stadium, he has been a leader in the effort to preserve one of the few remaining Negro League ballparks. Gillette lives in Detroit's historic Indian Village, two doors away from the house built for Chalmers Motors president Hugh Chalmers in 1910.

SOL GITTLEMAN graduated from Drew University in 1955. After a promising college baseball career, he was shown the scouting report written by a part-time bird dog covering colleges in northern New Jersey: "Too small; can't hit with power, weak arm, cheats on the infield." This led him to graduate school at Columbia and the University of Michigan, where he received his PhD in comparative literature. He has been at Tufts University since 1964, serving as provost for twenty-one years. Gittleman currently serves as the Alice and Nathan Gantcher University Professor. His *Reynolds, Raschi, and Lopat: New York's Big Three and the Great Yankee Dynasty of 1949–1953* was published in 2007. He has been a SABR member since 1986.

PETER M. GORDON joined SABR in 1984 and has written several biographies and articles for the website and various books. He has also published poems, feature articles, and a content development blog, *My Program Idea*, at blogspot.com. Peter has worked in the entertainment industry for more than thirty years. He was the Golf Channel's first head of programming, launched its international business, and still lives in Orlando, where he is a television producer and consultant.

CHIP GREENE is the grandson of Nelson Greene, who pitched for the Brooklyn Dodgers during parts of the 1924 and '25 seasons. For twenty years Chip lived in Gaithersburg, Maryland, just thirty miles south of Middletown. In the summer of 2008, he moved with his family to Waynesboro, Pennsylvania, just thirty miles north of Middletown. His biography of Hal Keller can be found on SABR's Baseball Biography Project.

DON HARRISON'S passion for newspapers coupled with a love of baseball and basketball provided the impetus for his career in sportswriting. They led to *Connecticut Baseball: The Best of the*

Nutmeg State, his book about one small state's myriad contributions to Major League Baseball, and his new book, *Hoops in Connecticut: The Nutmeg State's Passion for Basketball*, both published by the History Press. As sports editor of the *Waterbury Republican*, Harrison was a two-time selection as Connecticut Sportswriter of the Year. He chronicled nine World Series, including the New York Mets' improbable triumph over the Baltimore Orioles in 1969 and Reggie Jackson's three home runs in the finale of the 1977 fall classic. Don put his expertise to work as a contributor to two editions of *The Official Encyclopedia of Baseball*. He is a member of the Society for American Baseball Research. Harrison's freelance articles have appeared in the *Sporting News*, *Sports Quarterly-Baseball*, the *New York Times*, and dozens of other publications.

TOM HAWTHORN is a magazine writer and a columnist for the *Globe and Mail* newspaper. He lives in Victoria BC, Canada.

MIKE HUBER is a SABR member and the dean of academic life at Muhlenberg College in Allentown, Pennsylvania, where he regularly sponsors undergraduate work in sabermetrics. He has published his sabermetrics research in several journals, including the *Baseball Research Journal*, the *Journal of Statistics Education*, *Chance*, *Base Ball*, and the *Annals of Applied Statistics*, and he is the author of *West Point's Field of Dreams: Major League Baseball at Doubleday Field* (2004). He has been rooting for the Baltimore Orioles since 1968 and has two chapters in *Pitching, Defense, and Three-Run Homers* (University of Nebraska Press, 2012), a book about the 1970 world champion Orioles.

JIMMY KEENAN has been a SABR member since 2001. His grandfather Jimmy Lyston, along with his great-grandfather John M. Lyston and John's two brothers Marty and Bill were all professional baseball players. He is the author of the book *The Lystons: A Story of One Baltimore Family and Our National Pastime*. His biography of Cupid Childs was published in SABR's *The National Pastime* in 2009. In addition, he was the writer and historian for the Forgotten Birds documentary that chronicles the fifty-year history of the Minor League Baltimore Orioles. His prerecorded interview about the 1921 Baltimore Orioles can be heard at the "Second Inning" display at the Sports Legends Museum in Baltimore, Maryland. He has also written biographies for SABR's Baseball Biography Project and three Biography Project–related books. Jimmy is a 2010 inductee into the Oldtimers Baseball Association of Maryland's Hall of Fame and was elected chairman of the organization's board of governors in 2011.

CHRIS KEMMER was born into a baseball-obsessed family in Troy, New York. During the early 1950s when there were three teams in New York, Chris and Dad were Yankee fans, Mom was a Giants fan, and her brothers were Dodgers fans. Mom and the boys were crushed when their teams left town—Mom eventually became a real, die-hard Yankee's fan in spite of her previous opinion of the team Dad loved. Today, Chris works as a marketing consultant in the trucking industry, writing articles for trade magazines and publishing her own newsletter, the *Fleet Sentiment Report*. Baseball and the history of the game remain important components in the lives of Chris and her family.

TARA KRIEGER received her JD from New York Law School in May 2012. A member of SABR since 2005, she has spent time as a staff writer at *Newsday* and the *Poughkeepsie Journal*, as well as an editor for the official website of Major League Baseball. Freelance contributions include the *Seattle Times*, Maple Street Press's *Meet the*

Mets and *Bombers Broadside*, and *The Miracle Has Landed: The Amazin' Story of How the 1969 Mets Shocked the World*.

WALTER LECONTE has been an avid baseball researcher for about forty of his sixty-two years and has focused mostly on the New York Yankees. Walter has authored two Yankees books, *The Ultimate New York Yankees Record Book* and *The Yankee Encyclopedia* (coauthored with Mark Gallagher). He has recently researched in-season exhibition games, or ISEGs, for short. In fact, he has discovered almost five thousand of them, dating back to 1871. He has been dubbed "the ISEG King" by his wife, Kathy. A native New Orleanian, he has been a Yankees fan since his early childhood. He has been an ongoing member of the Society for American Baseball Research since the early 1980s and is a regular volunteer for Retrosheet. He resides in Lee's Summit, Missouri, with his wife and his special feline friends.

LEN LEVIN, a retired newspaper editor, a Red Sox fan, and an admirer of the Yankees, has seen many memorable contests between the two teams and expects to see many more. A resident of Providence, Rhode Island, he is a lifelong New Englander. Besides watching baseball games, he edits baseball books.

DAN LEVITT recently completed *The Battle That Forged Modern Baseball: The Federal League Challenge and Its Legacy*. He is also the author of *Ed Barrow: The Bulldog Who Built the Yankees' First Dynasty* (University of Nebraska Press, 2008), a Seymour Award finalist, and coauthor of *Paths to Glory: How Great Baseball Teams Got That Way* (2003), winner of the Sporting News/SABR Baseball Research Award. He lives in Minneapolis with wife and two boys.

RICK MALWITZ, a graduate of Rutgers University, worked for more than four decades for newspapers in New Jersey, prior to his retirement in 2011. He worked as a sports reporter, general assignment reporter, editorial page editor, and for twenty years as a columnist. As a member of the Baseball Writers Association of America, he cast one of forty-one write-in votes for Pete Rose for the Hall of Fame, the first year he would have been eligible had he not been barred from the game by Major League Baseball.

PETER MANCUSO has been a member of SABR since 1998 and has chaired SABR's Nineteenth-Century Committee since 2007. A native of Staten Island, New York, he ended a career in the NYPD when he retired in 1987 as the department's assistant director of training. Shortly after leaving the NYPD and while a part-time consultant to a U.S. Department of Justice program to improve responses to domestic violence crimes, he, along with his brother, cofounded a company producing antiques shows, book fairs, and quilting events. He holds a BA and MA in criminal justice from John Jay College (CUNY).

JEFFREY MARLETT teaches religious studies at the College of Saint Rose in Albany, New York. He is the author of *Saving the Heartland: Catholic Missionaries in Rural America, 1920–1960* (2002). Currently, he is working on a biography of Leo Durocher. He wrote the Durocher biography and an article about Leo's suspension for *The Team That Forever Changed Baseball and America: The 1947 Brooklyn Dodgers*.

JOHN MCMURRAY is chair of the Society for American Baseball Research's Deadball Era Committee. He contributed to SABR's 2006 book *Deadball Stars of the American League* and is a past chair of SABR's Ritter Award Subcommittee, which annually presents an award to the best book on Deadball Era baseball published during the prior year. He has contributed many interview-based player profiles to *Baseball Digest* in recent years.

JACK V. MORRIS is a corporate librarian for an environmental engineering company. He lives in East Coventry, Pennsylvania, with his wife and two daughters. He is the author of the Rube Melton biography in the book *The Team That Forever Changed Baseball and America: The 1947 Brooklyn Dodgers*.

ROB NEYER is SB Nation's national baseball editor and has written or cowritten six books about baseball, including *The Neyer/James Guide to Pitchers* and *Rob Neyer's Big Book of Baseball Legends*. Rob lives in Portland, Oregon, the largest city in America without a professional baseball team.

BILL NOWLIN has been vice president of SABR since 2004. Bill is one of the founders of Rounder Records. In 2011 he returned to his professorial days, teaching an online course, Baseball and Politics, at the University of Massachusetts and one on sportswriting at Lesley University in 2012. He is a lifelong Red Sox fan who has written or edited more than thirty Red Sox–related books. He has enjoyed a number of visits to Yankee Stadium, quietly rooting for the Red Sox, but this is his first appearance in a Yankees book.

ROYSE "CRASH" PARR was born in Elk City, Oklahoma, in 1935. He sold soda pop at the local semipro red-stone ballpark when his hometown team was a national contender. Parr is a retired oil-company attorney in Tulsa. He limits his baseball research, books, and articles to Oklahoma subjects. An admirer of the noble Indian athlete, his favorite bumper sticker is "Custer Had It Coming."

CHRISTINE L. PUTNAM was a freelance writer who specialized in American history. With the help of many presidential libraries, as well as the White House Office of the Curator, she published a book called *But the President Wants Meatloaf!* about the American presidents and their favorite foods. She was also the food critic at the *Burbank (CA) Leader* for several years. Christine passed away on December 8, 2011.

JAMES LINCOLN RAY served as the former features writer for Suite101Baseball from 2007 through 2011. During that time he authored more than four hundred articles that covered all aspects of the national pastime. He is also a major contributor to the Society of American Baseball Research's Baseball Biography Project, having authored the biographies of Lou Gehrig, Don Mattingly, Chuck Klein, Paul O'Neill, and Roy White. James lives with his wife, Cindy, and practices law in Philadelphia, Pennsylvania.

MIKE RICHARD is a lifelong Red Sox fan who got his first exposure to the team at a most appropriate time—when he was eleven years old—and fell in love with the 1967 Impossible Dream team. He has written two sports books on high school football: *Glory to Gardner: 100 Years of Football in the Chair City* and *Super Saturdays: The History of the Massachusetts High School Super Bowl*. He is a guidance counselor at Gardner (Massachusetts) High School and a columnist for the *Gardner News*. He is also working on a book about baseball markers, monuments, and gravestones of New England. He lives in Gardner with his wife, Peggy, and has two adult children, Casey and Lindsey.

RICHARD RIIS is a librarian and professional genealogist. He has written numerous articles on popular music and was a contributing editor to *Rock and Roll Disc* and *The All Music Guide*. He has written about baseball cards for *The Vintage* and *Classic Baseball Collector* and *Sports Collectors Digest* and contributed to the *Standard Catalog of Vintage Baseball Cards*. He lives in South Setauket, New York.

C. PAUL ROGERS III is the president of the Hall-Ruggles (Dallas-Fort Worth) chapter of SABR and is the coauthor of four baseball books, including *Lucky Me: My 65 Years in Baseball* (2011), with Eddie Robinson, and *The Whiz Kids and the 1950 Pennant* (1996), with boyhood hero Robin Roberts. His real job is as a law professor at Southern Methodist University in Dallas, Texas, where he served as dean of the law school for nine years.

MIKE ROSS, designer, artist, photographer, is founder-chairman of SABR UK and the SABR Origins Committee. A sometime author, Ross wrote *Baseball* for a burgeoning UK and Far Eastern consumption. Later he authored *Fenway Saved*, a photographic book including text primarily authored and edited with Jim Prime, preserving the ever-changing Boston park. Ross pioneered live UK TV World Series baseball for Screensport and founded the earliest baseball journals for UK fans now included in the Hall of Fame archives, as is his twenty-square-foot 3D construction of bat, ball, and painted wood depicting a version of the Ted "Williams (strike) Zone"; he was involved in a Bat and Ball brotherhood exhibition at Lords cricket grounds, later transferred to Cooperstown. His design archive (as "the Ritva Man") at London's Victoria and Albert Museum includes credited designs inspired by baseball uniforms. Mike, born in Maine, resides in London, England.

JOSEPH M. SCHUSTER is the author of *The Might Have Been* (2012). The chair of the Communications and Journalism Department at Webster University in St. Louis, Missouri, he has published articles in numerous magazines and newspapers, including the late, lamented SPORT magazine; the *St. Louis Post-Dispatch*; the St. Louis Cardinals' official team magazine, *Gameday*; and other periodicals. He is married and the father of five rabid baseball fans.

CURT SMITH says *USA Today* is "America's voice of authority on baseball broadcasting." His fifteen books include the classic *Voices of the Game, Pull Up a Chair, Storied Stadiums, A Talk in the Park*, and his newest, *Mercy!* a tribute to Fenway Park's centennial. Smith is a GateHouse Media and mlb.com columnist, National Public Radio affiliate commentator, frequent Smithsonian Institution and National Baseball Hall of Fame host, and senior lecturer at the University of Rochester. He wrote more speeches than anyone for former president George H. W. Bush.

ART SPANJER is a retired professor of library and information sciences. He likes to keep busy doing freelance writing, research, and tending to his small ranch in the hill country of Texas. The absolute loves of his life, other than his lovely wife, Lisa, are Major League Baseball and the pursuit of learning.

LYLE SPATZ has been a SABR member since 1973 and chairman of the Baseball Records Committee since 1991. He is the author of five books on baseball history and the editor of two baseball record books. His book *1921: The Yankees, the Giants, and the Battle for Baseball Supremacy in New York* (University of Nebraska Press), written with coauthor Steve Steinberg, won the Seymour Medal for the best book of baseball history or biography published in 2010. Lyle, who lives in Florida with his wife, Marilyn, edited the first book in Nebraska's team series, *The Team That Forever Changed Baseball and America: The 1947 Brooklyn Dodgers*.

MARK STEWART has spent twenty-five years as a sportswriter. He has profiled more than five hundred athletes in print and online and has written more than fifty nonfiction baseball books for children and adults. He has had the pleasure of meeting several of the players profiled in this book, including Joe DiMaggio, Tommy Henrich, Phil Rizzuto, Ralph Houk, and Yogi Berra. In 2004 he worked with Berra on the ten-CD project *Yogi Berra's Favorite Baseball Radio Shows*, helping the Hall of Famer through the selection process and producing the support material packaged with the set. Mark is a founding partner of the sports-information website JockBio.com.

CORT VITTY is a native of New Jersey and a graduate of Seton Hall University. A lifelong fan of the New York Yankees, he has been a SABR member (Bob Davids Chapter) since 1999. Vitty's work has appeared in the *National Pastime, Go-Go to Glory: The 1959 White Sox*, Seamheads.com, and PhiladelphiaAthletics.org. In addition to the Billy Johnson essay in this publication, Vitty has authored SABR biographies of Buzz Arlett, Lu Blue, Goose Goslin, Mickey Grasso, Babe Phelps, Dave Philley, and Harry "Suitcase" Simpson. Vitty resides in Maryland with his wife, Mary Anne.

JOHN VORPERIAN, a.k.a. Johnny V, is host and producer of *Beyond the Game*, a sports program cablecast in New York, also shown at http://www.wpcommunitymedia.org. Since 2002 the longtime SABR member has interviewed enough Mets, Yanks, Nats, Reds, Royals, Padres, Giants, Dodgers, Tigers, Bucs, and Sox to fill several dugouts. He teaches sports law at Concordia College in New York and is a featured columnist for http://www.boxscorenews.com. The card-carrying Sports Lawyer Association member owes his athletics obsession all to his mom, Martha Vorperian. Her passion for baseball and football knew no bounds. Their kitchen-table talk always focused on the latest concerning her beloved Fightin' Irish, New York football Giants, and Yankees. This contribution is dedicated to her with many thanks from a very appreciative son.

JOSEPH WANCHO lives in Westlake, Ohio, and is a lifelong Cleveland Indians fan. Working at AT&T since 1994 as a process and development manager, he has been a SABR member since 2005. He has made contributions to several Baseball Biography Projects as well as the website. Currently, he serves as cochairman of the Minor League Research Committee.

DAVE WILLIAMS was six years old in 1969 when the Amazin' Mets embarked on their miracle ride and made him a fan for life. He has been a SABR member since 2001 and has contributed to other SABR biography projects, including bios of Lou Brock, Tim McCarver, and Rube Walker. He lives in Glastonbury, Connecticut, with his wife, Julia, and daughter, Clara.

Printed in the USA
CPSIA information can be obtained
at www.ICGtesting.com
LVHW081701240124
769630LV00008B/1368

9 780803 240940